CIMA

STUDY TEXT

Stage 4 Paper 13

Strategic Financial Management

New in this July 1999 edition

- Revised chapter structure
- Updated on tax and economic changes
- Additional material on financial control, corporate failure, working capital management and capital reconstructions
- More concise coverage throughout, for easier learning

FOR EXAMS IN NOVEMBER 1999 AND THE YEAR 2000

BPP Publishing
July 1999

First edition 1994
Sixth edition July 1999

ISBN 0 7517 3127 7 (previous edition 0 7517 3112 9)

British Library Cataloguing-in-Publication Data
A catalogue record for this book
is available from the British Library

Published by

BPP Publishing Limited
Aldine House, Aldine Place
London W12 8AW

http://www.bpp.co.uk

Printed in Great Britain by WM Print
Frederick Street
Walsall
West Midlands WS2 9NF

We are grateful to the Chartered Institute of Management Accountants for permission to reproduce past examination questions. The suggested solutions to the illustrative questions have been prepared by BPP Publishing Limited.

Page

HOW TO USE THIS STUDY TEXT

Aims of this Study Text

To provide you with the knowledge and understanding, skills and application techniques that you need if you are to be successful in your exams

This Study Text has been written around the **Strategic Financial Management** syllabus (reproduced on pages (xi) to (xiii), and cross-referenced to where in the text each topic is covered) and the 1999-2000 syllabus guidance notes (which we set out on pages (xiv) to (xviii)).

- It is **comprehensive**. We do not omit sections of the syllabus as the examiner is liable to examine any angle of any part of the syllabus - and you do not want to be left high and dry.
- It keeps you **up-to-date** in developments in strategic financial management and in the way in which the examiner is examining the subject.
- And it is **on-target**. We do not include any material which is not examinable. You can therefore rely on the BPP Study Text as the stand-alone source of all your information for the exam, without worrying that any of the material is irrelevant.

To allow you to study in the way that best suits your learning style and the time you have available, by following your personal Study Plan (see page (ix))

You may be studying at home on your own until the date of the exam, or you may be attending a full-time course. You may like to (and have time to) read every word, or you may prefer to (or only have time to) skim-read and devote the remainder of your time to question practice. Wherever you fall in the spectrum, you will find the BPP Study Text meets your needs in designing and following your personal Study Plan.

To tie in with the other components of the BPP Effective Study Package to ensure you have the best possible chance of passing the exam (see page (vi))

Recommended period of use	Elements of the BPP Effective Study Package
Three to twelve months before the exam	**Study Text** Use the Study Text to acquire knowledge, understanding, skills and the ability to use application techniques.
One to six months before the exam	**Practice & Revision Kit** Attempt the tutorial questions and complete the interactive checklists which are provided for each topic area in the Kit. Then try the numerous examination questions, for which there are realistic suggested solutions prepared by BPP's own authors. May 2000 examinees will find the 2000 edition of the Kit invaluable for bringing them up-to-date as at 1 December 1999, the cut-off date for May 2000 examinable material.
From three 3 months before the exam until the last minute	**Passcards** Work through these short, memorable notes which are focused on what is most likely to come up in the exam you will be sitting.
One to six months before the exam	**Success Tapes** Cover the vital elements of your syllabus in less than 90 minutes per subject with these audio cassettes. Each tape also contains exam hints to help you fine tune your strategy.
Three to twelve months before the exam	**Breakthrough Videos** Use a Breakthrough Video to supplement your Study Text. They give you clear tuition on key exam subjects and allow you the luxury of being able to pause or repeat sections until you have fully grasped the topic.
Three to twelve months before the exam	**Master CD** Take advantage of an Interactive CD-ROM containing questions on all aspects of the syllabus, cross referenced to help topics.

Settling down to study

By this stage in your career you are probably very experienced at learning and taking exams. But have you ever thought about *how* you learn? Let's have a quick look at the key elements required for effective learning. You can then identify your learning style and go on to design your own approach to how you are going to study with this text - your personal Study Plan.

Key element of learning	Using the BPP Study Text
Motivation	You can rely on the comprehensiveness and technical quality of BPP material. You've chosen the right Study Text - so you're in pole position to pass your exam!
Clear objectives and standards	Do you want to be a prizewinner or simply achieve a moderate pass? Decide.
Feedback	Work through the examples in this text and do the Questions and the Quick quizzes. Evaluate your efforts critically - how are you doing?
Study Plan	You need to be honest with yourself about your progress - don't be over-confident, but don't be negative either. Make your Study Plan (see below) and try to stick to it. Focus on the short-term objectives - completing two chapters a night, say - but beware of losing sight of your study objectives.
Practice	Use the Quick quizzes and Chapter roundups to refresh your memory after you have completed your initial study of each chapter.

These introductory pages let you see exactly what you are up against. But however you study, you should:

- **read through the syllabus and syllabus guidance notes** - these will help you to identify areas you have already covered, perhaps at a lower level of detail, and areas that are totally new to you;
- **study the examination paper section**, where we show you the format of the exam (how many and what kind of questions) and analyse all the papers set so far under the syllabus, **including the one set in May 1999**.

Key study steps

The following steps are, in our experience, the ideal approach to studying for professional exams but you can of course adapt it for your particular learning style (see page (ix)). Tackle the chapters in the order you find them in the Study Text. Taking into account your individual learning style, follow these key study steps for each chapter.

Key study steps	Activity
Step 1 *Chapter topic list*	Study the list. Each numbered topic is a numbered section in the chapter.
Step 2 *Introduction*	Read through it. It is designed to show you *why* the topics in the chapter need to be studied - how they lead on from previous topics, and how they lead into subsequent ones.
Step 3 *Knowledge brought forward boxes*	In these we highlight information and techniques that it is assumed you have 'brought forward' with you from your earlier studies. If there are topics which have changed recently due to legislation for example, these topics are explained in full. Do not panic if you do not feel instantly comfortable with the content of the box - it should come back to you as we develop the subject for this paper. If you are really unsure, we advise you to go back to your previous notes.
Step 4 *Explanations*	Proceed methodically through the chapter, reading each section thoroughly and making sure you understand. Where a topic has been examined, we state the month and year of examination against the appropriate heading. You should pay particular attention to these topics.
Step 5 *Key terms* and *Exam focus points*	• **Key terms** can often earn you *easy marks* if you state them clearly and correctly in an appropriate exam answer (and they are indexed at the back of the text so you can check easily that you are on top of all of them when you come to revise). • **Exam focus points** give you a good idea of how the examiner tends to examine certain topics - and they also pinpoint *easy marks*.
Step 6 *Note taking*	Take brief notes if you wish, avoiding the temptation to copy out too much.
Step 7 *Examples*	Follow each through to its solution very carefully.
Step 8 *Case examples*	Study each one, and try to add flesh to them from your own experience - they are designed to show how the topics you are studying come alive (and often come unstuck) in the real world.
Step 9 *Questions*	Make a very good attempt at each one.
Step 10 *Answers*	Check yours against ours, and make sure you understand any discrepancies.
Step 11 *Chapter roundup*	Work through it very carefully, to make sure you have grasped the major points it is highlighting.

Key study steps	Activity
Step 12 *Quick quiz*	When you are happy that you have covered the chapter, use the **Quick quiz** to check how much you have remembered of the topics covered. The answers are in the paragraphs in the chapter that we refer you to.
Step 13 *Question(s) in the Question bank*	Either at this point, or later when you are thinking about revising, make a full attempt at the **Question(s)** suggested at the very end of the chapter. You can find these at the end of the Study Text, along with the **Answers** so you can see how you did. We highlight those that are introductory, and those which are of the standard you would expect to find in an exam.

Developing your personal Study Plan

Preparing a Study Plan (and sticking closely to it) is one of the key elements in learning success.

First you need to be aware of your style of learning. There are four typical learning styles. Consider yourself in the light of the following descriptions and work out which you fit most closely. You can then plan to follow the key study steps in the sequence suggested.

Learning styles	Characteristics	Sequence of key study steps in the BPP Study Text
Theorist	Seeks to understand principles before applying them in practice	1, 2, 3, 4, 7, 8, 5, 9/10, 11, 12, 13 (6 continuous)
Reflector	Seeks to observe phenomena, thinks about them and then chooses to act	
Activist	Prefers to deal with practical, active problems; does not have much patience with theory	1, 2, 9/10 (read through), 7, 8, 5, 11, 3, 4, 9/10 (full attempt), 12, 13 (6 continuous)
Pragmatist	Prefers to study only if a direct link to practical problems can be seen; not interested in theory for its own sake	9/10 (read through), 2, 5, 7, 8, 11, 1, 3, 4, 9/10 (full attempt), 12, 13 (6 continuous)

Next

Work out the time you have available per week, given the following.

- The standard you have set yourself
- The time you need to set aside later for work on the Practice & Revision Kit and Passcards
- The other exam(s) you are sitting
- Very importantly, practical matters such as work, travel, exercise, sleep and social life

Note your time available in box A. A [ ]

Now

- Take the time you have available per week for this Study Text show in box A, multiply it by the number of weeks available and insert the result in box B. B [ ]
- Divide the figure in Box B by the number of chapters in this text and insert the result in box C. C [ ]

Then

Set about studying each chapter in the time shown in box C, following the key study steps in the order suggested by your particular learning style.

This is your personal **Study Plan.**

Short of time?

Whatever your objectives, standards or style, you may find you simply do not have the time available to follow all the key study steps for each chapter, however you adapt them for your particular learning style. If this is the case, follow the Skim Study technique below (the icons in the Study Text will help you to do this).

Skim Study technique

Study the chapters in the order you find them in the Study Text. For each chapter, follow the key study steps 1-3, and then skim-read through step 4. Jump to step 11, and then go back to step 5. Follow through steps 7 and 8, and prepare outline answers to questions (steps 9/10). Try the Quick quiz (step 12), following up any items you can't answer, then do a plan for the Question (step 13), comparing it against our answers. You should probably still follow step 6 (note-taking), although you may decide simply to rely on the BPP Passcards for this.

Moving on...

However you study, when you are ready to embark on the practice and revision phase of the BPP Effective Study Package, you should still refer back to this Study Text, both as a source of **reference** (you should find the list of key terms and the index particularly helpful for this) and as a **refresher** (the Chapter roundups and Quick quizzes help you here).

And remember to keep careful hold of this Study Text - you will find it invaluable in your work.

SYLLABUS

The syllabus contains a weighting for each syllabus area, and a ranking of the level of ability required in each topic. The CIMA has published the following explanatory notes on these points.

Study weightings

A percentage weighting is shown against each topic in the syllabus; this is intended as a guide to the amount of study time each topic requires.

All topics in a syllabus must be studied, as a question may examine more than one topic, or carry a higher proportion of marks than the percentage study time suggested.

The weightings do not specify the number of marks which will be allocated to topics in the examination.

Abilities required in the examination

Each examination paper contains a number of topics. Each topic has been given a number to indicate the level of ability required of the candidate.

The numbers range from 1 to 4 and represent the following ability levels:

Appreciation (1)
To understand a knowledge area at an early stage of learning, or outside the core of management accounting, at a level which enables the accountant to communicate and work with other members of the management team.

Knowledge (2)
To have detailed knowledge of such matters as laws, standards, facts and techniques so as to advise at a level appropriate to a management accounting specialist.

Skill (3)
To apply theoretical knowledge, concepts and techniques to the solutions of problems where it is clear what technique has to be used and the information needed is clearly indicated.

Application (4)
To apply knowledge and skills where candidates have to determine from a number of techniques which is the most appropriate and select the information required from a fairly wide range of data, some of which might not be relevant; to exercise professional judgement and to communicate and work with members of the management team and other recipients of financial reports.'

Syllabus aims and content

Aims

To test the candidate's abilities to:

- evaluate the impact of different financial strategies on organisations
- select and evaluate funding choices in different organisations
- evaluate investment decisions
- identify and assess risk, using hedging methods to reduce such risks

Content

		Ability required	Covered in Chapter
13(a)	**Financial strategy formulation** *(study weighting 15%)*		
(i)	Identifying, quantifying and achieving the financial objectives of the organisation: the distinction between long and short term	4	1
(ii)	Objectives of 'not for profit' organisations	3	1
(iii)	Internal constraints to policy formulation and action: funding and gearing	4	1
(iv)	External constraints to policy formulation and action: government legislation, accounting concepts, regulatory bodies, other stakeholders	4	2
(v)	Using both financial and non-financial published information in the formulation of strategy, eg balanced scorecard	4	6, 9, 19
(vi)	Risk analysis and setting out possible contingencies: Simulation, sensitivity analysis, probabilities	4	4
(vii)	Illiquidity and corporate collapse	4	3
(viii)	Profit improvement schemes	3	4
13(b)	**Treasurership** *(study weighting 35%)*		
(i)	The efficient market hypothesis	2	9
(ii)	The operation of securities markets (stock exchanges); the role of merchant banks and other financial institutions	2	8
(iii)	The role of the treasury function	3	5
(iv)	Sources of capital and their advantages and disadvantages: equity, debt, mezzanine, leasing, venture capital, euro-finance	4	5-8, 21
(v)	Cost of capital: equity, debt, weighted average, marginal cost	4	10
(vi)	Capital structure: traditional theory, Modigliani and Miller	4	11
(vii)	Dividend policy: theories and strategies of dividend policy, scrip issues	4	6, 15
(viii)	Working capital management: aggressive/conservative strategies	3	5, 15, 16
(ix)	Cash management: cash forecasts and budgets, cash deficits, cash surpluses, cashflow models	4	17
(x)	Debtors management: factoring and invoice discounting	4	16
(xi)	Interest rate risk management	3	14
13(c)	**Investment decisions** *(study weighting 30%)*		
(i)	Evaluating and reporting on investment decisions: considering tax, inflation, all relevant cash flows, treatment of risk and post audit	4	18-20
(ii)	Evaluating the impact of different sources of finance on an investment decision: leasing, adjusted present value using an adjusted discount rate	4	7, 20
(iii)	Assessing investments as options on future cash flows, including the option to abandon	4	23
(iv)	Single period capital rationing eg use of profitability index	3	19
(v)	Selecting an appropriate discount rate (eg cost of capital) following consideration of project risk	4	4, 10, 20

		Ability required	Covered in Chapter
(vi)	Portfolio theory, the capital asset pricing model and the arbitrage pricing model: uses and limitations	3	12, 13, 20
(vii)	Valuation of businesses for mergers, acquisitions or disposal (eg management buyouts)	4	21
(viii)	Corporate restructuring and its impact on financial statements and financial performance	4	21

13(d) International financial management

(study weighting 20%)

(i)	Theoretical foreign exchange relationships	3	22
(ii)	Risks and methods of reducing risks related to foreign operations: translation, economic, transaction and political risk	4	22
(iii)	Use of hedging techniques to manage foreign exchange movements including derivatives	4	22, 23
(iv)	International capital budgeting and the impact of inflation and fluctuating exchange rates	4	24, 25

CIMA SYLLABUS GUIDANCE NOTES 1999-2000

The following Guidance Notes are published by the CIMA in the August 1999 CIMA Student as an aid to students and lecturers.

'The following guidance notes have been drafted by the Chief Examiner for each of the subjects. They are intended to inform candidates and lecturers about the scope of the syllabus, the emphasis that should be placed on various topics and the approach which the examination papers will adopt.

Most of these guidance notes are applicable immediately, insofar as they provide general guidance on each subject. Guidance specific to changes effective from the May 2000 examination will be applicable from that examination and are detailed at the end of these notes.

The syllabus is concerned with the planning, operating and monitoring of the finance function and with understanding the effect these activities have on the organisation as a whole.

The main objective of financial management is often cited as maximisation of shareholder wealth. However, many of the principles and procedures of financial management are just as relevant to the public sector and not-for-profit organisations (such as charities) as they are to privately owned or listed companies. The scenarios used in examinations may use all forms of organisation, although it is fair to say that the emphasis will be on companies in the private sector, whether small, family-owned businesses or large enterprises with a stock market quotation and widespread share ownership.

In an examination, candidates will be expected to have some recall of subjects studied at earlier Stages. It will be particularly useful for candidates to revise the syllabuses for Cost Accounting and Quantitative Methods (Paper 2) and Economic Environment (Paper 3) at Stage 1 and Business Taxation (Paper 12) at Stage 3. However, it is not expected that candidates should be able to produce detailed calculations of, for example, advance corporation tax liabilities, or calculate standard deviations. They should, however, be able to recall the main principles and purposes of such methods and procedures.

Although the syllabus aims to test for practical applications of financial management, much of it is underpinned by theoretical concepts which need to be studied. The uses and limitations of the theories and the difficulties in linking them to practical aspects of corporate finance should also be understood.

Detailed accounting procedures will not be tested, although candidates are expected to be familiar with the aims and purposes of all extant SSAP and FRSs. In particular, they should know how the contents might affect a company's ability to raise and use funds. These are part of the external constraints on policy formulation.

Financial strategy formulation

Syllabus reference 13 (a)

Study weighting 15%

Questions on this section will typically be asked in conjunction with aspects of one of the other three main syllabus areas. For example, objectives of not-for-profit organisations combined with an investment appraisal; the effect of internal and external constraints on policy formulation in combination with raising new capital; or illiquidity and corporate collapse combined with working capital management.

This section specifically refers to not-for-profit organisations. As noted in the introduction, the basic principles and procedures of financial management are relevant to all types of organisations. However, the objectives may differ as may the detailed activities involved in achieving the objectives. For example, the differences between financial management in the private and public sectors are diminishing as government tries to make the public sector more commercially aware.

The main differences are how the operation is financed, what returns are required and how these returns are measured. These issues could be examined under objectives of not-for-profit organisations in section (a) or under cost of capital in section (b). Similarly, evaluating and reporting on investment decisions, covered in section (c), is not limited to profit making organisations and the principles could be applied to not-for-profit organisations.

Section (e) on the SMM syllabus (corporate social responsibility and professional ethics) links closely to external constraints to policy formulation on the SFM syllabus. In SFM, the focus is likely to be on the issues surrounding the constraints on pursuing the maximisation of shareholder wealth as the sole objective of the firm.

Balanced scorecard is mentioned specifically in the syllabus. However, this subject, or aspects of it, could also feature in other papers, including MAA at Stage 3. The mention of balanced scorecard in SFM is useful for reminding students that financial strategy is not based solely on published and/or financial data.

In the examination, candidates may be required to:

- choose, and calculate, performance indicators to assess efficiency and effectiveness, including traditional measures such as profitability, liquidity etc, given a set of data. The ability to choose and interpret appropriate indicators will be given at least equal weighting with the ability to calculate the ratios correctly;
- understand the limitations of using historical data for forecasting purposes, and how non-financial data can influence forecasts;
- explain the principles of risk analysis, for example how sensitivity analysis and simulation exercises might be used to incorporate risk into an investment appraisal;
- explain how a company might manage a period of illiquidity;
- discuss the uses and limitations of models which can be used to predict corporate collapse, for example Altman's Z score;
- demonstrate some understanding of the issues involved in corporate governance;
- demonstrate an awareness of the Cadbury Report, its purpose and recommendations in outline.

The following items are **not** examinable:

- detailed knowledge of the contents of the Cadbury Report;
- large scale calculations of sensitivities or simulations.

Treasurership

Syllabus reference 13 (b)

Study weighting 35%

This section contains some of the most complex areas of financial management and requires careful study. In the examination, candidates may be required to:

- discuss and evaluate various sources of finance of varying durations, for example:

  Equity. This is the risk, and permanent, capital of a business, ie in balance sheet terms, ordinary share capital and reserves. The difference between book values, market values and nominal values of equity should be fully understood.

  Medium to long-term debt. This type of finance can take many forms, eg convertibles, debts with warrants, 'mezzanine' (which refers to unsecured loans often used in management buyouts), euro-bonds, government grants or assistance, and different types of leasing arrangements.

Venture capital. This is a specialised form of finance provided for new companies, buy-outs and small growth companies which are perceived as carrying above average risk.

- understand the factors which might affect the cost of funds, eg the size of the business under review, a company's existing capital structure or government economic policy;
- demonstrate the ability to match sources of capital to a company's requirements and circumstances;
- demonstrate knowledge of theoretical explanations of capital structure, including Modigliani and Miller's propositions 1, 2 and 3;
- calculate the cost of the various components of capital structure, demonstrating an understanding of the various models available, eg the Dividend Valuation Model, the Earnings Growth Model and the Capital Asset Pricing Model (CAPM). The weaknesses of these models for practical purposes should be understood as well as the arithmetic involved in their calculations;
- demonstrate an understanding of the effect of capital structure on equity beta and the relationship of asset to equity betas, including taxation adjustments;
- demonstrate an understanding of adjusted present value techniques. Formulae for calculating adjusted cost of capital are included in the CIMA Mathematical Tables;
- discuss the role of financial institutions and the regulatory authorities. Knowledge of how these institutions affect the ability of a business to raise and manage funds is required as well as knowledge of how they operate;
- on the subject of interest rate risk management, demonstrate an understanding of the theories of the determination of interest rates and how companies manage the risk;
- discuss dividend policy, demonstrating a working knowledge of the various dividend policies available to a company in practice, including the information content;
- demonstrate an understanding of the principles of Modigliani and Miller's theory of dividend irrelevancy;
- on the subject of working capital management, answer numerical questions as well as provide a discussion of policy issues, eg calculations on cost of credit or cash management;
- demonstrate a knowledge of cash management models and the use of probability in cash and credit management;
- demonstrate an understanding of the forms of the Efficient Markets Hypothesis, its usefulness and limitations. Also an awareness that many aspects of corporate finance theory assume efficient markets for their validity, eg the Capital Asset Pricing Model.

The following items are **not** examinable:

- Miller's theories on the effects of personal taxation on capital structure and the cost of capital;
- the mathematical or graphical proof of Modigliani and Miller's theory of dividend irrelevancy;
- memorised formulae for cash management models. These are provided in CIMA's *Mathematical Tables* and questions will normally simplify the calculations required.

Investment decisions

Syllabus reference 13 (c)

Study weighting 30%

There has been a large amount of empirical research into the use of various methods of investment appraisal over the past fifteen years. Although it is not essential for candidates to be familiar with the results of these studies, familiarity with one or two of the most well-known and widely quoted (eg Richard Pike's work) would be a distinct advantage.

In the examination, candidates may be required to:

- identify the correct variables to include in an investment appraisal, incorporate inflation in the cash flows and adjust for risk;
- understand the use of the CAPM to determine risk-adjusted discount rates;
- understand other methods of risk adjustment such as certainty equivalents;
- understand the advantages and disadvantages of procedures for evaluating capital investment decisions when the company faces a period of capital rationing, including the use of a profitability index, and mathematical programming;
- demonstrate the impact of taxation on the investment decision, for example capital allowances (in the UK);
- understand the need to consider and quantify the social or environmental costs and benefits of an investment where possible;
- understand the principles and practices of project control, continuous evaluation and post-audit;
- understand the uses of limitations and modern portfolio theory (MPT) and the CAPM;
- understand the difference between portfolio theory and the arbitrage pricing model (APM) and how APM could be developed by companies using internal information;
- understand the benefits and limitations of using the share price as a benchmark guide in the valuation of a public listed company;
- understand alternative methods of valuation of different types of businesses and the difficulties involved in their application;
- demonstrate an understanding of the main provisions of the relevant accounting standards that cover the accounting treatment of mergers and acquisitions.

The following items are **not** examinable:

- in the context of linear and integer programming, the formulation of the objective function and the performance of simplex calculations;
- calculations of: betas from raw data; a two-asset portfolio variance; the APM;
- detail on the accounting treatment of mergers and acquisitions.

International financial management

Syllabus reference 13 (d)

Study weighting 20%

In the examination, candidates may be required to:

- demonstrate a good knowledge of foreign exchange arithmetic, eg how to calculate the net cost to a company of using different hedging techniques, as well as an ability to discuss risk management techniques;

- understand what types of foreign exchange risk may affect a company and what methods are available to minimise the risks, eg foreign currency hedging techniques;
- demonstrate a knowledge of both internal and external hedging techniques, and of when and how they might be used;
- demonstrate an understanding of how foreign exchange markets operate and of foreign exchange terminology, eg the meaning of spot and futures markets and the theories of interest rate parity and purchasing power parity;
- understanding the meaning of the term 'derivatives', and the circumstances in which derivatives may be worthwhile, for example the use of options and swaps;
- understand the two methods of applying NPV techniques to international investment appraisal;
- demonstrate a general knowledge of recent events in the economies and financial markets of countries outside the UK: students are encouraged to read appropriate journals such as *The Economist.* Overseas candidates may use their knowledge and experience of their own country and institutions when answering questions which appear to be UK-specific.

The following items are **not** examinable:

- Black and Scholes Option Pricing Model;
- detailed knowledge of the economy and financial institutions of specific foreign countries.

THE EXAM PAPER

Format of the paper

The examination paper will be divided into two sections.

Section A will contain a compulsory case study-type question, normally for 60 marks. This compulsory question will cover a number of syllabus topics from more than one syllabus section. There will typically be four or five parts to the question. It will contain a substantial calculation element worth between 30% and 50% of the marks (ie between 18 and 30 marks) and a report section which requires candidates to provide detailed analysis and commentary on their calculations and on the implications for the organisation which is the subject of the case study.

Calculations not specifically requested in the question are often possible and incorporating appropriate additional ratios etc into the report may earn credit.

Section B will offer a choice of two from four questions, each normally carrying 20 marks. Usually at least one of the questions will require discussion only and will involve *no* calculations.

Time allowed: 3 hours

Analysis of past papers 1995-1999

The analysis below shows the topics which have been examined so far in the *Strategic Financial Management* paper and the CIMA Specimen paper. Throughout the Study Text we highlight topics that have been examined by cross-referencing the date.

May 1999

Section A (60 marks)

1 Working capital policy and calculations; managing exchange risk; currency of invoice

Section B (40 marks)

2 Share valuation methods; takeover bid evaluation
3 Evaluation of two alternative investments including non-financial factors, converting real cash flows to nominal terms
4 Balanced scorecard approach; stakeholder theory
5 NPV and sources of finance for an overseas project

November 1998

Section A (60 marks)

1 High technology company: contract evaluation; exchange and other risks; foreign investment decisions

Section B (40 marks)

2 Interest rate risk; investment of cash surpluses
3 Management of working capital: creditors
4 Financial objectives; role of treasury and financial control departments
5 Cost of capital; capital structure; methods of finance

May 1998

Section A (60 marks)

1 Company flotation: pricing of new issue and effect on shareholders. Raising finance by equity or convertible debt

Section B (40 marks)

2 Hedging and foreign exchange risk. Foreign currency arithmetic: interest rate parity and purchasing power parity
3 Capital investment decision, including inflation, working capital and selection of appropriate discount rate
4 Adjusted present value of an investment; evaluation of leasing; comparison of leasing and long-term debt
5 Costs incurred in periods of financial difficulty; business failure prediction models

November 1997

Section A (60 marks)

1 Plc diversifying by acquisition: evaluation of different options. Methods of valuation; assessment of the offer price; method of financing. Services of a merchant bank and stockbroker

Section B (40 marks)

2 Credit management problems in a small company. Credit control policy in a medium-sized manufacturing company
3 Corporate objectives in the public and private sectors compared; performance measures for the public sector
4 Hedging of foreign exchange risk for an importer/exporter; management of risks in trading with developing countries
5 Review of a portfolio of investments; convertible loan stock: explanations and calculations

May 1997

Section A (60 marks)

1 Case study of a growing small business, covering: problems in raising finance; cash flow and p&l forecasts; report on the company's prospects, its objectives and its methods of financial forecasting

Section B (40 marks)

2 NPV evaluation of a joint venture abroad; exchange rate relationships; currency swaps
3 Dividend policy; share repurchase
4 IRR and NPV methods compared; role of regulators of monopolistic industries
5 Electronic funds transfer; cash management models; application of the Miller-Orr model

November 1996

Section A (60 marks)

1 Case study of a family-owned company in financial difficulties, covering: the role of merchant banks; business valuation; financial controls; profit improvement

Section B (40 marks)

2 Decision to grant credit: evaluation using probabilities
3 Goals of companies; incorporation of environmental costs into investment appraisal
4 Discussion of interest rate swaps, currency swaps and hedging strategies
5 Leasing decision, from lessee's and lessor's viewpoints

May 1996

Section A (60 marks)

1 Case study of an AIM-quoted company, covering: CAPM and alternative methods; appraisal of alternative projects; risk and uncertainty; venture capital compared with other sources of finance.

Section B (40 marks)

2 Use of performance indicators; financial and non-financial factors in success
3 Investments in marketable securities by a company
4 Capital rationing with indivisible projects
5 The interest yield curve; statistical information sources; Monte Carlo simulation; sensitivity analysis

November 1995

Section A (60 marks)

1 Case study of a listed manufacturing company, covering: earnings per share; share and company valuations; alternative capital structures; P/E ratios; effects of directors' share options on decision making

Section B (40 marks)

2 Cash budget; cashflow improvements
3 Role of the financial manager in different types of organisation
4 Responsibilities of and separation of the treasury function
5 Calculation of NPV of a project overseas; methods of financing overseas operations

May 1995

Section A (60 marks)

1 Case study of a high technology company planning to invest in a developing country; the activities of a regulatory authority

Section B (40 marks)

2 Explanations on systematic, unsystematic and total risk, and market efficiency
3 Computations using share valuation methods; dividend policies
4 Valuation of shares in a proposed takeover, taking account of synergy effects
5 Discussions on the use of financial analysis to predict corporate collapse and the valuation of a company as a going concern versus its liquidation value

Specimen Paper

Section A (50 marks)

1 Case study of a business supplying horticultural products and planning to create a new retail subsidiary

Section B (50 marks)

2 Dividend policy of a company; scrip dividends
3 Lease or buy decision of a company
4 Calculations using forward exchange rates; discussions on exchange rate risks
5 Company's selection of marketable securities; comments on: interest rate influences; cash management

Tables and formulae

The CIMA Mathematical Tables for Students include tables and formulae for use in the exam. (See the Appendix in this Study Text.)

THE MEANING OF EXAMINERS' INSTRUCTIONS

The examinations department of the CIMA has asked the Institute's examiners to be precise when drafting questions. In particular, examiners have been asked to use precise instruction words. It will probably help you to know what instruction words may be used, and what they mean. With the Institute's permission, their list of recommended requirement words, and their meaning, is shown below.

Recommended requirement words are:

Advise/recommend	Present information, opinions or recommendations to someone to enable that recipient to take action
Amplify	Expand or enlarge upon the meaning of (a statement or quotation)
Analyse	Determine and explain the constituent parts of
Appraise/assess/evaluate	Judge the importance or value of
Assess	See 'appraise'
Clarify	Explain more clearly the meaning of
Comment (critically)	Explain
Compare (with)	Explain similarities and differences between
Contrast	Place in opposition to bring out difference(s)
Criticise	Present the faults in a theory or policy or opinion
Demonstrate	Show by reasoning the truth of
Describe	Present the details and characteristics of
Discuss	Explain the opposing arguments
Distinguish	Specify the differences between
Evaluate	See 'appraise'
Explain/interpret	Set out in detail the meaning of
Illustrate	Use an example - chart, diagram, graph or figure as appropriate - to explain something
Interpret	See 'explain'
Justify	State adequate grounds for
List (and explain)	Itemise (and detail meaning of)
Prove	Show by testing the accuracy of
Recommend	See 'advise'
Reconcile	Make compatible apparently conflicting statements or theories
Relate	Show connections between separate matters
State	Express
Summarise	State briefly the essential points (dispensing with examples and details)
Tabulate	Set out facts or figures in a table

Requirement words which will be avoided

Examiners have been asked to avoid instructions which are imprecise or which may not specifically elicit an answer. The following words will not be used.

Consider	As candidates could do this without writing a word
Define	In the sense of stating exactly what a thing is, as CIMA wishes to avoid requiring evidence of rote learning
Examine	As this is what the examiner is doing, not the examinee
Enumerate	'List' is preferred
Identify	
Justify	When the requirement is not 'to state adequate grounds for' but 'to state the advantage of'
List	On its own, without an additional requirement such as 'list and explain'
Outline	As its meaning is imprecise. The addition of the word 'briefly' to any of the suggested action words is more satisfactory
Review	
Specify	
Trace	

Part A

Financial strategy formulation

Chapter 1

FINANCIAL OBJECTIVES

Chapter topic list		Syllabus reference	Ability required
1	Objectives of companies	13 a(i), (iii)	Application
2	Stakeholders and objectives	13 a(i), (iv)	Application
3	Objectives of publicly owned and non-commercial bodies	13 a(ii)	Skill
4	Financial management decisions	13 a(iii)	Application

Introduction

In Part A of this Study Text, we are concerned with how **financial objectives** of different types of organisation are identified and formulated; the **constraints** on formulating financial strategy; **non-financial objectives** and non-financial information; and also the analysis of the **performance of organisations**.

Not-for-profit organisations are specifically mentioned in the syllabus. The differences between financial management in private and public sectors are lessening as the government seeks to increase commercial awareness in the public sector.

Exam focus point

The topics in Part A are most likely to be examined along with the syllabus areas covered later in the Study Text, but are no less important because of this.

1 OBJECTIVES OF COMPANIES 5/96, 11/96

Strategic financial management

KEY TERM

Strategic financial management is defined in the *CIMA Official Terminology* (OT) as 'the identification of the possible strategies capable of maximising an organisation's net present value, the allocation of scarce capital resources among the competing opportunities and the implementation and monitoring of the chosen strategy so as to achieve stated objectives'.

1.1 The above definition given indicates that **strategy** depends on stated **objectives** or **targets**. Therefore, an obvious starting point is the identification and formulation of these objectives.

Financial objectives of a company

1.2 The theory of company finance is based on the assumption that **the objective of management is to maximise the market value of the enterprise**. Specifically, the main objective of a company should be to maximise the wealth of its ordinary shareholders.

A company is financed by ordinary shareholders, preference shareholders, loan stock holders and other long-term and short-term creditors. All surplus funds, however, belong to the legal owners of the company, its ordinary shareholders. Any retained profits are undistributed wealth of these equity shareholders.

How are the wealth of shareholders and the value of a company measured?

1.3 If the financial objective of a company is to maximise the value of the company, and in particular the value of its ordinary shares, we need to be able to put values on a company and its shares. How do we do it?

1.4 Three possible methods of valuation of a company might occur to us.

(a) **A balance sheet valuation, with assets valued on a going concern basis**. Certainly, investors will look at a company's balance sheet. If retained profits rise every year, the company will be a profitable one. Balance sheet values are not a measure of 'market value', although retained profits might give some indication of what the company could pay as dividends to shareholders.

(b) **The valuation of a company's assets on a break-up basis**. This method of valuing a business is only of interest when the business is threatened with liquidation, or when its management is thinking about selling off individual assets (rather than a complete business) to raise cash.

(c) **Market values**. The market value is the price at which buyers and sellers will trade stocks and shares in a company. This is the method of valuation which is most relevant to the financial objectives of a company.

(i) When shares are traded on a recognised stock market, such as the Stock Exchange, the market value of a company can be measured by the price at which shares are currently being traded.

(ii) When shares are in a private company, and are not traded on any stock market, there is no easy way to measure their market value. Even so, the financial objective of these companies should be to maximise the wealth of their ordinary shareholders.

1.5 The **wealth of the shareholders** in a company comes from dividends received and the market value of the shares. A **shareholder's return** on investment is obtained in the form of dividends received and capital gains from increases in the market value of his or her shares.

1.6 **Dividends** are generally paid just twice a year (interim and final dividends), whereas a current market value is (for quoted shares) always known from share prices. There is also a theory, supported by empirical evidence and common sense, that market prices are influenced strongly by expectations of what future dividends will be. So we might conclude that the wealth of shareholders in quoted companies can be measured by the market value of the shares.

How is the value of a business increased?

1.7 If a company's shares are **traded on a stock market**, the wealth of shareholders is increased when the share price goes up. Ignoring day-to-day fluctuations in price caused by patterns of supply and demand, and ignoring fluctuations caused by 'environmental' factors such as changes in interest rates, the price of a company's shares will go up when the company makes attractive profits, which it pays out as dividends or re-invests in the business to achieve future profit growth and dividend growth. However, to increase the share price the company should achieve its profits without taking business risks and financial risks which worry shareholders.

1.8 If there is an increase in earnings and dividends, management can hope for an increase in the share price too, so that shareholders benefit from both higher revenue (dividends) and also capital gains (higher share prices).

Management should set **financial targets** for factors which they can influence directly, such as profits and dividend growth. And so a financial objective might be expressed as the aim of increasing profits, earnings per share and dividend per share by, say, 10% a year for each of the next five years.

1.9 Following Financial Reporting Standard (FRS) 3 **earnings** are the profits attributable to equity (that is, to ordinary shareholders) after tax and after extraordinary gains or losses. **Earnings per share** (EPS) are the earnings attributable to each equity share.

1.10 Dividends are the direct reward to shareholders that a company pays out, and so dividends are evidence of a company's ability to provide a return for its shareholders. Companies might therefore set targets for growth in dividend per share.

Other financial targets

1.11 In addition to targets for earnings, EPS, and dividend per share, a company might set **other financial** targets, such as:

(a) a restriction on the company's level of gearing, or debt. For example, a company's management might decide that:

  (i) the ratio of long-term debt capital to equity capital should never exceed, say, 1:1;

  (ii) the cost of interest payments should never be higher than, say, 25% of total profits before interest and tax;

(b) a target for profit retentions. For example, management might set a target that dividend cover (the ratio of distributable profits to dividends actually distributed) should not be less than, say, 2.5 times;

(c) a target for operating profitability. For example, management might set a target for the profit/sales ratio (say, a minimum of 10%) or for a return on capital employed (say, a minimum ROCE of 20%).

1.12 These financial targets are not primary financial objectives, but they can act as **subsidiary targets** or constraints which should help a company to achieve its main financial objective without incurring excessive risks.

Some **recently privatised companies** act within regulatory financial constraints imposed by 'consumer watchdog' bodies set up by government. For example, BT (British Telecom) is overseen by the telecommunications regulator (OFTEL), which restricts price rises to protect consumers.

Short-term and long-term objectives

1.13 Targets such as those mentioned in Paragraph 1.11 are usually measured over a year rather than over the long term, and it is the maximisation of shareholder wealth in the long term that ought to be the corporate objective.

Short-term measures of return can encourage a company to pursue short-term objectives at the expense of long-term ones, for example by deferring new capital investments, or spending only small amounts on research and development and on training.

Multiple financial targets

1.14 A major problem with setting a number of different financial targets, either primary targets or supporting secondary targets, is that they might not all be consistent with each other, and so might not all be achievable at the same time. When this happens, some compromises will have to be accepted.

1.15 EXAMPLE: FINANCIAL OBJECTIVES

Lion Grange Ltd has recently introduced a formal scheme of long range planning. At a meeting called to discuss the first draft plans, the following estimates emerged.

(a) Sales in the current year reached £10,000,000, and forecasts for the next five years are £10,600,000, £11,400,000, £12,400,000, £13,600,000 and £15,000,000.

(b) The ratio of net profit after tax to sales is 10%, and this is expected to continue throughout the planning period.

(c) Net asset turnover, currently 0.8 times, will remain more or less constant.

It was also suggested that:

(a) if profits rise, dividends should rise by at least the same percentage;

(b) an earnings retention rate of 50% should be maintained;

(c) the ratio of long-term borrowing to long-term funds (debt plus equity) is limited (by the market) to 30%, which happens also to be the current gearing level of the company.

Prepare a financial analysis of the draft long range plan and suggested policies for dividends, retained earnings and gearing.

1.16 SOLUTION

The draft financial plan, for profits, dividends, assets required and funding, can be drawn up in a table, as follows.

	Current year	Year 1	Year 2	Year 3	Year 4	Year 5
	£m	£m	£m	£m	£m	£m
Sales	10.0	10.6	11.4	12.4	13.6	15.0
Net profit after tax	1.0	1.06	1.14	1.24	1.36	1.5
Dividends (50% of profit after tax)	0.5	0.53	0.57	0.62	0.68	0.75
Net assets (125% of sales)	12.5	13.25	14.25	15.5	17.0	18.75
Equity (increased by retained earnings)	8.75*	9.28	9.85	10.47	11.15	11.9
Maximum debt (30% of assets)	3.75	3.97	4.27	4.65	5.10	5.62
	12.50	13.25	14.12	15.12	16.25	17.52
Funds available/ (Shortfalls in funds), given maximum gearing of 30% and no new issue of shares = funds available minus net assets required	0	0	(0.13)	(0.38)	(0.75)	(1.23)

* The current year equity figure is a balancing figure, equal to the difference between net assets and long-term debt, which is currently at the maximum level of 30% of net assets.

1.17 These figures show that the financial objectives of the company are not compatible with each other, and adjustments will have to be made.

(a) Given the assumptions about sales, profits, dividends and net assets required, there will be an increasing shortfall of funds from year 2 onwards, unless new shares are issued or the gearing level rises above 30%.

(b) In years 2 and 3, the shortfall can be eliminated by retaining a greater percentage of profits, but this may have a serious adverse effect on the share price. In year 4 and year 5, the shortfall in funds cannot be removed even if dividend payments are reduced to nothing.

(c) The net asset turnover appears to be low. The situation would be eased if investments were able to generate a higher volume of sales, so that fewer fixed assets and less working capital would be required to support the projected level of sales.

(d) If net asset turnover cannot be improved, it may be possible to increase the profit to sales ratio by reducing costs or increasing selling prices.

(e) If a new issue of shares is proposed to make up the shortfall in funds, the amount of funds required must be considered very carefully. Total dividends would have to be increased in order to pay dividends on the new shares. The company seems unable to offer prospects of suitable dividend payments, and so raising new equity might be difficult.

(f) It is conceivable that extra funds could be raised by issuing new debt capital, so that the level of gearing would be over 30%. It is uncertain whether investors would be prepared to lend money so as to increase gearing. If more funds were borrowed, profits after interest and tax would fall so that the share price might also be reduced.

Non-financial objectives 11/98

1.18 A company may have important **non-financial objectives**:

- **The welfare of employees**: trying to provide good wages and salaries, comfortable and safe working conditions, good training and career development, and good pensions
- **The welfare of management**: managers may seek to improve their own circumstances, eg with high salaries, company cars and other perks, even though their decisions will incur expenditure and so reduce profits

- **The welfare of society as a whole**: some managements are aware of the role that their company has to play in providing for the well-being of society, eg oil companies' awareness of their role as providers of energy for society, faced with the problems of protecting the environment and preserving the Earth's dwindling energy resources
- **The provision of a service**: the objectives of some companies include the provision to a particular standard of a service to the public, eg for many privatised utility companies such as British Telecom (BT) and British Gas and the regional electricity distribution companies, the regulatory regime imposed by government specifies certain service standards
- **The fulfilment of responsibilities towards customers and suppliers.**
  - Responsibilities towards customers include providing a product or service of a quality that customers expect, and dealing honestly and fairly with customers.
  - Responsibilities towards suppliers are expressed mainly in terms of trading relationships. A company's size could give it considerable power as a buyer. The company should not use its power unscrupulously.

Other non-financial objectives are **growth, diversification** and **leadership in research and development.**

The relationship between financial and non-financial objectives

1.19 Non-financial objectives do not negate financial objectives, but they do mean that the simple theory of company finance, that the objective of a firm is to maximise the wealth of ordinary shareholders, is too simplistic. Financial objectives may have to be compromised in order to satisfy non-financial objectives.

> *Stage 4 Topic Link.* The *development* of corporate objectives is covered in detail in the BPP Study Text for Paper 14 *Strategic Management Accountancy and Marketing.*

2 STAKEHOLDERS AND OBJECTIVES

Stakeholder groups 5/99

2.1 There is a variety of different groups or individuals whose interests are directly affected by the activities of a firm: the **stakeholders** in the firms:

- Common (equity) shareholders
- Preferred shareholders
- Trade creditors
- Holders of unsecured debt securities
- Holders of secured debt securities
- Intermediate (business) customers
- Final (consumer) customers
- Suppliers
- Employees
- Past employees
- Retirees
- Competitors
- Neighbours
- The immediate community
- The national society
- The world society
- Corporate management
- Organisational strategists
- The chief executive
- The board of directors
- Government
- Special interest groups

(Sharplin, *Strategic management*)

Objectives of stakeholder groups

2.2 The various groups of stakeholders in a firm will have different goals which will depend in part on the particular situation of the enterprise. Some of the more important aspects of these different goals are as follows.

Ordinary (equity) shareholders are the providers of the risk capital of a company and usually their goal will be to maximise the wealth which they have as a result of the ownership of the shares in the company.

Trade creditors have supplied goods or services to the firm. Trade creditors will generally be profit-maximising firms themselves and have the objective of being paid the full amount due by the date agreed. On the other hand, they usually wish to ensure that they continue their trading relationship with the firm and may sometimes be prepared to accept later payment to avoid jeopardising that relationship.

Long-term creditors, which will often be banks, have the objective of receiving payments of interest and capital on the loan by the due date for the repayments. Where the loan is secured on assets of the company, the creditor will be able to appoint a receiver to dispose of the company's assets if the company defaults on the repayments. To avoid the possibility that this may result in a loss to the lender if the assets are not sufficient to cover the loan, the lender will wish to minimise the risk of default and will not wish to lend more than is prudent.

Employees will usually want to maximise their rewards paid to them in salaries and benefits, according to the particular skills and the rewards available in alternative employment. Most employees will also want continuity of employment.

Government has objectives which can be formulated in political terms. Government agencies impinge on the firm's activities in different ways including through taxation of the firm's profits, the provision of grants, health and safety legislation, training initiatives and so on. Government policies will often be related to macroeconomic objectives such as sustained economic growth and high levels of employment.

Management has, like other employees (and managers who are not directors will normally be employees), the objective of maximising their own rewards. It is the duty of the directors and the managers to whom they delegate responsibilities to manage the company for the benefit of shareholders. The objective of reward maximisation might conflict with the exercise of this duty, in ways which will shall examine a little later.

Stakeholder groups and strategy

2.3 The actions of stakeholder groups in pursuit of their various goals can exert influence on strategy. The greater the power of the stakeholder, the greater his influence will be. Johnson and Scholes separate power groups into '**internal coalitions**' and '**external stakeholder groups**'. Internal coalitions will include the marketing department, the finance department, the manufacturing department, the chairman and board of directors and so on. Each internal coalition or external stakeholder group will have different expectations about what it wants, and the expectations of the various groups will conflict. Each group, however, will influence strategic decision-making.

Shareholders and management

2.4 Although ordinary shareholders (equity shareholders) are the owners of the company to whom the board of directors are accountable, the actual powers of shareholders tend to be restricted, except in companies where the shareholders are also the directors.

2.5 The day-to-day running of a company is the responsibility of the management, and although the company's results are submitted for shareholders' approval at the annual general meeting (AGM), there is often apathy and acquiescence in directors' recommendations. AGMs are often very poorly attended.

2.6 Shareholders have no right to inspect the books of account, and their forecasts of future prospects generally need to be gleaned from the annual report and accounts, stockbrokers, investment journals and daily newspapers.

Agency theory and the agency problem

2.7 The relationship between management and shareholders is sometimes referred to as an **agency relationship**, in which managers act as agents for the shareholders, using delegated powers to run the affairs of the company in the shareholders' best interests.

2.8 **Agency theory** (Fama and Jensen) proposes that, although individual members of the business team act in their own self-interest, the well-being of each individual depends on the well-being of other team members and on the performance of the team in competition with other teams. The firm is seen as constituted by contracts among the different factors of production.

2.9 The agency relationship arising from the separation of ownership from management is sometimes characterised as the **agency problem**. For example, if managers hold none or very little of the equity shares of the company they work for, what is to stop them from:

(a) working inefficiently?
(b) not bothering to look for profitable new investment opportunities?
(c) giving themselves high salaries and perks?

2.10 One power that shareholders possess is **the right to remove the directors from office**. But shareholders have to take the initiative to do this, and in many companies, the shareholders lack the energy and organisation to take such a step. Even so, directors will want the company's report and accounts, and the proposed final dividend, to meet with shareholders' approval at the AGM.

2.11 For management below director level, it is the responsibility of the directors to ensure that they perform well. Getting the best out of subordinates is one of the functions of management, and directors should be expected to do it as well as they can.

2.12 Another reason why managers might do their best to improve the financial performance of their company is that managers' pay is often related to the size or profitability of the company. Managers in very big companies, or in very profitable companies, will normally expect to earn higher salaries than managers in smaller or less successful companies.

Goal congruence

2.13 Agency theory sees employees of businesses, including managers, as individuals, each with his or her own objectives. Within a department of a business, there are departmental objectives. If achieving these various objectives leads also to the achievement of the objectives of the organisation as a whole, there is said to be **goal congruence**.

KEY TERM

Goal congruence: accordance between the objectives of agents acting within an organisation and the objectives of the organisation as a whole.

2.14 Goal congruence may be better achieved and the 'agency problem' better dealt with by giving managers some profit-related pay, or by providing incentives which are related to profits or share price, such as:

- pay or bonuses related to the size of profits (**profit-related pay**);
- rewarding managers with shares, eg when a private company 'goes public' and managers are invited to subscribe for shares in the company at an attractive offer price.
- rewarding managers with **share options**. In a share option scheme, selected employees are given a number of share options, each of which gives the holder the right after a certain date to subscribe for shares in the company at a fixed price. The value of an option will increase if the company is successful and its share price goes up. For example, an employee might be given 10,000 options to subscribe for shares in the company at a price of £2.00 per share. If the share price goes up to, say, £5 per share by the time that the exercise date for the options arrives, the employee will be able to profit by £30,000 (by buying £50,000 worth of shares for £20,000).

Stage 4 Topic Link. You will be aware of the different types of management incentive scheme from your studies for Paper 16 *Management Accounting Control Systems*.

2.15 Such measures might encourage management to adopt '**creative accounting**' methods which will distort the reported performance of the company in the service of the managers' own ends. However, creative accounting methods such as off-balance sheet finance present a temptation to management at all times given that they allow a more favourable picture of the state of the company to be presented than otherwise, to shareholders, potential investors, potential lenders and others.

2.16 An alternative approach is to attempt to monitor managers' behaviour, for example by establishing '**management audit**' procedures, to introduce additional reporting requirements, or to seek assurances from managers that shareholders' interests will be foremost in their priorities.

Why should managers bother to know who their shareholders are?

2.17 A company's senior management should remain aware of who its major shareholders are, and it will often help to retain shareholders' support if the chairman or the managing director meets occasionally with the major shareholders, to exchange views.

- The company's management might learn about shareholders' preferences for either high dividends or high retained earnings for profit growth and capital gain.
- For public companies, changes in shareholdings might help to explain recent share price movements.
- The company's management should be able to learn about shareholders' attitudes to both risk and gearing. If a company is planning a new investment, its management

might have to consider the relative merits of seeking equity finance or debt finance, and shareholders' attitudes would be worth knowing about before the decision is taken.

- Management might need to know its shareholders in the event of an unwelcome takeover bid from another company, to identify key shareholders whose views on the takeover bid might be crucial to the final outcome.

2.18 Having a wide range of shareholders has advantages.

- Likelihood of greater activity in the market in the firm's shares, ie greater 'market liquidity'.
- Less likelihood of one shareholder having a controlling interest.
- Since shareholdings are smaller on average, likelihood of less effect on the share price if one shareholder sells his holding.

(d) Greater likelihood of a takeover bid being frustrated.

Question

Before looking at what follows below, see if you can think of some **disadvantages** of a company having a large number of shareholders.

2.19 A large number of shareholders has disadvantages.

- **High administrative costs** eg the costs of sending out copies of the annual report and accounts, counting proxy votes, registering new shareholders and paying dividends.
- The **varying tax rates and objectives** of shareholder clientele groups, which make a dividend/retention policy more difficult for the management to decide upon.

Shareholder value analysis

2.20 **Shareholder value analysis** (SVA) was developed during the 1980s from the work of Rappaport and focuses on value creation using the net present value (NPV) approach. Thus, SVA assumes that the value of a business is the net present value of its future cash flows, discounted at the appropriate cost of capital. Many leading companies (including, for example, Pepsi, Quaker and Disney) have used SVA as a way of linking management strategy and decisions to the creation of value for shareholders.

KEY TERM

Shareholder value analysis. An approach to financial management which focuses on the creation of economic value for shareholders, as measured by share price performance and flow of dividends (OT).

2.21 SVA takes the following approach.

- Key decisions with implications for cash flow and risk are specified. These may be **strategic, operational, related to investment** or **financial**.
- **Value drivers** are identified as the factors having the greatest impact on shareholder value, and management attention is focused on the decisions which influence the value drivers. Value drivers include:

- sales growth and margin
- working capital and fixed capital investment
- the cost of capital

2.22 SVA may help managers to concentrate on activities which create value rather than on short-term profitability. A problem with the approach is that of specifying a terminal value at the end of the planning horizon, which will extend for perhaps five or ten years.

Shareholders, managers and the company's long-term creditors

2.23 The relationship between **long-term creditors** of a company, the **management** and the **shareholders** of a company encompasses the following factors.

(a) Management may decide to raise finance for a company by taking out long-term or medium term loans. They might well be taking risky investment decisions using outsiders' money to finance them.

(b) Investors who provide debt finance will rely on the company's management to generate enough net cash inflows to make interest payments on time, and eventually to repay loans.

However, long-term creditors will often take security for their loan, perhaps in the form of a fixed charge over an asset (such as a mortgage on a building). Debentures are also often subject to certain restrictive covenants, which restrict the company's rights to borrow more money until the debentures have been repaid.

If a company is unable to pay what it owes its creditors, the creditors may decide:

(i) to exercise their security; or
(ii) to apply for the company to be wound up.

(c) The money that is provided by long-term creditors will be invested to earn profits, and the profits (in excess of what is needed to pay interest on the borrowing) will provide extra dividends or retained profits for the shareholders of the company. In other words, shareholders will expect to increase their wealth using creditors' money.

3 OBJECTIVES OF PUBLICLY OWNED AND NON-COMMERCIAL BODIES 11/97

Nationalised industries

3.1 The framework of financial management in **state-owned** (or **nationalised**) **industries** consists of:

(a) strategic objectives;
(b) rules about investment plans and their appraisal;
(c) corporate plans, targets and aims;
(d) external financing limits.

Following the privatisation programme of the 1980s and early 1990s, the UK's nationalised industries are much fewer in number than they were. The largest nationalised industries remaining is the Post Office. Some other countries, however, have much more extensive state ownership of industries.

3.2 Nationalised industries are generally financed by government loans, and some borrowing from the capital markets. They do not have equity capital, and there is no stock exchange to give a day-by-day valuation of the business. The financial objective cannot be to maximise the wealth of its owners, the government or the general public, because this is not a concept which can be applied in practice. Nevertheless, there will be a financial objective, to contribute in a certain way to the national economy, possibly according to the political views of the government.

- There may be an objective to earn enough profits for the industry to provide for a certain proportion of its investment needs from its own resources.
- A very profitable state-owned industry may be expected to transfer surplus funds to the government.

3.3 Even so, the principal objective of a nationalised industry will in most cases not be a financial one at all. Financial objectives will be subordinated to a number of political and social considerations.

(a) A nationalised industry may be expected to provide a **certain standard of service** to all customers, regardless of the fact that some individuals will receive a service at a charge well below its cost. For example, the postal service must deliver letters to remote locations at standard prices.

(b) The need to provide a service may be of such overriding social and political importance that the government is prepared to **subsidise** the industry. There is a strong body of opinion, for example, which argues that public transport is a social necessity and a certain level of service must be provided, with losses made up by government subsidies.

3.4 Nationalised industries in the UK are generally expected to aim at a **rate of return** (before interest and tax) on their new investment programmes of **5% in real terms**. Such a target is applied so that the industries do not divert resources away from those areas where they could be used to best effect.

3.5 **Financial targets** vary from industry to industry, depending on how profitable or unprofitable it is expected to be. For profitable industries, the financial target has so far been set in terms of achieving a target real rate of return, generally of 5%. The return is measured as a current cost operating profit on the net replacement cost of assets employed.

3.6 **Performance aims** back up the financial targets, and may be expressed in terms of target cost reductions or efficiency improvements. Achieving cost reduction through efficiency improvements has been a prime target of nationalised industries in the UK in recent years. The Post Office, for example, has in the past had a target to reduce real unit costs in its mail business and in its counters business.

3.7 **External financing limits (EFLs)** control the flow of finance to and from nationalised industries. They set a limit on the amount of finance the industry can obtain from the government, and in the case of very profitable industries, they set requirements for the net repayment of finance to the government.

Not-for-profit organisations

3.8 Some organisations are set up with a prime objective which is not related to making profits. Charities and government organisations are examples. These organisations exist to pursue **non-financial aims**, such as providing a service to the community. However, there will be **financial constraints** which limit what any such organisation can do.

(a) A not-for-profit organisation needs finance to pay for its operations, and the major financial constraint is the amount of funds that it can obtain.

(b) Having obtained funds, a not-for-profit organisation should seek to use the funds:

(i) economically: not spending £2 when the same thing can be bought for £1;
(ii) efficiently: getting the best use out of what money is spent on;
(iii) effectively: spending funds so as to achieve the organisation's objectives.

3.9 The nature of financial objectives in a not-for-profit organisation can be explained in more detail, using government organisations in the UK as an illustration.

Government departments

3.10 Financial management in **government departments** is different from financial management in an industrial or commercial company for some fairly obvious reasons.

(a) Government departments do not operate to make a profit, and the objectives of a department or of a programme of spending cannot be expressed in terms of maximising the return on capital employed.

(b) Government services are provided without the commercial pressure of competition. There are no competitive reasons for controlling costs, being efficient or, when services are charged for (such as medical prescriptions), keeping prices down.

(c) Government departments have full-time professional civil servants as their managers, but decisions are also taken by politicians.

(d) The government gets its money for spending from taxes, other sources of income and borrowing (such as issuing gilts) and the nature of its fund-raising differs substantially from fund-raising by companies.

3.11 Since managing government is different from managing a company, a different framework is needed for planning and control. This is achieved by:

(a) setting objectives for each department;
(b) careful planning of public expenditure proposals;
(c) emphasis on getting value for money.

3.12 A development in recent years has been the creation of agencies to carry out specific functions (such as vehicle licensing). These **executive agencies** are answerable to the government for providing a certain level of service, but are independently managed on business principles.

4 FINANCIAL MANAGEMENT DECISIONS 11/95, 11/98

4.1 **Maximising the wealth of shareholders** generally implies maximising profits consistent with long-term stability. It is often found that short-term gains must be sacrificed in the interests of the company's long-term prospects. In the context of this overall objective of financial management, there are three main types of decisions facing financial managers: **investment decisions, financing decisions** and **dividend decisions**.

In practice, these three areas are interconnected and should not be viewed in isolation.

Investment decisions

4.2 Investment decisions involve committing funds to:

(a) **internal investment projects** (and withdrawing from such projects should they turn out to be unprofitable);

(b) **external investment decisions**, involving the takeover of another company or a merger;

(c) **disinvestment decisions**, involving selling a part of the business, such as an unwanted subsidiary company.

Financing decisions

4.3 The assets of a company must be financed by share capital and reserves, long-term liabilities or short-term liabilities. When a company is growing, it will need additional finance from one or more of these sources.

4.4 The financial manager must know:

(a) where additional funds can be obtained and at what cost;
(b) the effect on a company's profitability and value of using any particular source of funds;
(c) the effect on financial risk of using any particular source of funds.

4.5 A company ought to be profitable, but it must be 'liquid' too, so that it always has access to enough cash to pay creditors and employees. Financing decisions therefore include cash management.

The opportunity cost of finance

4.6 Financial management is concerned with obtaining funds for investment, and investing those funds profitably so as to maximise the value of the firm. It is not enough to invest at a profit; it is necessary to invest so that the profits are sufficient to pay lenders a satisfactory amount of interest. If a company cannot pay interest at the market rate demanded by lenders, the lenders will prefer to invest elsewhere on the capital market, where they can get this rate. There is a market **opportunity cost of funds** which a company must expect to pay for new finance.

4.7 Similarly, if a company cannot make big enough profits, shareholders will be dissatisfied. The company will not be able to raise funds from new issues of shares, because investors will not be attracted. Existing shareholders who wish to sell their shares will find that buyers, who can invest in whatever securities they choose, will offer a comparatively low price, and the market price of the shares will be depressed. Since investors have a wide range of shares available to them, there is a market opportunity cost of equity.

Dividend decisions

4.8 Ordinary shareholders expect to earn dividends, and the value of a company's shares will be related to the amount of dividends that a company has been paying, and also to prospects for future dividends.

4.9 **Dividend decisions** are also directly related to financing decisions, since retained profits are the most important source of new funds for companies. What a company pays as dividends out of profits cannot be retained in the business to finance future growth, and profits retained represent a withholding of dividends.

Financial management and control

4.10 Financial management can be defined as the management of the finances of an organisation in order to achieve the financial objectives of the organisation. This involves **financial control** as well as **financial planning**.

4.11 The financial control function is concerned with monitoring performance to determine the extent to which the various activities of the organisation are meeting their financial objectives. This involves the use of existing budgets, actual results and financial forecasts to evaluate performance.

4.12 The financial control department is therefore mainly concerned with investment policy, although it may also deal with financing policy in evaluating the way in which funds are being raised and used, and the relative costs of finance. The direct input of this department to **policy determination** is relatively low, but it does make an important contribution to the **achievement of policy**. Good financial control will mean that mistakes may be made once, but not repeated; that investments that are not achieving their objectives are identified and action taken to remedy the situation; and that forthcoming problems are identified quickly and dealt with appropriately.

Chapter roundup

- This chapter has set the scene for the study of strategic financial management. We have identified the **objectives of companies and other organisations**, and we will now go on to study both the **financial resources available** to achieve these objectives and the methods for doing so.
- We have also set out the **types of decision** a financial manager has to make, in seeking to attain the financial objectives of the organisation or enterprise.

Quick quiz

1 On what management objective is the theory of company finance primarily based? (see para 1.2)

2 What non-financial objectives might a company have? (1.18)

3 List six types of stakeholder group. (2.1)

4 What is meant by the agency relationship? (2.7)

5 What are the main elements in the relationship between a company and its long-term creditors? (2.23)

6 What might be the objectives of a publicly owned (nationalised) industry? (3.3, 3.4)

7 Investment decisions can be grouped into three categories. What are they? (4.1)

8 What does opportunity cost of finance mean? (4.6, 4.7)

Question to try	Level	Marks	Time
1	Introductory	n/a	20 mins

Chapter 2

EXTERNAL CONSTRAINTS

Chapter topic list		Syllabus reference	Ability required
1	Government and regulatory constraints	13 a(iv)	Application
2	Economic influences	13 a(iv)	Application
3	Published information	13 a(v)	Application

Introduction

We now examine the range of **external factors** which may influence the formulation of financial strategy.

It is important to see how changes or differences in these factors may influence strategy. For example, a **change in government legislation** may open up (or close up) opportunities. In seeking **investment opportunities in other countries**, the particular external factors which operate there will need to be considered.

Exam focus point

The topic of external constraints to policy formulation links to section (e) of the Paper 14 SMM syllabus, which deals with corporate social responsibility and professional ethics. The Examiner has indicated that in SFM, the focus is likely to be on constraints to maximisation of shareholder wealth.

1 GOVERNMENT AND REGULATORY CONSTRAINTS 5/95

The influence of government

1.1 The government does not have a direct interest in companies (except for those in which it actually holds shares). However, the government does often have a strong indirect interest in companies' affairs.

(a) **Taxation.** The government raises taxes on sales and profits and on shareholders' dividends. It also expects companies to act as tax collectors for income tax and VAT. The tax structure might influence investors' preferences for either dividends or capital growth.

(b) **Encouraging new investments.** The government might provide funds towards the cost of some investment projects. It might also encourage private investment by offering tax incentives.

(c) **Encouraging a wider spread of share ownership.** In the UK, the government has made some attempts to encourage more private individuals to become company shareholders, by means of attractive privatisation issues (such as in the electricity, gas and telecommunications industries) and tax incentives, such as ISAs (individual savings accounts), to encourage individuals to invest in shares.

(d) **Legislation.** The government also influences companies, and the relationships between shareholders, creditors, management, employees and the general public, through legislation, including the Companies Acts, legislation on employment, health and safety regulations, legislation on consumer protection and consumer rights and environmental legislation.

(e) **Economic policy.** A government's economic policy will affect business activity. For example, exchange rate policy will have implications for the revenues of exporting firms and for the purchase costs of importing firms. Policies on economic growth, inflation, employment, interest rates and so on are all relevant to business activities.

The encouragement of free market forces

1.2 Throughout the industrialised world, governments have tried to stimulate their economies by giving **encouragement to free market forces** through:

(a) greater liberalisation of markets, by removing regulations and legislative restrictions on them (deregulation);

(b) a reduction in the role of the government in industry and commerce;

(c) a simplified tax system, which encourages firms to take commercial decisions which are not influenced by tax advantages or disadvantages;

(d) the privatisation of state-owned assets (such as British Gas, British Telecom and the electricity industry in the UK);

(e) opening up state-controlled activities to competition from private firms;

(f) encouraging competition, by a judicious regulation of monopolies and mergers, and by giving encouragement to small firms;

(g) the removal or reduction of import restrictions, to open up domestic markets to greater foreign competition.

Financial reporting and accounting concepts

1.3 As you will be aware, limited companies and their directors are bound by the provisions of the Companies Act 1985 (CA 1985). This legislation governs the preparation and publication of the annual financial statements of companies.

1.4 The form and content of a company's accounts are regulated primarily by CA 1985, but must also comply with the accounting standards published by the Accounting Standards Board (ASB) - called FRSs (financial reporting standards) - and by the Accounting Standards Committee, which the ASB has now replaced.

1.5 The shorter term financial objectives of companies include targets for profitability. The measurement of profit under historical cost accounting follows the principles of the generally accepted fundamental accounting concepts (going concern, accruals, consistency and prudence) set out in the accounting standard SSAP 2. Although profits do matter, they are not the best measure of a company's achievements.

(a) Accounting profits are not the same as 'economic' profits. Accounting profits can be manipulated to some extent by choices of accounting policies.

Question 1

Can you give three examples of how accounting profits might be so manipulated?

Answer

Here are some examples you might have chosen.

(i) Provisions, such as provisions for depreciation or anticipated losses
(ii) The capitalisation of various expenses, such as development costs
(iii) Adding overhead costs to stock valuations

(b) A company might make an accounting profit without having used its resources in the most profitable way possible. There is a difference between the accounting concept of 'historical cost' and the economic concept of 'opportunity cost', which is the value that could have been obtained by using resources in their most profitable alternative way.

(c) Profits on their own take no account of the volume of investment that it has taken to earn the profit. Profits must be related to the volume of investment to have any real meaning. Hence measures of financial achievement include:

(i) accounting return on capital employed;

(ii) earnings per share;

(iii) yields on investment, for example dividend yield as a percentage of stock market value.

(d) Profits are reported every year (with half-year interim results for quoted companies). They are measures of **short-term** performance, whereas a company's performance should ideally be judged over a longer term.

Corporate governance and the Cadbury Report

1.6 Issues of **corporate governance** in the UK have been addressed recently in the report of the Cadbury Committee, which was formed in 1991. The terms of reference of the committee were to consider, along with any other relevant matters, the following issues:

(a) the responsibilities of executive and non-executive directors for reviewing and reporting on performance to shareholders and other financially interested parties; and the frequency, clarity and form in which information should be provided;

(b) the case for audit committees of the board, including their composition and role;

(c) the principal responsibilities of auditors and the extent and value of the audit;

(d) the links between shareholders, boards, and auditors.

1.7 The **Cadbury Report** defines corporate governance as '**the system by which companies are directed and controlled.**' The roles of those concerned with the financial statements are described.

(a) The **directors** are responsible for the corporate governance of the company.

(b) The **shareholders** are linked to the directors via the financial reporting system.

(c) The **auditors** provide the shareholders with an external objective check on the directors' financial statements.

(d) Other concerned **users**, particularly employees (to whom the directors owe some responsibility) are indirectly addressed by the financial statements.

1.8 The Cadbury Committee was set up because of the lack of confidence which was perceived in financial reporting and in the ability of auditors to provide the assurances required by the users of financial statements. The main difficulties were considered to be in the relationship between auditors and boards of directors. In particular, the commercial pressures on both directors and auditors caused pressure to be brought to bear on auditors by the board and the auditors often capitulated. Problems were also perceived in the ability of the board of directors to control their organisations. These problems have been debated for some time, but recent company collapses, often sudden and unexpected, intensified the worries of regulating bodies, the Stock Exchange and the government. The lack of board accountability in many of these company collapses intensified the perceived need for action.

1.9 The committee aims to set out the responsibilities of each group involved in the reporting process and to make recommendations on good practice.

Code of Best Practice

1.10 The **Code of Best Practice** included in the Cadbury Report is aimed at the directors of all UK public companies, but the directors of all companies are encouraged to use the Code for guidance. Pressure should be brought by all the relevant parties on the directors to ensure compliance with the Code. In particular, institutional investors will have a lot of power to influence the directors. Directors should state in the annual report and accounts whether they comply with the Code and give reasons for any non-compliance. Some of the key points in the Code are summarised in the following paragraphs.

The board of directors

1.11 The board must meet on a regular basis, retain full control over the company and monitor the executive management. A clearly accepted division of responsibilities is necessary at the head of the company, so no one person has complete power, answerable to no-one. (Compare this to the Robert Maxwell situation.) The report thus encourages the separation of the posts of chairman and chief executive.

Non-executive directors

1.12 The following points are made about **non-executive directors**, who are those directors not running the day to day operations of the company.

(a) They should bring independent judgement to bear on important issues, including key appointments and standards of conduct.

(b) There should be no business, financial or other connection between the non-executive directors and the company, apart from fees and shareholdings.

(c) Fees should reflect the time they spend on the business of the company, so extra duties could earn extra pay.

(d) They should not take part in share option schemes and their service should not be pensionable, to maintain their independent status.

(e) Appointments should be for a specified term and reappointment should not be automatic. The board as a whole should decide on their nomination and selection.

(f) Procedures should exist whereby non-executive directors may take independent advice, at the company's expense if necessary.

Executive directors

1.13 In relation to the directors who run companies on a day to day basis, the main points in the Code relate to service contracts (contracts of employment) and pay. The length of such contracts should be three years at most, unless the shareholders approve a longer contract. A remuneration committee of non-executive directors should decide on the level of executive pay.

The audit committee

1.14 A major recommendation in the Code is that all listed companies must establish effective **audit committees** if they have not already done so. The Code takes its example from countries such as Canada and the USA where audit committees for listed companies are compulsory.

1.15 The audit committees should have formal terms of reference dealing with their membership, authority and duties. They should meet at least three times every year and membership of the committee should be shown in the annual report.

The Greenbury Report

1.16 The controversy surrounding the pay of directors and managers in the former utilities - the 'fat cat' debate, led to the government appointing the **Greenbury Committee** to look at the issues involved and make various recommendations. The main recommendations, which went further than Cadbury, are as follows and compliance has been made a Stock Exchange listing requirement.

(a) The **remuneration committee** (already part of the Cadbury Code) should consist entirely of non-executive directors 'with no personal financial interest other than as shareholders in the matter to be decided' and no potential conflict of interest from cross-directorships.

(b) There should be an annual report to shareholders, which should be approved by the shareholders in annual general meeting.

1.17 Greenbury has also extended the Cadbury disclosure of directors' remuneration to 'full transparency' giving full details of each director's pay package. Non-mandatory recommendations included the following.

(a) Sensitivity to the wider pay scene, particularly within the company.

(b) Bonuses should be partly in shares/options:

(i) which should be held for a significant period (at least three years);
(ii) which should have challenging performance criteria attached; and
(iii) where options are not issued at a discount.

(c) The length of directors' contracts should be reduced to a year or less to avoid large pay-offs.

The method of disclosing directors' pension entitlements still needs to be decided. There is some discussion of whether the disclosure requirements ought to be incorporated into any future revision of company law.

Question 2

If you were on the main board of a large plc, would you be very happy about the **Greenbury** proposals?

1.18 There is a variety of problems to be faced with these recommendations, including the difficulty of assessing executive remuneration in what is acknowledged to be an imperfect market for executive skills. As well as assessing this market, the remuneration committee would have to consider:

(a) the differentials at management/director level (difficult with many layers of management);

(b) the ability of managers to leave, taking clients and knowledge to a competitor or their own new business;

(c) individual performance and additional work/effort;

(d) the company's overall performance.

The problem here, particularly with (c) and (d), is that it places the non-executive directors of the remuneration committee in charge of the executive directors, ie it goes further than simply providing 'transparency' as regards executive pay.

1.19 In view of scandals in other areas, it has been suggested that the **Greenbury** proposals should be extended to all types of quango and also to charities, building societies etc.

The Hampel Report

1.20 The **Hampel Committee on Corporate Governance** produced a final report in January 1998. The committee followed up matters raised in the Cadbury and Greenbury reports, aiming to restrict the regulatory burden on companies and substituting principles for detail whenever possible. The introduction to the report also states that whilst the Cadbury and Greenbury reports concentrated on the prevention of abuses, Hampel was equally concerned with the positive contribution good corporate governance can make.

1.21 Hampel proposed combining the various best practices, principles and codes of **Cadbury, Greenbury and Hampel** into one single '**supercode**'. The London Stock Exchange has now issued a combined corporate governance code, which was derived from the recommendations of the Cadbury, Greenbury and Hampel reports. In June 1998 the Stock Exchange Listing Rules were amended to make compliance with the new code obligatory for listed companies for **accounting period ending after 31 December 1998.**

1.22 The introduction to the report points out that the **primary duty of directors is to shareholders**, to enhance the value of shareholders' investment over time. Relationships with other stakeholders are important, but making the directors responsible to other stakeholders would mean there was no clear yardstick for judging directors' performance.

1.23 The Hampel Committee is also against treating the corporate governance codes as sets of prescriptive rules, and judging companies by whether they have complied. The report states that there can be guidelines which will normally be appropriate but the differing circumstances of companies mean that sometimes there are valid reasons for exceptions. The major recommendations of the report were as follows.

Directors

1.24 **Executive** and **non-executive directors** should continue to have the same duties under the law. New directors should be properly trained. The majority of non-executive directors should be independent, and boards should disclose in the annual report which of the non-executive directors are considered to be independent. Non-executive directors should comprise at least one third of the membership of the board. The roles of chairman and chief executive should generally be separate. Whether or not the roles of chairman and chief executive are combined, a senior non-executive director should be identified. All directors should submit themselves for **re-election** at least once every three years. Boards should assess the **performance** of individual directors and collective board performance.

Directors' remuneration

1.25 Boards should establish a **remuneration committee**, made up of independent non-executive directors, to develop policy on remuneration and devise remuneration packages for individual executive directors. Remuneration committees should use their judgement in devising schemes appropriate for the specific circumstances of the company. Total rewards from such schemes should not be excessive. Boards should try and reduce directors' contract periods to one year or less, but this cannot be achieved immediately. The accounts should include a general statement on remuneration policy, but this should not be the subject of an AGM vote.

Shareholders and the AGM

1.26 Companies should consider providing a business presentation at the **AGM**, with a question and answer session. Shareholders should be able to vote separately on each substantially separate issue; and that the practice of 'bundling' unrelated proposals in a single resolution should cease. The number of proxy votes for or against a resolution should be announced after votes on a show of hands. Companies should propose a resolution at the AGM relating to the report and accounts. Notice of the AGM and related papers should be sent to shareholders at least 20 working days before the meeting.

Accountability and audit

1.27 Each company should establish an **audit committee** of at least three non-executive directors, at least two of them independent. The audit committee should keep under review the overall financial relationship between the company and its auditors, to ensure a balance between the maintenance of objectivity and value for money. Directors should report on **internal control,** but should not be required to report on effectiveness of controls. Auditors should report privately on internal controls to directors. Directors should maintain and review controls relating to all relevant control objectives, and not merely financial controls. Companies which do not already have a separate internal audit function should consider the need for one.

Reporting

1.28 The accounts should contain a **statement** of how the company applies the corporate governance principles, and should **explain their policies**, including any circumstances justifying departure from best practice.

Criticisms of the Hampel report

1.29 Some commentators have criticised the Hampel report for stating that the debate on accountability has obscured the first responsibility of a board, to enhance the prosperity of a company over time. Critics have argued that accountability and prosperity should be seen as compatible. In addition, Hampel has been criticised for dropping the requirement for the board to report publicly on the effectiveness of internal controls and for the auditors to report publicly on the statement made by the board.

1.30 The government is contemplating certain **statutory changes** to reinforce the work of the corporate governance committees, but will otherwise leave the approach of **voluntary compliance** alone for now. However Margaret Beckett, the Trade and Industry Secretary, has stated that there should be an emphasis on **growth, investment, accountability** and **transparency.**

Regulation of markets

5/97

1.31 An important role of the government is the **regulation of private markets** where these fail to bring about an efficient use of resources. As you should be aware from your earlier studies in economics, **market failure** is said to occur when the market mechanism fails to result in economic efficiency, and therefore the outcome is sub-optimal. In response to the existence of market failure, and as an alternative to taxation and public provision of production, the state often resorts to regulating economic activity in a variety of ways. Of the various forms of market failure, the following are the cases where regulation of markets can often be the most appropriate policy response.

(a) **Imperfect competition** - where monopoly power is leading to inefficiency, the state will intervene through controls on, say, prices or profits in order to try to reduce the effects of the monopoly.

(b) **Externalities** - a possible means of dealing with the problem of external costs and benefits is via some form of regulation. Regulations might include, for example, controls on emissions of pollutants, restrictions on car use in urban areas, the banning of smoking in public buildings, compulsory car insurance and compulsory education.

(c) **Imperfect information** - regulation is often the best form of government action whenever informational inadequacies are undermining the efficient operation of private markets. This is particularly so when consumer choice is being distorted. Examples here would include legally enforced product quality/safety standards, consumer protection legislation, the provision of job centres and other means of improving information flows in the labour market and so on.

(d) **Equity** - the government may also resort to regulation to improve social justice. For example, legislation to prevent racial and/or sexual discrimination in the labour market; regulation to ensure equal access to goods such as health care, education and housing; minimum wage regulations and equal pay legislation.

Rôles of regulatory bodies

1.32 Regulation can be defined as any form of state interference with the operation of the free market. This could involve regulating demand, supply, price, profit, quantity, quality, entry, exit, information, technology, or any other aspect of production and consumption in the market.

Where privatisation has perpetuated natural monopolies, in the UK the regulatory authorities specific to each industry such as OFTEL (telecommunications), OFGAS (gas) and OFWAT (water), have the role of ensuring that consumers' interests are not subordinated to those of other stakeholders, such as employees, shareholders and tax authorities. The regulator's role is generally 'advisory' rather than statutory, and may extend only to a part of a company's business, necessitating a correct allocation of costs across different activities of the company.

1.33 The two main methods used to regulate monopoly industries are as follows.

(a) **Price control**: the regulator agreeing the output prices with the industry. Typically, the price is progressively reduced in real terms each year by setting price increases at a rate below that of inflation as measured by the Retail Prices Index (RPI). This has been used with success by regulators in the UK but can be confrontational.

(b) **Profit control**: the regulator agreeing the maximum profit which the industry can make. A typical method is to fix maximum profit at x% of capital employed, but this does not provide any incentive to making more efficient use of assets: the higher the capital employed, the higher the profit.

1.34 In addition the regulator will be concerned with:

(a) actively promoting competition by encouraging new firms in the industry and preventing unreasonable barriers to entry;

(b) addressing quality and safety issues and considering the social implications of service provision and pricing.

Self-regulation

1.35 In many areas, the participants may decide to maintain a system of voluntary self-regulation, possibly in order to try to avert the imposition of government controls. Areas where self-regulation often exists are the professions (eg the Law Society, the British Medical Association and other professional bodies), and financial markets (eg the Council of the Stock Exchange, the Take-over Panel and the Securities and Investments Board).

Costs of regulation

1.36 The potential costs of regulation include the following.

(a) **Enforcement costs** - regulation can, manifestly, only be effective if it is properly monitored and enforced. Direct costs of enforcement include the setting up and running of the regulatory agencies - employing specialist staff, monitoring behaviour, prosecuting offenders (or otherwise ensuring actions are modified in line with regulations). Indirect costs are those incurred by the regulated (eg the firms in the industry) in conforming to the restrictions.

(b) **Regulatory capture** refers to the process by which the regulator becomes dominated and controlled by the regulated firms, such that it acts increasingly in the latter's interests, rather than those of consumers. This is a phenomenon which has been observed in the USA (where economic regulation has always been more widespread).

(c) **Unintended consequences of regulation.** An example is the so-called 'Aversch-Johnson effect'. This refers to the tendency of rate-of-return (profit) regulation to encourage firms to become too capital-intensive. In other words, firms regulated in this way (which is a common method of economic regulation in the USA) have an incentive to choose a method of production which is not least-cost, because it involves too high a ratio of capital to labour.

Deregulation

1.37 **Deregulation** is, in general, the opposite of regulation. Deregulation can be defined as the removal or weakening of any form of statutory (or voluntary) regulation of free market activity. Deregulation allows free market forces more scope to determine the outcome. There was a shift in policy in the 1980s in the UK and in the USA towards greater deregulation of markets, in the belief that this would improve efficiency. Indeed, many politicians and commentators believed that it was state over-regulation of British industry that was largely responsible for Britain's comparatively uncompetitive and inefficient performance. Whether or not this was, or remains, true is an open question.

1.38 As with the appraisal of regulation, a rational assessment of a deregulatory measure or a programme of such measures should weigh up the potential **social** benefits against the **social** costs. If there will be a net gain to society, we can say that the deregulation should proceed. It would be simplistic to contend that **all** regulation is detrimental to the economy. As we have seen, where there is a clear case of market failure, then state regulation may be the most appropriate way of achieving a more socially efficient or equitable outcome.

1.39 More competition is however not always desirable and in some industries it could have certain disadvantages, including the following.

(a) **Loss of economies of scale.** If increased competition means that each firm produces less output on a smaller scale, unit costs will be higher. Liberalising a 'natural monopoly', for instance, is undesirable, and often not feasible.

(b) **Lower quality or quantity of service.** The need to reduce costs may lead firms to reduce quality or eliminate unprofitable but socially valuable services.

2 ECONOMIC INFLUENCES

Aggregate demand and inflation

2.1 **Aggregate demand** is the total expenditure in a national economy on goods and services. A growth in aggregate demand can have either or both of the following consequences.

(a) Firms will produce more to meet the demand. These firms could be either domestic firms or foreign suppliers.

(b) Firms will be unable to produce more to meet the demand, because of capacity limitations, and so prices will go up because of the strength of demand.

2.2 The rate of **price inflation** in the economy is important because it affects:

(a) costs of production and selling prices;

(b) interest rates;

(c) foreign exchange rates;

(d) demand in the economy. High rates of inflation seem to put a brake on real economic growth.

2.3 Companies faced with higher costs of production and higher interest rates will try to pass on their extra costs to customers by raising their selling prices. Some companies will be able

to raise prices more easily than others, depending on the nature of demand in the industry's markets.

Expectations of inflation and the effects of inflation

2.4 When managers evaluate a particular project, or when shareholders evaluate their investments, they can only guess at what the rate of inflation is going to be. Their expectations will probably be wrong, at least to some extent, because it is extremely difficult to forecast the rate of inflation accurately. The only way in which uncertainty about inflation can be allowed for in project evaluation is by risk and uncertainty analysis.

2.5 Inflation affects **asset values, costs and revenues** in the following ways.

(a) Since fixed assets and stocks will increase in money value, the same quantities of assets must be financed by increasing amounts of capital.

(i) If the future rate of inflation can be predicted, management can work out how much extra finance the company will need, and take steps to obtain it (for example by increasing retentions of earnings, or borrowing).

(ii) If the future rate of inflation cannot be predicted with accuracy, management should guess at what it will be and plan to obtain extra finance accordingly. However, plans should also be made to obtain 'contingency funds' if the rate of inflation exceeds expectations. For example, a higher bank overdraft facility might be negotiated, or a provisional arrangement made with a bank for a loan.

(b) Inflation means higher costs and higher selling prices. The effect of higher prices on demand is not necessarily easy to predict. A company that raises its prices by 10% because the general rate of inflation is running at 10% might suffer a serious fall in demand.

Interest rates

2.6 **Interest rates** are an important element in the economic environment, and are of particular relevance for financial managers. Under the rules introduced by the new UK Labour Government in 1997, short-term interest rates are set by the Bank of England, the central bank, to be consistent with the inflation target set by the Government.

(a) Interest rates measure the cost of borrowing. If a company wants to raise money, it must pay interest on its borrowing, and the rate of interest payable will be one which is 'current' at the time the borrowing takes place. When interest rates go up, companies will pay more interest on some of their borrowing (for example on bank overdrafts).

(b) Interest rates in a country influence the foreign exchange value of the country's currency.

(c) Interest rates act as a guide to the sort of return that a company's shareholders might want, and changes in market interest rates will affect share prices.

2.7 The interest rates in the UK financial markets which are most commonly quoted are as follows.

(a) The clearing banks' **base rates.** Banks will lend money to small companies and individual customers at certain margins above their base rate, which acts as a reference point. The base rate is set independently by each clearing bank, although in practice, an increase in the base rate of one bank will be followed by similar changes by other banks.

(b) The **inter-bank lending rate** on the London inter-bank money market. This interest rate is referred to as **LIBOR**, short for the London Inter-Bank Offered Rate. For large loans to big companies, banks will set interest rates at a margin above LIBOR rather than at a margin above base rate.

(c) The **Treasury bill rate**. This is the rate at which the Bank of England sells Treasury bills to the money market. It is an average rate, since institutions tender for bills and tender prices vary.

(d) The **yield on long-dated gilt-edged securities** (20 years to maturity). Gilt-edged securities are securities issued by the government.

2.8 There are many other different interest rates you might see quoted, for example:

(a) the yield on bank deposit accounts or building society accounts;

(b) the bank overdraft rate for personal customers;

(c) various money market rates, such as the yield on deposits with discount houses, the rate of discount on bank bills or 'fine' trade bills, the yield on sterling certificates of deposit, and the yield on local authority deposits;

(d) the rate of discount offered by the Bank of England for its purchase of different types of eligible bills from the discount market.

2.9 There are several reasons why interest rates differ in **different markets** and **market segments.**

(a) **Risk**. Higher risk borrowers must pay higher rates on their borrowing, to compensate lenders for the greater risk involved.

(b) **The need to make a profit on re-lending**. Financial intermediaries make their profits from re-lending at a higher rate of interest than the cost of their borrowing.

(c) **The duration of the lending**. Normally, long-term loans will earn a higher yield than short-term loans. The reasons for this term structure of interest rates are discussed later.

(d) **The size of the loan**. Deposits above a certain amount with a bank or building society might attract higher rates of interest than smaller deposits.

(e) **International interest rates**. The level of interest rates varies from country to country. The reasons for these variations are:

(i) differing rates of inflation from country to country;

(ii) government policies on interest rates and foreign currency exchange rates.

(f) **Different types of financial asset**. Different types of financial asset attract different rates of interest. This is largely because of the competition for deposits between different types of financial institution.

The term structure of interest rates: the yield curve 5/96

2.10 Suppose that an investor decides to buy some government securities (gilts). Since the securities represent borrowing by the government, it might seem reasonable to expect that the nominal rate of interest paid would be the same, no matter what the type of security.

2.11 Obviously, this is not the case. One reason why this is so is that the government borrows by issuing new securities from time to time, and the rate of interest offered on a new issue of securities will depend on conditions in the market at the time. This will explain why the nominal interest rate on new gilt-edged securities might be 12% on one occasion, 10% on another and 8% on another.

2.12 There is another important reason why interest rates on the same type of financial asset might vary. This is that interest rates depend on the term to maturity of the asset. For example, Treasury Stock might be short-dated, medium-dated, or long-dated. The **term structure of interest rates** refers to the way in which the yield on a security varies according to the term of the borrowing, that is the length of time until the debt will be repaid as shown by the **yield curve**. Normally, the longer the term of an asset to maturity, the higher the rate of interest paid on the asset.

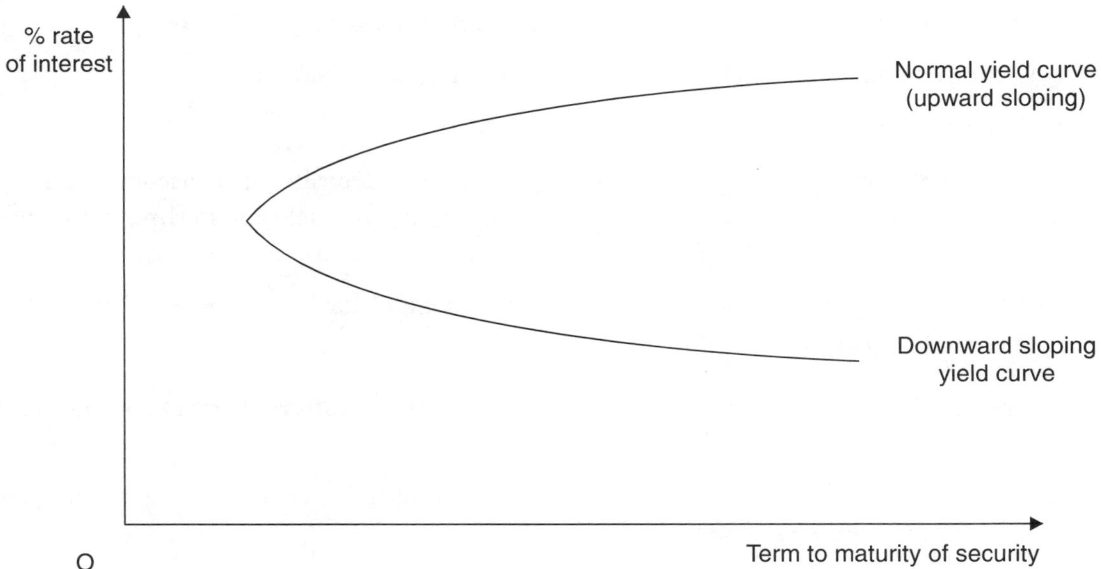

Yield curves

2.13 The reasons why, in theory, the yield curve will normally be upward sloping, so that long-term financial assets offer a higher yield than short-term assets, are as follows.

(a) The investor must be compensated for tying up his money in the asset for a longer period of time. In other words, if the government were to make two issues of 9% Treasury Stock on the same date, one with a term of five years and one with a term of 20 years (and if there were no expectations of changes in interest rates in the future) then the **liquidity preference** of investors would make them prefer the five year stock.

The only way to overcome the liquidity preference of investors is to compensate them for the loss of liquidity; in other words, to offer a higher rate of interest on longer dated stock.

(b) There is a greater risk in lending long-term than in lending short-term. To compensate investors for this risk, they might require a higher yield on longer dated investments.

2.14 So why might a yield curve slope downwards, with short-term rates higher than longer term rates?

(a) **Expectations** about the way that interest rates will move in the future also affects the term structure of interest rates. When interest rates are expected to fall, short-term rates might be higher than long-term rates, and the yield curve would be downward sloping. Thus, the shape of the yield curve gives an indication to the financial manager about how interest rates are expected to move in the future.

(b) **Government policy** on interest rates might be significant too. In the UK, government influence over interest rates is directed mainly towards short-term interest rates. A policy of keeping interest rates relatively high might therefore have the effect of forcing short-term interest rates higher than long-term rates.

(c) The **market segmentation theory** of interest rates suggests that the slope of the yield curve will reflect conditions in different segments of the market. This theory holds that the major investors are confined to a particular segment of the market and will not switch segment even if the forecast of likely future interests rates changes. For instance, banks, building societies and general insurance companies invest mainly at the 'short end' of the market (with short periods to maturity) while life assurance and pension funds invest mainly at the 'long end'. Although there may be some truth in this theory, the fact that the shape of the yield curve is used in practice to predict interest rate movements suggests that expectations of future interest rates must also have some significant influence on the slope of the yield curve.

Nominal rates and real rates of interest

2.15 **Nominal rates of interest** are the actual rates of interest paid. **Real rates of interest** are rates of interest adjusted for the rate of inflation. The real rate is therefore a measure of the increase in the real wealth, expressed in terms of buying power, of the investor or lender.

(a) The real rate of interest, with rates expressed as decimals, is:

$$\frac{1 + \text{nominal rate of interest}}{1 + \text{rate of inflation}} - 1$$

If the nominal rate of interest is 12% and the rate of inflation is 8%, the real rate of interest would be 1.12/1.08 – 1 = 0.037 = 3.7%.

(b) The real rate of interest is sometimes estimated (for arithmetical simplicity) as the difference between the nominal rate of interest and the rate of inflation. In our example, this would be 12% – 8% = 4%.

2.16 The real rate of interest will usually be positive, although when the rate of inflation is very high, the real rate of interest might become negative (the rate of inflation exceeding the nominal interest rate). Nominal rates of interest will tend to rise when the rate of inflation increases, because lenders will want to earn a real return and will therefore want nominal rates to exceed the inflation rate.

Interest rates, inflation and capital gains or losses

2.17 A positive real rate of interest adds to an investor's real wealth from the income he earns from his investments. However, when interest rates go up or down, perhaps due to a rise or fall in the rate of inflation, there will also be a potential capital loss or gain for the investor. In other words, the market value of interest-bearing securities will alter. Market values will fall when interest rates go up.

2.18 For example, when the Government issues long-term gilts at a coupon interest rate of, say, 10% and the market rate of interest is also 10%, the market value of the securities will be £100 per £100 face value of the stock (or '£100 per cent').

(a) Now if nominal interest rates in the market subsequently rise to, say, 14% the re-sale value of the gilts will fall to:

$$£100 \times \frac{10\%}{14\%} = £71.43 \text{ per £100 face value of the stock.}$$

An investor in the gilts will make a capital loss of £28.57 per cent (plus selling costs) if he decides to sell the securities.

(b) If nominal interest rates subsequently fall to, say, 8%, the re-sale value of the gilts will rise to:

$$£100 \times \frac{10\%}{8\%} = £125 \text{ per cent.}$$

An investor could then sell his asset for a capital gain of £25 per cent (less selling costs).

Interest rates and share prices

2.19 When interest rates change, the return expected by investors from shares will also change. For example, if interest rates fell from 14% to 12% on government securities, and from 15% to 13% on company debentures, the return expected from shares (dividends and capital growth) would also fall. This is because shares and debt are alternative ways of investing money. If interest rates fall, shares become more attractive to buy. As demand for shares increases, their prices rise too, and so the dividend return gained from them falls in percentage terms.

2.20 The fundamental theory of shares values is explained elsewhere in this Study Text. Basically, however, it is predicted that if a shareholder expects a 15% return on his investment in equities, and the annual dividend on one of his shares is 21p, then the market value of the share should be 21p/15% = £1.40 (ignoring any prospect of capital growth).

However, if interest rates fell, the shareholder would probably be satisfied with a lower return from his shares, say 14%, and the price of a share offering an annual dividend of 21p should then rise to 21p/14% = £1.50.

Equally, if interest rates went up, the shareholder would probably want a higher return from his shares, and share prices would fall. If, in our example, the investor wanted a 16% return, the predicted share price would fall to 21p/16% = £1.31.

Changes in interest rates and financing decisions

2.21 Interest rates are important for financial decisions by companies.

(a) **When interest rates are low**, it might be financially prudent:

- (i) to borrow more, preferably at a fixed rate of interest, and so increase the company's gearing;
- (ii) to borrow for long periods rather than for short periods;
- (iii) to pay back loans which incur a high interest rate, if it is within the company's power to do so, and take out new loans at a lower interest rate.

(b) **When interest rates are higher:**

- (i) a company might decide to reduce the amount of its debt finance, and to substitute equity finance, such as retained earnings;
- (ii) a company which has a large surplus of cash and liquid funds to invest might switch some of its short-term investments out of equities and into interest-bearing securities;
- (iii) a company might opt to raise new finance by borrowing short-term funds and debt at a variable interest rate (for example on overdraft) rather than long-term

funds at fixed rates of interest, in the hope that interest rates will soon come down again.

Interest rates and new capital investments

2.22 When interest rates go up, and so the cost of finance to a company goes up, the minimum return that a company will require on its own new capital investments will go up too. Some new capital projects might be in the pipeline, with purchase contracts already signed with suppliers, and so there will often be a time lag before higher interest rates result in fewer new investments.

2.23 A company's management should give close consideration, when interest rates are high, to keeping investments in assets, particularly unwanted or inefficient fixed assets, stocks and debtors, down to a minimum, in order to reduce the company's need to borrow.

Exchange rates

2.24 An **exchange rate** is the rate at which money in one currency can be exchanged for money in another currency. Exchange rates between different currencies on the world's foreign exchange markets are continually changing, and often by large amounts.

2.25 Foreign exchange rates are important for a business and its financial management because they affect:

(a) the cost of imports;
(b) the value of exports;
(c) the costs and benefits of international borrowing and lending.

2.26 Changes in the value of sterling will affect the cost of goods from abroad. For example, if a consignment of goods is shipped from the USA to the UK, and the invoice price is US$420,000:

(a) if the sterling-dollar exchange rate is £1 = $1.75, the cost of the imports would be £240,000;

(b) if sterling fell in value to £1 = $1.50, the cost of the imports would be higher, at £280,000.

2.27 Changes in the value of sterling affect buying costs for everyone in the UK, companies and households alike, because a large proportion of the raw materials, components and finished goods that we consume is imported.

2.28 Exchange rates affect **exporting companies**, for similar reasons, because changes in exchange rates affect the price of exported goods to foreign buyers.

(a) When sterling goes up in value, goods sold abroad by a UK exporter, and invoiced in sterling, will cost more to the foreign buyer (who must purchase sterling with his own currency in order to pay).

(b) When sterling falls in value, goods sold abroad by a UK exporter and invoiced in sterling will become cheaper to foreign buyers.

To the extent that demand is influenced by price, the demand for exports will therefore vary with changes in the exchange rate.

Exchange rate policies

2.29 Governments may choose to let currencies fluctuate completely freely (a 'free float'), or they can attempt to regulate the values of their national currencies. Under a system of **fixed or semi-fixed exchange rates**, a government acts to ensure that its currency keeps its value. This may be accomplished by market operations, or by legislation forbidding transactions at other than the official rate.

2.30 Under **managed floating**, a government will buy or sell its currency to prevent sharp fluctuations in its value, but will set no particular limits to the currency's value.

Exchange rate policies: the view of business

2.31 Businesses want both certainty and an exchange rate which will make them competitive. Fixed exchange rates offer the greatest certainty, followed by a managed float. However, rigidity of exchange rates can rapidly damage the competitiveness of exporting businesses in a country. While importers might benefit in the short term from fixed exchange rates if domestic inflation remained comparatively high, they could in the longer term find that foreign currency was simply not available.

International capital investments

2.32 Exchange rates can affect **international capital investments** significantly. Suppose that a UK company issues some shares. What is the likelihood that overseas investors will buy some of the shares? Obviously, prospects for capital growth and dividends will influence the investors' decision, but prospects of changes in the value of sterling will be important too. A 20% increase in the market value of UK company shares is worthless to a US investor if in the same period of time the value of sterling falls by a corresponding amount against the dollar, leaving no capital gain in dollars.

2.33 When a UK company wishes to finance operations overseas, there may be advantages in borrowing in the same currency as an investment. Assets and liabilities in the same currency can be 'matched' with one another, thus avoiding exchange losses on conversion in the group's annual accounts. Revenues in the foreign currency can be used to repay borrowings in the same currency, thus eliminating losses due to fluctuating exchange rates.

The Treasury economic model

2.34 The Treasury first developed an economic forecasting model in the late 1940s, and this came to be used by government as an aid to demand management policies. The forecasts are now published in the Financial Statement and Budget Report which accompanies the Budget. The model is run on desk-top computers and is used to simulate how a set of policy actions such as interest rate changes affect variables such as consumer spending or job vacancies. It consists of over 1,000 mathematical equations linking variables such as unemployment, the rate of inflation and the budget deficit.

2.35 A significant problem with constructing an economic forecast is that of making estimates of economic output (GDP) for the period from the last known figures to the month in which the forecast is made. For example, for a forecast prepared in February, only the GDP figures up to the previous September are known. The GDP estimate for the intervening period must be estimated from various indicators, including exports, imports, retail sales, industrial production and employment. Difficulties arise when these indicators give conflicting messages.

2.36 Once the base period figures have been established, the part of the forecast relating to the future can be built up. This task is assisted by the existence of a number of forward indicators which provide information on the prospects in particular sectors of the economy. For example, the Department of Trade and Industry compiles figures based on enquiries to businesses asking for estimates of percentage changes in expected investment. The Confederation of British Industry (CBI) also makes enquiries about its members' investment intentions. Figures for new orders received, wage settlements and government expenditure forecasts are also incorporated into the model. These various forms of data provide a fairly direct means of forecasting for the forthcoming 6 to 12 months. For the longer term, the Treasury's integrated econometric model must be employed.

2.37 The main product of the Treasury model is a detailed table of Gross Domestic Product (GDP) and its components, given on a quarterly basis for a period of two to three years.

2.38 An article published in the *Financial Times* in May 1993 drew attention to some of the problems involved in modelling the economy.

> 'Dozens, if not hundreds, of models are used worldwide to simulate activities in specific economies. They differ from each other largely in the way their equations link up variables and how easy they are to use.'

The performance of the UK economy itself acts as a **control** upon the validity of the model.

> 'The Treasury model has entered the spotlight partly because of the inadequacies of the Treasury's recent forecasts, which in common with many private-sector projections failed to spot either the 1986-88 boom or the seriousness of the recession before it was too late.
>
> Although the model can hardly take the full blame for the poor predictions - other important factors include the judgements made by Treasury economists and the political "spin" imparted to projections - by ministers - Treasury officials conceded the software in the model has not been kept sufficiently up to date.'

2.39 The Treasury publishes average errors for its calendar year forecasts; for example, these showed a mean absolute error of 1% for GDP for the ten year period to 1988. The errors in the forecasts for component expenditures tend to be greater than for the GDP itself.

2.40 The Treasury model is in a state of constant revision, and there must necessarily be some room left for judgement, for example when events of which the model does not take account, such as strikes and fuel shortages, occur.

3 PUBLISHED INFORMATION 5/96

3.1 Published sources provide financial and non-financial data which, in the process of formulating financial strategy, can supplement the information that management obtains from internal sources or from trade contacts.

Exam focus point

You should be broadly aware of the information sources outlined in this section, but you do not need to learn them in detail.

3.2 Planning and decision-making rely on accurate and complete information. Financial managers often rely on externally provided information systems as the source of much current information about other companies (which might be targets for takeover bids), certain markets (such as commodity and foreign exchange markets), share prices, or business and economic matters.

3.3 There are various sources of environmental data.

(a) Newspapers and periodicals contain relevant environmental information.

(b) Sometimes more detailed country information is needed than that supplied by the press. Export consultants might specialise in dealing with particular countries, and so can be a valuable source of information.

(c) Trade journals might give information about a wide variety of relevant issues to a particular industry. Trade associations, also, are good at spreading news.

(d) The government is a source of statistical data relating to the economy and society. Also, the government can be a source of specific advice to businesses. The Business in Europe programme of the DTI includes the following.

  (i) Single European Market information.
  (ii) Advice on overcoming trade barriers.
  (iii) Information on individual markets and opportunities.
  (iv) Expertise from private sector advisors.
  (v) Where to get further advice.
  (vi) A telephone hotline.

(e) Sources of technological information include the Patent Office, trade journals and universities.

(f) A firm's sales and marketing staff are aware of competitive data.

(g) Various databases can be accessed (see below).

3.4 Some companies specialise in providing an external 'electronic reference library' or **on-line information retrieval system** (OLIRS) to make this information available to subscribers. This is an externally supplied database. Subscribers can gain access to the supplier's information from a terminal in their office and pay a fee for access to the data.

A number of firms provide on line information systems on commercial and tax matters, such as Datastream, Data-Star, Extel and Butterworths. Reuters provides an OLIRS about money market interest rates and foreign exchange rates to firms involved in money and foreign exchange markets, and to the treasury departments of a large number of companies.

3.5 Large volumes of information are available through **databases held by public bodies**. Some newspapers offer computerised access to old editions, with search facilities looking for information on particular companies or issues. FT PROFILE, for example, provides on-line business information. Public databases are also available for inspection.

3.6 An example of a public database is *Spearhead*, run by the Department for Trade and Industry (DTI). This is an on-line database of information relating to the single European market programme of the European Union (EU).

3.7 The **government** provides a wealth of **statistical information**, which often provides the best indicators of the economic environment within which businesses must operate.

Question 3

Interpret the following indices of output, obtained from published government statistics.

Standard Industrial Classification	*19X1*	*19X2*	*19X3*	*19X4*	*19X5*	*19X6*	*19X7*	*19X8*	*19X9*
Rubber products	107.8	111.4	113.8	113.1	100.0	86.4	79.2	81.3	79.1
Processing of plastics	95.2	102.3	106.5	110.6	100.0	94.7	99.0	110.1	121.0

(Source: Annual Abstract of Statistics)

Answer

These figures show that over the decade the plastics processing industry had expanded strongly, with a temporary setback in the years 19X5-19X7. In contrast, the rubber products industry fell into serious recession in 19X5-19X7 and by 19X9 had failed to recover. These figures would have implications for firms planning investment in these industries.

Price indices

3.8 Statistics about **prices** are presented in the form of price indices, including the following.

(a) **General Index of Retail Prices or Retail Prices Index (RPI).** This measures monthly changes in retail prices of goods and services bought by UK households. Separate indices are published for groups, and sub-groups of goods and services;

(b) **Tax and Price Index (TPI).** This index measures the change in gross taxable income needed to compensate taxpayers for any increase in retail prices, taking into account both changes in retail prices and also changes in individuals' liability to income tax and National Insurance contributions;

(c) **Producer price indices.** Index numbers are calculated for:

(i) groups of commodities;

(1) produced in the UK;
(2) imported into the UK;

(ii) materials purchased by certain sectors of industry;

(iii) output of certain sectors of industry.

3.9 (a) If the Retail Prices Index is rising, a company's own costs may be rising at a comparable rate, and we should expect:

(i) the workforce to demand wage increases that are at least in line with increases in the RPI;

(ii) unit costs of output to rise;

(iii) interest rates to be somewhat higher than the rate of increase in the RPI;

(iv) that a company will have some scope for putting up its own prices in line with increases in the RPI, without provoking adverse customer reaction.

(b) Sometimes, increases in a specific producer price index or commodity price index might help to explain a company's particular problems. For example, if a company uses timber as a major raw material, and the price index for timber rises at an exceptionally high rate, the company will expect:

(i) the rate of inflation in its own industry to be particularly high;

(ii) unit costs to rise substantially, so that selling prices have to be raised by a large amount too;

(iii) customer demand to fall in response to exceptionally high price increases.

Interest rates and yields on securities

3.10 Statistics on interest rates and other security yields are available from a variety of sources, not just the government. The *Financial Times* provides daily information on dividend yields and interest rates, for example, but the best historical record of interest rates and yields is probably provided in the *Bank of England Quarterly Bulletin*. The most important statistics are also published in the government's monthly Financial Statistics booklet.

Exchange rates

3.11 The main government sources of **exchange rate statistics** are the monthly Financial Statistics and the Bank of England Quarterly Bulletin. Exchange rates are also published daily in the Financial Times. Exchange rates between currencies are continually changing. Statistics are available giving monthly closing 'spot' and 'three month forward' rates. There is also a sterling index, which expresses the value of sterling against a basket of other currencies.

Balance of payments statistics

3.12 UK balance of payments statistics, which cover transactions between the UK and the rest of the world, are published annually in a booklet called 'The United Kingdom Balance of Payments', also called the 'Pink Book'. Monthly information is also available in Financial Statistics, the Monthly Digest of Statistics and Economic Trends.

3.13 Information that is available includes:

(a) trade in goods (formerly called 'visible trade'):

   (i) UK exports, analysed by sections and divisions;
   (ii) UK imports, analysed by sections and divisions;
   (iii) the surplus or deficit on trade in goods (the balance of trade);

(b) trade in services (formerly called invisible trade);

(c) investment income (interest, profits and dividends);

(d) transfers (by individuals and governments);

(e) capital transactions;

(f) official financing, that is, the use of the government's 'official reserves'.

(Items (a) to (d) make up what is called the current account of the balance of payments, although the term 'current account' is soon to be dropped. Capital transactions and movements in the official reserves are shown as net transactions in external assets and liabilities).

3.14 For trade in goods, there are also published indices for:

(a) the volume of exports;
(b) the volume of imports;
(c) the unit value of exports;
(d) the unit value of imports.

3.15 Monthly statistics for the UK's balance of trade are monitored closely by the Stock Exchange, because of the possible implications for:

(a) the state of the UK economy;

(b) the value of sterling;

(c) interest rates.

Sources of published statistics

3.16 Here is a summary list of some of the important sources of published statistics.

(a) **Government sources**

(i) The *Monthly Digest of Statistics* is a collection of various statistics from all government departments.

(ii) *Financial Statistics* is a monthly series of financial statistics, many supplied by the Bank of England.

(iii) The *Annual Abstract of Statistics* is similar to the *Monthly Digest*, except published annually and containing more statistics.

(iv) *Business Monitors* are produced for each industry every quarter (sometimes monthly) and includes statistics on sales figures, production, exports and imports.

(v) *Overseas Trade Statistics* is published monthly. There is also the annual 'Pink Book' on the UK balance of payments which was mentioned above.

(b) **Non-government sources**

(i) The London Business School, which produces regular economic reports.

(ii) Stockbroking companies, which provide regular financial forecasting services, with particular emphasis on investment-related topics.

(iii) The National Institute of Economic and Social Research, the Confederation of British Industry (CBI) and other bodies, which produce occasional reports.

(iv) Daily newspapers, such as the Financial Times; also weekly and monthly specialist magazines.

(v) Banks, which can provide customers with some business information, particularly about economic conditions and customers in overseas countries.

(vi) Occasional reports of trade associations or local Chambers of Commerce.

Exam focus point

As with Chapter 1, topics in Chapter 2 may well feature in questions in conjunction with topics from the rest of the syllabus.

Chapter roundup

- This chapter has covered the environment within which businesses must operate. **Environmental factors** can be very significant for businesses, but are outside their control.
- The environment can **change** unexpectedly, with serious consequences for many businesses. It is therefore essential both to allow for such possible changes when making plans and to monitor the relevant economic statistics, so that changes can be anticipated as far as possible and responded to with minimal disruption.
- The **Cadbury Report** has clarified many of the contentious issues of corporate governance and sets standards of best practice in relation to financial reporting and accountability, while the **Greenbury Code** has made recommendations on directors' pay. The **Hampel Report** has reviewed the Cadbury and Greenbury recommendations.

Quick quiz

1 Give reasons why profitability is not the best measure of a company's achievements. (see para 1.5)

2 What were the main recommendations of the Hampel report? (1.24 - 1.28)

3 What broadly is the role of an industry regulatory authority in a monopoly industry? (1.32-1.34)

4 What is the 'yield curve'? (2.12)

5 How are interest rates likely to affect share prices? (2.19, 2.20)

6 How do changes in exchange rates affect the price of exported goods to foreign buyers? (2.28)

7 Why are price indices significant for businesses? (3.9)

Question to try	Level	Marks	Time
2	Introductory	n/a	25 mins

Chapter 3

ANALYSIS OF FINANCIAL PERFORMANCE

Chapter topic list		Syllabus reference	Ability required
1	Ratio analysis	13 a(v)	Application
2	Comparisons of accounting figures	13 a(v)	Application
3	Predicting business failure	13 a(vii)	Application
4	Other information from companies' accounts	13 a(v)	Application
5	The balanced scorecard approach	13 a(v)	Application

Introduction

The purpose of this chapter is to look at how **accounting reports** and **other items of information** should be interpreted so as to assess a **company's financial position**.

You will already be familiar with from **ratio analysis** from Paper 5 and Paper 9.

The syllabus makes specific mention of the **balanced scorecard** approach.

1 RATIO ANALYSIS

5/96

1.1 As part of the system of financial control in an organisation, it will be necessary to have ways of measuring the progress of the enterprise and of individual subsidiaries, so that managers know how well the company concerned is doing. The financial situation of a company will also obviously affect its share price. Is the company profitable? Is it growing? Does it have satisfactory liquidity? Is its gearing level acceptable? What is its dividend policy?

1.2 The answers to some of these questions can be obtained from accounting reports produced by the company. The usual way of interpreting accounting reports is to calculate and then to analyse certain ratios (**ratio analysis**).

Stage 4 Topic Link. The technique of ratio analysis is also relevant to Paper 14 and, particularly in the context of control of divisions of an enterprise, to Paper 16.

Broad categories of ratios

1.3 Ratios can be grouped into the following four categories:

(a) profitability and return;
(b) debt and gearing;

(c) liquidity: control of cash and other working capital items;
(d) shareholders' investment ratios (or 'stock market ratios').

Within each heading we will identify a number of standard measures or ratios that are normally calculated and generally accepted as meaningful indicators. It must be stressed however that each individual business must be considered separately, and a ratio that is meaningful for a manufacturing company may be completely meaningless for a financial institution. Also, ratios need to be compared over a number of periods if the analysis is to be of value.

Try not to be too mechanical when working out ratios, and constantly think about what you are trying to achieve.

1.4 The Du Pont system of ratio analysis involves constructing a pyramid of interrelated ratios like that below.

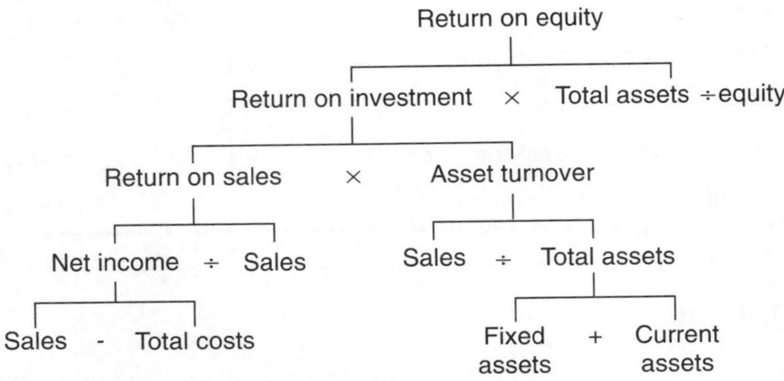

Such **ratio pyramids** help in providing for an overall management plan to achieve profitability, and allow the interrelationships between ratios to be checked.

1.5 The key to obtaining meaningful information from ratio analysis is **comparison**: comparing ratios over time within the same business to establish whether the business is improving or declining, and comparing ratios between similar businesses to see whether the company you are analysing is better or worse than average within its own business sector.

1.6 Ratio analysis on its own is not sufficient for interpreting company accounts, and there are other items of information which should be looked at. These include the following.

(a) Comments in the Chairman's report and the directors' report.

(b) The age and nature of the company's assets.

(c) Current and future developments in the company's markets, at home and overseas.

(d) Recent acquisitions or disposals of a subsidiary by the company.

(e) The cash flow statement (where required by FRS 1).

(f) Other features of the report and accounts, such as post balance sheet events, contingent liabilities, a qualified auditors' report, the company's taxation position, and so on.

Profitability

1.7 A company ought of course to be profitable, and obvious checks on **profitability** are:

(a) whether the company has made a profit or a loss on its ordinary activities;
(b) by how much this year's profit or loss is bigger or smaller than last year's profit or loss.

It is probably better to consider separately the profits or losses on extraordinary items if there are any. An extraordinary gain would obviously be a good bonus and an extraordinary loss might cause concern. However, such gains or losses should not be expected to occur again, unlike profits or losses on normal trading.

1.8 **Profit on ordinary activities before taxation** is generally thought to be a better figure to use than profit after taxation, because there might be unusual variations in the tax charge from year to year which would not affect the underlying profitability of the company's operations.

1.9 Another profit figure that should be calculated is **PBIT**: profit before interest and tax. This is the amount of profit which the company earned before having to pay interest to the providers of loan capital. By providers of loan capital, we usually mean longer term loan capital, such as debentures and medium-term bank loans, which will be shown in the balance sheet as 'Creditors: amounts falling due after more than one year.' This figure is of particular importance to bankers and lenders.

1.10 Profit before interest and tax is therefore:

(a) the profit on ordinary activities before taxation; **plus**
(b) interest charges on long term loan capital.

1.11 To calculate PBIT, in theory, all we have to do is to look at the interest payments in the relevant note to the accounts. Do not take the net interest figure in the profit and loss account itself, because this represents interest payments less interest received, and PBIT is profit including interest received but before interest payments.

1.12 The note to the accounts on interest charges, unfortunately, does not give us the exact figure we want, and we have to take the most suitable figure available. Company law requires companies to show the amount of interest in respect of:

(a) bank loans and bank overdrafts, and other loans which are repayable within five years;
(b) loans repayable by instalments (for example finance leases) beyond five years;
(c) all other loans (for example long-term debentures).

1.13 The interest cost we want is (c) plus (b) and probably a part of (a) (for interest on loans repayable within one to five years which are 'Creditors: amounts falling due after more than one year'). Unless a company gives clear details of its interest costs, it is probably simplest to approximate the interest for PBIT as the total of (a), (b) and (c).

Profitability and return: the return on capital employed (ROCE)

1.14 It is impossible to assess profits or profit growth properly without relating them to the amount of funds (the capital) employed in making the profits. An important profitability ratio is therefore **return on capital employed (ROCE)**, which states the profit as a percentage of the amount of capital employed.

1.15 Profit is usually taken as PBIT, and capital employed is shareholders' capital plus long-term liabilities and debt capital. This is the same as total assets less current liabilities. The underlying principle is that we must compare like with like, and so if capital means share capital and reserves plus long-term liabilities and debt capital, profit must mean the profit earned by all this capital together. This is PBIT, since interest is the return for loan capital.

$$\text{Thus ROCE} = \frac{\text{Profit on ordinary activities before interest and taxation BPBIT)}}{\text{Capital employed}}$$

Capital employed = Shareholders' funds plus 'creditors: amounts falling due after more than one year" plus any long-term provisions for liabilities and charges.

Evaluating the ROCE

1.16 What does a company's ROCE tell us? What should we be looking for? There are three comparisons that can be made.

(a) The change in ROCE from one year to the next.

(b) The ROCE being earned by other companies, if this information is available. Here it is not available.

(c) A comparison of the ROCE with current market borrowing rates.

(i) What would be the cost of extra borrowing to the company if it needed more loans, and is it earning an ROCE that suggests it could make high enough profits to make such borrowing worthwhile?

(ii) Is the company making an ROCE which suggests that it is making profitable use of its current borrowing?

Analysing profitability and return in more detail: the secondary ratios

1.17 We may analyse the ROCE, to find out why it is high or low, or better or worse than last year. There are two factors that contribute towards a return on capital employed, both related to turnover.

(a) **Profit margin**. A company might make a high or a low profit margin on its sales. For example, a company that makes a profit of 25p per £1 of sales is making a bigger return on its turnover than another company making a profit of only 10p per £1 of sales.

(b) **Asset turnover**. Asset turnover is a measure of how well the assets of a business are being used to generate sales. For example, if two companies each have capital employed of £100,000, and company A makes sales of £400,000 a year whereas company B makes sales of only £200,000 a year, company A is making a higher turnover from the same amount of assets and this will help company A to make a higher return on capital employed than company B. Asset turnover is expressed as 'x times' so that assets generate x times their value in annual turnover. Here, company A's asset turnover is 4 times and company B's is 2 times.

1.18 Profit margin and asset turnover together explain the ROCE, and if the ROCE is the primary profitability ratio, these other two are the secondary ratios. The relationship between the three ratios is as follows.

Profit margin × Asset turnover = ROCE

$$\frac{\text{PBIT}}{\text{Sales}} \times \frac{\text{Sales}}{\text{Capital employed}} = \frac{\text{PBIT}}{\text{Capital employed}}$$

1.19 It is also worth commenting on the **change in turnover** from one year to the next. Strong sales growth will usually indicate volume growth as well as turnover increases due to price rises, and volume growth is one sign of a prosperous company.

The gross profit margin, the net profit margin and profit analysis

1.20 Depending on the format of the profit and loss account, you may be able to calculate the gross profit margin as well as the net profit margin. Looking at the two together can be quite informative.

1.21 EXAMPLE: PROFITABILITY

A company has the following summarised profit and loss accounts for two consecutive years.

	Year 1	*Year 2*
	£	£
Turnover	70,000	100,000
Less cost of sales	42,000	55,000
Gross profit	28,000	45,000
Less expenses	21,000	35,000
Net profit	7,000	10,000

Although the net profit margin is the same for both years at 10%, the gross profit margin is not.

In year 1 it is: $\frac{28,000}{70,000} = 40\%$

and in year 2 it is: $\frac{45,000}{100,000} = 45\%$

1.22 Is this good or bad for the business? An increased profit margin must be good because this indicates a wider gap between selling price and cost of sales. However, given that the net profit ratio has stayed the same in the second year, expenses must be rising. In year 1 expenses were 30% of turnover, whereas in year 2 they were 35% of turnover. This indicates that administration, selling and distribution expenses or interest costs require tight control.

1.23 A percentage analysis of profit between year 1 and year 2 is as follows.

	Year 1	*Year 2*
	%	%
Cost of sales as a % of sales	60	55
Gross profit as a % of sales	40	45
	100	100
Expenses as a % of sales	30	35
Net profit as a % of sales	10	10
Gross profit as a % of sales	40	45

Debt and gearing ratios 11/98

1.24 Debt ratios are concerned with how much the company owes in relation to its size and whether it is getting into heavier debt or improving its situation.

(a) When a company is heavily in debt, and seems to be getting even more heavily into debt, the thought that should occur to you is that this cannot continue. If the company carries on wanting to borrow more, banks and other would-be lenders are very soon likely to refuse further borrowing and the company might well find itself in trouble.

(b) When a company is earning only a modest profit before interest and tax, and has a heavy debt burden, there will be very little profit left over for shareholders after the interest charges have been paid. And so if interest rates were to go up or the company were to borrow even more, it might soon be incurring interest charges in excess of PBIT. This might eventually lead to the liquidation of the company.

1.25 These are the two main reasons why companies should keep their debt burden under control. Four ratios that are particularly worth looking at are the **debt ratio, gearing, interest cover** and the **cash flow ratio**.

1.26 The **debt ratio** is the ratio of a company's total debts to its total assets.

(a) Assets consist of fixed assets at their balance sheet value, plus current assets.

(b) Debts consist of all creditors, whether amounts falling due within one year or after more than one year.

You can ignore long-term provisions and liabilities, such as deferred taxation.

1.27 There is no absolute rule on the maximum safe debt ratio, but as a very general guide, you might regard 50% as a safe limit to debt. In practice, many companies operate successfully with a higher debt ratio than this, but 50% is nonetheless a helpful benchmark. In addition, if the debt ratio is over 50% and getting worse, the company's debt position will be worth looking at more carefully.

KEY TERM

Financial leverage/gearing: The use of debt finance to increase the return on equity by deploying borrowed funds in such a way that the return generated is greater than the cost of servicing the debt. If the reverse is true, and the return on deployed funds is less than the cost of servicing the debt, the effect of gearing is to reduce the return on equity (*OT*).

1.28 **Capital gearing** is concerned with the amount of debt in a company's **long-term** capital structure, which we have been concerned with earlier in this Study Text. **Gearing ratios** provide a long-term measure of liquidity.

$$\text{Gearing ratio} = \frac{\text{Prior charge capital (long-term debt)}}{\text{Long-term debt + equity (shareholders' funds)}}$$

1.29 **Operating gearing** is concerned with the relationship in a company between its variable/fixed cost operating structure and its profitability. It can be calculated as the ratio of contribution (sales minus variable costs of sales) to PBIT. The possibility of rises or falls in sales revenue and volumes means that operating gearing has possible implications for a company's business risk.

1.30 The **interest cover** ratio shows whether a company is earning enough profits before interest and tax to pay its interest costs comfortably, or whether its interest costs are high in relation to the size of its profits, so that a fall in profit before interest and tax (PBIT) would then have a significant effect on profits available for ordinary shareholders.

$$\text{Interest cover} = \frac{\text{PBIT}}{\text{Interest charges}}$$

1.31 An interest cover of 2 times or less would be low, and it should really exceed 3 times before the company's interest costs can be considered to be within acceptable limits. Note that although preference share capital is included as prior charge capital for the gearing ratio, it is usual to exclude preference dividends from 'interest' charges. We also look at all interest payments, even interest charges on short-term debt, and so interest cover and gearing do not quite look at the same thing.

1.32 The **cash flow ratio** is the ratio of a company's net annual cash inflow to its total debts:

$$\frac{\text{Net annual cash inflow}}{\text{Total debts}}$$

(a) Net annual cash inflow is the amount of cash which the company has coming into the business each year from its operations. This will be shown in a company's cash flow statement for the year.

(b) Total debts are short-term and long-term creditors, together with provisions for liabilities and charges.

1.33 Obviously, a company needs to earn enough cash from operations to be able to meet its foreseeable debts and future commitments, and the cash flow ratio, and changes in the cash flow ratio from one year to the next, provides a useful indicator of a company's cash position.

Liquidity ratios: cash and working capital

1.34 Profitability is of course an important aspect of a company's performance, and debt or gearing is another. Neither, however, addresses directly the key issue of liquidity. A company needs liquid assets so that it can meet its debts when they fall due.

1.35 **Liquidity** is the amount of cash a company can obtain quickly to settle its debts (and possibly to meet other unforeseen demands for cash payments too). Liquid funds consist of:

(a) cash;

(b) short-term investments for which there is a ready market, such as investments in shares of other companies. (Short-term investments are distinct from investments in shares in subsidiaries or associated companies);

(c) fixed term deposits with a bank or building society, for example six month deposits with a bank;

(d) trade debtors. These are not cash, but ought to be expected to pay what they owe within a reasonably short time;

(e) bills of exchange receivable. Like ordinary trade debtors, these represent amounts of cash due to be received soon.

1.36 Some assets are more liquid than others. Stocks of goods are fairly liquid in some businesses. Stocks of finished production goods might be sold quickly, and a supermarket will hold consumer goods for resale that could well be sold for cash very soon. Raw materials and components in a manufacturing company have to be used to make a finished product before they can be sold to realise cash, and so they are less liquid than finished goods. Just how liquid they are depends on the speed of stock turnover and the length of the production cycle.

1.37 Fixed assets are not liquid assets. A company can sell off fixed assets, but unless they are no longer needed, or are worn out and about to be replaced, they are necessary to continue the company's operations. Selling fixed assets is certainly not a solution to a company's cash needs, and so although there may be an occasional fixed asset item which is about to be sold off, probably because it is going to be replaced, it is safe to disregard fixed assets when measuring a company's liquidity.

1.38 In summary, liquid assets are current asset items that will or could soon be converted into cash, and cash itself. Two common definitions of liquid assets are **all current assets** or **all current assets with the exception of stocks.**

1.39 The main source of liquid assets for a trading company is sales. A company can obtain cash from sources other than sales, such as the issue of shares for cash, a new loan or the sale of fixed assets. But a company cannot rely on these at all times, and in general, obtaining liquid funds depends on making sales and profits.

1.40 A company must be able to pay its debts when they fall due, and in the balance sheet, foreseeable creditors to be paid are represented by current liabilities, that is, amounts falling due within one year. There are of course other payments that a company might want to make as well, such as the purchase of new fixed assets for cash.

Why does profit not provide an indication of liquidity?

1.41 If a company makes profits, it should earn money, and if it earns money, it might seem that it should receive more cash than it pays out. In fact, profits are not always a good guide to liquidity. Two examples will show why this is so.

(a) Suppose that company X makes all its sales for cash, and pays all its running costs in cash without taking any credit. Its profit for the year just ended was as follows.

	£	£
Sales		400,000
Less costs: running costs	200,000	
depreciation	50,000	
		250,000
Profit		150,000
Less dividends (all paid)		80,000
Retained profits		70,000

During the year, the company purchased a fixed asset for £180,000 and paid for it in full.

Depreciation is not a cash outlay, and so the company's 'cash profits' less dividends were sales less running costs less dividends = £120,000. However, the fixed asset purchase required £180,000, and so the company's cash position worsened in the year by £60,000, in spite of the profit.

(b) Suppose that company Y buys three items for cash, each costing £5,000, and resells them for £7,000 each. The buyers of the units take credit, and by the end of the company's accounting year, they were all still debtors.

(i) The profit on the transactions is £2,000 per unit and £6,000 in total.

(ii) The company has paid £15,000 to buy the goods, but so far it has received no cash back from selling them, and so its cash position is so far £15,000 worse off from the transactions.

(iii) The effect so far of the transactions is:

Reduction in cash	£15,000
Increase in debtors	£21,000
Increase in profit	£6,000

The increase in assets is £6,000 in total, to match the £6,000 increase in profit, but the increase in assets is the net change in cash (reduced balance) and debtors (increased balance).

1.42 Both of these examples show ways in which a company can be profitable but at the same time get into cash flow problems. If an analysis of a company's published accounts is to give us some idea of the company's liquidity, profitability ratios are not going to be appropriate for doing this. Instead, we look at liquidity ratios and working capital turnover ratios.

The current ratio and the quick ratio

1.43 The standard test of liquidity is the **current ratio**. It can be obtained from the balance sheet, and is:

$$\frac{\text{Current assets}}{\text{current liabilities}}$$

A company should have enough current assets that give a promise of 'cash to come' to meet its commitments to pay its current liabilities. Obviously, a ratio in excess of 1 should be expected. Otherwise, there would be the prospect that the company might be unable to pay its debts on time. In practice, a ratio comfortably in excess of 1 should be expected, but what is 'comfortable' varies between different types of businesses.

1.44 Companies are not able to convert all their current assets into cash very quickly. In particular, some manufacturing companies might hold large quantities of raw material stocks, which must be used in production to create finished goods. Finished goods might be warehoused for a long time, or sold on lengthy credit. In such businesses, where stock turnover is slow, most stocks are not very liquid assets, because the cash cycle is so long. For these reasons, we calculate an additional liquidity ratio, known as the quick ratio or acid test ratio.

1.45 The **quick ratio**, or **acid test ratio**, is:

$$\frac{\text{Current assets less stocks}}{\text{Current liabilities}}$$

This ratio should ideally be at least 1 for companies with a slow stock turnover. For companies with a fast stock turnover, a quick ratio can be less than 1 without suggesting that the company is in cash flow difficulties.

1.46 Do not forget the other side of the coin. The current ratio and the quick ratio can be bigger than they should be. A company that has large volumes of stocks and debtors might be over-investing in working capital, and so tying up more funds in the business than it needs to. This would suggest poor management of debtors or stocks by the company.

Turnover periods

1.47 We can calculate **turnover periods** for stock, debtors and creditors (debtor and creditor days) - the Question below revises these calculations. If we add together the stock days and the debtor days, this should give us an indication of how soon stock is convertible into cash. Both debtor days and stock days therefore give us a further indication of the company's liquidity.

Question

Calculate liquidity and working capital ratios from the accounts of a manufacturer of products for the construction industry, and comment on the ratios.

	19X8	19X7
	£m	£m
Turnover	2,065.0	1,788.7
Cost of sales	1,478.6	1,304.0
Gross profit	586.4	484.7
Current assets		
Stocks	119.0	109.0
Debtors (note 1)	400.9	347.4
Short-term investments	4.2	18.8
Cash at bank and in hand	48.2	48.0
	572.3	523.2
Creditors: amounts falling due within one year		
Loans and overdrafts	49.1	35.3
Corporation taxes	62.0	46.7
Dividend	19.2	14.3
Creditors (note 2)	370.7	324.0
	501.0	420.3
Net current assets	71.3	102.9

Notes

		19X8	19X7
		£m	£m
1	Trade debtors	329.8	285.4
2	Trade creditors	236.2	210.8

Answer

	19X8	19X7
Current ratio	$\frac{572.3}{501.0} = 1.14$	$\frac{523.2}{420.3} = 1.24$
Quick ratio	$\frac{453.3}{501.0} = 0.90$	$\frac{414.2}{420.3} = 0.99$
Debtors' payment period	$\frac{329.8}{2{,}065.0} \times 365 = 58$ days	$\frac{285.4}{1{,}788.7} \times 365 = 58$ days
Stock turnover period	$\frac{119.0}{1{,}478.6} \times 365 = 29$ days	$\frac{109.0}{1{,}304.0} \times 365 = 31$ days
Creditors' turnover period	$\frac{236.2}{1{,}478.6} \times 365 = 58$ days	$\frac{210.8}{1{,}304.0} \times 365 = 59$ days

As a manufacturing group serving the construction industry, the company would be expected to have a comparatively lengthy debtors' turnover period, because of the relatively poor cash flow in the construction industry. It is clear that the company compensates for this by ensuring that they do not pay for raw materials and other costs before they have sold their stocks of finished goods (hence the similarity of debtors' and creditors' turnover periods).

The company's current ratio is a little lower than average but its quick ratio is better than average and very little less than the current ratio. This suggests that stock levels are strictly controlled, which is reinforced by the low stock turnover period. It would seem that working capital is tightly managed, to avoid the poor liquidity which could be caused by a high debtors' turnover period and comparatively high creditors.

Creditors' turnover is ideally calculated by the formula:

$$\frac{\text{Average stock}}{\text{Purchases}} \times 365$$

However, it is rare to find purchases disclosed in published accounts and so cost of sales serves as an approximation. The creditors' turnover ratio often helps to assess a company's liquidity; an increase in creditor days is often a sign of lack of long-term finance or poor management of current assets, resulting in the use of extended credit from suppliers, increased bank overdraft and so on.

Exam focus point

In allocating marks, the examiner will give at least as much weighting to the ability to choose and to interpret appropriate indicators as to the ability to calculate ratios correctly.

Stock market ratios

1.48 The final set of ratios to consider are the ratios which help equity shareholders and other investors to assess the value and quality of an investment in the ordinary shares of a company. These ratios (described in Chapter 7) are:

- the **earnings per share**
- the **dividend cover**
- the **price/earnings (P/E) ratio**
- the **dividend yield**
- the **earnings yield**

The value of an investment in ordinary shares in a listed company is its market value, and so investment ratios must have regard not only to information in the company's published accounts, but also to the current share price, and ratios (c), (d) and (e) all involve using the share price.

2 COMPARISONS OF ACCOUNTING FIGURES

2.1 Useful information is obtained from ratio analysis largely by means of comparisons. As we have seen, comparisons that might be made are:

(a) between the company's results in the most recent year and its results in previous years;
(b) between the company's results and the results of other companies in the same industry;
(c) between the company's results and the results of other companies in other industries.

Results of the same company over successive accounting periods

2.2 Although a company might present useful information in its five year or ten year summary, it is quite likely that the only detailed comparison you will be able to make is between the current year's and the previous year's results. The comparison should give you some idea of whether the company's situation has improved, worsened or stayed much the same between one year and the next.

2.3 Useful comparisons over time include:

(a) the percentage growth in profit (before and after tax) and the percentage growth in turnover;

(b) increases or decreases in the debt ratio and the gearing ratio;

(c) changes in the current ratio, the stock turnover period and the debtors' payment period;

(d) increases in the EPS, the dividend per share, and the market price.

2.4 The principal advantage of making comparisons over time is that they give some indication of progress: are things getting better or worse? However, there are some weaknesses in such comparisons.

(a) The effect of **inflation** should not be forgotten.

(b) The progress a company has made needs to be set in the context of what other companies have done, and whether there have been any special environmental or economic influences on the company's performance.

Allowing for inflation

2.5 Ratio analysis is not usually affected by **price inflation**, except as follows.

(a) **Return on capital employed** (ROCE) can be misleading if fixed assets, especially property, are valued at historical cost net of depreciation rather than at current value. As time goes by and if property prices go up, the fixed assets would be seriously undervalued if they were still recorded at their historical cost, and so the return on capital employed would be misleadingly high.

(b) Some growth trends can be misleading, in particular the **growth in sales turnover**, and the **growth in profits or earnings**.

2.6 For example, suppose that a company achieved the following results.

	19X8	*19X7*	*% growth*
	£m	£m	
Turnover	46	43	7.0
Profit	12	11	9.1

However, if price inflation from 19X7 to 19X8 was 10%, the performance of the company would show a drop in turnover and profit in real terms, of about 3% in turnover and of about 0.9% in profit.

Putting a company's results into context

2.7 The financial and accounting ratios of one company should be looked at in the context of what other companies have been achieving, and also any special influences on the industry or the economy as a whole. Here are two examples.

(a) If a company achieves a 10% increase in profits, this performance taken in isolation might seem commendable, but if it is then compared with the results of rival companies, which might have been achieving profit growth of 30% the performance might in comparison seem very disappointing.

(b) An improvement in ROCE and profits might be attributable to a temporary economic boom, and an increase in profits after tax might be attributable to a cut in the rate of corporation tax. When improved results are attributable to factors outside the control of the company's management, such as changes in the economic climate and tax rates other companies might be expected to benefit in the same way.

Comparisons between different companies in the same industry

2.8 Making comparisons between the results of different companies in the same industry is a way of assessing which companies are outperforming others.

(a) Even if two companies are in the same broad industry (for example, retailing) they might not be direct competitors. For example, in the UK, the Kingfisher group (including Woolworths/B&Q/Comet) does not compete directly with the Burton/Debenhams group. Even so, they might still be expected to show broadly similar performance, in terms of growth, because a boom or a depression in retail markets will affect all retailers. The results of two such companies can be compared, and the company with the better growth and accounting ratios might be considered more successful than the other.

(b) If two companies are direct competitors, a comparison between them would be particularly interesting. Which has achieved the better ROCE, sales growth, or profit growth? Does one have a better debt or gearing position, a better liquidity position or better working capital ratios? How do their P/E ratios, dividend cover and dividend yields compare? And so on.

2.9 Comparisons between companies in the same industry can help investors to rank them in order of desirability as investments, and to judge relative share prices or future prospects. It is important, however, to make comparisons with caution: a large company and a small company in the same industry might be expected to show different results, not just in terms of size, but in terms of:

(a) percentage rates of growth in sales and profits;

(b) percentages of profits re-invested. Dividend cover will be higher in a company that needs to retain profits to finance investment and growth;

(c) fixed assets. Large companies are more likely to have freehold property in their balance sheet than small companies.

Comparisons between companies in different industries

2.10 Useful information can also be obtained by comparing the financial and accounting ratios of companies in different industries. An investor ought to be aware of how companies in one industrial sector are performing in comparisons with companies in other sectors. For example, it is important to know:

(a) whether sales growth and profit growth is higher in some industries than in others. For example how does growth in the financial services industry compare with growth in heavy engineering, electronics or leisure?

(b) how the return on capital employed and return on shareholder capital compare between different industries;

(c) how the P/E ratios and dividend yields vary between industries. For example, if a publishing company has a P/E ratio of, say, 20, which is average for its industry, whereas an electronics company has a P/E ratio of, say, 14, do the better growth performance and prospects of the publishing company justify its higher P/E ratio?

Exam focus point

You could be expected to reconcile profit statements to cash flow statements, a skill you should have acquired in earlier studies.

3 PREDICTING BUSINESS FAILURE 5/95, 5/98

3.1 The analysis of financial ratios is largely concerned with the efficiency and effectiveness of the use of resources by a company's management, and also with the financial stability of the company. Investors will wish to know:

(a) whether additional funds could be lent to the company with reasonable safety;
(b) whether the company would fail without additional funds.

3.2 One method of predicting business failure is the use of **liquidity ratios** (the current ratio and the quick ratio). A company with a current ratio well below 2:1 or a quick ratio well below 1:1 might be considered illiquid and in danger of failure. Research seems to indicate, however, that the current ratio and the quick ratio and trends in the variations of these ratios for a company, are poor indicators of eventual business failure.

Z scores

3.3 E I Altman researched into the simultaneous analysis of several financial ratios as a combined **predictor of business failure**. Altman analysed 22 accounting and non-accounting variables for a selection of failed and non-failed firms in the USA and from these, five key indicators emerged. These five indicators were then used to derive a **Z score**. Firms with a Z score above a certain level would be predicted to be financially sound, and firms with a Z score below a certain level would be categorised as probable failures. Altman also identified a range of Z scores in between the non-failure and failure categories in which eventual failure or non-failure was uncertain.

KEY TERM

Z-score: a single figure, produced by a financial model, which combines a number of variables (generally financial statements ratios), whose magnitude is intended to aid the prediction of failure (*OT*).

3.4 Altman's Z score model (derived in 1968) emerged as:

$$Z = 1.2X_1 + 1.4X_2 + 3.3X_3 + 0.6X_4 + 1.0X_5$$

where

X_1 = working capital/total assets
X_2 = retained earnings/total assets
X_3 = earnings before interest and tax/total assets
X_4 = market value of equity/book value of total debt (a form of gearing ratio)
X_5 = sales/total assets.

Exam focus point

It is not necessary for you to memorise this formula, which would be given in the exam if needed.

3.5 In Altman's model, a Z score of 2.7 or more indicated non-failure, and a Z score of 1.8 or less indicated failure.

3.6 Altman's sample size was small, and related to US firms in a particular industry. Subsequent research based on the similar principle of identifying a Z score predictor of business failure has produced different prediction models, using a variety of financial ratios and different Z score values as predictors of failure. It would be argued, for example, that different ratios and Z score values would be appropriate for conditions in the UK.

The value of Z scores

3.7 A current view of the link between financial ratios and business failure would appear to be as follows.

(a) The financial ratios of firms which fail can be seen in retrospect to have deteriorated significantly prior to failure, and to be worse than the ratios of non-failed firms. In retrospect, financial ratios can be used to suggest why a firm has failed.

(b) No fully accepted model for **predicting** future business failures has yet been established, although some form of Z score analysis would appear to be the most promising avenue for progress. In the UK, several Z score-type failure prediction models exist.

(c) Because of the use of X_4: market value of equity/book value of debt, Z score models cannot be used for unquoted companies which lack a market value of equity.

3.8 Z score models are used widely in the banking sector, in risk assessment, loan grading and corporate finance activities. They are also used by accountancy firms, fund management houses, stockbrokers and credit insurers (such as Trade Indemnity).

Other corporate failure models

3.9 **Beaver** conducted a study which showed that:

(a) the worst predictor of failure is the current ratio (current assets/current liabilities); and
(b) the best predictor of failure is cash flow borrowings.

3.10 Other writers have put forward alternative models designed to predict whether a business will fail.

Taffler's approach is based on the following measures.

(a) earnings before tax/current liabilities
(b) current assets/total liabilities
(c) current liabilities/total assets
(d) sales/total assets

3.11 From historical data on a wide range of actual cases, **Argenti** developed a model which is intended to predict the likelihood of company failure. The model is based on calculating scores for a company based on (a) defects of the company; (b) management mistakes and (c) the symptoms of failure. For each of the scores (a), (b) and (c) there is a 'danger mark'.

3.12 Among the most important factors in the model are:

(a) defects:
  (i) autocratic Chief Executive (Robert Maxwell is an example here);
  (ii) passive board;
  (iii) lack of budgetary control;

(b) mistakes:
  (i) over-trading (expanding faster than cash funding);
  (ii) gearing - high bank overdrafts/loans;
  (iii) failure of large project jeopardises the company (eg Laker Airways);

(c) symptoms:
  (i) deteriorating ratios;

(ii) creative accounting - signs of window-dressing;
(iii) declining morale and declining quality.

Weaknesses of corporate failure models and prediction methods

3.13 Weaknesses of corporate failure models include the following.

(a) In common with all correlation models, they relate to the past, without taking into account the current state of the macroeconomic environment (the level of inflation and interest rates, and so on).

(b) The models share the limitations of the accounting model (including the accounting concepts and conventions) on which they are based.

(c) The publication of accounting data by companies is subject to a delay. Failure might occur before the data becomes available.

(d) If the measures incorporated in the models become used as objectives, as some suggest, then the model is likely to become less useful as a predictive tool, as the measures will be subject to manipulation.

(e) The definition of corporate failure is not clear, given that various forms of rescue or restructuring are possible, short of liquidation, for a company which is in trouble.

3.14 There are the following problems in using available **financial information** to predict failure.

(a) **Significant events** can take place between the end of the financial year and the publication of the accounts. An extreme example of this would be the collapse of the Barings merchant bank. A further feature of the Barings case that is worthy of comment is the fact that the factors that led up to the collapse were essentially internal to the business and would never have become apparent in the published accounts.

(b) The information is essentially **backward looking** and takes no account of current and future situations. An extreme example would be the Central American banana producers. There would be nothing in their published accounts to predict the effect on their businesses of Hurricane Mitch.

3.15 The use of **creative, or even fraudulent, accounting** can be significant in situations of corporate failure. Polly Peck was the fastest growing company in the UK at one time, but eventually and catastrophically it failed when accounting manipulation could no longer conceal its true financial position. Similarly, the pressure to deliver earnings growth may result in companies making poor decisions that eventually lead to their downfall. It is arguable that a recent deterioration in the performance of BTR (now Invensys) is attributable to its policy of aggressive acquisition followed by price increases and stringent cost reduction. Although this delivered growth in earnings for a while and made it a highly regarded company in which to invest, the effects of this policy are now being felt in a shrinking customer base and the consequences of a lack of investment in the underlying businesses.

Business is not an exact science, and the use of apparently objective models can foster the illusion that it can be reduced to a set of numerical ratios. Businesses must always operate under conditions of inadequate and imperfect information. It is thus not surprising that deterministic models of failure prediction only ever appear to meet with partial success.

Other indicators of financial difficulties

3.16 You should not think that **ratio analysis of published accounts** and **Z score analysis** are the only ways of spotting that a company might be running into financial difficulties. There are other possible indicators too.

(a) **Other information in the published accounts**

Some information in the published accounts might not lend itself readily to ratio analysis, but still be an indicator of financial difficulties, for example:

(i) very large increases in intangible fixed assets;
(ii) a worsening net liquid funds position, as shown by the funds flow statement;
(iii) very large contingent liabilities;
(iv) important post balance sheet events.

(b) **Information in the chairman's report and the directors' report**

The report of the chairman or chief executive that accompanies the published accounts might be very revealing. Although this report is not audited, and will no doubt try to paint a rosy picture of the company's affairs, any difficulties the company has had and not yet overcome will probably be discussed in it. There might also be warnings of problems to come in the future.

The directors' report is usually restricted to the minimum information required by law, but it might be interesting to check whether there have been any changes in the composition of the board since last year. Have many of last year's directors gone? Are there many new directors, and if so, what are their qualifications?

(c) **Information in the press**

Newspapers and financial journals are a source of information about companies, and the difficulties or successes they are having. There may be reports of strikes, redundancies and closures.

There are often articles in newspapers which focus on particular companies. If a company is in financial difficulty, adverse comments might well appear in one of these articles.

(d) **Published information about environmental or external matters**

There will also be published information about matters that will have a direct influence on a company's future, although the connection may not be obvious. Examples of external matters that may affect a company adversely are:

(i) new legislation, for example on product safety standards or pollution controls, which affect a company's main products;

(ii) international events, for example political disagreements with a foreign country, leading to a restriction on trade between the countries. The foreign country concerned might be a major importer of a company's products;

(iii) new and better products being launched on to the market by a competitor;

(iv) a big rise in interest rates, which might affect a highly-geared company seriously;

(v) a big change in foreign exchange rates, which might affect a major importer or exporter seriously.

4 OTHER INFORMATION FROM COMPANIES' ACCOUNTS

Fixed assets

4.1 Two features of a company's fixed assets which can be looked at are:

(a) how the company has accounted for the revaluation of fixed assets;
(b) the amount of intangible fixed assets in the balance sheet.

The revaluation of fixed assets

4.2 Fixed assets may be stated in the balance sheet at cost less accumulated depreciation. They may also be revalued from time to time to a current market value. When this happens:

(a) the increase in the balance sheet value of the fixed asset is matched by an increase in the **revaluation reserve**;

(b) depreciation in subsequent years is based on the revalued amount of the asset, its estimated residual value and its estimated remaining useful life.

4.3 It has been usual for companies to revalue their land and buildings periodically, but not their other fixed assets such as plant and machinery. There has been nothing to stop companies revaluing all their fixed assets regularly, but land and buildings have been an obvious example of fixed assets that can increase substantially in value. To avoid a serious understatement of their balance sheet value, companies have therefore revalued their land and buildings from time to time, typically every two or three years.

Intangible fixed assets

4.4 **Intangible fixed assets** are assets which do not have any physical substance, but are of use to a business over a number of years in helping to provide goods or services. Intangible assets include trademarks, patents, copyrights, development expenditure and goodwill.

4.5 Companies are allowed to include intangible fixed assets in their balance sheet, but if they do, they must depreciate them over their estimated useful lives. Instead of having intangible fixed assets, many companies write off the cost of intangible items in the year of acquisition.

4.6 An important area of recent debate is the extent to which companies should be allowed to include the values of brand names in their balance sheets. Valuations of such assets are likely to be highly subjective.

Share capital and reserves

4.7 The **capital and reserves** section of a company's accounts contains information which appears to be mainly the concern of the various classes of shareholder. However, because the shareholders' interest in the business acts as a buffer for the creditors in the event of any financial problems, this section is also of some importance to creditors.

4.8 The nature of any increase in reserves will be of some interest. For example, if a company has increased its total share capital and reserves in the year:

(a) did it do so by issuing new shares resulting in a higher allotted share capital and share premium account?

(b) did it do so by revaluing some fixed assets, resulting in a higher revaluation reserve?

(c) did it make a substantial profit and retain a good proportion of this profit in the business resulting in a higher profit and loss account balance?

4.9 A scrip issue might also be of some interest. It will result in a fall in the market price per share. If it has been funded from a company's profit and loss account reserves, a scrip issue would indicate that the company recognised and formalised its long-term capital needs by now making some previously distributable reserves non-distributable.

4.10 If a company has issued shares in the form of a dividend, are there obvious reasons why this should be so? For example, does the company need to retain capital within the business because of poor trading in the previous year, making the directors reluctant to pay out more cash dividend than necessary?

Debentures, loans and other liabilities

4.11 Two points of interest about debentures, loans and other liabilities are:

(a) whether or not loans are secured;
(b) the redemption dates of loans.

Secured loans

4.12 For debentures and loan stock which are secured, the details of the security are usually included in the terms of a trust deed. Details of any **fixed or floating charges against assets** must be disclosed in a note to the accounts.

Redemptions of debentures and loan stock

4.13 In analysing a set of accounts, particular attention should be paid to some significant features concerning **debenture or loan stock redemption**. These are:

(a) the closeness of the redemption date, which would indicate how much finance the company has to find in the immediate future to repay its loans. It is not unusual, however, to repay one loan by taking out another, and so a company does not necessarily have to find the money to repay a loan from its own resources;

(b) the percentage interest rate on the loans being redeemed, compared with the current market rate of interest. This would give some idea, if a company decides to replace loans by taking out new loans, of the likely increase (or reduction) in interest costs that it might face, and how easily it might accommodate any interest cost increase.

4.14 There are classes of debentures which do not have a redemption date attached. This does not mean that they will never be redeemed because a company can always buy back its own debentures in the market. The holder of an **irredeemable debenture** does not, however, have a date by which redemption must take place, so he cannot demand repayment. Consequently, not being very attractive to investors, this is a rare form of finance.

Geographical analysis of trading

4.15 When you study a company's published accounts, a useful item of information to look for might be the analysis of the company's turnover in each part of the world. It could show in which markets the company is making good progress, and where it is losing ground to competitors.

Post balance sheet events

4.16 **Post balance sheet events** are those events both favourable and unfavourable which occur between the balance sheet date and the date on which the financial statements are approved by the board of directors. The following are examples of post balance sheet events which should normally be disclosed.

(a) Mergers and acquisitions.
(b) The issue of new shares and debentures.
(c) The purchase and sales of major fixed assets and investments.
(d) Losses of fixed assets or stocks as a result of a catastrophe such as fire or flood.
(e) The opening of new trading activities.
(f) The closure of a significant part of the trading activities.
(g) A decline in the value of property and investments held as fixed assets.
(h) Changes in exchange rates (if there are significant overseas interests).
(i) Government action, such as nationalisation.
(j) Strikes and other labour disputes.
(k) The augmentation of pension benefits to employees.

Contingencies

4.17 **Contingencies** are conditions which exist at the balance sheet date where the outcome will be confirmed only on the occurrence or non-occurrence of one or more uncertain future events.

4.18 Contingencies can result in contingent gains or contingent losses. The fact that the condition exists at the balance sheet date distinguishes a contingency from a post balance sheet event, which arises between the balance sheet date and the date of the formal approval of the financial statements by the board of directors.

The usual types of reported contingencies

4.19 Some of the principal types of contingencies disclosed by companies are as follows.

- Guarantees given by the company
- Discounted bills of exchange
- Uncalled liabilities on shares or loan stock
- Lawsuits or claims pending
- Tax on profits where the basis on which the tax should be computed is unclear

5 THE BALANCED SCORECARD APPROACH 5/99

> *Stage 4 Topic link.* You will also cover this topic at Stage 4 in Paper 14 and Paper 16.

5.1 The **balanced scorecard** is a way of measuring performance, already being used by organisations such as Apple and National Westminster Bank, which integrates traditional financial measures with operational, customer and staff issues which are vital to the long-term competitiveness of an organisation.

5.2 The technique was developed by Robert Kaplan and publicised in the January-February 1992 edition of the *Harvard Business Review*. The balanced scorecard is:

> 'a set of measures that gives top managers a fast but comprehensive view of the business. The balanced scorecard includes financial measures that tell the results of actions already taken. And

it complements the financial measures with operational measures on customer satisfaction, internal processes, and the organisation's innovation and improvement activities - operational measures that are the drivers of future financial performance.'

The reason for using such a system is that 'traditional financial accounting measures like return on investment and earnings per share can give misleading signals for continuous improvement and innovation - activities today's competitive environment demands'.

5.3 The balanced scorecard allows managers to look at the business from four important perspectives and to answer four basic questions, as detailed by Rod Newing ('Wake up to the balanced scorecard', *Management Accounting,* March 1995).

Perspective	*Question*
Customer	What do existing and new customers value from us?
Internal	What processes must we excel at to achieve our financial and customer objectives?
Innovation and learning	Can we continue to improve and create future value?
Financial	How do we create value for our shareholders?

Rather than by lengthy discussions by management, the answers to these questions are found by talking to people outside the organisation.

Once those factors that are important to the organisation's success have been established, performance measures and targets for improvement are set. The measures and targets must be clearly communicated to all levels of management and employees so that they understand how their own efforts can impact upon the targets set. The balanced scorecard can then become the most important monthly management report.

The four perspectives

5.4 (a) **Customer perspective.** This section of the balanced scorecard requires customers themselves to identify a specific set of goals and performance measures relating to what actually matters to them.

(i) Time
(ii) Quality
(iii) Performance of the product
(iv) Service

In order to view the firm's performance through customers' eyes, firms hire market researchers to assess how it is performing. Higher service and quality may cost more at the outset, but savings can be made.

(b) **Internal business perspective.** Measures from the customer's perspective need to be translated into the actions the firm must take to meet these expectations. The internal business perspective of the balanced scorecard identifies the business processes that have the greatest impact on customer satisfaction, such as quality and employee skills. The organisation's overall goals have to be broken down into unit, departmental or workgroup measures which can be influenced by employee actions.

(c) **Innovation and learning perspective.** Whilst the customer and internal process perspectives identify the current parameters for competitive success, the company needs to learn, innovate and improve to satisfy future needs. The organisation must produce new products, reduce costs and add value. Performance measures must emphasise continuous improvement in meeting customers' needs. Examples of measures might be these.

(i) How long does it take to create new products?
(ii) How quickly does the firm climb the learning curve to make new products?
(iii) What percentage of revenue comes from new products?
(iv) How many suggestions are made by staff and are acted upon?

(d) **Financial perspective.** The financial perspective includes traditional measures such as profitability and growth but the measures are set through talking to the shareholders direct. The financial perspective looks at whether the other three perspectives will result in financial improvement.

Chapter roundup

- The **ratios** covered in this chapter provide various tools with which you can analyse financial statements. Comments on a company based on such ratios are far more likely to be right than comments based on a casual read through a set of accounts. However, you should also make use of whatever other information can be gleaned from a company's accounts.
- It is important to bear in mind that **historical (past) data** has limitations for the purpose of **forecasting** what will happen in future periods. A firm's profitability may have risen steadily over the past five years, but we cannot simply extrapolate this trend into the future.
- The **balanced scorecard** approach attempts to integrate traditional financial measures with operational, customer and staff perspectives.

Quick quiz

1 Define return on capital employed. (see paras 1.14, 1.15)
2 What is the debt ratio? (1.26)
3 How can a profitable company run out of cash? (1.41)
4 What is the quick ratio? (1.45)
5 How does inflation affect ratio analysis? (2.5)
6 What is a Z score? (3.3)
7 Outline the weaknesses of corporate failure models. (3.13)
8 Why should creditors be interested in a company's share capital and reserves? (4.7)
9 What types of contingencies might be disclosed in a company's accounts? (4.19)
10 Identify the four perspectives which the balanced scorecard approach focuses upon. (5.4)

Question to try	Level	Marks	Time
3	Exam standard	20	36 mins

Chapter 4

PROFIT IMPROVEMENT, VALUE FOR MONEY AND ANALYSING RISK

Introduction

Profits can of course be improved either by improving sales revenue or by reducing costs. In the first part of this chapter, we shall be looking at several approaches to **cost reduction**. These include **value analysis**.

In this chapter, we also look at how **economy**, **efficiency** and **effectiveness** - of particular relevance in the public sector but also relevance in the private sector - can be assessed and monitored.

Various methods of analysing **risk** and **uncertainty**, the final topic area covered in the chapter, can be used for capital budgeting decisions. The problem of risk is acute with capital budgeting because of the timescale involved. The **choice of discount rate** is important since it provides a useful method of adjusting for risk.

1 PROFIT IMPROVEMENT SCHEMES 11/96

Exam focus point

Although not likely to appear in the SFM paper often, this topic should not be neglected. Note that it was examined in 11/96.

Cost reduction and cost control

1.1 Cost reduction should not be confused with cost control.

KEY TERMS

Cost control is the regulation of the costs of operating a business and is concerned with keeping costs within acceptable limits. These limits will usually be specified as a standard cost or target cost limit in a formal operational plan or budget. If actual costs differ from planned costs by an excessive amount, cost control action will be necessary.

Cost reduction, in contrast, starts with an assumption that current cost levels, or planned cost levels, are too high, even though cost control might be good and efficiency levels high. Cost reduction is a planned and positive approach to reducing expenditure and thus to profit improvement.

1.2 Cost control action ought to lead to a **reduction in excessive spending** (for example when material wastage is higher than budget or productivity levels below agreed standards.) However, a cost reduction programme can be directed towards reducing expected cost levels by cutting costs to below current budgeted or standard levels by purchasing new equipment, or changing methods of working and so on. Both budgets and standards reflect current costs and conditions, and not necessarily the cost and conditions which would minimise costs.

Planning for cost reduction

1.3 There are two basic approaches to cost reduction.

(a) **Crash programmes to cut spending levels**. If an organisation is having problems with its profitability or cash flow, the management might decide on an immediate programme to reduce spending to a minimum. Some current projects might be abandoned, capital expenditures deferred, employees made redundant or new recruitment stopped and so on.

(b) **Planned programmes to reduce costs**. Many companies tend to introduce crash programmes for cost reduction in times of crisis and ignore the problem completely in times of prosperity. A far better approach is to introduce continual assessments of an organisation's entire products, production methods, services, internal administration systems and so on.

1.4 Cost reduction exercises are planned campaigns to cut expenditure; they should preferably be continuous, long-term campaigns, so that short-term cost reductions are not soon reversed and 'forgotten'. The major difficulties with cost reduction programmes are as follows.

(a) Resistance by employees to pressure to reduce costs, usually because the nature and purpose of the campaign has not been properly explained to them, and they feel threatened by the change.

(b) They may be limited to a small area of the business with the result that costs are reduced in one cost centre only to reappear as an extra cost in another cost centre.

(c) Cost reduction campaigns are often introduced as a rushed, desperate measure instead of a carefully organised, well thought-out exercise.

1.5 Cost reduction does not happen of its own accord, and managers must make positive decisions to reduce costs.

(a) A planned programme of cost reduction will begin with an assumption that some costs can be reduced significantly. The benefits of cost savings must be worthwhile, and should exceed the costs of achieving them.

(b) Areas for potential cost reduction should be investigated, and unnecessary costs identified.

(c) Cost reduction measures should be proposed, agreed, implemented and then monitored.

The scope of cost reduction campaigns

1.6 The scope of a cost reduction campaign should embrace the activities of the entire company, which in a manufacturing company would span purchasing and distribution and all levels within the organisation from the shop floor upwards. Non-manufacturing industries and public sector organisations should equally look at all areas of their activities for ways of reducing costs. A cost reduction campaign should have a long-term aim as well as short-term objectives.

(a) In the short term only variable costs, for the most part, are susceptible to cost reduction efforts. Many fixed costs (for example depreciation, rent) are unavoidable.

(b) Some fixed costs are avoidable in the short term (for example advertising or sales promotion expenditure). These are called **discretionary fixed costs**.

(c) In the long term most costs can be either reduced or avoided. This includes fixed cost as well as variable cost expenditure items.

Improving efficiency and efficiency standards

1.7 One way of reducing costs is to improve the efficiency of materials usage, the productivity of labour, or the efficiency of machinery or other equipment. There are several ways in which this might be done.

(a) **Improved materials usage** might be achieved by reducing levels of wastage, where wastage is currently high.

(b) **Labour productivity** can possibly be improved by the following methods.

- (i) Giving pay incentives for better productivity.
- (ii) Changing work methods to eliminate unnecessary procedures.
- (iii) Improving co-operation between groups or departments.
- (iv) Setting more challenging standards of efficiency to aim for.
- (v) Introducing standards where they did not exist before.

(c) **Improving the efficiency of equipment usage** might involve the following.

- (i) Making better use of equipment resources.
- (ii) Achieving a better balance between preventive maintenance and machine 'down-time' for repairs.

1.8 Once improved standards of efficiency have been set, as a means of reducing costs, it is then obviously important that **cost control** should be applied by management.

Other methods of reducing materials costs

1.9 We have seen that materials costs can be reduced by attacking the costs of wastage, if wastage costs in production are high. Other ways of reducing materials costs are as follows.

(a) **Obtaining lower prices** for purchases of materials and components. Bulk purchase discounts might be obtainable at favourable rates. Alternatively, a more cost-conscious approach to buying, with a system of putting all major purchase contracts out to tender, might help to reduce prices.

(b) **Improving stores control** and stores costs. You should be familiar with the concept of the economic ordering quantity, which is the size of order that will minimise the combined costs of ordering items for stock and stockholding costs. Holding costs can be reduced by dealing with problems of obsolescence, deterioration of items in store or theft.

(c) **Using alternative materials.** Cheaper substitute materials might be available. Examples of cost reduction by using alternative materials are given later in the context of value analysis.

(d) **Standardisation of parts.** Standardisation of parts and components might offer enormous cost reduction potential for some manufacturing industries.

Methods of reducing labour costs

1.10 The key to reducing labour costs might be as follows.

(a) **Improving efficiency/productivity**, which was mentioned earlier.

(b) **Changing the methods of work**. A **work study** or **organisation and methods (O & M)** programme might be set up to look for cost savings from improved work methods.

(c) **Replacing humans with machinery**. The substitution of labour by automatic equipment might reduce costs substantially, as the well publicised experiences of the newspaper industry showed.

Other aspects of cost reduction

Reducing finance costs

1.11 **Finance costs** might offer some scope for savings.

(a) There might be a finance cost in taking credit from suppliers, in the form of an opportunity cost of failing to take advantage of discounts for early payment that suppliers might be offering.

(b) Similarly, a company should give some thought to the credit terms it offers to customers. Finance tied up in working capital involves a cost. (This might be the interest charges on a bank overdraft, the cost of borrowing long-term finance, or the opportunity cost of the capital tied up.) Costs might be reduced by reassessing policies for offering early payment discounts to credit customers, or discounting bills of exchange receivable.

(c) A company might wish to reassess its sources of finance. Is it borrowing at the lowest obtainable rates? Is its gearing too high and does it rely too much on debt capital?

(d) Savings might be achievable from improved foreign exchange dealings, for companies involved in buying and selling abroad.

Rationalisation measures

1.12 Where organisations grow, especially by means of mergers and takeovers, there is a tendency for work to be duplicated in different parts of the organisation. Two or three factories, for example, might make the same product, when it would be more economical to concentrate all production in one factory. The elimination of unnecessary duplication and the concentration of resources is a form of **rationalisation**. The end result of such rationalisation is therefore to reduce costs through greater efficiency.

Reducing expenses

1.13 Expense items, other than materials and labour, may be a significant part of total costs, and these too should be controlled. Management should continually question the need for any cost item, for example whether accommodation (and rent) can be reduced.

1.14 With sharp increases in energy costs in recent years (and with the prospect of limited energy resources in the near future) some attention has been given to reducing energy consumption. **Energy audits** can be conducted as follows.

(a) Employees should be educated into a concern for energy saving.

(b) All fuel costs should be identified, and areas of high cost should receive most attention.

(c) Analysis should identify needless energy consumption (the excessive heating of industrial buildings in particular having been heavily criticised).

(d) Areas for investment in energy-saving equipment should be identified, and the potential value of the investment evaluated (for example insulation schemes and re-processing of waste heat).

1.15 Cost reduction might be achieved if senior managers ensure that proper control over spending decisions is exercised. All too often, costly spending decisions are taken by junior managers without proper consideration of the long-term cost.

Value analysis and value engineering

1.16 One approach to cost reduction, which embraces many of the techniques already mentioned in this chapter, is value analysis and value engineering. Value analysis is a planned, scientific approach to cost reduction, which reviews the material composition of a product and production design so that modifications and improvements can be made which **do not reduce the value of the product to the customer or the user**. The value of the product must therefore be kept the same or else improved, at a reduced cost. The administration of a value analysis exercise should perhaps be the responsibility of a cost reduction committee.

KEY TERMS

Value analysis is defined in the CIMA *Official Terminology* as 'a systematic inter-disciplinary examination of factors affecting the cost of a product or service, in order to devise means of achieving the specified purpose most economically at the required standard of quality and reliability' (BS3138).

Value engineering is defined as 'an activity which helps to design products which meet customer needs at the lowest cost while assuring the required standard of quality and reliability'.

What is different about value analysis?

1.17 There are two features of value analysis that distinguish it from other approaches to cost reduction.

(a) It encourages innovation and a more radical outlook for ways of reducing costs.

(b) It recognises the various types of value which a product or service provides, analyses this value, and then seeks ways of improving or maintaining aspects of this value but at a lower cost.

1.18 Value analysis involves the systematic investigation of every source of cost and technique of production with the aim of getting rid of all unnecessary costs. An unnecessary cost is an additional cost incurred without adding use, exchange or esteem value to a product.

1.19 Typical considerations in value analysis are as follows.

(a) Can a cheaper substitute material be found which is as good as, if not better than, the material currently used?

(b) Can unnecessary weight or embellishments be removed without reducing the product's attractions or desirability?

(c) Is it possible to use standardised components thereby reducing the variety of units used and produced? Variety reduction through standardisation facilitates longer production runs at lower unit costs.

(d) Is it possible to reduce the number of components? For example could a product be assembled safely with fewer screws?

Advanced manufacturing technology

1.20 The advent of **advanced manufacturing technology (AMT)** has provided scope for many more approaches to cost reduction, some of which can also be applied in a traditional manufacturing environment.

1.21 For example, **Just in time (JIT)** is a system of manufacturing and a workflow control technique that aims to eliminate waste. Wasteful activities include the following.

(a) Inspection of goods
(b) Shopfloor queues
(c) Re-working of defective items
(d) Excessive storage
(e) Unnecessary movement of materials

1.22 Two main aspects of JIT systems can be identified.

(a) **Just in time purchasing** seeks to match the usage of raw materials in production as closely as possible with the delivery of the materials from external suppliers.

Raw material stocks are thus kept at a near-zero level. For JIT purchasing to work, a firm must be able:

(i) to place frequent (and if necessary small) orders for materials;
(ii) to rely on the supplier to deliver on time;
(iii) to be confident that the supplier will deliver materials of acceptable quality.

(b) **Just in time production**. Production only takes place when there is actual customer demand for the output. The aim is on-time production to order, therefore levels of work in progress and finished goods stocks are minimised.

1.23 **Manufacturing resource planning (MRP II)** developed out of material requirements planning (MRP). MRP was devised in the late 1960s as a system for calculating the total quantities of materials required to manufacture finished products. The aim was stock control: making sure that the materials would be available in sufficient quantities to meet production demand, but that excessive quantities of unwanted items would not be held.

1.24 MRP II is used by many companies for manufacturing planning, but with the advent of Just in Time manufacturing (JIT) it has been criticised as a planning system. It allows for, rather than seeking to eliminate, long leadtimes, shopfloor queues, large batch sizes, scrap and quality problems. Even so, MRP II has advantages as a system for planning and controlling manufacturing systems, especially when JIT methods are unsuitable.

1.25 A **flexible manufacturing system (FMS)** is a highly automated manufacturing system, which is computer controlled and capable of producing a broad range of parts in a flexible manner. It is characterised by small batch production, the ability to change quickly from one job to another and very fast response times, so that output can be produced quickly in response to specific orders that come in.

2 VALUE FOR MONEY

2.1 **Value for money (VFM)** means providing a service in a way which is economical, efficient and effective.

(a) **Economy** means doing things cheaply.
(b) **Efficiency** means doing things well.
(c) **Effectiveness** means doing the right things.

These are the **3 Es** of VFM.

2.2 The assessment of economy, efficiency and effectiveness should be a part of the normal management process of any organisation, public or private.

(a) Management should carry out **performance reviews** as a regular feature of their control responsibilities.

(b) Independent assessments of management performance can be carried out by 'outsiders', perhaps an internal audit department, as value for money audits (**VFM audits**).

2.3 The term 'value for money' is used to cover all three aspects of measuring performance - economy, efficiency and effectiveness. Public sector organisations are now under considerable pressure to prove that they operate economically, efficiently and effectively, and are encouraged from many sources to draw up action plans to achieve value for money as part of the continuing process of good management.

2.4 Value for money is important whatever level of expenditure is being considered. Negatively it may be seen as an approach to spreading cuts in public expenditure fairly across services but more positively it is necessary to ensure that the desired impact is achieved with the minimum use of resources.

The three Es

2.5 In 1990, the CCAB issued an Audit Brief on VFM audit and this defines the **three Es** as follows.

(a) **Economy**: attaining the appropriate quantity and quality of physical, human and financial resources (**inputs**) at lowest cost. An activity would not be economic, if, for example, there was over-staffing or failure to purchase materials of requisite quality at the lowest available price.

(b) **Efficiency**: this is the relationship between goods or services produced (**outputs**) and the resources used to produce them. An efficient operation produces the maximum output for any given set of resource inputs; or it has minimum inputs for any given quantity and quality of product or service provided.

(c) **Effectiveness**: this is concerned with how well an activity is achieving its policy objectives or other intended effects.

2.6 In a profit-making organisation, objectives can be expressed financially in terms of target profit or return. The organisation, and profit centres within it, can be judged to have operated effectively if they have achieved a target profit within a given period. In NFP (**not-for-profit) organisations**, effectiveness cannot be measured this way, because the organisation has non-financial objectives. The effectiveness of performance in NFPs could be measured in terms of whether targeted non-financial objectives have been achieved, but there are several problems involved in trying to do this.

2.7 Value for money can often only be judged by **comparison**. In searching for value for money, present methods of operation and uses of resources must be compared with alternatives. Usually there will exist some alternative that gives better value for money. It is important that present arrangements are challenged and seen to be justified in the face of proposed alternatives. Alternatives to present arrangements can be uncovered and critically evaluated by a process of performance review by management.

Stage 4 Topic Link. Performance measurement in not-for-profit organisations is included in the syllabus for Paper 16 *Management Accounting Control Systems.*

Studying and measuring the three Es

2.8 Economy, efficiency and effectiveness can be studied and measured with reference to the following.

(a) **Inputs**, which means **money**, or **resources** - the labour, materials, time and so on consumed, and their cost. For example, a VFM audit into state secondary education would look at the efficiency and economy of the use of resources for education (the use of schoolteachers, school buildings, equipment, cash) and whether the resources are being used for their purpose: what is the pupil/teacher ratio and are trained teachers being fully used to teach the subjects they have been trained for?

(b) **Outputs**, in other words the results of an activity, measurable as the services actually produced, and the quality of the services. In the case of a VFM audit of secondary education, outputs would be measured as the number of pupils taught and the number of subjects taught per pupil; how many examination papers are taken and what is the pass rate; what proportion of students go on to further education at a university or college.

(c) **Impacts**, which are the effect that the outputs of an activity or programme have in terms of achieving policy objectives. Policy objectives might be to provide a minimum level of education to all children up to the age of 16, and to make education relevant for the children's future jobs and careers. This might be measured by the ratio of jobs vacant to unemployed school leavers. A VFM audit could assess to what extent this objective is being achieved.

2.9 **Economy** is concerned with the cost of inputs, and it is achieved by obtaining those inputs at the lowest acceptable cost. Economy does not mean straightforward cost-cutting, because resources must be acquired which are of a suitable quality to provide the service to the desired standard. Cost-cutting should not sacrifice quality to the extent that service standards fall to an unacceptable level. Economising by buying poor quality materials, labour or equipment is usually a false economy.

2.10 **Efficiency** means the following.

(a) Maximising output for a given input, for example maximising the number of transactions handled per employee or per £1 spent.

(b) Achieving the minimum input for a given output. For example, the Department of Social Security is currently required to pay Child Benefit to over 10 million parents. Efficiency will be achieved by making these payments with the minimum labour and computer time.

2.11 **Effectiveness** means ensuring that the outputs of a service or programme have the desired impacts, in other words, finding out whether they succeed in achieving objectives, and if so, to what extent. In a VFM audit, the objectives of a particular programme or activity need to be specified and understood in order for the auditor to make a proper assessment of whether value for money has been achieved.

2.12 An example which has been cited is a decision by the government that hill farmers should be paid an allowance or subsidy. The allowances or subsidies could be paid economically and efficiently, but an auditor in a VFM audit would need to know why the allowance or subsidy is being paid to decide whether value for money has been achieved. Suppose that the purpose of the subsidy was to encourage farmers to continue farming in hill areas so as to provide employment for the rural population. Farmers might use their allowance to buy labour-saving machinery, with the 'impact' that jobs are lost in hill farming. In such a situation, a VFM audit would reveal that value for money had not been achieved because the objective of the programme of subsidies or allowance payments had not achieved the stated objective, and even had an opposite effect.

Performance measurement in the public sector 11/97

2.13 Many of the distinctions between the private and public sector are becoming blurred as the government tries to inject elements of competition and market forces. Conversely, the private sector's new focus on customers and quality of service has much in common with the aims of public sector bodies. The problems of performance measurement in the public sector are to a great extent the problems of performance measurement generally, in particular with regard to non-financial indicators. In the past, however, the public sector has been perceived as presenting special difficulties. Why is this so?

2.14 A central theme of many of the governments pronouncements on the public sector throughout the 1980s and 1990s has been the need to improve performance, but basic control theory tells us that in order to improve we first need to know where we are going wrong and how far we are going wrong.

2.15 With public sector services, there has rarely been any market competition and no profit motive. In the private sector, these two factors help to guide the process of fixing proper prices and managing resources economically, efficiently and effectively. Since most public sector organisations cannot be judged by their success against competition nor by profitability, some other methods of assessing performance have to be used.

2.16 In the public sector, performance measures are difficult to define. Measures of output quantity and output quality, by themselves, provide insufficient evidence of how well the community is served by a programme.

2.17 Public sector services are characterised by the following facts.

(a) Centralised decisions about spending are made by the Treasury, the Cabinet and Parliament.
(b) The implementation of spending decisions is done by government departments.
(c) The beneficiaries of the spending decisions are the public, not the 'spenders'.

Therefore there are mainly three groups involved in public spending.

2.18 Measures of a programme's importance and quality (ultimate effectiveness) should therefore be obtained from the following sources:

(a) the policymakers (elected or appointed members and senior officers);
(b) the departments involved (especially the 'professionals');
(c) the 'constituents', those who provide the resources and those who receive the services.

To fulfil the requirements of accountability the policymakers must provide information about the aims and results of public spending to their constituents and obtain their views. If efficiency is to be 'proved' it must be demonstrated to others and this requires a better dialogue with the public.

What is performance?

2.19 **Performance** can be measured by:

(a) progress towards objectives;
(b) progress in improving efficiency;
(c) control over spending.

Objectives must be justified as appropriate and worthwhile and the activities undertaken must be properly defined at the outset. It is no use making progress towards inappropriate objectives or becoming more efficient in achieving unjustified activities. In the public sector multiple objectives are pursued, including economic, technical, regulatory and social objectives.

2.20 **Efficiency** is a ratio measure relating inputs to outputs. Inputs are the human material and other resources transformed through activities to produce outputs. Inputs are usually translated into monetary costs by taking the price paid, but often what is most useful is the 'opportunity cost' (ie value in 'next best use'). Outputs are most often expressed in physical units, eg tonnes of refuse collected. Generally it has been the absence of reasonable measures of output that has hindered the development of efficiency measurement in the public sector, but the lack of sophisticated management accounting systems has also contributed.

2.21 Efficiency measurement is illustrated in three different situations as follows.

(a) **Where input is, or can be, fixed**

$$\frac{\text{Actual output}}{\text{Maximum output obtainable}} \text{ for a given output}$$

$$\frac{25}{30} \text{ miles per gallon} = 83.3\% \text{ efficiency}$$

(b) **Where output is, or can be, fixed**

$$\frac{\text{Minimum input needed}}{\text{Actual input}} \text{ for a given output}$$

$$\frac{\text{55 hours}}{\text{60 hours}} \text{ to erect scaffolding} = 91.7\% \text{ efficiency}$$

(c) **Where input and output are variable**

$$\frac{\text{Actual output}}{\text{Actual input}} \text{ compared with } \frac{\text{Standard output}}{\text{Standard input}}$$

$$\frac{7{,}000}{\pounds 9{,}030} = \pounds 1.29\text{p per meal compared with } \frac{7{,}500}{\pounds 9{,}600} \text{ meals} = \pounds 1.28\text{p per meal}$$

$\therefore$ 99.2% efficiency

Executive agencies

2.22 In 1992 the Treasury published a guide entitled *Executive Agencies - A guide to setting targets and measuring performance.* The following are some of the salient points.

(a) The targets will usually fall under one or other of the following broad headings.

(i) Financial performance
(ii) Volume and output
(iii) Quality of service (embracing timeliness, quality of 'product', and availability)
(iv) Efficiency

(b) No agency should set more than a handful of key targets.

(c) It is important that an explicit balance should be decided between the targets set for quality of service and those covering volume of output and efficiency.

(d) Consistent terminology should be used to avoid confusion when different terms are used to describe the same phenomenon.

2.23 Regarding point (d) the annex to the guide includes the following table.

Term	Definition	Example
Effectiveness	An effectiveness measure reveals the extent to which objectives have been met: it makes no reference to cost.	Total hip replacement operations are associated with a mortality rate of less than 2 per cent.
Efficiency	An efficiency measure describes the relationship between the output of an agency and the associated inputs.	Average total hip replacement costs (unit cost of output) is £5,000.
Quality	A quality measure describes the usefulness or value of a service. Relates to the delivery of that service to the recipient.	The average waiting time for a total hip replacement operation is 4 months.
Target	A target is a quantified objective set by management to be attained at a specified date.	Output target: Average number of total hip replacement operations per week next year to be 10.5 or above. Quality target: Waiting time for a first appointment next year to be no more than 2 weeks.

Nationalised industries

2.24 The basis on which the remaining nationalised industries are currently judged is found mainly in a White Paper dating back to 1978, *The Nationalised Industries* Cmnd 3137.

Three sets of criteria were provided by which performance would be judged.

(a) A financial target, decided industry by industry. For industries which are unlikely to make a profit this target is set in terms of an amount of grant or deficit. The financial target is seen as the 'primary expression of financial performance.'

(b) An investment criterion. This takes the form of a required rate of return (RRR), on new investment as a whole.

(c) Non-financial performance indicators to supplement the financial targets.

The financial targets are clearly a critical measure of performance and correspond closely to the financial measures used in the private sector but they need to be linked to the performance in non-financial terms that is achieved by the industries.

Question 1

Listed below are eight of the nine National Charter Standards from the Hospital Patient's Charter.

(a) Respect for privacy, dignity and religious and cultural beliefs.
(b) Arrangements to ensure everyone, including people with special needs, can use services.
(c) Information to relatives and friends.
(d) Waiting time for an ambulance service.
(e) Waiting time for initial assessment in accident and emergency departments.
(f) Waiting time in outpatient clinics.
(g) Cancellation of operations.
(h) A named qualified nurse, midwife, or health visitor responsible for each patient.

Required

Devise performance measures that would enable each of these aims to be expressed in quantitative terms and explain how the information could be obtained.

To help you, here are some suggestions for the first three, derived directly from the Patient's Charter.

(a) Number and availability of private areas for confidential discussions with relatives; range and proportion of non-standard meals served.

(b) Availability of facilities for children compared with demand for such facilities; number of entrances accessible for wheelchairs.

(c) Number of staff available to deal with calls; calls handled per person; average time waiting for a call to be answered; number of complaints about lack of information or misinformation.

The Charter's standard for (g) is that operations should not be cancelled on the day the patient is due to arrive in hospital, and that if an operation is cancelled twice the patient will be admitted to hospital within one month of the second cancellation.

Don't forget to explain how the information would be obtained - from questionnaires, random observations, hospital logs and records or whatever you think is appropriate.

---

3 RISK ANALYSIS 5/96, 11/98

Stage 4 Topic Link. Techniques to aid decision-making in uncertainty come in to your Stage 4 studies for Papers 14 and 15 as well.

Risk and uncertainty

KEY TERM

Risk: A condition in which there exists a quantifiable dispersion in the possible outcomes from any activity (OT).

3.1 Risk as described here is the **business risk** of an **investment** in the business. This is in contrast to financial risk which is the risk that a geared company may not make enough profit, after paying the interest on its borrowings, to finance a satisfactory dividend. Business risk can be defined as the potential volatility of profits caused by the nature and type of business operations involved.

3.2 There are three elements in business risk.

(a) The **inherent risk of the industry or market itself**. For example, the fashion industry is a higher risk industry than the food processing industry; and to a UK firm, export markets in the Third World are likely to be higher risk markets than the UK market.

(b) The **stage in the product's life cycle**. Every product has a life cycle, and the 'classical' product life cycle consists of four stages.

- Introduction
- Growth
- Maturity
- Decline

When an investment is made in a product which is in its introductory phase, there is a high risk that it will fail to win market acceptance, and will have a very short market life. When an investment is made in a declining product, the risk of a rapid decline in sales is high.

(c) The **proportion of fixed costs in total costs**. When an investment involves a high proportion of fixed costs, it will need to achieve a high sales volume just to break even, and so the business risk will be high.

3.3 There are basically two ways of analysing risk and uncertainty.

(a) One approach takes the view that estimates of future costs, sales demand and revenues will at best be based on rational opinions and assumptions, and actual results might easily be better or worse than estimated. Just how much better or worse than estimated they might be is unquantifiable.

(b) Another approach takes the view that we can provide **quantified estimates** of how the future outcomes might vary. These quantified estimates will often be expressed as probabilities that a particular outcome will occur. For example, estimates of future sales demand might be made as follows.

Sales demand	*Probability*
Units	
10,000	0.2
12,000	0.5
15,000	0.2
20,000	0.1

3.4 Analysing possible future outcomes can be done using either approach (a) or approach (b). Approach (a) might be described as **uncertainty analysis**, whereas the more quantifiable approach (b) might be described in contrast as **risk analysis**. The distinction between **uncertainty** and **risk**, if you are called on to make one, is basically a matter of whether or not the variability of future outcomes can be quantified or not.

3.5 The methods or techniques of analysing uncertainty and risk, and of taking uncertainty and risk into consideration when reaching a decision, include the following.

(a) Conservative estimates can be made. Here outcomes are estimated in a conservative manner in order to provide a built-in safety factor. However, the method fails to consider explicitly a range of outcomes and, by concentrating only on conservative figures, may also fail to consider the expected or most likely outcomes.

(b) We can look at the worst possible and best possible outcomes, as well as the most likely outcome, and reach a decision which takes these into account.

(c) Sensitivity analysis can be used.

(d) We can assess probabilities and calculate for each decision alternative:

(i) the expected value of costs or benefits and also, possibly, the standard deviation of the possible outcomes;

(ii) a probability distribution of the possible outcomes.

Decision trees might be used to show the alternatives facing the decision maker. Computerised decision models might also be used.

(e) We can assess the value of having more information to help the decision maker to reach a decision.

Adjusting the discount rate 5/96

3.6 With this method of allowing for risk, a premium is added to the discount rate used in appraising investments as a safety margin. Marginally profitable projects are then less likely to have a positive NPV. For example, if a company's cost of capital is say 10%, a very risky project might be discounted at, say, 15% and a less risky project might be evaluated at a discount rate of, say, 12%.

3.7 This method recognises that risky investments ought to earn a higher return as reward for the risks that are taken. The problem with the method is that the size of the risk premium to be added is chosen arbitrarily.

Applying a time limit to the payback period

3.8 Estimates of future cash flows are difficult to make at the best of times, and estimates of cash flows several years ahead are quite likely to be inaccurate. It is also difficult to control capital projects over a long period of time, to ensure that the expected benefits are fully realised.

3.9 A method of limiting the risk on a capital project is to apply a **payback time limit**, so that a project should not be undertaken unless it pays back within, say, four years. There are two ways of applying a payback time limit.

(a) A project might be expected to pay back within a certain time limit, and in addition show a positive NPV from its net cash flows.

(b) Alternatively, a project might be expected to pay back **in discounted cash flow terms** within a certain time period. For example, a project might be required to have a positive NPV on its cumulative cash flows by year 4.

3.10 EXAMPLE: DISCOUNTED PAYBACK

A company plans to spend £700,000 now on a project that is expected to last for 15 years. The annual cash benefits are expected to be £150,000. The target DCF rate of return is 12%. In addition, the company requires all capital projects to have achieved payback in DCF terms by year 5. Should the project be undertaken?

3.11 SOLUTION

The NPV of the project over a 15 year period is positive.

Year	*Cash flow*	*Discount factor*	*Present value*
	£	12%	£
0	(700,000)	1.000	(700,000)
1-15	150,000	6.811	1,021,650
			321,650

However, the project does not pay back in DCF terms by year 5.

Year	*Cash flow*	*Discount factor*	*Present value*	*Cumulative NPV*
	£		£	£
0	(700,000)	1.000	(700,000)	(700,000)
1	150,000	0.893	133,950	(566,050)
2	150,000	0.797	119,550	(446,500)
3	150,000	0.712	106,800	(339,700)
4	150,000	0.636	95,400	(244,300)
5	150,000	0.567	85,050	(159,250)

Since it fails to pay back in discounted cash flow terms and by year 5, the project should be rejected.

In this example, the project NPV would become positive between year 7 and year 8. This can be confirmed by looking at the cumulative discount tables to see where the discount factor at 12% exceeds $\frac{£700{,}000}{£150{,}000} = 4.667$.

The reason for rejecting the project would be that since it fails to pay back within five years, it relies too heavily on the estimates of cash flows in the later years of the project's life to be considered a safe enough investment.

Sensitivity analysis 5/96

3.12 One method of incorporating risk in an investment appraisal is to apply sensitivity analysis tests to the project. This can be done by re-calculating the NPV in a number of different situations, for example:

(a) if the initial cost of the investment were 5% higher than expected;
(b) if running costs were 10% higher or savings were 10% lower than expected;
(c) if costs were 5% higher and savings 5% lower than expected.

3.13 If the NPV is negative when costs are increased a little, or benefits are reduced a little, the project would be rejected on the grounds that it is too sensitive to variations in one or more key cost or revenue items.

Measuring the margin of error

3.14 With this method of sensitivity analysis, the forecast variables are adjusted to see what changes would be necessary before a project would only just break even.

3.15 EXAMPLE: MEASURING THE MARGIN OF ERROR

Nevers Ure Ltd is considering a project with the following cash flows.

Year	*Purchase of plant*	*Running costs*	*Savings*
	£	£	£
0	(7,000)		
1		2,000	6,000
2		2,500	7,000

The cost of capital is 8%. Measure the sensitivity of the project to changes in the levels of expected costs and savings.

3.16 SOLUTION

The PV of the cash flows is as follows.

Year	*Discount factor*	*PV of plant cost*	*PV of running costs*	*PV of savings*	*PV of net cash flow*
	8%	£	£	£	£
0	1.000	(7,000)			(7,000)
1	0.926		(1,852)	5,556	3,704
2	0.857		(2,143)	5,999	3,856
		(7,000)	(3,995)	11,555	560

The project has a positive NPV and would appear to be worthwhile. The changes in cash flows which would need to occur before the project only just breaks even (NPV = 0) are as follows.

(a) Plant costs would need to increase by a PV of £560, $\frac{560}{7,000} = 8.0\%$

(b) Running costs would need to increase by a PV of £560, $\frac{560}{3,995} = 14.0\%$

(c) Savings would need to fall short by a PV of £560, $\frac{560}{11,555} = 4.8\%$

Question 2

A project has a net present value at 12% of £4,270. There is, however, uncertainty about a cost at year 2 which is estimated to be £50,000. What percentage increase in this cost would make the project non-viable?

Answer

The present value of the cost is £50,000 × 0.797 = £39,850.

The required increase is £4,270/£39,850 = 0.10715 = 10.715%, or about 11%.

3.17 The **weaknesses of sensitivity analysis** are as follows.

(a) In spite of the possibility of checking the sensitivity of a project's NPV to changes in the cash flows from two or more items in conjunction, it is more usual for sensitivity analysis to be applied to each cost or revenue item individually. This is often unrealistic, because items are often interdependent.

(b) Sensitivity analysis does not examine the probability that any particular variation in costs or revenues might occur. For example how likely is it that running costs will be 5% or 10% higher than expected?

Exam focus point

Note that mathematical techniques and statistical methods will not be examined in isolation from other topics on the syllabus, and you will not be expected to carry out detailed sensitivity analysis in the examination.

The certainty equivalent approach

3.18 Another method is the **certainty equivalent approach**. By this method, the expected cash flows of the project are converted to equivalent riskless amounts. The greater the risk of an expected cash flow, the smaller the certainty equivalent value (for receipts) or the larger the certainty equivalent value (for payments). The disadvantage of the certainty equivalent approach is that the amount of the adjustment to each cash flow is decided subjectively by management.

KEY TERM

Certainty equivalent approach: a method of risk analysis in which the expected cash flows of a project are converted to equivalent riskless amounts. The greater the risk of an expected cash flow, the smaller the certainty equivalent value for receipts and the larger the certainty equivalent value for payments.

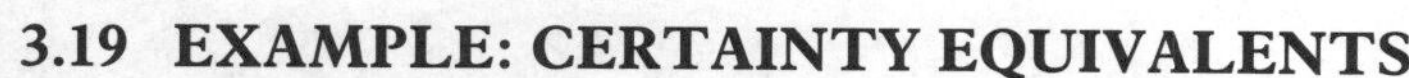

3.19 EXAMPLE: CERTAINTY EQUIVALENTS

Dark Ages Ltd, whose cost of capital is 10%, is considering a project with the following expected cash flows.

Year	Cash flow	Discount factor	Present value
	£	10%	£
0	(9,000)	1.000	(9,000)
1	7,000	0.909	6,363
2	5,000	0.826	4,130
3	5,000	0.751	3,755
		NPV	5,248

The project would seem to be worthwhile. However, because of the uncertainty about the future cash flows, the management decides to reduce them to certainty equivalents by taking only 70%, 60% and 50% of the years 1, 2 and 3 cash flows respectively. (Note that this method of risk adjustment allows for different risk factors in each year of the project.) Is the project worthwhile?

3.20 SOLUTION

The risk-adjusted NPV of the project would be as follows.

Year	Cash flow	PV factor	PV
	£		£
0	(9,000)	1.000	(9,000)
1	4,900	0.909	4,454
2	3,000	0.826	2,478
3	2,500	0.751	1,878
		NPV	(190)

The project is too risky and should be rejected.

Probability estimates of cash flows 11/98

3.21 A probability distribution of expected cash flows can often be estimated, and this may be used:

(a) to calculate an expected value of the NPV;

(b) to measure risk, for example:

(i) by calculating the worst possible outcome and its probability;
(ii) by calculating the probability that the project will fail to achieve a positive NPV.

3.22 EXAMPLE: PROBABILITY ESTIMATES OF CASH FLOWS

A company is considering a project involving the outlay of £300,000 which it estimates will generate cash flows over its two year life at the probabilities shown in the following table.

Cash flows for project

Year 1	*Cash flow*	*Probability*
	£	
	100,000	0.25
	200,000	0.50
	300,000	0.25
		1.00

If cash flow in Year 1 is:	*there is a probability of:*	*that cash flow in Year 2 will be:*
£		£
100,000	0.25	0
	0.50	100,000
	0.25	200,000
	1.00	
200,000	0.25	100,000
	0.50	200,000
	0.25	300,000
	1.00	
300,000	0.25	200,000
	0.50	300,000
	0.25	350,000
	1.00	

The company's investment criterion for this type of project is 10% DCF. What is the expected value (EV) of the project's NPV, and what is the probability that the NPV will be negative?

3.23 SOLUTION

The present value of the cash flows is as follows.

Year	*Cash flow*	*Discount factor*	*Present value*
	£'000	10%	£'000
1	100	0.909	90.9
1	200	0.909	181.8
1	300	0.909	272.7
2	100	0.826	82.6
2	200	0.826	165.2
2	300	0.826	247.8
2	350	0.826	289.1

The possible cash flows and their probabilities are as follows.

Year 1 PV of cash flow £'000	*Probability*	*Year 2 PV of cash flow* £'000	*Probability*	*Joint Prob*	*Total PV of cash inflows* £'000	*EV of PV of cash inflows* £'000
(1)	(a)	(2)	(b)	(a)×(b)	(1)+(2)	
90.9	0.25	0.0	0.25	0.0625	90.9	5.681
90.9	0.25	82.6	0.50	0.1250	173.5	21.688
90.9	0.25	165.2	0.25	0.0625	256.1	16.006
181.8	0.50	82.6	0.25	0.1250	264.4	33.050
181.8	0.50	165.2	0.50	0.2500	347.0	86.750
181.8	0.50	247.8	0.25	0.1250	429.6	53.700
272.7	0.25	165.2	0.25	0.0625	437.9	27.369
272.7	0.25	247.8	0.50	0.1250	520.5	65.063
272.7	0.25	289.1	0.25	0.0625	561.8	35.113
			EV of PV of cash inflows			344.420

* Project cash inflows have PV of less than £300,000.

	£
EV of PV of cash inflows	344,420
Project cost	300,000
EV of NPV	44,420

Since the EV of the NPV is positive, the project should go ahead unless the risk element is unacceptably high.

The probability that the project will fail to break even is the probability that the total PV of cash inflows is less than £300,000. From the table of figures, we can establish that this probability is 0.0625 + 0.125 + 0.0625 + 0.125 = 0.375 or 37.5%. This might be considered an unacceptably high risk.

Constructing models 5/96, 5/97

3.24 It might be possible to use a financial model to decide what plan will optimise the achievement of the organisation's financial objectives. One type of **optimising model** is a linear programming model, which you should recall is a model for maximising or minimising an objective function, subject to certain constraints. In the case of financial modelling, a linear programming model might be formulated:

(a) to maximise shareholders' wealth (expressed, perhaps, as the share value);

(b) subject to certain constraints, which might be:

(i) financial (such as shortage of funds); or
(ii) non-financial such as:

(1) resource productivity, such as maximum output per employee per year;

(2) environmental, such as maximum consumption of raw materials;

(3) social, such as employee welfare, for example maximum or minimum retirement age.

3.25 In a **financial planning model**, the variables might include:

(a) fixed assets;
(b) current assets;
(c) liabilities;
(d) revenues from the sale of different products;
(e) payments for various items of operating cost;
(f) taxation;
(g) sources of funds (equity, loans, preference shares);
(h) dividends and interest rates.

3.26 The inter-relationships between the variables will be specified in the model. For example, an increase in sales will affect the cost of sales, debtors, creditors, cash, fixed assets, profits, taxation and dividends in a way specified by the model, according to assumptions about the contribution/sales ratio, price inflation for various cost items, asset turnover ratios, taxation rates and capital allowances and dividend cover.

3.27 The model can be used to plan ahead, and the future profitability of the company can be estimated. If the company needs extra funds, the amount required can be assessed, and steps taken at an early stage to ensure that they will be available. If the model forecasts unsatisfactory profits and dividends, management will be aware that they need to devise long-term strategies now to improve results in future years.

Simulation: the Monte Carlo method

3.28 The **Monte Carlo simulation** method involves the use of random numbers and can be employed in the study of a dynamic system over time, where the relationships between variables, or the values of variables, are not constant. In the business environment it can be used to examine forecasting problems and also inventory and scheduling problems. A simulation model is designed so that the analyst can observe the behaviour of the 'system' over time and gather useful information about it. The technique is basically experimental in nature in the sense that a simulation 'run' can often be regarded as a sample in a statistical experiment.

3.29 Carrying out a properly controlled simulation is, in essence, much the same as observing the real system. In simulation, however, the researcher is able to control the system rather than being controlled by it. This means that he can experiment with the system by altering its parameters and decision rules at will. Such experiments are, of course, rarely possible when observing a real system in action. Another major advantage is that the actual time span over which the system is simulated can be compressed. For example the performance of a system over a year could be examined in a few minutes on a computer.

3.30 EXAMPLE: SIMULATION AND PROJECT APPRAISAL

The following probability estimates have been prepared for a proposed investment project.

	Year	*Probability*	£
Cost of equipment	0	1.00	(40,000)
Annual revenue	1-5	0.15	40,000
		0.40	50,000
		0.30	55,000
		0.15	60,000
Annual running costs	1-5	0.10	25,000
		0.25	30,000
		0.35	35,000
		0.30	40,000

The cost of capital is 12%. How might a simulation model be used to assess the project's NPV?

3.31 SOLUTION

A simulation model could be constructed by assigning a range of random numbers to each possible value for each of the uncertain variables, as follows.

Annual revenue £	*Probability*	*Random numbers*	*Annual running costs* £	*Probability*	*Random numbers*
40,000	0.15	00 - 14	25,000	0.10	00 - 09
50,000	0.40	15 - 54	30,000	0.25	10 - 34
55,000	0.30	55 - 84	35,000	0.35	35 - 69
60,000	0.15	85 - 99	40,000	0.30	70 - 99

The model would then be used in the same way as any simulation model. Random numbers would be generated, probably by computer, and these would be used to assign values to each of the uncertain variables. (Some pocket calculators also have the facility to generate random numbers.)

For example, if random numbers 378420015689 were generated, the values assigned to the variables would be as follows.

	Revenue		*Costs*	
Calculation	*Random No*	*Value*	*Random No*	*Value*
		£		£
1	37	50,000	84	40,000
2	20	50,000	01	25,000
3	56	55,000	89	40,000

The NPV would be calculated many times over using the values established in this way with more random numbers, and the results would be analysed to provide:

(a) an average expected NPV for the project;

(b) a statistical distribution pattern for the possible variation in the NPV above or below this average.

The decision to go ahead with the project or not would then be made on the basis of expected return and risk.

Decision trees

3.32 Decision trees are a way of illustrating the choices facing a decision maker (whether in making an investment or some other decision) and the possible consequences of each choice. The following example will be used to help you to revise the technique. If you think you know the technique already, attempt your own solution.

3.33 EXAMPLE: A DECISION TREE

Elsewhere Ltd is considering the production of a new consumer item with a five year product lifetime. In order to manufacture this time it would be necessary to build a new plant. After having considered several alternative strategies, management are left with the following three possibilities.

Strategy A: build a large plant at an estimated cost of £600,000

This strategy faces two types of market conditions: high demand with a probability of 0.7 or low demand with a probability of 0.3. If the demand is high the company can expect to receive a net annual cash inflow of £250,000 for each of the next five years. If the demand is low there would be a net annual cash outflow of £50,000.

Strategy B: build a small plant at an estimated cost of £350,000

This strategy also faces two types of market conditions: high demand with a probability of 0.7 or low demand with a probability of 0.3. The net annual cash inflow of the five-year period for the small plant is £25,000 if the demand is low and is £150,000 if the demand is high.

Strategy C: do not build a plant initially

This strategy consists of leaving the decision for one year whilst more information is collected. The resulting information can be positive or negative with estimated probabilities of 0.8 and 0.2 respectively. At the end of this time management may decide to build either a large plant or a small plant at the same costs as at present providing the information is positive. If the resulting information is negative, management would decide to build no plant at all. Given positive information the probabilities of high and low demand change to 0.9 and 0.1 respectively, regardless of which plant is built. The net annual cash inflows for the remaining four-year period for each type of plant are the same as those given in strategies A and B.

All costs and revenues are given in present value terms and should not be discounted.

Required

(a) Draw a decision tree to represent the alternative courses of action open to the company.

(b) Determine the expected return for each possible course of action and hence decide the best course of action for the management of Elsewhere Ltd.

3.34 SOLUTION

(a) *Decision tree for a possible new plant*

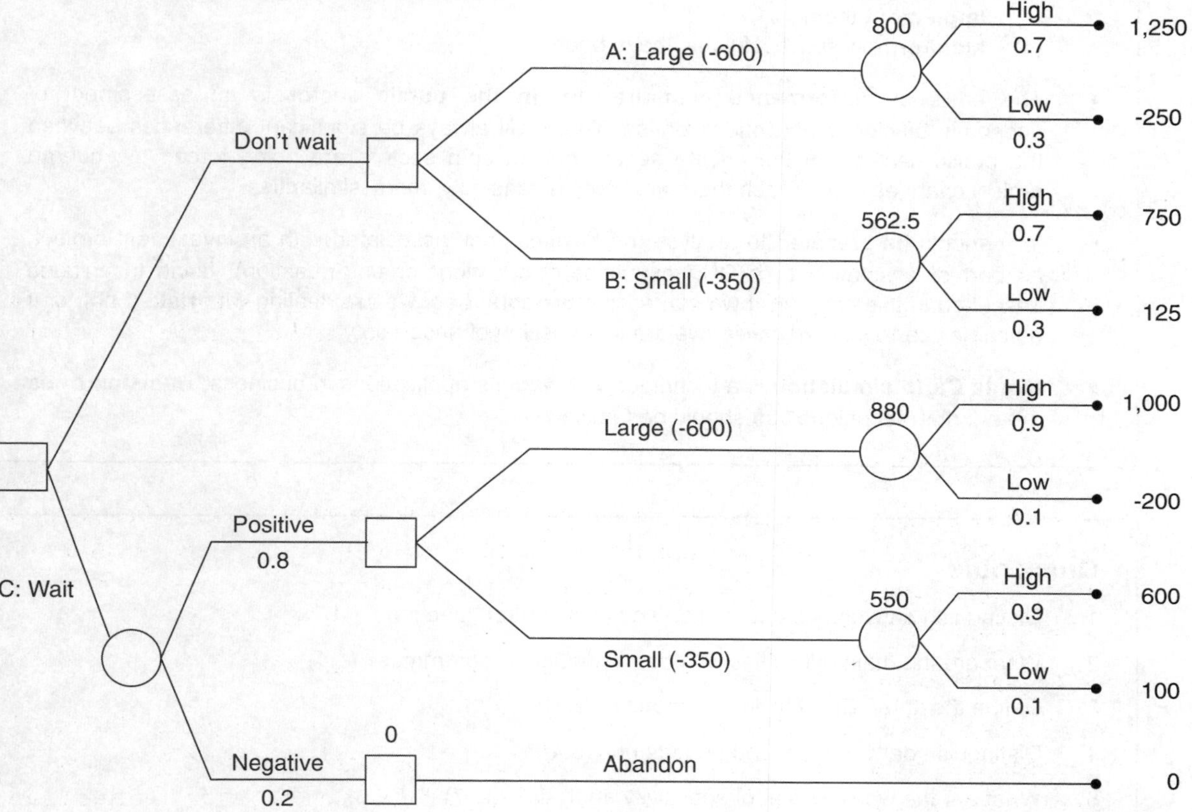

Key
□ Decision point
○ Outcome point

(b) Evaluation of the decision tree (see above) shows that the best course of action is to wait a year, and then build a large plant if positive information is received, but abandon the project if negative information is received.

Expected values (in thousands of pounds) are calculated as follows.

Large plant now (A)	$(0.7 \times 5 \times 250) - (0.3 \times 5 \times 50) - 600$	= 200
Small plant now (B)	$(0.7 \times 5 \times 150) + (0.3 \times 5 \times 25) - 350$	= 212.5
Large plant following positive information		
	$(0.9 \times 4 \times 250) - (0.1 \times 4 \times 50) - 600$	= 280
Small plant following positive information		
	$(0.9 \times 4 \times 150) + (0.1 \times 4 \times 25) - 350$	= 200

Positive information: higher of 280 and 180, ie 280

Waiting (C)	$(0.8 \times 280) + (0.2 \times 0)$	= 224

224 is higher than either 200 or 212.5, hence the recommendation to wait.

Chapter roundup

- There are a number of **cost reduction measures** that can be taken to improve profitability. Cost reduction measures ought to be a planned programme rather than the result of panic action. **Value analysis** is one type of formal cost reduction programme.
- Cost reduction calls for decisions about how **costs** should be reduced. Like all decisions, the task of management is as follows.

  (a) **Identify decision options**: the ways of saving costs
  (b) **Evaluate** them
  (c) **Implement** them
  (d) **Monitor** how successful they have been

- The basis of **performance measurement in the public sector** is an assessment of economy, efficiency and effectiveness. There will always be significant differences between the public sector and the private sector, but as both sectors are being forced to undergo radical changes in approach there are also, increasingly, many similarities.
- You should be prepared to analyse the business risk associated with an investment project, as part of a solution to a DCF examination question (or part-question), using techniques described in this chapter. If we can assign **probabilities**, we are dealing with **risk**. If not, or if outcomes cannot be identified, we are in a position of uncertainty.
- **Monte Carlo simulation** is a technique with various applications in business. **Decision trees** are a further technique you should be familiar with.

Quick quiz

1 Distinguish between cost reduction and cost control. (see para 1.1)

2 What are the main difficulties with cost reduction programmes? (1.4)

3 Define the 'three Es' of 'value for money'. (2.1)

4 Distinguish between risk and uncertainty. (3.4)

5 What are the weaknesses of sensitivity analysis? (3.17)

6 What is a certainty equivalent? (3.18)

7 Explain how a simulation using random numbers is carried out. (3.31)

Question to try	Level	Marks	Time
4	Exam standard	25	45 mins

Part B

Treasurership

Chapter 5

THE TREASURY FUNCTION

Chapter topic list	Syllabus reference	Ability required
1 Treasury departments	13 b(iii)	Skill
2 Capital structure and cash flow planning	13 b(viii)	Skill
3 Sources of funds	13 b(iv)	Application

Introduction

The section of the syllabus we now move on to, entitled 'Treasurership', covers a wide variety of topics.

In this chapter, we discuss the work of the **treasury function**, which in larger companies will form a separate department. More specific aspects of treasury work - for example **cash management techniques** - are covered later in this Study Text.

1 TREASURY DEPARTMENTS 11/95, 5/96, 11/98

1.1 Large companies, including multinationals, often rely heavily for both long-term and short-term funds on the financial and currency markets. These markets are volatile, with interest rates and foreign exchange rates changing continually and by significant amounts. Many large companies have set up separate treasury departments to manage cash and foreign currency.

KEY TERM

The CIMA *Official Terminology* (1996) gives the Association of Corporate Treasurers' definition of **treasury management**, which is 'the corporate handling of all financial matters, the generation of external and internal funds for business, the management of currencies and cash flows, and the complex strategies, policies and procedures of corporate finance'.

1.3 A treasury department, even in a large company, is likely to be quite small, with perhaps a staff of three to six qualified accountants, bankers or corporate treasurers working under a Treasurer, who is responsible to the Finance Director. In some cases, where the company or organisation handles very large amounts of cash or foreign currency dealings, and often has large cash surpluses, the treasury department might be larger.

The role of the treasurer

1.3 The **Association of Corporate Treasurers** has listed the experience it will require from its student members before they are eligible for full membership of the Association. This list of required experience gives a good indication of the roles of treasury departments.

(a) **Corporate financial objectives**

(i) financial aims and strategies;
(ii) financial and treasury policies;
(iii) financial and treasury systems.

(b) **Liquidity management**: making sure the company has the liquid funds it needs, and invests any surplus funds, even for very short terms.

(i) working capital and money transmission management;
(ii) banking relationships and arrangements;
(iii) money management.

Cash management and liquidity management are probably the most obvious responsibilities of a treasurer. In some organisations, the task is largely one of controlling stocks, debtors, creditors and bank overdrafts. In cash-rich companies, the treasurer will invest surplus funds to earn a good yield until they are required again for another purpose. A good relationship with one or more banks is desirable, so that the treasurer can negotiate overdraft facilities, money market loans or longer term loans at reasonable interest rates.

(c) **Funding management**

(i) funding policies and procedures;
(ii) sources of funds;
(iii) types of funds.

Funding management is concerned with all forms of borrowing, and alternative sources of funds, such as leasing and factoring.

The treasurer needs to know:

(i) where funds are obtainable;
(ii) for how long;
(iii) at what interest rate;
(iv) whether security would be required;
(v) whether interest rates would be fixed or variable.

If a company borrows, say, £10,000,000, even a difference of ¼% in the interest cost of the loan obtained would be worth £25,000 in interest charges each year.

(d) **Currency management**

(i) exposure policies and procedures;
(ii) exchange dealing, including futures and options;
(iii) international monetary economics and exchange regulations.

Currency dealings can save or cost a company considerable amounts of money, and the success or shortcomings of the corporate treasurer can have a significant impact on the profit and loss account of a company which is heavily involved in foreign trade.

(e) **Corporate finance**

(i) equity capital management;
(ii) business acquisitions and sales;
(iii) project finance and joint ventures.

Corporate finance is concerned with matters such as raising share capital, its form (ordinary or preference, or different classes of ordinary shares), obtaining a stock exchange listing, dividend policy, financial information for management, mergers, acquisitions and business sales.

(f) **Related subjects**

(i) corporate taxation (domestic and foreign tax);
(ii) risk management and insurance;
(iii) pension fund investment management.

Centralised or decentralised cash management?

1.4 A large company may have a number of subsidiaries and divisions. In the case of a multinational, these will be located in different countries. It will be necessary to decide whether the treasury function should be centralised.

1.5 With **centralised cash management**, the central Treasury department effectively acts as the bank to the group. The central Treasury has the job of ensuring that individual operating units have all the funds they need at the right time.

1.6 The following are advantages of having a centralised specialist treasury department.

(a) Centralised liquidity management avoids having a mix of cash surpluses and overdrafts in different localised bank accounts. With bulk cash flows, lower bank charges can probably be negotiated.

(b) Larger volumes of cash are available to invest, giving better short-term investment opportunities (for example money markets, high-interest accounts and Certificates of Deposit).

(c) Any borrowing can be arranged in bulk, at lower interest rates than for smaller borrowings, and perhaps on the eurocurrency or eurobond markets.

(d) Foreign currency risk management is likely to be improved in a group of companies. A central treasury department can match foreign currency income earned by one subsidiary with expenditure in the same currency by another subsidiary. In this way, the risk of losses on adverse exchange rate movements can be avoided without the expense of forward exchange contracts or other hedging methods.

(e) A specialist treasury department will employ experts with knowledge of dealing in forward contracts, futures, options, eurocurrency markets, swaps and so on. Localised departments could not have such expertise.

(f) The centralised pool of funds required for precautionary purposes will be smaller than the sum of separate precautionary balances which would need to be held under decentralised treasury arrangements.

(g) Through having a separate profit centre, attention will be focused on the contribution to group profit performance that can be achieved by good cash, funding, investment and foreign currency management.

1.7 If cash management is decentralised:

(a) sources of finance can be diversified and can match local assets;

(b) greater autonomy can be given to subsidiaries and divisions because of the closer relationships they will have with the decentralised cash management function;

(c) the decentralised Treasury function may be able to be more responsive to the needs of individual operating units;

(d) since cash balances will not be aggregated at group level, there will be more limited opportunities to invest such balances on a short-term basis.

Centralised cash management in the multinational firm

1.8 If cash management within a **multinational firm** is centralised, each subsidiary holds only the minimum cash balance required for transaction purposes. All excess funds will be remitted to the central Treasury department.

1.9 Funds held in the central pool of funds can be returned quickly to the local subsidiary by telegraphic transfer or by means of worldwide bank credit facilities. The firm's bank can instruct its branch office in the country in which the subsidiary is located to advance funds to the subsidiary. Multinationals' central pools of funds are generally maintained in major financial centres such as London, New York, Tokyo and Zurich.

The treasury department as cost centre or profit centre

Exam focus point

The concepts 'profit centre' and 'cost centre' are covered in your Paper 16 *Management Accounting Control Systems* Study Text.

1.10 A treasury department might be managed either as a **cost centre** or as a **profit centre**. For a group of companies, this decision may need to be made for treasury departments in separate subsidiaries as well as for the central corporate treasury department.

1.11 In a cost centre, managers have an incentive only to keep the costs of the department within budgeted spending targets. The cost centre approach implies that the treasury is there to perform a service of a certain standard to other departments in the enterprise. The treasury is treated much like any other service department.

1.12 However, some companies (including BP, for example) are able to make significant profits from their treasury activities. Treating the treasury department as a profit centre recognises the fact that treasury activities such as speculation may earn revenues for the company, and may as a result make treasury staff more motivated. The profit centre approach is probably going to be appropriate only if the company has a high level of foreign exchange transactions. Such companies may choose **not** to hedge against fluctuating exchange rates, depending on their perception of the current and future economic environment, in the hope of making higher-risk speculative gains.

1.13 If a profit centre approach is being considered, the following issues should be addressed.

(a) **Competence of staff**. It may be unreasonable to expect local managers to have sufficient expertise in the area of treasury management to carry out speculative treasury operations competently. Mistakes in this specialised field may be costly. It may only be appropriate to operate a larger centralised treasury as a profit centre, and additional specialist staff demanding high salaries may need to be recruited.

(b) **Controls**. Adequate controls must be in place to prevent costly errors and overexposure to risks such as foreign exchange risks. It is possible to enter into a very large foreign exchange deal over the telephone.

(c) **Information**. A treasury team which trades in futures and options or in currencies is competing with other traders employed by major financial institutions who may have better knowledge of the market because of the large number of customers they deal with. In order to compete effectively, the team needs to have detailed and up-to-date market information.

(d) **Attitudes to risk**. The more aggressive approach to risk-taking which is characteristic of treasury professionals may be difficult to reconcile with the more measured approach to risk which may prevail within the board of directors. The recognition of treasury operations as profit making activities may not fit well with the main business operations of the company.

(e) **Internal charges**. If the department is to be a true profit centre, then market prices should be charged for its services to other departments. It may be difficult to put realistic prices on some services, such as arrangement of finance or general financial advice.

(f) **Performance evaluation**. Even with a profit centre approach, it may be difficult to measure the success of a treasury team for the reason that successful treasury activities sometimes involve **avoiding** the incurring of costs, for example when a currency devalues. For example, a treasury team which hedges a future foreign currency receipt over a period when the domestic currency undergoes devaluation (as sterling did in 1992 when it left the European exchange rate mechanism) may avoid a substantial loss for the company.

2 CAPITAL STRUCTURE AND CASH FLOW PLANNING

Capital structure considerations

2.1 The assets of a business must be financed somehow, and when a business is growing, the additional assets must be financed by additional capital. As you will by now be aware, **capital structure** refers to the way in which an organisation is financed, by a combination of long-term capital (ordinary shares and reserves, preference shares, debentures, bank loans, convertible loan stock and so on) and short-term liabilities such as a bank overdraft and trade creditors.

2.2 There are different ways in which the funding of current and fixed assets can be achieved by employing long and short-term sources of funding. The diagram below illustrates three alternative types of policy A, B and C. The dotted lines A, B and C are the cut-off levels between short-term and long-term financing for each of the policies A, B and C respectively: assets above the relevant dotted line are financed by short-term funding while assets below the dotted line are financed by long-term funding.

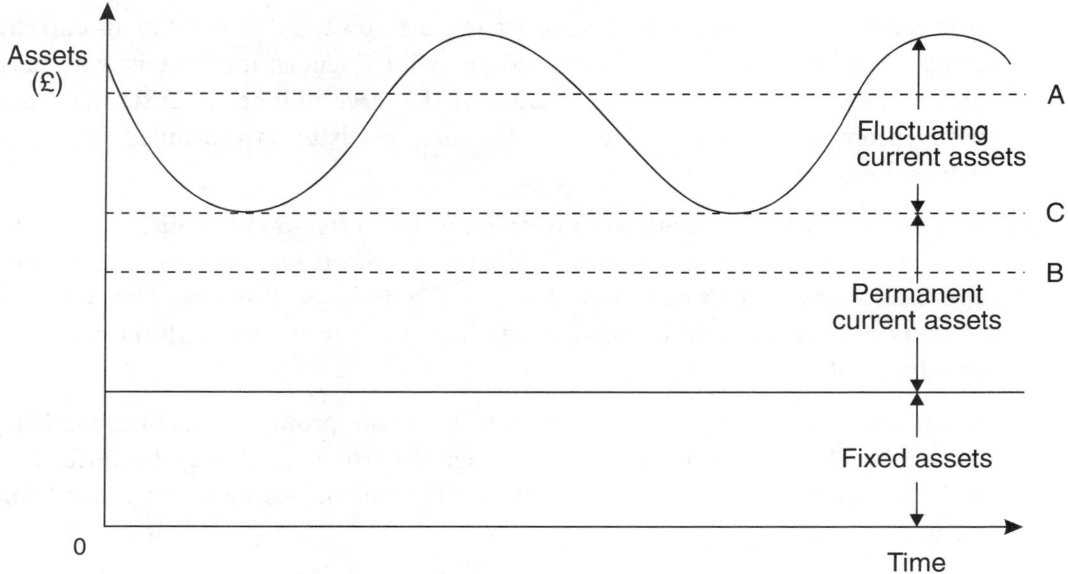

2.3 Fluctuating current assets together with permanent current assets form part of the working capital of the business, which may be financed by either long-term funding (including equity capital) or by current liabilities (short-term funding). This can be seen in terms of policies A, B and C.

(a) Policy A can be characterised as a **conservative approach** to financing working capital. All fixed assets and permanent current assets, as well as part of the fluctuating current assets, are financed by long-term funding. There is only a need to call upon short-term financing at times when fluctuations in current assets push total assets above the level of dotted line A. At times when fluctuating current assets are low and total assets fall below line A, there will be surplus cash which the company will be able to invest in marketable securities.

(b) Policy B is a more **aggressive approach** to financing working capital. Not only are fluctuating current assets all financed out of short-term sources, but so are some of the permanent current assets. This policy represents an increased risk of liquidity and cash flow problems, although potential returns will be increased if short-term financing can be obtained more cheaply than long-term finance.

(c) A **balance** between risk and return might be best achieved by policy C, a policy of maturity matching in which long-term funds finance permanent assets while short-term funds finance non-permanent assets.

Cash flow planning

2.4 A business must maintain an adequate inflow of cash in order to survive. If a business owes money and cannot pay its debts when they fall due, it can be put into liquidation by its creditors, even if it is making profits. Since a company must have adequate cash inflows to survive, management should plan and control cash flows as well as profitability.

2.5 Cash budgeting is an important element in short-term cash flow planning. Cash budget periods might be for one year, or less (for example monthly budgets). The purpose of cash budgets is to make sure that the organisation will have enough cash inflows to meet its cash outflows. If a budget reveals that a short-term cash shortage can be expected, steps will be taken to meet the problem and avoid the cash crisis (perhaps by arranging a bigger bank overdraft facility).

2.6 Cash budgets and cash flow forecasts on their own do not give full protection against a cash shortage and enforced liquidation of the business by creditors. There may be unexpected changes in cash flow patterns. When unforeseen events have an adverse effect on cash inflows, a company will only survive if it can maintain adequate cash inflows despite the setbacks. **Strategic fund management** is an extension of cash flow planning, which takes into consideration the ability of a business to overcome unforeseen problems with cash flows.

2.7 Strategic fund management recognises that the assets of a business can be divided into three categories.

(a) Assets which are needed to carry out the 'core' activities of the business. A group of companies will often have one or several main activities, and in addition will carry on several peripheral activities. The group's strategy should be primarily to develop its main activities, and so there has to be enough cash to maintain those activities and to finance their growth.

(b) Assets which are not essential for carrying out the main activities of the business, and which could be sold off at fairly short notice. These assets will consist mainly of short-term marketable investments.

(c) Assets which are not essential for carrying out the main activities of the business, and which could be sold off to raise cash, although it would probably take time to arrange the sale, and the amount of cash obtainable from the sale might be uncertain. These assets would include:

(i) long-term investments (for example, substantial shareholdings in other companies);

(ii) subsidiary companies engaged in 'peripheral' activities, which might be sold off to another company or in a management buyout;

(iii) land and buildings.

2.8 If an unexpected event takes place which threatens a company's cash position, the company could meet the threat by:

(a) working capital management to improve cash flows by reducing stocks and debtors, taking more credit, or negotiating a higher bank overdraft facility;

(b) changes to dividend policy;

(c) arranging to sell off non-essential assets. The assets in category (b) above would be saleable at short notice, and arrangements could also be made to dispose of the assets in category (c), should the need arise and provided that there is enough time to arrange the sale.

Strategic cash flow planning

2.9 It is essential for the survival of any business to have an adequate inflow of cash. Cash flow planning at a strategic level is similar to normal cash budgeting, with the following exceptions.

(a) The **planning horizon** is longer.

(b) The **uncertainties about future cash inflows and cash outflows** are much greater.

(c) The business should be able to respond, if necessary, to an unexpected need for cash. Where could extra cash be raised, and in what amounts?

(d) A company should have planned cash flows which are consistent with:

  (i) its dividend payment policy; and
  (ii) its policy for financial structuring, debt and gearing.

Question

Suppose that WXY plc had the following balance sheet as at 31 December 19X8.

	£
Fixed assets	3,500,000
Current assets less current liabilities	500,000
	4,000,000
Share capital	500,000
Reserves	1,600,000
Long-term 10% debt	1,900,000
	4,000,000

The company's strategic planners have formulated the following policies.

(a) By the end of the next year (31 December 19X9), gearing should not exceed 100% - ie long term debt should not exceed the total of share capital and reserves.

(b) The company shall pay out 50% of its profits as dividend to shareholders.

The following estimates have been made.

(a) Each £10,000 of assets generates profits of £2,000 pa, before interest.
(b) The current market cost of debt capital is 10% pa.

The company would like to invest a further £500,000 but does not intend to make a share issue to raise the finance. Advise its management. Could it borrow the money and still achieve its strategic targets by the end of 19X9?

Ignore taxation and fixed asset depreciation.

Answer

The company's strategic aims *can* all be achieved, without a new share issue, even though it is already near the gearing limit it has set itself, of 100%.

A further £500,000 investment in capital would yield extra annual profits of £100,000 p.a. before interest.

Without a share issue, the £500,000 would have to be raised as a loan at 10%, raising the total company debt to £2,400,000 and total assets at the beginning of the year to £4,500,000.

	£
Profits before interest in 19X9 (£4,500,000 × 20%)	900,000
Interest (10% of £2,400,000)	240,000
Profits before dividend	660,000
Dividend (NB: taxation ignored)	330,000
Retained profits	330,000

Balance sheet at 31 December 19X9

	£
Total assets (depreciation ignored)	
At 31.12.X8	4,000,000
New investment	500,000
Retained profits	330,000
	4,830,000
Financed by	
Share capital	500,000
Reserves	1,930,000
Debt capital	2,400,000
	4,830,000

The company's gearing would just about remain below the maximum target limit of 100%.

3 SOURCES OF FUNDS

3.1 A business needs funds to finance its activities.

(a) New funds might be raised **internally** (from retained profits) or **externally** from other sources of funds.

(b) Externally raised funds might be:

(i) **short-term,** repayable within a short period of time, say one year;

(ii) **long-term,** repayable only after a long period of time, or not necessarily repayable at all (for example equity funds and irredeemable debt capital).

(c) The source of external funds might be **equity capital** or **debt capital**.

(d) Debt capital, long-term or short-term, can be raised from a number of different sources, including trade credit, a bank overdraft, a bank loan or debt instruments such as debentures or loan stock and (in the case of some large companies) **eurobonds**.

Capital markets

3.2 Capital markets are markets for trading in long-term finance, in the form of long-term financial instruments such as equities and debentures.

3.3 The capital markets are distinguished from the money markets, which are markets for (i) trading **short-term** financial instruments such as bills of exchange and Certificates of Deposit and (ii) **short-term** lending and borrowing.

3.4 (a) Short-term capital is capital which is borrowed for a period which might range from as short as overnight up to about one year.

(b) Long-term capital is capital borrowed for a period of about five years or more.

There is a 'grey area' between long-term and short-term capital, which is lending and borrowing for a period from about a year up to about five years, which is not surprisingly sometimes referred to as medium-term capital. In the UK, the bulk of medium-term borrowing by firms is done through the banks.

3.5 Companies obtain long-term or medium-term capital in one of the following ways.

(a) **Share capital.** Most new issues of share capital are in the form of ordinary share capital (as distinct from preference share capital) and ordinary shareholders are the owners or 'members' of the company. Companies which issue ordinary share capital are inviting investors to take an equity stake in the business, or to increase their existing equity stake.

(b) **Loan capital.** Long-term loan capital might be raised in the form of a mortgage or a debenture. The lender will usually want some security for the loan, and the mortgage deed or debenture deed will specify the security. Most loans have a fixed term, and the difference between medium-term and long-term loans is simply the length of their term to maturity. Debenture stock, like shares, can be issued on the stock market and then bought and sold in subsequent trading. Interest is paid on the stock and the loan is repaid when the stock reaches its maturity date.

The role of the capital markets

3.6 The capital markets serve two main purposes.

(a) **They enable organisations to raise new finance**, for example by issuing new shares or new debentures. In the UK, a company must be a public company (a plc) to be allowed to raise finance from the public on a capital market.

Capital markets make it easier for companies to raise new long-term finance than if they had to raise funds 'privately' from investors.

(b) **They enable existing investors to sell their investments**, should they want to do so. For example, a shareholder in a listed company can sell his shares whenever he wants to on the Stock Exchange.

The marketability of securities is a very important feature of the capital markets.

(i) Investors are more willing to buy stocks and shares if they know that they could sell them easily, should they want to.

(ii) Market prices have a share valuation function.

(iii) Most trading of stocks and shares on the capital markets is in secondhand securities, rather than new issues.

Capital markets in the UK

3.7 There are several capital markets in the UK.

(a) **The Stock Exchange** provides the main market where:

(i) listed companies (large public limited companies whose shares are listed in the Stock Exchange's Official List) can raise new funds by issuing new shares or loan stock;

(ii) investors can buy and sell existing stocks and shares of listed companies.

(b) **The 'gilts' or gilt-edged market** is the market for the government's long-term debt securities. The government can raise new funds by issuing gilt-edged loan stock, and issued gilts are also traded secondhand.

(c) **The Alternative Investment Market (AIM)** is a relatively new market regulated by the Stock Exchange where companies that are not big enough to obtain a full listing on the Stock Exchange can raise new capital by issuing shares. Like the main market of the Stock Exchange, the AIM is also a market for trading existing shares.

(d) **Over-the-counter (OTC) markets** involve dealing firms which organise and 'make' markets which are not regulated or controlled by an official stock exchange.

(e) **Banks** can be approached directly for medium-term loans as well as short-term loans or overdrafts. The major clearing banks, many merchant banks and foreign banks operating in the UK are often willing to lend medium-term capital, especially to well established companies.

Chapter roundup

- In this chapter we have seen the importance of **cash** to a business, and we have looked at the skills needed to ensure its availability (**treasurership**) and at its proper control (**cash planning**).
- We have also outlined the main domestic **sources of funds**.
- In the rest of this Part of the Study Text, we will consider **particular sources of finance** in more detail, the viewpoints of **suppliers of finance** and the detailed **management of working capital**.

Quick quiz

1 What are the functions of a treasurer? (see para 1.3)

2 What are the advantages of having a centralised specialist treasury department? (1.6)

3 What factors should be considered in converting a treasury department into a profit centre? (1.13)

4 Indicate how 'conservative', 'aggressive' and 'balanced' approaches to funding may be characterised. (2.3)

5 What unforeseen changes could lead to a business's running out of cash? (2.6)

6 What are the main capital markets in the UK? (3.7)

Question to try	Level	Marks	Time
5	Introductory	n/a	20 mins

Chapter 6

SOURCES OF FINANCE I

Chapter topic list		Syllabus reference	Ability required
1	Share capital	13 b(iv); (vii)	Application
2	Loan stock	13 b(iv)	Application
3	Convertibles and warrants	13 b(iv)	Application

Introduction

Share capital is the foundation of most businesses' finance. We will therefore look first at the types of share capital. Methods of issuing shares are considered in Chapter 8. We also look in this chapter at **loan stock**, another source of long-term funding for businesses.

Convertibles and **warrants** are forms of hybrid financial instruments based upon loan stock and shares.

Exam focus point

In case study questions, you are free to say in your answer if more information is required. Then, make reasonable assumptions and state them clearly.

1 SHARE CAPITAL 11/98

Ordinary shares (equity)

1.1 Ordinary shares are issued to the owners of a company. The ordinary shares of UK companies have a nominal or 'face' value at which they are shown in the balance sheet. This is typically £1 or 50p, but shares with a nominal value of say 5p, 10p or 25p are not uncommon. The market value of a quoted company's shares bears **no relationship** whatsoever to their **nominal value**, except that when ordinary shares are issued, the issue price will be equal to or (more usually) **more than** the nominal value of the shares. Outside the UK it is not uncommon for a company's shares to have no nominal value.

1.2 Some companies have different classes of ordinary shares with different rights and voting powers laid down by the Articles of Association. The Stock Exchange discourages the use of different classes of ordinary shares and will not, except in highly unusual circumstances, allow a new issue of shares by a quoted company with rights inferior to those of another class already in issue.

1.3 A new issue of shares might be made in a variety of different circumstances.

(a) The company might want to raise more cash. When this happens, should the shares be issued *pro rata* to existing shareholders, so that control or ownership of the company is not affected? For example, if a company with 200,000 ordinary shares in issue decides to issue 50,000 new shares to raise cash, should it offer the new shares to existing shareholders, or should it sell them to new shareholders instead?

   (i) If a company sells the new shares to existing shareholders in proportion to their existing shareholding in the company, we have a rights issue. In the example above, the 50,000 shares could be issued as a one for four rights issue, by offering shareholders one new share for every four shares they currently hold. This is the method preferred by the London Stock Exchange as it avoids dilution of existing interests.

   (ii) If the number of new shares being issued is small compared to the number of shares already in issue, it might be decided instead to sell them to new shareholders, since ownership of the company would only be minimally affected.

(b) The company might want to issue new shares partly to raise cash but more importantly to 'float' its shares on a stock market. When a UK company joins the Stock Exchange, at least a minimum proportion of its shares must be made available to the general investing public if the shares are not already widely held.

(c) The company might issue new shares to the shareholders of another company, in order to take it over.

Retained profits

1.4 New issues of shares can be an important method of funding for a company at certain times in its development. However, by far the most significant source of new funding for companies on the whole is retained profits although borrowing is significant too. Raising new funds through equity issues is relatively insignificant as a source of company finance, except as a means of financing the takeover of other companies.

Preference shares

1.5 **Preference shareholders** are entitled to a fixed percentage dividend before any dividend is paid to the ordinary shareholders. As with ordinary shares, a preference dividend can only be paid if sufficient distributable profits are available, although with **cumulative preference shares** the right to an unpaid dividend is carried forward to later years. The arrears of dividend on cumulative preference shares must be paid before any dividend is paid to the ordinary shareholders. Depending on the Articles of Association, preference shareholders may be entitled to receive the nominal value of their shares in the event of winding up before any payments are made to the ordinary shareholders. The stated dividend (such as 7%) on preference shares is the cash dividend, not grossed up.

1.6 In recent years preference shares have formed a negligible part of new capital issues. The main reason for this from the viewpoint of companies is that their dividends, unlike interest on loans, are not allowable for corporation tax.

1.7 From the point of view of the investor, preference shares are less attractive than loan stock because they **cannot be secured** on the company's assets and the **dividend yield** traditionally offered on preference dividends has been much too low to provide an attractive investment compared with the interest yields that can be earned by investing in loan stock.

Rights issues

1.8 A **rights issue** is a method of raising new share capital by means of an offer to existing shareholders, inviting them to subscribe cash for new shares in proportion to their existing holdings.

For example, a rights issue on a one for four basis at 280p per share would mean that a company is inviting its existing shareholders to subscribe for one new share for every four shares they hold, at a price of 280p per new share. A rights issue may be made by any type of company, private or public, listed or unlisted. The analysis below, however, applies primarily to listed companies.

1.9 The major advantages of a rights issue are as follows.

(a) Rights issues are cheaper than offers for sale to the general public (discussed in the next chapter). This is partly because no prospectus is required, partly because the administration is simpler and partly because the cost of underwriting will be less.

(b) Rights issues are more beneficial to existing shareholders than issues to the general public. New shares are issued at a discount to the current market price, to make them attractive to investors. If the shares are issued to the general public, the benefit of the discount will be enjoyed by whoever buys the shares. A rights issue secures the discount on the market price for existing shareholders.

(c) Relative voting rights are unaffected if shareholders all take up their rights.

Deciding the issue price for a rights issue

1.10 The offer price in a rights issue will be lower than the current market price of existing shares. The size of the discount will vary, and will be larger for difficult issues.

1.11 The offer price must also be at or above the nominal value of the shares, so as not to contravene company law. Where the current market price of shares is below the nominal value, or only very slightly above it, a rights issue would therefore be impracticable.

1.12 A company making a rights issue must set a price which is low enough to secure the acceptance of shareholders, who are being asked to provide extra funds, but not too low, so as to avoid excessive dilution of the earnings per share.

The market price of shares after a rights issue: the theoretical ex rights price

1.13 After the announcement of a rights issue, there is a tendency for share prices to fall, although the extent and duration of the fall may depend on the number of shareholders and the size of their holdings. This temporary fall is due to uncertainty in the market about the consequences of the issue, with respect to future profits, earnings and dividends. After the issue has actually been made, the market price per share will normally fall, because there are more shares in issue and the new shares were issued at a discount price.

1.14 When a rights issue is announced, all existing shareholders have the right to subscribe for new shares, and so there are rights attached to the existing shares. The shares are therefore described as being 'cum rights' (with rights attached) and are traded cum rights. On the first day of dealings in the newly issued shares, the rights no longer exist and the old shares are now 'ex rights' (without rights attached).

1.15 In theory, the new market price will be the consequence of an adjustment to allow for the discount price of the new issue, and a theoretical ex rights price can be calculated.

1.16 EXAMPLE: RIGHTS ISSUE (1)

Fundraiser plc has 1,000,000 ordinary shares of £1 in issue, which have a market price on 1 September of £2.10 per share. The company decides to make a rights issue, and offers its shareholders the right to subscribe for one new share at £1.50 each for every four shares already held. After the announcement of the issue, the share price fell to £1.95, but by the time just prior to the issue being made, it had recovered to £2 per share. This market value just before the issue is known as the cum rights price. What is the theoretical ex rights price?

1.17 SOLUTION

In theory, the market price will fall after the issue, as follows.

	£
1,000,000 shares have a 'cum rights' value of (× £2)	2,000,000
250,000 shares will be issued to raise (× £1.50)	375,000
Theoretical value of 1,250,000 shares	2,375,000

The theoretical ex rights price is $\frac{£2,375,000}{1,250,000} = £1.90$ per share.

The same calculation is often shown as follows.

	£
Four shares have a cum rights value of (× £2)	8.00
One new share is issued for	1.50
The value of five shares is theoretically	9.50

The theoretical ex rights price is £9.50/5 = £1.90 per share.

This is the basis of the following formula included in the CIMA *Mathematical Tables*, in which the cum rights price is described as the 'rights-on price' and N is the number of rights required to buy one share.

EXAM FORMULA

$$\text{Ex rights price} = \frac{1}{N+1}((N \times \text{rights-on price}) + \text{issue price})$$

1.18 We would alternatively use the first formula given in the CIMA *Mathematical Tables* as below.

EXAM FORMULA

If N is the number of rights required to buy one share, the value of a right is:

$$\frac{\text{Rights - on price} - \text{issue price}}{N+1} = \frac{\text{Ex - rights price} - \text{issue price}}{N}$$

In this example:

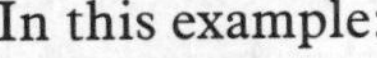

$$\frac{£2.00 - £1.50}{4+1} = \frac{\text{Ex rights price} - £1.50}{4}$$

Ex rights price – £1.50 = 4 × £0.50 ÷ 5

Ex rights price = £1.50 + £0.40 = £1.90

Exam focus point

In this Study Text, 'EXAM FORMULA' boxes like those above show formulae that are included in the CIMA *Mathematical Tables* which will be available to you in the exam.

The value of rights

1.19 The value of rights is the theoretical gain a shareholder would make by exercising his rights.

(a) Using the above example, if the price offered in the rights issue is £1.50 per share, and the market price after the issue is expected to be £1.90, the value attaching to a right is £1.90 – £1.50 = £0.40. A shareholder would therefore be expected to gain 40 pence for each new share he buys. If he does not have enough money to buy the share himself, he could sell the right to subscribe for a new share to another investor, and receive 40 pence from the sale. This other investor would then buy the new share for £1.50, so that his total outlay to acquire the share would be £0.40 + £1.50 = £1.90, the theoretical ex rights price.

(b) The value of rights attaching to existing shares is calculated in the same way. If the value of rights on a new share is 40 pence, and there is a one for four rights issue, the value of the rights attaching to each existing share is 40 ÷ 4 = 10 pence.

Using the formula from the CIMA *Mathematical Tables:*

$$\text{Value of a right} = \frac{\text{Ex rights price} - \text{issue price}}{\text{N}}$$

$$= (£1.90 - £1.50) \div 4 = 10 \text{ pence}$$

The theoretical gain or loss to shareholders

1.20 The possible courses of action open to shareholders are:

(a) to 'take up' or 'exercise' the rights, that is, to buy the new shares at the rights price. Shareholders who do this will maintain their percentage holdings in the company by subscribing for the new shares;

(b) to 'renounce' the rights and sell them on the market. Shareholders who do this will have lower percentage holdings of the company's equity after the issue than before the issue, and the total value of their shares will be less (on the assumption that the actual market price after the issue is close to the theoretical ex rights price);

(c) to renounce part of the rights and take up the remainder. For example, a shareholder may sell enough of his rights to enable him to buy the remaining rights shares he is entitled to with the sale proceeds, and so keep the total market value of his shareholding in the company unchanged;

(d) to do nothing at all. Shareholders may be protected from the consequences of their inaction because rights not taken up are sold on a shareholder's behalf by the company. The Stock Exchange rules state that if new securities are not taken up, they should be sold by the company to new subscribers for the benefit of the shareholders who were entitled to the rights. However, if the amount involved is small the shares can be sold for the benefit of the company. The shareholder (or the company) gets the difference between the issue price and the market price after the issue.

Unless a shareholder exercises all his rights, his proportion of the total equity of the company will decline.

Question

Gopher plc has issued 3,000,000 ordinary shares of £1 each, which are at present selling for £4 per share. The company plans to issue rights to purchase one new equity share at a price of £3.20 per share for every three shares held. A shareholder who owns 900 shares thinks that he will suffer a loss in his personal wealth because the new shares are being offered at a price lower than market value. On the assumption that the actual market value of shares will be equal to the theoretical ex rights price, what would be the effect on the shareholder's wealth if:

(a) he sells all the rights;
(b) he exercises half of the rights and sells the other half;
(c) he does nothing at all?

Answer

	£
Three shares 'cum rights' are worth (× £4)	12.00
One new share will raise	3.20
Four new shares will have a theoretical value of	15.20

The theoretical ex rights price is $\frac{£15.20}{4}$ = £3.80 per share

	£
Theoretical ex rights price	3.80
Price per new share	3.20
Value of rights per new share	0.60

The value of the rights attached to each existing share is $\frac{£0.60}{3}$ = £0.20.

We will assume that a shareholder is able to sell his rights for £0.20 per existing share held.

(a) If the shareholder sells all his rights:

	£
Sale value of rights (900 × £0.20)	180
Market value of his 900 shares, ex rights (× £3.80)	3,420
Total wealth	3,600
Total value of 900 shares cum rights (× £4)	£3,600

The shareholder would neither gain nor lose wealth. He would not be required to provide any additional funds to the company, but his shareholding as a proportion of the total equity of the company will be lower.

(b) If the shareholder exercises half of the rights (buys 450/3 = 150 shares at £3.20) and sells the other half:

	£
Sale value of rights (450 × £0.20)	90
Market value of his 1,050 shares, ex rights (× £3.80)	3,990
	4,080
Total value of 900 shares cum rights (× £4)	3,600
Additional investment (150 × £3.20)	480
	4,080

The shareholder would neither gain nor lose wealth, although he will have increased his investment in the company by £480.

(c) If the shareholder does nothing, but all other shareholders either exercise their rights or sell them, he would lose wealth as follows.

	£
Market value of 900 shares cum rights (× £4)	3,600
Market value of 900 shares ex rights (× £3.80)	3,420
Loss in wealth	180

It follows that the shareholder, to protect his existing investment, should either exercise his rights or sell them to another investor. If he does not exercise his rights, the new securities he was

entitled to subscribe for might be sold for his benefit by the company, and this would protect him from losing wealth.

The actual market price after a rights issue

1.21 The actual market price of a share after a rights issue may differ from the theoretical ex rights price. This will occur when the expected earnings yield from the new funds raised is different from the earnings yield from existing funds in the business. The market will take a view of how profitably the new funds will be invested, and will value the shares accordingly. An example will illustrate this point.

1.22 EXAMPLE: RIGHTS ISSUE (2)

Musk plc currently has 4,000,000 ordinary shares in issue, valued at £2 each, and the company has annual earnings equal to 20% of the market value of the shares. A one for four rights issue is proposed, at an issue price of £1.50. If the market continues to value the shares on a price/earnings ratio of 5, what would be the value per share if the new funds are expected to earn, as a percentage of the money raised,

(a) 15%?
(b) 20%?
(c) 25%?

How do these values in (a), (b) and (c) compare with the theoretical ex rights price? Ignore issue costs.

1.23 SOLUTION

The theoretical ex rights price will be calculated first.

	£
Four shares have a current value (× £2) of	8.00
One new share will be issued for	1.50
Five shares would have a theoretical value of	9.50

The theoretical ex rights price is $\frac{£9.50}{5}$ = £1.90.

1.24 The new funds will raise 1,000,000 × £1.50 = £1,500,000.

Earnings as a % of money raised	*Additional earnings*	*Current earnings*	*Total earnings after the issue*
	£	£	£
15%	225,000	1,600,000	1,825,000
20%	300,000	1,600,000	1,900,000
25%	375,000	1,600,000	1,975,000

1.25 If the market values shares on a P/E ratio of 5, the total market value of equity and the market price per share would be as follows.

Total earnings	*Market value*	*Price per share (5,000,000 shares)*
£	£	£
1,825,000	9,125,000	1.825
1,900,000	9,500,000	1.900
1,975,000	9,875,000	1.975

1.26 If the additional funds raised are expected to generate earnings at the **same** rate as existing funds, the actual market value will probably be the same as the theoretical ex rights price. If the new funds are expected to generate earnings at a **lower** rate, the market value will fall below the theoretical ex rights price. If this happens, shareholders will lose. If the new funds are expected to earn at a **higher** rate than current funds, the market value should be above the theoretical ex rights price. If this happens, shareholders will profit by taking up their rights.

1.27 The decision by individual shareholders as to whether they take up the offer will depend on the expected rate of return on the investment (and the risk associated with it) and the return obtainable from other investments (allowing for the associated risk).

2 LOAN STOCK 5/95, 11/97, 11/98

KEY TERM

Loan stock is long-term debt capital raised by a company for which interest is paid, usually half yearly and at a fixed rate. Holders of loan stock are therefore long-term creditors of the company.

2.1 Loan stock has a nominal value, which is the debt owed by the company, and interest is paid at a stated **coupon** on this amount. For example, if a company issues 10% loan stock, the coupon will be 10% of the nominal value of the stock, so that £100 of stock will receive £10 interest each year. The rate quoted is the gross rate, before tax. Unlike shares, debt is often issued at par, ie with £100 payable per £100 nominal value. Where the coupon rate is fixed at the time of issue, it will be set according to prevailing market conditions given the credit rating of the company issuing the debt. Subsequent changes in the market (and company) conditions will cause the market value of the bond to fluctuate, although the coupon will stay at the fixed percentage of the nominal value.

KEY TERM

Coupon: The rate of gross interest on loan stock expressed as a percentage of the nominal value of the stock.

2.2 **Debentures** are a form of loan stock, legally defined as the written acknowledgement of a debt incurred by a company, normally containing provisions about the payment of interest and the eventual repayment of capital. A debenture trust deed would empower a trustee (such as an insurance company or a bank) to intervene on behalf of debenture holders if the conditions of borrowing under which the debentures were issued are not being fulfilled. This might involve:

(a) failure to pay interest on the due dates;

(b) an attempt by the company to sell off important assets contrary to the terms of the loan;

(c) a company taking out additional loans and thereby exceeding previously agreed borrowing limits in the Articles or the debenture trust deed. (A trust deed might well place restrictions on the company's ability to borrow more from elsewhere until the debentures have been redeemed.)

Debentures with a floating rate of interest

2.3 These are debentures for which the coupon rate of interest can be changed by the issuer, in accordance with changes in market rates of interest. They may be attractive to both lenders and borrowers when interest rates are volatile, and preferable to fixed interest loan stock or debentures. Floating rate debentures protect borrowers from having to pay high rates of interest on their debentures when market rates of interest have fallen. On the other hand, they allow lenders to benefit from higher rates of interest on their debentures when market rates of interest go up.

Deep discount bonds

2.4 **Deep discount bonds** are loan stock issued at a price which is at a large discount to the face value or nominal value of the stock, and which will be redeemable at par (or above par) when they eventually mature.

2.5 For example a company might issue £1,000,000 of loan stock in 1999, at a price of £50 per £100 of stock, and redeemable at par in the year 2019.

2.6 For a company with specific cash flow requirements, the low servicing costs during the currency of the bond may be an attraction, coupled with a high cost of redemption at maturity.

2.7 Investors might be attracted by the large capital gain offered by the bonds, which is the difference between the issue price and the redemption value. However, deep discount bonds will carry a much lower rate of interest than other types of loan stock. The only tax advantage is that the gain gets taxed (as **income**) in one lump on maturity or sale, not as amounts of interest each year. The borrower can, however, deduct notional interest each year in computing profits.

Zero coupon bonds

2.8 **Zero coupon bonds** are bonds that are issued **at a discount** to their redemption value, but no interest is paid on them. The investor gains from the difference between the issue price and the redemption value, and there is an implied interest rate in the amount of discount at which the bonds are issued (or subsequently re-sold on the market).

(a) The advantage for borrowers is that zero coupon bonds can be used to raise cash immediately, and there is no cash repayment until redemption date. The cost of redemption is known at the time of issue, and so the borrower can plan to have funds available to redeem the bonds at maturity.

(b) The advantage for lenders is restricted, unless the rate of discount on the bonds offers a high yield. The only way of obtaining cash from the bonds before maturity is to sell them, and their market value will depend on the remaining term to maturity and current market interest rates.

The tax advantage of zero coupon bonds is the same as that for deep discount bonds (see Paragraph 2.7 above).

Security

2.9 Loan stock and debentures will often be secured. Security may take the form of either a **fixed charge** or a **floating charge**.

(a) **Fixed charge.** Security would be related to a specific asset or group of assets, typically land and buildings. The company would be unable to dispose of the asset without providing a substitute asset for security, or without the lender's consent.

(b) **Floating charge.** With a floating charge on certain assets of the company (for example stocks and debtors), the lender's security in the event of a default of payment is whatever assets of the appropriate class the company then owns (provided that another lender does not have a prior charge on the assets). The company would be able, however, to dispose of its assets as it chose until a default took place. In the event of default, the lender would probably appoint a receiver to run the company rather than lay claim to a particular asset.

Unsecured loan stock

2.10 Not all loan stock is secured. Investors are likely to expect a higher yield with **unsecured loan stock** to compensate them for the extra risk. The rate of interest on unsecured loan stock may be around 1% or more higher than for secured debentures.

The redemption of loan stock

2.11 Loan stock and debentures are usually **redeemable**. They are issued for a term of ten years or more, and perhaps 25 to 30 years. At the end of this period, they will 'mature' and become redeemable (at par or possibly at a value above par).

2.12 Most redeemable stocks have an earliest and a latest redemption date. For example, 12% Debenture Stock 2007/09 is redeemable at any time between the earliest specified date (in 2007) and the latest date (in 2009). The issuing company can choose the date. The decision by a company when to redeem a debt will depend on how much cash is available to the company to repay the debt, and on the nominal rate of interest on the debt. If the debentures pay 12% nominal interest and current interest rates are lower, say 9%, the company may try to raise a new loan at 9% to redeem debt which costs 12%. On the other hand, if current interest rates are 14%, the company is unlikely to redeem the debt until the latest date possible, because the debentures would be a cheap source of funds.

2.13 Some loan stock does not have a redemption date, and is **irredeemable** or 'undated'. Undated loan stock might be redeemed by a company that wishes to pay off the debt, but there is no obligation on the company to do so.

Companies that are unable to repay debt capital

2.14 A company might get into difficulties and be unable to pay its debts. When this occurs, the debenture holders or loan stock holders could exercise their right to appoint a receiver and make use of whatever security they have. Occasionally, perhaps because the secured assets have fallen in value and would not realise much in a forced sale, or perhaps out of a belief that the company can improve its position soon, unpaid debenture holders might be persuaded to surrender their debentures in exchange for an equity interest in the company or possibly convertible debentures, paying a lower rate of interest, but carrying the option to convert the debentures into shares at a specified time in the future.

Tax relief on loan interest

2.15 For companies, debt capital is a potentially attractive source of finance because interest charges reduce the profits chargeable to corporation tax. Companies might also wish to avoid dilution of shareholdings and increase their gearing (the ratio of fixed interest capital to equity capital) in order to improve their earnings per share by benefiting from tax relief on interest payments.

2.16 Why do companies not borrow up to the hilt to get as much debt finance as they can? What restricts their ability or their willingness to borrow? There are various reasons why a company might be unwilling or unable to borrow more.

(a) Interest charges have been very high in recent years, making debt capital quite expensive, even after tax relief. Interest yields are higher than dividend yields on equity shares.

(b) Heavy borrowing increases the financial risks for ordinary shareholders. A company must be able to pay the interest charges and eventually repay the debt from its cash resources, and at the same time maintain a healthy balance sheet which does not deter would-be creditors. There might be insufficient security for a new loan.

(c) There might be restrictions on a company's power to borrow.

(i) The company's Articles of Association may limit borrowing. These borrowing limits cannot be altered except with the approval of the shareholders at a general meeting of the company.

(ii) Trust deeds of existing loan stock may limit borrowing. These limits can only be overcome by redeeming the loan stock.

Reverse yield gap

2.17 Because debt involves lower risk than equity investment, we might expect yields on debt to be lower than yields on shares. In fact, the opposite has applied in recent years, so that the yields on shares are lower than on low-risk debt: this situation is known as a **reverse yield gap**. A reverse yield gap can occur because shareholders may be willing to accept lower returns on their investment in the short term, in anticipation that they will make capital gains in the future.

Mortgages

2.18 **Mortgages** are a specific type of secured loan. Companies place the title deeds of freehold or long leasehold property as security with a lender and receive cash on loan, usually repayable over a specified period, with interest payable at a fixed or floating rate. Most organisations owning property which is unencumbered by any charge should be able to obtain a mortgage up to two-thirds of the value of the property.

3 CONVERTIBLES AND WARRANTS 11/97, 5/98

Convertible loan stock

3.1 Convertible securities are fixed return securities that may be converted, on pre-determined dates and at the option of the holder, into ordinary shares of the company at a predetermined rate. Once converted they cannot be converted back into the original fixed return security. Conversion terms often vary over time. For example, the conversion terms of convertible stock might be that on 1 April 2000, £2 of stock can be converted into one ordinary share, whereas on 1 April 2001, the conversion price will be £2.20 of stock for one ordinary share.

3.2 The current market value of ordinary shares into which a unit of stock may be converted is known as the **conversion value**. The conversion value will be below the value of the stock at the date of issue, but will be expected to increase as the date for conversion approaches on the assumption that a company's shares ought to increase in market value over time. The difference between the issue value of the stock and the conversion value at as the date of issue is the implicit **conversion premium**.

3.3 EXAMPLE: CONVERTIBLE LOAN STOCK

The 10% convertible loan stock of Starchwhite plc is quoted at £142 per £100 nominal. The earliest date for conversion is in four years time, at the rate of 30 ordinary shares per £100 nominal loan stock. The share price is currently £4.15. Annual interest on the stock has just been paid.

(a) What is the average annual growth rate in the share price that is required for the stockholders to achieve an overall rate of return of 12% a year compound over the next four years, including the proceeds of conversion?

(b) What is the implicit conversion premium on the stock?

3.4 SOLUTION

(a)

Year	*Investment*	*Interest*	*Discount factor*	*Terminal value*
	£	£	12%	£
0	(142)		1.000	(142.00)
1		10	0.893	8.93
2		10	0.797	7.97
3		10	0.712	7.12
4		10	0.636	6.36
				(111.62)

The 30 shares on conversion at the end of year 4 must have a present value of at least £111.62, to provide investors with a 12% return.

The money value at the end of year 4 needs to be £111.62 ÷ 0.636 = £175.50.

The current market value of 30 shares is (× £4.15) £124.50.

The growth factor in the share price over four years needs to be:

$$\frac{175.50}{124.50} = 1.4096$$

If the annual rate of growth in the share price, expressed as a proportion, is g, then:

$$(1 + g)^4 = 1.4096$$
$$1 + g = 1.0896$$
$$g = 0.0896, \text{ say } 0.09$$

Conclusion. The rate of growth in the share price needs to be 9% a year (compound).

(b) The conversion premium can be expressed as an amount per share or as a percentage of the current conversion value.

(i) As an amount per share: $\frac{£142-£(30\times4.15)}{30} = £0.583$ per share

(ii) As a % of conversion value: $\frac{£0.583}{£4.15} \times 100\% = 14\%$

The issue price and the market price of convertible loan stock

3.5 A company will aim to issue loan stock with the greatest possible conversion premium as this will mean that, for the amount of capital raised, it will, on conversion, have to issue the lowest number of new ordinary shares. The premium that will be accepted by potential investors will depend on the company's growth potential and so on prospects for a sizeable increase in the share price.

3.6 Convertible loan stock issued at par normally has a lower coupon rate of interest than straight debentures. This lower yield is the price the investor has to pay for the conversion rights. It is, of course, also one of the reasons why the issue of convertible stock is attractive to a company.

3.7 When convertible loan stock is traded on a stock market, its **minimum** market price will be the price of straight debentures with the same coupon rate of interest. If the market value falls to this minimum, it follows that the market attaches no value to the conversion rights.

3.8 The actual market price of convertible stock will depend not only on the price of straight debt but also on the current conversion value, the length of time before conversion may take place, and the market's expectation as to future equity returns and the risk associated with these returns. If the conversion value rises above the straight debt value then the price of convertible stock will normally reflect this increase.

3.9 Most companies issuing convertible stocks expect them to be converted. They view the stock as **delayed equity**. They are often used either because the company's ordinary share price is considered to be particularly depressed at the time of issue or because the issue of equity shares would result in an immediate and significant drop in earnings per share. There is no certainty, however, that the security holders will exercise their option to convert; therefore the stock may run its full term and need to be redeemed.

Warrants (or subscription rights)

3.10 A **warrant** is a right given by a company to an investor, allowing him to buy new shares at a future date at a fixed, pre-determined price known as the exercise price. Warrants are usually issued as part of a package with unsecured loan stock: an investor who buys stock will also acquire a certain number of warrants. The purpose of warrants is to make the loan stock more attractive.

3.11 Once issued, warrants are detachable from the stock and can be sold and bought separately before or during the 'exercise period' (the period during which the right to use the warrants to subscribe for shares is allowed). The market value of warrants will depend on expectations of actual share prices in the future.

3.12 During the exercise period, the price of a warrant should not fall below the higher of:

(a) nil; and
(b) the 'theoretical value', which equals:

(Current share price – Exercise price) × Number of shares obtainable from each warrant

3.13 If, for example, a warrant entitles the holder to purchase two ordinary shares at a price of £3 each, when the current market price of the shares is £3.40, the minimum market value (or 'theoretical value') of a warrant would be (£3.40 – £3) × 2 = 80p.

3.14 If the price fell below the theoretical value during the exercise period, then arbitrage would be possible. For example, suppose the share price is £2.80 and the warrant exercise price is £2.20. The warrants are priced at 50p with each entitled to one share. Ignoring transactions costs, investors could make an instant gain of 10p per share by buying the warrant, exercising it and then selling the share.

3.15 For a company with good growth prospects, the warrant will usually be quoted at a premium above the minimum prior to the exercise period. This premium is known as the warrant conversion premium. It is sometimes expressed as a percentage of the current share price.

3.16 EXAMPLE: WARRANT CONVERSION PREMIUM

An investor holds some warrants which can be used to subscribe for ordinary shares on a one for one basis at an exercise price of £2.50 during a specified future period. The current share price is £2.25 and the warrants are quoted at 50p. What is the warrant conversion premium?

3.17 SOLUTION

The easiest way of finding the premium is to deduct the current share price from the cost of acquiring a share using the warrant, treating the warrant as if it were currently exercisable:

	£
Cost of warrant	0.50
Exercise price	2.50
	3.00
Current share price	2.25
Premium	0.75

3.18 You may be wondering why an investor would prefer to buy warrants at 50p when this means that it will cost him more to get the ordinary shares than if he bought them directly. The attractions of warrants to the investor are:

(a) low initial outlay - he only has to spend 50p per share as opposed to £2.25. This means that he could buy 4½ times as many warrants as shares or, alternatively, he could invest the remaining £1.75 in other, less risky investments;

(b) lower downside potential - his maximum loss per share is 50p instead of £2.25. Of course the risk of the loss of 50p is much greater than the risk of losing £2.25. The share price of £2.25 is below the exercise price. If it remained at this level until the beginning of the exercise period, the warrants would become worthless as it would not be worthwhile exercising them; and

(c) high potential returns - see below.

The gearing effect of warrants

3.19 In a similar way to share options, warrants offer the investor the possibility of making a high profit as a percentage of initial cost. This is because the price of the warrants will tend to move more or less in line with the price of the shares. Thus, if the share price rises by 50p the increase in the value of the warrant will be similar. Using the previous prices, a 50p increase in share price is about 22% but a 50p increase in the warrant price is 100%. This illustrates the gearing effect of warrants.

3.20 Let us now recalculate the premium, assuming a 50p rise in the share price and a 50p rise in the warrant price.

	£
Cost of warrant (50p + 50p)	1.00
Exercise price	2.50
	3.50
Current share price (£2.25 + 50p)	2.75
Premium	0.75

The premium has stayed the same. The share price is now above the exercise price. The warrants now have an 'intrinsic' value of 25p (ie 275p – 250p).

3.21 In the short run, the warrant price and share price normally move fairly closely in line with each other. In the longer term, the price of the warrant and hence the premium will depend on:

(a) the length of time before the warrants may be exercised;
(b) the current price of the shares compared with the exercise price; and
(c) the future prospects of the company.

As the exercise period approaches, any premium will reduce. Towards the end of the exercise period the premium will disappear because, if there were a premium, it would be cheaper to buy the shares directly rather than via the warrant.

Advantages of warrants

3.22 The main advantages of warrants to the company are as follows.

(a) Warrants themselves do not involve the payment of any interest or dividends. Furthermore, when they are initially attached to loan stock, the interest rate on the loan stock will be lower than for a comparable straight debt.

(b) Warrants make a loan stock issue more attractive and may make an issue of unsecured loan stock possible where adequate security is lacking.

(c) They provide a means of generating additional equity funds in the future without any immediate dilution in earnings per share.

3.23 The main advantages to the investor are as follows.

(a) As warrants provide no income all profits are in the form of capital gains which will be attractive to higher-rate taxpayers who have not used up their annual £5,800 tax-free allowance.

(b) As we have seen, there is potential for a high, though speculative, profit on a relatively low initial outlay.

Chapter roundup

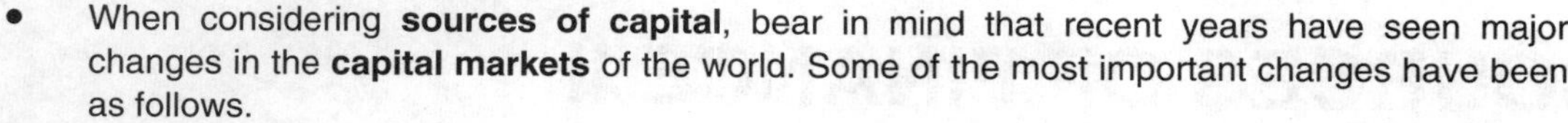

- In this chapter, we have looked at **share capital**, **loan stock**, **convertibles** and **warrants** as sources of business capital.
- When considering **sources of capital**, bear in mind that recent years have seen major changes in the **capital markets** of the world. Some of the most important changes have been as follows.
    - **Globalisation**. The capital markets of each country have become internationally integrated. Securities issued in one country can now be traded in capital markets around the world.
    - **Securitisation of debt**. Securitisation of debt refers to international borrowing by large companies, not from a bank, but by issuing securities instead. This has been possible because of the deregulation of capital markets, and the opening of overseas markets to borrowers since the abolition of exchange controls. Examples of securitised debt are eurobonds and commercial paper (see the next chapter).
    - **Risk management**. Various techniques have been developed for companies to manage their financial risk, such as swaps and options.
    - **Competition**. There is much fiercer competition between financial institutions for business. Foreign banks have competed successfully in the UK with the big clearing banks.

Quick quiz

1 What actions are open to a shareholder when there is a rights issue of shares? (see para 1.14)

2 What are deep discount bonds? (2.4)

3 What is the significance of tax relief on loan interest? (2.15)

4 Distinguish between convertible loan stock and warrants. (3.1, 3.10)

Question to try	Level	Marks	Time
6	Exam standard	25	45 mins

Chapter 7

SOURCES OF FINANCE II

	Chapter topic list	Syllabus reference	Ability required
1	Government assistance	13 b(iv)	Application
2	Bank borrowing	13 b(iv)	Application
3	Leasing and hire purchase	13 b(iv); c(ii)	Application
4	International borrowing and equity markets	13 b(iv)	Application
5	Smaller businesses	13 b(iv)	Application

Introduction

In this chapter, we look at the government assistance which may be available for firm's long-term finance needs, at bank borrowing and leasing, at international aspects of financing and at the special problems of smaller businesses seeking sources of finance.

You need to appreciate that different sources of finance are suitable for different sizes of enterprise. For example, you should not suggest eurobonds (discussed in this chapter) as a possible source of a finance for a small company.

1 GOVERNMENT ASSISTANCE

1.1 The UK government has provided finance to companies in cash grants and other forms of direct assistance, as part of its policy of helping to develop the national economy, especially in high technology industries and in areas of high unemployment.

1.2 Government incentives might be offered on:

(a) a **regional basis**, giving help to firms that invest in an economically depressed area of the country that has been officially designated as a 'development area' or 'assisted area';

(b) a **selective national basis**, giving help to firms that invest in an industry that the government would like to see developing more quickly, such as robotics or fibre optics.

1.3 The European Commission has acted against industrial aid for modernisation and development because it distorts competition. The UK government's powers to grant such aid are limited.

The Enterprise Initiative

1.4 The Enterprise Initiative is a package of measures offered by the Department of Trade and Industry (DTI) to businesses in the UK, including some regional selective grant assistance. Also provided is a network of 'Business Links', which are local business advice centres.

1.5 **Regional selective assistance** is available for investment projects undertaken by firms in **Assisted Areas**. The project must be commercially viable, create or safeguard employment, demonstrate a need for assistance and offer a distinct regional and national benefit. The amount of grant will be negotiated as the minimum necessary to ensure the project goes ahead.

1.6 The **Regional Enterprise Grants** scheme is specially geared to help small firms employing fewer than 25 in one of the Development Areas to expand and diversify. Regional enterprise grants can help finance viable projects for:

(a) investment - grants of 15% of the cost of fixed assets up to a maximum of £15,000 are available;

(b) innovation - grants of 50% of the agreed project cost up to a maximum grant of £25,000 are available.

European Regional Development Fund

1.7 The **European Regional Development Fund (ERDF)** is financed from the general budget of the European Union (EU). The funds are given directly to EU member governments. In the ERDF's first 15 years of operation, the UK received £3.6 billion from the fund. Approximately 80% of the funds available are allocated to the four poorest countries in the EU.

1.8 Although ERDF assistance is intended to supplement the regional aid programme of the EU countries, there has been criticism that, under the quota system used to allocate the funds, the money has been used to replace governments' own aid rather than to supplement it. In an effort to meet this criticism, 5% of ERDF payments are linked to specific projects put forward by member governments rather than being allocated on a quota basis.

2 BANK BORROWING 5/99

2.1 Borrowings from banks are an important source of finance to companies. Bank lending is still mainly short-term, although medium-term lending has grown considerably in recent years. **Overdraft finance** may carry a higher rate of interest than a medium-term loan, but it has the major advantage of flexibility: as cash flows into the business, the overdraft will reduce and the business will only be paying for the finance it needs from day to day. A medium-term loan is, on the other hand, likely to be for a fixed amount, and there are likely to be penalties for early repayment.

2.2 The rate of interest charged on medium-term bank lending to large companies will typically be set at a margin above the London Inter-Bank Offer Rate (LIBOR), with the size of the margin depending on the credit standing and riskiness of the borrower. The rate of interest charged will be adjusted every 3, 6, 9 or 12 months in line with recent movements in the LIBOR. Fixed rates of interest are also available, for up to five years. Lending to smaller companies will usually be at a margin above the bank's base rate. Fixed rates may also be available.

2.3 Longer term bank loans will sometimes be available, usually for the purchase of property, where the loan takes the form of a **mortgage**.

The factors that a banker will consider

2.4 When a banker is asked by a business customer for a loan or overdraft facility, he will consider several factors. Banking students are often taught to remember the main factors by the mnemonic PARTS.

- Purpose
- Amount
- Repayment
- Term
- Security

(a) The purpose of the loan. A loan request will be refused if the purpose of the loan is not acceptable to the bank.

(b) The amount of the loan. The customer must state exactly how much he wants to borrow. The banker must verify, as far as he is able to do so, that the full amount required has been estimated correctly.

(c) How will the loan be repaid? Will the customer be able to obtain sufficient income to make the necessary repayments? If not, the loan request will be refused.

(d) What would be the duration (term) of the loan? Traditionally, banks have offered short-term loans or overdrafts, although longer-term lending is increasing.

(e) Does the loan require security? If so, is the proposed security adequate?

3 LEASING AND HIRE PURCHASE 11/96, 5/98

Sale and leaseback arrangements

3.1 A company which owns its own premises can obtain finance by selling the property to an insurance company or pension fund for immediate cash and renting it back, usually for at least 50 years with rent reviews every few years. The property itself will probably need to be non-specialised, modern, and situated in a geographical area with good long-term prospects for increases in property value, otherwise it would offer a poor investment to the institution, in the event that the tenant went out of business, or stopped renting the property for some other reason.

3.2 A company would raise more cash from a **sale and leaseback agreement** than from a mortgage, but it should only make such an agreement if it cannot raise sufficient funds any other way. **Disadvantages** of sale and leaseback are as follows.

(a) The company loses ownership of a valuable asset which is almost certain to appreciate over time.

(b) The future borrowing capacity of the firm will be reduced, since the property if owned could be used to provide security for a loan.

(c) The company is contractually committed to occupying the property for many years ahead, and this can be restricting.

(d) The real cost is likely to be high, particularly as there will be frequent rent reviews.

Leasing

3.3 You will be familiar with leasing and **SSAP 21** from your accounting studies. Leasing in the UK is historically associated with leasehold property, but our concern here is with leasing arrangements for equipment. A lease is an agreement between two parties, the **lessor** and the **lessee**.

(a) The lessor owns a capital asset, but grants the lessee use of it. **Finance houses** (often subsidiaries of banks) act as the lessor in such arrangements;

(b) The lessee does not own the asset, but has the use of it, and in return makes payments under the terms of the lease to the lessor, for a specified period of time.

3.4 Leasing is therefore a form of rental. Leased assets often include plant and machinery, and cars and commercial vehicles, but might also be computers, ships, aeroplanes, oil production equipment and office equipment.

There are two basic forms of lease, operating (or **part-payout**) leases and finance (or **full payout**) leases.

Operating leases

3.5 Operating leases are rental agreements between a lessor and a lessee whereby:

(a) the lessor supplies the equipment to the lessee;

(b) the lessor is responsible for servicing and maintenance of the leased equipment;

(c) the period of the lease is fairly short, less than the economic life of the asset, so that at the end of one lease agreement, the lessor can lease the same equipment to someone else.

Finance leases

3.6 Finance leases are lease agreements between the user of the leased asset (the lessee) and a provider of finance (the lessor) for most or all of the asset's expected useful life.

KEY TERMS

Finance lease: a lease that transfers substantially all the risks and rewards of ownership of an asset to the lessee (*OT*).

Operating lease: a lease other than a finance lease. The lessor retains most of the risk and rewards of ownership (*OT*).

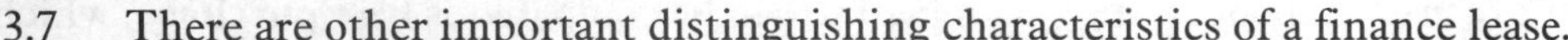

3.7 There are other important distinguishing characteristics of a finance lease.

(a) The lessee is responsible for the upkeep, servicing and maintenance of the asset. The lessor is not involved in this at all.

(b) The lease has a primary period, which covers all or most of the useful economic life of the asset. At the end of this primary period, the lessor would not be able to lease the asset again because it would be worn out or obsolete. The lessor must therefore ensure that the lease payments during the primary period pay for the full cost of the asset as well as providing the lessor with a suitable return on his investment.

(c) It is usual at the end of the primary period to allow the lessee the option to continue to lease the asset for an indefinite secondary period, in return for a very low rent, sometimes called a 'peppercorn rent'. Alternatively, the lessee might be allowed to sell the asset on a lessor's behalf (since the lessor is the legal owner) and to keep most of the sale proceeds, paying only a small percentage (perhaps 10%) to the lessor.

3.8 Under some schemes, a lessor leases equipment to the lessee for most of the equipment's life, and at the end of the lease period sells the equipment himself, with none of the sale proceeds going to the lessee.

Why might leasing be popular?

3.9 What are the attractions of leases to the supplier of the equipment, the lessee and the lessor?

(a) The **supplier of the equipment** is paid in full at the beginning. The equipment is sold to the lessor, and apart from obligations under guarantees or warranties, the supplier is free from all further financial concern about the asset.

(b) The **lessor** invests finance by purchasing assets from suppliers and makes a return out of the lease payments received from the lessee. Provided that a lessor can find lessees willing to pay the amounts he wants to make his return, the lessor will make good profits on his deals. He will also get capital allowances on his purchase of the equipment.

(c) Leasing might be attractive to the **lessee**:

(i) if the lessee does not have enough cash to pay for the asset, and may be having difficulty obtaining a bank loan to buy it, and so has to rent it in one way or another if he is to have use of the asset at all;

(ii) if finance leasing is cheaper than a bank loan. The cost of payments under a loan might exceed the cost of a lease.

The lessee may find a finance lease attractive from the point of view of taxation (see later example).

3.10 Operating leases have further advantages.

(a) The leased equipment does not have to be shown in the lessee company's published balance sheet, and so the lessee's balance sheet shows no increase in the gearing ratio.

(b) The equipment is leased for a shorter period than its expected useful life. In the case of high technology equipment, if the equipment becomes out-of-date before the end of its expected life, the lessee does not have to keep on using it, and it is the lessor who must bear the risk of being unable to sell out-of-date equipment.

Hire purchase

3.11 Another form of credit finance with which leasing can be compared is **hire purchase**, which is a form of instalment credit. There are two basic forms of instalment credit, whereby an individual or business purchases goods on credit and pays for them by instalments.

(a) **Lender credit** is when the buyer borrows money from a lender and uses the money to purchase goods outright.

(b) **Vendor credit** is when the buyer obtains goods on credit from a seller (vendor) and agrees to pay the vendor by instalments. Hire purchase is an example of vendor credit.

Hire purchase is similar to leasing, with the exception that ownership of the goods passes to the hire purchase customer on payment of the final credit instalment, whereas a lessee never becomes the legal owner of the goods. The HP payments consist partly of 'capital' payments towards the purchase of the asset, and partly of interest charges.

KEY TERM

Hire purchase: a contract for the hire of an asset which contains a provision giving the hirer an option to acquire legal title to the asset upon the fulfilment of certain conditions stated in the contract (SSAP 21).

3.12 Hire purchase agreements nowadays usually involve a **finance house** or **finance company**.

(a) The supplier sells the goods to the finance house.
(b) The supplier delivers the goods to the customer who will eventually purchase them.
(c) The hire purchase arrangement exists between the finance house and the customer.

3.13 For example, if a company buys a car costing £10,000 under an HP agreement, the car supplier might provide HP finance over a three year period at an interest cost of 10%, and the HP payments might be, say, as follows.

	Capital element £	*Interest element* £	*Total HP payment* £
Year 0: down payment	2,540	0	2,540
Year 1	2,254	746	3,000
Year 2	2,479	521	3,000
Year 3	2,727	273	3,000
Total	10,000	1,540	11,540

3.14 The **tax position** on a hire purchase arrangement is as follows.

(a) The buyer obtains whatever capital allowances are available, based on the capital element of the cost. Capital allowances on the full capital element of the cost can be used from the time the asset is acquired.

(b) In addition, interest payments within the HP payments are an allowable expense against tax, spread over the term of the HP agreement.

(c) Capital payments within the HP payments, however, are not allowable against tax.

3.15 In the example of the arrangement for the car given above, the car buyer would obtain whatever capital allowances are obtainable on motor vehicles, from the time of obtaining the car, plus allowances for the interest costs of £746 in year 1, £521 in year 2 and £273 in year 3.

Lease or buy decisions

3.16 There are several ways of evaluating a decision whether to lease an asset, or to purchase it by another means of finance.

3.17 The traditional method is to take the view that a decision to lease is a financing decision, which can only be made after a decision to acquire the asset has already been taken. It is therefore necessary to make a two-stage decision, as follows.

(a) An acquisition decision is made on whether the asset is worth having. The present values of operational costs and benefits from using the asset are found to derive a **net present value (NPV).**

(b) A financing decision is then made if the acquisition is justified by a positive NPV. This is the decision on whether to lease or buy.

3.18 The traditional method is complicated by the need to **choose a discount rate** for each stage of the decision. In the case of a non-taxpaying organisation, the method is applied as follows.

(a) The cost of capital that should be applied to the cash flows for the acquisition decision is the cost of capital that the organisation would normally apply to its project evaluations, typically its weighted average cost of capital (discussed later in this Study Text).

(b) The cost of capital that should be applied to the (differential) cash flows for the financing decision is the cost of borrowing.

   (i) We assume that if the organisation decided to purchase the equipment, it would finance the purchase by borrowing funds (rather than out of retained funds).

   (ii) We therefore compare the cost of borrowing with the cost of leasing (or hire purchase) by applying this cost of borrowing to the financing cash flows.

3.19 In the case of a tax-paying organisation, taxation should be allowed for in the cash flows, so that the traditional method would recommend:

(a) discounting the cash flows of the acquisition decision at the firm's after-tax cost of capital;

(b) discounting the cash flows of the financing decision at the after-tax cost of borrowing.

3.20 The tax treatment of finance leases in the UK under Finance Act 1991 rules is:

(a) to allow depreciation as an expense;

(b) to allow the interest element of the finance charge as an expense over the period of the lease.

This treatment leads to some calculations complex, while the result may not be materially different from that obtained if we assume that the lease payments are allowable for tax in full.

Exam focus point

It will be acceptable to make this latter assumption (that lease payments are tax-allowable) in the exam, provided that you state it in your answer and provided that the question does not direct otherwise.

3.21 EXAMPLE: LEASE OR BUY DECISIONS (1)

Mallen and Mullins Ltd has decided to install a new milling machine. The machine costs £20,000 and it would have a useful life of five years with a trade-in value of £4,000 at the end of the fifth year. Additional cash profits from the machine would be £8,000 a year for five years. A decision has now to be taken on the method of financing the project. Three methods of finance are being considered.

(a) The company could purchase the machine for cash, using bank loan facilities on which the current rate of interest is 14% before tax.

(b) The company could lease the machine under an agreement which would entail payment of £4,800 at the end of each year for the next five years.

(c) The company could purchase the machine under a hire purchase agreement. This would require an initial deposit of £6,500 and payments of £4,400 per annum at the end of each of the next five years. The interest part of the payments, for tax purposes, would be £2,100 at the end of year 1 and £1,800, £1,400, £1,000 and £700 at the end of each of years 2, 3, 4 and 5 respectively.

The company's weighted average cost of capital is 12% after tax. The rate of corporation tax is 30%. If the machine is purchased, the company will be able to claim an annual writing down allowance of 25% of the reducing balance.

Advise the management on whether to acquire the machine, on the most economical method of finance and on any other matter which should be considered before finally deciding which method of finance should be adopted.

3.22 SOLUTION

The traditional method begins with the acquisition decision. The cash flows of the project should be discounted at 12%. The first writing down allowance is assumed to be claimed in the first year resulting in a saving of tax at year 2.

Capital allowances

Year		*Allowance*
		£
1	25% of £20,000	5,000
2	25% of £(20,000 – 5,000)	3,750
3	25% of £(15,000 – 3,750)	2,813
4	25% of £(11,250 – 2,813)	2,109
		13,672
5	£(20,000 – 13,672 – 4,000)	2,328
		16,000

Taxable profits and tax liability

Year	*Cash profits*	*Capital allowance*	*Taxable profits*	*Tax at 30%*
	£	£	£	£
1	8,000	5,000	3,000	1,000
2	8,000	3,750	4,250	1,275
3	8,000	2,813	5,187	1,556
4	8,000	2,109	5,891	1,767
5	8,000	2,328	5,672	1,702

NPV calculation for the acquisition decision

Year	*Equipment*	*Cash profits*	*Tax*	*Net cash flow*	*Discount factor*	*Present value*
	£	£	£	£	12%	£
0	(20,000)			(20,000)	1.000	(20,000)
1		8,000		8,000	0.893	7,144
2		8,000	(1,000)	7,000	0.797	5,579
3		8,000	(1,275)	6,725	0.712	4,788
4		8,000	(1,556)	6,444	0.636	4,098
5	4,000	8,000	(1,767)	10,233	0.567	5,802
6			(1,702)	(1,702)	0.507	(863)
					NPV	6,548

3.23 The net present value (NPV) is positive, and so we conclude that the machine should be acquired, regardless of the method used to finance the acquisition.

3.24 The second stage is the financing decision, and cash flows are discounted at the after-tax cost of borrowing, which is at 14% × 70% = 9.1%, say 9%. The only cash flows that we need to consider are those which will be affected by the choice of the method of financing.

(a) *The present value (PV) of purchase costs*

Year	Item	Cash flow	Discount factor	PV
		£	9%	£
0	Equipment cost	(20,000)	1.000	(20,000)
5	Trade-in value	4,000	0.650	2,600
	Tax savings, from allowances			
2	30% × £5,000	1,500	0.842	1,263
3	30% × £3,750	1,125	0.772	869
4	30% × £2,813	844	0.708	598
5	30% × £2,110	633	0.650	411
6	30% × £2,327	698	0.596	416
			NPV of purchase	(13,843)

(b) *The PV of leasing costs*

It is assumed that the lease payments are fully tax-allowable.

Year	Lease payment	Savings in tax (30%)	Discount factor	PV
	£	£	9%	£
1-5	(4,800) pa		3.890	(18,672)
2-6		1,440 pa	3.569	5,139
			NPV of leasing	(13,533)

(c) *The PV of hire purchase*

Year	HP payments	Capital allowances - tax saved	Tax saved re interest on HP payments	Net cash flow	Discount factor at 9%	PV
	£	£	30%	£		£
0	(6,500)			(6,500)	1.000	(6,500)
1	(4,400)			(4,400)	0.917	(4,035)
2	(4,400)	1,500	630	(2,270)	0.842	(1,911)
3	(4,400)	1,125	540	(2,735)	0.772	(2,111)
4	(4,400)	844	420	(3,136)	0.708	(2,220)
5	(400)*	633	300	533	0.650	346
6		698	210	908	0.596	541
				NPV of hire purchase		(15,890)

* £4,400 less £4,000 trade-in value.

3.25 The cheapest option would be to lease the machine. However, other matters to be considered include the following.

(a) **Running expenses**. The calculations assume that the running costs are the same under each alternative. This may not be so. Expenses like maintenance, consumable stores, insurance and so on may differ between the alternatives.

(b) **The effect on cash flow**. Purchasing requires an immediate outflow of £20,000 compared to nothing for leasing. This effect should be considered in relation to the company's liquidity position, which in turn will affect its ability to discharge its debts and to pay dividends.

(c) **Alternative uses of funds**. The proposed outlay of £20,000 for purchase should be considered in relation to alternative investments.

(d) **The trade-in value**. The net present value of purchase is affected by the trade-in the fifth year. This figure could be very inaccurate.

(e) **The effect on reported profits**. Annual profits are reported on an accrual basis (ie after the deduction of depreciation). The effect of the three alternatives on reported profits should be considered since this could, if significant, affect dividend policy and the valuation of the company's shares.

3.26 A disadvantage of the traditional approach to making a lease or buy decision is that if there is a negative NPV when the operational cash flows of the project are discounted at the firm's cost of capital, the investment will be rejected out of hand, with no thought given to how the investment might be financed. It is conceivable, however, that the costs of leasing might be so low that the project would be worthwhile provided that the leasing option were selected. This suggests that an investment opportunity should not be rejected without first giving some thought to its financing costs.

3.27 Other methods of making lease or buy decisions are as follows.

(a) Compare the cost of leasing with the cost of purchase, and select the cheaper method of financing; then calculate the NPV of the project on the assumption that the cheaper method of financing is used. In other words, make the financing decision first and the acquisition decision afterwards.

(b) Calculate an NPV for the project under each of two assumptions about financing.

(i) The machine is purchased.
(ii) The machine is leased.

Select the method of financing which gives the higher NPV, provided that the project is viable (that is, has a positive NPV). In other words, combine the acquisition and financing decisions together into a single-stage decision. This method is illustrated in the following example.

3.28 EXAMPLE: LEASE OR BUY DECISIONS (2)

In the case of Mallen and Mullins Ltd, the NPV with purchase would be + £6,548. This was calculated above (Paragraph 3.28). The NPV with leasing would be as follows. A discount rate of 12% is used here.

Year	*Profit less leasing cost*	*Tax at 30%*	*Net cash flow*	*Discount factor*	*PV*
	£	£	£	12%	£
1	3,200		3,200	0.893	2,858
2	3,200	(960)	2,240	0.797	1,785
3	3,200	(960)	2,240	0.712	1,595
4	3,200	(960)	2,240	0.636	1,425
5	3,200	(960)	2,240	0.567	1,270
6		(960)	(960)	0.507	(487)
				NPV	8,446

According to this method, leasing is preferable, because the NPV is £1,898 higher.

Operating leases

3.29 Since operating leases are a form of renting, the only cash flows to consider for this type of leasing are:

(a) the lease payments;
(b) tax saved: operating lease payments are allowable expenses for tax purposes.

Question 1

The management of a company has decided to acquire Machine X which costs £63,000 and has an operational life of four years. The expected scrap value would be zero.

Tax is payable at 30% on operating cash flows one year in arrears. Capital allowances are available at 25% a year on a reducing balance basis.

Suppose that the company has the opportunity either to purchase the machine or to lease it under a finance lease arrangement, at an annual rent of £20,000 for four years, payable at the end of each year. The company can borrow to finance the acquisition at 11%. Should the company lease or buy the machine?

Answer

Working

Capital allowances

Year		£
1	(25% of £63,000)	15,750
2	(75% of £15,750)	11,813
3	(75% of £11,813)	8,859
		36,422
4	(£63,000 - £36,422)	26,578

The financing decision will be appraised by discounting the relevant cash flows at the after-tax cost of borrowing, which is 11% × 67% = 7.37%, say 7%.

(a) *Purchase option*

Year	*Item*	*Cash flow* £	*Discount factor* 7%	*Present value* £
0	Cost of machine	(63,000)	1.000	(63,000)
	Tax saved from capital allowances			
2	30% × £15,750	4,725	0.873	4,125
3	30% × £11,813	3,544	0.816	2,892
4	30% × £8,859	2,658	0.763	2,028
5	30% × £26,578	7,973	0.713	5,685
				(48,270)

(b) *Leasing option*

It is assumed that the lease payments are tax-allowable in full.

Year	*Item*	*Cash flow*	*Discount factor* 7%	*Present value* £
1-4	Lease costs	(20,000)	3.387	(67,740)
2-5	Tax savings on lease costs (× 30%)	6,000	3.165	18,990
				(48,750)

The purchase option is marginally cheaper, using a cost of capital based on the after-tax cost of borrowing.

On the assumption that investors would regard borrowing and leasing as equally risky finance options, the purchase option is recommended.

The position of the lessor

3.31 So far, we have looked at examples of leasing decisions from the viewpoint of the lessee. You may, as in the November 1996 *SFM* paper, be asked to evaluate a leasing arrangement **from the position of the lessor**. This is rather like a mirror image of the lessee's position.

Assuming that it is purchasing the asset, the lessor will receive capital allowances on the expenditure, and the lease payments will be taxable income.

3.31 EXAMPLE: LEASE OR BUY DECISIONS (3)

Continuing the same case of Mallen and Mullins Ltd, suppose that the lessor's required rate of return is 12% after tax. The lessor's cash flows will be as follows.

	Cash flow	*Discount factor*	*PV*
	£	12%	£
Purchase costs (see paragraph 3.24)			
Year 0	(20,000)	1.000	(20,000)
Year 5 (trade-in)	4,000	0.567	2,268
Tax savings			
Year 2	(1,500)	0.797	1,196
Year 3	1,125	0.712	801
Year 4	844	0.636	537
Year 5	633	0.567	359
Year 6	698	0.507	354
Lease payments: years 1-5	4,800	3.605	17,304
Tax on lease payments: years 2-6	(1,440)	3.218	(4,634)
NPV			(1,815)

3.32 *Conclusion.* The proposed level of lease payments are not justifiable for the lessor if it seeks a required rate of return of 12%, since the resulting NPV is negative.

4 INTERNATIONAL BORROWING AND EQUITY MARKETS

4.1 Borrowing and equity markets are becoming increasingly internationalised, particularly for larger companies. Companies are able to borrow funds on the eurocurrency (money) markets and on the markets for eurobonds and eurocommercial paper. These markets are collectively called 'euromarkets'.

Eurocurrency markets

4.2 A UK company might borrow money from a bank or from the investing public, in sterling. But it might also borrow in a foreign currency, especially if it trades abroad, or if it already has assets or liabilities abroad denominated in a foreign currency. When a company borrows in a foreign currency, the loan is known as a **eurocurrency loan.** (It is not only European foreign currencies which are involved, and so the 'euro-' prefix is a misnomer.) For example, if a UK company borrows US $50,000 from its bank, the loan will be a 'eurodollar' loan. London is a centre for eurocurrency lending and companies with foreign trade interests might choose to borrow from their bank in another currency.

4.3 The eurocurrency markets involve the depositing of funds with a bank outside the country of the currency in which the funds are denominated and re-lending these funds for a fairly short term, typically three months, normally at a floating rate of interest. **Eurocredits** are medium to long-term international bank loans which may be arranged by individual banks or by syndicates of banks.

International capital markets

4.4 Large companies may arrange borrowing facilities from their bank, in the form of bank loans or bank overdrafts. Instead, however, they might prefer to borrow from private investors. In other words, instead of obtaining a £10,000,000 bank loan, a company might issue 'bonds', or 'paper' in order to borrow directly from investors, with:

(a) the bank merely arranging the transaction, finding investors who will take up the bonds or paper that the borrowing company issues;

(b) interest being payable to the investors themselves, not to a bank.

4.5 In recent years, a strong market has built up which allows very large companies to borrow in this way, long-term or short-term.

Eurobonds

KEY TERM

A **eurobond** is a bond denominated in a currency which differs from that of the country of issue.

4.6 Eurobonds are long-term loans raised by international companies or other institutions and sold to investors in several countries at the same time. Such bonds can be sold by one holder to another. The term of a eurobond issue is typically 10 to 15 years. Although eurobond funds may be raised at lower cost than direct borrowing from banks, issue costs are generally higher than the costs of using the eurocurrency markets. Eurobonds may be the most suitable source of finance for a large organisation with an excellent credit rating, such as a large successful multinational company, which:

(a) requires a long-term loan to finance a big capital expansion programme (with a loan for at least 5 years and up to 20 years);

(b) requires borrowing which is not subject to the national exchange controls of any government (a company in country X could raise funds in the currency of country Y by means of a eurobond issue, and thereby avoid any exchange control restrictions which might exist in country X). In addition, domestic capital issues may be regulated by the government or central bank, with an orderly queue for issues. In contrast, eurobond issues can be made whenever market conditions seem favourable.

4.7 The interest rate on a bond issue may be fixed or variable. Many variable rate issues have a minimum interest rate which the bond holders are guaranteed, even if market rates fall even lower. These bonds convert to a fixed rate of interest when market rates do fall to this level. For this reason, they are called 'drop lock' floating rate bonds.

Eurobond issues and foreign exchange risk

4.8 A borrower contemplating a eurobond issue must consider the **foreign exchange risk** of a long-term foreign currency loan. If the money is to be used to purchase assets which will earn revenue in a currency different to that of the bond issue, the borrower will run the risk of exchange losses if the currency of the loan strengthens against the currency of the revenues out of which the bond (and interest) must be repaid. If the money is to be used to purchase assets which will earn revenue in the same currency, the borrower can match these revenues with payments on the bond, and so remove or reduce the exchange risk.

Eurobonds and the investor

4.9 An investor subscribing to a bond issue will be concerned about the following factors.

(a) **Security**. The borrower must be of high quality. A standard condition of a bond issue is a 'negative pledge clause' in which the borrower undertakes not to give any prior charge over its assets, during the life of the bond issue, that would rank ahead of the rights of the investors in the event of a liquidation. Bond issues are risk-rated by independent agencies such as Standard and Poors, Moodies and IBCA to denote what risk the investor faces.

(b) **Marketability**. Investors will wish to have a ready market in which bonds can be bought and sold. If the borrower is of high quality the bonds or notes will be readily negotiable.

(c) **Anonymity**. Investors in eurobonds tend to be attracted by the anonymity of this type of issue as the bonds are generally issued to bearer.

(d) **The return on the investment**. This is paid tax-free.

Euro-equity issues

4.10 A **euro-equity issue** may be defined as an issue of equity in a market outside the company's own domestic market. The euro-equity (international equity) market has not developed to such an extent as the comparable eurobond market. The market started in 1965 when bonds were issued with the option to convert them into equity. Later, bonds were issued with warrants attached, meaning that the bond does not have to be surrendered if the warrant is used to obtain shares. Furthermore, the warrant can be traded separately from the bond.

4.11 Conventional share issues have also been made on the euro-equity markets, as for example when there were attempts to place large numbers of shares of US corporations and of Japanese companies in Europe. These attempts were largely unsuccessful: the absence of a sufficiently liquid after-market or secondary market in such shares is the main limitation on such euro-equity issues.

4.12 'Sweeteners' are often added to the shares issued on the market, to make the issue more attractive to investors. For example, a 'rolling put option' might be added to a convertible preference share, giving the purchaser the right to sell the convertible preference share back to the company at any time between, say, five and ten years after the issue.

4.13 A company may find it appropriate to raise funds by selling shares outside its domestic capital market if this is too small for its needs. Another reason why a company may seek a euro-equity issue is to attract shareholders based in the markets in which it trades overseas. The liquidity of the company's shares and the international standing of the firm can be improved. The wider spread of shareholdings which might be achieved could act as a defence against hostile takeovers. An issue overseas may also be convenient if compliance with domestic capital market listing requirements is a complex or lengthy process.

Case example

To give one example of the sale of shares in overseas markets, the flotation of British Telecom involved an international issue alongside the main issue of shares on the UK stock market.

Commercial paper

4.14 A large company can raise short-term finance by issuing **commercial paper**. Businesses were first allowed to issue sterling commercial paper (SCP) in 1986, following the success of euro-commercial paper (ECP) in the early 1980s. Commercial paper (CP) is a short-term financial instrument:

(a) issued in the form of unsecured promissory notes with a fixed maturity of up to one year, but typically between seven days and three months. (A promissory note is a written promise to pay);

(b) issued in bearer form;

(c) issued on a discount basis (so the rate of interest on the CP is implicit in its sale value).

KEY TERM

Commercial paper: Unsecured short-term loan note issued by companies, and generally maturing within nine months (*OT*).

The term **eurocommercial paper** refers to CP issued in any currency (often US dollars).

Similar instruments issued with a maturity of over one and up to five years at a rate of interest rather than a discount are known as **medium term notes** ('MTNs'). The credit risk of the counterparty presents a problem with this form of finance.

4.15 Commercial paper is an example of **securitisation** - the raising of loans in the form of debt securities. With securitisation, banks raise finance for their customers by packaging and selling the customers' securities, such as commercial paper, rather than by lending them money.

4.16 The following organisations are entitled to issue commercial paper and medium term notes.

(a) Companies with net assets of at least £25 million

(b) Overseas public sector bodies (as long as the relevant government's debt securities are traded on a Stock Exchange or equivalent exchange)

(c) Certain UK local authorities

Qualifying companies can now issue CP and MTNs in any currency. The minimum amount is £100,000 or currency equivalent, although a minimum of £1,000,000 is more usual. The market is most active among multinationals and very large domestic companies, frequently involving very large sums on a revolving or standby basis.

Issues are 'investor-driven' in that CP is only issued to meet demand from specific investors.

4.17 The flexibility of commercial paper arises because the borrower is able to choose the period to maturity (in practice, between 7 and 364 days). For example, a company might decide that it wants to issue some new paper at the end of November, with maturity in the middle of March. However, if the interest rates that would be payable are not attractive enough at the time for this term of borrowing, the borrower can decide instead to issue paper with a maturity in (say) mid-February. Corporate borrowers are therefore able to schedule borrowing for when they expect interest rates to be most favourable to themselves.

4.18 Other advantages of commercial paper include the following.

(a) Interest rates are determined by market conditions but companies which issue commercial paper can hope to obtain slightly lower interest rates on their borrowing than if they borrowed direct from a bank.

(b) A company that issues CP does not have to be formally 'rated'. However, companies that are rated will be able to issue paper at finer rates.

(c) If a company has surplus cash, it can invest it in commercial paper rather than in a bank deposit, and hope to earn a slightly higher interest rate on its short-term investment.

(d) The 'paper' is tradeable.

(*Note*. These are among the advantages of dispensing with financial intermediaries, ie financial disintermediation, of which CP is an example.)

KEY TERM

Disintermediation: the bypassing of financial intermediaries in order to arrange lending and borrowing directly between the ultimate parties to the transaction.

Syndicated credits

4.19 A 'credit' in this context is a facility whereby a borrower can borrow funds when required, but might in fact not take up the full amount of the facility. This differs from a loan, which involves an actual transaction for a specified sum for a particular period of time.

4.20 The **syndicated credit market** provides credit facilities at relatively high rates of interest, typically at a substantial margin above LIBOR. The market is frequently used by highly geared companies.

(a) Such a company might need such a facility if it is involved in a takeover bid, in which case it will use the standby credit to fund the acquisition if the bid is successful.

(b) The market is used in the re-financing of debts incurred in past takeovers in cases where the company has been unable to obtain alternative funds to pay off the debt.

(c) The market is also used for local and overseas governmental borrowing, and for project financing (eg Eurotunnel).

4.21 Because much of the takeover activity of the late 1980s was of US corporations, the majority of syndicated credits relating to mergers was denominated in US dollars.

Multiple option facilities

4.22 **Multiple option facilities** (MOFs) comprise a variety of instruments through which companies can raise funds. Such instruments gained popularity in the late 1980s, and include Note Issuance Facilities (NIFs) and Revolving Underwriting Facilities (RUFs). In a typical MOF arrangement, the company may get a bank to put together a panel of banks who agree to provide an amount of 'standby' loans over a period of, say, five years, perhaps at an interest rate set to vary by reference to LIBOR. Another 'tender panel' of banks is set up and is invited to bid to provide loans when the company requires cash. The company is able to choose the lowest bid, or alternatively use the standby facility.

4.23 MOFs allow short-term loans (say, for three months) to be arranged in succession, effectively enabling medium-term finance to be obtained, if required, at competitive rates of interest. As implied by their name, MOFs allow the money required to be raised in various different forms, including foreign currency loans and bills of exchange.

Should a company borrow on the euromarkets or domestic markets?

Question 2

See if you can identify the main issues which will be relevant to this question before reading the following paragraph.

4.24 The following factors are relevant to choosing between borrowing on euromarkets or domestic markets.

(a) Spreads between borrowing and lending rates are likely to be lower on the euromarket, because domestic banking systems are generally subject to tighter regulation and more stringent reserve requirements.

(b) Euromarket loans generally require no security, while borrowing on domestic markets is quite likely to involve fixed or floating charges on assets as security.

(c) Availability of euromarket funds is enhanced by the fact that euromarkets are attractive to investors as interest is paid gross without the deduction of withholding tax which occurs in many domestic markets.

(d) With interest normally at floating rates on euromarkets, draw-down dates can be flexible, although there may be early redemption penalties, and commitment fees to pay if the full amount of the loan is not drawn down.

(e) It is often easier for a large multinational to raise very large sums on the euromarkets than in a domestic financial market.

5 SMALLER BUSINESSES 5/97

5.1 Some of the various sources of finance for companies that have been mentioned so far such as stock market flotation or eurobonds, are suitable only for fairly large companies. Compared to large companies, small companies and non-corporate businesses have great difficulty in obtaining funds. Smaller businesses are perceived as being more risky, and investors either refuse to invest or expect a higher return on their investment, which the borrowing firm must then be able to pay.

5.2 Small businesses and unquoted companies do not have ready access to new long-term funds, except for:

(a) internal funds, from retained earnings;
(b) perhaps, extra finance obtained by issuing more shares to private shareholders;
(c) some bank borrowing.

So how are small businesses to overcome financial restrictions and achieve a good rate of growth?

5.3 The problems of finance for small businesses have received much publicity in recent years, and some efforts have been made to provide them with access to sources of funds. Most of these sources are referred to as 'venture capital'. Venture capital is discussed later in this Study Text.

Government assistance for small businesses

Exam focus point

Availability of government assistance is country-specific. For the exam, at a minimum, you should be aware of the possibilities of such assistance and the major schemes operating in at least one country.

5.4 The UK government has introduced a number of assistance schemes to help businesses, and several of these are designed to encourage lenders and investors to make finance available to small and unquoted businesses. They include the Loan Guarantee Scheme, the Enterprise Initiative, development agencies, the Enterprise Investment Scheme and venture capital trusts.

The Loan Guarantee Scheme

5.5 The **Loan Guarantee Scheme** was introduced by the government in 1981. It is intended to help small businesses to get a loan from the bank, when a bank would otherwise be unwilling to lend because the business cannot offer the security that the bank would want. The borrower's annual turnover must not exceed a limit which depends on the type of business.

5.6 Under the scheme, which was revised in 1993, the bank can lend up to £250,000 without security over **personal** assets or a personal guarantee being required of the borrower. However, all available **business** assets must be used as security if required. The government will guarantee the bulk of the loan, while the borrower must pay an annual premium on the guaranteed part of the loan. The scheme is not open to 'local service' businesses such as small retailers.

5.7 Most types of business can apply for such a loan through their bank. This includes sole traders and partnerships as well as limited companies. Some business activities, however, are excluded (for example agriculture, banking, education, forestry, estate agents, insurance companies, medical services, night clubs, postal and tele-communications services).

The Enterprise Initiative

5.8 The Regional Enterprise Grants offered as part of the DTI's Enterprise Initiative (described earlier in this chapter) are directed at smaller firms (with 25 employees or fewer).

Development agencies

5.9 The UK government has set up the **Scottish and Welsh Development Agencies** which have been given the task of trying to encourage the development of trade and industry in their areas. The strategy of the agencies has been mainly to encourage the start-up and development of small companies, although they will also give help to larger companies too.

5.10 The assistance that a development agency might give to a firm could include:

(a) free factory accommodation, or factory accommodation at a low rent;

(b) financial assistance, in the form of:

(i) an interest relief grant for a bank loan. A company developing its business in an area might obtain a bank loan, and the development agency will agree to compensate the bank for providing the loan at a low rate of interest;

(ii) direct financial assistance in the form of equity finance or loans.

The Enterprise Investment Scheme

5.11 The **Enterprise Investment Scheme (EIS)** replaces the Business Expansion Scheme (which ended in 1993). The EIS is intended to encourage investment in the ordinary shares of unquoted companies. When a qualifying individual subscribes for eligible shares in a qualifying company, the individual saves tax at 20% on the amount subscribed (including any share premium) up to a limit of £1,000,000 per company (or £5,000,000 if the company's trade is ship chartering). A **qualifying individual** is one who is not connected with the company at any time in the period from two years before the issue (or from incorporation if later) to five years after the issue. The maximum total investment that can qualify in a tax year is £100,000 per individual. Investments in private rented housing are excluded. Capital gains generated by individual investors in the EIS are tax-free provided the investment is held for five years.

5.12 The scheme includes a measure to encourage 'business angels' who introduce finance to small companies which allows them to become paid directors of the companies they invest in without loss of tax relief.

Venture capital trusts

5.13 Venture capital providers have been around for many years, but in the November 1993 Budget, the Chancellor of the Exchequer Mr Kenneth Clarke also announced a second measure to encourage equity investment in the form of a new kind of investment trust called a **venture capital trust (VCT)** which came into being in 1995. This followed criticism from banks and small business groups that small companies were too dependent on short-term finance.

5.14 The new type of investment trust is to invest a large proportion of assets in unquoted companies, with investors gaining 20% income tax relief on dividends, provided shares are held in the VCT for five years, and capital gains rollover relief if the gain is invested in a VCT. There will be an investment ceiling per person of £100,000. The maximum investment that VCTs are permitted to make in each unquoted company is £1,000,000.

Franchising

5.15 Franchising is a method of expanding a business on less capital than would otherwise be needed. For suitable businesses, it is an alternative to raising extra capital for growth. Franchisors include Budget Rent-a-car, Dyno-rod, Express Dairy, Kall-Kwik Printing, Kentucky Fried Chicken, Prontaprint, Sketchley Cleaners and Wimpy.

5.16 Under a franchising arrangement, a franchisee pays a franchisor for the right to operate a local business, under the franchisor's trade name. The franchisor must bear certain costs (possibly for architect's work, establishment costs, legal costs, marketing costs and the costs of other support services) and will charge the franchisee an initial franchise fee to cover set-up costs, relying on the subsequent regular payments by the franchisee for an operating profit. These regular payments will usually be a percentage of the franchisee's turnover.

5.17 Although the franchisor will probably pay a large part of the initial investment cost of a franchisee's outlet, the franchisee will be expected to contribute a share of the investment himself. The franchisor may well help the franchisee to obtain loan capital to provide his share of the investment cost.

5.18 The advantages of franchises to the **franchisor** are as follows.

(a) The capital outlay needed to expand the business is reduced substantially.

(b) The image of the business is improved because the franchisees will be motivated to achieve good results and will have the authority to take whatever action they think fit to improve results.

5.19 The advantage of a franchise to the **franchisee** is that he obtains ownership of a business for an agreed number of years (including stock and premises, although premises might be leased from the franchisor) together with the backing of a large organisation's marketing effort and experience. The franchisee is able to avoid some of the mistakes of many small businesses, because the franchisor has already learned from his own past mistakes and developed a scheme that works.

Reduction of capital

5.20 We have assumed so far that a company will want to raise extra finance. This is not always true. Occasionally, a company might have funds surplus to requirements, and choose to use them to:

(a) repay a bank loan;
(b) redeem some loan capital;
(c) pay off other debts;
(d) re-purchase its own shares (discussed in Chapter 16).

5.21 Paying off loans will save loan interest, and if a company cannot earn a bigger return with its funds than it is having to pay in interest, it is sensible to reduce lending by redeeming loans, where possible.

Chapter roundup

- **Government grants and other assistance** should not be neglected as a source of finance, although this source is less significant in the UK than it used to be.
- **Bank borrowing** can be used as a financial source over short-term periods as well as longer periods. **Overdraft finance** is very flexible, because interest will only be charged on the daily balance.
- The factors a bank will consider regarding business lending can be summarised as: **P**urpose, **A**mount, **R**epayment, **T**erms, **S**ecurity.
- **Leasing** is an important source of medium-term and long-term funding for some companies. The position of the lessor is like a mirror image of the lessee's position, but depends upon the lessor's required rate of return.
- **International money and capital markets** are possible sources of finance for larger companies.
- The sources of finance available to **smaller companies** are more limited in range than for the larger enterprise. (You will lose marks in an exam if you suggest a financial source which is unsuited to the size of company in question.)

Quick quiz

1 What is the Enterprise Initiative in outline? (see para 1.4)

2 What factors will a banker consider when thinking of lending to a company? (2.4)

3 What is sale and leaseback? (3.1)

4 What are the advantages of leasing equipment rather than purchasing it? (3.9, 3.10)

5 What are the eurocurrency markets? (4.2, 4.3)

6 What are eurobonds? (4.6)

7 What is meant by a euro-equity issue? (4.10)

8 What are commercial paper and medium term notes? (4.14)

9 What is the Enterprise Investment Scheme? (5.11, 5.12)

Question to try	Level	Marks	Time
7	Introductory	25	45 mins

Chapter 8

SECURITIES MARKETS

Chapter topic list		Syllabus reference	Ability required
1	The Stock Exchange and regulatory bodies	13 b(ii)	Knowledge
2	New share issues	13 b(ii)	Knowledge
3	Merchant banks	13 b(ii)	Knowledge
4	Institutional investors	13 b(ii)	Knowledge
5	Venture capital	13 b(iv)	Application

Introduction

The syllabus requires you to have knowledge of the workings of a **stock exchange** and the role of **merchant banks** and **other financial institutions**, and we now turn to these topics. We also look at **venture capital**, an important source of capital for new enterprises.

1 THE STOCK EXCHANGE AND REGULATORY BODIES

1.1 London together with Tokyo and New York make up the so-called 'golden triangle' of stock market cities. The London Stock Exchange is a primary capital market in which companies and other institutions can raise funds by issuing shares or loan stock, but it is more important as a secondary market for buying and selling existing securities. The London Stock Exchange governs and regulates two markets.

(a) The main market deals in shares of 'fully listed' companies.
(b) There is a second-tier market called the **Alternative Investment Market (AIM).**

Exam focus point
Past examiners' reports show that many students are unaware that not all public limited companies (plcs) are listed on the Stock Exchange.

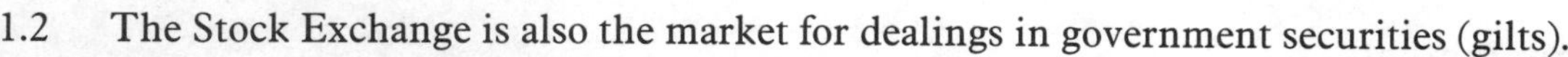

1.2 The Stock Exchange is also the market for dealings in government securities (gilts).

The functions of the stock market

1.3 The main functions of the stock market are:

(a) to bring companies and investors together, so that:

(i) investors can put risk capital into companies;
(ii) companies can use the capital that they raise to invest in new capital projects;

(b) to provide investors with a means of selling their investment, should they wish to do so, by offering a ready market in the buying and selling of existing shares and loan stock.

1.4 These are the main functions of a stock market, but we can add two more important ones.

(a) When a company comes to the stock market for the first time, and 'floats' its shares on the market, the owners of the company can realise some of the value of their shares in cash, because they will offer a proportion of their personally held shares for sale to new investors.

(b) When one company wants to take over another, it is common to do so by issuing shares to finance the takeover. For example, if ABC plc wants to take over XYZ plc, it might offer XYZ plc shareholders, say, three new shares in ABC plc for every two shares held in XYZ plc. Takeovers by means of a share exchange are only feasible if the shares that are offered can be readily traded on a stock market, and so have an identifiable market value.

1.5 (a) The UK stock market has sometimes failed badly in recent years to provide a source of investment finance for companies. Research has shown that:

(i) companies which have needed money to finance new investments have obtained their funds mainly from retained profits. The next most significant source of funds has been borrowing, in particular borrowing from banks;

(ii) the stock market in the UK have provided companies with only very small amounts of risk capital for new investments by companies.

(b) The UK stock markets have been relatively successful in:

(i) providing investors with a market for buying and selling listed securities. The holder of even a large quantity of shares in a listed company will find it relatively easy to sell his shares whenever he wants to at the current market price;

(ii) allowing companies to float their shares on the market and so giving the companies' owners the chance to sell some of their shareholdings for cash;

(iii) providing a means by which companies can issue new shares to finance the takeover of other companies.

1.6 The Stock Exchange also has another important function - that of market regulation. The proponents of the UK system argue that one of its strengths is that regulation is carried out by the market itself rather than by some government department. By international standards there is an extraordinary degree of trust, particularly in the way in which contracts are made. Deals are made by verbal agreement (backed by documentation later). The Stock Exchange's motto is 'My word is my bond'.

The main market

1.7 A company wishing to have some or all of its shares listed on the Stock Exchange must agree to obey the Stock Exchange rules. For companies with a listing on the main market, these rules are contained in the so-called Yellow Book 'Admission of Securities to Listing'.

1.8 Some of the rules in the Yellow Book are as follows.

(a) To obtain a full listing, the company should normally have traded successfully for at least three years but from January 1999 a rule was introduced allowing this criteria to be relaxed subject to a review the case concerned.

(b) Enough shares should be made available to the investing public so that a ready market exists, and there is no shortage of supply for would-be investors.

(c) Enough shares must be available on the Stock Exchange launch to create a free market.

Thus it is more appropriate to issue 2,000,000 shares with a nominal value of £1 each than to issue only 2,000 shares with a nominal value of £1,000 each.

(d) The company's listed securities would be expected to have a minimum total value. Although the Stock Exchange will accept shares of a company valued at this minimum, currently under £1,000,000, for quotation, except in very special circumstances a prospective market capitalisation of £6,000,000 is considered to be a reasonable minimum. This would normally mean minimum annual profits before tax of between £750,000 and £1,200,000. In addition to the size qualification, a company must have a satisfactory trading record and be in a financially stable position.

(e) The company must undertake to obey the rules of the Stock Exchange, for example about the provision of information such as the announcement of half-year (interim) results.

(f) Shares in the company must be traded on the Stock Exchange by **market makers**.

The advantages and disadvantages of flotation on the main market

1.9 Flotation is the process of making shares available to the general public by obtaining a quotation on the Stock Exchange. Flotation is sometimes referred to as 'going public' or 'obtaining a Stock Exchange listing'. Why should a company want to be floated on the stock market?

1.10 The advantages of flotation to the existing shareholders are as follows.

(a) They can sell some of their shares.

(b) A wider market is created for their remaining shares.

(c) From the fact of flotation, shares may be perceived as a less risky investment.

(d) A quotation provides a ready share price, which lessens the uncertainties of inheritance tax by avoiding the problems of valuing unquoted shares.

1.11 The advantages of flotation to the company are as follows.

(a) New funds are obtained if the flotation involves the issue of new shares.

(b) A better credit standing is obtained, so that it may be easier to borrow money.

(c) Buying another company with a new issue of shares is much more practicable for a quoted company than for an unquoted company.

(d) Shares can be issued more easily at a later date. It is difficult for companies to expand beyond a certain size without getting a quotation, because of the difficulty of raising enough funds.

(e) The reduction in the perceived risk for shareholders and the greater marketability of shares may lead to a lower cost of equity.

(f) The extra status and prominence given to public companies might help the company to generate new business by attracting new customers.

(g) A public company with a main market or second tier listing can offer its top employees the tax benefits of an approved share option scheme. A share option scheme might help the company to retain the services of these staff.

1.12 The disadvantages of flotation include the following.

(a) The costs of flotation must be borne by the company.

(b) The company must comply with the stringent Stock Exchange regulations.

(c) A dilution of control will result from the wider holding of the company's shares.

(d) Other ways of raising finance might be better.

(e) The company may not be big enough, or growing fast enough, for its shares to perform well on the stock market.

(f) Listed company status will put extra administrative burdens on the management.

(g) The profits and performance of a listed company are much more in the public eye and the company cannot afford to show poor results without attracting considerable criticism.

(h) The company's share price may become vulnerable to campaigns to drive it down by selling shares. Several companies have been victims of such 'bear raids'.

(i) The company may become the target of unwelcome bidders.

A private company which goes public often first seeks a listing on the second-tier market, to progress later to a full Stock Exchange listing after a few more years of growth.

The Alternative Investment Market (AIM)

1.13 The London Stock Exchange launched the AIM in June 1995 as a market for smaller, growing, companies that cannot qualify for or do not wish to join the Official List. It was not a direct replacement for the previous second-tier market, the Unlisted Securities Market (USM), since the AIM has more lax entry requirements and regulation than either the USM or the Official List. The new market is however regulated, in contrast to share trading under 'Rule 4.2' which developed into a semi-official alternative market over the years. The Exchange removed Rule 4.2 from its rulebook at the end of September 1995.

1.14 The key characteristics of the AIM are as follows.

(a) No eligibility criteria for new entrants, whether in size, profitability or length of track record.

(b) Any type of security can be offered, provided there are no restrictions on transferability.

(c) No Stock Exchange requirements for the percentage of shares in public hands or the number of shareholders, although if too few shares are freely available, then there will be no market maker and no realistic market price.

(d) Fewer obligations to issue shareholder circulars; public announcements will generally be sufficient.

(e) Documents produced for admission to the AIM are the responsibility of the directors and are not reviewed by the Exchange.

(f) Every company whose securities trade on the AIM must have (at all times) a Nominated Adviser chosen from an official list and a Nominated Broker which must be a member firm of the Exchange. The Adviser's role is to advise the directors of the issuer on their obligations under AIM rules. The Broker's role is to support trading if there is no market maker and to act as a point of contact for investors.

(g) AIM securities are subject to the Exchange's Market Supervision and Surveillance Department in the same way as the companies on the Official List. Unusual price movements and market imperfections will be scrutinised.

(h) AIM shares are treated as unquoted for tax purposes, meaning that a number of reliefs are available to investors.

1.15 To gain entry to the AIM, companies must normally issue a prospectus in accordance with the Public Offer of Securities (POS) Regulations, 1995. The Stock Exchange will not examine this prospectus, for which directors must take responsibility. AIM companies will have to publish interim reports and details of directors' dealings, and price-sensitive information must be released promptly. The Stock Exchange plans to fine companies that breach AIM rules.

Exemptions from the POS rules apply for:

(a) offers restricted to a small circle of knowledgeable persons;

(b) offers raising less than around £25,000;

(c) some larger offers with a minimum subscription of more than about £25,000 per subscriber;

(d) issues by charities, housing associations and similar bodies;

(e) succeeding issues where a POS prospectus has already been issued.

1.16 AIM companies might be new business 'start-ups' or well established family businesses, from high technology firms to traditional manufacturers. It has been estimated that the AIM could raise approximately £2 billion annually, and it is also expected to attract companies on the USM and the main market which wish to cut the cost of a stock market quotation. The Stock Exchange hopes that the failure rate among AIM companies will be minimised as a result of its careful vetting of Nominated Advisers, each of which might be approved by the Exchange.

1.17 In conclusion, the AIM would appear to offer the advantages of wider access to capital, enhanced credibility among financial institutions and a higher public profile, at a much lower cost than a full listing. By May 1997, about two years after its launch, the AIM had attracted 280 entrants, with a combined capitalisation of almost £6 billion.

Market operators on the Stock Exchange

1.18 The traditional distinction between stockbroker and stockjobber was abolished in 1986. All Stock Exchange member firms are now **broker/dealers** and deal by telephone using the computerised price display system rather than on the trading floor. A broker/dealer can apply to the Stock Exchange to register as a **market maker**, dealing on their own account in certain securities. These market makers are allowed to trade in a **dual capacity**:

(a) handling the market dealings in shares of a company (the role previously performed by stockjobbers) and acting as **principals** - by dealing on their own account; and also

(b) dealing directly with clients/investors (stockbroking) - by dealing as **agents** on behalf of clients.

1.19 Brokers/dealers who only deal for clients on a commission basis and not on their own account are known as **agency brokers**.

1.20 To prevent unfair and unscrupulous advantage of dual capacity being taken by employees, broker/dealers who act both as market makers and as brokers are required to set up so-called 'Chinese walls', meaning organisational arrangements which separate the two activities.

1.21 As indicated above, market makers are broker/dealers in securities who buy and sell the securities on their own account (ie as principals), and who may also buy and sell securities on behalf of clients. It is thus possible for a firm to act as a stockbroker on behalf of a client and buy or sell shares on the client's behalf, when they also trade as market makers on their own account in the same shares.

1.22 Market makers have not eliminated stockbroking, even though dual capacity trading has eliminated the old role of the stockjobber. Firms can still act as agency brokers for clients without being at the same time market makers in the shares they buy and sell on their behalf. A market maker **must** undertake to make two-way prices (for selling and for buying) in the securities for which he is registered as market maker, under **any** trading conditions.

The new **SETS** system (covering major stocks) represents a change from the 'quote-driven' market maker system to an 'order-driven' share trading system in which the orders of buyers and sellers of shares are matched directly instead of via the market maker system.

1.23 Market makers in gilt-edged securities are often referred to using the abbreviation GEMMs **(gilt-edged market makers).**

1.24 **Inter-dealer brokers** (IDBs) act as intermediaries between market makers rather like a kind of 'wholesaler', although they do not normally hold large blocks of shares. They operate without disclosing the name of the counterparty and their services can therefore be useful to protect the exposed position of a client, for example a client who is oversold (ie has contracted to sell more shares than he owns and therefore must buy to make up the difference). Approximately 90% of IDBs' turnover is in gilt-edged securities.

1.25 Market liquidity is facilitated by the existence of **Stock Exchange money brokers** (SEMBs). SEMBs allow market operators to delay payment for deals by borrowing or lending money and stocks. SEMBs are able to borrow stock from long-term shareholders such as insurance companies, who charge fees for providing the stocks.

The regulatory framework

1.26 The Financial Services Act 1986 has established regulations for firms in the investment services industry, including the buying and selling of stocks and shares. The Treasury has overall responsibility for regulation under the Act. Operational powers are delegated to the **Financial Services Authority (FSA)**, formerly the Securities and Investments Board (SIB).

1.27 Under the terms of the 1986 Act, only 'authorised persons' are allowed to carry on investment business. Authorisation will be granted by the FSA, and methods by which the FSA can grant authorisation include:

(a) direct authorisation of individual firms;

(b) authorisation for all members of a recognised **Self-Regulatory Organisation (SRO)**. This is an organisation which is approved by the FSA, and issues a code of regulations to its members.

1.28 The Financial Services Act puts heavy reliance on self-regulation by City firms, and:

(a) the willingness of firms to obey the regulations of the SRO to which they belong;
(b) the SRO's ability to enforce its regulations without the backing of statutory powers.

1.29 Any firm which belongs to an SRO will be authorised to carry on investment business, but only business within the scope of the SRO itself.

The following organisations have been recognised as Self-Regulatory Organisations (SROs) under the Act.

(a) **The Securities and Futures Authority (SFA).** The SFA regulates activities of broker/dealers and market makers on the London Stock Exchange, and of other dealers not on the Stock Exchange such as US brokers trading in the UK. It is also responsible for dealers on LIFFE and other commodity exchanges.

(b) **The Investment Management Regulatory Organisation (IMRO).** IMRO regulates those who manage investment portfolios. IMRO members include banks, pension funds and investment trusts. IMRO is the principal or 'lead' regulator for the banks where conflicts arise with rules of other SROs.

(c) **The Personal Investment Authority (PIA).** This SRO was set up in 1994 to take over the functions of LAUTRO (the Life And Unit Trust Regulatory Organisation) and FIMBRA (the Financial Intermediaries, Managers and Brokers Regulatory Association). The PIA regulates the marketing of various financial products to individuals.

1.30 Where an institution belongs to more than one SRO, the SIB provides for the appointment of a **lead regulator**, which is regarded as the principal regulatory authority to be followed. Normally the lead regulator is one of the SROs. In the special case of banks, the lead regulator is the Bank of England.

RPBs and other bodies

1.31 The framework of the Financial Services Act encompasses **recognised professional bodies (RPBs)**, such as the Law Society (the solicitors' professional body) and the Institute of Chartered Accountants in England and Wales, which are empowered to authorise their members to conduct investment business. The various RPBs are within the scope of the Act, because their members sometimes advise clients on their investments. There are also recognised secondary investment exchanges and clearing houses. Lloyds (the insurance market) is regulated under its own Act. The company secretary may also find that he has dealings with bodies, such as the National Association of Pension Funds (NAPF) and the Institutional Shareholders Committee (ISC), which put forward the collective views of their members as institutional investors in the securities issued by companies.

1.32 The Financial Services Act also grants official recognition to investment exchanges. An investment exchange is an organised market within which investment business can be carried out. To become a **Recognised Investment Exchange (RIE)** under the Act, there must be adequate clearing facilities for settling investment transactions. The Stock Exchange is an RIE and its Yellow Book Rules are its regulations as an RIE for listed companies.

Licensed securities dealers

1.33 Not every dealer in shares is a member of the Stock Exchange. Market makers in shares of companies on the over-the-counter markets (see below) are not members of the Stock Exchange, although they must be licensed dealers, under the requirements of the Financial Services Act.

Over-the-counter (OTC) markets

1.34 Shares and other financial instruments are also bought and sold outside the supervised and regulated official exchanges in **'over-the-counter' (OTC) markets**. Regulators are reported to be increasingly concerned about the growth of OTC markets. It is feared that dealers on the OTC markets could manipulate prices on the official markets, and that some may be using the secrecy of these markets to conceal illegal insider dealing and other illicit transactions. However, shares are dealt 'off the market' to reduce costs as well as to maintain secrecy.

Crossing networks

1.35 Unofficial trading systems include 'Global Posit', which started operating in the UK during 1993, and Instinet, a subsidiary of Reuters. These systems provide 'crossing networks', which electronically match buyers and sellers, offering for larger institutional investors an alternative to the system of market-makers which is at the heart of the Stock Exchange. The trading on these networks is off-market insofar as it is outside the normal market-making system, but on-market in that the volumes of trades are included in Stock Exchange totals.

1.36 In the US, crossing networks are well established and account for up to half of all share trading. Although the networks are growing in the UK, they still account for only a small proportion of share trading overall. Market-makers complain that the development of these networks will take away volume, and therefore liquidity, from the main market in which they operate.

1.37 Another example of one of the variety of trading platforms being established in the UK is **Tradepoint**, which was approved as a **Recognised Investment Exchange** under the Financial Services Act in 1995. Tradepoint is allowed to operate a screen-based order-matching system for a selection of London equities.

2 NEW SHARE ISSUES 5/98

2.1 A company seeking to obtain additional equity funds may be:

(a) an unquoted company wishing to obtain a Stock Exchange main market or AIM quotation;

(b) an unquoted company wishing to issue new shares, but without obtaining a main market or AIM quotation;

(c) a company which is already listed on the main market or the AIM wishing to issue additional new shares.

2.2 The methods by which an unquoted company can obtain a quotation on the stock market are an **offer for sale**, a **prospectus issue**, a **placing**, or an **introduction**. Of these, the offer for sale and placing are the most common.

Offers for sale

2.3 An **offer for sale** is a means of selling the shares of a company to the public at large.

(a) An unquoted company may issue new shares, and sell them on the Stock Exchange, to raise cash for the company. All the shares in the company, not just the new ones, would then become marketable.

(b) Shareholders in an unquoted company may sell some of their existing shares to the general public. When this occurs, the company is not raising any new funds, but is merely providing a wider market for its existing shares (all of which would become marketable), and giving existing shareholders the chance to cash in some or all of their investment in their company.

KEY TERM

Offer for sale: An invitation to apply for shares in a company based on information contained in the prospectus *(OT)*.

2.4 When companies 'go public' for the first time, a large issue will probably take the form of an offer for sale (or occasionally an offer for sale by tender). A smaller issue is more likely to be a placing, since the amount to be raised can be obtained more cheaply if the issuing house or other sponsoring firm approaches selected institutional investors privately. A company whose shares are **already listed** might issue new shares to the general public. It is likely, however, that a new issue by a quoted company will be either a placing or a rights issue, which are described later.

Issuing houses and sponsoring member firms

2.5 When an unquoted company applies for a Stock Exchange listing, it must be sponsored by a firm that is a member of the Stock Exchange. This sponsoring member firm has the responsibility of ensuring that the company meets the requirements for listing, and carries out the necessary procedures. The company will also employ the services of an issuing house, which might well be the sponsoring member firm itself. An issuing house has the job of trying to ensure a successful issue for the company's shares, by advising on an issue price for the shares, and trying to interest institutional investors in buying some of the shares.

The issue price and offers for sale

2.6 The price at which shares are offered will be critical to the success of the issue. The offer price must be advertised a short time in advance, so it is fixed without certain knowledge of the condition of the market at the time applications are invited. In order to safeguard the success of an issue, share prices are often set lower than they might otherwise be. It is normal practice for an issuing house to try to ensure that a share price rises to a premium above its issue price soon after trading begins. A target premium of 20% above the issue price would be fairly typical.

2.7 Companies will be keen to avoid over-pricing an issue, so that the issue is under-subscribed, leaving underwriters with the unwelcome task of having to buy up the unsold shares. On the other hand, if the issue price is too low then the issue will be oversubscribed and the company would have been able to raise the required capital by issuing fewer shares.

Offers for sale by tender

2.8 It is often very difficult to decide upon the price at which the shares should be offered to the general public. One way of trying to ensure that the issue price reflects the value of the shares as perceived by the market is to make an offer for sale by tender.

(a) A minimum price will be fixed and subscribers will be invited to tender for shares at prices equal to or above the minimum.

(b) The shares will be allotted at the highest price at which they will all be taken up. This is known as the striking price.

2.9 Offers by tender are less common than offers for sale.

The reasons why offers for sale by tender might not be preferred are as follows.

(a) It is sometimes felt that the decision to made an offer by tender reflects badly on the issuing house's ability to determine the issue price.

(b) It is claimed that the use of tenders leaves the determination of prices to the 'uninformed public' rather than the City 'experts'. However, in practice the major influence on the striking price will be the tenders of the institutional investors.

(c) An offer for sale is more certain in the amount of finance that will be raised.

(d) Some potential investors may be deterred from applying for shares as they do not wish to have to decide on a price.

2.10 EXAMPLE: OFFER FOR SALE BY TENDER

Byte Henderson plc is a new company that is making its first public issue of shares. It has decided to make the issue by means of an offer for sale by tender. The intention is to issue up to 4,000,000 shares (the full amount of authorised share capital) at a minimum price of 300 pence. The money raised, net of issue costs of £1,000,000, would be invested in projects which would earn benefits with a present value equal to 130% of the net amount invested.

The following tenders have been received. (Each applicant has made only one offer.)

Price tendered per share	*Number of shares applied for at this price*
£	
6.00	50,000
5.50	100,000
5.00	300,000
4.50	450,000
4.00	1,100,000
3.50	1,500,000
3.00	2,500,000

(a) How many shares would be issued, and how much in total would be raised, if Byte Henderson plc chooses:

(i) to maximise the total amount raised?
(ii) to issue exactly 4,000,000 shares?

(b) Harvey Goldfinger, a private investor, has applied for 12,000 shares at a price of £5.50 and has sent a cheque for £66,000 to the issuing house that is handling the issue. In both cases (a)(i) and (ii), how many shares would be issued to Mr Goldfinger, assuming that any partial acceptance of offers would mean allotting shares to each accepted applicant in proportion to the number of shares applied for? How much will Mr Goldfinger receive back out of the £66,000 he has paid?

(c) Estimate the likely market value of shares in the company after the issue, assuming that the market price fully reflects the investment information given above and that exactly 4,000,000 shares are issued.

2.11 SOLUTION

(a) We begin by looking at the cumulative tenders.

Price	Cumulative number of shares applied for	Amount raised if price is selected, before deducting issue costs
£		£
6.00	50,000	300,000
5.50	150,000	825,000
5.00	450,000	2,250,000
4.50	900,000	4,050,000
4.00	2,000,000	8,000,000
3.50	3,500,000	12,250,000
3.00	6,000,000	12,000,000

(i) To maximise the total amount raised, the issue price should be £3.50. The total raised before deducting issue costs would be £12,250,000.

(ii) To issue exactly 4,000,000 shares, the issue price must be £3.00. The total raised would be £12,000,000, before deducting issue costs.

(b) (i) Harvey Goldfinger would be allotted 12,000 shares at £3.50 per share. He would receive a refund of 12,000 × £2 = £24,000 out of the £66,000 he has paid.

(ii) If 4,000,000 shares are issued, applicants would receive two thirds of the shares they tendered for. Harvey Goldfinger would be allotted 8,000 shares at £3 per share and would receive a refund of £42,000 out of the £66,000 he has paid.

(c) The net amount raised would be £12,000,000 minus issue costs of £1,000,000, £11,000,000.

The present value of the benefits from investment would be 130% of £11,000,000, £14,300,000. If the market price reflects this information, the price per share would rise

to $\frac{£14{,}300{,}000}{4{,}000{,}000}$ = £3.575 per share.

A prospectus issue

2.12 In a **prospectus issue**, or public issue, a company offers its own shares to the general public. An issuing house or merchant bank may act as an agent, but not as an underwriter. This type of issue is therefore risky, and is very rare. Well known companies making a large new issue may use this method, and the company would almost certainly already have a quotation on the Stock Exchange.

KEY TERM

Prospectus: a description of a company's operations, financial background, prospects and the detailed terms and conditions relating to an offer for sale or placing of its shares by notice, circular, advertisement or any form of invitation which offers securities to the public *(OT)*.

A placing

2.13 A **placing** is an arrangement whereby the shares are not all offered to the public, but instead, the sponsoring market maker arranges for most of the issue to be bought by a small number of investors, usually institutional investors such as pension funds and insurance companies.

A Stock Exchange introduction

2.14 By this method of obtaining a quotation, no shares are made available to the market, neither existing nor newly created shares; nevertheless, the Stock Exchange grants a quotation. This will only happen where shares in a large company are already widely held, so that a market can be seen to exist. A company might want an introduction to obtain greater marketability for the shares, a known share valuation for inheritance tax purposes and easier access in the future to additional capital.

Underwriters

2.15 A company about to issue new securities in order to raise finance might decide to have the issue underwritten. **Underwriters** are financial institutions which agree (in exchange for a fixed fee, perhaps 2.25% of the finance to be raised) to buy at the issue price any securities which are not subscribed for by the investing public.

2.16 Underwriters remove the risk of a share issue's being under-subscribed, but at a cost to the company issuing the shares. It is not compulsory to have an issue underwritten.

(a) It is unnecessary to underwrite a placing since a purchaser for the shares is arranged in the issue process.

(b) An offer for sale by tender would only need underwriting if there is a risk that there will be under-subscription even at the minimum price.

(c) A rights issue should in theory not require underwriting, since new shares are being offered to existing shareholders. However, the underwriting of rights issues is common practice.

With underwriting, the company making the issue is sure of receiving the funds it wants to raise, net of expenses.

2.17 As an alternative to **underwriting** an issue, a company could choose to issue its share at a **deep discount**, that is, at a price well below the current market price, to ensure the success of the issue. This is less common. A major disadvantage of issuing shares at a deep discount is that, since companies try to avoid reducing the dividends paid out per share, the total amount required for dividends in future years will be that much higher, since more shares would have to be issued at the low price to raise the amount of finance required. If the company expects only moderate growth in total earnings and dividends, the company's shareholders might even suffer a fall in earnings per share.

Because of the costs of underwriting, there has been a trend in recent years for companies with marketable securities to adopt the practice known as the 'bought deal', whereby a major investment bank buys the whole of a new issue at a very small discount to the market.

Pricing shares for a stock market launch

2.18 Pricing shares for a stock market launch is a task for the company's sponsor.

Factors that the sponsor will take into account are as follows.

(a) Are there similar companies already quoted, whose P/E ratios can be used for comparison? The chosen P/E ratio can be multiplied by the company's most recent EPS, as shown in the prospectus, to arrive at a draft share price. This price can be negotiated with the company's current owners.

    A company which is coming to the AIM will obtain a lower P/E ratio than a similar company on the main market.

(b) What are current market conditions?

(c) With what accuracy can the company's future trading prospects be forecast?

(d) It is usual to set a price which gives an immediate premium when the launch takes place. A sponsor will usually try to ensure that the market price rises to a premium of about 20% over the launch price on the day that the launch takes place.

(e) A steady growth in the share price year by year should be achievable.

2.19 EXAMPLE: PRICING SHARES FOR A STOCK MARKET LAUNCH

Launchpad plc is proposing to obtain a Stock Exchange listing, to raise £10,000,000 from a placing of new shares. Issue costs will be 8% of the gross receipts.

The company already has 4,000,000 shares in issue. The company expects to earn a post-tax profit of £4,000,000 in its next year of operations, plus a 15% post-tax return on the newly-raised funds, and to pay out 50% of its profits as dividends. Dividend growth would be 3% a year.

For the issue to be successful, Launchpad plc would have to issue shares at a 20% discount to what it considers the market value of the shares ought to be. Shareholders will expect a net dividend yield (that is, net of the tax credit) of 12%.

Calculate a suitable issue price for the shares, and the number of shares that would have to be issued.

2.20 SOLUTION

(a) Receipts net of issue costs from the new issue = 92% of £10,000,000
= £9,200,000

(b) Post-tax profits on the newly raised funds in year 1 = 15% of £9,200,000
= £1,380,000

(c) Total post-tax profits in year 1 = £4,000,000 + £1,380,000
= £5,380,000

(d) Dividends in year 1 = 50% of £5,380,000
= £2,690,000

(e) Market value, based on the dividend growth model, expected dividend growth of 3% a year from year 1 and a required return of 12%

$$= \frac{d_1}{(r-g)} = \frac{£2,690,000}{(0.12-0.03)}$$

$$= \frac{£2,690,000}{0.09}$$

$$= £29,888,888$$

(f) Let the number of shares issued be X.

Total number of shares	= 4,000,000 + X
Let the share price after the issue be P.	
Total market value	= £29,888,888
(4,000,000 + X) × P	= £29,888,888

(g) Let P_d be the discount price at which the new shares must be issued, which is 20% below what the share price P ought to be.

$P_d = 0.8P$

From (f) it follows that:

$$\frac{(4{,}000{,}000+X)P_d}{0.8} = £29{,}888{,}888$$

$$4{,}000{,}000P_d + XP_d = £29{,}888{,}888 \times 0.8 = £23{,}911{,}110$$

(h) XP_d = number of new shares issued × issue price = £10,000,000

(i) Taking (g) and (h) together,

$$4{,}000{,}000P_d + 10{,}000{,}000 = £23{,}911{,}110$$

$$4{,}000{,}000\ P_d = £13{,}911{,}110$$

$$P_d = \frac{£13{,}911{,}110}{4{,}000{,}000} = £3.48$$

(j) Since XP_d = £10,000,000

$$X = \frac{£10{,}000{,}000}{£3.48}$$

$$= 2{,}873{,}563$$

Conclusions

1 2,873,563 shares should be issued at a price of £3.48 to raise £10,000,000.

2 The price of £3.48 is at a 20% discount to the market value after the issue. The market value will be £3.48 ÷ 0.8 = £4.35 per share.

3 After the issue, there will be 6,873,563 shares valued at £4.35 each or £29,899,999 in total. Allowing for rounding errors, this is the total valuation of £29,888,888 given in (g) above.

New issues of shares by quoted companies

2.21 When a quoted company makes an issue of new shares to raise capital, it could make an offer for sale, but it is more likely to issue the shares by means of a **rights issue**.

Rights issues or issuing shares for cash to new investors?

2.22 When shares are issued for cash to outside buyers, existing shareholders forfeit their **pre-emptive rights** to a rights issue. Arguably, pre-emptive rights are a form of restrictive practice which runs contrary to the modern trend towards market deregulation. Companies can issue shares for cash without obtaining prior approval from shareholders for each such share issue, provided that they have obtained approval from shareholders within the past 12 months to make new issues of shares for cash which are not rights issues. (This shareholder approval could be obtained at the company's AGM.)

2.23 Companies can thus issue shares for cash without having to bear the high costs of a rights issue, for example by placing shares for cash at a higher price than they might have been able to obtain from a rights issue. (We looked at the valuation of rights issues in the last chapter.)

Vendor placings

2.24 A **vendor placing** occurs when there is an issue of shares by one company to take over another, and these shares are then sold in a placing to raise cash for the shareholders in the target company, who are selling their shares in the takeover.

2.25 EXAMPLE: VENDOR PLACING

AB plc wants to take over Z Ltd. AB plc wants to finance the purchase by issuing more equity shares, and the shareholders of Z Ltd want to sell their shares for cash. AB plc can arrange a vendor placing whereby:

(a) AB plc issues new shares to finance the takeover;

(b) these shares are placed by AB plc's stockbrokers (market makers) with institutional investors, to raise cash;

(c) the cash that is raised is used to pay the shareholders in Z Ltd for their shares.

Other methods of issuing shares

2.26 There are some other methods of issuing shares on the Stock Exchange, as follows.

(a) An **open offer** is an offer to existing shareholders to subscribe for new shares in the company but, unlike a rights issue:

   (i) the offer is not necessarily pro rata to existing shareholdings;

   (ii) the offer is not allotted on renounceable documents. (With rights issues the offer to subscribe for new shares must be given on a renounceable letter, so that the shareholder can sell his rights if he so wishes.)

(b) A **capitalisation issue** is a 'scrip issue' of shares which does not raise any new funds. It is made to 'capitalise' reserves of the company: in effect, to change some reserves into share capital. Shareholders receive new shares pro rata to their existing shareholdings.

(c) A **vendor consideration issue** is an issue of shares whereby one company acquires the shares of another in a takeover or merger. For example, if A plc wishes to take over B plc, A might make a 'paper' offer to B's shareholders, try to buy the shares of B by offering B's shareholders newly issued shares of A. This is now a common form of share issue, because mergers and takeovers are fairly frequent events.

(d) **Employee share option schemes** are schemes for awarding shares to employees. For example, in an employee share option scheme, a company awards its employees share options, which are rights to subscribe for new shares at a later date at a predetermined price (commonly, the market price of the shares when the options are awarded, or the market price less a discount). When and if the options are eventually exercised, the employees will receive the newly issued shares at a price that ought by then to be below the market price.

The timing and costs of new equity issues

2.27 New equity issues in general (offers for sale and placings as well as rights issues) will be more common when share prices are high than when share prices are low.

(a) When share price are high, investors' confidence will probably be high, and investors will be more willing to put money into companies with the potential for growth.

(b) By issuing shares at a high price, a company will reduce the number of shares it must issue to raise the amount of capital it wants. This will reduce the dilution of earnings for existing shareholders.

(c) Following on from (b), the company's total dividend commitment on the new shares, to meet shareholders' expectations, will be lower.

(d) If share prices are low, business confidence is likely to be low too. Companies may not want to raise capital for new investments until expectations begin to improve.

2.28 Typical costs of a share issue include:

(a) underwriting costs;
(b) the Stock Exchange listing fee (the initial charge) for the new securities;
(c) fees of the issuing house, solicitors, auditors and public relations consultants;
(d) charges for printing and distributing the prospectus;
(e) advertising, which must be done in national newspapers.

2.29 Costs vary according to whether equity or debt capital is being issued and whether the issue is a rights issue, an offer for sale or placing. With a placing, a full prospectus is not needed, advertising is cheaper and underwriting is not needed. Some costs of flotation are variable (for example commission payable to an issuing house) but many costs are fixed (for example the costs of a prospectus, including professional fees, printing and advertising). The greater the amount of capital raised, the lower will be the costs of flotation as a percentage of the funds raised, because fixed costs are spread more thinly. High fixed costs help to explain why small companies have found it difficult and often undesirable to raise new funds through the Stock Exchange.

3 MERCHANT BANKS 11/96, 11/97

3.1 The term **merchant banking** is difficult to define because merchant banks engage in diverse activities, with individual banks having their specialised areas of expertise and interest, and also because some of the services of merchant banks are also provided by traditional clearing banks. The alternative term **investment bank** is now becoming more common. Merchant banking is perhaps best thought of in terms of its customers, who are generally corporate clients wanting particular financial services. The clearing banks carry out some merchant banking activities themselves.

The range of merchant banking activities

3.2 Merchant or investment banking activities are various. The following list gives some examples.

(a) Granting acceptance credits (described in a later chapter).

(b) Involvement in the issue and underwriting of shares on the Stock Exchange.

(c) Taking 'wholesale' deposits of funds, both in sterling and foreign currencies. (Merchant banks created the 'eurodollar' market for US dollar loans to borrowers outside the USA).

(d) Large scale term lending to corporate borrowers.

(e) Dealing in foreign exchange.

(f) Dealing in the gold and silver bullion markets.

(g) Handling Stock Exchange business on behalf of clients.

(h) Managing investments on behalf of clients, including investment trusts, unit trusts, insurance companies, pension funds and charities.

(i) Acting as trustees.

(j) Advising business customers generally, but in particular providing advice about pursuing or resisting company takeovers or mergers.

(k) Providing venture capital.

(l) Share registration.

(m) Dealing in stocks and shares as a market maker or stockbroker, through a subsidiary company.

Medium-term lending

3.3 Merchant banks compete for deposits of larger customers, and make large medium-term loans to borrowers. There is intense competition between banks in this area of activity with merchant banks, foreign banks and clearing banks vying with each other for 'wholesale' deposits and medium-term lending business.

Business advice on mergers and takeovers

3.4 All the major banks offer corporate advice to customers, but merchant banks or 'investment banks', and the merchant banking divisions of clearing banks, have become increasingly involved in providing advice on business mergers and takeovers. If company A, for example, wants to take over company B by bidding for its shares, one merchant bank might advise the board of directors of company A in proceeding with the bid, and another bank might advise the board of company B, possibly on ways of contesting the takeover. Another function of a merchant bank might be to identify suitable candidates for a takeover by a customer.

Merchant banks and new capital issues by companies

3.5 The role of merchant banks in the issue of new share and loan capital is a major element of merchant banking. The banks provide not just advice but also the organisation for capital issues. Capital issues business is not the exclusive preserve of merchant banks, however, and organisations other than merchant banks undertake capital issues. The regulatory body for capital issues is the Issuing Houses Association, and its members are known as issuing houses. (All the accepting houses are members.) The task of an issuing house is to supervise the issue of a company's stocks or shares.

3.6 Whenever an issuing house sponsors a capital issue, its reputation is at stake. It must therefore satisfy itself as to the integrity of the company and its long term business stability and strength. It must be satisfied in particular that the accounting information about the company, prepared by a firm of reporting accountants, is satisfactory. It must also advise the company carefully about the offer price of the shares.

4 INSTITUTIONAL INVESTORS

4.1 **Institutional investors** are institutions which have large amounts of funds which they want to invest, and they will invest in stocks and shares or any other assets (such as gold or works of art) which offer satisfactory returns and security. The institutional investors are now the biggest investors on the stock market but they might also invest venture capital, or lend directly to companies.

Question

Before looking at the following paragraph, see if you can list the major types of institutional investor in the UK.

Pension funds as institutional investors

4.2 Pension funds comprise funds set aside to provide for retirement pensions. They are financed from pension contributions paid into a fund by a company and its employees, and by private individuals.

4.3 Pension funds are continually receiving large amounts of money from pension contributions. They are also likely to be paying out money for pensions, as lump sums, and regular pension payments to beneficiaries. Money coming in can be diverted to meet payment obligations, but there will usually be an excess of contributions coming in over pensions going out, and this excess must be invested.

4.4 A fund manager is the person who makes the investment decisions, buying and selling securities. Fund managers must attempt to ensure that their investments will provide enough income to meet future pension commitments. Generally speaking, most holdings are considered to be long-term. Few fund managers would expect to make a substantial profit from short term speculation as such dealing is highly risky. Often a portion of the fund is invested in high yield securities, such as gilts which will, hopefully, give enough income to meet current commitments, and the balance is invested in growth assets such as equities or property.

Insurance companies

4.5 Insurance companies sell various types of insurance policy (life assurance policies, car insurance, house insurance, pension policies and so on). They need cash to pay out for claims or other entitlements under the terms of their policies, but they will have substantial cash income to invest. The investment strategy of insurance companies is comparable to the investment strategy of pension fund managers.

(a) They invest in a portfolio of company stocks and shares, government securities (gilts), direct loans and mortgages and other investments.

(b) They limit investment risks, investing most of their funds in secure companies.

(c) They deal in large blocks of stocks and shares, because the potential return from small investments is often not worth the trouble.

Investment trusts

4.6 Investment trusts are companies whose business is to invest in the securities of a wide range of other companies. Their portfolios may change continually, as circumstances require.

(a) Having a capital structure like any other company, they pay dividends to shareholders from profits which arise from their investment income. An investment trust company with a Stock Exchange listing must have a clause in its Memorandum or Articles prohibiting the distribution as dividend of any surpluses arising from the sale of investments it holds.

(b) Most of the funds of investment trusts are invested directly through the Stock Exchange, and little money goes into unquoted shares. Normally they are only interested in larger unquoted companies but some investment trusts might be prepared to take a block of shares in a smaller unquoted company.

Unit trusts

4.7 **Unit trusts** cater for small investors who wish to spread their investment risk over a wide range of securities, but have insufficient funds to create such a portfolio by themselves. A 'unit' is a portfolio of shares or other investments managed by a unit trust company in which individual investors are invited to take a stake (sub-unit).

4.8 The unit trust is based on a trust deed. Unit holders receive their income as a proportionate share of the investment income from the securities in the unit after deducting expenses of the management company. When a unit holder wants to realise his investment, he can sell his unit. Unit prices vary in market value according to the value of the shares or other securities which make up the unit's portfolio.

5 VENTURE CAPITAL 5/96

KEY TERM

Venture capital: risk capital, normally provided in return for an equity stake.

Venture capital organisations

5.1 Venture capital organisations have been operating for many years. There are now quite a large number of such organisations. The British Venture Capital Association is a regulatory body for all the institutions that have joined it as members.

5.2 Examples of venture capital organisations are:

(a) Investors in Industry plc (the 3i group);
(b) Equity Capital for Industry;
(c) venture capital subsidiaries of the clearing banks.

The 3i group

5.3 Investors in Industry plc, or the 3i group as it is more commonly known, is the biggest and oldest of the venture capital organisations. It is involved in many venture capital schemes.

The 3i group was owned by the clearing banks and the Bank of England until its flotation on the stock market during 1994.

5.4 Like other venture capitalists, the 3i group want to invest in companies that will be successful. The group's publicity material states that successful investments have three common characteristics.

- A good basic idea, a product or service which meets real customer needs.
- Finance, in the right form, to turn the idea into a solid business.
- Commitment and drive of an individual or group, and determination to succeed.

5.5 The types of venture that the 3i group might invest in include the following.

(a) **Business start-ups**. When a business has been set up by someone who has already put time and money into getting it started, the group may be willing to provide finance to enable it to get off the ground. With start-ups, the 3i group often prefers to be one of several financial institutions putting in venture capital.

(b) **Business development**. The group may be willing to provide development capital for a company which wants to invest in new products or new markets or to make a business acquisition, and so which needs a major capital injection.

(c) **Management buyouts**. A management buyout is the purchase of all or parts of a business from its owners by its managers.

(d) Helping a company where one of its owners wants to **realise all or part of his investment**. The 3i group may be prepared to buy some of the company's equity.

Venture capital funds

5.6 Some other organisations are engaged in the creation of **venture capital funds**, whereby the organisation raises venture capital funds from investors and invests in management buyouts or expanding companies. The venture capital fund managers usually reward themselves by taking a percentage of the portfolio of the fund's investments.

5.7 **Venture capital trusts** are a special type of fund giving investors tax reliefs.

The clearing banks and venture capital

5.8 In one sense, the clearing banks have been venture capitalists for many years, providing loans and overdrafts to small companies, often without security. However, an overdraft or loan is not venture capital, in the sense that the bank does not take an equity stake in the business. Even so, virtually all businesses, old, new, small and large, rely to some extent on financial assistance from their bank. The banks also provide venture capital in return for an equity stake through their venture capital subsidiaries.

Finding venture capital

5.9 When a company's directors look for help from a venture capital institution, they must recognise that:

(a) the institution will want an equity stake in the company;

(b) it will need convincing that the company can be successful (management buyouts of companies which already have a record of successful trading have been increasingly favoured by venture capitalists in recent years);

(c) it may want to have a representative appointed to the company's board, to look after its interests.

5.10 A venture capital organisation will only give funds to a company that it believes can succeed, and before it will make any definite offer, it will want from the company's management:

(a) a business plan;

(b) details of how much finance is needed and how it would be used;

(c) the most recent trading figures for the company, a balance sheet, a cash flow forecast and a profit forecast;

(d) details of the management team, with evidence of a wide range of management skills;

(e) details of major shareholders;

(f) details of the company's current banking arrangements and any other sources of finance;

(g) any sales literature or publicity material that the company has issued.

A survey has indicated that around 75% of requests for venture capital are rejected on an initial screening, and only about 3% of all requests survive both this screening and further investigation and result in actual investments.

5.11 The venture capital organisation ('VC' below) will take account of various factors, as follows, in deciding whether to not to invest.

- **The nature of the company's product.** The VC will consider whether the good or service can be produced viably and has potential to sell, in the light of any market research which the company has carried out.
- **Expertise in production**. The VC will want to be sure that the company has the necessary technical ability to implement production plans with efficiency.
- **Expertise in management**. Venture capitalists pay much attention to the quality of management, since they believe that this is crucial to the success of the enterprise. Not only should the management team be committed to the enterprise; they should also have appropriate skills and experience.
- **The market and competition**. The nature of the market for the product will be considered including the threat which rival producers or future new entrants to the market may present.
- **Future prospects**. The VC will want to be sure that the possible prospects of profits in the future compensate for the risks involved in the enterprise. The VC will expect the company to have prepared a detailed business plan detailing its future strategy.
- **Board membership.** The VC is likely to require a place on the Board of Directors. Board representation will ensure that the VC's interests will be taken account of, and that the VC has a say in matters relating to the future strategy of the business.
- **The risk borne by the existing owners.** The VC is likely to wish to ensure that the existing owners of the business bear a significant part of the investment risk relating to the expansion. If they are owner-managers, bearing part of the risk will provide an incentive for them to ensure the success of the venture.

5.12 The ways in which the venture capitalist can eventually realise its investment are called **exit routes.** Ideally the VC will try to ensure that there are a number of exit routes, such as the following.

(a) The sale of shares to the public or to institutional investors following a flotation of the company's shares on a recognised stock exchange, or on the Alternative Investment Market (or its equivalent in other countries).

(b) The sale of shares to another business in a takeover.

(c) The sale of shares to the original owners, if they later have the resources to make such a purchase.

Chapter roundup

- This chapter has covered the practicalities of **issuing shares** in some detail. When the **Stock Exchange** is used, large amounts are generally involved, so the financial manager does need to consider all alternatives carefully, looking to the possible long-term effects on the company.
- We have also looked at **merchant banks**, which can play a key role in the raising of new equity, and at possible sources of equity investment. When suggesting such sources, it is important to bear in mind the investors' objectives.
- **Venture capitalists** are prepared to take risks with moderate amounts of finance, but other investors may wish to concentrate on very large investments with much lower risk.

Quick quiz

1 What are the roles of the stock market? (see paras 1.3 - 1.6)

2 What is a 'market maker'? (1.18)

3 What is an offer for sale? (2.3)

4 What is a placing? (2.13)

5 What is the role of underwriters? (2.15)

6 What is a vendor placing? (2.24)

7 What are the different types of cost of an issue of shares on the stock market? (2.28)

8 Give examples of the activities of merchant banks. (3.2)

9 How might a merchant bank be involved in a takeover? (3.4)

10 Identify three types of 'exit route' for a venture capitalist. (5.12)

Question to try	Level	Marks	Time
9	Introductory	n/a	20 mins

Chapter 9

VALUATION OF SECURITIES AND MARKET EFFICIENCY

Chapter topic list		Syllabus reference	Ability required
1	Share prices and investment returns	13 b(i)	Knowledge
2	The fundamental analysis theory of share values	13 b(i)	Knowledge
3	Charting or technical analysis	13 b(i)	Knowledge
4	Random walk theory	13 b(i)	Knowledge
5	The efficient market hypothesis	13 b(i)	Knowledge
6	Stock market ratios	13 a(v)	Application

Introduction

In this chapter, we look at methods of **valuing individual shares**, and then at aspects of the **efficiency of stock markets**. We also look at the yardsticks by which **stock market analysts** generally judge **company performance**.

1 SHARE PRICES AND INVESTMENT RETURNS

1.1 Investors will buy shares to obtain an income from dividends and/or to make a capital gain from an increase in share prices. The market price of a security will depend on the return that investors expect to get from it.

1.2 The return from an **ordinary share** consists of dividends plus any capital gain.

(a) **Dividends.** In the UK these carry a tax credit equal to the lower rate of income tax 10% (in the tax year 1999/2000).

(b) The **capital gain (or loss)** is the difference between the price at which the investor bought the share, and the share's current market value. Capital gains are not taxable until the shareholder sells his or her shares, and realises the capital gain.

1.3 Returns on **fixed interest securities** consist of:

(a) interest payments;

(b) either:

(i) changes in the market value of the security, if the investor sells it before maturity; or

(ii) the redemption value of the security when it eventually matures, less the price paid.

1.4 Generally speaking, investors who buy ordinary shares are taking a bigger financial risk than investors in fixed interest securities. This is because holders of debt receive interest out of pre-tax profits and have a prior claim over shareholders in the event that the company goes into liquidation. Ordinary shareholders, in contrast, can only receive dividends if the company has enough distributable profits and might suffer capital losses if the share price goes down.

1.5 If the purpose of investing is to earn dividend income, an investor will try to buy shares which are expected to provide a satisfactory dividend in relation to their market value. The movement in share prices, which occurs from day to day on the stock market, means that an investor can improve his return by **buying at the right time**. For example, if the share price is £1.50 on day 1, rising to £1.55 on day 2, falling to £1.48 on day 3 and rising to £1.50 on day 4, the investor will obtain the best return if he buys shares on day 3. However, if he predicts that the share price will fall even lower than £1.48 in one or two weeks time, he will prefer to wait until then before buying.

1.6 Similarly, the prediction of share price movements may help an investor to maximise his capital gain from buying and selling shares. Shares should be bought when prices are at their lowest and sold when they are at their highest. Since stockbrokers and investment advisers give advice to clients about when to buy and sell shares, they need a method of foretelling which way share prices will move, up or down, and when. It is therefore useful to consider the extent to which share prices and share price movements can be predicted.

Theories of share price behaviour

1.7 There are differing views about share price movements, which may be broadly classified as:

(a) **the fundamental analysis theory;**
(b) **technical analysis (chartist theory)**;
(c) **random walk theory.**

These different theories about how share prices are reached in the market, especially fundamental analysis, have important consequences for financial management.

2 THE FUNDAMENTAL ANALYSIS THEORY OF SHARE VALUES

5/95, 11/97

2.1 The fundamental theory of share values is based on the theory that the 'realistic' market price of a share can be derived from a valuation of estimated future dividends. The value of a share will be the discounted present value of all future expected dividends on the share, discounted at the shareholders' cost of capital.

Exam focus point

You need to learn the two formulae given below for use in the exam.

2.2 (a) When the company is expected to pay constant dividends every year into the future, 'in perpetuity':

$$p_o = \frac{d}{r}$$

where p_o is the market price of the share ex div, that is, excluding any current dividend that might be payable d is the expected annual dividend per share in the future

r is the shareholders' cost of capital (the required rate of return).

(b) When the company is expected to pay a dividend which increases at a constant rate, g, every year into the future, the following **dividend growth model** may be used:

$$p_o = \frac{d_0(1+g)}{(r-g)} = \frac{d_1}{(r-g)}$$

where d_0 is the dividend in the current year (year 0) and so $d_0(1+g)$ is the expected future dividend in year 1 (d_1).

2.3 EXAMPLE: CONSTANT DIVIDEND

Hocus plc expects to pay a constant dividend of £450,000 at the end of every year for ever (in perpetuity). Assuming that a dividend has just been paid, calculate what the market value of Hocus plc's shares ought to be if its shareholders' cost of capital is 15%.

2.4 SOLUTION

$$p_o = \frac{£450{,}000}{(1.15)} + \frac{£450{,}000}{(1.15)^2} + \frac{£450{,}000}{(1.15)^3} + \text{.... and so on, in perpetuity.}$$

The present value of £1 a year for ever at a rate of interest r% (r expressed as a proportion) is 1/r.

Therefore, the present value of £450,000 a year at a rate of interest of 15%

is $£450{,}000 \frac{1}{0.15} = £3{,}000{,}000$.

The value of Hocus plc's shares will be £3,000,000.

2.5 EXAMPLE: DIVIDEND GROWTH

Pocus plc paid a dividend this year of £3,000,000. The company expects the dividend to rise by 2% a year in perpetuity. This expectation is shared by the investors in the stock market. The current return expected by investors from shares in the same industry as Pocus plc is 11%.

(a) What would you expect the total market value of the shares of Pocus plc to be?

(b) If it is now rumoured in the stock market that interest rates are about to rise and so shareholders will want to earn an extra 1% on their shares. What change would you expect in the value of the shares of Pocus plc?

(c) What conclusion do you draw from this example?

2.6 SOLUTION

$$p_o = \frac{d_0(1+g)}{r-g}$$

(a) Predicted share value (return of 11%) $= \frac{£3{,}000{,}000(1.02)}{(0.11-0.02)} = £34{,}000{,}000$

(b) Predicted share value (return of 12%) $= \dfrac{£3{,}000{,}000(1.02)}{(0.12-0.02)} = £30{,}600{,}000$

The value of the company's shares would fall by £3,400,000.

(c) When interest rates are expected to go up, there may well be a fall in share prices. Similarly, expectations of a fall in interest rates may well result in an increase in share prices. This is because the required return on shares is likely to move approximately in step with changes in rates of interest on other investments.

Question 1

The management of Crocus plc are trying to decide on the dividend policy of the company.

There are two options that are being considered.

(a) The company could pay a constant annual dividend of 8p per share.

(b) The company could pay a dividend of 6p per share next year, and use the retained earnings to achieve an annual growth of 3% in dividends for each year after that.

The shareholders' cost of capital is thought to be 18%. Which dividend policy would maximise the wealth of shareholders, by maximising the share price?

Answer

(a) With a constant annual dividend

$$\text{Share price} = \frac{8p}{0.18} = 44.4p$$

(b) With dividend growth

$$\text{Share price} = \frac{6p(1.03)}{(0.18-0.03)} = \frac{6.18}{0.15} = 41.2p$$

The constant annual dividend would be preferable.

The value of debentures

2.7 The same valuation principle can be applied to the valuation of debentures and other loan stock. However, the future income from fixed interest debentures is predictable, which should make the process of valuation more straightforward.

(a) For irredeemable debentures or loan stock, where the company will go on paying interest every year in perpetuity, without ever having to redeem the loan:

$$p_o = \frac{i}{r}$$

where p_o the market price of the stock ex interest, that is, excluding any interest payment that might soon be due

i is the annual interest payment on the stock

r is the return required by the loan stock investors.

(b) For redeemable debentures or loan stock, the market value is the discounted present value of future interest receivable, up to the year of redemption, **plus** the discounted present value of the redemption payment.

2.8 EXAMPLE: DEBENTURES

A company has issued some 9% debentures, which are now redeemable at par in three years time. Investors now require an interest yield of 10%. What will be the current market value of £100 of debentures?

2.9 SOLUTION

Year		*Cash flow*	*Discount factor*	*Present value*
		£	10%	£
1	Interest	9	0.909	8.18
2	Interest	9	0.826	7.43
3	Interest	9	0.751	6.76
3	Redemption value	100	0.751	75.10
				97.47

£100 of debentures will have a market value of £97.47.

The importance of the fundamental theory of share values

2.10 If the fundamental analysis theory of share values is correct, the price of any share will be predictable, provided that all investors have the same information about a company's expected future profits and dividends, and a known cost of capital. So is it correct? Are share prices predictable? And if not, why not?

2.11 In general terms, fundamental analysis seems to be valid. This means that if an investment analyst can foresee before anyone else that:

(a) a company's future profits and dividends are going to be different from what is currently expected; or

(b) shareholders' cost of capital will rise or fall (for example in response to interest rate changes)

then the analyst will be able to predict a future share price movement, and so recommend clients to buy or sell the share before the price change occurs.

2.12 In practice however, share price movements are affected by day to day fluctuations, reflecting supply and demand in a particular period, investor confidence, market interest rate movements, and so on. Investment analysts want to be able to predict these fluctuations in prices, but fundamental analysis might be inadequate as a technique. Some analysts, known as **chartists**, therefore rely on technical analysis of share price movements.

3 CHARTING OR TECHNICAL ANALYSIS

3.1 **Chartists** or '**technical analysts**' attempt to predict share price movements by assuming that past price patterns will be repeated. There is no real theoretical justification for this approach, but it can at times be spectacularly successful. Studies have suggested that the degree of success is greater than could be expected merely from chance. Nevertheless not even the most extreme chartist would claim that every major price movement can be predicted accurately and sufficiently early to make correct investment decisions.

3.2 Chartists do not attempt to predict every price change. They are primarily interested in trend reversals, for example when the price of a share has been rising for several months but suddenly starts to fall. There are several features of charts that are considered important.

These include **resistance levels, double tops** and **double bottoms**, and '**head and shoulders' patterns**.

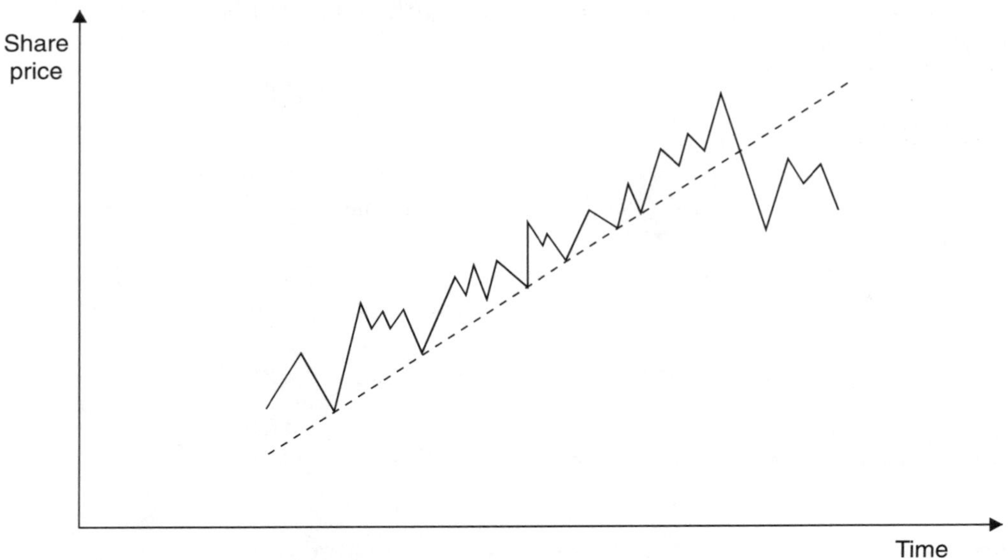

Figure 1 Resistance level

3.3 The dotted line in Figure 1 represents the lower resistance level on a rising trend. It will be noticed that many of the troughs lie on this line, but only at the end is it breached. The chartist would claim that this breach is a good indication that the trend has been reversed.

3.4 Let us now look at a resistance level on a double top. Suppose that the price of a share has been rising steadily for some time. Recently the price fell as some investors sold to realise profits and it then rose to its maximum level for a second time before starting to fall again. This is known as a double top and based on experience the chartist would predict that the trend has reversed. A typical double top might appear as in Figure 2. (Double bottoms can be interpreted in a similar but opposite way.)

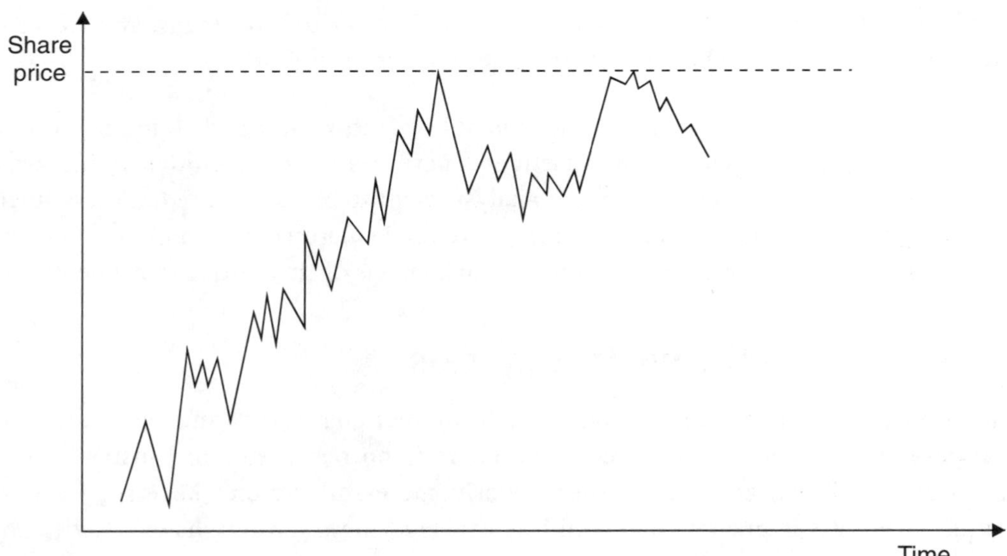

Figure 2 Double top

3.5 Another indication of a trend reversal is the 'head and shoulders'. In Figure 3, the price has been rising for some time before, at the left shoulder, profit taking has caused the price to drop. The price has then risen steeply again to the head before more profit taking causes the price to drop to more or less the same level as before (the neck). Although the price rises again the gains are not as great as at the head. The level of the right shoulder together with the frequent dips down towards the neck would suggest to the chartist that the upward trend previously observed is over and that a fall is imminent. The breach of the neckline is the indication to sell. An inverse head and shoulders can be interpreted in a similar manner.

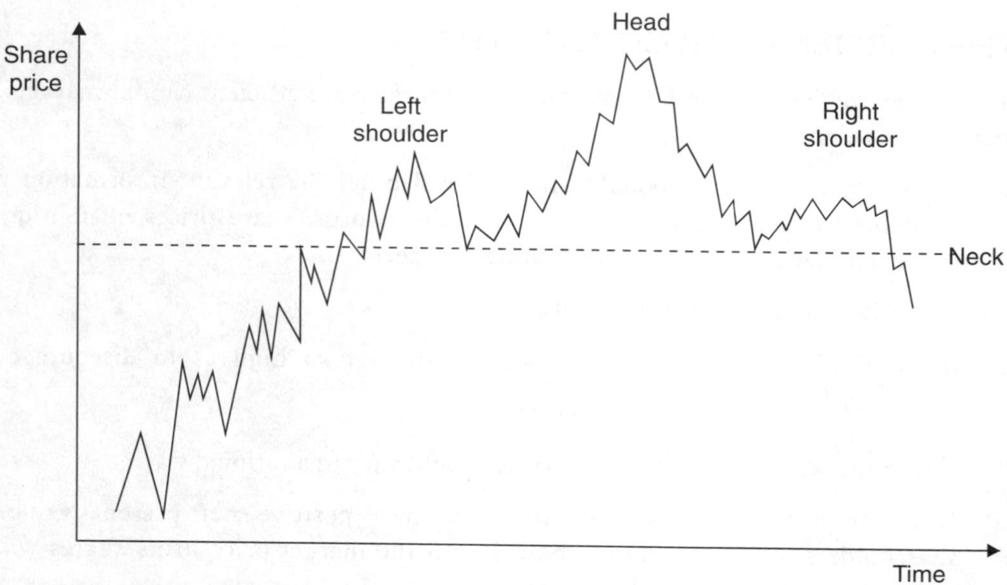

Figure 3 Head and shoulders

3.6 Moving averages help the chartist to examine overall trends. For example, he may calculate and plot moving averages of share prices for 20 days, 60 days and 240 days. The 20 day figures will give a reasonable representation of the actual movement in share prices after eliminating day to day fluctuations. The other two moving averages give a good idea of longer term trends.

4 RANDOM WALK THEORY

4.1 Random walk theory is consistent with the fundamental theory of share values. It accepts that a share should have an intrinsic price dependent on the fortunes of the company and the expectations of investors. One of its underlying assumptions is that all relevant information about a company is available to all potential investors who will act upon the information in a rational manner. The key feature of random walk theory is that although share prices will have an intrinsic or fundamental value, this value will be altered as new information becomes available, and that the behaviour of investors is such that the actual share price will fluctuate from day to day around the intrinsic value.

4.2 Random walk theory emerged in the late 1950s as an attempt to disprove chartist theory. H V Roberts challenged the idea that share price movements were systematic, and showed how sequences of random numbers can exhibit the same pattern as actual recorded changes of share prices on the Stock Exchange. Roberts was able to duplicate the 'head and shoulders' pattern of share price movements with random numbers, and he concluded that such 'patterns' are illusory and of no value for predicting share prices.

Random walks and an efficient stock market

4.3 Research was carried out in the late 1960s to explain why share prices in the stock market display a random walk phenomenon. This research led to the development of the efficient market hypothesis. It can be shown that random movements in share prices will occur if the stock market operates 'efficiently' and makes information about companies, earnings, dividends and so on, freely (or cheaply) available to all customers in the market. In displaying efficiency, the stock market also lends support to the fundamental analysis theory of share prices.

5 THE EFFICIENT MARKET HYPOTHESIS 5/95

5.1 It has been argued that the UK and US stock markets are efficient capital markets, that is, markets in which:

(a) the prices of securities bought and sold reflect all the relevant information which is available to the buyers and sellers. In other words, share prices change quickly to reflect all new information about future prospects;

(b) no individual dominates the market;

(c) transaction costs of buying and selling are not so high as to discourage trading significantly.

5.2 If the stock market is efficient, share prices should vary in a rational way.

(a) If a company makes an investment with a positive net present value (NPV), shareholders will get to know about it and the market price of its shares will rise in anticipation of future dividend increases.

(b) If a company makes a bad investment shareholders will find out and so the price of its shares will fall.

(c) If interest rates rise, shareholders will want a higher return from their investments, so market prices will fall.

The definition of efficiency

5.3 Different types of efficiency can be distinguished in the context of the operation of financial markets.

(a) If financial markets allow funds to be directed towards firms which make the most productive use of them, then there is **allocative efficiency** in these markets. Allocative efficiency will be at its maximum or 'optimum' level if there is no alternative allocation of funds, channelled from savings, which would result in higher economic prosperity.

(b) Transaction costs are incurred by participants in financial markets, for example commissions on share transactions, margins between interest rates for lending and for borrowing, and loan arrangement fees. Financial markets have **operational efficiency** if transaction costs are kept as low as possible. Transaction costs are kept low where there is open competition between brokers and other market participants.

(c) The **information processing efficiency** of a stock market means the ability of a stock market to price stocks and shares fairly and quickly. An efficient market in this sense is one in which the market prices of all the securities traded on it reflect all the available information. There is no possibility of 'speculative bubbles' in which share prices are pushed up or down, by speculative pressure, to unrealistically high or low levels.

Varying degrees of information processing efficiency

5.4 There are three degrees or 'forms' of **'information processing' efficiency**: **weak form, semi-strong form** and **strong form**.

5.5 Tests can be carried out on the workings of a stock market to establish whether the market operates with a particular form of efficiency.

(a) **Weak form tests** are made to assess whether a stock market shows at least weak form efficiency.

(b) **Semi-strong form tests** are made to assess whether a market shows at least semi-strong form efficiency.

(c) **Strong form tests** are made to assess whether a market shows strong form efficiency.

Weak form tests and weak form efficiency

5.6 The weak form hypothesis of market efficiency explains changes in share prices as the result of new information which becomes available to investors. In other words, share prices only change when new information about a company and its profits have become available. Share prices do **not** change **in anticipation** of new information being announced.

5.7 Since new information arrives unexpectedly, changes in share prices should occur in a random fashion: a weak form test seeks to prove the validity of the random walk theory of share prices. In addition, since the theory states that current share prices reflect all information available from past changes in the price, if it is correct then chartist or technical analysis cannot be based on sound principles.

5.8 Research to prove that the stock market displays weak form efficiency has been based on the principle that if share price changes are random, and if there is no connection between past price movements and new share price changes, then there should be no correlation between successive changes in the price of a share. That is, that trends in prices cannot be detected. Proofs of the absence of trends have been claimed in the work of various writers.

Semi-strong form tests and semi-strong form efficiency

5.9 Semi-strong form tests attempt to show that the stock market displays semi-strong efficiency, by which we mean that current share prices reflect both:

(a) all relevant information about past price movements and their implications; and
(b) all knowledge which is available publicly.

5.10 Tests to prove semi-strong efficiency have concentrated on the ability of the market to anticipate share price changes before new information is formally announced. For example, if two companies plan a merger, share prices of the two companies will inevitably change once the merger plans are formally announced. The market would show semi-strong efficiency, however, if it were able to **anticipate** such an announcement, so that share prices of the companies concerned would change in advance of the merger plans being confirmed.

5.11 Research in both the UK and the USA has suggested that market prices anticipate mergers several months before they are formally announced, and the conclusion drawn is that the stock markets in these countries **do** exhibit semi-strong efficiency. It has also been argued that the market displays sufficient efficiency for investors to see through 'creative accounting' or 'window dressing' of accounts by companies which use loopholes in accounting standards to overstate profits.

5.12 Suppose that a company is planning a rights issue of shares in order to invest in a new project. A semi-strong form efficient market hypothesis (unlike the weak form hypothesis) would predict that if there is public knowledge before the issue is formally announced, of the issue itself and of the expected returns from the project, then the market price (cum rights) will change to reflect the anticipated profits before the issue is announced.

Strong form tests and strong form efficiency

5.13 A strong form test of market efficiency attempts to prove that the stock market displays a strong form of efficiency, by which we mean that share prices reflect all information available:

(a) from past price changes;
(b) from public knowledge or anticipation; and
(c) from specialists' or experts' insider knowledge (eg investment managers).

It would follow that in order to maximise the wealth of shareholders, management should concentrate simply on maximising the net present value of its investments and it need not worry, for example, about the effect on share prices of financial results in the published accounts because investors will make allowances for low profits or dividends in the current year if higher profits or dividends are expected in the future.

5.14 In theory an expert, such as an investment manager, should be able to use his privileged access to additional information about companies to earn a higher rate of return than an ordinary investor. Unit trusts should in theory therefore perform better than the average investor. Research has suggested, however, that this expert skill does not exist (or at least, that any higher returns earned by experts are offset by management charges).

KEY TERM

Efficient market hypothesis: hypothesis that the stock market responds immediately to all available information, with the effect that an individual investor cannot, in the long run, expect to obtain greater than average returns from a diversified portfolio of shares *(OT)*.

How efficient are stock markets?

5.15 Evidence so far collected suggests that stock markets show efficiency that is at least weak form, but tending more towards a semi-strong form. In other words, current share prices reflect all or most publicly available information about companies and their securities. However, it is very difficult to assess the market's efficiency in relation to shares which are not usually actively traded.

5.16 Fundamental analysis and technical analysis, which are carried out by analysts and investment managers, play an important role in creating an efficient stock market. This is because an efficient market depends on the widespread availability of cheap information about companies, their shares and market conditions, and this is what the firms of market makers and other financial institutions **do** provide for their clients and for the general investing public.

5.17 If the strong form of the efficient market hypothesis is correct, a company's real financial position will be reflected in its share price. Its real financial position includes both its current position and its expected future profitability. If the management of a company attempts to maximise the net present value of their investments and to make public any relevant information about those investments then current share prices will in turn be maximised.

5.18 The **implication for an investor** is that if the market shows strong form or semi-strong form efficiency, he can rarely spot shares at a bargain price that will soon rise sharply in value. This is because the market will already have anticipated future developments, and will have reflected these in the share price. All the investor can do, instead of looking for share bargains, is to concentrate on building up a good spread of shares (a portfolio) in order to achieve a satisfactory balance between risk and return.

5.19 EXAMPLE: EFFICIENT MARKET HYPOTHESIS

Company X has 3,000,000 shares in issue and company Y 8,000,000.

(a) On day 1, the market value per share is £3 for X and £6 for Y.

(b) On day 2, the management of Y decide, at a private meeting, to make a takeover bid for X at a price of £5 per share. The takeover will produce large operating savings with a present value of £8,000,000.

(c) On day 5, Y publicly announces an unconditional offer to purchase all shares of X at a price of £5 per share with settlement on day 20. Details of the large savings are not announced and are not public knowledge.

(d) On day 10, Y announces details of the savings which will be derived from the takeover.

Ignoring tax and the time value of money between day 1 and 20, and assuming the details given are the only factors having an impact on the share price of X and Y, determine the day 2, day 5 and day 10 share price of X and Y if the market is:

(a) semi-strong form efficient;
(b) strong form efficient;

in each of the following *separate* circumstances.

(i) The purchase consideration is cash as specified above.

(ii) The purchase consideration, decided on day 2 and publicly announced on day 5, is five newly issued shares of Y for six shares of X.

5.20 SOLUTION

(a) **Semi-strong form efficient market (i) cash offer**

With a semi-strong form of market efficiency, shareholders know all the relevant historical data and publicly available current information.

(i) Day 1 Value of X shares: £3 each, £9,000,000 in total.

Value of Y shares: £6 each, £48,000,000 in total.

(ii) Day 2 The decision at the **private** meeting does not reach the market, and so share prices are unchanged.

(iii) Day 5 The takeover bid is announced, but no information is available yet about the savings.

(1) The value of X shares will rise to their takeover bid price of £5 each, £15,000,000 in total.

(2) The value of Y shares will be as follows.

	£
Previous value (8,000,000 × £6)	48,000,000
Add value of X shares to be acquired, at previous market worth (3,000,000 × £3)	9,000,000
	57,000,000
Less purchase consideration for X shares	15,000,000
New value of Y shares	42,000,000
Price per share	£5.25

The share price of Y shares will fall on the announcement of the takeover.

(iv) Day 10 The market learns of the potential savings of £8,000,000 (present value) and the price of Y shares will rise accordingly to:

$$\frac{£42{,}000{,}000 + £8{,}000{,}000}{8{,}000{,}000 \text{shares}} = £6.25 \text{ per share.}$$

The share price of X shares will remain the same as before, £5 per share.

Semi-strong form efficient market (ii) share exchange offer

(i) The share price will not change until the takeover is announced on day 5, when the value of the combined company will be perceived by the market to be (48 + 9) £57,000,000.

The number of shares in the enlarged company Y would be as follows.

Current	8,000,000
Shares issued to former X shareholders (3,000,000 × 5/6)	2,500,000
	10,500,000

The value per share in Y would change to reflect what the market expects the value of the enlarged company to be.

$$\frac{£57{,}000{,}000}{10{,}500{,}000} = £5.43 \text{ per share}$$

The value per share in X would reflect this same price, adjusted for the share exchange terms.

$$\frac{5}{6} \text{ of } £5.43 = £4.52$$

(ii) Day 10 The value of the enlarged company would now be seen by the market to have risen by £8,000,000 to £65,000,000 and the value of Y shares would rise to:

$$\frac{£65{,}000{,}000}{10{,}500{,}000} = £6.19 \text{ per share}$$

The value per X share would be:

$$\frac{5}{6} \text{ of } £6.19 = £5.16$$

(b) **Strong form efficient market (i) cash offer**

In a strong form efficient market, the market would become aware of **all** the relevant information when the private meeting takes place. The value per share would change as early as **day 2** to:

(i) X: £5
(ii) Y: £6.25

The share prices would then remain unchanged until day 20.

Strong form efficient market (ii) share exchange offer

In the same way, for the same reason, the value per share would change **on day 2** to:

(i) X: £5.16
(ii) Y: £6.19

and remain unchanged thereafter until day 20.

5.21 The different characteristics of a semi-strong form and a strong form efficient market thus affect the timing of share price movements, in cases where the relevant information becomes available to the market eventually. The difference between the two forms of market efficiency concerns when the share prices change, not by how much prices eventually change.

You should notice, however, that in neither case would the share prices remain unchanged until day 20. In a **weak form** efficient market, the price of Y's shares would not reflect the expected savings until after the savings had been achieved and reported, so that the takeover bid would result in a fall in the value of Y's shares for a considerable time to come.

Explaining share price movements

5.22 Events such as the 'crash' of October 1987, in which share prices fell suddenly by 20% to 40% on the world's stock markets, raise serious questions about the validity of random walk theory, the fundamental theory of share values and the efficient market hypothesis. If these theories are correct, how can shares that were valued at one level on one day suddenly be worth 40% less the next day, without any change in expectations of corporate profits and dividends? On the other hand, a widely feared crash late in 1989 failed to happen, suggesting that stock markets may not be altogether out of touch with the underlying values of companies.

5.23 Various types of anomaly appear to support the views that irrationality often drives the stock market, including the following.

(a) Seasonal month-of-the-year effects, day-of-the-week effects and also hour-of-the-day effects seem to occur, so that share prices might tend to rise or fall at a particular time of the year, week or day.

(b) There may be a short-run overreaction to recent events.

(c) Individual shares or shares in small companies may be neglected.

5.24 According to **speculative bubble theory,** stock market behaviour is non-linear and based on inflating and bursting speculative bubbles, rather than economic forecasts. Security prices rise above their intrinsic prices reflecting expected cash returns because some investors believe that others will pay more for them in the future. This behaviour feeds upon itself and prices rise for a period, producing a bull market. However, at some point, investors will eventually react to all the information which they have previously ignored, losing confidence that prices can rise still further, and a market crash then occurs.

5.25 Zeeman (1974) divided all investors into two (non-mutually exclusive) classes: '**fundamentalists**', who are guided in their investment strategies by economic analyses to construct forecasts based on rational expectations, and '**speculators**', whose decisions reflect adaptive behaviour in response to technical analysis of recent stock market patterns. Instability in financial markets occurs if there is a substantial proportion of speculators, amplifying changes in market indices. If the index begins to rise/fall, there will be a rapid move into a bull/bear phase respectively.

The 'coherent market hypothesis'

5.26 A recent approach, developed by Vaga in a 1991 publication and drawing upon catastrophe theory, is that known as the **coherent market hypothesis** (CMH). The CMH holds that financial markets may be in one of four states depending on the combination of economic fundamentals and group sentiment or crowd behaviour:

(a) random walks (an efficient market with neutral fundamentals);
(b) unstable transition (an inefficient market with neutral fundamentals);
(c) coherence (crowd behaviour with bullish fundamentals);
(d) chaos (crowd behaviour with mildly bearish fundamentals).

5.27 According to Vaga, the 1987 crash was pure crowd behaviour characteristic of a chaotic market and had little to do with information on economic fundamentals.

6 STOCK MARKET RATIOS 11/95

6.1 Investors are interested in:

(a) the value (market price) of the securities that they hold;
(b) the return that the security has obtained in the past;
(c) expected future returns;
(d) whether their investment is reasonably secure.

6.2 Information that is relevant to market prices and returns is available from published stock market information, and in particular from certain **stock market ratios**.

The dividend yield

6.3 The dividend yield is given by $\frac{\text{Gross dividend per share}}{\text{Market price per share}} \times 100\%$

The gross dividend is the dividend paid plus the appropriate tax credit. The gross dividend yield is used in preference to a net dividend yield, so that investors can make a direct comparison with (gross) interest yields from loan stock and gilts.

6.4 EXAMPLE: DIVIDEND YIELD

A company pays a dividend of 15p (net) per share. The market price is 240p. What is the dividend yield if the tax credit is at 10%?

$$\text{Gross dividend per share} = 15\text{p} \times \frac{100}{(100-10)} = 16.67\text{p}$$

$$\text{Dividend yield} = \frac{16.67\text{p}}{240\text{p}} \times 100\% = 6.95\%$$

Interest yield

6.5 Interest yield = $\frac{\text{Gross interest}}{\text{Market value of loan stock}} \times 100\%$

6.6 EXAMPLE: INTEREST YIELD

An investor buys £1,000 (nominal value) of a bond with a coupon of 8% for the current market value of £750.

$$\text{Interest yield} = \frac{1{,}000 \times 8\%}{750} \times 100\% = 10.67\%$$

Exam focus point

Note that the interest yield, which is the investor's rate of return, is different from the coupon rate of 8%. (Many students confuse these.)

Dividend yield and interest yield

6.7 In practice, we usually find with quoted companies that the dividend yield on shares is less than the interest yield on debentures and loan stock (and also less than the yield paid on gilt-edged securities). The share price generally rises in most years, giving shareholders capital gains. In the long run, shareholders will want the return on their shares, in terms of dividends received plus capital gains, to exceed the return that investors get from fixed interest securities.

Earnings per share (EPS)

Exam focus point

The Examiner has commented that many candidates do not know how to calculate earnings per share correctly. Make sure that you do.

6.8 EPS is widely used as a measure of a company's performance and is of particular importance in comparing results over a period of several years. A company must be able to sustain its earnings in order to pay dividends and re-invest in the business so as to achieve future growth. Investors also look for **growth** in the EPS from one year to the next.

6.9 EPS is defined (in Financial Reporting Standard 3) as the profit in pence attributable to each equity (ordinary) share, based on:

(a) the profit (or in the case of a group the consolidated profit) of the period after tax, minority interests and extraordinary items, and after deducting preference dividends;

(b) divided by the number of equity shares in issue and ranking for dividend.

Extraordinary items are unusual, non-repeating items that affect profit but have effectively been outlawed by FRS 3. The detailed requirements of FRS 3 were covered in Paper 9 *Financial Reporting*.

Question 2

Walter Wall Carpets plc made profits before tax in 19X8 of £9,320,000. Tax amounted to £2,800,000.

The company's share capital is as follows.

	£
Ordinary share (10,000,000 shares of £1)	10,000,000
8% preference shares	2,000,000
	12,000,000

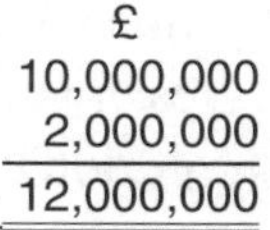

Required

Calculate the EPS for 19X8.

Answer

	£
Profits before tax	9,320,000
Less tax	2,880,000
Profits after tax	6,520,000
Less preference dividend (8% of £2,000,000)	160,000
Earnings	6,360,000
Number of ordinary shares	10,000,000
EPS	63.6p

6.10 EPS on its own does not really tell us anything. It must be seen in the context of several other matters.

(a) EPS is used for comparing the results of a company over time. Is its EPS growing? What is the rate of growth? Is the rate of growth increasing or decreasing?

(b) Is there likely to be a significant dilution of EPS in the future, perhaps due to the exercise of share options or warrants, or the conversion of convertible loan stock into equity?

(c) EPS should not be used blindly to compare the earnings of one company with another. For example, if A plc has an EPS of 12p for its 10,000,000 10p shares and B plc has an EPS of 24p for its 50,000,000 25p shares, we must take account of the numbers of shares. When earnings are used to compare one company's shares with another, this is done using the P/E ratio or perhaps the earnings yield.

(d) If EPS is to be a reliable basis for comparing results, it must be calculated consistently. The EPS of one company must be directly comparable with the EPS of others, and the EPS of a company in one year must be directly comparable with its published EPS figures for previous years. Changes in the share capital of a company during the course of a year cause problems of comparability.

6.11 Note that EPS is a figure based on past data, and it is easily manipulated by changes in accounting policies and by mergers or acquisitions. The use of the measure in calculating management bonuses makes it particularly liable to manipulation. The attention given to EPS as a performance measure by City analysts is arguably disproportionate to its true worth. Investors should be more concerned with future earnings, but of course estimates of these are more difficult to reach than the readily available figure.

6.12 A **fully diluted EPS** (FDEPS) can be measured where the company has issued securities that might be converted into ordinary shares at some future date, such as convertible loan stock, share warrants or share options. The FDEPS gives investors an appreciation of by how much EPS might be affected if and when the options, warrants or conversion rights are exercised.

6.13 Total earnings are increased by:

(a) the savings in interest (net of tax) from the conversion of loan stock into shares;

(b) in the case of share options or warrants, the addition to profits (net of tax) from investing the cash obtained from their exercise (estimated on the assumption that the cash is invested in 2½% Consolidated Stock at their market price on the first day of the period).

$$\text{FDEPS} = \frac{\text{Adjusted earnings}}{\text{Maximum number of ordinary shares}}$$

6.14 EXAMPLE: FULLY DILUTED EARNING PER SHARE

Suppose that Walter Wall Carpets plc (see Question 2 above) has in issue £4,000,000 of 8% convertible unsecured loan stock, convertible in three years' time, with a conversion ratio of 5 shares per £100 of loan stock. The company pays tax at 30%. What is the fully diluted EPS?

6.15 SOLUTION

Undiluted EPS is 63.6 pence, as shown in Question 2 above. If all holders of the convertible stock convert their holding to ordinary shares, an additional 200,000 (=4,000,000/100 × 5) shares will be issued in three years' time. The interest saving on conversion is:

£4,000,000 × 8% × 0.70 = £224,000.

Therefore:

$$\text{FDEPS} = \frac{6{,}360{,}000 + 224{,}000}{10{,}000{,}000 + 200{,}000} = \frac{6{,}574{,}400}{10{,}200{,}000} = 64.5 \text{ pence}$$

The price earnings (P/E) ratio

6.16 The P/E ratio is the most important yardstick for assessing the relative worth of a share. It is:

$$\frac{\text{Market price in pence}}{\text{EPS in pence}}$$

which is the same as:

$$\frac{\text{Total market value of equity}}{\text{Total earnings}}$$

6.17 The value of the P/E ratio reflects the market's appraisal of the shares' future prospects. In other words, if one company has a higher P/E ratio than another it is because investors either expect its earnings to increase faster than the other's or consider that it is a less risky company or in a more 'secure' industry. The P/E ratio is, simply, a measure of the relationship between the market value of a company's shares and the earnings from those shares.

6.18 It is an important ratio because it relates two key considerations for investors, the market price of a share and its earnings capacity. It is significant only as a measure of this relationship between earnings and value.

6.19 EXAMPLE: PRICE EARNINGS RATIO

A company has recently declared a dividend of 12p per share. The share price is £3.72 cum div and earnings for the most recent year were 30p per share. Calculate the P/E ratio.

6.20 SOLUTION

$$\text{P/E ratio} = \frac{\text{MV ex div}}{\text{EPS}} = \frac{£3.60}{30\text{p}} = 12$$

Changes in EPS: the P/E ratio and the share price

6.21 The dividend valuation model or fundamental theory of share values is the theory that share prices are related to expected future dividends on the shares.

6.22 Another approach to assessing what share prices ought to be, which is often used in practice, is a P/E ratio approach. It is a commonsense approach to share price assessment (although not as well founded in theory as the dividend valuation model), which is that:

(a) the relationship between the EPS and the share price is measured by the P/E ratio;

(b) there is no reason to suppose, in normal circumstances, that the P/E ratio will vary much over time;

(c) so if the EPS goes up or down, the share price should be expected to move up or down too, and the new share price will be the new EPS multiplied by the constant P/E ratio.

6.23 For example, if a company had an EPS last year of 30p and a share price of £3.60, its P/E ratio would have been 12. If the current year's EPS is 33p, we might expect that the P/E ratio would remain the same, 12, and so the share price ought to go up to 12 × 33p = £3.96.

6.24 EXAMPLE: EFFECTS OF A RIGHTS ISSUE

Annette Cord Sports Goods plc has 6,000,000 ordinary shares in issue, and the company has been making regular annual profits after tax of £3,000,000 for some years. The share price is £5. A proposal has been made to issue 2,000,000 new shares in a rights issue, at an issue price of £4.50 per share. The funds would be used to redeem £9,000,000 of 12% debenture stock. The rate of corporation tax is 30%.

What would be the predicted effect of the rights issue on the share price, and would you recommend that the issue should take place?

6.25 SOLUTION

If the stock market shows semi-strong form efficiency, the share price will change on announcement of the rights issue, in anticipation of the change in EPS. The current EPS is 50p per share, and so the current P/E ratio is 10.

	£	£
Current annual earnings		3,000,000
Increase in earnings after rights issue		
Interest saved (12% × £9,000,000)	1,080,000	
Less tax on extra profits (30%)	324,000	
		756,000
Anticipated annual earnings		3,756,000

Number of shares (6,000,000 + 2,000,000)	8,000,000
EPS	469.5 pence
Current P/E ratio	10
The anticipated P/E ratio is assumed to be the same.	
Anticipated share price	£4.695

The proposed share issue is a one for three rights issue, and we can estimate the theoretical ex rights price.

	£
Current value of three shares (× £5)	15.00
Rights issue price of one share	4.50
Theoretical value of four shares	19.50

Theoretical ex rights price $\frac{£19.50}{4} = £4.875$

6.26 The anticipated share price after redeeming the debentures would be £469.5 per share, which is less than the theoretical ex rights price. If the rights issue goes ahead and the P/E ratio remains at 10, shareholders should expect a fall in share price below the theoretical ex rights price, which indicates that there would be a capital loss on their investment. The rights issue is for this reason not recommended.

Changes in the P/E ratio over time

6.27 Changes in the P/E ratios of companies over time will depend on several factors.

(a) If interest rates go up, investors will be attracted away from shares and into debt capital. Share prices will fall, and so P/E ratios will fall.

Similarly, if interest rates go down, shares will become relatively more attractive to invest in, so share prices and P/E ratios will go up.

(b) If prospects for company profits improve, share prices will go up, and P/E ratios will rise. Share prices depend on expectations of future earnings, not historical earnings, and so a change in prospects, perhaps caused by a substantial rise in international trade, or an economic recession, will affect prices and P/E ratios.

(c) Investors' confidence might be changed by a variety of circumstances, such as:

(i) the prospect of a change in government;

(ii) the prospects for greater exchange rate stability between currencies.

The dividend cover

6.28 The dividend cover is the number of times the actual dividend could be paid out of current profits.

The dividend cover is equal to:

$$\frac{\text{Maximum possible equity dividend that could be paid out of current profits}}{\text{Actual dividend for ordinary shareholders}}$$

The figures for the maximum dividend and the actual dividend may be either both gross or both net.

6.29 The dividend cover indicates:

(a) the **proportion** of distributable profits for the year that is being **retained** by the company;

(b) the level of **risk** that the company will **not be able to maintain the same dividend** payments in future years, should earnings fall.

6.30 A high dividend cover means that a high proportion of profits are being retained, which might indicate that the company is investing to achieve earnings growth in the future.

6.31 EXAMPLE: DIVIDEND COVER

The EPS of York plc is 20p. The dividend was 20% on the 25p ordinary shares. Calculate the dividend cover.

6.32 SOLUTION

$$\text{Dividend cover} = \frac{20\text{p}}{20\% \text{ of } 25\text{p}} = 4$$

A dividend cover of 4 means that the company is retaining 75% of its earnings for reinvestment.

Chapter roundup

- In this chapter, we have seen how **share values** may be arrived at. We may then start to see how a financial manager should act, in order to **maximise shareholders' wealth**.
- In aiming to maximise the share value, and hence shareholders' wealth, the financial manager must face the need to convince the **stock market** of the worth of the company. It is therefore important to appreciate the meaning and importance of the various **stock market ratios**.

Quick quiz

1 What is the fundamental theory of share values? (see para 2.1) State the formulae for the valuation of shares, assuming (a) no dividend growth (b) a constant rate of dividend growth in perpetuity. (see para 2.2)

2 What is chartism? (3.1)

3 What is random walk theory? (4.1 - 4.2) How is this theory related to the efficient market hypothesis? (4.3)

4 What does efficiency mean, in the context of the efficient market hypothesis? (5.3)

5 What is: (a) weak form efficiency? (5.6)
 (b) semi-strong form efficiency? (5.9)
 (c) strong form efficiency? (5.13)

6 How does the difference between weak form and semi-strong form efficiency matter, in terms of by how much or when share prices change? (5.21)

7 How is dividend yield calculated? (6.3)

8 How might EPS be used to judge the returns that a company is making for its equity investors? (6.10)

9 What is the P/E ratio? (6.16) Why is it significant? (6.18)

10 What makes a share's P/E ratio change over time? (6.28)

11 What is the dividend cover? (6.28) What does it indicate? (6.29, 6.30)

Question to try	Level	Marks	Time
10	Introductory	n/a	25 mins

Chapter 10

THE COST OF FUNDS

	Chapter topic list	Syllabus reference	Ability required
1	Investment decisions, financing and the cost of capital	13 b(v); c(v)	Application
2	The costs of different sources of finance	13 b(v)	Application
3	Special problems	13 b(v)	Application
4	The weighted average cost of capital	13 b(v)	Application

Introduction

This chapter and the next chapter assume a basic understanding of **discounted cash flow** techniques, which will be revised in Part C of this Study Text.

1 INVESTMENT DECISIONS, FINANCING DECISIONS AND THE COST OF CAPITAL 5/96

1.1 The cost of capital has two aspects to it. It is the **cost of funds** that a company raises and uses, and the return that investors expect to be paid for putting funds into the company. It is thus the **minimum return** that a company should make its own investments, to earn the cash flows out of which investors can be paid their return. The cost of capital can therefore be measured by studying the returns required by investors, and used to derive a discount rate for DCF analysis and investment appraisal.

KEY TERM

Cost of capital: The minimum acceptable return on an investment, generally computed as a hurdle rate for use in investment appraisal exercises. The computation of the optimal cost of capital can be complex, and many ways of determining this opportunity cost have been suggested *(OT)*.

The cost of capital as an opportunity cost of finance

1.2 The cost of capital, however it is measured, is an **opportunity cost of finance,** because it is the minimum return that investors require. If they do not get this return, they will transfer some or all of their investment somewhere else. Here are two examples.

(a) If a bank offers to lend money to a company, the interest rate it charges is the yield that the bank wants to receive from investing in the company, because it can get just as good a return from lending the money to someone else. In other words, the interest rate is the opportunity cost of lending for the bank.

(b) When shareholders invest in a company, the returns that they can expect must be sufficient to persuade them not to sell some or all of their shares and invest the money somewhere else. The yield on the shares is therefore the opportunity cost to the shareholders of not investing somewhere else.

The cost of capital and risk

1.3 The cost of capital has three elements.

(a) The **risk-free rate of return** is the return which would be required from an investment if it were completely free from risk. Typically, a risk-free yield would be the yield on government securities.

(b) The **premium for business risk** is an increase in the required rate of return due to the existence of uncertainty about the future and about a firm's business prospects. The actual returns from an investment may not be as high as they are expected to be. Business risk will be higher for some firms than for others, and some types of project undertaken by a firm may be more risky than other types of project that it undertakes.

(c) The **premium for financial risk** relates to the danger of high debt levels (high gearing). For ordinary shareholders, financial risk is evident in the variability of earnings after deducting payments to holders of debt capital. The higher the gearing of a company's capital structure, the greater will be the financial risk to ordinary shareholders, and this should be reflected in a higher risk premium and therefore a higher cost of capital.

1.4 Because different companies are in different types of business (varying business risk) and have different capital structures (varying financial risk) the cost of capital applied to one company may differ radically from the cost of capital of another.

2 THE COSTS OF DIFFERENT SOURCES OF FINANCE

2.1 Where a company uses a mix of equity and debt capital its overall cost of capital might be taken to be the weighted average of the cost of each type of capital, but before discussing this we must look at the cost of each source of capital: equity, preference shares, debt capital and so on.

The cost of ordinary share capital

2.2 New funds from equity shareholders are obtained either from **new issues of shares** or from **retained earnings**. Both of these sources of funds have a cost.

(a) Shareholders will not be prepared to provide funds for a new issue of shares unless the return on their investment is sufficiently attractive.

(b) Retained earnings also have a cost. This is an opportunity cost, the dividend forgone by shareholders.

The dividend valuation model

2.3 If we begin by ignoring share issue costs, the cost of equity, both for new issues and retained earnings, could be estimated by means of a **dividend valuation model**, on the assumption that the market value of shares is directly related to expected future dividends on the shares.

2.4 If the future dividend per share (d) is expected to be **constant** in amount then the ex dividend share price (p_o) will be calculated by the formula:

$$p_o = \frac{d}{(1+r)} + \frac{d}{(1+r)^2} + \frac{d}{(1+r)^3} + \ldots = \frac{d}{r}, \text{ so } r = \frac{d}{p_o}$$

where r is the shareholders' cost of capital

d is the annual dividend per share, starting at year 1 and then continuing annually in perpetuity.

Assumptions in the dividend valuation model

2.5 The dividend valuation model is based on certain assumptions.

(a) The dividends from projects for which the funds are required will be of the same risk type or quality as dividends from existing operations.

(b) There would be no increase in the cost of capital, for any other reason besides (a) above, from a new issue of shares.

(c) All shareholders have perfect information about the company's future, there is no delay in obtaining this information and all shareholders interpret it in the same way.

(d) Taxation can be ignored.

(e) All shareholders have the same marginal cost of capital.

(f) There would be no issue expenses for new shares.

Share issue costs and the cost of equity

2.6 The issue of shares, whether to the general public or as a rights issue, costs money and these costs should be considered in investment appraisal. Two approaches have been suggested.

(a) One approach is to deduct issue costs as a year 0 cash outflow of the project or projects for which the share capital is being raised. The issue costs would not affect the cost of equity capital.

(b) An alternative approach you might come across is to calculate the cost of new equity with the formula:

$$r = \frac{d}{p_o - X}$$

where X represents the issue costs. Thus, if the issue price of a share is £2.50, issue costs are 20p per share, and new shareholders expect constant annual dividends of 46p, the cost of new equity would be:

$$\frac{46}{(250-20)} = 0.2 = 20\%$$

Approach (a) is recommended.

The dividend growth model

2.7 Shareholders will normally expect dividends to increase year by year and not to remain constant in perpetuity. The fundamental theory of share values states that the market price of a share is the present value of the discounted future cash flows of revenues from the share, so the market value given an expected constant annual growth in dividends would be:

$$p_o = \frac{d_0(1+g)}{(1+r)} + \frac{d_0(1+g)^2}{(1+r)^2} + ...$$

where p_o is the current market price (ex div)
d_0 is the current net dividend
r is the shareholders' cost of capital
g is the expected annual growth in dividend payments
and both r and g are expressed as proportions.

2.8 This formula assumes a constant growth rate in dividends, but it could easily be adapted for uneven growth. Capital growth through increases in the share price will arise from changed expectations about future dividend growth, or changes in the required return, r.

2.9 It is often convenient to assume a constant expected dividend growth rate in perpetuity. The formula in Paragraph 2.7 then simplifies to:

$$p_o = \frac{d_0(1+g)}{(r-g)}$$

2.10 Re-arranging this, we get a formula for the ordinary shareholders' cost of capital.

$$r = \frac{d_0(1+g)}{p_o} + g$$

2.11 Some text books give an alternative formula, which comes to the same thing.

EXAM FORMULA

$$r = \frac{d_1}{p_o} + g$$

where d_1 is the dividend in year 1, so that:

$$d_1 = d_0(1+g)$$

The growth model is sometimes called Gordon's growth model.

Question 1

A share has a current market value of 96p, and the last dividend was 12p. If the expected annual growth rate of dividends is 4%, calculate the cost of equity capital.

Answer

Cost of capital $= \frac{12(1+0.04)}{96} + 0.04$

$= 0.13 + 0.04$
$= 0.17$
$= 17\%$

Estimating the growth rate

2.12 If an examination question requires you to calculate a cost of equity using the growth model, it is likely that you will be expected to predict the future growth rate from an analysis of the growth in dividends over the past few years.

2.13 EXAMPLE: COST OF CAPITAL (1)

The dividends and earnings of Hall Shores plc over the last five years have been as follows.

Year	*Dividends*	*Earnings*
	£	£
19X1	150,000	400,000
19X2	192,000	510,000
19X3	206,000	550,000
19X4	245,000	650,000
19X5	262,350	700,000

The company is financed entirely by equity and there are 1,000,000 shares in issue, each with a market value of £3.35 ex div. What is the cost of equity?

What implications does dividend growth appear to have for earnings retentions?

2.14 SOLUTION

The dividend growth model will be used.

(a) Dividends have risen from £150,000 in 19X1 to £262,350 in 19X5. The increase represents four years growth. (Check that you can see that there are four years growth, and not five years growth, in the table.) The average growth rate, g, may be calculated as follows.

$$\text{Dividend in 19X1} \times (1+g)^4 = \text{Dividend in 19X5}$$

$$(1+g)^4 = \frac{\text{Dividend in 19X5}}{\text{Dividend in 19X1}}$$

$$= \frac{£262{,}350}{£150{,}000}$$

$$= 1.749$$

$$1 + g = \sqrt[4]{1.749} = 1.15$$

$$g = 0.15\text{, ie } 15\%$$

(b) The growth rate over the last four years is assumed to be expected by shareholders into the indefinite future, so the cost of equity, r, is:

$$\frac{d_0(1+g)}{p_o} + g$$

$$= \frac{0.26235(1.15)}{3.35} + 0.15 = 0.24\text{, ie } 24\%$$

(c) Retained profits will earn a certain rate of return and so growth will come from the yield on the retained funds. It might be assumed that g = bR where b is the yield on new investments and R is the proportion of profits retained for reinvestment. In our example, if we applied this assumption the future annual growth rate would be 15% if bR continued to be 15%. If the rate of return on new investments averages 24% (which is the cost of equity) and if the proportion of earnings retained is 62.5% (which it has been, approximately, in the period 19X1 – 19X5) then g = bR = 24% × 62.5% = 15%.

The cost of debt capital and the cost of preference shares

2.15 Estimating the cost of fixed interest or fixed dividend capital is much easier than estimating the cost of ordinary share capital because the interest received by the holder of the security is fixed by contract and will not fluctuate. The cost of debt capital already issued is the rate of interest (the internal rate of return) which equates the current market price with the discounted future cash receipts from the security.

2.16 Ignoring taxation for the moment, in the case of **irredeemable** debt (or preference shares) the future cash flows are the interest (or dividend) payments in perpetuity so that:

$$p_o = \frac{i}{(1+r)} + \frac{i}{(1+r)^2} + \frac{i}{(1+r)^3} \ldots\ldots$$

where p_o is the current market price of debt capital after payment of the current interest (dividend)
i is the interest (dividend) received
r is the cost of debt (preference share) capital

$$\frac{1}{(1+r)} + \frac{1}{(1+r)^2} + \frac{1}{(1+r)^3} \ldots\ldots$$

simplifies to $\frac{1}{r}$

so:

$$p_o = \frac{i}{r} \qquad \text{and} \qquad r = \frac{i}{p_o}$$

2.17 If the debt is **redeemable** then in the year of redemption the interest payment will be received by the holder as well as the amount payable on redemption, so:

$$p_o = \frac{i}{(1+r)} + \frac{i}{(1+r)^2} + \ldots\ldots + \frac{i+p_n}{(1+r)^n}$$

where p_n = the amount payable on redemption in year n.

2.18 The above equation cannot be simplified, so 'r' will have to be calculated by trial and error, as an IRR. The best trial and error figure to start with in calculating the cost of redeemable debt is to take the cost of debt capital as if it were irredeemable and then add the annualised capital profit that will be made from the present time to the time of redemption.

2.19 EXAMPLE: COST OF CAPITAL (2)

Owen Allot plc has in issue 10% debentures of a nominal value of £100. The market price is £90 ex interest. Calculate the cost of this capital if the debenture is:

(a) irredeemable;
(b) redeemable at par after 10 years.

Ignore taxation.

2.20 SOLUTION

The cost of irredeemable debt capital is $\frac{i}{p_o} = \frac{£10}{£90} \times 100\% \quad = \quad 11.1\%$

2.21 **The cost of redeemable debt capital**. The cost of debt capital is 11.1% if irredeemable. The capital profit that will be made from now to the date of redemption is £10 (£100 – £90). This profit will be made over a period of ten years which gives an annualised profit of £1 which is about 1% of current market value. The best trial and error figure to try first is therefore 12%.

Year		*Cash flow*	*Discount factor*	*PV*	*Discount factor*	*PV*
			12%	£	11%	£
0	Market value	(90)	1.000	(90.00)	1.000	(90.00)
1-10	Interest	10	5.650	56.50	5.889	58.89
10	Capital repayment	100	0.322	32.20	0.352	35.20
				(1.30)		+4.09

The approximate cost of debt capital is, therefore, $(11 + \frac{4.09}{(4.09 - -1.30)} \times 1) = 11.76\%$

2.22 The cost of debt capital estimated above represents the cost of continuing to use the finance rather than redeem the securities at their current market price. It would also represent the cost of raising additional fixed interest capital if we assume that the cost of the additional capital would be equal to the cost of that already issued. If a company has not already issued any fixed interest capital, it may estimate the cost of doing so by making a similar calculation for another company which is judged to be similar as regards risk.

Debt capital and taxation

2.23 The interest on debt capital is an allowable deduction for purposes of taxation and so the cost of debt capital and the cost of share capital are not properly comparable costs. This tax relief on interest ought to be recognised in DCF computations. One way of doing this is to include tax savings due to interest payments in the cash flows of every project. A simpler method, and one that is normally used, is to allow for the tax relief in computing the cost of debt capital, to arrive at an 'after-tax' cost of debt. The after-tax cost of irredeemable debt capital is:

$$r = \frac{i}{p_o}(1-T)$$

where	r	is the cost of debt capital
	i	is the annual interest payment
	p_o	is the current market price of the debt capital ex interest (that is, after payment of the current interest)
	T	is the rate of corporation tax.

2.24 Therefore if a company pays £10,000 a year interest on irredeemable debenture stock with a nominal value of £100,000 and a market price of £80,000, and the rate of corporation tax is 30%, the cost of the debentures would be:

$$\frac{10,000}{80,000}(1 - 0.30) = 0.0875 = 8.75\%.$$

2.25 The higher the rate of corporation tax is, the greater the tax benefits in having debt finance will be compared with equity finance. In the example above, if the rate of tax had been 50%, the cost of debt would have been, after tax:

$$\frac{10{,}000}{80{,}000}(1 - 0.50) = 0.0625 = 6.25$$

2.26 In the case of **redeemable debentures**, the capital repayment is not allowable for tax. To calculate the cost of the debt capital to include in the weighted average cost of capital, it is necessary to calculate an internal rate of return which takes account of tax relief on the interest.

2.27 EXAMPLE: COST OF CAPITAL (3)

(a) A company has outstanding £660,000 of 8% debenture stock on which the interest is payable annually on 31 December. The stock is due for redemption at par on 1 January 19X6. The market price of the stock at 28 December 19X2 was 103 cum interest. Ignoring any question of personal taxation, what do you estimate to be the current market rate of interest?

(b) If a new expectation emerged that the market rate of interest would rise to 12% during 19X3 and 19X4 what effect might this have in theory on the market price at 28 December 19X2?

(c) If the effective rate of corporation tax was 30% what would be the percentage cost to the company of debenture stock in (a) above? Tax is paid each 31 December on profits earned in the year ended on the previous 31 December.

2.28 SOLUTION

(a) The current market rate of interest is found by calculating the pre-tax internal rate of return of the cash flows shown in the table below. We must subtract the current interest (of 8% per £100 of stock) from the current market price, and use this 'ex interest' market value. A discount rate of 10% is chosen for a trial-and-error start to the calculation.

Item and date		*Year*	*Cash flow*	*Discount factor*	*Present value*
			£	10%	£
Market value					
(ex int)	28.12.X2	0	(95)	1.000	(95.0)
Interest	31.12.X3	1	8	0.909	7.3
Interest	31.12.X4	2	8	0.826	6.6
Interest	31.12.X5	3	8	0.751	6.0
Redemption	1.1.X6	3	100	0.751	75.1
NPV					0.0

By coincidence, the market rate of interest is 10% since the NPV of the cash flows above is zero.

(b) If the market rate of interest is expected to rise in 19X3 and 19X4 it is probable that the market price in December 19X2 will fall to reflect the new rates obtainable. The probable market price would be the discounted value of all future cash flows up to 19X6, at a discount rate of 12%.

Item and date		*Year*	*Cash flow*	*Discount factor*	*Present value*
			£	*12%*	£
Interest	31.12.X2	0	8	1.000	8.0
Interest	31.12.X3	1	8	0.893	7.1
Interest	31.12.X4	2	8	0.797	6.4
Interest	31.12.X5	3	8	0.712	5.7
Redemption	1.1.X6	3	100	0.712	71.2
NPV					98.4

The estimated market price would be £98.4 per cent **cum** interest.

(c) Again we must deduct the current interest payable and use ex interest figures.

At a market value of 103

Item and date		*Year*	*Cash flow ex int*	*PV 5%*	*PV 8%*
			£	£	£
Market value		0	(95.0)	(95.0)	(95.0)
Interest	31.12.X3	1	8.0	7.6	7.4
Tax saved	31.12.X4	2	(2.4)	(2.2)	(2.1)
Interest	31.12.X4	2	8.0	7.3	6.9
Tax saved	31.12.X5	3	(2.4)	(2.1)	(2.0)
Interest	31.12.X5	3	8.0	6.9	6.4
Tax saved	31.12.X6	4	(2.4)	(2.0)	(1.8)
Redemption	1. 1.X6	3	100.0	86.4	79.4
NPV				6.9	(0.8)

The estimated cost of capital is:

$$5\% + \left(\frac{6.9}{(6.9 - -0.8)} \times 3\%\right) = 7.7\%$$

The cost of floating rate debt

2.29 If a firm has floating rate debt, then the cost of an equivalent fixed interest debt should be substituted. 'Equivalent' usually means fixed interest debt with a similar term to maturity in a firm of similar standing, although if the cost of capital is to be used for project appraisal purposes, there is an argument for using debt of the same duration as the project under consideration.

The cost of convertible securities

2.30 The cost of fixed interest securities which are convertible into ordinary shares is found as follows, allowing for taxation and assuming that conversion will take place.

$$P_0 = \frac{I(1-T)}{(1+r)} + \frac{I(1-T)}{(1+r)^2} + \ldots.. + \frac{I(1-T)}{(1+r)^n} + \frac{V_n C}{(1+r)^n}$$

where
- P_0 is the current market price of the convertible security, convertible in year n, after paying the current year's interest
- I is the annual interest payment
- T is the rate of corporation tax
- r is the cost of capital of the convertible security holders
- V_n is the market value of an ordinary share in year n
- C is the conversion ratio, that is the number of shares into which the security is convertible.

The cost of capital, r, would be calculated by finding the IRR which equates P_0 with the present value of the future cash flows.

If the cost of capital found by treating the convertibles as non-convertible debentures is higher, that higher cost should be used on the basis that the debenture holders will choose not to convert, so as to secure the higher rate of return for themselves.

2.31 EXAMPLE: COST OF CAPITAL (4)

Some 8% convertible debentures have a current market value of £106 per cent. An interest payment was made recently. The debentures will be convertible into equity shares in three years time, at a rate of four shares per £10 of debentures. The shares are expected to have a market value of £3.50 each at that time, and all the debenture holders are expected to convert their debentures.

What is the cost of capital to the company for the convertible debentures? Corporation tax is at 30%. Assume that tax savings occur in the same year that the interest payments arise.

2.32 SOLUTION

			Try 12 %		*Try 15%*	
Year	*Item*	*Cash flow*	*Discount factor*	*PV*	*Discount factor*	*PV*
				£		£
0	Current MV	(106.00)	1.000	(106.00)	1.000	(106.00)
1-3	Interest less tax (I(1 – T))	5.60	2.402	13.45	2.283	12.78
3	Value of shares on conversion (40 × £3.5)	140.00	0.712	99.68	0.658	92.12
				7.13		(1.10)

$$\text{Cost of capital} = 12\% + \left[\frac{7.13}{(7.13 - -1.10)} \times (15-12)\right]\%$$

$$= 12\% + 2.6\%$$

$$= 14.6\%$$

The cost of short-term funds

2.33 The cost of short-term funds such as bank loans and overdrafts is the current interest being charged on such funds.

Depreciation

2.34 Depreciation, being a non-cash item of expense, is ignored in our cost of capital computations, but depreciation is a means of retaining funds within a business for new investments or replacements. For our purposes, it is sufficient to say that **the cost of funds retained by depreciation is ignored**, because it is argued that they should be taken as having a cost equal to the company's weighted average cost of capital, and so are irrelevant to the calculation of the cost of capital.

3 SPECIAL PROBLEMS

Private companies and the cost of equity

3.1 The cost of capital cannot be calculated from market values for **private companies** in the way that has been described so far, because the shares in a private company do not have a quoted market price. Since private companies do not have a cost of equity that can be readily estimated, it follows that a big problem for private companies which want to use DCF for evaluating investment projects is how to select a cost of capital for a discount rate.

3.2 Suitable approaches might be:

(a) to estimate the cost of capital for similar public companies, but then add a further premium for additional business and financial risk;

(b) to build up a cost of capital by adding estimated premiums for business risk and financial risk to the risk-free rate of return.

Government organisations and the cost of capital

3.3 The same problem faces government organisations. Government organisations do not have a market value, and most of them do not pay interest on much or all of the finance they receive. Government activities do not involve business risk, and there is no financial risk either for the investor, which is mainly the government itself. It is therefore impossible to calculate a cost of capital for government organisations. The problem is overcome in their case by using a target 'real' rate of return set by the Treasury.

The cost of equity capital: gross dividend or net dividend yield?

3.4 We have seen that the cost of equity is calculated on the basis of net dividends (perhaps with dividend growth). This selection of net dividends rather than gross dividends for the cost of equity requires some explanation. The net dividend is the appropriate choice because the cost of capital is used as the discount rate for the evaluation of capital projects by a company, and the company must have sufficient profits from its investments to pay shareholders the net dividends they require out of after-tax profits.

3.5 The taxation on profits is allowed for in the cash flows of each project. The discount rate is therefore applied to the cash flows of the project after tax. If a company were to make a payment of dividends out of profits, the amount available would be the net dividend, related to the after-tax profits earned. Since the company's cost of equity is connected with the net dividends payable by the company, the company need not be concerned with the net dividends received by the shareholders after personal taxation has been deducted from the shareholders' gross dividend income. The cash return to a shareholder from his investment in the shares may well differ from the cash which the company pays out. That is, the cost of equity to the company will differ from the required net return of the shareholder.

3.6 Different shareholders have different tax positions, and may therefore have different preferences as to the amount of dividends they receive and the amount of retained earnings kept within the business for capital growth.

4 THE WEIGHTED AVERAGE COST OF CAPITAL 5/98, 11/98

Computing a discount rate

4.1 We have looked at the costs of individual sources of capital for a company. But how does this help us to work out the cost of capital as a whole, or the discount rate to apply in DCF investment appraisals?

4.2 In many cases it will be difficult to associate a particular project with a particular form of finance. A company's funds may be viewed as a pool of resources. Money is withdrawn from this pool of funds to invest in new projects and added to the pool as new finance is raised or profits are retained. Under these circumstances it might seem appropriate to use an average cost of capital as the discount rate.

4.3 The correct cost of capital to use in investment appraisal is the marginal cost of the funds raised (or earnings retained) to finance the investment. The weighted average cost of capital (WACC) might be considered the most reliable guide to the marginal cost of capital, but only on the assumption that the company continues to invest in the future, in projects of a standard level of business risk, by raising funds in the same proportions as its existing capital structure.

KEY TERM

Weighted average cost of capital: the average cost of the company's finance (equity, debentures, bank loans) weighted according to the proportion each element bears to the total pool of capital. Weighting is usually based on market valuations, current yields and costs after tax *(OT)*.

General formula for the WACC

4.4 A general formula for the weighted average cost of capital (WACC) is:

$$r_D\left(\frac{D}{E+D}\right) + r_E\left(\frac{E}{E+D}\right)$$

where r_E is the cost of equity
r_D is the cost of debt
E is the market value of equity in the firm
D is the market value of debt in the firm

4.5 The above formula ignores taxation. Bringing in corporation tax, we should calculate the cost of debt net of tax, where the marginal tax rate is T_c, giving the WACC as:

EXAM FORMULA

$$r_D(1-T_C)\left(\frac{E}{E+D}\right)+r_E\left(\frac{E}{E+D)}\right)$$

Exam focus point

This formula is included in the CIMA *Mathematical Tables* provided in the exam. Note that this is the only formula in the *Mathematical Tables* where the cost of capital is shown as r_E. Elsewhere in the *Cost of capital* section of the tables, r is used to signify the cost of equity.

4.6 The formula above works only for irredeemable debt. If you are given a pre-tax cost of debt and no details about the nature of the debt, then you can assume that it is irredeemable. If you need to calculate a WACC where debt is redeemable, you should calculate the after-tax cost of debt using the techniques set out earlier in this chapter and substitute this into the formula in place of $r_D(1 - T_c)$.

4.7 EXAMPLE: WEIGHTED AVERAGE COST OF CAPITAL (1)

Prudence plc is financed partly by equity and partly by debentures. The equity proportion is always kept at two thirds of the total. The cost of equity is 18% and that of debt 12%. A new project is under consideration which will cost £100,000 and will yield a return before interest of £17,500 a year in perpetuity. Should the project be accepted? Ignore taxation.

4.8 SOLUTION

Since the company will maintain its gearing ratio unchanged, it is reasonable to assume that its marginal cost of funds equals its WACC. The weighted average cost of capital is as follows.

	Proportion	*Cost*		*Cost × proportion*
Equity	$\frac{2}{3}$	18%		12%
Debt	$\frac{1}{3}$	12%		4%
			WACC	16%

4.9 The present value of the future returns in perpetuity can be found using the WACC as the discount rate, as follows.

$$\text{Present value of future cash flows} = \frac{\text{Annual cash flow}}{\text{Discount rate}} = \frac{£17{,}500}{0.16} = £109{,}375$$

The NPV of the investment is £109,375 – £100,000 = £9,375.

4.10 Another way of looking at the investment shows how using the WACC as the discount rate ensures that equity shareholders' wealth is increased by undertaking projects with a positive NPV when discounted at the WACC.

The amount of finance deemed to be provided by the debenture holders will be $^1/_3$ × £100,000 = £33,333. The interest on this will be 12% × £33,333 = £4,000, leaving £13,500 available for the equity shareholders. The return they are receiving based on their 'investment' of £66,667 will be as follows.

$$\text{Return to equity} = \frac{£13{,}500}{£66{,}667} = 0.2025 \text{ or } 20.25\%$$

As this return exceeds the cost of equity capital, the project is acceptable.

Weighting

4.11 In the last example, we simplified the problem of weighting the different costs of capital by giving the proportions of capital. Two methods of weighting could be used.

(a) Weights could be based on **market values** (by this method, the cost of retained earnings is implied in the market value of equity).

(b) Weights could be based on **book values**.

Although the latter are often easier to obtain they are of doubtful economic significance. It is, therefore, more meaningful to use market values when data are available. For unquoted companies estimates of market values are likely to be extremely subjective and consequently book values may be used. When using market values it is not possible to split the equity value between share capital and reserves and only one cost of equity can be used. This removes the need to estimate a separate cost of retained earnings.

Question 2

The management of Custer Ackers plc are trying to decide on a cost of capital to apply to the evaluation of investment projects.

The company has an issued share capital of 500,000 ordinary £1 shares, with a current market value cum div of £1.17 per share. It has also issued £200,000 of 10% debentures, which are redeemable at par in two years time and have a current market value of £105.30 per cent, and £100,000 of 6% preference shares, currently priced at 40p per share. The preference dividend has just been paid, and the ordinary dividend and debenture interest are due to be paid in the near future.

The ordinary share dividend will be £60,000 this year, and the directors have publicised their view that earnings and dividends will increase by 5% a year into the indefinite future.

The fixed assets and working capital of the company are financed by the following.

	£
Ordinary shares of £1	500,000
6% £1 Preference shares	100,000
Debentures	200,000
Reserves	380,000
	1,180,000

Required

Advise the management. Ignore inflation, and assume corporation tax of 30%. Assume also that tax savings occur in the same year as the interest payments to which they relate.

Note. The cost of capital of a security is the IRR which equates the current market value of the security with its expected future cash flows. The balance sheet (accounting) values of the securities and reserves should be ignored.

Answer

(a) **Equity**. Given a 5% annual increase in dividend in perpetuity, the cost of equity capital may be estimated as

$$\frac{60{,}000(1+0.05)}{585{,}000-60{,}000\ ^*}+0.05=0.17,\ \text{ie } 17\%$$

* Market value ex div

(b) **Preference shares**. The cost of capital is $\frac{6\text{p}}{40\text{p}}\times 100\% = 15\%$

(c) **Debentures**. The cost of capital is the IRR of the following cash flows.

Year	*Cost*	*Interest*	*Tax relief*	*Net cash flows*
	£	£	£	£
0	(95.30)			(95.30)
1		10	(3.00)	7.00
2	100.00	10	(3.00)	107.00

Net cash flow	*Discount factor*	*Try 10%* *PV*	*Discount factor*	*Try 8%* *PV*
£		£		£
(95.30)	1.000	(95.30)	1.000	(95.30)
7.00	0.909	6.36	0.926	6.48
107.00	0.826	88.38	0.857	91.70
		(0.56)		2.88

The IRR is approx $8\% + \frac{2.88}{(2.88--0.56)}\times(10-8)\% = 9.67\%$

(d) **Weighted average cost of capital**

Item	*Market value*	*Cost of capital*	*Product*
	£		£
Ordinary shares*	525,000	17%	89,250
Preference shares	40,000	15%	6,000
Debentures*	190,600	9%	17,154
	755,600		112,404

* ex div and ex interest

$$\text{WACC} = \frac{112,404}{755,600} = 0.149 = 14.9\%, \text{ say } 15\%$$

(e) The management of Custer Ackers plc may choose to add a premium for risk on top of this 15% and apply a discount rate of, say, 18% to 20% in evaluating projects.

Using the WACC in investment appraisal

4.12 The weighted average cost of capital can be used in investment appraisal if we make the following assumptions:

(a) new investments must be financed by new sources of funds: retained earnings, new share issues, new loans and so on;

(b) the cost of capital to be applied to project evaluation must reflect the marginal cost of new capital; and

(c) the weighted average cost of capital reflects the company's long-term future capital structure, and capital costs. If this were not so, the current weighted average cost would become irrelevant because eventually it would not relate to any actual cost of capital.

Arguments against using the WACC

4.13 The arguments against using the WACC as the cost of capital for investment appraisal (as follows) are based on criticisms of the assumptions that are used to justify use of the WACC.

(a) New investments undertaken by a company might have different **business risk** characteristics from the company's existing operations. As a consequence, the return required by investors might go up (or down) if the investments are undertaken, because their business risk is perceived to be higher (or lower).

(b) The finance that is raised to fund a new investment might substantially change the capital structure and the perceived **financial risk** of investing in the company. Depending on whether the project is financed by equity or by debt capital, the perceived financial risk of the entire company might change. This must be taken into account when appraising investments.

(c) Many companies raise **floating rate** debt capital as well as fixed interest debt capital. With floating rate debt capital, the interest rate is variable, and is altered every three or six months or so in line with changes in current market interest rates. The cost of debt capital will therefore fluctuate as market conditions vary. Floating rate debt is difficult to incorporate into a WACC computation, and the best that can be done is to substitute an 'equivalent' fixed interest debt capital cost in place of the floating rate debt cost.

Marginal cost of capital approach

4.14 The marginal cost of capital approach involves calculating a marginal cut-off rate for acceptable investment projects by:

(a) establishing rates of return for each component of capital structure, except retained earnings, based on its value if it were to be raised under current market conditions;

(b) relating dividends or interest to these values to obtain a marginal cost for each component;

(c) applying the marginal cost to each component depending on its proportionate weight within the capital structure and adding the resultant costs to give a weighted average.

4.15 It can be been argued that the current weighted average cost of capital should be used to evaluate projects, where a company's capital structure changes only very slowly over time; then the marginal cost of new capital should be roughly equal to the weighted average cost of current capital.

If this view is correct, then by undertaking investments which offer a return in excess of the WACC, a company will increase the market value of its ordinary shares in the long run. This is because the excess returns would provide surplus profits and dividends for the shareholders.

4.16 Where gearing levels fluctuate significantly, or the finance for new project carries a significantly different level of risks to that of the existing company, there is good reason to seek an alternative marginal cost of capital.

4.17 Note that the marginal cost of capital approach outlined above only takes into account the incremental financing costs of the new project. The financing of a major project may change the risk profile of the existing capital structure, in which case the **adjusted present value (APV) method**, discussed later in this Study Text, is likely to be more appropriate.

Chapter roundup

- As you will see from this chapter, every **source of finance** has a **cost**. In deciding how to finance a company, the costs of all sources must be considered.
- Financial managers need a **cost of capital** to use in making decisions. A **weighted average** might seem a reasonable cost to use, but you should appreciate the arguments against, as well as those for, using it.

Quick quiz

1 A cost of capital can be said to consist of three elements. What are they? (see para 1.3)

2 What is the dividend valuation model formula for the cost of equity:

(a) with no dividend growth? (2.4)
(b) with dividend growth? (2.7 - 2.10)

3 How is the after-tax cost of debt capital calculated? (2.23 - 2.26)

4 How is the cost of convertible securities calculated? (2.30)

5 What are the main arguments against using the WACC as the discount rate? (4.13)

Question to try	Level	Marks	Time
11	Exam standard	25	45 mins

Chapter 11

THE EFFECT OF CAPITAL STRUCTURE

Chapter topic list		Syllabus reference	Ability required
1	Gearing, financial risk and the cost of capital	13 b(vi)	Application
2	Traditional and net operating income views of WACC	13 b(vi)	Application
3	Modigliani-Miller (MM) theory without taxation	13 b(vi)	Application
4	Modigliani-Miller theory adjusted for taxation	13 b(vi)	Application

Introduction

This chapter should be read after the topics in **Chapter 10** have been covered.

1 GEARING, FINANCIAL RISK AND THE COST OF CAPITAL 11/95

1.1 A high level of debt creates financial risk. The financial risk of a company's capital structure can be measured by a gearing ratio. The method of calculating a gearing ratio which is appropriate for investment evaluation is one based on market values. Gearing can be measured as:

$$\frac{\text{Market value of debt (including preference shares)}}{\text{Market value of equity + Market value of debt}} \quad \text{or} \quad \frac{D}{D+E}$$

1.2 Because of the financial risk associated with gearing, higher gearing will increase the rate of return required by ordinary shareholders, and may also affect the yield required by long-term creditors. It follows that a company's gearing level could have a bearing on its weighted average cost of capital.

Gearing, project appraisal and the source of funds to finance a new project

1.3 It can be suggested that a project which has a positive NPV when its cash flows are discounted at the WACC might be financially harmful to shareholders if it is financed in the wrong way. This suggestion can be taken one step further. If a project is viable (has a positive NPV) when it is discounted at the current WACC, then it would be worthwhile provided that the new funds which are raised to finance it leave the company's WACC unchanged.

Gearing and shareholders' investment decisions

1.4 The value of equity is related, not only to the size of dividends and the cost of equity, but also to the weighted average cost of capital. This connection will now be investigated in some detail. We will assume that a shareholder would be prepared to accept a change in the gearing of a company, and therefore a change in the required rate of return for equity, provided that the effect of this change in gearing would be to increase the value of his shares, or at the very least to leave them unchanged.

2 TRADITIONAL AND NET OPERATING INCOME VIEWS OF WACC

2.1 There are two main theories about the effect of changes in gearing on the weighted average cost of capital (WACC) and share values. These are:

(a) the '**traditional' view**;
(b) the **net operating income approach (Modigliani and Miller).**

2.2 The assumptions on which these theories are based are as follows.

(a) The company pays out all its earnings as dividends.

(b) The gearing of the company can be changed immediately by issuing debt to repurchase shares, or by issuing shares to repurchase debt. There are no transaction costs for issues.

(c) The earnings of the company are expected to remain constant in perpetuity and all investors share the same expectations about these future earnings.

(d) Business risk is also constant, regardless of how the company invests its funds.

(e) Taxation, for the time being, is ignored.

The traditional view of WACC

2.3 The traditional view is as follows.

(a) As the level of gearing increases the cost of debt remains unchanged up to a certain level of gearing. Beyond this level, the cost of debt will increase.

(b) The cost of equity rises as the level of gearing increases.

(c) The weighted average cost of capital does not remain constant, but rather falls initially as the proportion of debt capital increases, and then begins to increase as the rising cost of equity (and possibly of debt) becomes more significant.

(d) The optimum level of gearing is where the company's weighted average cost of capital is minimised.

2.4 The traditional view about the cost of capital is illustrated in Figure 1. It shows that the weighted average cost of capital will be minimised at a particular level of gearing P. The traditional view is that the weighted average cost of capital, when plotted against the level of gearing, is saucer shaped. The optimum capital structure is where the weighted average cost of capital is lowest, at point P.

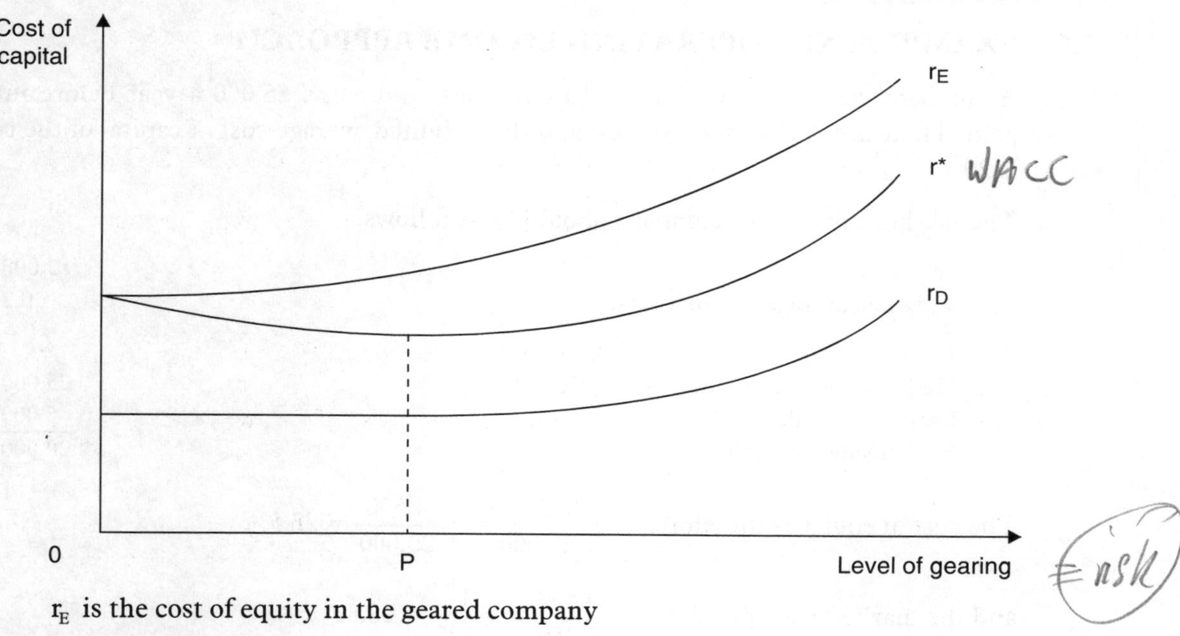

r_E is the cost of equity in the geared company

r_D is the cost of debt

r^* is the weighted average cost of capital

Figure 1

The net operating income view of WACC

2.5 The net operating income approach takes a different view of the effect of gearing on WACC. It assumes that the weighted average cost of capital is unchanged, regardless of the level of gearing, because of the following two factors.

(a) The cost of debt remains unchanged as the level of gearing increases.

(b) The cost of equity rises in such a way as to keep the weighted average cost of capital constant.

This would be represented on a graph as shown in Figure 2.

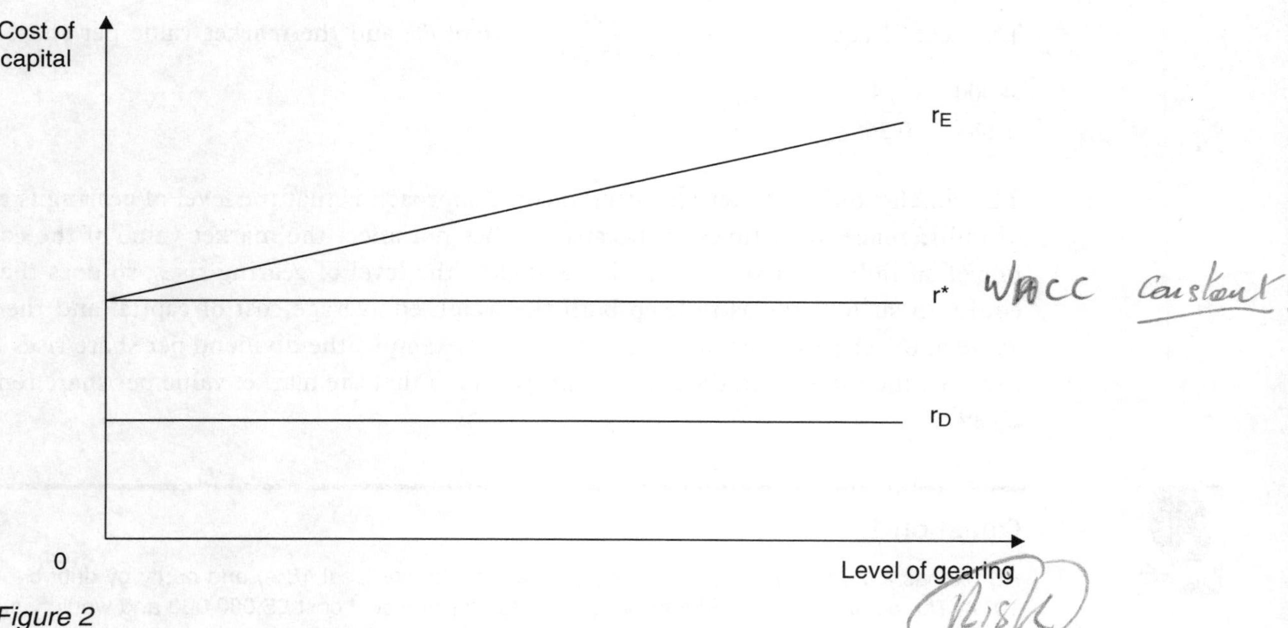

Figure 2

2.6 EXAMPLE: NET OPERATING INCOME APPROACH

A company has £5,000 of debt at 10% interest, and earns £5,000 a year before interest is paid. There are 2,250 issued shares, and the weighted average cost of capital of the company is 20%.

The market value of the company should be as follows.

Earnings	£5,000
Weighted average cost of capital	0.2
	£
Market value of the company (£5,000 ÷ 0.2)	25,000
Less market value of debt	5,000
Market value of equity	20,000

The cost of equity is therefore $\frac{5,000-500}{20,000} = \frac{4,500}{20,000} = 22.5\%$

and the market value per share is $\frac{4,500}{2,250} \times \frac{1}{0.225} = £8.89$

2.7 Suppose that the level of gearing is increased by issuing £5,000 more of debt at 10% interest to repurchase 562 shares (at a market value of £8.89 per share) leaving 1,688 shares in issue.

The weighted average cost of capital will, according to the net operating income approach, remain unchanged at 20%. The market value of the company should still therefore be £25,000.

Earnings	£5,000
Weighted average cost of capital	0.2
	£
Market value of the company	25,000
Less market value of debt	10,000
Market value of equity	15,000

Annual dividends will now be £5,000 – £1,000 interest = £4,000.

The cost of equity has risen to $\frac{4,000}{15,000} = 26.667\%$ and the market value per share is still:

$\frac{4,000}{1,688} \times \frac{1}{0.2667} = £8.89$

2.8 The conclusion of the net operating income approach is that the level of gearing is a matter of indifference to an investor, because it does not affect the market value of the company, nor of an individual share. This is because as the level of gearing rises, so does the cost of equity in such a way as to keep both the weighted average cost of capital and the market value of the shares constant. Although, in our example, the dividend per share rises from £2 to £2.37, the increase in the cost of equity is such that the market value per share remains at £8.89.

Question 1

AB plc has a WACC of 16%. It is financed partly by equity (cost 18%) and partly by debt capital (cost 10%). The company is considering a new project which would cost £5,000,000 and would yield annual profits of £850,000 before interest charges. It would be financed by a loan at 10%. As a consequence of the higher gearing, the cost of equity would rise to 20%. The company pays out all profits as dividends, which are currently £2,250,000 a year.

(a) What would be the effect on the value of equity of undertaking the project?

(b) To what extent can you analyse the increase or decrease in equity value into two causes, the NPV of the project at the current WACC and the effect of the method of financing?

Ignore taxation. The traditional view of WACC and gearing is assumed in this exercise.

Answer

(a)

	£
Current profits and dividends	2,250,000
Increase in profits and dividends	
(£850,000 less extra interest 10% x £5,000,000)	350,000
New dividends, if project is undertaken	2,600,000
New cost of equity	20%

	£
New MV of equity	13,000,000
Current MV of equity	
(£2,250,000 ÷ 0.18)	12,500,000
Increase in shareholder wealth from project	500,000

(b) (i) NPV of project if financed at current WACC

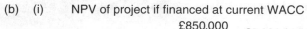

$$= \frac{£850{,}000}{0.16} - £5{,}000{,}000 = +£312{,}500$$

(ii) The effect of financing on share values must be to increase the MV of equity by the remaining £187,500, which indicates that the effect of financing the project in the manner proposed will be to increase the company's gearing, but to reduce its WACC.

3 MODIGLIANI-MILLER (MM) THEORY WITHOUT TAXATION

3.1 Modigliani and Miller developed a defence of the net operating income approach to the effect of gearing on the cost of capital. Their view was that investors would use **arbitrage** to keep the weighted average cost of capital constant when changes in a company's gearing occur.

> **KEY TERM**
>
> **Arbitrage:** the simultaneous purchase and sale of a security in different markets, with the aim of making a risk-free profit through the exploitation of any price difference between the markets *(OT)*.

3.2 EXAMPLE: ARBITRAGE

Consider two companies, Ordinary plc and Levered plc, in the same risk class, which are identical in all respects except that Ordinary plc is financed entirely by equity whereas the capital structure of Levered plc includes £40,000 of debt at 8% interest.

We will assume that the annual earnings of both companies (before interest) are the same, £20,000, and we will begin by considering the traditional view of the cost of capital, and suppose that the cost of equity in the unlevered company is 13½%, and in the levered company, it is higher at 14%.

The market valuation of each company, according to the traditional view, would be as follows.

	Ordinary plc	*Levered plc*
	£	£
Annual earnings	20,000	20,000
Less interest	-	3,200
Available for equity (earnings = dividends)	20,000	16,800
Cost of equity	0.135	0.14
	£	£
Market value of equity	148,148	120,000
Market value of debt	-	40,000
Market value of company	148,148	160,000
Weighted average cost of capital (PBIT÷market value)	13.5%	12.5%
Gearing ratio	0%	25%

3.3 The two companies, identical in every respect except their gearing, are therefore assumed by the traditional view to have different market values. MM argue that this situation could not last for long because investors in Levered plc would soon see that they could get the same return for a smaller investment by investing in Ordinary plc. Exercising arbitrage, they would sell their shares in Levered plc and buy shares in Ordinary plc.

This sale would:

(a) drive up the price of Ordinary plc shares (thereby lowering the cost of its equity capital); and

(b) force down the price of Levered plc shares (thereby raising the cost of its equity capital); until the total market value of each company is the same. Arbitrage would then cease.

3.4 Arbitrage would occur as follows. Suppose Mr Onepercent owns 1% of the equity in Levered plc. These would have a market value of (1% × £120,000)= £1,200. He would notice that Ordinary plc makes the same annual earnings as Levered plc (£20,000) but with a smaller investment (£148,148 compared to £160,000). He would therefore take the following steps.

(a) He would sell his shares in Levered plc for £1,200.

(b) He would borrow £400 at 8% interest. This amount is equivalent to 1% of the debt of Levered plc (£40,000 at 8%). In this way, Mr Onepercent would have substituted personal gearing for the corporate gearing of Levered plc. His assets would be as follows.

£	
1,200	from the sale of his shares
400	borrowed at 8%
1,600	which is 1% of the value of Levered plc

His personal gearing ratio (400/1,600 = 25%) is the same as the gearing ratio of Levered plc, and so MM would argue that his financial risk is in no way changed by this process of arbitrage.

(c) He would then buy 1% of the equity of Ordinary plc for £148,148 × 1% = £1,481.48. To do this, he would use the borrowed £400 plus £1081.48 of his own money.

(d) His annual earnings from Ordinary plc would be as follows.

	£
1% of £20,000	200
Less the interest he must repay on his personal loan (8% of £400)	32
Net earnings	168

This is exactly the same as he would earn from keeping 1% of the equity of Levered plc (1% of £16,800) but he can earn this from a smaller net investment of £1,081.48 rather than £1,200.

(e) Alternatively, if he spends the entire £1,600 in purchasing shares of Ordinary plc, his annual earnings would be a dividend of:

$\frac{1,600}{148,148} \times £20,000 = £216$ less loan repayments of £32, leaving him with £184, which is £16 more than he currently earns from his Levered plc investment.

3.5 Rational investors will continue to substitute personal gearing for corporate gearing, and buy shares in Ordinary plc, until the price of these shares has risen, the price of Levered plc shares has fallen, and the market values of the two companies are the same. At this point:

(a) the cost of equity in the company with the higher gearing (Levered plc) will be higher than the cost of equity in the other company;

(b) because both the market values and the annual earnings of the companies are the same, the weighted average costs of capital must be the same, despite the difference in gearing.

Exam focus point

Be prepared to explain in the exam how arbitrage works.

The Modigliani-Miller propositions, ignoring taxes

3.6 We can now set out the propositions of Modigliani and Miller, ignoring tax relief on the interest charged on debt capital.

3.7 The following symbols will be used.

V_u	=	the market value of an ungeared (all equity) company
D	=	the market value of the debt capital in a geared company which is similar in every respect to the ungeared company (same profits before interest and same business risk) except for its capital structure. The debt capital is assumed, for simplicity, to be irredeemable.
E	=	the market value of the equity in the geared company
r	=	the cost of equity in an ungeared company
r_E	=	the cost of equity in the geared company
r_D	=	the cost of debt capital

The total market value of the geared company V_g is then equal to (E + D).

The total market value of a company and the WACC (ignoring taxation)

3.8 MM suggested that the total market value of any company is independent of its capital structure, and is given by discounting its expected return at the appropriate rate. The value of a geared company is therefore as follows.

$$V_g = V_u$$

$$V_g = \frac{\text{Profit before interest}}{\text{WACC}}$$

$$V_u = V_g = \frac{\text{Earnings in an ungeared company}}{r}$$

The cost of equity in a geared company (ignoring taxation)

3.9 MM went on to argue that the expected return on a share in a geared company equals the expected cost of equity in a similar but ungeared company, plus a premium related to financial risk.

3.10 The premium for financial risk can be calculated as the debt/equity ratio multiplied by the difference between the cost of equity for an ungeared company and the risk-free cost of debt capital.

$$r_E = r + [(r - r_D) \times \frac{D}{E}]$$

Note the following points.

(a) The part of the formula to the right of the plus sign is the value of the premium for financial risk.

(b) The formula requires the debt ratio (debt: equity) to be used rather than the more common debt: (debt + equity).

(c) Market values are used, not book values.

3.11 EXAMPLE: MM, IGNORING TAXATION (1)

The cost of equity in Minehead plc, an all equity company, is 15%. The WACC is therefore also 15%.

Another company, Dunster plc, is identical in every respect to the first, except that it is geared, with a debt: equity ratio of 1:4. The cost of debt capital is 5% and this is a risk-free cost of debt. What is Dunster plc's WACC?

3.12 SOLUTION

r_E = 15% + ((15 – 5)% × ¼) = 17.5%.

	Weighting	*Cost*	*Product*
Equity	80%	17.5%	14%
Debt	20%	5.0%	1%
		WACC =	15%

The WACC in the geared company is the same as in the ungeared company.

3.13 EXAMPLE: MM, IGNORING TAXATION (2)

Loesch plc is an all equity company and its cost of equity is 12%.

Berelco plc is similar in all respects to Loesch plc, except that it is a geared company, financed by £1,000,000 of 3% debentures (current market price £50 per cent) and 1,000,000 ordinary shares (current market price £1.50 ex div).

What is Berelco's cost of equity and weighted average cost of capital?

3.14 SOLUTION

$$r_D = 3\% \times \frac{100}{50} = 6\%$$

$$r_E = 12\% + [(12\% - 6\%) \times \frac{500}{1,500}] = 14\%$$

	Market value		*Cost*		
	£'000				£'000
Equity	1,500	×	0.14	=	210
Debt	500	×	0.06	=	30
	2,000				240

$$\text{WACC} = \frac{240}{2,000} = 0.12 = 12\%$$

This is the same as Loesch plc's WACC. As gearing is introduced, the cost of equity rises, but in such a way that the WACC does not change.

Weaknesses in MM theory

3.15 MM theory has been criticised on four main grounds.

(a) The risks for the investor may differ between personal gearing and corporate gearing. In the example in Paragraphs 3.2 to 3.4, Mr Onepercent stands to lose financially no more than £1,200, which is in his stake in a company (Levered plc) with limited liability. If he practises arbitrage, he would stand to lose his personal investment in Ordinary plc (£1,481.48 – £400 = £1,081.48) plus his debt repayment (£400), a total of £1,481.48. The financial risk is consequently greater.

(b) The cost of borrowing for an individual is likely to be higher than the cost of borrowing for a company. MM assume that the cost is the same for personal and corporate borrowers.

(c) Transaction costs will restrict the arbitrage process.

(d) MM theory initially ignored tax implications (discussed below).

3.16 Further weaknesses in the MM theory are as follows.

(a) In practice, it may be impossible to identify firms with identical business risk and operating characteristics.

(b) Some earnings may be retained and so the simplifying assumption of paying out all earnings as dividends would not apply.

(c) Investors are assumed to act rationally which may not be the case in practice.

3.17 MM also acknowledge that when the level of gearing gets high, the cost of debt will rise. They argue, however, that this does not affect the weighted average cost of capital because the cost of equity falls at the same time as risk-seeking investors are attracted to buying shares in the company.

3.18 When a company's gearing reaches very high levels, it may be perceived as being in danger of insolvency, and its market value will be very low (instead of being very high, as MM would predict). MM ignored the possibility of bankruptcy, and so their theory may not be valid at very high levels of gearing.

4 MODIGLIANI-MILLER THEORY ADJUSTED FOR TAXATION

Exam focus point

Remember, follow any assumptions about taxation given in questions carefully. Tax rates assumed will not necessarily be those which currently apply in the real world.

4.1 Allowing for taxation reduces the cost of debt capital by multiplying it by a factor $(1 - T_c)$ where T_c is the rate of corporation tax (assuming the debt to be irredeemable). So far, our analysis of MM theory has ignored the tax relief on debt interest, which makes debt capital cheaper to a company, and therefore reduces the weighted average cost of capital where a company has debt in its capital structure.

4.2 MM modified their theory to admit that tax relief on interest payments does lower the weighted average cost of capital. They claimed that the weighted average cost of capital will continue to fall, up to gearing of 100%.

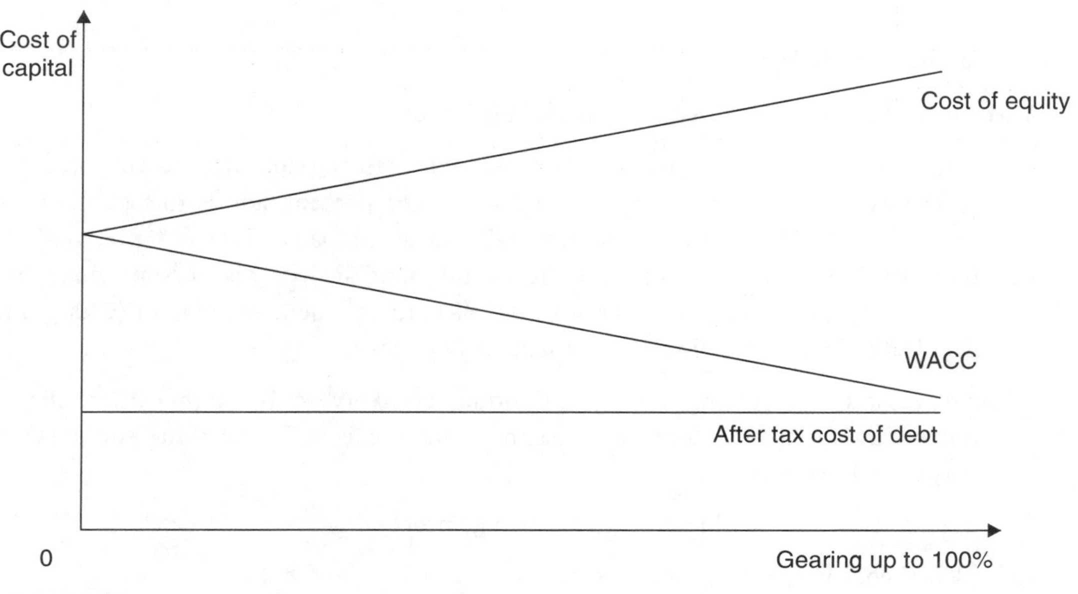

Figure 3

Adjustment to the MM cost of equity formula to allow for taxes

4.3 The formula for the cost of equity in a geared company becomes:

$$r_E = r + (1 - T_c)[(r - r_D) \times \frac{D}{E}]$$

where T_c is the corporation tax rate and r_D is the pre-tax (gross) cost of debt capital.

The financial risk premium is adjusted by a factor of $(1 - T_c)$.

4.4 From this formula we can derive the following formula:

$WACC_g = r(1 - T^*L)$

where $WACC_g$ is the weighted average cost of capital of a geared company

r is the cost of equity and the WACC of a similar ungeared company

T^* is the tax saving due to interest payments expressed as a decimal, usually equal to the corporation tax rate

L is equivalent to $\frac{D}{D+E}$

(You are not expected to know the derivation, and so this is not given here.)

4.5 EXAMPLE (CONTINUED)

Thus, assuming a corporation tax rate of 30%, Dunster plc's cost of equity, using the information in Paragraphs 3.12 and 3.13, would be:

$15\% + (1 - 0.30)\,[(15\% - 5\%) \times {}^1/_4] = 16.75\%$

and its WACC would be:

$$15\% \left[1 - \frac{0.30 \times 1}{(1+4)}\right] = 15\% \times 0.94 = 14.1\%$$

4.6 This is below the ungeared company's WACC which is 15%. So higher gearing reduces the WACC.

Question 2

Apply the formula given in Paragraphs 4.3 and 4.4 to find the cost of equity and WACC for Berelco plc (using the information given in Paragraph 3.13). The corporation tax rate is 30%.

Answer

Berelco plc's cost of equity would be

$$12\% + (1 - 0.30)[(12 - 6)\% \times \frac{500}{1{,}500}]$$

$= 13.4\%$

and its WACC would be

$$12\% \left[1 - \frac{0.30 \times 500}{1{,}500 + 500}\right] = 12\% \times 0.925 = 11.1\%$$

This is below Loesch plc's WACC of 12%.

Is there an optimum level of gearing?

4.7 We have now seen that MM modified their theory to say that when taxation is taken into account, the WACC will continue to fall as the level of gearing increases. The arbitrage process still operates, although the actions of investors will be influenced by their personal rates of taxation.

4.8 MM argued that since WACC falls as gearing rises, and the value of a company should rise as its WACC falls, the value of a geared company will always be greater than its ungeared counterpart, but only by the amount of the debt-associated tax saving of the geared company, assuming a permanent change in gearing.

$$V_g = V_u + DT_c$$

where V_g is the value of the similar geared company.

4.9 However, the positive tax effects of debt finance will be exhausted where there is insufficient tax liability to use the tax relief which is available. This is known as **tax shield exhaustion.**

4.10 EXAMPLE: MM, WITH TAXES

Notnil plc and Newbegin plc are companies in the same industry. They have the same business risk and operating characteristics, but Notnil is a geared company whereas Newbegin is all equity financed. Notnil plc earns three times as much profit before interest as Newbegin plc. Both companies pursue a policy of paying out all their earnings each year as dividends.

The market value of each company is currently as follows.

		Notnil plc		*Newbegin plc*
		£m		£m
Equity	(10m shares)	36	(20m shares)	15
Debt	(£12m of 12% loan stock)	14		
		50		15

The annual profit before interest of Notnil is £3,000,000 and that of Newbegin is £1,000,000. The rate of corporation tax is 30%. It is thought that the current market value per ordinary share in Newbegin plc is at the equilibrium level, and that the market value of Notnil's debt capital is also at its equilibrium level. There is some doubt, however, about whether the value of Notnil's shares is at its equilibrium level.

Apply the MM formula to establish the equilibrium price of Notnil's shares.

4.11 SOLUTION

$V_g = V_u + DT_c$

V_u = the market value of an ungeared company. Since Notnil earnings (before interest) are three times the size of Newbegin's, V_u is three times the value of Newbegin's equity:

3 × £15,000,000 = £45,000,000.

DT_c = £14,000,000 × 30% = £4,200,000

V_g = £45,000,000 + £4,200,000 = £49,200,000.

Since the market value of debt in Notnil plc is £14,000,000, it follows that the market value of Notnil's equity should be £49,200,000 – £14,000,000 = £35,200,000.

$$\text{Value per share} = \frac{£35{,}200{,}000}{10{,}000{,}000} = £3.52 \text{ per share}$$

Since the current share price is £3.60 per share, MM would argue that the shares in Notnil are currently over-valued by the market, but only by £800,000 in total or 8p per share.

4.12 Now let us relate the MM company valuation formula to the process of **arbitrage**.

4.13 EXAMPLE: MM AND ARBITRAGE

Lenox plc and Groves plc are two companies operating in the same industry. They have the same business risk, and are identical in most other respects. The annual earnings before interest and tax are £40,000 for each company. The only differences between the companies are in their financial structures and their market values. Details of these are given below.

Lenox plc

	£
Ordinary shares of £1	30,000
Share premium account	10,000
Profit and loss account	110,000
Shareholders' funds	150,000
12% loan stock (newly issued)	100,000
	250,000

Lenox's ordinary shares have a market value of 600 pence, and the 12% loan stock is trading at £100.

Groves plc

	£
Ordinary shares of £1	50,000
Share premium account	16,000
Profit and loss account	100,000
Shareholders' funds	166,000

Groves' shares have a market value of 400 pence. Corporation tax is at 30%.

Suppose that you are the owner of 1% of the equity of Lenox plc. If you agreed with the propositions of Modigliani and Miller, would you retain your shares in Lenox or could you improve your financial position? Ignore personal taxes.

4.14 SOLUTION

A difficulty with this problem is the need to allow for tax relief on corporate debt, when working out how an investor should gear himself up so as to achieve personal gearing which is the same as the geared company. Check the solution carefully on this point.

According to MM theory, where there are corporate taxes, the value of a geared company will always be greater than the value of its ungeared counterpart, but only by the amount of the debt-associated tax saving of the geared company. This is expressed by the formula

$$V_g = V_u + DT_c$$

If actual market values do not conform to this formula, it would follow that one company is incorrectly valued by the market relative to the other.

4.15 Let us assume that the shares of Groves, the ungeared company, are correctly valued by the market at 400 pence. We would then predict that the total market value of Lenox, the geared company, should be $V_u + DT_c$.

	£
Market value of Groves shares (50,000 × £4)	200,000
Market value of Lenox debt multiplied by tax rate (100,000 × 30%)	30,000
Correct market value of Lenox plc	230,000

Actual market value of Lenox

	£
Market value of Lenox shares (30,000 × £6)	180,000
Market value of Lenox debt capital	100,000
	280,000

4.16 We can conclude that Lenox plc is over-valued by the market and so an investor in Lenox shares can improve his or her financial position by:

(a) selling all his or her shares in Lenox;

(b) gearing, by personal borrowing, so as to achieve the same personal gearing as Lenox;

(c) buying shares in Groves.

This action will increase the investor's income without any change in the investor's business or financial risk. This process of arbitrage should continue until the equilibrium of $V_g = V_u + DT_c$ is restored.

4.17 1% of the equity of Lenox has a current market value of 1% × £180,000 = £1,800.

	£
Sell 1% holding of shares in Lenox to receive	1,800
Borrow, through personal borrowing*, an amount equal to 1% of the market value of Lenox's debt capital, adjusted to allow for the tax relief that Lenox gets on the debt interest (1% × £100,000 × 0.70)	700
	2,500

(* The rate of interest on personal borrowing is assumed to be the same as the market rate of interest on corporate debt, which is 12%).

The investor should now invest £2,500 in the equity of Groves plc, and can buy £2,500 ÷ £200,000 = 1.25% of Groves' shares.

4.18 The investor's income will now be higher than before, but because personal gearing has been substituted for corporate gearing, there is no change in the investor's financial risk. The increase in income can be illustrated as follows.

	Holding 1% shares in Lenox plc	*Holding 1.25% of shares in Groves plc with personal gearing*
	£	£
Earnings before interest and tax	40,000	40,000
Less interest charge for the company	12,000	0
	28,000	40,000
Less tax (30%)	8,400	12,000
Earnings, assumed equal to dividends	19,600	28,000
Investor's share (1% of Lenox/1.25% of Groves)	196.00	350.00
Less interest on personal debt (12% × £700)	0	84.00
Investor's net income	196.00	266.00

The investor can increase his or her annual income by £(266.00 – 196.00) = £70.00 through this arbitrage process.

Empirical testing and conclusion

4.19 It might be imagined that empirical testing should have been carried out by now either to prove or to disprove MM theory. Given, however, that MM accept that the weighted average cost of capital declines after allowing for tax, and that traditional theorists argue in favour of a flattish bottom to the weighted average cost of capital curve, it is very difficult to prove that one theory is preferable to the other.

Question 3

The cost of equity in an ungeared company is 18%. The cost of risk free debt capital is 8%.

(a) What is the cost of equity in a similar geared company, according to MM, which is 75% equity financed and 25% debt financed, assuming corporation tax at a rate of 30%?

(b) What is the WACC of the geared company, allowing for taxation?

Answer

(a) $r_g = 18\% + (1-0.30)[(18-8)\% \times \frac{25}{75}] = 20.333\%$

(b) $r^* = r\left[1 - \frac{T^*D}{(E+D)}\right] = 18\%[1 - \frac{0.30 \times 25}{(75+25)}]$

$= 18\% \times 0.925 = 16.7\%$

Question 4

CD plc and YZ are identical in every respect except for their gearing. The market value of each company is as follows.

CD plc		*YZ plc*	
	£m		£m
Equity (5m shares)	?	(8m shares)	24
Debt (£20m of 5% loan stock)	10		
	?		24

According to MM theory, what is the value of CD plc shares, given a corporation tax rate of 30%?

Answer

Value of CD plc in total $V_g = (V_u + DT_c)$ where V_u is the value of YZ plc.

V_g = £24,000,000 + £10,000,000 × 30% = £27,000,000.

CD plc's equity is valued at £27,600,000 – debt of £10,000,000 = £17,000,000, or £3.40 per share.

Chapter roundup

- Some of the theories discussed in this chapter may seem to be far removed from the realities of day-to-day decision making. However, the directors of a company have a duty to act in the company's interests, and if there is an **optimum level of gearing** they should do their best to estimate and achieve it.

Quick quiz

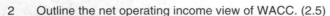

1 Outline the traditional view of WACC. (see para 2.3)

2 Outline the net operating income view of WACC. (2.5)

3 What is the basis on which Modigliani and Miller (MM) defended the net operating income view of WACC? (3.1)

4 What weaknesses are there in MM's theory? (3.15, 3.16)

5 Taking taxation into account in MM's theory, is there an optimum level of gearing? (4.7 - 4.9)

Question to try	Level	Marks	Time
12	Exam standard	25	45 mins

Chapter 12

PORTFOLIO MANAGEMENT

Chapter topic list		Syllabus reference	Ability required
1	Portfolios and portfolio theory	13 c(vi)	Skill
2	Investors' preferences	13 c(vi)	Skill
3	Portfolio theory and financial management	13 c(vi)	Skill

Introduction

The **diversification of portfolios** is an important concept in financial management. In this chapter, we examine the benefits of portfolio diversification. **Modern portfolio theory**, which has gained much popularity since 1970, concludes that a well diversified portfolio is optimal. We explain here some key aspects of portfolio theory, its relevance and its limitations.

1 PORTFOLIOS AND PORTFOLIO THEORY 5/96, 11/97

1.1 A portfolio is the collection of different investments that make up an investor's total holding. A portfolio might be:

(a) the investments in stocks and shares of an investor;
(b) the investments in capital projects of a company.

1.2 Portfolio theory, which originates from the work of Markowitz, is concerned with establishing guidelines for building up a portfolio of stocks and shares, or a portfolio of projects. The same theory applies to both stock market investors and to companies with capital projects to invest in.

Factors in the choice of investments

1.3 There are five major factors to be considered when an investor chooses investments, no matter whether the investor is an institutional investor, a company making an investment or a private individual investor.

(a) **Security**. Investments should at least maintain their capital value.

(b) **Liquidity**. Where the investments are made with short-term funds, they should be convertible back into cash at short notice.

(c) **Return**. The funds are invested to make money. The highest return compatible with safety should be sought.

(d) **Spreading risks**. The investor who puts all his funds into one type of security risks everything on the fortunes of that security. If it performs badly, his entire investment will make a loss. A better (and more secure) policy is to spread investments over several types of security, so that losses on some may be offset by gains on others.

(e) **Growth prospects**. The most profitable investments are likely to be in businesses with good growth prospects.

Portfolios: expected return and risk

1.4 When an investor has a portfolio of securities, he will expect the portfolio to provide a certain return on his investment.

1.5 The **expected return of a portfolio** will be a weighted average of the expected returns of the investments in the portfolio, weighted by the proportion of total funds invested in each.

The expected return $\bar{r}_p$ of a two-asset portfolio can thus be stated as the following formula:

$$\bar{r}_p = x\bar{r}_a + (1 - x)\bar{r}_b$$

where x is the proportion of investment A in the portfolio

$\bar{r}_a$, $\bar{r}_b$ are the expected returns of investments A and B

For example, if 70% of the portfolio relates to a security which is expected to yield 10% and 30% to a security expected to yield 12%, the portfolio's expected return is (70% × 10%) + (30% × 12%) = 10.6%.

1.6 The **risk** in an investment, or in a portfolio of investments, is the risk that the actual return will not be the same as the expected return. The actual return may be higher, but it may be lower. A prudent investor will want to avoid too much risk, and will hope that the actual returns from his portfolio are much the same as what he expected them to be.

1.7 The risk of a security, and the risk of a portfolio, can be measured as the standard deviation of expected returns, given estimated probabilities of actual returns.

1.8 EXAMPLE: PORTFOLIOS (1)

Suppose that the return from an investment has the following probability distribution.

Return	*Probability*	*Expected value*
x	p	px
%		
8	0.2	1.6
10	0.2	2.0
12	0.5	6.0
14	0.1	1.4
		11.0

The expected return is 11%, and the standard deviation of the expected return is as follows. The symbol $\bar{x}$ refers to the expected value of the return, 11%.

Return			
x	$x - \bar{x}$	p	$p(x - \bar{x})^2$
%	%		
8	−3	0.2	1.8
10	−1	0.2	0.2
12	1	0.5	0.5
14	3	0.1	0.9
		Variance	3.4

Standard deviation = $\sqrt{3.4}$ = 1.84%

Thus, the expected return is 11% with a standard deviation of 1.84%.

1.9 The risk of an investment might be high or low, depending on the nature of the investment.

(a) Low risk investments usually give low returns.

(b) High risk investments might give high returns, but with more risk of disappointing results.

So how does holding a **portfolio of investments** affect expected returns and investment risk?

Diversification as a means of reducing risk

1.10 Portfolio theory states that individual investments cannot be viewed simply in terms of their risk and return. The relationship between the return from one investment and the return from other investments is just as important.

1.11 The relationship between investments can be one of three types.

(a) **Positive correlation**. When there is positive correlation between investments, if one investment does well (or badly) it is likely that the other will perform likewise. Thus if you buy shares in one company making umbrellas and in another which sells raincoats you would expect both companies to do badly in dry weather.

(b) **Negative correlation**. If one investment does well the other will do badly, and vice versa. Thus if you hold shares in one company making umbrellas and in another which sells ice cream, the weather will affect the companies differently.

(c) **No correlation**. The performance of one investment will be independent of how the other performs. If you hold shares in a mining company and in a leisure company, it is likely that there would be no relationship between the profits and returns from each.

1.12 This relationship between the returns from different investments is measured by the correlation coefficient. A figure close to +1 indicates high positive correlation, and a figure close to –1 indicates high negative correlation. A figure of 0 indicates no correlation.

1.13 If investments show high negative correlation, then by combining them in a portfolio overall risk would be reduced. Risk will also be reduced by combining in a portfolio investments which have no significant correlation.

1.14 EXAMPLE: PORTFOLIOS (2)

Security A and Security B have the following expected returns.

	Security A	*Security B*
Probability	*Return*	*Return*
0.1	15%	10%
0.8	25%	30%
0.1	35%	50%

1.15 The expected return from each security is as follows.

	Security A		*Security B*	
Probability	*Return*	*EV*	*Return*	*EV*
	%	%	%	%
0.1	15	1.5	10	1
0.8	25	20.0	30	24
0.1	35	3.5	50	5
	Expected return =	25.0	Expected return =	30

1.16 The variance of the expected return for each security is $\sum p(x - \bar{x})^2$.

	Security A			Security B		
Probability	*Return*			*Return*		
p	*x*	$x - \bar{x}$	$p(x - \bar{x})^2$	*y*	$y - \bar{y}$	$p(y - \bar{y})^2$
0.1	15	(10)	10	10	(20)	40
0.8	25	0	0	30	0	0
0.1	35	10	10	50	20	40
	$\bar{x}$ =25	Variance =	20	$\bar{y}$ =30	Variance =	80

1.17 The standard deviation is the square root of the variance.

Security A: $\sqrt{20} = 4.472\%$

Security B: $\sqrt{80} = 8.944\%$

Security B therefore offers a higher return than security A, but at a greater risk.

1.18 Let us now assume that an investor acquires a portfolio consisting of 50% A and 50% B. The **expected return from the portfolio** will be 0.5 × 25% + 0.5 × 30% = 27.5%. This is less than the expected return from security B alone, but more than that from security A. The combined portfolio should be less risky than security B alone (although in this example of just a two-security portfolio, it will be more risky than security A alone except when returns are negatively correlated).

1.19 We can work out the standard deviation of the expected return:

(a) if there is perfect positive correlation between the returns from each security, so that if A gives a return of 15%, then B will give a return of 10% and so on;

(b) if there is perfect negative correlation between the returns from each security, so that if A gives a return of 15%, B will yield 50%, if A gives a return of 35%, B will yield 10%, and if A gives a return of 25%, B will yield 30%;

(c) if there is no correlation between returns, and so the probability distribution of returns is as follows.

A	B		p
%	%		
15	10	(0.1 × 0.1)	0.01
15	30	(0.1 × 0.8)	0.08
15	50	(0.1 × 0.1)	0.01
25	10	(0.8 × 0.1)	0.08
25	30	(0.8 × 0.8)	0.64
25	50	(0.8 × 0.1)	0.08
35	10	(0.1 × 0.1)	0.01
35	30	(0.1 × 0.8)	0.08
35	50	(0.1 × 0.1)	0.01
			1.00

Perfect positive correlation

1.20 The standard deviation of the portfolio may be calculated as follows, given an expected return of 27.5%.

Probability	*Return from 50% A*	*Return from 50% B*	*Combined portfolio return*		
p			x	$(x - \bar{x})$	$p(x - \bar{x})^2$
	%	%	%		
0.1	7.5	5	12.5	(15)	22.5
0.8	12.5	15	27.5	0	0
0.1	17.5	25	42.5	15	22.5
				Variance =	45.0

The standard deviation is √45 = 6.71%

Perfect negative correlation

1.21 The standard deviation of the portfolio, given an expected return of 27.5%, is as follows.

Probability p	*Return from 50% A*	*Return from 50% B*	*Combined portfolio return* x	$(x - \bar{x})$	$p(x - \bar{x})^2$
	%	%	%		
0.1	7.5	25	32.5	5	2.5
0.8	12.5	15	27.5	0	0
0.1	17.5	5	22.5	(5)	2.5
				Variance =	5.0

The standard deviation is √5 = 2.24%

No correlation

1.22 The standard deviation of the portfolio, given an expected return of 27.5%, is as follows.

Probability p	*Return from 50%* A	*Return from 50%* B	*Combined portfolio return* x	$(x - \bar{x})$	$p(x - \bar{x})^2$
	%	%	%		
0.01	7.5	5	12.5	(15)	2.25
0.08	7.5	15	22.5	(5)	2.00
0.01	7.5	25	32.5	5	0.25
0.08	12.5	5	17.5	(10)	8.00
0.64	12.5	15	27.5	0	0.00
0.08	12.5	25	37.5	10	8.00
0.01	17.5	5	22.5	(5)	0.25
0.08	17.5	15	32.5	5	2.00
0.01	17.5	25	42.5	15	2.25
				Variance =	25.00

The standard deviation is √25 = 5%

Conclusion

1.23 You should notice that for the same expected return of 27.5%, the standard deviation (the risk):

(a) is highest when there is perfect positive correlation between the returns of the individual securities in the portfolio;

(b) is lower when there is no correlation;

(c) is lowest when there is perfect negative correlation. The risk is then less than for either individual security taken on its own.

Another way of calculating the standard deviation of a portfolio

1.24 The **standard deviation of the returns from a portfolio** of two investments can be calculated using the following formula.

$$\sigma_p = \sqrt{\sigma_a^2 x^2 + \sigma_b^2 (1-x)^2 + 2x(1-x)p_{ab}\,\sigma_a\,\sigma_b}$$

where:

σ_p is the standard deviation of a portfolio of two investments, A and B

σ_a is the standard deviation of the returns from investment A

σ_b is the standard deviation of the returns from investment B

σ_a^2, σ_b^2 are the variances of returns from investment A and B (the squares of the standard deviations)

x is the weighting or proportion of investment A in the portfolio

p_{ab} is the correlation coefficient of returns from investment A and B

$$= \frac{\text{Covariance of investments A and B}}{\sigma_a \times \sigma_b}$$

1.25 EXAMPLE: PORTFOLIOS (3)

We will use the previous example of the portfolio of 50% security A and 50% security B.

(a) When there is perfect positive correlation between the returns from A and B, r = 1.

$$\sigma_p^2 = 20 \times 0.5^2 + 80 \times 0.5^2 + 2 \times 0.5 \times 0.5 \times 1 \times \sqrt{20} \times \sqrt{80}$$
$$= 5 + 20 + 0.5 \times 4.472 \times 8.944$$
$$= 45$$

The standard deviation of the portfolio is $\sqrt{45} = 6.71\%$

(b) When there is perfect negative correlation between returns from A and B, r = –1.

$$\sigma_p^2 = 20 \times 0.5^2 + 80 \times 0.5^2 + 2 \times 0.5 \times 0.5 \times -1 \times \sqrt{20} \times \sqrt{80}$$
$$= 5 + 20 - 0.5 \times 4.472 \times 8.944$$
$$= 5$$

The standard deviation of the portfolio is $\sqrt{5} = 2.24\%$

(c) When there is no correlation between returns from A and B, r = 0.

$$\sigma_p^2 = 20 \times 0.5^2 + 80 \times 0.5^2 + 2 \times 0.5 \times 0.5 \times 0 \times \sqrt{20} \times \sqrt{80}$$
$$= 5 + 20 + 0$$
$$= 25$$

The standard deviation of the portfolio is $\sqrt{25} = 5\%$

1.26 These are exactly the same figures for standard deviations that were calculated earlier.

Exam focus point

The Examiner has stated that if the calculation of a two-asset portfolio variance is tested, formulae will be given.

2 INVESTORS' PREFERENCES

2.1 Investors must choose a portfolio which gives them a satisfactory balance between:

(a) the expected returns from the portfolio; and

(b) the risk that actual returns from the portfolio will be higher or lower than expected. Some portfolios will be more risky than others.

2.2 Traditional investment theory suggests that rational investors wish to maximise return and minimise risk. Thus if two portfolios have the same element of risk, the investor will choose the one yielding the higher return. Similarly, if two portfolios offer the same return the investor will select the portfolio with the lesser risk. This is illustrated by Figure 1.

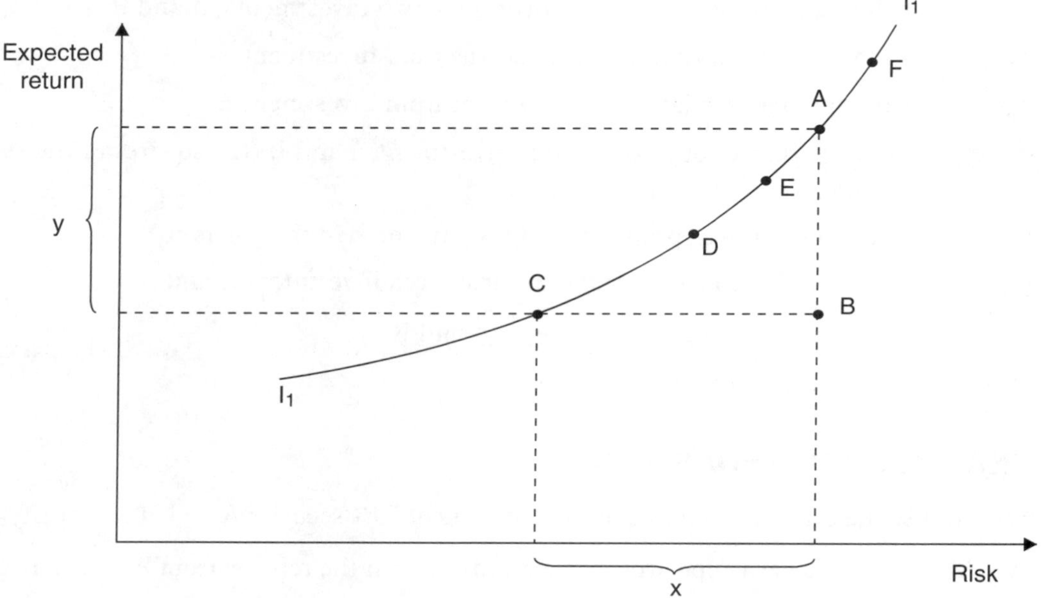

Figure 1 An investor's indifference curve

2.3 Portfolio A will be preferred to portfolio B because it offers a higher expected return for the same level of risk. Similarly, portfolio C will be preferred to portfolio B because it offers the same expected return for lower risk. (A and C are said to **dominate** portfolio B). But whether an investor chooses portfolio A or portfolio C will depend on the individual's attitude to risk: whether he wishes to accept a greater risk for a greater expected return.

2.4 The curve I_1 is an investor's indifference curve. The investor will have no preference between any portfolios which give a mix of risk and expected return which lies on the curve, since he derives **equal utility** from each of them. Thus, to the investor the portfolios A, C, D, E and F are all just as good as each other, and all of them are better than portfolio B. Remembering that the risk of a portfolio can be measured as the standard deviation of expected returns, this may be expressed by saying that portfolio B is dispreferred on grounds of **mean-variance inefficiency**.

2.5 An investor would prefer combinations of return and risk on indifference curve A to those on curve B (Figure 2) because curve A offers higher returns for the same degree of risk (and less risk for the same expected returns). For example, for the same amount of risk x, the expected return on curve A is y_1, whereas on curve B it is only y_2.

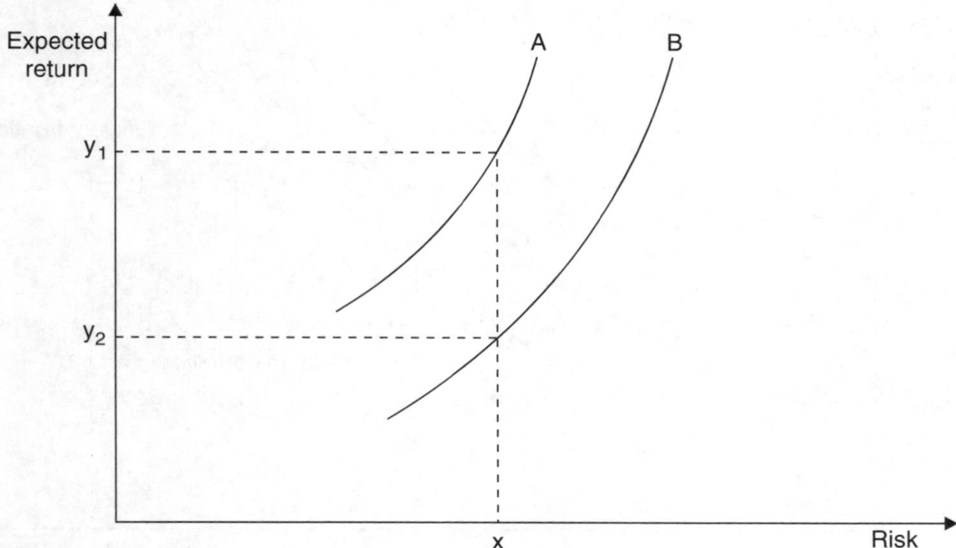

Figure 2 Indifference curves compared

Efficient portfolios

2.6 If we drew a graph (Figure 3) to show the expected return and the risk of the many possible portfolios of investments, we could (according to portfolio theory) plot an egg-shaped cluster of dots on a scattergraph as follows.

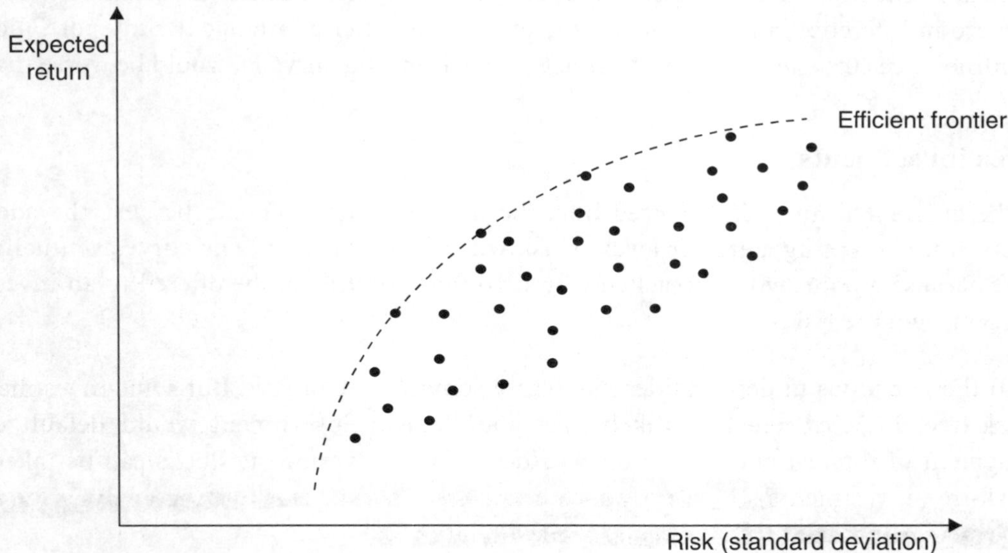

Figure 3 The efficient frontier of available investment portfolios

In this graph, there are some portfolios which would not be as good as others. However, there are other portfolios which are neither better nor worse than each other, because they have either a higher expected return but a higher risk, or a lower expected return but a lower risk. These portfolios lie along the so-called 'efficient frontier' of portfolios which is shown as a dotted line in Figure 3. Portfolios on this efficient frontier are called 'efficient' portfolios.

2.7 We can now place an investor's indifference curves on the same graph as the possible portfolios of investments (the egg-shaped scatter graph), as in Figure 4.

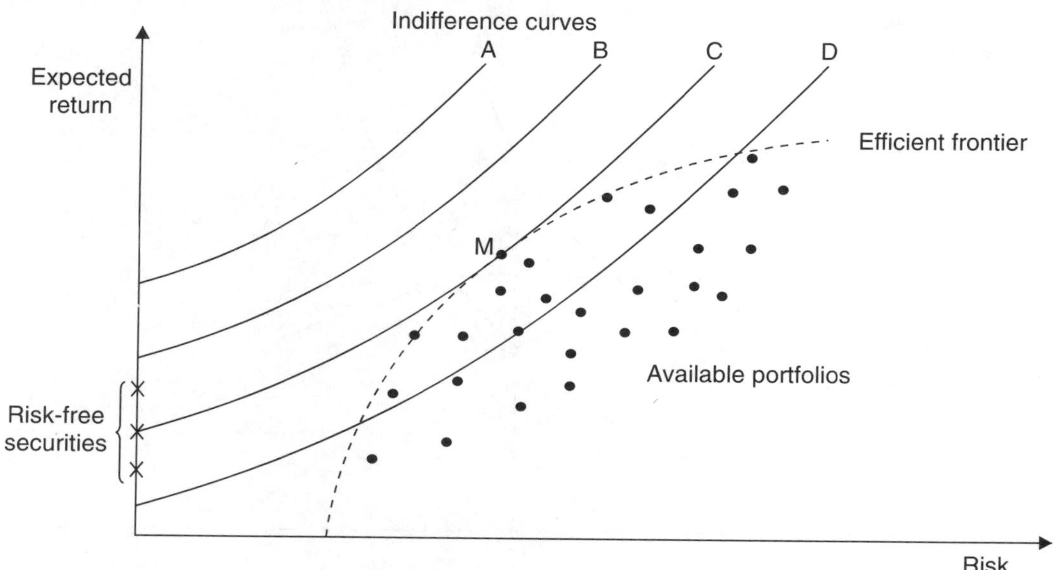

Figure 4 The optimum portfolio (ignoring risk-free securities)

An investor would prefer a portfolio of investments on indifference curve A to a portfolio on curve B, which in turn is preferable to a portfolio on curve C which in turn is preferable to curve D. No portfolio exists, however, which is on curve A or curve B.

2.8 The optimum portfolio (or portfolios) to select is one where an indifference curve touches the efficient frontier of portfolios at a tangent. In Figure 4, this is the portfolio marked M, where indifference curve C touches the efficient frontier at a tangent. Any portfolio on an indifference curve to the right of curve C, such as one on curve D, would be worse than M.

Risk-free investments

2.9 The efficient frontier is a curved line, not a straight line. This is because the additional return for accepting a greater level of risk will not be constant. The curve eventually levels off because a point will be reached where no more return can be offered to an investor for accepting more risk.

2.10 All the portfolios under consideration carry some degree of risk. But some investments are risk-free. It is extremely unlikely that the British Government would default on any payment of interest and capital on its stocks. Thus government stocks can be taken to be risk-free investments. If we introduce a risk-free investment into the analysis we can see that the old efficient frontier is superseded (Figure 5).

2.11 The straight line XZME is drawn at a tangent to the efficient frontier and cuts the y axis at the point of the risk-free investment's return. The line (known as the 'capital market line' (CML)) becomes the new efficient frontier.

2.12 Portfolio M is the same as in Figure 4. It is the efficient portfolio which will appeal to the investor most, ignoring risk-free investments. Portfolio Z is a mixture of the investments in portfolio M and risk-free investments. Investors will prefer portfolio Z (a mixture of risky portfolio M and the risk-free investment) to portfolio P because a higher return is obtained for the same level of risk. The only portfolio consisting entirely of **risky investments** a rational investor should want to hold is portfolio M. All other risky portfolios are inefficient (because they are below the CML).

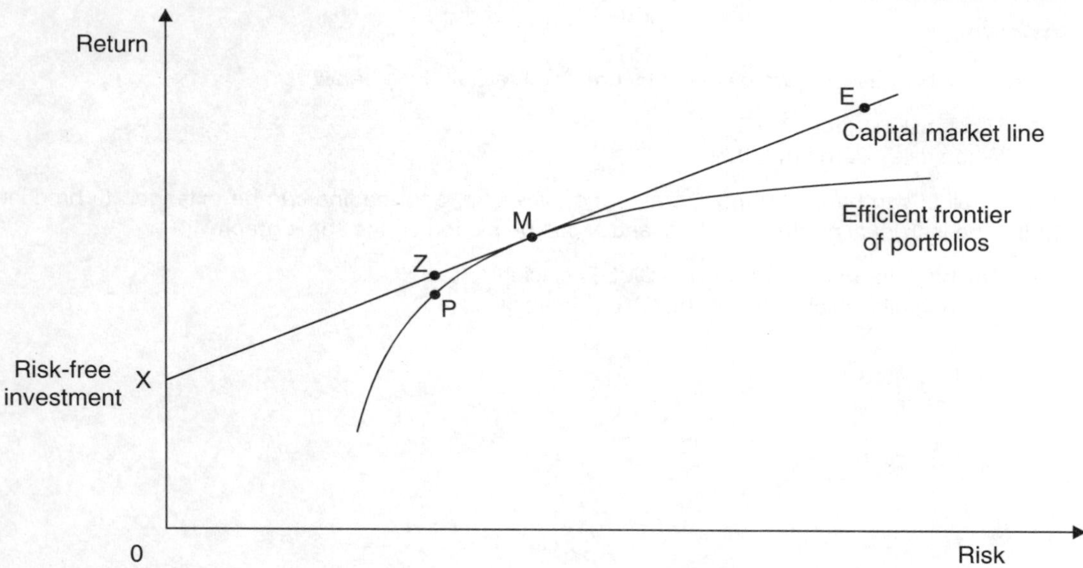

Figure 5 The capital market line

2.13 As with the curvilinear frontier, one portfolio on the capital market line is as attractive as another to a rational investor. One investor may wish to hold portfolio Z, which lies 2/3 of the way along the CML between risk-free investment X and portfolio M (that is, a holding comprising 2/3 portfolio M and 1/3 risk-free securities). Another investor may wish to hold portfolio E, which entails putting all his funds in portfolio M and borrowing money at the risk-free rate to acquire more of portfolio M.

2.14 We have said that investors will only want to hold one portfolio of risky investments: portfolio M. This may be held in conjunction with a holding of the risk-free investment (as with portfolio Z). Alternatively, an investor may borrow funds to augment his holding of M (as with portfolio E). Therefore:

(a) since all investors wish to hold portfolio M; and
(b) all shares quoted on the Stock Exchange must be held by investors; it follows that
(c) all shares quoted on the Stock Exchange must be in portfolio M.

2.15 Thus **portfolio M is the market portfolio** and each investor's portfolio will contain a proportion of it. (Although in the real world, investors do not hold every quoted security in their portfolio, in practice a well diversified portfolio will 'mirror' the whole market in terms of weightings given to particular sectors, high income and high capital growth securities, and so on.) However, in practice, investors **might** be able to build up a small portfolio that 'beats the market' or might have a portfolio which performs worse than the market average. The following question illustrates this.

Question

The following data relate to four different portfolios of securities.

Portfolio	*Expected rate of return* %	*Standard deviation of return on the portfolio %*
K	11	6.7
L	14	7.5
M	10	3.3
N	15	10.8

The expected rate of return on the market portfolio is 8.5% with a standard deviation of 3%. The risk-free rate is 5%.

Identify which of these portfolios could be regarded as 'efficient'.

Answer

To answer this question, we can start by drawing the CML (see below).

(a) When risk = 0, return = 5.
(b) When risk = 3, return = 8.5.

These points can be plotted on a graph and joined up, and the line can be extended to produce the CML. The individual portfolios K, L, M and N can be plotted on the same graph.

(a) Any portfolio which is above the CML is efficient.
(b) Any portfolio which is below the CML is inefficient.

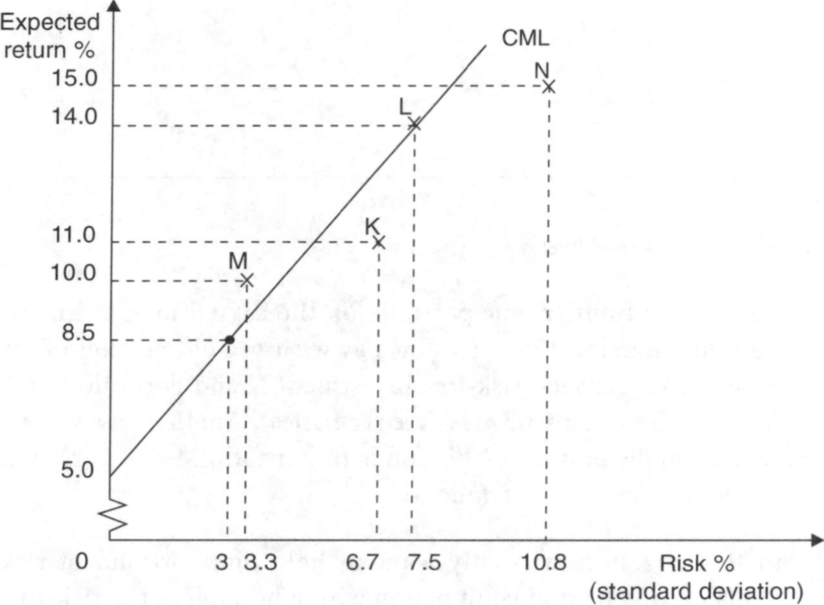

(a) Portfolio M is very efficient.
(b) Portfolio L is also efficient.
(c) Portfolios K and N are inefficient.

If you prefer numbers to graphs, we can tackle the problem in a slightly different way, by calculating the equation of the CML.

Let the standard deviation of a portfolio be x.

Let the return from a portfolio be y.

The CML equation is $y = r_f + bx$.

where r_f is the risk-free rate of return. Here, this is 5.

To calculate b, we can use the high-low method.

When $x = 3, y = 8.5$
When $x = 0, y = 5$

Therefore $b = \frac{(8.5-5)}{(3-0)} = \frac{3.5}{3} = 1.16667$

The CML is $y = 5 + 1.16667x$

Portfolio	*Standard deviation x*	*CML return*	*%*	*Actual return %*	*Efficient or inefficient portfolio*
K	6.7	(5 + 1.16667 × 6.7)	12.8	11	Inefficient
L	7.5	(5 + 1.16667 × 7.5)	13.8	14	Efficient
M	3.3	(5 + 1.16667 × 3.3)	8.9	10	Very efficient
N	10.8	(5 + 1.16667 × 10.8)	17.6	15	Inefficient

If the actual return exceeds the CML return for the given amount of risk, the portfolio is efficient.

Here, L is efficient and M is even more efficient, but K and N are inefficient.

The return on the market portfolio M

2.16 The expected returns from portfolio M will be higher than the return from risk-free investments because the investors expect a greater return for accepting a degree of investment risk. The size of the risk premium will increase as the risk of the market portfolio increases. We can show this with an analysis of the capital market line (CML) as in Figure 6.

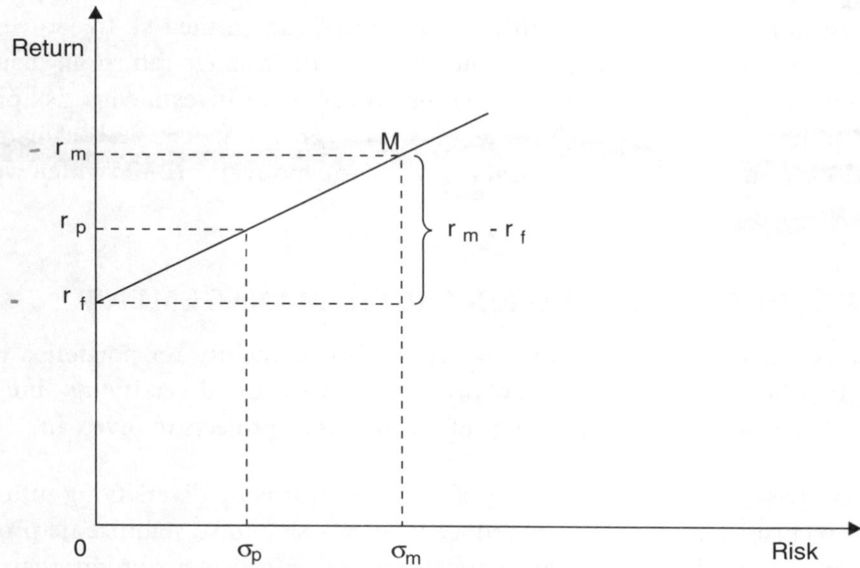

r_m = return from portfolio M
r_f = risk-free return
σ_m = risk of the portfolio M

Figure 6 The risk premium in required returns from a portfolio

2.17 Let r_f = the risk-free rate of return
r_m = the return on market portfolio M
r_p = the return on portfolio P, which is a mixture of investments in portfolio M and risk-free investments
σ_m = the risk (standard deviation) of returns in portfolio M
σ_p = the risk (standard deviation) of returns in portfolio P

The gradient of the CML can be expressed as $\dfrac{r_m - r_f}{\sigma_m}$

This represents the extent to which the required returns from a portfolio should exceed the risk-free rate of return, to compensate investors for risk.

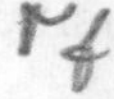

The beta factor

2.18 The equation of the CML can be expressed as: $r_p = r_f + \left(\dfrac{r_m - r_f}{\sigma_m}\right)\sigma_p$

where $\left(\dfrac{r_m - r_f}{\sigma_m}\right)\sigma_p$ is the risk premium that the investor should require as compensation for accepting portfolio risk σ_p.

2.19 The risk premium can be arranged into:

$$\frac{\sigma_p}{\sigma_m}(r_m - r_f)$$

The expression $\frac{\sigma_p}{\sigma_m}$ is referred to as a **beta factor**, so that an investor's required return from a portfolio can be stated as $r_p = r_f + (r_m - r_f)\,\beta$

2.20 The beta factor (β) can therefore be used to measure the extent to which a portfolio's return (or indeed an individual investment's return) should exceed the risk-free rate of return. The beta factor is multiplied by the difference between the average return on market securities (r_m) and the risk-free return (r_f) to derive the portfolio's or investment's risk premium. This risk premium will include both a business risk and a financial risk element in it. This equation forms the basis of the **capital asset pricing model (CAPM)**, which we shall look at in the next chapter.

3 PORTFOLIO THEORY AND FINANCIAL MANAGEMENT

3.1 Our discussion of portfolio theory has concentrated mainly on portfolios of stocks and shares. Investors can reduce their investment risk by diversifying, but what about individual companies choosing a range of businesses or projects to invest in?

3.2 Just as an investor can reduce the risk of variable returns by diversifying into a portfolio of different securities, a company can reduce its own risk and so stabilise its profitability if it invests in a portfolio of different projects or operations, assuming that any positive correlation between returns is weak.

(a) If a company which manufactures garden tables diversifies into manufacturing umbrellas for garden tables, it is unlikely that the diversification will reduce risk, because the returns from trading in garden tables and garden table umbrellas will be positively correlated, both depending on the strength of demand for garden furniture.

(b) On the other hand, if a company which manufactures and sells computer equipment were to diversify into trading in video recorders, children's clothing, industrial paints, domestic plumbing and electrical services, it is probable that its risk of variable profits would be reduced.

Should companies try to diversify?

3.3 The answer to this question is not clear-cut, and you can probably think of examples of large companies today which concentrate mainly on a single industry or product range (for example, British Telecom) and **conglomerates** which are **widely diversified** (for example, the 'guns-to-buns' Tomkins group, which is however proposing a demerger of its Rank Hovis McDougall subsidiary in late 1999 which will reduce its degree of diversification).

KEY TERM

Conglomerate: An entity comprising a number of dissimilar businesses *(OT)*.

3.4 There are a number of reasons why a company should not try to diversify too far.

(a) A company may employ people with particular skills, and it will get the best out of its employees by allowing them to stick to doing what they are good at. A manager with expert knowledge of the electronics business, for example, might not be any good at managing a retailing business. Some managers can adapt successfully to running a diversified business, and a company can acquire employees with the necessary skills by taking over other companies. Even so, diversification will not necessarily succeed, because a company may lack the skills and expertise to be a successful diversified business.

(b) When companies try to grow, they will often find the best opportunities to make extra profits in industries or markets with which they are familiar. If a market opens up for say, a new electronic consumer product, the companies which are likely to exploit the market most profitably are those which already have experience in producing electronic consumer products.

(c) Conglomerates are vulnerable to takeover bids where the buyer plans to 'unbundle' the companies in the group and sell them off individually at a profit. The reason why conglomerates are vulnerable to takeover bids is that their returns will often be mediocre rather than high, and so the stock market will value the shares on a fairly low P/E ratio. Separate companies within the group would be valued according to their individual performance and prospects, often at P/E ratios that are much higher than for the conglomerate as a whole.

(d) A company can reduce its business risk by diversifying and lower business risk would protect the company's shareholders; however, a shareholder does not need the company to reduce investment risk on his behalf. The shareholder can reduce risk himself by diversifying into shares in a range of different companies. Why should a company try to reduce risk when investors can do this themselves?

(e) Investors can probably reduce investment risk more efficiently than companies. They have a wider range of investment opportunities. Investments with uncorrelated or negatively correlated returns will be easier to identify. Estimates of beta factors will be more reliable for quoted companies' shares than for companies' capital expenditure projects.

3.5 These arguments suggest that a company should not necessarily diversify widely into completely different products and markets. On the other hand, it would be against the interests of shareholders if a company were to be so unprofitable that it went into liquidation. Companies should try to obtain some protection against short-term profit changes, and some diversification will help to provide this protection.

Limitations of portfolio analysis for the financial manager

3.6 **Portfolio analysis** offers a way in which the financial manager can deal with risk by diversifying through the investment decisions which are made by the firm. However, portfolio theory applied to the selection of investment proposals has a number of limitations.

(a) In practice, it may require guesswork to estimate probabilities of different outcomes, for example when a new product is to be developed. In other cases, such as machine replacement, sufficient information may however be available to make relatively good probability estimates.

(b) It will be difficult in practical cases to know what are shareholders' preferences between risk and return and therefore to reflect these preferences in decision-making.

(c) The agency problem in management's relationship to the company (see Chapter 1) is relevant. Portfolio theory is based on the notion of managers assessing the relevant probabilities and deciding the combination of activities that a business will be involved in. Managers have the security of their jobs to consider, while the shareholder can easily buy and sell securities. It is arguable that managers are as a result more risk-averse than shareholders, and this may distort managers' investment decisions.

(d) Projects may be of such a size that they are not easy to divide in accordance with recommended diversification principles.

(e) The theory assumes that there are constant returns to scale, in other words that the percentage returns provided by a project are the same however much is invested in it. In practice, there may be economies of scale to be gained from making a larger investment in a single project.

(f) Other aspects of risk not covered by the theory may need to be considered, eg bankruptcy costs.

Chapter roundup

- Both individuals and firms diversify their investments. Individuals have **portfolios of shares** and firms have **portfolios of business operations**.
- **Portfolio theory** takes account of the fact that many investors have a range of investments which are unlikely all to changes values in step. The investor should be concerned with his or her overall position, not with the performance of individual investments.
- **Diversification** is equally an important consideration for the financial manager in making investment decisions. Portfolio theory has limitations in its use by the financial manager, although it provides the basis of the more sophisticated **CAPM** approach to making investment decisions under risk, which we turn to in the next chapter.

Quick quiz

1 What are the factors in choosing a portfolio of investments? (see para 1.3)

2 How is the expected return from a portfolio measured? (1.5)

3 Returns from investments might be positively correlated, negatively correlated, or uncorrelated. How does correlation of returns from individual investments affect the risk of a portfolio? (1.23)

4 How are the expected returns and risks of portfolios on the efficient frontier related to each other? (2.6)

5 Give an example of a risk-free investment. (2.10)

6 What is the equation of the capital market line? (2.18) Use this to derive an expression for the beta factor. (2.19)

7 How is the beta factor used? (2.20)

8 What limitations are there in using portfolio analysis in financial management decisions? (3.6)

Question to try	Level	Marks	Time
13	Introductory	n/a	6 mins

Chapter 13

THE CAPITAL ASSET PRICING MODEL

Chapter topic list		Syllabus reference	Ability required
1	Risk and the CAPM	13 c(vi)	Skill
2	Calculating a beta factor	13 c(vi)	Skill
3	CAPM and portfolio management	13 c(vi)	Skill
4	Gearing and the β values of companies' equity	13 c(vi)	Skill
5	Practical implications of the CAPM	13 c(vi)	Skill
6	The arbitrage pricing model	13 c(vi)	Skill

Introduction

The **Capital Asset Pricing Model** (CAPM) brings together aspects of topics covered in earlier chapters: **portfolio theory**, **share valuations**, the **cost of capital** and **gearing**. Towards the end of the chapter, we discuss a possible replacement for the CAPM - the **arbitrage pricing model** (APM). Detailed knowledge of the APM is not required for your examination.

1 RISK AND THE CAPM 5/95, 5/96, 11/97

1.1 The uses of the **capital asset pricing model (CAPM)** include:

(a) trying to establish the 'correct' equilibrium market value of a company's shares;

(b) trying to establish the cost of a company's equity (and the company's average cost of capital), taking account of the risk characteristics of a company's investments, both business and financial risk.

The CAPM thus provides an approach to establishing a cost of equity capital which is an alternative to the dividend valuation model.

Systematic risk and unsystematic risk

1.2 Whenever an investor invests in some shares, or a company invests in a new project, there will be some risk involved. The actual return on the investment might be better or worse than that hoped for. To some extent, risk is unavoidable (unless the investor settles for risk-free securities such as gilts). Investors must take the rough with the smooth and for reasons outside their control, returns might be higher or lower than expected. Provided that the investor diversifies his investments in a suitably wide portfolio, the investments which perform well and those which perform badly should tend to cancel each other out, and much risk can be diversified away. In the same way, a company which invests in a number of projects will find that some do well and some do badly, but taking the whole portfolio of investments, average returns should turn out much as expected.

1.3 Risks that can be diversified away are referred to as **unsystematic risk**. But there is another sort of risk too. Some investments are by their very nature more risky than others. This has nothing to do with chance variations up or down in actual returns compared with what an investor should expect. This **inherent risk** - the **systematic risk** or **market risk** - cannot be diversified away (see Figure 1).

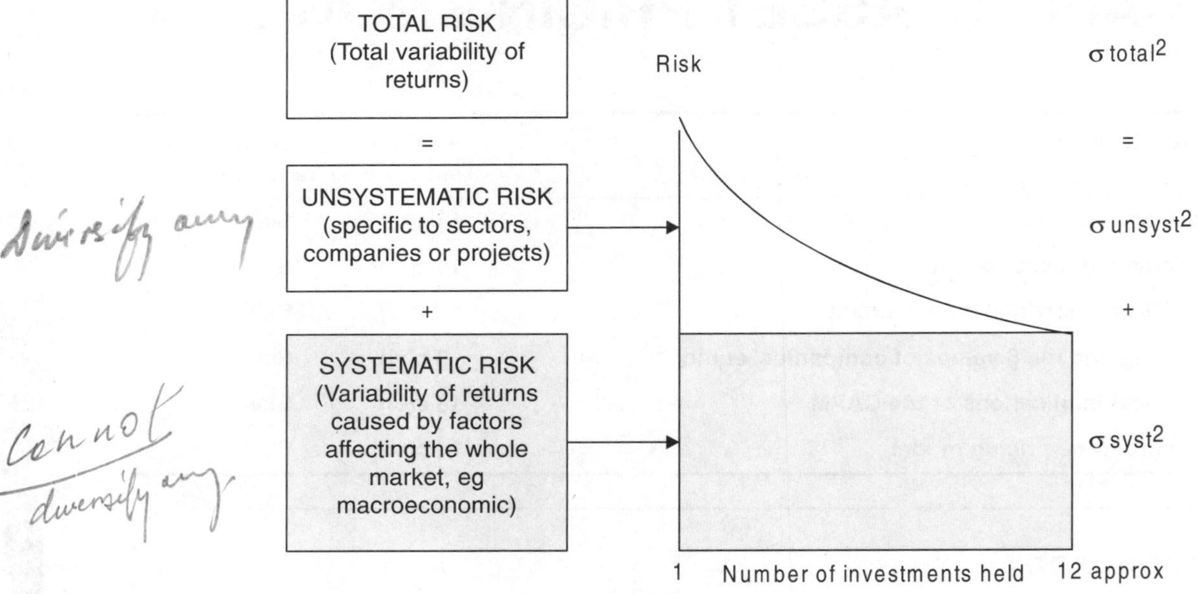

Figure 1

1.4 Systematic risk must therefore be accepted by any investor, unless he invests entirely in risk-free investments. In return for accepting systematic risk, an investor will expect to earn a return which is higher than the return on a risk-free investment.

1.5 The amount of systematic risk in an investment varies between different types of investment.

(a) Some industries by their nature are more risky than others. For example, it might be that the systematic risk in the operating cash flows of a company in a high technology industry is greater than the systematic risk for a company which operates a chain of supermarkets.

(b) In the same way, some individual projects will be more risky than others and so the systematic risk involved in an investment to develop a new product would be greater than the systematic risk of investing in a replacement asset.

Systematic risk and unsystematic risk: implications for investments

1.6 The implications of systematic risk and unsystematic risk are as follows.

(a) If an investor wants to avoid risk altogether, he must invest entirely in risk-free securities.

(b) If an investor holds shares in just a few companies, there will be some unsystematic risk as well as systematic risk in his portfolio, because he will not have spread his risk enough to diversify away the unsystematic risk. To eliminate unsystematic risk, he must build up a well-diversified portfolio of investments.

(c) If an investor holds a balanced portfolio of all the stocks and shares on the stock market, he will incur systematic risk which is exactly equal to the average systematic risk in the stock market as a whole.

(d) Shares in individual companies will have systematic risk characteristics which are different to this market average. Some shares will be less risky and some will be more risky than the stock market average. Similarly, some investments will be more risky and some will be less risky than a company's 'average' investments.

Systematic risk and the CAPM

1.7 The capital asset pricing model is mainly concerned with how systematic risk is measured, and how systematic risk affects required returns and share prices. **Systematic risk** is measured using **beta factors**.

KEY TERM

Beta factor: in portfolio theory, a measure of the volatility of the price of a security, and thus of its **systematic risk**, used to calculate appropriate discount rates in the capital asset pricing model. If a share price will rise or fall at double the market rate, the beta factor is 2.

1.8 CAPM theory includes the following propositions.

(a) Investors in shares require a return in excess of the risk-free rate, to compensate them for systematic risk.

(b) Investors should not require a premium for unsystematic risk, because this can be diversified away by holding a wide portfolio of investments.

(c) Because systematic risk varies between companies, investors will require a higher return from shares in those companies where the systematic risk is bigger.

1.9 The same propositions can be applied to capital investments by companies.

(a) Companies will want a return on a project to exceed the risk-free rate, to compensate them for systematic risk.

(b) Unsystematic risk can be diversified away, and so a premium for unsystematic risk should not be required.

(c) Companies should want a bigger return on projects where systematic risk is greater.

Market risk and returns

1.10 The CAPM was first formulated for investments in stocks and shares on the market, rather than for companies' investments in capital projects. It is based on a comparison of the systematic risk of individual investments (shares in a particular company) and the risk of all shares in the market as a whole. Market risk (systematic risk) is the average risk of the market as a whole. Taking all the shares on a stock market together, the total expected returns from the market will vary because of systematic risk. The market as a whole might do well or it might do badly.

Risk and returns from an individual security

1.11 In the same way, an individual security may offer prospects of a return of x%, but with some risk (business risk and financial risk) attached. The return (the x%) that investors will require from the individual security will be higher or lower than the market return, depending on whether the security's systematic risk is greater or less than the market average. A major **assumption in CAPM** is that there is a linear relationship between the return obtained from an individual security and the average return from all securities in the market.

1.12 EXAMPLE: CAPM (1)

The following information is available about the performance of an individual company's shares and the stock market as a whole.

	Individual company	*Stock market as a whole*
Price at start of period	105.0	480.0
Price at end of period	110.0	490.0
Dividend during period	7.6	39.2

1.13 The expected return on the company's shares $E(r_j)$ and the expected return on the 'market portfolio' of shares $E(r_m)$ may be calculated as:

$$\frac{\text{Capital gain (or loss) + dividend}}{\text{Price at start of period}}$$

$$E(r_j) = \frac{(110-105)+7.6}{105} = 0.12 \qquad E(r_m) = \frac{(490-480)+39.2}{480} = 0.1025$$

1.14 A statistical analysis of 'historic' returns from a security and from the 'average' market may suggest that a linear relationship can be assumed to exist between them. A series of comparative figures could be prepared (month by month) of the return from a company's shares and the average return of the market as a whole. The results could be drawn on a scattergraph and a 'line of best fit' drawn (using linear regression techniques) as shown in Figure 1.

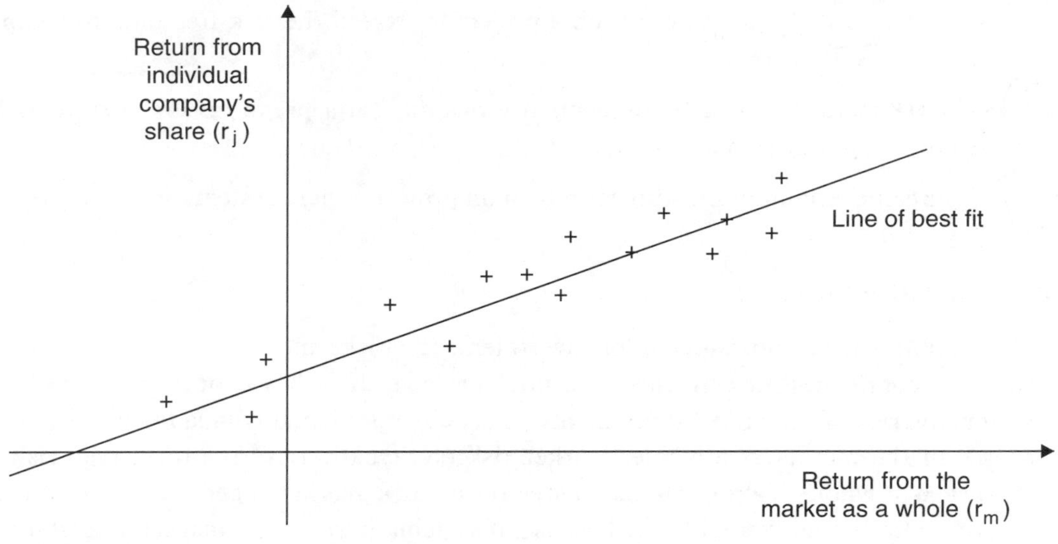

Figure 1

1.15 This analysis would show three things.

(a) The return from the security and the return from the market as a whole will tend to rise or fall together.

(b) The return from the security may be higher or lower than the market return. This is because the systematic risk of the individual security differs from that of the market as a whole.

(c) The scattergraph may not give a good line of best fit, unless a large number of data items are plotted, because actual returns are affected by unsystematic risk as well as by systematic risk.

Note that returns can be negative. A share price fall represents a capital loss, which is a negative return.

1.16 The conclusion from this analysis is that individual securities will be either more or less risky than the market average in a fairly predictable way. The measure of this relationship between market returns and an individual security's returns, reflecting differences in systematic risk characteristics, can be developed into a beta factor for the individual security.

The beta factor and the market risk premium

KEY TERM

A share's **beta factor** is the measure of its volatility in terms of market risk. The beta factor of the market as a whole is 1.0. Market risk makes market returns volatile and the beta factor is simply a basis or yardstick against which the risk of other investments can be measured.

1.17 Suppose that returns on shares in XYZ plc tend to vary twice as much as returns from the market as a whole, so that if market returns went up 3%, say, returns on XYZ plc shares would be expected to go up by 6% and if market returns fell by 3%, returns on XYZ plc shares would be expected to fall by 6%. The beta factor of XYZ plc shares would be 2.0.

1.18 Thus if the average market return rises by, say, 2%, the return from a share with a beta factor of 0.8 should rise by 1.6% in response to the **same conditions** which have caused the market return to change. The **actual return** from the share might rise by, say, 2.5%, or even fall by, say, 1%, but the difference between the actual change and a change of 1.6% due to general market factors would be attributed to unsystematic risk factors unique to the company or its industry.

1.19 It is an essential principle of CAPM theory that unsystematic risk can be cancelled out by diversification. In a well-balanced portfolio, an investor's gains and losses from the unsystematic risk of individual shares will tend to cancel each other out. In other words, if shares in X plc do worse than market returns and the beta factor of X's shares would predict, shares in Y plc will do better than predicted, and the net effect will be self-cancelling elimination of the specific (unsystematic) risk from the portfolio, leaving the average portfolio return dependent only on changes in the average market return, and the beta factors of shares in the portfolio.

Excess returns over returns on risk-free investments

1.20 The CAPM also makes use of the principle that returns on shares in the market as a whole are expected to be higher than the returns on risk-free investments. The difference between market returns and risk-free returns is called an excess return. For example, if the return on British Government stocks is 9% and market returns are 13%, the **excess** return on the market's shares as a whole is 4%.

1.21 The difference between the risk-free return and the expected return on an individual security can be measured as the excess return for the market as a whole multiplied by the security's beta factor. Thus, if shares in DEF plc have a beta of 1.5 when the risk-free return is 9% and the expected market return is 13%, then the expected return on DEF plc shares would exceed the risk-free return by 1.5(13 – 9)% = 6% and the total expected return on DEF shares would be (9 + 6)% = 15%. If the market returns fall by 3% to 10%, say, the expected return on DEF plc shares would fall by 1.5 × 3% = 4.5% to 10.5%, being 9% + 1.5(10 – 9)% = 10.5%.

The CAPM formula

1.22 The capital asset pricing model is a statement of the principles explained above. It can be stated as follows.

EXAM FORMULA

$$E(r_j) - r_f = [E(r_m) - r_f]\,\beta_j$$

where $E(r_j)$ is the expected return from an individual security
r_f is the risk-free rate of return
r_m is the return from the market as a whole
β_j is the beta factor of the individual security

Exam focus point

Don't be put off balance by the fact that the *Mathematical Tables* provided in the exam also include another version of the CAPM formula above using different notation:

$$r - r_f = \beta(r_m - r_f)$$

KEY TERM

Capital asset pricing model (CAPM): a theory which predicts that the expected risk premium for an indivdiual stock will be proportional to its beta, such that:

Expected risk premium on a stock = beta × expected risk premium in the market.

Risk premium is defined as the expected incremental return for making a risky investment rather than a safe one (*OT*).

Alpha values

1.23 A share's **alpha value** is a measure of its abnormal return, which is the amount by which the share's returns are currently above or below what would be expected, given its systematic risk. The alpha value can be seen as a measure of how wrong the CAPM is!

1.24 EXAMPLE: CAPM (2)

ABC plc's shares have a beta value of 1.2 and an alpha value of +2%. The market return is 10% and the risk-free rate of return is 6%.

Expected return 6% + (10 – 6) × 1.2% = 10.8%

Current return = Expected return ± alpha value
= 10.8% + 2% = 12.8%

1.25 Alpha values:

- reflect only temporary, abnormal returns
- can be positive or negative
- over time, will tend towards zero for any individual share, and for a well diversified portfolio taken as a whole will be 0
- if positive, might attract investors into buying the share to benefit from the abnormal return, so that the share price will temporarily go up

The CAPM and share prices

1.26 The CAPM can be used not only to estimate expected returns from securities with differing risk characteristics, but also to predict the value of shares.

1.27 EXAMPLE: CAPM (3)

Company X and company Y both pay an annual cash return to shareholders of 34.048 pence per share and this is expected to continue in perpetuity. The risk-free rate of return is 8% and the current average market rate of return is 12%. Company X's β coefficient is 1.8 and company Y's is 0.8. What is the expected return from companies X and Y respectively, and what would be the predicted market value of each company's shares?

1.28 SOLUTION

(a) The expected return for X is 8% + (12% – 8%) × 1.8 = 15.2%

(b) The expected return for Y is 8% + (12% – 8%) × 0.8 = 11.2%

The dividend valuation model can now be used to derive expected share prices.

(c) The predicted value of a share in X is $\frac{34.048\text{p}}{0.152}$ = 224 pence

(d) The predicted value of a share in Y is $\frac{34.048\text{p}}{0.112}$ = 304 pence

The actual share prices of X and Y might be higher or lower than 224p and 304p. If so, CAPM analysis would conclude that the share is currently either overpriced or underpriced.

Question 1

The risk-free rate of return is 7%. The average market return is 11%.

(a) What will be the return expected from a share whose β factor is 0.9?

(b) What would be the share's expected value if it is expected to earn an annual dividend of 5.3p, with no capital growth?

Answer

(a) 7% + (11% – 7%) × 0.9 = 10.6%

(b) $\frac{5.3\text{p}}{10.6\%}$ = 50 pence

2 CALCULATING A BETA FACTOR

2.1 The beta factor for a particular security can be calculated by plotting its return against the market return and drawing the line of best fit. The equation of this line can be derived by regression analysis. The beta factor is the gradient of the line. The beta factor of security can be calculated by using the following formula.

EXAM FORMULA

$$\beta_i = \frac{Cov_{i,m}}{\sigma_m^2}$$

where $Cov_{i,m}$ is the covariance between stock i's return and the market return and σ_m^2 is the variance of the market return.

2.2 EXAMPLE: CAPM (4)

The risk-free rate of return is 6% and the market rate of return is 11%. The standard deviation of returns for the market as a whole is 40%. The covariance of returns for the market with returns for the shares of Peapod plc is 19.2%. Since the variance is the square of a standard deviation, the beta value for Peapod plc is:

$$\frac{0.192}{0.4^2} = \frac{0.192}{0.16} = 1.20$$

The cost of equity capital for Peapod plc would therefore be 6% + (11 – 6) × 1.2% = 12%.

2.3 Another formula for calculating a share's beta factor is:

$$\beta = \frac{\sigma_s \rho_{sm}}{\sigma_m}$$

where

σ_s is the standard deviation of returns on the shares of a company

σ_m is the standard deviation of returns on equity for the market as a whole

ρ_{sm} is the correlation coefficient between total returns on equity for the stock market as a whole and total returns on the shares of the individual company.

2.4 EXAMPLE: CAPM (5)

We are given the following information.

The average stock market return on equity	=	15%
The risk-free rate of return (pre-tax)	=	8%
Company X: dividend yield	=	4%
Company X: share price rise (capital gain)	=	12%
Standard deviation of total stock market return on equity	=	9%
Standard deviation of total return on equity of Company X	=	10.8%
Correlation coefficient between Company X return on equity and average stock market return on equity	=	0.75

What is the beta factor for Company X shares, and what does this information imply for the actual returns and actual market value of Company X shares?

2.5 SOLUTION

(a) $\beta = \dfrac{\sigma_s \rho_{sm}}{\sigma_m}$

$= \dfrac{10.8\% \times 0.75}{9\%}$

$= 0.9$

(b) The cost of Company X equity should therefore be:

$r_s = 8\% + (15 - 8) \times 0.9\% = 14.3\%$

2.6 The actual returns on Company X equity are 4% + 12% = 16%. This implies that:

(a) the actual returns include extra returns due to unsystematic risk factors; or

(b) if there are no unsystematic risk factors, the price of Company X shares is currently lower than it should be.

Question 2

The standard deviation of market returns is 50%, and the expected market return ($E(r_m)$) is 12%. The risk-free rate of return is 9%. The covariance of returns for the market with returns on shares in Anxious plc has been 20%. Calculate a beta value and a cost of capital for Anxious plc equity.

Answer

(a) The variance of market returns is $0.50^2 = 0.25$.

$\beta = \dfrac{0.20}{0.25} = 0.8$

(b) Cost of Anxious equity = 9% + (12 – 9) × 0.8% = 11.4%

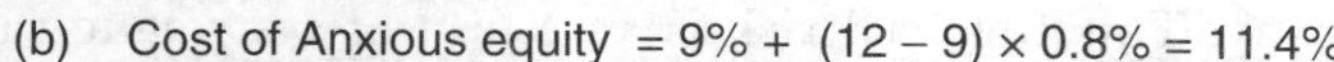

Exam focus point

You will not be expected to calculate beta factors from raw data in the exam.

3 CAPM AND PORTFOLIO MANAGEMENT

3.1 Just as an individual security has a beta factor, so too does a portfolio of securities.

(a) A portfolio consisting of all the securities on the stock market (in the same proportions as the market as a whole), excluding risk-free securities, will have an expected return equal to the expected return for the market as a whole, and so will have a beta factor of 1.

(b) A portfolio consisting entirely of risk-free securities will have a beta factor of 0.

(c) The beta factor of an investor's portfolio is the weighted average of the beta factors of the securities in the portfolio.

3.2 EXAMPLE: CAPM (6)

A portfolio consisting of five securities could have its beta factor computed as follows.

Security	*Percentage of portfolio*	*Beta factor of security*	*Weighted beta factor*
A plc	20%	0.90	0.180
B plc	10%	1.25	0.125
C plc	15%	1.10	0.165
D plc	20%	1.15	0.230
E plc	35%	0.70	0.245
	100%	Portfolio beta =	0.945

3.3 If the risk-free rate of return is 12% and the average market return is 20%, the expected return from the portfolio would be 12% + (20 – 12) × 0.945% = 19.56%

3.4 The calculation could have been made as follows.

Security	*Beta factor*	*Expected return* $E(r_j)$	*Weighting* %	*Weighted return*
A plc	0.90	19.2	20	3.84
B plc	1.25	22.0	10	2.20
C plc	1.10	20.8	15	3.12
D plc	1.15	21.2	20	4.24
E plc	0.70	17.6	35	6.16
			100	19.56

4 GEARING AND THE β VALUES OF COMPANIES' EQUITY

4.1 The gearing of a company will affect the risk of its equity. If a company is geared and its financial risk is therefore higher than the risk of an all-equity company, then the β value of the geared company's equity will be higher than the β value of a similar ungeared company's equity.

4.2 The CAPM is consistent with the propositions of Modigliani and Miller. MM argue that as gearing rises, the cost of equity rises to compensate shareholders for the extra financial risk of investing in a geared company. This financial risk is an aspect of systematic risk, and ought to be reflected in a company's beta factor.

Beta values and the effect of gearing: geared betas and ungeared betas

4.3 The connection between MM theory and the CAPM means that it is possible to establish a mathematical relationship between the β value of an ungeared company and the β value of a similar, but geared, company. The β value of a geared company will be higher than the β value of a company identical in every respect except that it is all-equity financed. This is because of the extra financial risk. The mathematical relationship between the 'ungeared' and 'geared' betas is as follows.

$$\beta_a = \beta_e \frac{E}{E+D(1-T_c)} + \beta_d \frac{D(1-T_c)}{E+D(1-T_c)}$$

where β_a is the beta factor of an ungeared company: the ungeared beta

β_e is the beta factor of equity in a similar, but geared company: the geared beta

β_d is the beta factor of debt in the geared company

D is the market value of the debt capital in the geared company

E is the market value of the equity capital in the geared company

T_c is the rate of corporation tax

4.4 Debt is often assumed to be risk-free and its beta (β_d) is then taken as zero, in which case the formula above reduces to the following form.

$$\beta_a = \beta_e \times \frac{E}{E+D(1-T_c)}$$

4.5 Re-arranging this, we have:

$$\beta_e = \beta_a \times \frac{E+D(1-T_c)}{E}$$

$$= \beta_a \left(1 + \frac{D(1-T_c)}{E}\right) = \beta_a + \beta_a \times \left(\frac{D(1-T_c)}{E}\right)$$

Note that the geared beta is equal to the ungeared beta plus a premium for financial risk which equals:

$$\beta_a \left[\frac{D(1-T_c)}{E}\right]$$

4.6 EXAMPLE: CAPM (7)

Two companies are identical in every respect except for their capital structure. Their market values are in equilibrium, as follows.

	Geared plc	*Ungeared plc*
	£'000	£'000
Annual profit before interest and tax	1,000	1,000
Less interest (4,000 × 8%)	320	0
	680	1,000
Less tax at 30%	204	300
Profit after tax = dividends	476	700
Market value of equity	3,900	6,600
Market value of debt	4,180	0
Total market value of company	8,080	6,600

The total value of Geared plc is higher than the total value of Ungeared plc, which is consistent with MM's proposition that $V_g = V_u + DT_c$.

All profits after tax are paid out as dividends, and so there is no dividend growth. The beta value of Ungeared plc has been calculated as 1.0. The debt capital of Geared plc can be regarded as risk-free.

Calculate:

(a) the cost of equity in Geared plc;
(b) the market return r_m;
(c) the beta value of Geared plc.

4.7 SOLUTION

(a) Since its market value (MV) is in equilibrium, the cost of equity in Geared plc can be calculated as:

$$\frac{d}{MV} = \frac{476}{3{,}900} = 12.20\%$$

(b) The beta value of Ungeared plc is 1.0, which means that the expected returns from Ungeared plc are exactly the same as the market returns, and the r_m = 700/6,600 = 10.6%.

(c) $$\beta_e = \beta_a \times \frac{E + D(1 - T_c)}{E}$$

$$= 1.0 \times \frac{3{,}900 + (4{,}180 \times 0.70)}{3{,}900} = 1.75$$

The beta of Geared plc, as we should expect, is higher than the beta of Ungeared plc.

Using the geared and ungeared beta formula to estimate a beta factor for a company

4.8 Another way of estimating a beta factor for a company's equity is to use data about the returns of other quoted companies which have similar operating characteristics: that is, to use the beta values of other companies' equity to estimate a beta value for the company under consideration. The beta values estimated for the firm under consideration must be adjusted to allow for differences in gearing from the firms whose equity beta values are known. The formula for geared and ungeared beta values can be applied.

4.9 EXAMPLE: CAPM

The management of Crispy plc wish to estimate their company's equity beta value. The company, which is an all-equity company, has only recently gone public and insufficient data is available at the moment about its own equity's performance to calculate the company's equity beta. Instead, it is thought possible to estimate Crispy's equity beta from the beta values of quoted companies operating in the same industry and with the same operating characteristics as Crispy.

Details of three similar companies are as follows. The tax rate is 30%.

(a) Snapp plc has an observed equity beta of 1.15. Its capital structure at market values is 70% equity and 30% debt. Snapp plc is very similar to Crispy plc except for its gearing.

(b) Crackle plc is an all-equity company. Its observed equity beta is 1.25. It has been estimated that 40% of the current market value of Crackle is caused by investment in projects which offer high growth, but which are more risky than normal operations and which therefore have a higher beta value. These investments have an estimated beta of 1.8, and are reflected in the company's overall beta value. Crackle's normal operations are identical to those of Crispy.

(c) Popper plc has an observed equity beta of 1.35. Its capital structure at market values is 60% equity and 40% debt. Popper has two divisions, X and Y. The operating characteristics of X are identical to those of Crispy but those of Y are thought to be

50% more risky than those of X. It is estimated that X accounts for 75% of the total value of Popper, and Y for 25%.

Required

(a) Assuming that all debt is virtually risk-free, calculate three estimates of the equity beta of Crispy, from the data available about Snapp, Crackle and Popper respectively.

(b) Now assume that Crispy plc is not an all-equity company, but instead is a geared company with a debt:equity ratio of 2:3 (based on market values). Estimate the equity beta of Crispy from the data available about Snapp.

4.10 SOLUTION

(a) **Snapp plc - based estimate**

$$\beta_e = \beta_a \times \frac{E + D(1 - T_c)}{E}$$

$$1.15 = \beta_a \times \frac{70 + 30(1 - 0.30)}{70}$$

$$1.15 = 1.3\beta_u$$

$$\beta_u = 0.88$$

(b) **Crackle plc - based estimate**

If the beta value of normal operations of Crackle is β_n, and we know that the high-risk operations have a beta value of 1.8 and account for 40% of Crackle's value, we can estimate a value for β_n.

Overall beta = 0.4(high risk beta) + 0.6(normal operations beta)

$$1.25 = 0.4(1.8) + 0.6\,\beta_n$$

$$\beta_n = 0.88$$

Since Crackle is an all-equity company, this provides the estimate of Crispy's equity beta.

(c) **Popper plc - based estimate**

It is easiest to arrive at an estimate of Crispy's equity beta by calculating the equity beta which Popper would have had if it had been an all-equity company instead of a geared company.

$$\beta_e = \beta_a \times \frac{E + D(1 - T_c)}{E}$$

$$1.35 = \beta_a \times \frac{0.6 + 0.4(1 - 0.30)}{0.6}$$

$$\beta_a = \frac{1.35}{1.47} = 0.92$$

This equity beta estimate for Popper plc is a weighted average of the beta values of divisions X and Y, so that:

$$0.92 = 0.75\beta_x + 0.25\beta_y$$

where β_x and β_y are the beta values for divisions X and Y respectively. We also know that Y is 50% more risky than X, so that $\beta_y = 1.5\beta_x$.

$$0.92 = 0.75\beta_x + 0.25(1.5\beta_x)$$

$\beta_x = 0.82$

Since Crispy plc is similar in characteristics to division X, the estimate of Crispy's equity beta is 0.82.

4.11 If Crispy plc is a geared company with a market-value based gearing ratio of 2:3, we can use the geared and ungeared beta formula again. The ungeared beta value, based on data about Snapp, was 0.88. The geared beta of Crispy would be estimated as:

$$\beta_e \quad = \quad 0.88 \times \frac{3+2(1-0.30)}{3} \quad = 1.29$$

Weaknesses in the formula

4.12 The problems with using the geared and ungeared beta formula for calculating a firm's equity beta from data about other firms are as follows.

(a) It is difficult to identify other firms with identical operating characteristics.

(b) Estimates of beta values from share price information are not wholly accurate. They are based on statistical analysis of historical data, and as the previous example shows, estimates using one firm's data will differ from estimates using another firm's data. The beta values for Crispy estimated from Snapp, Crackle and Popper are all different.

(c) There may be differences in beta values between firms caused by:

(i) different cost structures (eg, the ratio of fixed costs to variable costs);
(ii) size differences between firms;
(iii) debt capital not being risk-free;

(d) If the firm for which an equity beta is being estimated has opportunities for growth that are recognised by investors, and which will affect its equity beta, estimates of the equity beta based on other firms' data will be inaccurate, because the opportunities for growth will not be allowed for.

4.13 Perhaps the most significant simplifying assumption is that to link MM theory to the CAPM, it must be assumed that the cost of debt is a risk-free rate of return. This could obviously be unrealistic. Companies may default on interest payments or capital repayments on their loans. It has been estimated that corporate debt has a beta value of 0.2 or 0.3.

4.14 The consequence of making the assumption that debt is risk-free is that the formulae tend to **overstate** the financial risk in a geared company and to **understate** the business risk in geared and ungeared companies by a compensating amount. In other words, β_u will be slightly higher and β_g will be slightly lower than the formulae suggest.

5 PRACTICAL IMPLICATIONS OF THE CAPM

5.1 Practical implications of CAPM theory for an investor are as follows.

(a) He should decide what beta factor he would like to have for his portfolio. He might prefer a portfolio beta factor of greater than 1, in order to expect above-average returns when market returns exceed the risk-free rate, but he would then expect to lose heavily if market returns fall. On the other hand, he might prefer a portfolio beta factor of 1 or even less.

(b) He should seek to invest in shares with low beta factors in a bear market, when average market returns are falling. He should then also sell shares with high beta factors.

(c) He should seek to invest in shares with high beta factors in a bull market, when average market returns are rising.

An investor can measure the beta factor of his portfolio by obtaining information about the beta factors of individual securities. These are obtainable from a variety of investment analysts, or from the London Business School's Risk Management Service.

Limitations of the CAPM for the selection of a portfolio of securities

5.2 Under the CAPM, the return required from a security is related to its systematic risk rather than its total risk. If we relax some of the assumptions upon which the model is based, as follows, then the total risk may be important.

(a) The model assumes that the costs of insolvency are zero, or in other words, that all assets can be sold at going concern prices and that there are no selling, legal or other costs. In practice, the costs of insolvency cannot be ignored. Furthermore, the risk of insolvency is related to a firm's total risk rather than just its systematic risk.

(b) The model assumes that the investment market is efficient. If it is not, this will limit the extent to which investors are able to eliminate unsystematic risk from their portfolios.

(c) The model also assumes that portfolios are well diversified and so need only be concerned with systematic risk. However, this is not necessarily the case, and undiversified or partly diversified shareholders should also be concerned with unsystematic risk and will seek a total return appropriate to the total risk that they face.

5.3 The major sources of difficulty in applying the CAPM in practice are:

(a) the need to determine the excess return $(E(r_m) - r_f)$. Expected, rather than historical, returns should be used, although historical returns are used in practice;

(b) the need to determine the risk-free rate. A risk-free investment might be a government security. However, interest rates vary with the term of the lending;

(c) errors in the statistical analysis used to calculate β values.

5.4 Beta factors based on historical data may be a poor basis for future decision-making. Evidence from a US study suggests that stocks with high or low betas tend to be fairly stable over time, but this may not always be so. Financial managers should preferably use betas for industrial sectors rather than individual company betas, as measurement errors will tend to cancel each other out. Beta values may change over time, for example if luxury items produced by a company become regarded as necessities, or if the cost structure (eg the proportion of fixed costs) of a business change. The CAPM is also unable to forecast accurately returns for companies with low price/earnings ratios and to take account of seasonal 'month-of-the-year' effects and 'day-of-the-week' effects that appear to influence returns on shares.

CAPM and international investment decisions 11/98

5.5 The CAPM is based on three elements:

- **The beta factor,** which measures the systematic risk of the company, that is, the risk attaching to the company's operations that cannot be eliminated through diversification.

- **The risk-free rate of return** in the country in which the company operates.

- **The market rate of return** in the country in which the company operates.

5.6 Problems in using the model for investment appraisal in an international context arise from the fact that where the company is raising funds and operating in a number of countries, it may be difficult to establish exactly what the risk-free and market rates of return are. Even within one country, the return on government securities (which is used to estimate the risk-free rate) varies according to their term to maturity, and the problems of estimation increase when the economic situation in more than one country has to be taken into account. Similarly it can be hard to estimate an equity beta for the operations of the firm as a whole. In practice, an international company will normally base its calculations on conditions in its home country, even though it may raise capital and operate in many different countries.

6 THE ARBITRAGE PRICING MODEL

Exam focus point

What is important here is to be aware that there are other models apart from the CAPM, and to know the benefits and limitations of the arbitrage pricing model (APM) relative to the CAPM. *Detailed* knowledge of the APM and calculations based on it will not be required.

6.1 The CAPM is seen as a useful analytical tool by financial managers as well as by financial analysts. However, critics suggest that the relationship between risk and return is more complex than is assumed in the CAPM. One model which could replace the CAPM in the future is the **arbitrage pricing model (APM)**.

6.2 Unlike the CAPM, which analyses the returns on a share as a function of a single factor - the return on the market portfolio - the APM assumes that the return on each security is based on a number of independent macroeconomic factors. The actual return r on any security is shown as:

$$r = E(r_j) + \beta_1 F_1 + \beta_2 F_2 ... + e$$

where $E(r_j)$ is the expected return on the security
β_1 is the sensitivity to changes in factor 1
F_1 is the difference between actual and expected values of factor 1
β_2 is the sensitivity to changes in factor 2
F_2 is the difference between actual and expected values of factor 2
e is a random term

KEY TERM

Arbitrage pricing theory: a model which assumes that the return on a security is based on a number of independent factors, to each of which a particular risk premium is attached.

6.3 Factor analysis is used to ascertain the factors to which security returns are sensitive. Four key factors identified by researchers have been:

(a) unanticipated inflation;
(b) changes in the expected level of industrial production;
(c) changes in the risk premium on bonds (debentures);
(d) unanticipated changes in the term structure of interest rates.

6.4 If a certain combination of securities is expected to produce higher returns than is indicated by its risk sensitivities, then traders will engage in arbitrage trading to improve the expected returns. It has been demonstrated that when no further arbitrage opportunities exist, the expected return $E(r_j)$ can be shown as:

$$E(r_j) = r_f + \beta_1(r_1 - r_f) + \beta_2(r_2 - r_f) \ldots$$

where r_f is the risk-free rate of return

r_1 is the expected return on a portfolio with unit sensitivity to factor 1 and no sensitivity to any other factor

r_2 is the expected return on a portfolio with unit sensitivity to factor 2 and no sensitivity to any other factor

6.5 This implies that the expected rate of return on a security is a function of the risk-free rate of return plus risk premiums ($(r_1 - r_f)$, $(r_2 - r_f)$ etc) depending on the sensitivity of the security to various factors such as the four factors identified in Paragraph 6.3 above.

6.6 With the APM, the CAPM's problem of identifying the market portfolio is avoided, but this is replaced with the problem of identifying the macroeconomic factors and their risk sensitivities. As with the CAPM, the available empirical evidence is inconclusive and neither proves nor disproves the theory of the APM. Both the CAPM and the APM do however provide a means of analysing how risk and return may be determined in conditions of competition and uncertainty.

Chapter roundup

- The **capital asset pricing model** has many applications. However, you should not think of it as the only approach to the cost of equity, or to project appraisal. You should learn the formulae, not only to be able to use them but also to be able to criticise the CAPM.
- The **risk** involved in holding securities (shares) divides into risk specific to the company and risk due to variations in market activity.
- **Unsystematic or business risk** can be diversified away, while **systematic or market risk** cannot. Investors may mix a diversified market portfolio with risk-free assets to achieve a preferred mix of risk and return on the **Capital Market Line** (see Chapter 12).
- In the future, the **arbitrage pricing model** could replace the capital asset pricing model as a tool for analysing the **determination of risk and return**.

Quick quiz

1. Distinguish between systematic risk and unsystematic risk. (see paras 1.3, 1.4)
2. State the formula for the CAPM (the security market line). (1.22)
3. What is meant by a share's alpha value? (1.23)
4. Which portfolios will have a beta factor of (a) one and (b) zero? (3.1)
5. Explain briefly how the gearing of a company affects its beta value. (4.1)
6. Outline the main practical problems in using the CAPM in capital investment decisions. (5.2 - 5.4)
7. Outline the main features of the arbitrage pricing model. (6.2 - 6.5)

Question to try	Level	Marks	Time
13(b)-(d)	Introductory	n/a	15 mins

Chapter 14

INTEREST RATE RISK

Chapter topic list		Syllabus reference	Ability required
1	Interest rate risk	13 b(xi)	Skill
2	Interest rate futures	13 b(xi)	Skill
3	Interest rate swaps	13 b(xi)	Skill
4	Interest rate options	13 b(xi)	Skill
5	Hedging strategy alternatives: example	13 b(xi)	Skill

Introduction

Here we consider **interest rate risk** and some of the financial instruments which are now available for managing financial risks, including **'derivatives'** such as **options** and **swaps**. The risk of interest rate changes is however less significant in most cases than the risk of currency fluctuations which, in some circumstances, can fairly easily wipe out profits entirely if it is not hedged. **Currency risk** or **foreign exchange risk** is considered later in the Study Text.

1 INTEREST RATE RISK 11/98

Managing a debt portfolio

1.1 There are three important considerations for corporate treasurers in managing a debt portfolio, that is, in deciding how a company should obtain its short-term funds so as to be able to repay debts as they mature and to minimise any inherent risks, notably foreign exchange risk, in the debts the company owes and is owed. These three considerations are as follows.

(a) **Maturity mix**. The treasurer must avoid having too much debt becoming repayable within a short period.

(b) **Currency mix**. Foreign currency debts create a risk of losses through adverse movements in foreign exchange rates before the debt falls due for payment. Foreign currency management involves hedging against foreign currency risks, for example by means of forward exchange contracts, or having debts in several currencies, some of which will strengthen and some of which will weaken over time.

(c) **The mix of fixed interest and floating rate debts**

(i) Too much fixed interest rate debt creates an unnecessary cost when market interest rates fall. A company might find itself committed to high interest costs that it could have avoided.

(ii) Too much borrowing at a variable rate of interest (such as bank overdrafts and medium-term bank lending) leads to high costs when interest rates go up.

Interest rate exposure and hedging

1.2 The variability of interest rates over time can be appreciated from the table below.

Selected UK interest rates

	Treasury bill yield	*Selected retail bank base rates*	*Inter-bank 3 month offer rate*	*Sterling certificates of deposit 3 months offer rate*	*Euro-dollar 3 month rate*	*Long dated (20 years) UK gilts yields*
1990	13.50	14.00	14.00	13.88	7.50	11.08
1991	10.45	10.50	11.00	10.88	4.19	9.92
1992	6.44	7.00	7.19	6.91	3.32	9.13
1993	4.95	5.50	5.31	5.25	3.28	7.87
1994	6.00	6.25	6.56	6.44	6.44	8.05
1995	6.31	6.50	6.50	6.47	5.54	8.26
1996	6.26	6.00	6.44	6.41	5.50	8.10
1997	7.13	7.25	7.63	7.59	5.69	7.09

(Source: Economic Trends)

1.3 There are a number of situations in which a company might be exposed to risk from interest rate movements.

(a) **Fixed rate versus floating rate debt.** A company can get caught paying higher interest rates by having fixed rather than floating rate debt, or floating rather than fixed rate debt, as market interest rates change.

(b) **Currency of debt.** This is also a foreign currency exposure. A company can face higher costs if it borrows in a currency for which exchange rates move adversely against the company's domestic currency. The treasurer should seek to match the currency of the loan with the currency of the underlying operations/assets that generate revenue to pay interest/repay the loans.

(c) **Term of loan.** A company can be exposed by having to repay a loan earlier than it can afford to, resulting in a need to re-borrow, perhaps at a higher rate of interest.

(d) **Term loan or overdraft facility?** A company might prefer to pay for borrowings only when it needs the money as with an overdraft facility: the bank will charge a commitment fee for such a facility. Alternatively, a term loan might be preferred, but this will cost interest even if it is not needed in full for the whole term.

1.4 Where the magnitude of the risk is immaterial in comparison with the company's overall cash flows, one option is to do nothing and to accept the effects of any movement in interest rates which occur.

Exam focus point

Bear in mind this possibility - the decision *not* to take action to reduce interest rate risk - when answering questions in the exam.

Hedge efficiency

KEY TERM

Hedge: a transaction to reduce or eliminate an exposure to risk *(OT)*.

1.5 **Hedging** is the process of financial risk management. Hedging has a cost, either a fee to a financial institution or a reduction in profit, but companies might well consider the costs to be justified by the reduction in financial risks that the hedging achieves. The degree to which the exposure is covered is termed the **hedge efficiency**: a perfect hedge has 100% efficiency.

Interest rate risk management

1.6 Methods of reducing interest rate risk include forward rate interest agreements (FRAs), interest rate futures, interest rate options (or interest rate guarantees), interest rate swaps and options on interest rate swaps ('swaptions'). In the remainder of this section, we look at FRAs, before considering interest rate futures, options and swaps.

Forward interest rate agreements (FRAs)

1.7 FRAs are agreements, typically between a company and a bank, about the interest rate on future borrowing or bank deposits. For example, a company can enter into a FRA with a bank that fixes the rate of interest for borrowing at a certain time in the future. If the actual interest rate proves to be higher than the rate agreed, the bank pays the company the difference. If the actual interest rate is lower than the rate agreed, the company pays the bank the difference.

1.8 One limitation on FRAs is that they are usually only available on loans of at least £500,000. They are also likely to be difficult to obtain for periods of over one year.

1.9 An advantage of FRAs is that, for the period of the FRA at least, they protect the borrower from adverse market interest rate movements to levels above the rate negotiated for the FRA. With a normal variable rate loan (for example linked to a bank's base rate or to LIBOR) the borrower is exposed to the risk of such adverse market movements. On the other hand, the borrower will similarly not benefit from the effects of favourable market interest rate movements.

1.10 The interest rates which banks will be willing to set for FRAs will reflect their current expectations of interest rate movements. If it is expected that interest rates are going to rise during the term for which the FRA is being negotiated, the bank is likely to seek a higher fixed rate of interest than the variable rate of interest which is current at the time of negotiating the FRA.

Question 1

Explain what is meant by hedging in the context of interest rate risk.

Answer

Hedging is a means of reducing risk. Hedging involves coming to an agreement with another party who is prepared to take on the risk that you would otherwise bear. The other party may be willing to take on that risk because he would otherwise bear an opposing risk which may be 'matched' with your risk; alternatively, the other party may be a speculator who is willing to bear the risk in return for the prospect of making a profit. In the case of interest rates, a company with a variable rate loan clearly faces the risk that the rate of interest will increase in the future as the result of changing market conditions which cannot now be predicted.

Many financial instruments have been introduced in recent years to help corporate treasurers to hedge the risks of interest rate movements. These instruments include forward rate agreements, financial futures, interest rate swaps, options, and options on interest rate swaps ('swaptions').

Gap analysis of interest rate risk

1.11 The degree to which a firm is exposed to interest rate risk can be identified by using the method of **gap analysis**.

1.12 Some of the interest rate risks to which a firm is exposed may cancel each other out, where there are both assets and liabilities with which there is exposure to interest rate changes. If interest rates rise, more interest will be payable on loans and other liabilities, but this will be compensated for by higher interest received on assets such as money market deposits.

1.13 The effect of interest rate changes depends upon whether interest rates for the assets and liabilities are floating or fixed. Floating interest rates, of course, move up and down according to general market conditions. With fixed interest rates, the interest on the asset or liability will only be repriced at the date of maturity in the light of prevailing market conditions. If a fixed interest rate liability matures at the same time as a fixed rate asset, then the interest rate risks arising from the repricing of the two instruments will cancel each other out.

1.14 Gap analysis is based on the principle of grouping together assets and liabilities which are sensitive to interest rate changes according to their maturity dates. Two different types of 'gap' may occur.

(a) **A negative gap**. A negative gap occurs when a firm has a larger amount of interest-sensitive liabilities maturing at a certain time or in a certain period than it has interest-sensitive assets maturing at the same time. The difference between the two amounts indicates the net exposure.

(b) **A positive gap**. There is a positive gap if the amount of interest-sensitive assets maturing in a particular time exceeds the amount of interest-sensitive liabilities maturing at the same time.

1.15 With a negative gap, the company faces exposure if interest rates rise by the time of maturity. With a positive gap, the company will lose out if interest rates fall by maturity. The company's interest rate hedge should be based on the size of the gap.

Duration analysis

1.16 In the case of bonds, the return is comprised of both interest and a capital gain or loss accruing during the bond's life. Therefore, it is not possible simply to match bonds on the basis of a period to maturity. What can be done is to base the analysis on the 'notional' time to maturity or the **duration** of the bond.

Exam focus point

The calculations necessary for duration analysis are beyond the scope of the syllabus, and you need only be aware of the general principles.

1.17 The duration of the bond is calculated as the weighted average period to maturity of the cashflows of a bond, the weights being the present value of the cashflows arising from the bond. Note that:

(a) for a zero coupon bond, the duration is the same as the period to actual maturity;
(b) for coupon bearing bonds, the duration is less than the period to maturity.

2 INTEREST RATE FUTURES 11/98

2.1 Most LIFFE (London International Financial Futures and Options Exchange) futures contracts involve interest rates (interest rate futures), and these offer a means of hedging against the risk of interest rate movements. Such contracts are effectively a gamble on whether interest rates will rise or fall. Like other futures contracts, interest rate futures offer a way in which speculators can 'bet' on market movements just as they offer others who are more risk-averse a way of hedging risks.

KEY TERM

A **futures contract** is an agreement to buy or sell a standard quantity of a particular financial instrument at a specified future date at an agreed price - the price being determined by trading on the floor of a futures exchange.

2.2 For example, a company can contract to buy (or sell) £100,000 of a notional 30-year Treasury bond bearing an 8% coupon, in say, 6 months time, at an agreed price.

(a) The futures price is likely to vary with changes in interest rates, and this acts as a hedge against adverse interest rate movements.

(b) The outlay to buy futures is much less than for buying the financial instrument itself, and so a company can hedge large exposures of cash with a relatively small initial employment of cash.

2.3 LIFFE provides a market for futures contracts in long-dated, medium-dated and short-dated gilt-edged stocks, American, German and Japanese government bonds, short-term sterling and eurocurrency interest rates. The **Chicago Mercantile Exchange (CME)** and the **Chicago Board of Trade (CBOT)** are other important exchanges for the trading of interest rate futures.

2.4 Interest rate futures are similar in effect to FRAs, except that the terms, the amounts and the periods are standardised. The pricing of an interest rate futures contract is determined by prevailing interest rates. For example, if three month eurodollar time deposit interest rates are 8%, a three month eurodollar futures contract will be priced at 92 (100 – 8). If interest rates are 11%, the contract price will be 89 (100 – 11). As with currency futures, the minimum amount by which the price of a interest rate futures contract can move is called a **tick**.

The effects of price movements

2.5 A tick or point of price has a known, measurable value. Here are some examples.

(a) In the case of 3-month eurodollar futures, the amount of the underlying instrument is a 3-month deposit of $1,000,000. As a tick is 0.01 (or one-hundredth of one per cent), the value of a tick is $25 (0.01% × $1,000,000 × 3/12).

(b) In the case of long gilt futures, the underlying instrument is £50,000 of notional gilts. Given that a tick is 1/32 of one per cent, the value of one tick is £15.625 (1/32 × 1% × £50,000).

2.6 Interest rate futures are not all priced in the same way.

(a) Prices of short-term interest rate futures, which, as already indicated, reflect the interest rates on the underlying financial instrument, are quoted at a discount to a par value of 100. For example, a price of 93.40 indicates that the underlying money market deposit is being traded at a rate of 6.6% (100 – 93.40).

(b) Pricing for long-term bond futures is as a percentage of par value, similarly to the pricing of bonds themselves.

   (i) In the case of US Treasury bond futures and Notional UK gilt futures, prices are quoted in 32nds of each full percentage point of price. The number of 32nds is shown as a number following a hyphen. For example, 91-23 denotes a price of $91^{23}/_{32}$ per 100 nominal value and 91-16 denotes a price of $91^{1}/_{2}$ per 100 nominal value.

   (ii) For other types of bond future, decimal pricing is used, so that if Italian government bond futures are quoted at 92.75, this indicates a price of $92^{3}/_{4}$ per 100 nominal value.

2.7 EXAMPLE: FUTURES PRICE MOVEMENTS (1)

June 3-month ecu futures fell in price on a particular day from 96.84 to 96.76. Privet plc has purchased June futures, having a long position on five contracts. Calculate the change in value of the contracts on the day concerned.

2.8 SOLUTION

The fall in price represents 8 ticks (96.84 – 96.76 = 0.08 and the tick size is 0.01%). The value of one tick is 25 ecus. Each contract has fallen in value by 25 × 8 = 200 ecus. Privet plc has bought five contracts and so the day's price movement represents for the company a loss on the contracts of 200 × 5 = 1,000 ecus.

2.9 EXAMPLE: FUTURES PRICE MOVEMENTS (2)

September long gilts sterling futures fell in price on a particular day from 99-9 to 98-27. Privet plc has sold September futures, having a short position of 10 contracts. Calculate the change in value of the contract on the day concerned.

2.10 SOLUTION

The fall in price represents 14 ticks ($99^{9}/_{32}$ – $98^{27}/_{32}$ = $^{14}/_{32}$ and the tick size is $^{1}/_{32}$ of 1%). The value of one tick for long gilts sterling futures is £15.625. Each contract has fallen in value by £15.625 × 14 = £218.75. For Privet plc, which has sold 10 contracts, the day's price movement represents a profit of £218.75 × 10 = £2,187.50.

Question 2

The following futures price movements were observed during a week in October.

Contract	*Price at start of week*	*Price at end of week*
December short sterling	90.40	91.02
December US Treasury bonds	92-16	92-06
December Japanese government bond	93.80	94.25

Hawthorn plc has the following positions in these contracts:

(a) a short position (seller) of ten December short sterling contracts;

(b) a long position (buyer) of six December US Treasury bonds contracts;
(c) a long position of eight December Japanese government bonds contracts.

See the table earlier in this section giving notional deposit amounts and tick sizes and values.

Required

Calculate the profit or loss to the company on the futures contracts.

Answer

Short sterling

Increase in price (91.02 – 90.40 = 0.62)	62 ticks
Value per tick	£12.50
Increase in value of one contract (62 × £12.50)	£775

The company is a seller of ten contracts and would lose £7,750 (£775 × 10)

US Treasury bond futures

Fall in price ($92^{16}/_{32}$ – $92^{6}/_{32}$ = 10/32)	10 ticks
Value per tick	$31.25
Fall in value of one contract (10 × $31.25)	$312.50

The company is a buyer of six contracts and would lose $1,875 ($312.50 × 6)

Japanese government bonds

Increase in price (94.25 – 93.80 = 0.45)	45 ticks
Value per tick	Y10,000
Increase in value of one contract (45 × Y10,000)	Y450,000

The company is a buyer of eight contracts and would gain Y3,600,000 (Y450,000 × 8)

2.11 EXAMPLE: INTEREST RATE HEDGE USING FUTURES

Yew plc has taken a 3 month $1,000,000 eurodollar deposit with interest payable of 8%, the loan being due for rollover on 31 March. At 1 January, the company treasurer considers that interest rates are likely to rise in the near future. The futures price is 91 representing a yield of 9%. Given a standard contract size of $1,000,000 the company sells a eurodollar three month contract to hedge against interest on the three month loan required at 31 March (to sell a contract is to commit the seller to take a deposit). At 31 March the spot interest rate is 11%.

(a) What is the cost saving to Yew plc?
(b) Calculate the hedge efficiency.

2.12 SOLUTION

(a) The company can buy back the future at 89 (100 – 11). The cost saving is the profit on the futures contract.

$$\$1,000,000 \times (91 - 89) \times {}^{3}/_{12} = \$5,000$$

(b) The additional interest cost resulting from the increase in interest rates is $1,000,000 × 3% × ³/₁₂ = $7,500. Hedge efficiency = $5,000 ÷ 7,500 = 66.7%.

The hedge has effectively reduced the new interest cost by 2%. Instead of a cost of 11% at 31 March ($27,500) for a three month deposit, the net cost is $22,500 ($27,500 – 5,000).

Use of interest rate futures

2.13 The standardised nature of interest rate futures is a limitation on their use by the corporate treasurer as a means of hedging, because they cannot always be matched with specific interest rate exposures. However, their use if growing. Global trading in interest rate futures rose from around 20,000 contracts in 1975 to 156 million contracts by 1988, and by 1988 interest rate futures made up of 42% of the total volume of futures trading. Futures contracts are frequently used by banks and other financial institutions as a means of hedging their portfolios: such institutions are often not concerned with achieving an exact match with their underlying exposure.

2.14 The seller of a futures contract does not have to own the underlying instrument, but may need to deliver it on the contract's delivery date if the buyer requires it. Many, but not all, interest rate contracts are settled for cash rather than by delivery of the underlying instrument.

2.15 Interest rate futures offer an attractive means of speculation for some investors, because there is no requirement that buyers and sellers should actually be lenders and borrowers (respectively) of the nominal amounts of the contracts. A relatively small investment can lead to substantial gains, or alternatively to substantial losses. The speculator is in effect 'betting' on future interest rate movements.

Basis risk

2.16 The concept of hedge efficiency was introduced earlier. There are two reasons why it is often not possible to achieve a perfect (100%) hedge with currency futures or interest rate futures, as follows.

(a) The fact that futures are available only in certain standard sizes means that the contracts may not fit exactly the company's needs.

(b) There is also **basis risk,** which we mentioned earlier in the context of currency futures, arising from the fact that the price of the futures contract may not move as expected in relation to the value of the instrument which is being hedged. There are two main reasons for basis risk.

  (i) Cashflow requirements may differ, altering the relative values of the underlying financial instrument and the derivative futures contract. This is because usually no payment is required when a forward contract is entered into, while an initial margin must be deposited for a futures contract.

  (ii) The financial instrument which the firm is seeking to hedge may be different from the financial instrument which underlies the futures contract. For example, a firm may wish to hedge interest rates which are linked to bank base interest rates using a futures contract which is based on the London Inter-Bank Offer Rate (LIBOR). This type of hedge is called cross hedging, and there will be basis risk because LIBOR will not always move exactly in line with bank base interest rates.

Hedge ratio

2.17 The **hedge ratio** is the ratio of the amount of the futures contracts bought or sold to the amount of the underlying financial instrument being hedged. For example, if a company is exposed to interest rate risk on a loan of £210,000 and it takes a position in futures contracts for £200,000, the hedge ratio is:

$$\frac{200,000}{210,000} = 95.2\%$$

3 INTEREST RATE SWAPS 11/96

KEY TERM

Swap: An arrangement whereby two organisations contractually agree to exchange payments on different terms, eg in different currencies or one at a fixed rate and the other at a floating rate *(OT)*.

3.1 **Interest rate swaps** are transactions that exploit different interest rates in different markets for borrowing, to reduce interest costs for either fixed or floating rate loans.

KEY TERM

An **interest rate swap** is an arrangement whereby two companies, or a company and a bank, swap interest rate commitments with each other. In a sense, each simulates the other's borrowings, with the following effects.

(a) A company which has debt at a fixed rate of interest can make a swap so that it ends up paying interest at a variable rate.

(b) A company which has debt at a variable rate of interest (floating rate debt) ends up paying a fixed rate of interest.

3.2 Note that the parties to a swap retain their obligations to the original lenders. This means that the parties must accept **counterparty risk**. An example is illustrated in Figure 1.

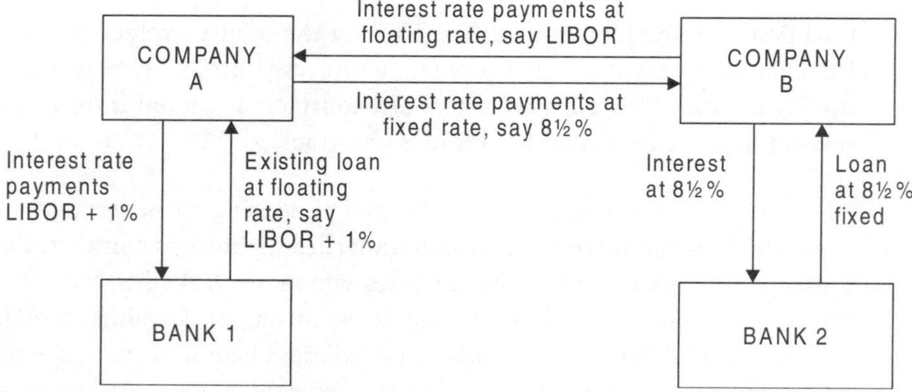

Figure 1 Interest rate swap

3.3 In this example, company A can use a swap to change from paying interest at a floating rate of LIBOR + 1% to one of paying fixed interest of (8½% + 1%) = 9½%.

3.4 A swap may be arranged with a bank, or a counterparty may be found through a bank or other financial intermediary.

3.5 Interest rate swaps could be arranged in different currencies, for example between a fixed rate in US dollars and a floating rate in sterling. Where this happens, the swaps are normally reversed with the principal eventually swapped back at the original exchange rate. For example, a UK company and a US company can arrange a back-to-back loan and currency swap (Figure 2).

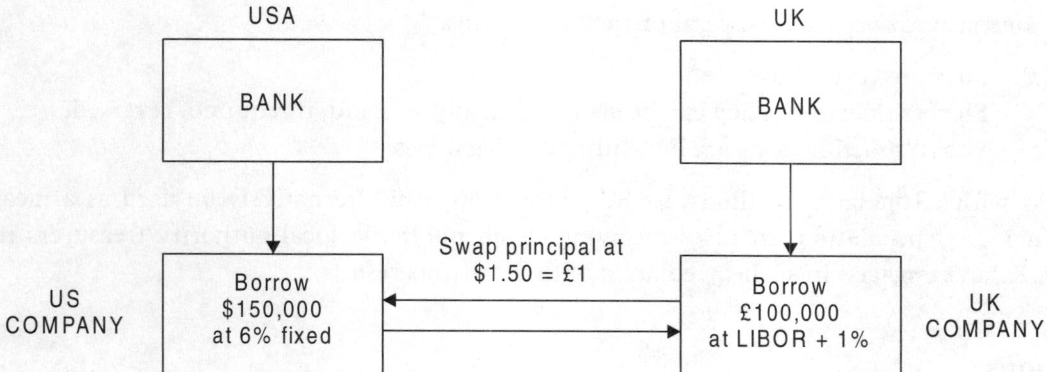

Figure 2 Back-to-back loan and currency swap

3.6 The companies can service each other's debt (interest rate swap) and also exchange the principal, with the UK company taking $150,000 and the US company taking £100,000 (currency swap). Each company will eventually repay the principal on each other's loans at a rate of $1.50 = £1.

3.7 EXAMPLE: INTEREST RATE SWAPS

Goodcredit plc has been given a high credit rating. It can borrow at a fixed rate of 11%, or at a variable interest rate equal to LIBOR, which also happens to be 11% at the moment. It would like to borrow at a variable rate.

Secondtier plc is a company with a lower credit rating, which can borrow at a fixed rate of 12½% or at a variable rate of LIBOR plus ½%. It would like to borrow at a fixed rate.

(a) Without a swap, Goodcredit would borrow at LIBOR which is currently 11%, and Secondtier would borrow at 12½% fixed.

(b) With a swap,

  (i) Goodcredit would borrow at a fixed rate (11%);

  (ii) Secondtier would borrow at a variable rate (LIBOR plus ½%), currently 11½%.

  (iii) They would then agree a rate for swapping interest, perhaps with:

    (1) Goodcredit paying Secondtier variable rate interest, at LIBOR;
    (2) Secondtier paying Goodcredit fixed rate interest, say at 11½%.

3.8 The net result is as follows.

Goodcredit plc		*Secondtier plc*	
Pays		Pays	
to bank	(11%)	to bank	(LIBOR plus ½%)
in swap	(LIBOR)	in swap	(11½%)
Receives		Receives	
in swap	11½%	in swap	LIBOR
Net interest cost	LIBOR less ½%	Net interest cost	12%

The results of the swap are that Goodcredit ends up paying variable rate interest, but at a lower cost than it could get from a bank, and Secondtier ends up paying fixed rate interest, also at a lower cost than it could get from investors or a bank.

Other advantages of swaps

3.9 Interest rate swaps have several further attractions.

(a) They are easy to arrange.
(b) They are flexible. They can be arranged in any size and, if required, reversed.
(c) The transaction costs are low, limited to legal fees.

As with all hedging methods, interest rate swaps can alternatively be used as a means of financial speculation. In cases receiving much publicity, local authority treasurers in the UK have engaged in such speculation with disastrous results.

Swaptions

3.10 Among the various 'hybrid' hedging instruments available which combine the features of different financial instruments is the **swaption.** A swaption is an instrument which is traded on a market in the writing/purchasing of **options to buy an interest rate swap**. For example, A Ltd might buy a swaption from a bank, giving A Ltd the right, but not the obligation, to enter into an interest rate swap arrangement with the bank at or before a specified time in the future.

3.11 A swaption offers a borrower protection against rises in interest rates and at the same time allows it to take advantage of falls in rates. A '**European-style**' **swaption** is exercisable only on the maturity date while an '**American-style**' **swaption** is exercisable on any business day during the exercise period.

3.12 EXAMPLE: SWAPTIONS

It is now 1 January 19X6. Towyn plc pays a variable rate of interest on a $1,000,000 eurodollar loan which is due to mature on 30 June 19X9. The interest rate currently payable on this loan is 6.75% per annum. The company treasurer is now concerned about the possibility of interest rates rises over the near future.

The company's bank has indicated that an American-style dollar swaption is available with the following features.

Interest rate 7.5%
Exercise period 1 July 19X6 to 31 December 19X6
Maturity date 30 June 19X9
Premium $20,000

Required

Assess under what circumstances Towyn plc will gain from exercising the swaption. (Ignore the time value of money.)

3.13 SOLUTION

The swaption would be likely to be exercised if interest rates rose above 7.5% during the next nine months. To evaluate the benefit of the swaption, ignoring the time value of money, it is first necessary to evaluate its cost over the remaining three year period of the loan.

	$
Interest: $1,000,000 × 7.5% × 3	225,000
Premium	20,000
Total cost	245,000

This represents an effective annual rate of interest of 8.17% ($245,000/($1,000,000 × 3)). The average rate of interest payable by the company without the swap would therefore have to exceed 8.17% for the swaption to be beneficial. If interest rates fall, the swaption will not be exercised and the company will be able to advantage of the lower interest payments.

The company should also take into account the fact that if it does not enter into the agreement the premium will be payable whether or not the swaption was exercised. The premium is effectively the price paid for the possibility of taking advantage of lower interest rates.

4 INTEREST RATE OPTIONS 11/98

Over-the-counter interest rate options

4.1 An **interest rate option** grants the buyer of it the right, but not the obligation, to deal at an agreed interest rate (strike rate) at a future maturity date. On the date of expiry of the option, the buyer must decide whether or not to exercise the right. Clearly, a buyer of an option to borrow will not wish to exercise it if the market interest rate is now below that specified in the option agreement. Conversely, an option to lend will not be worth exercising if market rates have risen above the rate specified in the option by the time the option has expired.

The term **interest rate guarantee (IRG)** refers to an interest rate option which hedges the interest rate for a single period of up to one year.

4.2 Tailor-made **'over-the-counter' interest rate options** can be purchased from major banks, with specific values, periods of maturity, denominated currencies and rates of agreed interest. The cost of the option is the 'premium'. Interest rate options offer more flexibility than and are more expensive than FRAs.

Caps, floors and collars

4.3 Various **cap** and **collar** agreements are possible. An interest rate **cap** is an option which sets an interest rate ceiling. A **floor** is an option which sets a lower limit to interest rates. Using a 'collar' arrangement, the borrower can buy an interest rate cap and at the same time sell an interest rate floor which fixes a minimum cost for the company. The cost is lower than for a cap alone. However, the borrowing company forgoes the benefit of movements in interest rates below the floor limit in exchange for this cost reduction. A **zero cost collar** can even be negotiated sometimes, if the premium paid for buying the cap equals the premium received for selling the floor.

4.4 EXAMPLE: CAP AND COLLAR

Suppose the prevailing interest rate for a company's borrowing is 10%. The company treasurer considers that a rise in rates above 12% will cause serious financial difficulties for the company. How can the treasurer make use of a 'cap and collar' arrangement?

4.5 SOLUTION

The company can buy an interest rate cap from the bank. The bank will reimburse the company for the effects of a rise in rates above 12%. As part of the arrangements with the bank, the company can agree that it will pay at least 9%, say, as a 'floor' rate. The bank will pay the company for agreeing this. In other words, the company has sold the floor to the bank, which partly offsets the costs of the cap. The bank benefits if rates fall below the floor level.

Traded interest rate options

4.6 Exchange-traded interest rate options are available as **options on interest rate futures,** which give the holder the right to buy (call option) or sell (put option) one futures contract on or before the expiry of the option at a specified price. The best way to understand the pricing of interest rate options is to look at a schedule of prices. The schedule below (from the *Financial Times*) is for 8 August in a particular year.

Long gilt futures options (LIFFE) £50,000 64th of 100%

Strike	*Calls*				*Puts*			
price	*Sep*	*Oct*	*Nov*	*Dec*	*Sep*	*Oct*	*Nov*	*Dec*
106	0-61	1-09	1-34	1-54	0-31	1-13	1-38	1-58
107	0-29	0-46	1-05	1-25	0-63	1-50	2-09	2-29
108	0-11	0-26	0-47	1-01	1-45	2-30	2-51	3-05

4.7 The tick size (minimum price movement) is $^1/_{64}$% and the tick value is thus $^1/_{64}$% × 50,000 = £7.8125.

4.8 The price of an October call contract at a strike price of 106 is $1^9/_{64}$% × 50,000 = £570.31. This means that an investor could pay £570.31 and buy one long gilt futures option which would allow him to purchase a notional 9% UK gilt in October at a price of £106 per £100 stock.

4.9 Here is another schedule of prices for options on interest rate futures (again, for 8 August).

Short sterling options (LIFFE) £500,000 points of 100%

Strike	*Calls*			*Puts*		
Price	*Sep*	*Dec*	*Mar*	*Sep*	*Dec*	*Mar*
9300	0.19	0.31	0.38	0.05	0.21	0.40
9325	0.05	0.17	0.26	0.16	0.32	0.53
9350	0.01	0.09	0.17	0.37	0.49	0.69

4.10 This schedule shows that an investor could pay 0.19 × £500,000 = £950 to purchase the right to buy a three-month sterling futures contract in September at a price of 93.00.

4.11 EXAMPLE: TRADED INTEREST RATE OPTIONS

The following traded option on interest rate futures is available: **LIFFE Short sterling options £500,000 points of 100%.** On a day in April, a September put option with a strike price of 9300 was quoted at a premium of 0.69.

4.12 This shows that the purchaser of the option has the right to sell one £500,000 3-month sterling futures contract in September at a price of 93.00 on the futures market for a premium of 0.69%.

The total premium on one contract would be £500,000 × 0.69/100 = £3,450.

If, say, in June, September 3-month sterling futures are priced **below** 93.00 (reflecting an interest rate **rise**), the option will be exercised. In calculating any gain from the option, the premium cost must also be taken into account.

The profit for each contract is:

(93 – current futures price – 0.69) × 100 ticks

To evaluate a hedge, this profit will be set against extra interest costs incurred due to the interest rate increase.

4.13 If the futures price moves **higher,** as it is likely to if interest rates **fall,** the option will not be exercised. To evaluate a hedge, there is only the option premium to set against the interest saving from the lower interest rates.

5 HEDGING STRATEGY ALTERNATIVES: EXAMPLE

5.1 Different hedging instruments often offer alternative ways of managing risk in a specific situation. In this section, we work through an example in which different ways in which a company can hedge interest rate risk are evaluated, covering both interest rate futures and interest rate options (interest rate guarantees).

5.2 EXAMPLE: HEDGING STRATEGY (1)

It is 31 December. Octavo plc needs to borrow £6 million in three months' time for a period of six months. For the type of loan finance which Octavo would use, the rate of interest is currently 13% per year and the Corporate Treasurer is unwilling to pay a higher rate.

The treasurer is concerned about possible future fluctuations in interest rates, and is considering the following possibilities:

(a) forward rate agreements (FRAs);
(b) interest rate futures;
(c) interest rate guarantees or short-term interest rate caps.

5.3 The Corporate Treasurer of Octavo decides to hedge the interest rate risk by using interest rate futures. Her expectation is that interest rates will increase by 2% over the next three months.

The current price of March sterling three months time deposit futures is 87.25. The standard contract size is £500,000, while the minimum price movement is one tick, the value of which is 0.01% per year of the contract size.

Set out calculations of the effect of using the futures market to hedge against movements in the interest rate and estimate the hedge efficiency:

(a) if interest rates increase by 2% and the futures market price moves by 2%;
(b) if interest rates increase by 2% and the futures market price moves by 1.75%;
(c) if interest rates fall by 1.5% and the futures market price moves by 1.25%.

The time value of money, taxation and margin requirements can be ignored.

5.4 SOLUTION

(a) One tick has a value of:

$0.0001 \times 500{,}000 \times {}^{3}/_{12} = £12.50$

2% ≡ 200 ticks.

If interest rates rise by 2%, the extra interest over 6 months is:

£6,000,000 × 2% × 6/12 = £60,000

Therefore a £60,000 gain from the futures contracts is required.

2% (200 ticks) movement on one contract would produce a gain of:

200 × £12.50 = £2,500.

Therefore, to hedge £60,000, 24 contracts are required for the hedge.

£500,000 March sterling time deposit contracts to be sold at 87.25 (effectively 12.75% interest) on 31 December.

24 to be bought in March or when interest rates change at 85.25 (effectively 14.75% interest), closing out the position.

Gain: 24 × 200 ticks @ £12.50 = £60,000

There is 100% hedge efficiency (the perfect hedge).

(b) In this case, the futures gain will be:

24 × 175 ticks @ £12.50 = £52,500

The hedge efficiency is £52,500 ÷ £60,000 = 87.5%

(c) In this case, there is a gain on the cash market arising from the fall in interest rates, and a loss on the futures market.

Cash market gain: £6,000,000 × 1.5% × 6/12 = £45,000

A futures market loss arises from selling at 87.25 and closing out the position at 88.50.

Futures market loss: 24 × 125 ticks @ £12.50 = £37,500

ie £6m × 1.25% × 6/12 = £37,500

The hedge efficiency is $\frac{£45,000}{£37,500}$ = 120%

5.5 EXAMPLE: HEDGING STRATEGY (2)

We now extend the example to look at an alternative hedging method.

Required

Calculate, for situations (a) to (c) in Paragraph 5.3 above, whether the total cost of the loan after hedging would have been lower with the futures hedge chosen by the treasurer or with an interest rate guarantee which she could have purchased at 13% for a premium of 0.25% of the size of the loan to be guaranteed.

Again, the time value of money, taxation and margin requirements are to be ignored.

5.6 Futures hedge costs

(a) Interest £6m × 15% × 6/12 = £450,000
Less gain £60,000 = £390,000

(b) Interest (as in (i)) £450,000
Less gain £52,500 = £397,500

(c) Interest £6m × 11.5% × 6/12 =£345,000
Add loss £37,500 = £382,500

The premium for the guarantee is:

£6m × 0.25% = £15,000.

The guarantee would be used in cases (a) and (b) when interest rates increase.

Then, total cost limiting interest rates to 13% is:

£6m × 13% × 6/12 = £390,000
Plus premium £15,000 equals £405,000.

This costs more than the futures contracts hedge in cases (a) and (b).

In case (c), the guarantee is not used.

Interest costs at 11.5% are:

£6m × 11.5% × 6/12 = £345,000
Plus £15,000 premium = £360,000.

This costs less than the futures hedge, reflecting the fact that declining to take up the interest rate option in the case of the guarantee has allowed the company to take advantage of the lower interest rates in the cash market.

Chapter roundup

- **Interest rates**, like **exchange rates**, can be very volatile.
- Factors involving **interest rate risk** include the following.
  - Fixed rates versus floating rate debt
  - The term of the loan
- A variety of financial instruments are available for reducing exposure to interest rate risk, including **FRAs**, **futures**, **swaps** and **options**.
- An **interest rate guarantee** is a form of interest rate option.

Quick quiz

1 Define 'hedge efficiency'. (see para 1.5)

2 What is a forward interest rate agreement? (1.7)

3 Who might use interest rate futures? (2.13, 2.15)

4 What is a 'swaption'? (3.10, 3.11)

5 Explain what is meant by a 'zero cost collar'. (4.3)

Question to try	Level	Marks	Time
14	Introductory	20	36 mins

Chapter 15

CASH FLOW AND DIVIDEND POLICY

	Chapter topic list	Syllabus reference	Ability required
1	Working capital and its management	13b(viii)	Skill
2	The operating cycle and cash flow	13b(viii)	Skill
3	Dividends and retentions	13b(viii)	Application
4	Dividend policy	13b(viii)	Application
5	Repurchase of shares	13b(viii)	Application

Introduction

In this chapter, we consider the management of **working capital** in general terms. In the two following Chapters 16 and 17 we shall be looking at **specific aspects** of the management of stocks, debtors, creditors and cash.

We also deal with the question of how much should be paid out by a company to its shareholders in the form of dividends. What is the effect of **dividend policy** on share prices? What are the practical influences on dividend policy, including the effects of **taxation**?

1 WORKING CAPITAL AND ITS MANAGEMENT 11/95

What is working capital?

KEY TERM

Working capital: the capital available for conducting the day-to-day operations of an organisation; normally, the excess of current assets over current liabilities *(OT)*.

1.1 Every business needs adequate liquid resources to maintain day-to-day cash flow. It needs enough to pay wages and salaries as they fall due and enough to pay creditors if it is to keep its workforce and ensure its supplies. Maintaining adequate working capital is not just important in the short term. Sufficient liquidity must be maintained in order to ensure the survival of the business in the long term as well. Even a profitable company may fail if it does not have adequate cash flow to meet its liabilities as they fall due.

What is working capital management?

1.2 Ensuring that sufficient liquid resources are maintained is a matter of **working capital management**. This involves achieving a balance between the requirement to minimise the risk of insolvency and the requirement to maximise the return on assets. An excessively conservative approach to working capital management resulting in high levels of cash holdings will harm profits because the opportunity to make a return on the assets tied up as cash will have been missed.

The need for funds for investment in current assets

1.3 Current assets may be financed either by long-term funds or by current liabilities. The 'ideal' current ratio (current assets: current liabilities) is generally accepted to be 2:1 (half of current assets should be financed by long-term funds), but this proportion can obviously be varied in practice, depending on the circumstances of an individual company. Similarly, the 'ideal' quick ratio or acid test ratio (current assets minus stocks: current liabilities) is 1:1, although in practice, companies often have much lower quick ratios than this.

1.4 These liquidity ratios are a guide to the risk of cash flow problems and insolvency. If a company suddenly finds that it is unable to renew its short-term liabilities (for example, if the bank suspends its overdraft facilities, or creditors start to demand earlier payment), there will be a danger of insolvency unless the company is able to turn enough of its current assets into cash quickly. A current ratio of 2:1 and a quick ratio of 1:1 are thought to indicate that a company is reasonably well protected against the danger of insolvency.

1.5 Current liabilities are often a cheap method of finance (trade creditors do not usually carry an interest cost) and companies may therefore consider that in the interest of higher profits, it is worth accepting some risk of insolvency by increasing current liabilities, taking the maximum credit possible from suppliers.

The volume of current assets required

1.6 The volume of current assets required will depend on the nature of the company's business. For example, a manufacturing company may require more stocks than a company in a service industry. As the volume of output by a company increases, the volume of current assets required will also increase.

1.7 Even assuming efficient stock holding, debt collection procedures and cash management, there is still a certain degree of choice in the total volume of current assets required to meet output requirements. Policies of low stock-holding levels, tight credit and minimum cash holdings may be contrasted with policies of high stocks (to allow for safety or buffer stocks) easier credit and sizeable cash holdings (for precautionary reasons).

Over-capitalisation and working capital

1.8 If there are excessive stocks, debtors and cash, and very few creditors, there will be an over-investment by the company in current assets. Working capital will be excessive and the company will be in this respect over-capitalised. The return on investment will be lower than it should be, and long-term funds will be unnecessarily tied up when they could be invested elsewhere to earn profits.

1.9 Over-capitalisation with respect to working capital should not exist if there is good management, but the warning signs of excessive working capital would be unfavourable accounting ratios. The ratios which can assist in judging whether the investment in working capital is reasonable include the following.

(a) **Sales/working capital.** The volume of sales as a multiple of the working capital investment should indicate whether, in comparison with previous years or with similar companies, the total volume of working capital is too high.

(b) **Liquidity ratios.** A current ratio in excess of 2:1 or a quick ratio in excess of 1:1 may indicate over-investment in working capital.

(c) **Turnover periods**. Excessive turnover periods for stocks and debtors, or a short period of credit taken from suppliers, might indicate that the volume of stocks or debtors is unnecessarily high, or the volume of creditors too low.

The turnover periods may be calculated approximately as follows.

(i) Raw materials stock turnover = $\dfrac{\text{Average raw material stock} \times 365 \text{ days}}{\text{Purchases per annum}}$

(ii) WIP turnover (production cycle) = $\dfrac{\text{Average WIP} \times 365 \text{ days}}{\text{Cost of production* per annum}}$

* Cost of sales (or even sales) may be a necessary alternative to cost of production in an examination question.

(iii) Finished goods stock turnover = $\dfrac{\text{Average finished goods stock} \times 365 \text{ days}}{\text{Cost of sales per annum}}$

(iv) Debtors turnover period = $\dfrac{\text{Average debtors} \times 365 \text{ days}}{\text{Sales per annum}}$

(v) Creditors turnover period = $\dfrac{\text{Average trade creditors} \times 365 \text{ days}}{\text{Purchases per annum}}$

Exam focus point

You should be fully proficient in calculating working capital ratios for the exam.

Overtrading

1.10 In contrast with over-capitalisation, overtrading happens when a business tries to do too much too quickly with too little long-term capital, so that it is trying to support too large a volume of trade with the capital resources at its disposal. Even if an overtrading business operates at a profit, it could easily run into serious trouble because it is short of money. Such liquidity problems stem from the fact that it does not have enough capital to provide the cash to pay its debts as they fall due.

KEY TERM

Overtrading: the condition of a business which enters into commitments in excess of its available short-term resources. This can arise even if the company is trading profitably, and is typically caused by financing strains imposed by a lengthy operating cycle or production cycle *(OT)*.

1.11 EXAMPLE: OVERTRADING

Great Ambition Ltd appoints a new managing director who has great plans to expand the company. He wants to increase turnover by 100% within two years, and to do this he employs extra sales staff. He recognises that customers do not want to have to wait for deliveries, and so he decides that the company must build up its stock levels. There is a substantial increase in the company's stocks. These are held in additional warehouse space which is now rented. The company also buys new cars for its extra sales representatives.

The managing director's policies are immediately successful in boosting sales, which double in just over one year. Stock levels are now much higher, but the company takes longer credit from its suppliers, even though some suppliers have expressed their annoyance at the length of time they must wait for payment. Credit terms for debtors are unchanged, and so the volume of debtors, like the volume of sales, rises by 100%.

In spite of taking longer credit, the company still needs to increase its overdraft facilities with the bank, which are raised from a limit of £40,000 to one of £80,000. The company is profitable, and retains some profits in the business, but profit margins have fallen.

(a) Gross profit margins are lower because some prices have been reduced to obtain extra sales.

(b) Net profit margins are lower because overhead costs are higher. These include sales representatives' wages, car expenses and depreciation on cars, warehouse rent and additional losses from having to write off out-of-date (obsolete) and slow-moving stock items.

1.12 The balance sheet of the company might change over time from (A) to (B).

		Balance Sheet (A)			*Balance Sheet (B)*	
	£	£	£	£	£	£
Fixed assets			160,000			210,000
Current assets						
Stock		60,000			150,000	
Debtors		64,000			135,000	
Cash		1,000			-	
		125,000			285,000	
Current liabilities						
Bank	25,000			80,000		
Creditors	50,000			200,000		
		75,000			280,000	
			50,000			5,000
			210,000			215,000
Share capital			10,000			10,000
Profit and loss account			200,000			205,000
			210,000			215,000
Sales			£1,000,000			£2,000,000
Gross profit			£200,000			£300,000
Net profit			£50,000			£20,000

In situation (B), the company has reached its overdraft limit and has four times as many creditors as in situation (A) but with only twice the sales turnover. Stock levels are much higher, and stock turnover is lower.

The company is overtrading. If it had to pay its next trade creditor, or salaries and wages, before it received any income, it could not do so without the bank allowing it to exceed its overdraft limit. The company is profitable, although profit margins have fallen, and it ought to expect a prosperous future. But if it does not sort out its cash flow and liquidity, it will not survive to enjoy future profits.

1.13 Suitable solutions to the problem would be measures to reduce the degree of overtrading. **New capital** from the shareholders could be injected. **Better control** could be applied to stocks and debtors. The company could **abandon ambitious plans** for increased sales and more fixed asset purchases until the business has had time to consolidate its position, and build up its capital base with retained profits.

1.14 **Symptoms of overtrading** can be summarised as follows.

(a) There is a rapid increase in turnover.

(b) There is a rapid increase in the volume of current assets and possibly also fixed assets. Stock turnover and debtors turnover might slow down, in which case the rate of increase in stocks and debtors would be even greater than the rate of increase in sales.

(c) There is only a small increase in proprietors' capital (perhaps through retained profits). Most of the increase in assets is financed by credit, especially:

 (i) trade creditors. The payment period to creditors is likely to lengthen;

 (ii) a bank overdraft, which often reaches or even exceeds the limit of the facilities agreed by the bank.

(d) Some debt ratios and liquidity ratios alter dramatically.

 (i) The proportion of total assets financed by proprietors' capital falls, and the proportion financed by credit rises.

 (ii) The current ratio and the quick ratio fall.

 (iii) The business might have a liquid deficit, that is, an excess of current liabilities over current assets.

The causes of overtrading

1.15 Emphasis has been given so far to the danger of overtrading when a business seeks to increase its turnover too rapidly without an adequate capital base. In other words, overtrading is brought upon the business by the ambition of management. This is not the only **cause of overtrading**, however. Other causes are as follows.

(a) When a business repays a loan, it often replaces the old loan with a new one. However a business might repay a loan without replacing it, with the consequence that it has less long-term capital to finance its current level of operations.

(b) A business might be profitable, but in a period of inflation, its retained profits might be insufficient to pay for replacement fixed assets and stocks, which now cost more because of inflation. The business would then rely increasingly on credit, and find itself eventually unable to support its current volume of trading with a capital base that has fallen in real terms.

2 THE OPERATING CYCLE AND CASH FLOW

The operating cycle

2.1 The connection between investment in working capital and cash flow may be illustrated by means of the **cash cycle**, **operating cycle** or **trading cycle**. The operating cycle may be expressed as the (average) number of days between the outlay on raw materials, wages and other expenses and the inflow of cash from the sale of the company's product. In a manufacturing business, this equals:

The average time that raw materials remain in stock
less the period of credit taken from supplies
plus the time taken to produce the goods
plus the time taken by customers to pay for the goods

2.2 If the turnover periods for stocks and debtors lengthen, or the payment period to creditors shortens:

(a) the operating cycle will lengthen;

(b) the investment in working capital will increase.

The working capital requirement

2.3 Computing the working capital requirement is a matter of calculating the value of current assets less current liabilities, perhaps by taking averages over a one year period.

2.4 EXAMPLE: WORKING CAPITAL REQUIREMENTS (1)

The following data relate to Corn Ltd, a manufacturing company.

Turnover for the year	£1,500,000
Costs as percentages of sales	%
Direct materials	30
Direct labour	25
Variable overheads	10
Fixed overheads	15
Selling and distribution	5

On average:

(a) debtors take 2.5 months before payment;
(b) raw materials are in stock for three months;
(c) work-in-progress represents two months worth of half produced goods;
(d) finished goods represents one month's production;
(e) credit is taken as follows:

(i)	Direct materials	2 months
(ii)	Direct labour	1 week
(iii)	Variable overheads	1 month
(iv)	Fixed overheads	1 month
(v)	Selling and distribution	0.5 months

Work-in-progress and finished goods are valued at material, labour and variable expense cost. Compute the working capital requirement of Corn Ltd assuming the labour force is paid for 50 working weeks a year.

2.5 SOLUTION

(a) The annual costs incurred will be as follows.

		£
Direct materials	30% of £1,500,000	450,000
Direct labour	25% of £1,500,000	375,000
Variable overheads	10% of £1,500,000	150,000
Fixed overheads	15% of £1,500,000	225,000
Selling and distribution	5% of £1,500,000	75,000

(b) The average value of current assets will be as follows.

			£	£
Raw materials	3/12	× 450,000		112,500
Work-in-progress:				
Materials (50% complete)	1/12	× 450,000	37,500	
Labour (50% complete)	1/12	× 375,000	31,250	
Variable overheads (50% complete)	1/12	× 150,000	12,500	
				81,250
Finished goods				
Materials	1/12	× 450,000	37,500	
Labour	1/12	× 375,000	31,250	
Variable overheads	1/12	× 150,000	12,500	
				81,250
Debtors	2.5/12	× 1,500,000		312,500
				587,500

(c) Average value of current liabilities will be as follows.

Materials	2/12	× 450,000	75,000	
Labour	1/50	× 375,000	7,500	
Variable overheads	1/12	× 150,000	12,500	
Fixed overheads	1/12	× 225,000	18,750	
Selling and distribution	0.5/12	× 75,000	3,125	
				116,875

(d) Working capital required £587,500 – £116,875 = £470,625

It has been assumed that all the direct materials are allocated to work-in-progress when production starts.

Question 1

When unforeseen events have an adverse effect on cash inflows, a company will only survive if it can maintain adequate cash inflows. Give examples of unforeseen changes which may affect cash flow patterns.

Answer

Your list probably included some of the following:

(a) a change in the general economic environment. An economic recession will cause a slump in trade;

(b) a new product, launched by a competitor, which takes business away from a company's traditional and established product lines;

(c) new cost-saving product technology, which forces the company to invest in the new technology to remain competitive;

(d) moves by competitors which have to be countered (for example a price reduction or a sales promotion);

(e) changes in consumer preferences, resulting in a fall in demand;

(f) government action against certain trade practices or against trade with a country that a company has dealings with;

(g) strikes or other industrial action;

(h) natural disasters, such as floods or fire damage, which curtail an organisation's activities.

3 DIVIDENDS AND RETENTIONS

5/97

3.1 Cash flow generated from retained earnings is the single most important source of finance for UK companies. For any company, the amount of earnings retained within the business has a direct impact on the amount of dividends. Profit re-invested as retained earnings is profit that could have been paid as a dividend.

3.2 The major reasons for using cash generated from retained earnings to finance new investments, rather than to pay higher dividends and then raise new equity funds for the new investments, are as follows.

(a) The management of many companies believe that cash from retained earnings are funds which do not cost anything, although this is not true. However, it is true that the use of retained earnings as a source of funds does not lead to a payment of cash.

(b) The dividend policy of a company is in practice determined by the directors. From their standpoint, cash from retained earnings are an attractive source of finance because investment projects can be undertaken without involving either the shareholders or any outsiders.

(c) The use of cash from retained earnings as opposed to new shares or debentures avoids issue costs.

(d) The use of cash from retained earnings avoids the possibility of a change in control resulting from an issue of new shares.

3.3 Another factor that may be of importance is the financial and taxation position of the company's shareholders. If, for example, because of taxation considerations, they would rather make a capital profit (which will only be taxed when the shares are sold) than receive current income, then finance through retained earnings would be preferred to other methods.

3.4 A company must restrict its self-financing through retained profits because shareholders should be paid a reasonable dividend, in line with realistic expectations, even if the directors would rather keep the funds for re-investing.

At the same time, a company that is looking for extra funds will not be expected by investors (such as banks) to pay generous dividends, nor over-generous salaries to owner-directors.

Exam focus point

Don't make the mistake that many students make of equating reserves with cash. Remember: they are on different sides of the balance sheet. A company might have substantial reserves, but no cash.

Legal and procedural aspects of dividend payments

3.5 Dividends are usually paid by UK public companies twice a year. An **interim dividend** is paid after the publication of the interim results of the company for the first half year. A final dividend is paid after the annual accounts for the year have been published, and after the proposed dividend has been agreed by shareholders at the AGM.

3.6 It is usual for shareholders to have the power to vote to **reduce** the size of the final (proposed) dividend at the Annual General Meeting, but not the power to increase the dividend. The directors of the company are therefore in a strong position, with regard to shareholders, when it comes to determining dividend policy. For practical purposes, shareholders will usually be obliged to accept the dividend policy that has been decided on by the directors.

Scrip dividends, scrip issues and stock splits

3.7 A **scrip dividend** is a dividend payment which takes the form of new shares instead of cash. Effectively, it converts profit reserves into issued share capital. When the directors of a company would prefer to retain funds within the business but consider that they must pay at least a certain amount of dividend, they might offer equity shareholders the choice of:

(a) a cash dividend; or
(b) a scrip dividend of more shares in the company.

3.8 In recent years, **enhanced scrip dividends** have been offered by a number of companies. With enhanced scrip dividends, the value of the shares offered is much greater than the cash alternative, giving investors an incentive to choose the shares.

3.9 A **scrip issue** (or **bonus issue**) is an issue of new shares to existing shareholders, by converting equity reserves into issued share capital. For example, if a company with issued share capital of 100,000 ordinary shares of £1 each made a one for five scrip issue, 20,000 new shares would be issued to existing shareholders, one new share for every five old shares held. Issued share capital would be increased by £20,000, and reserves (probably share premium account, if there is one) reduced by this amount.

3.10 By creating more shares in this way, a scrip issue does not raise new funds, but does have the advantage of making shares cheaper and therefore (perhaps) more easily marketable on the Stock Exchange. For example, if a company's shares are priced at £6 on the Stock Exchange, and the company makes a one for two scrip issue, we should expect the share price after the issue to fall to £4 each. Shares at £4 each might be more easily marketable than shares at £6 each.

3.11 This advantage of a scrip issue is also the reason for a **stock split**. A stock split occurs where, for example, each ordinary share of £1 each is split into two shares of 50p each, thus creating cheaper shares with greater marketability. There is possibly an added psychological advantage, in that investors should expect a company which splits its shares in this way to be planning for substantial earnings growth and dividend growth in the future. As a consequence, the market price of shares may benefit. For example, if one existing share of £1 has a market value of £6, and is then split into two shares of 50p each, the market value of the new shares might settle at, say, £3.10 instead of the expected £3, in anticipation of strong future growth in earnings and dividends.

3.12 The difference between a stock split and a scrip issue is that a scrip issue converts equity reserves into share capital, whereas a stock split leaves reserves unaffected. Both are popular with investors as they are seen as likely to lead to increased dividends. Scrip dividends can, however, lead to tax complications for individual investors.

Dividends and share prices

3.13 The purpose of a dividend policy should be to maximise shareholders' wealth, which depends on both current dividends and capital gains. Capital gains can be achieved by retaining some earnings for reinvestment and dividend growth in the future.

Growth in dividends

3.14 The rate of growth in dividends is sometimes expressed, theoretically, as:

$$g = rb$$

where g is the annual growth rate in dividends
r is the rate of return on new investments
b is the proportion of profits that are retained.

3.15 EXAMPLE: DIVIDEND GROWTH

(a) If a company has a payout ratio of 40%, and retains the rest for investing in projects which yield 15%, the annual rate of growth in dividends could be estimated as 15% × 60% = 9%.

(b) If a company pays out 80% of its profits as dividends, and retains the rest for reinvestment at a rate of return of 15%, the current dividend would be twice as big as in (a), but annual dividend growth would be only 15% × 20% = 3%.

Approach to dividend policy, based on fundamental analysis of share values

3.16 A theoretical approach to dividend and retentions policy can be based on the fundamental theory of share values. We will make the following assumptions.

(a) The market value of a company's shares depends on:

(i) the size of dividends paid;
(ii) the rate of growth in dividends;
(iii) the shareholders' required rate of return.

(b) The rate of growth in dividends depends on how much money is reinvested in the company, and so on the rate of earnings retention.

(c) Shareholders will want their company to pursue a retentions policy that maximises the value of their shares.

3.17 The basic dividend-based formula for the market value of shares is:

$$p_o = \frac{d_1}{r}$$

where d_1 is a constant annual dividend, and r is the shareholders' required rate of return. This formula assumes a **constant** dividend, and no dividend growth at all, so an assumption on which this formula is based is that all earnings are paid out as dividends.

3.18 Using the dividend growth model, we have:

$$p_o = \frac{d_0(1+g)}{(r-g)}$$

where d_0 is the current year's dividend (year 0) and g is the growth rate in earnings and dividends, so $d_0(1 + g)$ is the expected dividend in one year's time. p_o is the market value excluding any dividend currently payable ('**ex div**').

KEY TERMS

- **Cum**: 'With', as in **cum dividend**, where security purchases include rights to the next dividend payment, and **cum rights**, where shares are traded with rights, such as to a scrip issue, attached (*OT*).
- **Ex**: 'Without', as in **ex dividend**, where security purchases do not include rights to the next dividend payment, and **ex rights**, where rights attaching to share ownership, such as a scrip issue, are not transferred to a new purchaser (*OT*).

3.19 EXAMPLE: DIVIDEND GROWTH MODEL

Tantrum plc has achieved earnings of £800,000 this year. The company intends to pursue a policy of financing all its investment opportunities out of retained earnings. There are considerable investment opportunities, which are expected to be available indefinitely. However, if Tantrum plc does not exploit any of the available opportunities, its annual earnings will remain at £800,000 in perpetuity. The following figures are available.

Proportion of earnings retained	*Growth rate in earnings*	*Required return on all investments by shareholders*
%	%	%
0	0	14
25	5	15
40	7	16

The rate of return required by shareholders would rise if earnings are retained, because of the risk associated with the new investments. What is the optimum retentions policy for Tantrum plc? The full dividend payment for this year will be paid in the near future in any case.

3.20 SOLUTION

Since: MV ex div $= \dfrac{d_o(1+g)}{(r-g)}$

Then: MV cum div $= \dfrac{d_o(1+g)}{(r-g)} + d_o$

We are trying to maximise the value of shareholder wealth, which is currently represented by the **cum div** market value, since a dividend will soon be paid.

(a) If retentions are 0%:

$$\text{MV cum div} = \frac{800{,}000}{0.14} + 800{,}000$$

$$= £6{,}514{,}286$$

(b) If retentions are 25%, the current dividend will be £600,000 and:

$$\text{MV cum div} = \frac{600{,}000(1.05)}{(0.15-0.05)} + 600{,}000$$

$$= £6{,}900{,}000$$

(c) If retentions are 40%, the current dividend will be £480,000 and:

$$\text{MV cum div} = \frac{480{,}000(1.07)}{(0.16 - 0.07)} + 480{,}000$$

$$= £6{,}186{,}667$$

The best policy (out of the three for which figures are provided) would be to retain 25% of earnings.

Dividend policy and shareholders' personal taxation

3.21 The market value of a share has been defined as the sum of all future dividends, discounted at the shareholder's marginal cost of capital. When constant dividends are expected, we have:

$$p_o = \frac{d_1}{r}$$

3.22 The cost of capital is generally taken to be a tax-free rate, ignoring the actual rates of personal taxation paid on dividends by different shareholders. To each individual shareholder, however, the dividends are subject to income tax at a rate which depends on his own tax position, and it is possible to re-define his valuation of a share as:

$$p_o = \frac{d_g(1-t)}{r_t}$$

where d_g = gross dividend (assumed to be constant each year)
t = rate of personal tax on the dividend
r_t = the shareholder's after tax marginal cost of capital.

3.23 Presumably, a company should choose between dividend payout and earnings retention so as to maximise the wealth of its shareholders; however, if not all shareholders have the same tax rates and after tax cost of capital, there might not be an optimum policy which satisfies all shareholders. By a **clientele effect**, companies may attract particular types of shareholders seeking particular dividend policies.

KEY TERM

Clientele effect: the tendency of companies to attract particular types of shareholder because of their management organisation and policies, particularly dividend policies.

3.24 A further problem occurs when income from dividends might be taxed either more or less heavily than capital gains. In the UK, individuals have an annual capital gains exemption which is not available for setting against income, and companies are taxed on capital gains but not on dividend income.

3.25 Since the purpose of a dividend policy should be to maximise the wealth of shareholders, it is important to consider whether it would be better to pay a dividend now, subject to tax on income, or to retain earnings so as to increase the shareholders' capital gains (which will be subject to capital gains tax when the shareholders eventually sell their shares).

4 DIVIDEND POLICY

Residual theory

4.1 The **residual theory of dividend policy** can be summarised as follows.

(a) If a company can identify projects with positive NPVs, it should invest in them.
(b) Only when these investment opportunities are exhausted should dividends be paid.

Traditional view

4.2 An alternative 'traditional' view of dividend policy, as outlined above, is to focus on the effects on share price. According to this view, the price of a share depends upon the mix of dividends, given shareholders' required rate of return, and growth.

$$r = \frac{d_1}{p_0} + g \quad \therefore p_0 = \frac{d_1}{(r-g)} = \frac{d_0(1+g)}{(r-g)}$$

Accordingly, the rate at which dividends are paid does matter to shareholders.

Irrelevancy theory

4.3 In contrast to the traditional view, Modigliani and Miller (MM) proposed that in a tax-free world, shareholders will be indifferent between dividends and capital gains, and the value of a company is determined solely by the 'earning power' of its assets and investments.

4.4 MM argued that if a company with investment opportunities decides to pay a dividend, so that retained earnings are insufficient to finance all its investments, the shortfall in funds will be made up by obtaining additional funds from outside sources. The consequent loss of value in the existing shares, as a result of obtaining outside finance instead of using retained earnings, is exactly equal to the amount of the dividend paid. A company should therefore be indifferent between paying a dividend (and obtaining new outside funds) and retaining earnings.

4.5 In answer to criticisms that certain shareholders will show a preference either for high dividends or for capital gains, MM argued that if a company pursues a consistent dividend policy, 'each corporation would tend to attract to itself a clientele consisting of those preferring its particular payout ratio, but one clientele would be entirely as good as another in terms of the valuation it would imply for the firm.'

The case in favour of the relevance of dividend policy (and against MM's views)

4.6 There are strong arguments against MM's view that dividend policy is irrelevant as a means of affecting shareholder's wealth.

(a) Differing rates of taxation on dividends and capital gains can create a preference for a high dividend or one for high earnings retention.

(b) Dividend retention should be preferred by companies in a period of capital rationing.

(c) Due to imperfect markets and the possible difficulties of selling shares easily at a fair price, shareholders might need high dividends in order to have funds to invest in opportunities outside the company.

(d) Markets are not perfect. Because of transaction costs on the sale of shares, investors who want some cash from their investments should prefer to receive dividends rather than to sell some of their shares to get the cash they want.

(e) Information available to shareholders is imperfect, and they are not aware of the future investment plans and expected profits of their company. Even if management were to provide them with profit forecasts, these forecasts would not necessarily be accurate or believable. As a consequence of imperfect information:

  (i) companies are normally expected at least to maintain the same level of dividends from one year to the next. Failure to maintain the dividend level would undermine investors' confidence;

  (ii) in practice, undertaking a new investment project with a positive NPV will not immediately increase the market value of shares by the amount of the NPV because markets do not show strong-form efficiency. It is only gradually, as the profits from the investment begin to show up in the profits and dividends in historical financial statements, that the market value of the shares will rise.

(f) Perhaps the strongest argument against the Modigliani-Miller view is that shareholders will tend to prefer a current dividend to future capital gains (or deferred dividends) because the future is more uncertain.

Practical aspects of dividend policy 5/95

4.7 So far, we have concentrated on theoretical approaches to establishing an optimal dividend and retentions policy. A practical approach to dividends and retentions should take various factors into consideration.

(a) The need to remain profitable. Dividends are paid out of profits, and an unprofitable company cannot for ever go on paying dividends out of retained profits made in the past.

(b) The law on distributable profits.

(c) Any dividend restraints which might be imposed by loan agreements.

(d) The effect of inflation, and the need to retain some profit within the business just to maintain its operating capability unchanged.

(e) The company's gearing level. If the company wants extra finance, the sources of funds used should strike a balance between equity and debt finance. Retained earnings are the most readily available source of growth in equity finance.

(f) The company's liquidity position. Dividends are a cash payment, and a company must have enough cash to pay the dividends it declares.

(g) The ease and cost with which the company could raise extra finance from sources other than retained earnings. Small companies which find it hard to raise finance might have to rely more heavily on retained earnings than large companies.

Dividends as a signal to investors

4.8 Investors usually expect a consistent dividend policy from the company, with stable dividends each year or, even better, steady dividend growth. A large rise or fall in dividends in any year can have a marked effect on the company's share price. Stable dividends or steady dividend growth are usually needed for share price stability. A cut in dividends may be treated by investors as **signalling** that the future prospects of the company are weak.

Thus, the dividend which is paid acts, possibly without justification, as a 'signal' of the future prospects of the company.

4.9 The signalling effect of a company's dividend policy may also be used by management of a company which faces a possible takeover. The dividend level might be increased as a defence against the takeover: investors may take the increased dividend as a signal of improved future prospects, thus driving the share price higher and making the company more expensive for a potential bidder to take over.

Question 2

Cavan plc is a company that is still managed by the two individuals who set it up 12 years ago. In the current year, the company acquired plc status and was launched on the second tier Alternative Investment Market. Previously, all of the shares had been owned by its two founders and certain employees. Now, 40% of the shares are in the hands of the investing public.

The company's profit growth and dividend policy are set out below. Will a continuation of the same dividend policy as in the past be suitable now that the company is quoted on the AIM?

Year	*Profits* £'000	*Dividend* £'000	*Shares in issue*
4 years ago	176	88	800,000
3 years ago	200	104	800,000
2 years ago	240	120	1,000,000
1 year ago	290	150	1,000,000
Current year	444	222 (proposed)	1,500,000

Answer

Year	*Dividend per share*	*Dividend as % of profit*
4 years ago	11.0	50%
3 years ago	13.0	52%
2 years ago	12.0	50%
1 year ago	15.0	52%
Current year	14.8	50%

The company appears to have pursued a dividend policy of paying out half of after-tax profits in dividend.

This policy is only suitable when a company achieves a stable EPS or steady EPS growth. Investors do not like a fall in dividend from one year to the next, and the fall in dividend per share in the current year is likely to be unpopular, and to result in a fall in the share price.

The company would probably serve its shareholders better by paying a dividend of at least 15p per share, possibly more, in the current year, even though the dividend as a percentage of profit would then be higher.

5 REPURCHASE OF SHARES 5/97

Why buy back the company's shares?

5.1 As you will know from Paper 9 *Financial Reporting* at Stage 3, companies are permitted to buy back shares from shareholders who are willing to sell them, subject to certain conditions. For a company with surplus cash, share repurchase serves as an alternative to paying the cash out as dividends. For a smaller private company with few shareholders, the reason for buying back the company's own shares may be that there is no immediate willing purchaser at a time when a shareholder wishes to sell shares.

5.2 Among the possible benefits of a share repurchase scheme are the following.

(a) Finding a use for surplus cash, which may be a 'dead asset'.

(b) Increase in earnings per share through a reduction in the number of shares in issue. This should lead to a higher share price than would otherwise be the case, and the company should be able to increase dividend payments on the remaining shares in issue.

(c) Increase in gearing. Repurchase of a company's own shares allows debt to be substituted for equity, so raising gearing. This will be of interest to a company wanting to increase its gearing without increasing its total long-term funding.

(d) Readjustment of the company's equity base to more appropriate levels, for a company whose business is in decline.

(e) Share repurchase may also fulfil special purposes, such as preventing a takeover or enabling a quoted company to withdraw from the stock market.

There are also disadvantages.

(a) It can be hard to arrive at a price which will be fair both to the vendors and to any shareholders who are not selling shares to the company.

(b) A repurchase of shares could be seen as an admission that the company cannot make better use of the funds than the shareholders.

(c) Some shareholders may suffer from being taxed on a capital gain following the purchase of their shares rather than receiving dividend income.

5.3 Repurchase of a company's own shares is common among US companies and is also now common in the UK. However, the practice remains rare in the rest of Europe. Share buybacks are indeed illegal in a number of European countries including Germany and in Scandinavia.

Chapter roundup

- In this chapter, **working capital** has been described in general terms.
- The **amount tied up in working capital** is equal to the value of raw materials, work in progress, finished goods stocks and debtors less creditors. The size of this net figure has a direct effect on the liquidity of an organisation.
- Empirical evidence suggests that investors consider **dividends** to be important; accordingly dividend policy should be of concern to company directors and financial managers. Companies generally **smooth out** dividend payments by adjusting only gradually to changes in earnings: large fluctuations might undermine public confidence.
- Modigliani and Miller showed that **dividend policy** was irrelevant to shareholder wealth in perfect capital markets. Given the imperfections in real-world markets and in taxation policies, the position is not so clear.
- **Repurchase of shares** (share buy-backs) have become increasingly common in recent years.

Quick quiz

1 What is over-capitalisation? (see paras 1.8, 1.9)

2 What are the causes of overtrading? (1.15)

3 What is the operating cycle? (2.1)

4 What reasons are there for using retained earnings to finance new investments? (3.2, 3.3)

5 How does a stock split differ from a scrip issue? (3.12)

6 Outline Modigliani and Miller's views on the irrelevance of dividend policy. (4.3 - 4.6)

7 What are the practical factors to be taken into consideration in deciding dividend policy? (4.7)

8 What are the possible advantages of a company repurchasing its own shares? (5.2)

Question to try	Level	Marks	Time
15	Introductory	n/a	25 mins

Chapter 16

THE MANAGEMENT OF DEBTORS, CREDITORS AND STOCKS

Introduction

This chapter, which deals with **specific techniques in working capital management**, should be studied after studying Chapter 15. **Debtors** are of particular importance. A 1995 survey of small and medium-sized enterprises in the UK found that trade debtors account for almost one-third of total corporate assets. **Bad debts** cause 7% of UK corporate failures.

Exam focus point

CIMA guidance on this subject has mentioned that credit management is likely to be tested more fully in the SFM paper than stock management.

1 THE MANAGEMENT OF DEBTORS 11/96, 11/97, 5/99

1.1 Several factors should be considered by management when a policy for credit control is formulated. These include:

(a) the administrative costs of debt collection;

(b) the procedures for controlling credit to individual customers and for debt collection;

(c) the amount of extra capital required to finance an extension of total credit. There might be an increase in debtors, stocks and creditors, and the net increase in working capital must be financed;

(d) the cost of the additional finance required for any increase in the volume of debtors (or the savings from a reduction in debtors). This cost might be bank overdraft interest, or the cost of long-term funds (such as loan stock or equity);

(e) any savings or additional expenses in operating the credit policy (for example the extra work involved in pursuing slow payers);

(f) the ways in which the credit policy could be implemented. For example:

(i) credit could be eased by giving debtors a longer period in which to settle their accounts. The cost would be the resulting increase in debtors;

   (ii) a discount could be offered for early payment. The cost would be the amount of the discounts taken;

(g) the effects of easing credit, which might be:

   (i) to encourage a higher proportion of bad debts;
   (ii) an increase in sales volume.

   Provided that the extra gross contribution from the increase in sales exceeds the increase in fixed cost expenses, bad debts, discounts and the finance cost of an increase in working capital, a policy to relax credit terms would be profitable.

Some of the factors involved in credit policy decisions will now be considered in more detail.

The debt collection policy

1.2 The overall debt collection policy of the firm should be such that the administrative costs and other costs incurred in debt collection do not exceed the benefits from incurring those costs.

Some extra spending on debt collection procedures might:

(a) reduce bad debt losses;

(b) reduce the average collection period, and therefore the cost of the investment in debtors.

Beyond a certain level of spending, however, additional expenditure on debt collection would not have enough effect on bad debts or on the average collection period to justify the extra administrative costs.

1.3 EXAMPLE: DEBTOR MANAGEMENT (1)

Couttes Purse Ltd requires advice on its debt collection policy. Should the current policy be discarded in favour of Option 1 or Option 2?

	Current policy	*Option 1*	*Option 2*
Annual expenditure on debt collection procedures	£240,000	£300,000	£400,000
Bad debt losses (% of sales)	3%	2%	1%
Average collection period	2 months	1 1/2 months	1 month

Current sales are £4,800,000 a year, and the company requires a 15% return on its investments.

1.4 SOLUTION

	Current policy £	*Option 1* £	*Option 2* £
Average debtors	800,000	600,000	400,000
Reduction in working capital	-	200,000	400,000
(a) Interest saving (15% of reduction)		30,000	60,000
Bad debt losses (sales value)	144,000	96,000	48,000
(b) Reduction in losses	-	48,000	96,000
Benefits of each option (a) + (b)	-	78,000	156,000
Extra costs of debt collection	-	60,000	160,000
Benefit/(loss) from option		18,000	(4,000)

Option 1 is preferable to the current policy, but Option 2 is worse than the current policy.

Assessing creditor worthiness

1.5 Credit control involves the initial investigation of potential credit customers and the continuing control of outstanding accounts.

The main points to note are as follows.

(a) New customers should give two good references, including one from a bank, before being granted credit.

(b) Credit ratings might be checked through a credit rating agency.

(c) A new customer's credit limit should be fixed at a low level and only increased if his payment record subsequently warrants it.

(d) For large value customers, a file should be maintained of any available financial information about the customer. This file should be reviewed regularly. Information is available from:

   (i) an analysis of the company's annual report and accounts;

   (ii) Extel cards (sheets of accounting information about public companies in the UK, and also major overseas companies, produced by Extel).

(e) The Department of Trade and Industry and the Export Credit Guarantee Department will both be able to advise on overseas companies.

(f) Press comments may give information about what a company is currently doing (as opposed to the historical results in Extel cards or published accounts which only show what the company has done in the past).

(g) The company could send a member of staff to visit the company concerned, to get a first-hand impression of the company and its prospects. This would be advisable in the case of a prospective major customer.

(h) Aged lists of debts should be produced and reviewed at regular intervals.

(i) The credit limit for an existing customer should be periodically reviewed, but it should only be raised if the customer's credit standing is good.

(j) It is essential to have procedures which ensure that further orders are not accepted from nor goods sent to a customer who is in difficulties. If a customer has exceeded his credit limit, or has not paid debts despite several reminders, or is otherwise known to be in difficulties, sales staff and warehouse staff must be notified immediately (and not, for example, at the end of the week, by which time more goods might have been supplied).

1.6 An organisation might devise a credit-rating system for new individual customers that is based on characteristics of the customer (such as whether the customer is a home owner, and the customer's age and occupation). Points would be awarded according to the characteristics of the customer, and the amount of credit that is offered would depend on his or her credit score.

Debt collection procedures

1.7 Sales paperwork should be dealt with promptly and accurately.

(a) Invoices should be sent out immediately after delivery.

(b) Checks should be carried out to ensure that invoices are accurate.

(c) The investigation of queries and complaints and, if appropriate, the issue of credit notes should be carried out promptly.

(d) If practical, monthly statements should be issued early so that all items on the statement might then be included in customers' monthly settlements of bills.

The level of credit

1.8 To determine whether it would be profitable to extend the level of total credit, it is necessary to assess:

(a) the extra sales that a more generous credit policy would stimulate;
(b) the profitability of the extra sales;
(c) the extra length of the average debt collection period;
(d) the required rate of return on the investment in additional debtors.

Discount policies

1.9 Varying the discount allowed for early payment of debts affects the **average collection period** and the **volume of demand** (and possibly, therefore, indirectly affects bad debt losses). To see whether the offer of a discount for early payment is financially worthwhile we must compare the cost of the discount with the benefit of a reduced investment in debtors. We shall begin with examples where the offer of a discount for early payment does not affect the volume of demand.

1.10 EXAMPLE: DEBTOR MANAGEMENT (2)

Lowe and Price Ltd has annual credit sales of £12,000,000, and three months are allowed for payment. The company decides to offer a 2% discount for payments made within ten days of the invoice being sent, and to reduce the maximum time allowed for payment to two months. It is estimated that 50% of customers will take the discount. If the company requires a 20% return on investments, what will be the effect of the discount? Assume that the volume of sales will be unaffected by the discount.

1.11 SOLUTION

We can calculate:

(a) the profits forgone by offering the discount;
(b) the interest saved or incurred as a result of the changes in the company cash flows.

1.12 (a) The volume of debtors, if the company policy remains unchanged, would be:

$$3/12 \times £12{,}000{,}000 = £3{,}000{,}000.$$

(b) If the policy is changed the volume of debtors would be:

$$(\frac{10}{365} \times 50\% \times £12{,}000{,}000) + (\frac{2}{12} \times 50\% \times £12{,}000{,}000)$$

$$= £164{,}384 + £1{,}000{,}000 = £1{,}164{,}384.$$

(c) There will be a reduction in debtors of £1,835,616.

(d) Since the company can invest at 20% a year, the value of a reduction in debtors (a source of funds) is 20% of £1,835,616 each year in perpetuity, that is, £367,123 a year.

(e) **Summary**

	£
Value of reduction in debtors each year	367,123
Less discounts allowed each year (2% × 50% × £12,000,000)	120,000
Net benefit of new discount policy each year	247,123

1.13 An extension of the payment period allowed to debtors may be introduced in order to increase sales volume.

Question

Ashfin Ltd currently expects sales of £50,000 a month. Variable costs of sales are £40,000 a month (all payable in the month of sale). It is estimated that if the credit period allowed to debtors were to be increased from 30 days to 60 days, sales volume would increase by 20%. All customers would be expected to take advantage of the extended credit. If the cost of capital is $12\frac{1}{2}$ % a year (or approximately 1% a month), is the extension of the credit period justifiable in financial terms?

Answer

	£
Current debtors (1 month)	50,000
Debtors after implementing the proposal (2 months)	120,000
Increase in debtors	70,000

	£
Financing cost (× $12\frac{1}{2}$%)	8,750
Annual contribution from additional sales	
(12 months x 20% x £10,000)	24,000
Annual net benefit from extending credit period	15,250

Bad debt risk

1.14 Different credit policies are likely to have differing levels of bad debt risk. The higher turnover resulting from easier credit terms should be sufficiently profitable to exceed the cost of:

(a) bad debts; plus
(b) the additional investment necessary to achieve the higher sales.

1.15 EXAMPLE: DEBTOR MANAGEMENT (3)

A company achieves current annual sales of £1,800,000. The cost of sales is 80% of this amount, but bad debts average 1% of total sales, and the annual profit is as follows.

	£
Sales	1,800,000
Less cost of sales	1,440,000
	360,000
Less bad debts	18,000
Profit	342,000

The current debt collection period is one month, and the management consider that if credit terms were eased (Option A), the effects would be as follows.

	Present policy	*Option A*
Additional sales (%)	–	25%
Average collection period	1 month	2 months
Bad debts (% of sales)	1%	3%

The company requires a 20% return on its investments. If the costs of sales are 75% variable and 25% fixed, and on the assumptions that:

(a) there would be no increase in fixed costs from the extra turnover;
(b) there would be no increase in average stocks or creditors;

what is the preferable policy, Option A or the present one?

1.16 SOLUTION

The increase in profit before the cost of additional finance for Option A can be found as follows.

(a)

	£
Increase in contribution from additional sales	
25% × £1,800,000 × 40%*	180,000
Less increase in bad debts	
(3% × £2,250,000) – £18,000	49,500
Increase in annual profit	130,500

* The C/S ratio is (100% – (75% × 80%)) = 40%

(b)

	£
Proposed investment in debtors	
£2,250,000 × 1/6	375,000
Less current investment in debtors	
£1,800,000 × 1/12	150,000
Additional investment required	225,000
Cost of additional finance at 20%	£45,000

(c) As the increase in profit exceeds the cost of additional finance, Option A should be adopted.

Credit insurance

1.17 Companies might be able to obtain **credit insurance** against certain approved debts going bad through a specialist credit insurance firm. A company cannot insure against all its bad debt losses, but may be able to insure against losses above the normal level.

1.18 When a company arranges credit insurance, it must submit specific proposals for credit to the insurance company, stating the name of each customer to which it wants to give credit and the amount of credit it wants to give. The insurance company will accept, amend or refuse these proposals, depending on its assessment of each of these customers.

1.19 Credit insurance is normally available for only up to about 75% of a company's potential bad debt loss. The remaining 25% of any bad debt costs are borne by the company itself. This is to ensure that the company does not become slack with its credit control and debt collection procedures, for example by indulging in overtrading and not chasing slow payers hard enough.

Factoring

KEY TERM

Factoring: the sale of debts to a third party (the factor) at a discount, in return for prompt cash. A factoring service may be **with recourse**, in which case the supplier takes the risk of the debt not being paid, or **without recourse** when the factor takes the risk *(OT)*.

1.20 The main aspects of factoring are:

(a) administration of the client's invoicing, sales accounting and debt collection service;

(b) credit protection for the client's debts, whereby the factor takes over the risk of loss from bad debts and so 'insures' the client against such losses. This service is also referred to as 'debt underwriting' or the 'purchase of a client's debts'. The factor usually purchases these debts 'without recourse' to the client, which means that if the client's debtors do not pay what they owe, the factor will not ask for his money back from the client;

(c) making payments to the client in advance of collecting the debts. This is sometimes referred to as 'factor finance' because the factor is providing cash to the client against outstanding debts.

The debts administration service of factoring companies

1.21 A company might be struggling just to do the administrative tasks of recording credit sales, sending out invoices, sending out monthly statements and reminders, and collecting and recording payments from customers. If the company's turnover is growing rapidly, or if its sales are changing from largely cash sales to largely credit sales, the accounting administration might be unable to cope with the extra work. A factoring organisation can help.

1.22 The administration of a client's debts by the factor covers:

(a) keeping the books of account for sales;
(b) sending out invoices to customers;
(c) collecting the debts;
(d) credit control (ensuring that customers pay on time) and chasing late payers.

1.23 For the client the advantages are that:

(a) the factor takes on a job of administration which saves staff costs for the client;

(b) the factor performs the service economically, by taking advantage of economies of scale for a large debts administration organisation. This should enable the factor to price his services reasonably.

1.24 The factor's service fee for debt administration varies according to the size of the client's operation, but it is typically between 0.75% and 2% of the book value of the client's debts. A business might be considered too small for factoring if its annual turnover were less than £250,000.

1.25 Many companies do not have the information or the capability to assess credit risks properly. Factors, however, do have this capability, and can therefore carry out the credit

control function for a client, vetting individual customers and deciding whether to grant credit and how much credit to allow. Because they control credit in this way, they will also underwrite their client's debts.

1.26 Most factors provide a debts administration service in which credit protection is an integral part. This is because the service is usually without recourse to the client in the event of non-payment by the customer. **Without recourse or non-recourse factoring** effectively means that the factor buys the client's debts from him and so the client is guaranteed protection against bad debts.

1.27 Under a 'without recourse' arrangement, the factor assumes full responsibility for credit control, because he now bears the credit risk.

(a) The factors will approve the amount of credit to be allowed to individual customers by the client.

(b) The factor will keep a continuous watch over customers' accounts.

(c) If a payment becomes overdue, the factor will consult the client. The client may decide to take over the bad debt risk from the factor, rather than incur badwill from the customer if the factor were to take legal action to recover the debt. Otherwise the factor is free to take non-payers to court to obtain payment.

1.28 Not every factoring organisation will purchase approved debts without recourse and **with recourse factoring** might be provided, for example for very large debts.

Making advances on debts (factor finance)

1.29 Some companies have difficulty in financing their debtors. There are two main reasons for this.

(a) If a company's turnover is rising rapidly, its total debtors will rise quickly too. Selling more on credit will put a strain on the company's cash flow. The company, although making profits, might find itself in difficulties because it has too many debtors and not enough cash.

(b) If a company grants long credit to its customers, it might run into cash flow difficulties for much the same reason. Exporting companies must often allow long periods of credit to foreign buyers.

1.30 Factors offer their clients a debt financing service to overcome these problems, and will be prepared to advance cash to the client against the security of the client's debtors. The client will assign his debtors to the factor.

The advantages of factoring

1.31 The benefits of factoring for a business customer include the following.

(a) The business can pay its suppliers promptly, and so be able to take advantage of any early payment discounts that are available.

(b) Optimum stock levels can be maintained, because the business will have enough cash to pay for the stocks it needs.

(c) Growth can be financed through sales rather than by injecting fresh external capital.

(d) The business gets finance linked to its volume of sales. In contrast, overdraft limits tend to be determined by historical balance sheets.

(e) The managers of the business do not have to spend their time on the problems of slow paying debtors.

(f) The business does not incur the costs of running its own sales ledger department.

1.32 An important disadvantage is that debtors will be making payments direct to the factor, which is likely to present a negative picture of the firm.

Factoring and bank finance

1.33 If a company arranges with a factor for advances to be made against its debts, the debts will become the security for the advance. This may require the consent of any bank which has a charge over the company. If the same company already has a bank overdraft facility, the bank may be relying on the debts as a form of security (perhaps not legal security, in the form of a floating charge over stocks and debtors, but as an element in the decision about how much overdraft to allow the company). The bank may therefore wish to reduce the company's overdraft limit. Certainly, a company should inform its bank when it makes an agreement with a factor for advances against debts.

1.34 EXAMPLE: FACTORING

A company makes annual credit sales of £1,500,000. Credit terms are 30 days, but its debt administration has been poor and the average collection period has been 45 days with 0.5% of sales resulting in bad debts which are written off.

A factor would take on the task of debt administration and credit checking, at an annual fee of 2.5% of credit sales. The company would save £30,000 a year in administration costs. The payment period would be 30 days. The factor would also provide an advance of 80% of invoiced debts at an interest rate of 14% (3% over the current base rate). The company can obtain an overdraft facility to finance its debtors at a rate of 2.5% over base rate.

Should the factor's services be accepted? Assume a constant monthly turnover.

1.35 SOLUTION

It is assumed that the factor would advance an amount equal to 80% of the invoiced debts, and the balance 30 days later.

(a) The current situation is as follows, using the company's debt collection staff and a bank overdraft to finance all debts.

Credit sales	£1,500,000 pa
Average credit period	45 days

The annual cost is as follows.

	£
$\frac{45}{365} \times £1,500,000 \times 13.5\%$	24,966
Bad debts: 0.5% × £1,500,000	7,500
Total cost	32,466

(b) **The cost of the factor**

80% of credit sales financed by the factor would be 80% of £1,500,000 = £1,200,000. For a consistent comparison, we must assume that 20% of credit sales would be financed by a bank overdraft.

The average credit period would be only 30 days.

The annual cost would be as follows.

		£
Factor's finance	$\left(\frac{30}{365} \times £1,200,000 \times 14\%\right)$	13,808
Overdraft	$\left(\frac{30}{365} \times £300,000 \times 13.5\%\right)$	3,329
		17,137
Cost of factor's services: 2.5% × £1,500,000		37,500
Less savings in company's administration costs		(30,000)
Net cost of the factor		24,637

(c) **Conclusion**

The factor is cheaper. In this case, the factor's fees exactly equal the savings in bad debts (£7,500) and administration costs (£30,000). The factor is then cheaper overall because it will be more efficient at collecting debts. The advance of 80% of debts is not needed, however, if the company has sufficient overdraft facility because the factor's finance charge of 14% is higher than the company's overdraft rate of 13.5%.

Invoice discounting

1.36 **Invoice discounting** is related to factoring and many factors will provide an invoice discounting service. It is the purchase of a selection of invoices, at a discount. The invoice discounter does not take over the administration of the client's sales ledger, and the arrangement is purely for the advance of cash. A client should only want to have some invoices discounted when he has a temporary cash shortage, and so invoice discounting tends to consist of one-off deals.

KEY TERM

Invoice discounting: the sale of debts to a third party at a discount, in return for prompt cash. The administration is managed in such a way that the debtor is generally unaware of the discounter's involvement and continues to pay the supplier *(OT)*.

1.37 **Confidential invoice discounting** is an arrangement whereby a debt is confidentially assigned to the factor, and the client's customer will only become aware of the arrangement if he does not pay his debt to the client.

1.38 If a client needs to generate cash, he can approach a factor or invoice discounter, who will offer to purchase selected invoices and advance up to 75% of their value. At the end of each month, the factor will pay over the balance of the purchase price, less charges, on the invoices that have been settled in the month. (Receipts from the paid invoices belong to the invoice discounter or factor).

1.39 There is an element of **credit protection** in the invoice discounting service, but its real purpose is to improve the client's cash flow. Since the invoice discounter does not control debt administration, and relies on the client to collect the debts for him, it is a more risky operation than normal factoring and so a factor might only agree to offer an invoice discounting service to reliable, well established companies.

2 THE MANAGEMENT OF CREDITORS AND SHORT-TERM FINANCE

11/98

Management of trade creditors

2.1 The management of creditors involves:

(a) attempting to obtain satisfactory credit from suppliers;
(b) attempting to extend credit during periods of cash shortage;
(c) maintaining good relations with regular and important suppliers.

If a supplier offers a discount for the early payment of debts, the evaluation of the decision whether or not to accept the discount is similar to the evaluation of the decision whether or not to **offer** a discount. One problem is the mirror image of the other. The methods of evaluating the offer of a discount to customers were described earlier.

Standard terms of trade for suppliers

2.2 The introduction of standard terms of trade for suppliers has a number of merits.

- Administrative processes for dealing with supplier invoice are greatly simplified.
- Cash flow forecasting becomes more straightforward.
- If the terms are communicated clearly to suppliers and formally agreed, the customer/supplier relationship will be smoother, and the number of payment queries reduced.

2.3 The terms should be both reasonable and flexible and not imposed unilaterally. Possible problems that could arise include the following.

- There will always be some suppliers for whom different terms will be required, for example, telephone accounts normally have to be settled within ten days, and there must be procedures for dealing with these situations.
- The company must ensure that it does not forgo valuable settlement discount opportunities in the process. Where such opportunities exist, they must be evaluated in financial terms, and the system must be able to deal with earlier payments if necessary.
- There must be procedures in place to ensure that even within the policy, credit opportunities are maximised, for example, credit notes should be taken immediately where they relate to earlier invoices, and not also held for the standard credit period.

Sources of short-term finance

2.4 Taking trade credit from suppliers is one way in which a company can obtain some **short-term finance**, in addition to its longer term sources. Short-term finance can also be obtained:

(a) with a bank overdraft;

(b) by raising finance from a bank or other organisation against the security of trade debtors, for example through factoring or invoice discounting (both described earlier in this chapter);

(c) for larger companies, by issuing short-term debt instruments, such as commercial paper.

Trade credit

2.5 Taking credit from suppliers is a normal feature of business. Nearly every company has some trade creditors waiting for payment. Trade credit is a source of short-term finance because it helps to keep working capital down. It is usually a cheap source of finance since suppliers rarely charge interest. However, trade credit *will* have a cost, whenever a company is offered a discount for early payment, but opts instead to take longer credit.

Trade credit and the cost of lost early payment discounts

2.6 Trade credit from suppliers is a major source of finance. It is particularly important to small and fast growing firms. The costs of making maximum use of trade credit include:

(a) the loss of suppliers' goodwill;
(b) the loss of any available cash discounts for the early payment of debts.

2.7 The cost of lost cash discounts can be estimated by the formula:

$$\frac{d}{100-d} \times \frac{365}{t}$$

where d is the size of the discount (for a 5% discount, d = 5)
t is the reduction in the payment period in days which would be necessary to obtain the early payment discount.

2.8 EXAMPLE: TRADE CREDIT

X Ltd has been offered credit terms from its major supplier of 2/10, net 45. That is, a cash discount of 2% will be given if payment is made within ten days of the invoice, and payments must be made within 45 days of the invoice. The company has the choice of paying 98p per £1 on day 10 (to pay before day 10 would be unnecessary), or to invest the 98p for an additional 35 days and eventually pay the supplier £1 per £1. The decision as to whether the discount should be accepted depends on the opportunity cost of investing 98p for 35 days. What should the company do?

2.9 SOLUTION

If the company refuses the cash discount, and pays in full after 45 days, the implied cost of interest per annum would be approximately

$$\frac{2}{100-2} \times \frac{365}{35} = 21.3\%$$

2.10 Suppose that X Ltd can invest cash to obtain an annual return of 25%, and that there is an invoice from the supplier for £1,000. The two alternatives are as follows.

	Refuse discount	*Accept discount*
	£	£
Payment to supplier	1,000.0	980
Return from investing £980 between day 10 and day 45:		
$£980 \times \frac{35}{365} \times 25\%$	23.5	-
Net cost	976.5	980

It is cheaper to refuse the discount because the investment rate of return on cash retained, in this example, exceeds the saving from the discount.

2.11 Although a company may delay payment beyond the final due date, thereby obtaining even longer credit from its suppliers, such a policy would be inadvisable (except where an unexpected short-term cash shortage has arisen). Unacceptable delays in payment will worsen the company's credit rating, and additional credit may become difficult to obtain.

Problems with taking too long a credit period

2.12 Problems may arise when credit periods taken regularly **exceed the terms of trade**. Many suppliers now impose a cost for the additional credit taken, as demonstrated above, and this should be compared with the cost of alternative short-term sources of funds to ensure that the cost of trade credit is not in fact greater than that of other funds. Further disadvantages to taking long credit periods include the following.

- The company's credit rating will be reduced.
- It may be difficult to obtain additional credit from suppliers.
- The company may rank behind other customers due to its payment record if shortages of materials arise.
- The goodwill between the company and its suppliers will be eroded. This may damage the business in other ways, for example, it may be difficult to get extra goods at short notice.
- Extra administrative costs will arise from the fact that suppliers will be continually chasing for payment.
- Staff morale may be eroded if those who are regularly deal with suppliers feel that they are unable to do an efficient job due to the payment policy in place.

Bills of exchange

KEY TERM

Bill of exchange: An unconditional written order given by one party (the drawer of the bill) to another (the drawee).

2.13 **Bills of exchange** are a form of IOU. When A sells goods to B, the settlement of the debt might be arranged by means of a bill of exchange (called a **trade bill** as B is a trader). A will draw a bill on B (asking B to pay a certain sum of money on a certain date in the future, such as 90 days after the date of the bill). B then accepts the bill, by signing it, and returns it to A. By accepting the bill, B is acknowledging its debt to A and is giving a promise to pay. After the credit period (the term of the bill) has expired, B will pay A the money owed. A trade bill is therefore a form of trade credit.

Trade bills and obtaining finance against the security of debtors

2.14 When a company obtains payment from its customers through trade bills, it can arrange to obtain finance from its bank against the security of the bill.

2.15 For example, if A Ltd sells goods to B Ltd for £50,000, the terms of payment might be agreed so that A Ltd draws a 90 day bill of exchange on B Ltd for £50,000, which B Ltd 'accepts'. A Ltd can then ask its bank to discount the bill, and A Ltd will receive payment (less discount) now from the bank instead of in 90 days from B Ltd. After 90 days, B Ltd must pay the holder of the bill which might still be the bank.

The rate of discount on the bill, which is the cost to A Ltd of discounting, will depend on the 'quality' of the bill. A higher discount applies to trade bills (bills drawn on and accepted by companies such as B Ltd) than to bank bills (bills drawn on and accepted by a bank). A lower discount is called a 'finer' discount.

Trade debts and obtaining short-term finance

2.16 Banks might agree to accept bills on a customer's behalf, provided that arrangements are made for the customer to reimburse the bank. Both trade bills and bank bills (also called acceptance credits - see below) are used quite commonly in international trade.

For example, suppose that Hexham Ltd in the UK sells goods to a company in Singapore. The terms of payment might be for Hexham Ltd to draw a bill of exchange on the Singapore company's bank (in the UK or Singapore). The bank bill could then be used by Hexham Ltd to raise finance, with the bill attracting a finer rate of discount because it has been accepted by a reputable bank.

Acceptance credits

2.17 **Acceptance credits** are a source of finance from banks for large companies, which are an alternative to bank overdrafts.

2.18 Acceptance credits have much in common with bills of exchange, but they are different. They are not the acceptance of bills of exchange by a bank on a customer's behalf, but are a development from this service. Acceptance credits are drawn by a company on a bank. An acceptance credit facility, which is offered by clearing banks as well as merchant banks, operates as follows.

(a) A bank and a large corporate customer agree a facility which allows the customer to draw bills of exchange on the bank, which the bank will accept. The bills are normally payable after 60 or 90 days, but might have a term as long as 180 days. They can be denominated in sterling or in a foreign currency.

(b) The accepted bills are then sold (discounted) by the bank in the discount market on behalf of the customer, and the money obtained from the sale, minus the bank's acceptance commission, is made available to the customer. Because of the bank's standing and reputation, bills accepted by it can be sold in the market at a low rate of discount.

(c) When a bill matures, the company will pay the bank the value of the bill and the bank will use the money in turn to pay the bill holder.

2.19 A bank will only agree to provide an acceptance credit facility to a corporate customer of good standing, because the bank must be confident that its money is safe. The length of time over which the acceptance credit facility is available will be subject to agreement between the bank and the customer, but may be as long as five years. The customer can draw bills on the bank throughout this period, up to the credit limit.

2.20 Acceptance credits are attractive to customers for the following reasons.

(a) They provide companies with alternative finance to a bank overdraft, with the money being obtained from a source outside the bank (the purchaser of the discounted bills).

(b) The amount of credit is promised to the customer for a stated period of time.

(c) There may be a cost advantage to the customer, because the rate of discount on bank bills in the discount market might be lower than the interest rate on a bank loan, or overdraft, which is related to the bank base rate or LIBOR. The reason for this is mainly that the interest rate on a discounted bill is fixed for the life of the bill (typically 90 days) because this rate is inherent in the discounted sale price of the bill. If market interest rates are rising during this period, and overdraft rates are going up, it would be more costly to maintain an overdraft than to have an acceptance credit facility.

(d) The company can assess the cost of its credit facility with more certainty, because costs are fixed over the life of a bill.

3 THE MANAGEMENT OF STOCKS

3.1 Almost every company carries stocks of some sort, even if they are only stocks of consumables such as stationery. For a manufacturing business, stocks (sometimes called inventories), in the form of raw materials, work in progress and finished goods, may amount to a substantial proportion of the total assets of the business.

3.2 Some businesses attempt to control stocks on a scientific basis by balancing the costs of stock shortages against those of stock holding. The 'scientific' control of stocks may be analysed into three parts.

(a) The economic order quantity (EOQ) model can be used to decide the optimum order size for stocks which will minimise the costs of ordering stocks plus stockholding costs.

(b) If discounts for bulk purchases are available, it may be cheaper to buy stocks in large order sizes so as to obtain the discounts.

(c) Uncertainty in the demand for stocks and/or the supply lead time may lead a company to decide to hold buffer stocks (thereby increasing its investment in working capital) in order to reduce or eliminate the risk of 'stock-outs' (running out of stock).

Stock costs

3.3 Stock costs can be conveniently classified into four groups.

(a) **Holding costs** comprise the cost of capital tied up, warehousing and handling costs, deterioration, obsolescence, insurance and pilferage.

(b) **Procuring costs** depend on how the stock is obtained but will consist of **ordering costs** for goods purchased externally, such as clerical costs, telephone charges and delivery costs.

(c) **Shortage costs** may be:

(i) the loss of a sale and the contribution which could have been earned from the sale;

(ii) the extra cost of having to buy an emergency supply of stocks at a high price;

(iii) the cost of lost production and sales, where the stock-out brings an entire process to a halt.

(d) **The cost of the stock itself**, the supplier's price or the direct cost per unit of production, will also need to be considered when the supplier offers a discount on orders for purchases in bulk.

Stock models

3.4 There are several different types of stock model, and these can be classified under the following headings.

(a) A **deterministic model** is one in which all the 'parameters' are known with certainty. In particular, the rate of demand and the supply lead time are known.

(b) A **stochastic model** is one in which the supply lead time or the rate of demand for an item is not known with certainty. However, the demand or the lead time follows a known probability distribution (probably constructed from a historical analysis of demand or lead time in the past).

In a deterministic system, since the demand and the lead time are known with certainty, there is no need for a safety stock. However, in a stochastic model, it may be necessary to have a buffer stock to limit the number of stock-outs or to avoid stock-outs completely.

3.5 Stochastic models are sometimes classified as follows.

(a) A **P system is a periodic review system** in which the requirement for stock is reviewed at fixed time intervals, and varying quantities are ordered on each occasion, according to the current level of stocks remaining.

(b) A **Q system is a re-order level system** in which a fixed quantity is ordered at irregular intervals, when stock levels have fallen to a re-order level specified on the store-keeper's records or 'bin card'.

A deterministic model: the basic EOQ formula

3.6 The economic order quantity (EOQ) is the optimal ordering quantity for an item of stock which will minimise costs.

Let D = the usage in units for one year (the demand)
C_o = the cost of making one order } relevant costs only
C_h = the holding cost per unit of stock for one year } relevant costs only
Q = the re-order quantity

Assume that:

(a) demand is constant;
(b) the lead time is constant or zero;
(c) purchase costs per unit are constant (ie no bulk discounts).

The total annual cost of having stock (T) is:

Holding costs + ordering costs

$$\frac{QC_h}{2} + \frac{C_oD}{Q}$$

The objective is to minimise $T = \frac{QC_h}{2} + \frac{C_oD}{Q}$

3.7 The order quantity, Q, which will minimise these total costs is:

$$Q = \sqrt{\frac{2C_oD}{C_h}}$$

Exam focus point

Derivation of the above EOQ formula is unlikely to be required, but it is useful to be aware of the components of the formula.

3.8 EXAMPLE: ECONOMIC ORDER QUANTITY

The demand for a commodity is 40,000 units a year, at a steady rate. It costs £20 to place an order, and 40p to hold a unit for a year. Find the order size to minimise stock costs, the number of orders placed each year, and the length of the stock cycle.

3.9 SOLUTION

$$Q = \sqrt{\frac{2C_oD}{C_h}} = \sqrt{\frac{2 \times 20 \times 40{,}000}{0.4}}$$

$$= 2{,}000 \text{ units}$$

This means that there will be

$\frac{40{,}000}{2{,}000}$ = 20 orders placed each year, so that the stock cycle is once every 52 ÷ 20 = 2.6 weeks.

Total costs will be $(20 \times £20) + (\frac{2{,}000}{2} \times 40p) = £800$ a year.

Uncertainties in demand and lead times: a re-order level system

3.10 When the volume of demand is uncertain, or the supply lead time is variable, there are problems in deciding what the re-order level should be. By holding a 'safety stock', a company can reduce the likelihood that stocks run out during the re-order period (due to high demand or a long lead time before the new supply is delivered). The average annual cost of such a safety stock would be:

Quantity of safety stock (in units)	×	Stock holding cost per unit per annum

3.11 The behaviour of the system would appear in a diagram as in Figure 1.

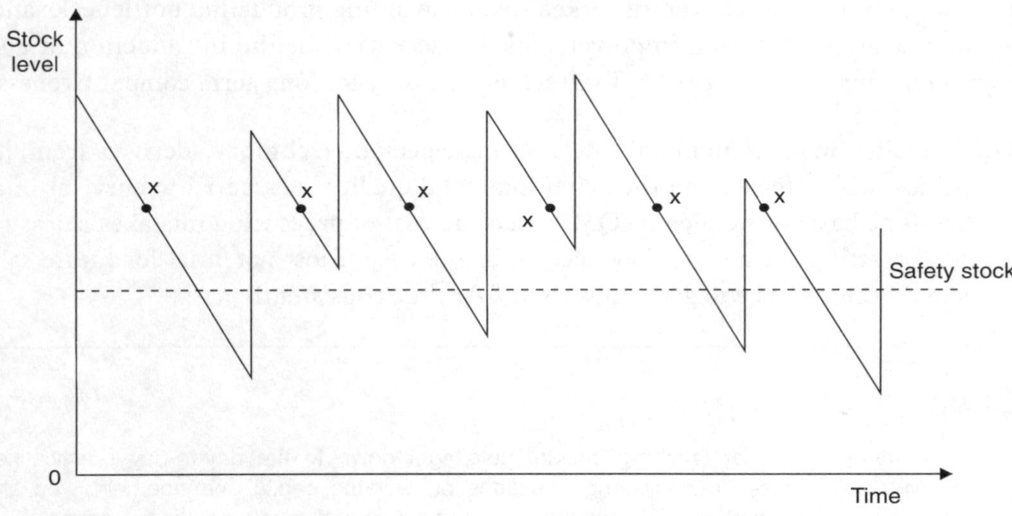

Figure 1

Points marked 'X' show the re-order level at which a new order is placed. The number of units ordered each time is the EOQ. Actual stock levels sometimes fall below the safety stock level, and sometimes the re-supply arrives before stocks have fallen to the safety level, but on average, extra stock holding amounts to the volume of safety stock. The size of the safety stock will depend on whether stock-outs (running out of stock) are allowed.

Just-in-time (JIT) procurement

3.12 In recent years, there have been developments in the inventory policy of some manufacturing companies which have sought to reduce their inventories of raw materials and components to as low a level as possible. This approach differs from other models, such as the EOQ model, which seek to minimise **costs** rather than inventory levels.

3.13 **Just-in-time procurement** and **stockless production** are terms which describe a policy of obtaining goods from suppliers at the latest possible time (ie when they are needed) and so avoiding the need to carry any materials or components stock.

3.14 Introducing JIT might bring the following potential benefits.

(a) Reduction in stock holding costs
(b) Reduced manufacturing lead times
(c) Improved labour productivity
(d) Reduced scrap/rework/warranty cost
(e) Price reductions on purchased materials
(f) Reduction in the number of accounting transactions

Reduced stock levels mean that a lower level of investment in working capital will be required.

3.15 JIT will not be appropriate in some cases. For example, a restaurant might find it preferable to use the traditional economic order quantity approach for staple non-perishable food stocks but adopt JIT for perishable and 'exotic' items. In a hospital, a stock-out could quite literally be fatal and JIT would be quite unsuitable.

Total quality management

3.16 A system of just-in-time procurement depends for its success on a smooth and predictable production flow, and so a JIT policy must also be aimed at improving production systems, eliminating waste (rejects and reworked items), avoiding production bottlenecks and so on. Many now argue that such improvements are necessary for the introduction of **advanced manufacturing technology** (AMT) which is necessary for long-term competitiveness.

3.17 **Total quality management** (TQM) is a management technique, derived from Japanese companies, which focuses on the belief that 'total quality is essential to survival in a global market'. The basic principle of TQM is that the cost of preventing mistakes is less than the cost of correcting them once they occur plus the cost of lost potential for future sales. The aim should therefore be to get things right first time consistently.

Chapter roundup

- The **management of working capital** gets right down to the day-to-day practicalities of running a business. In answering questions on working capital management, you should always consider whether any proposed course of action really makes business sense.

Quick quiz

1. What factors should be considered by management in the formulation of a policy for credit control? (see para 1.1)
2. How might the creditworthiness of a potential new customer be checked? (1.5, 1.6)
3. What is credit insurance? (1.17)
4. What services do factors provide? (1.20)
5. What is invoice discounting? (1.36)
6. What are acceptance credits? (2.17 - 2.20)
7. What is meant by JIT procurement? (3.13)
8. What is meant by total quality management? (3.17)

Question to try	Level	Marks	Time
16	Introductory	n/a	15 mins

Chapter 17

CASH MANAGEMENT

Chapter topic list		Syllabus reference	Ability required
1	Cash management techniques	13 b(ix)	Application
2	Short-term investments	13 b(ix)	Application
3	Payment methods	13 b(ix)	Application

Introduction

As with other aspects of working capital management, you must be prepared for **numerical questions** as well as discussions of policy issues in this area. The Examiner has stressed that knowledge of **cash management models** and the **use of probabilities** in this area is essential, as is familiarity with the **impact of new technology on payment systems**.

1 CASH MANAGEMENT TECHNIQUES 5/97

The need for cash management

1.1 How much cash should a company keep on hand or 'on short call' at a bank? The more cash which is on hand, the easier it will be for the company to meet its bills as they fall due and to take advantage of discounts. However, holding cash or near equivalents to cash has a cost in terms of the loss of earning which would otherwise have been obtained by using the funds in another way. The financial manager must try to balance liquidity with profitability.

1.2 We have already introduced the operating cycle, which connects investment in working capital with cash flows. Cash flow problems can arise in several ways.

(a) **Making losses**. If a business is continually making losses, it will eventually have cash flow problems. Just how long it will take before a loss-making business runs into cash flow trouble will depend on how big the losses are, and whether the depreciation charge is enough to create a loss despite a cash flow surplus. In such a situation, the cash flow troubles might only begin when the business needs to replace fixed assets.

(b) **Inflation**. In a period of inflation, a business needs ever-increasing amounts of cash just to replace used-up and worn-out assets. A business can be making a profit in historical cost accounting terms, but still not be receiving enough cash to buy the replacement assets it needs.

(c) **Growth**. When a business is growing, it needs to acquire more fixed assets, and to support higher amounts of stocks and debtors. These additional assets must be paid for somehow (or financed by creditors).

(d) **Seasonal business**. When a business has seasonal or cyclical sales, it may have cash flow difficulties at certain times of the year, when (i) cash inflows are low, but (ii) cash outflows are high, perhaps because the business is building up its stocks for the next period of high sales.

(e) **One-off items of expenditure**. There might occasionally be a single non-recurring item of expenditure that creates a cash flow problem, such as:

(i) the repayment of loan capital on maturity of the debt. Businesses often try to finance such loan repayments by borrowing again;

(ii) the purchase of an exceptionally expensive item. For example, a small or medium-sized business might decide to buy a freehold property which then stretches its cash resources for several months or even years.

Methods of easing cash shortages

1.3 The steps that are usually taken by a company when a need for cash arises, and when it cannot obtain resources from any other source such as a loan or an increased overdraft, are as follows.

(a) **Postponing capital expenditure**

Some capital expenditure items are more important and urgent than others.

(i) It might be imprudent to postpone expenditure on fixed assets which are needed for the development and growth of the business.

(ii) On the other hand, some capital expenditures are routine and might be postponable without serious consequences. The routine replacement of motor vehicles is an example. If a company's policy is to replace company cars every two years, but the company is facing a cash shortage, it might decide to replace cars every three years.

(b) **Accelerating cash inflows which would otherwise be expected in a later period**

The most obvious way of bringing forward cash inflows would be to press debtors for earlier payment. Often, this policy will result in a loss of goodwill and problems with customers. There will also be very little scope for speeding up payments when the credit period currently allowed to debtors is no more than the norm for the industry. It might be possible to encourage debtors to pay more quickly by offering discounts for earlier payment.

(c) **Reversing past investment decisions by selling assets previously acquired**

Some assets are less crucial to a business than others and so if cash flow problems are severe, the option of selling investments or property might have to be considered.

(d) **Negotiating a reduction in cash outflows, so as to postpone or even reduce payments**

There are several ways in which this could be done.

(i) Longer credit might be taken from suppliers. However, if the credit period allowed is already generous, creditors might be very reluctant to extend credit even further and any such extension of credit would have to be negotiated carefully. There would be a serious risk of having further supplies refused.

(ii) Loan repayments could be rescheduled by agreement with a bank.

(iii) A deferral of the payment of corporation tax could be agreed with the Inland Revenue. Corporation tax is payable nine months after a company's year end, but

it might be possible to arrange a postponement by a few months. When this happens, the Inland Revenue will charge interest on the outstanding amount of tax.

(iv) Dividend payments could be reduced. Dividend payments are discretionary cash outflows, although a company's directors might be constrained by shareholders' expectations, so that they feel obliged to pay dividends even when there is a cash shortage.

Deviations from expected cash flows

1.4 Cash budgets, whether prepared on an annual, monthly, weekly or even a daily basis, can only be estimates of cash flows. Even the best estimates will not be exactly correct, so deviations from the cash budget are inevitable.

1.5 This uncertainty about actual cash flows ought to be considered when the cash budget is prepared. It is desirable to prepare additional cash budgets based on different assumptions about sales levels, costs, collection periods, bad debts and so on. A cash budget model could be constructed, using a microcomputer and a spreadsheet package, and the sensitivity of cash flow forecasts to changes in estimates of sales, costs and so on could be analysed. By planning for different eventualities, management should be able to prepare contingency measures in advance and also appreciate the key factors in the cash budget.

1.6 A knowledge of the probability distribution of possible outcomes for the cash position will allow a more accurate estimate to be made of the minimum cash balances, or the borrowing power necessary, to provide a satisfactory margin of safety. Unforeseen deficits can be hard to finance at short notice, and advance planning is desirable.

Cash management services: computerised cash management

1.7 A relatively recent development in banking services is a cash management service for corporate customers. A company with many different bank accounts can obtain information about the cash balance in each account through a computer terminal in the company's treasury department linked to the bank's computer. The company can then arrange to move cash from one account to another and so manage its cash position more efficiently and make optimal use of its funds deposited with banks or in various money market investments. A cash management service can be provided to a company with several bank accounts in the UK, or, through an international network of banks, to a multinational company with accounts in different currencies in various countries.

1.8 The cash management services provided by the banks comprise three basic services.

(a) **Account reporting**

(i) Information is given about the balances on sterling or currency accounts whether held in the UK or overseas, including details of the cleared balance for the previous day and any uncleared items.

(ii) Forecast balance reports, which take into account uncleared items and automated entries (BACS credits and debits, standing orders and direct debits) can be obtained.

(iii) Reports giving details of individual transactions can be obtained.

(b) **Funds transfer** The customer can initiate sterling and currency payments through his terminal. Banks will also give customers with substantial cash floats the opportunity to get in touch with money market dealers directly and deposit funds in the money markets.

(c) **Decision support services.** A rates information service, giving information on foreign exchange rates and money market (sterling deposit) interest rates, can be used.

Float

1.9 The term 'float' is sometimes used to describe the amount of money tied up between:

(a) the time when a payment is initiated (for example when a debtor sends a cheque in payment, probably by post); and

(b) the time when the funds become available for use in the recipient's bank account.

1.10 There are three reasons why there might be a lengthy float.

(a) **Transmission delay**. When payment is sent through the post, it will take a day or longer for the payment to reach the payee.

(b) **Delay in banking the payments received (lodgement delay).** The payee, on receipt of a cheque or cash, might delay presenting the cheque or the cash to his bank. The length of this delay will depend on administrative procedures in the payee's organisation.

(c) **The time needed for a bank to clear a cheque (clearance delay).** A payment is not available for use in the payee's bank account until the cheque has been cleared. This will usually take two or three days for cheques payable in the UK. For cheques payable abroad, the delay is much longer.

1.11 There are several measures that could be taken to reduce the float.

(a) The payee should ensure that the **lodgement delay** is kept to a minimum. **Cheques** received should be presented to the bank on the day of receipt.

(b) The payee might, in some cases, arrange to **collect cheques** from the payer's premises. This would only be practicable, however, if the payer is local. The payment would have to be large to make the extra effort worthwhile.

(c) The payer might be asked to pay through his own branch of a bank. The payer can give his bank detailed payment instructions, and use the credit clearing system of the bank giro. The **bank giro** is a means of making credit transfers for customers of other banks and other branches. The payee may include a bank giro credit slip on the bottom of his invoice, to help with this method of payment.

(d) **BACS** (Bankers' Automated Clearing Services Ltd) is a system which provides for the computerised transfer of funds between banks. In addition, BACS is available to corporate customers of banks for making payments. The customer must supply a magnetic tape or disk to BACS, which contains details of payments, and payment will be made in two days. BACS is now commonly used by companies for salary payments.

(e) For regular payments **standing orders** or **direct debits** might be used.

(f) **CHAPS** (Clearing House Automated Payments System) is a computerised system for banks to make same-day clearances (that is, immediate payment) between each other. Each member bank of CHAPS can allow its own corporate customers to make immediate transfers of funds through CHAPS. However, there is a large minimum size for payments using CHAPS.

1.12 EXAMPLE: CASH MANAGEMENT

Ryan Coates owns a chain of seven clothes shops in the London area. Takings at each shop are remitted once a week on Thursday evening to the head office, and are then banked at the start of business on Friday morning. As business is expanding, Ryan Coates has hired an accountant to help him. The accountant gave him the following advice.

'Turnover at the seven shops totalled £1,950,000 last year, at a constant daily rate, but you were paying bank overdraft charges at a rate of 11%. You could have reduced your overdraft costs by banking the shop takings each day, except for Saturday's takings. Saturday takings could have been banked on Mondays.'

Comment on the significance of this statement, stating your assumptions. The shops are closed on Sundays.

1.13 SOLUTION

(a) A bank overdraft rate of 11% a year is approximately 11/365 = 0.03% a day

(b) Annual takings of £1,950,000 would be an average of £1,950,000/312 = £6,250 a day for the seven shops in total, on the assumption that they opened for a 52 week year of six days a week (312 days).

(c) Using the approximate overdraft cost of 0.03% a day, the cost of holding £6,250 for one day instead of banking it is 0.03% × £6,250 = £1.875.

(d) Banking all takings up to Thursday evening of each week on Friday morning involves an unnecessary delay in paying cash into the bank. The cost of this delay would be either:

(i) the opportunity cost of investment capital for the business; or
(ii) the cost of avoidable bank overdraft charges.

It is assumed here that the overdraft cost is higher and is therefore more appropriate to use. It is also assumed that, for interest purposes, funds are credited when banked.

Takings on	*Could be banked on*	*Number of days delay incurred by Friday banking*
Monday	Tuesday	3
Tuesday	Wednesday	2
Wednesday	Thursday	1
Thursday	Friday	0
Friday	Saturday	6
Saturday	Monday	4
		16

In one week, the total number of days delay incurred by Friday banking is 16. At a cost of £1.875 a day, the weekly cost of Friday banking was £1.875 × 16 = £30.00, and the annual cost of Friday banking was £30.00 × 52 = £1,560.

(e) *Conclusion*. The company could have saved about £1,560 a year in bank overdraft charges last year. If the overdraft rate remains at 11% and turnover continues to increase, the saving from daily banking would be even higher next year.

Inventory approach to cash management

1.14 There a number of different formal cash management models designed to indicate the optimum amount of cash that a company should hold. One such model, **Baumol's model**, is based on the idea that deciding on optimum cash balances is a similar question to deciding on optimum stock levels.

1.15 We can distinguish two types of cost which are involved in obtaining cash:

(a) the **fixed cost** represented for example, by the issue cost of equity finance or the cost of negotiating an overdraft;

(b) the **variable cost** (opportunity cost) of keeping the money in the form of cash.

1.16 The inventory approach uses an equation of a similar form to the EOQ formula for stock management which we looked at earlier.

1.17 The average total cost incurred for a period in holding a certain average level of cash (C) is:

$$\frac{Qi}{2} + \frac{FS}{Q}$$

Where S = the amount of cash to be used in each time period
F = the fixed cost of obtaining new funds (cost per sale/purchase of securities)
i = the interest cost of holding cash or near cash equivalents
Q = the total amount to be raised to provide for S

EXAM FORMULA

$$\text{Optimum amount of securities sold} = \sqrt{\frac{2 \times \text{annual cash disbursements} \times \text{cost per sale of securities}}{\text{interest rate}}}$$

$$\text{ie: } Q = \sqrt{\frac{2FS}{i}}$$

1.18 EXAMPLE: INVENTORY APPROACH TO CASH MANAGEMENT

Finder Limited faces a fixed cost of £4,000 to obtain new funds. There is a requirement for £24,000 of cash over each period of one year for the foreseeable future. The interest cost of new funds is 12% per annum; the interest rate earned on short-term securities is 9% per annum. How much finance should Finder Limited raise at a time?

1.19 SOLUTION

The cost of holding cash is 12% – 9% = 3%
The optimum level of Q (the 're-order quantity') is:

$$\sqrt{\frac{2 \times 4{,}000 \times 24{,}000}{0.03}} = £80{,}000$$

The optimum amount of new funds to raise is £80,000.

This amount is raised every 80,000 ÷ 24,000 = $3^1/_3$ years.

Drawbacks of the inventory approach

1.20 The inventory approach has the following drawbacks.

(a) In reality, amounts required over future periods will be difficult to predict with much certainty.

 BPP PUBLISHING

(b) There may be costs associated with running out of cash.

(c) There may be other normal costs of holding cash which increase with the average amount held.

(d) The model works satisfactorily for a firm which uses up its cash inventory at a steady rate, but not if there are larger inflows and outflows of cash from time to time.

The Miller-Orr model

1.21 In an attempt to produce a more realistic approach to cash management, various models more complicated than the inventory approach have been developed. One of these, the **Miller-Orr model**, manages to achieve a reasonable degree of realism while not being too elaborate.

1.22 We can begin looking at the Miller-Orr model by asking what will happen if there is no attempt to manage cash balances. Clearly, the cash balance is likely to 'meander' upwards or downwards. The Miller-Orr model imposes limits to this meandering. If the cash balance reaches an upper limit (point A in Figure 1) the firm buys sufficient securities to return the cash balance to a normal level (called the 'return point'). When the cash balance reaches a lower limit (point B in Figure 1), the firm sells securities to bring the balance back to the return point.

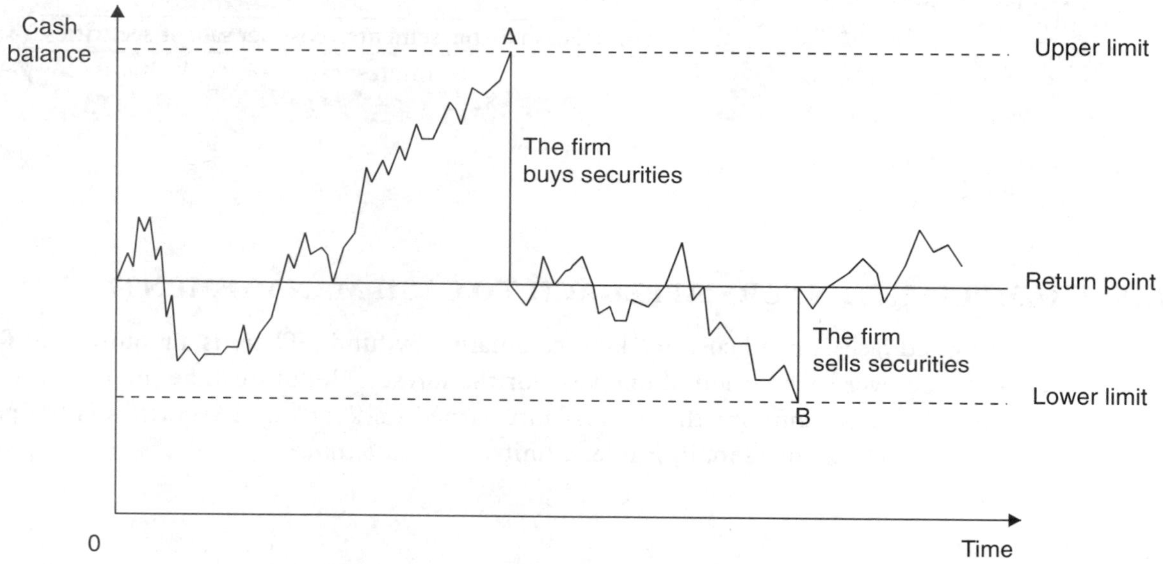

Figure 1 Applying the Miller-Orr model

1.23 How are the upper and lower limits and the return point set? Miller and Orr showed that the answer to this question depends on three factors:

(a) the variance of cash flows
(b) transaction costs
(c) interest rates

If the day-to-day variability of cash flows is high or the transaction cost in buying or selling securities is high, then wider limits should be set. If interest rates are high, the limits should be closer together.

1.24 To keep the interest costs of holding cash down, the return point is set at one-third of the distance (or 'spread') between the lower and the upper limit.

Return point = Lower limit + $^1/_3 \times$ spread

EXAM FORMULA

Spread between upper and lower cash balance limits.

$$= 3\left(\frac{3}{4} \times \frac{\text{transaction cost} \times \text{variance of cash flows}}{\text{interest rate}}\right)^{\frac{1}{3}}$$

1.25 To use the Miller-Orr model, it is necessary to follow the steps below.

(a) Set the lower limit for the cash balance. This may be zero, or it may be set at some minimum safety margin above zero.

(b) Estimate the variance of cash flows, for example from sample observations over a 100-day period.

(c) Note the interest rate and the transaction cost for each sale or purchase of securities (the latter is assumed to be fixed).

(d) Compute the upper limit and the return point from the model and instruct an employee to implement the limits strategy.

1.26 Now try applying the Miller-Orr equations yourself in the following exercise.

Question 1

The following data applies to a company.

(a) The minimum cash balance is £8,000.

(b) The variance of daily cash flows is 4,000,000, equivalent to a standard deviation of £2,000 per day.

(c) The transaction cost for buying or selling securities is £50.

(d) The interest rate is 0.025 per cent per day.

Required

Formulate a decision rule using the Miller-Orr model.

Answer

The spread between the upper and the lower cash balance limits is calculated as follows.

$$\text{Spread} = 3\left(\frac{3}{4} \times \frac{\text{transaction cost} \times \text{variance of cash flows}}{\text{interest rate}}\right)^{\frac{1}{3}}$$

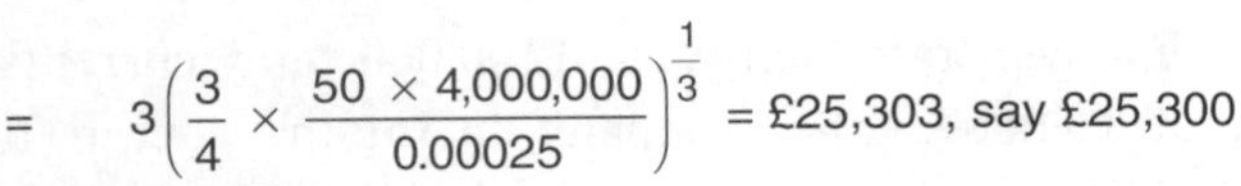

$$= 3\left(\frac{3}{4} \times \frac{50 \times 4{,}000{,}000}{0.00025}\right)^{\frac{1}{3}} = £25{,}303\text{, say } £25{,}300$$

The upper limit and return point are now calculated.

Upper limit = Lower limit + £25,300 = £8,000 + £25,300 = £33,300

Return point = lower limit + $^1/_3 \times$ spread

= £8,000 + $^1/_3 \times$ £25,300 = £16,433, say £16,400

The decision rule is as follows. If the cash balance reaches £33,300, buy £16,900 (= 33,300 – 16,400) in marketable securities. If the cash balance falls to £8,000, sell £8,400 of marketable securities for cash.

Advantages and disadvantages of the Miller-Orr model

1.27 The usefulness of the Miller-Orr model is limited by the assumptions on which it is based. In practice, cash inflows and outflows are unlikely to be entirely unpredictable as the model assumes: for example, for a retailer, seasonal factors are likely to affect cash inflows; for any company, dividend and tax payments will be known well in advance. However, the Miller-Orr model may save management time which might otherwise be spent in responding to those cash inflows and outflows which cannot be predicted.

Use of cash management models in practice

1.28 Some banks in the USA make cash management models available to their customers. These models vary from relatively simple spreadsheet-based models to more sophisticated systems such as those provided for multinational companies by the Chemical Bank. Like the basic Miller-Orr model, such models are designed to indicate minimum and maximum levels of cash holding in order to minimise the costs of holding idle cash balances and maximise interest earned on surplus funds.

1.29 As you might expect, such models require accurate inputs if they are to be effective. Sophisticated models, such as that used by the Chemical Bank, can take account of user's risk preferences by allowing limits to be set on the amount of funds allocated to any single investment. Users can manipulate variables to trace the effect on the short-term plan, which can help them to increase their awareness of the factors affecting day-to-day management decisions and the liquidity/profitability trade-off.

Exam focus point

You could be asked to discuss advantages and disadvantages of cash management models, but any formulae required to apply them would be provided in the exam.

Applying probabilities in cash management problems

Exam focus point

As mentioned in the Introduction to this chapter, the SFM examiner's guidance notes stress the importance of knowing how probabilities can be applied to cash management problems. The following example illustrates a use of this approach.

1.30 EXAMPLE: PROBABILITIES IN CASH MANAGEMENT

Sinkos Wim Ltd has an overdraft facility of £100,000, and currently has an overdraft balance at the bank of £34,000. The company maintains a cash float of £10,000 for transactions and precautionary purposes. It is unclear whether a long awaited economic recovery will take place, and the company has prepared cash budgets as set out below for the next three months using two different assumptions about economic events. The cash flow in months 2 and 3 depend on the cash flows in the previous month.

Estimated net cash flows

Month 1		*Month 2*		*Month 3*	
Probability	*Cash flow* £'000	*Probability*	*Cash flow* £'000	*Probability*	*Cash flow* £'000
		0.8	25	0.5	30
0.7	(40)			0.5	20
		0.2	10	0.5	10
				0.5	0
		0.8	0	0.5	(10)
0.3	(60)			0.5	(20)
		0.2	(10)	0.5	(40)
				0.5	(50)

Required

If the company intends to maintain a cash float of £10,000 at the end of each month, what is the probability that this will be possible at the end of each of months 1, 2 and 3 given the current overdraft limit?

1.31 SOLUTION

The opening balance at the beginning of month 1 is £10,000.

Month 1				*Month 2*				*Month 3*			
Prob.	*Cash flow* £'000	*Clos. bal.* £'000	*Over-draft* £'000	*Prob.*	*Cash flow* £'000	*Clos. bal.* £'000	*Over-draft* £'000	*Prob.*	*Cash flow* £'000	*Clos. bal.* £'000	*Over-draft* £'000
								0.28	30	10	19
				0.56	25	10	49	0.28	20	10	29
0.7	(40)	10	74								
								0.07	10	10	54
				0.14	10	10	64	0.07	0	10	64
								0.12	(10)	6	100
				0.24	0	10	94	0.12	(20)	(4)	100
0.3	(60)	10	94								
								0.03	(40)	(34)	100
				0.06	(10)	6	100	0.03	(50)	(44)	100

The probabilities that the cash float of £10,000 can be maintained at the end of each month are as follows.

Month 1: $0.7 + 0.3 = 1.0$
Month 2: $0.56 + 0.14 + 0.24 = 0.94$
Month 3: $0.28 + 0.28 + 0.07 + 0.07 = 0.7$

Question 2

Using the figures in the above example, state the probabilities that the company completely runs out of cash at the end of each month.

Answer

Under none of the projected outcomes for months 1 and 2 does the company run out of cash.

For month 3, the probability of the company running out of cash is:

0.12 + 0.03 + 0.03 = 0.18

Multilateral netting

1.32 Where there is a large number of separate transactions in different currencies between different subsidiaries, in a multinational company the obligations of different subsidiaries may be netted off against each other on a multilateral basis. This may bring the advantage of reduced transaction costs because there will be a reduced level of transfers between different currencies. However, in some countries, such as France and Italy, there are regulations limiting or prohibiting **netting**.

1.33 EXAMPLE: MULTILATERAL NETTING

A group of companies controlled from the USA has subsidiaries in the UK, South Africa and France. Below, these subsidiaries are referred to as UK, SA and FR respectively. At 30 June 19X5, inter-company indebtedness is as follows.

Debtor	*Creditor*	*Amount*
UK	SA	1,200,000 South African rand (R)
UK	FR	480,000 French francs (FF)
FR	SA	800,000 South African rand
SA	UK	£74,000 sterling
SA	FR	375,000 French francs

It is the company's policy to net off inter-company balances to the greatest extent possible. The central treasury department is to use the following exchange rates for this purpose.

US$1 equals R 6.126 / £0.6800 / F 5.880.

You are required to calculate the net payments to be made between the subsidiaries after netting off of inter-company balances.

1.34 SOLUTION

The first step is to convert the balances into US dollars as a common currency.

Debtor	*Creditor*	*Amount in US dollars*
UK	SA	1,200,000 ÷ 6.126 = $195,886
UK	FR	480,000 ÷ 5.880 = $81,633
FR	SA	800,000 ÷ 6.126 = $130,591
SA	UK	£74,000 ÷ 0.6800 = $108,824
SA	FR	375,000 ÷ 5.880 = $63,776

Receiving subsidiaries		*Paying subsidiaries*		
	UK	*SA*	*FR*	*Total*
	$	$	$	$
UK	-	108,824	-	108,824
SA	195,886	-	130,591	326,477
FR	81,633	63,776	-	145,409
Total payments	(277,519)	(172,600)	(130,591)	580,710
Total receipts	108,824	326,477	145,409	
Net receipt/(payment)	(168,695)	153,877	14,818	

The UK subsidiary should make payments of $153,877 to the South African subsidiary and $14,818 to the French subsidiary.

2 SHORT-TERM INVESTMENTS 5/96

2.1 Companies and other organisations sometimes have a surplus of cash and become 'cash rich'. A cash surplus is likely to be temporary, but while it exists the company should seek to obtain a good return by investing or depositing the cash, without the risk of a capital loss (or at least, without the risk of an excessive capital loss).

2.2 Possible reasons for a cash surplus are:

(a) profitability from trading operations;

(b) low capital expenditure, perhaps because of an absence of profitable new investment opportunities;

(c) receipts from selling parts of the business.

The board of directors might keep the surplus in liquid form:

(a) to benefit from high interest rates that might be available from bank deposits, when returns on re-investment in the company appear to be lower;

(b) to have cash available should a strategic opportunity arise, perhaps for the takeover of another company for which a cash consideration might be needed;

(c) to buy back shares from shareholders in the near future;

(d) to pay an increased dividend to shareholders.

2.3 Temporary cash surpluses are likely to be:

(a) deposited with a bank or similar financial institution;

(b) invested in short-term debt instruments. Debt instruments are debt securities which can be traded;

(c) invested in longer term debt instruments, which can be sold on the stock market when the company eventually needs the cash;

(d) invested in shares of listed companies, which can be sold on the stock market when the company eventually needs the cash.

2.4 The problem with (c) and (d) is the risk of capital losses due to a fall in the market value of the securities. With short-term debt instruments (item (b)) any capital losses should not be large, because of the short term to maturity. With bank deposits (item (a)) the risk of capital losses is minimal.

Short-term deposits

2.5 Cash can of course be put into a **bank deposit** to earn interest. The rate of interest obtainable depends on the size of the deposit, and varies from bank to bank. There are other types of deposit, as follows.

(a) **Money market deposits**. There is a very large money market in the UK for inter-bank lending, with banks lending to each other and borrowing from each other for short terms ranging from as little as overnight up to terms of a year or more. The international money markets, as mentioned elsewhere in this Text, provide a way of earning interest on deposits for periods from overnight up to five years. The interest

rates in the market are related to the London Interbank Offered Rate (LIBOR) and the London Interbank Bid Rate (LIBID).

(i) A large company will be able to lend surplus cash directly to a borrowing bank in the market.

(ii) A smaller company with a fairly large cash surplus will usually be able to arrange to lend money on the interbank market, but through its bank, and possibly on condition that the money can only be withdrawn at three months notice.

Deposits may be made in other currencies (**eurocurrency deposits**).

KEY TERM

Eurocurrency: currency which is held by individuals and institutions outside the country of issue of that currency.

(b) **Local authority deposits**. Local authorities often need short-term cash, and investors can deposit funds with them for periods ranging from overnight up to one year or more.

(c) **Finance house deposits**. These are time deposits with finance houses (usually subsidiaries of banks).

2.6 Deposits with banks, local authorities and finance houses are non-negotiable, which means that the investor who deposits funds cannot sell the deposit to another investor, should an unexpected need for cash arise. The deposit will only be released back to the investor when its term ends.

Short-term debt instruments

2.7 There are a number of short-term debt instruments which an investor can re-sell before the debt matures and is repaid, including:

(a) certificates of deposit (CDs);
(b) Treasury bills;
(c) bank bills, also called sterling bankers' acceptances;
(d) trade bills (discussed earlier);
(e) local authority bonds;
(f) commercial paper (discussed earlier).

Certificates of Deposit (CDs)

2.8 A **Certificate of Deposit** is a security that is issued by a bank, acknowledging that a certain amount of money has been deposited with it for a certain period of time (usually, a short term). The CD is issued to the depositor, and attracts a stated amount of interest. The depositor will be another bank or a large commercial organisation. CDs are negotiable and traded on the CD market (a money market), so if a CD holder wishes to obtain immediate cash, he can sell the CD on the market at any time. This secondhand market in CDs makes them attractive, flexible investments for organisations with excess cash.

> **KEY TERM**
>
> **Certificate of deposit:** a negotiable instrument which provides evidence of a fixed-term deposit with a bank. Maturity is normally within 90 days, but can be longer *(OT)*.

2.9 A company with surplus cash can:

(a) deposit a certain amount of cash with a bank for a fixed period, and receive a certificate of deposit from the bank; or

(b) buy an existing CD, which may have a much shorter period to maturity, on the CD market.

Treasury bills

2.10 **Treasury bills** are issued weekly by the government to finance short-term cash deficiencies in the government's expenditure programme. They are IOUs issued by the government, giving a promise to pay a certain amount to their holder on maturity. Treasury bills have a term of 91 day to maturity, after which the holder is paid the full value of the bill. A company can arrange through its bank to invest in Treasury bills. Since they are negotiable, they can be re-sold, if required, on the discount market before their maturity date.

2.11 Treasury bills do not pay interest, but the purchase price of a Treasury bill is less than its face value, the amount that the government will eventually pay on maturity. There is thus an implied rate of interest in the price at which the bills are traded. The secondhand value of Treasury bills in the discount market (the money market in which they are traded) varies with current interest rates but will never exceed their face value.

Eligible bank bills (sterling bankers' acceptances)

2.12 **Bank bills** are IOUs issued by a bank. Eligible bank bills are bills issued by 'eligible' banks: top-rated banks whose bills the Bank of England will agree to buy on the money market. They are denominated in sterling and are short-term. Like Treasury bills, they are negotiable. Most purchasers of bank bills are other banks, including the Bank of England.

Local authority bonds

2.13 These are short-term securities issued by local authorities to raise cash. They carry interest, and are repayable on maturity. They are traded secondhand in the money market, and so, like CDs, are a flexible investment for organisations with excess cash. They are not always available, however.

3 PAYMENT METHODS 5/97

3.1 The ease with which payments can be transferred between enterprises and between enterprises and its customers who are private individuals has been enhanced by the development of various electronic funds transfer operations. These include SWIFT and BACS.

> *Stage 4 Topic Link.* Knowledge of electronic payment methods may be useful for Paper 15 as well as Paper 13.

SWIFT

3.2 **SWIFT** (Society for Worldwide Interbank Financial Telecommunications) provides an electronic funds transfer (EFT) and payment system for its shareholder banks worldwide. Most major North American and Western European banks are members. Since its establishment, non-banks have been admitted as eligible users, and users include securities houses, recognised exchanges, central clearing institutions, moneybrokers and fund managers.

3.3 SWIFT is a secure telecommunications network which facilitates rapid international transfers between the member banks. SWIFT now handles about one and three-quarter million messages a day. To do so, it imposes standard formats on certain types of message to facilitate **Electronic Data Interchange (EDI).** These include purchase and sales orders, clearing instructions, foreign exchange confirmations, balance reporting, securities statements and trade confirmations.

Visa International

3.4 Visa's system allows individuals and small companies to make payments across European borders, and focuses on low value cross-border payments. Visa uses its existing data network, currently used by member banks to debit each other for credit card payments. Under the new system, banks are able to transmit credits as well. Visa expect the service to be used primarily by individuals, although small companies, such as retailers making VAT refunds to overseas customers, may also be a source of business.

CHAPS

3.5 **CHAPS** (Clearing House Automated Payment System) is a system whereby the participating banks in the UK can make large payments in sterling for settlement on the same day.

BACS

3.6 **BACS** (Bankers Automated Clearance Services) is used to transfer funds electronically between accounts in the UK banking system. This system is best known for processing payrolls. Instead of handing each employee a cheque at the end of each period, the employer will send the payment data coded on a magnetic medium to a bank participating in BACS and the payment is made electronically.

Factors to consider in making international payments

3.7 The various methods of payment which can be used in international trade each have their own distinguishing features, and will now be described in turn.

Payment by cheque

3.8 Payment by cheque is a **slow** method of settlement, because the payee must wait for the cheque to be returned to the drawer's bank for clearance before his own account is credited. The exporter will arrange for his bank to collect the payment. (In international trade, cheques must always be sent for collection.) The collection procedures for a cheque are as follows.

(a) If a foreign buyer draws a cheque in favour of a UK exporter:

(i) the buyer will post the cheque to the UK exporter;

(ii) the exporter will present the cheque to his bank in the UK;

(iii) the bank in the UK will send the cheque to the buyer's bank in the buyer's own country, which will then pay the amount of the cheque and debit its customer's account, ie the buyer's account;

(iv) on receiving payment from the buyer's bank, the bank in the UK will pay the exporter (or credit his account) after deducting collection charges.

(b) If the foreign buyer writes a cheque for an amount in sterling, he will have to arrange with his bank to have his account debited with an appropriate amount of his local currency. If the cheque is written in the buyer's own currency (or a third currency):

(i) the UK exporter may have a foreign currency bank account in that currency with a bank in the UK. He would then arrange to have this account credited with the cheque payment;

(ii) otherwise the exporter will have to arrange with his UK bank to have his sterling account credited with an appropriate amount of sterling. The bank would buy the foreign currency in exchange for sterling.

3.9 If a UK importer wished to pay an overseas supplier by cheque, much the same procedures operate in reverse.

3.10 Payment by cheque of a debt in international trade might be unsatisfactory for the following reasons.

(a) The long time it takes to collect payment by cheque is a serious inconvenience. Cheques are often payable in the buyer's country, and so the exporter must arrange for the money to be collected through his bank from abroad.

(b) The exporter (payee) will have to ask his bank to arrange to collect the payment for him, and the bank will make a **collection charge**.

(c) The cheque might contravene the exchange control regulations of the buyer's country, so that settlement would be delayed until the necessary authorisation to make payment has been obtained.

(d) Many companies are unaware that they are receiving an advance if their account is credited immediately in domestic currency when they present a cheque drawn on an overseas bank to their bank. The bank will charge interest on their advance.

(e) The cheque might not be paid when presented. If the cheque is unpaid, the bank will reclaim the advance, converting the domestic currency into the currency of the cheque at the prevailing exchange rate, possibly resulting in an exchange loss.

Speeding up settlement by cheque: lock boxes

3.11 In spite of there being quicker ways of getting paid, such as electronic transfer, a large proportion of trade in Europe is still settled by cheque. Cheque payment is often preferred by buyers as it helps to delay payment. After it is received by the creditor, the cheque must be presented to a local banks branch which will then forward it to the national head office of the bank of the creditor company, which must in turn present it to the debtor's bank overseas. This process can take up to 28 days to be completed.

3.12 If electronic transfer is not possible and payment by cheque must be accepted, it is possible to reduce the time taken for the payment process to only five days instead of 28 using a '**lock**

box' arrangement. Suppose you export to a customer which is a German company. You set up a 'lock box' bank account with a reputable German bank. You then ask the German customer to present the cheque to the German bank, providing full account details for the 'lock box'. Clearance of the cheque is then as fast as for a domestic cheque, with the funds being remitted electronically to your bank account. Lock box arrangements are possible in Europe and North America. Within North America, lock boxes are used to help overcome delays in the postal service resulting from the large distances involved.

Payment by bill of exchange

3.13 **Bills of exchange** are a fairly commonly used method of settlement in international trade.

3.14 The advantages of payment by means of a bill of exchange are as follows.

(a) They provide a convenient method of collecting payments from foreign buyers.

(b) The exporter can seek immediate finance, using term bills of exchange, instead of having to wait until the period of credit expires (ie until the maturity of the bill). At the same time, the foreign buyer is allowed the full period of credit before payment is made.

(c) On payment, the foreign buyer keeps the bill as evidence of payment, so that a bill of exchange also serves as a receipt.

(d) If a bill of exchange is dishonoured, it may be used by the drawer to pursue payment by means of legal action in the drawee's country.

(e) The buyer's bank might add its name to a term bill, to indicate that it *guarantees* payment at maturity. On the continent of Europe, this procedure is known as 'avalising' bills of exchange.

Payment by banker's draft

3.15 A **banker's draft** is a cheque drawn by a bank on one of its own bank accounts. For example, a banker's draft might be issued by a UK bank instructing payment out of its own bank account with a 'correspondent' bank in an overseas country. The draft may be denominated in a foreign currency but alternatively a banker's draft could be issued authorising payment in sterling, in which case the overseas supplier would present the draft to his bank in France and ask the bank to collect the payment.

3.16 Banker's drafts are fairly commonly used, but they are a **slow** method of payment and would not be used when quick payment is required. An advantage of a banker's draft is that the exporter receives direct notification that the payment is now available to him. If the draft is for an advance payment, and the exporter is waiting to receive it before shipping the goods abroad, this direct notification to the exporter might help to speed up the shipment.

Mail transfer (mail payment orders)

3.17 A mail transfer (MT) is:

(a) a payment order in writing;

(b) sent by one bank to another bank (overseas);

(c) which can be **authenticated** as having been authorised by a proper official in the sending bank;

(d) and which instructs the other bank to pay a certain sum of money;

(e) to a **specified beneficiary** (or on application by a specified beneficiary).

The payment order is sent from the instructing bank to the overseas bank by airmail.

3.18 As is the case with banker's drafts, the overseas bank will have an account in the name of the instructing bank, and it is this account which will be debited with the amount paid to the beneficiary. Unlike a banker's draft, a mail transfer is sent by the bank itself to another bank, not by the bank's customer to the overseas supplier.

3.19 Because mail transfer (MT) involves airmail communication between one bank and another, it is a quicker method of payment than a banker's draft at no extra cost. However, there is always a possibility that instructions sent by airmail will be delayed or lost in the post, and there are quicker methods of arranging payment.

Telegraphic transfer (TT): cable or telex payment orders

3.20 Telegraphic transfers (TT) or 'cable payment orders' are the same as mail transfers, except that instructions are sent by cable or telex instead of by airmail. TT is therefore slightly more costly to the paying bank's customer than mail transfer, but it speeds up payment. Large payments should be made by TT or by SWIFT (see below) because the marginal extra cost of TT over MT might be outweighed by the extra interest earnings or savings in interest costs which would be achievable if TT were used. A further advantage of TT over MT is that there is no danger of instructions being delayed or lost in the post.

Using SWIFT: IMTs and EIMTs

3.21 As more and more banks become members of SWIFT, the use of mail transfer and telegraphic transfer will decline because SWIFT (introduced earlier in this section) uses its own comparable methods of payment.

(a) A 'SWIFT message' is a payment equivalent to one by **mail** transfer, where the paying bank and correspondent bank overseas are both members of SWIFT. A SWIFT message is referred to as an **International Money Transfer** (IMT).

(b) Similarly a 'priority SWIFT message' is a payment equivalent to one by telegraphic transfer. A priority SWIFT message is referred to as an Express International Money Transfer (EIMT).

The distinction between non-urgent and urgent SWIFT messages is the speed of taking action to make the settlement, not the time that it takes for the message to be transmitted.

International money orders

3.22 An **international money order** is a means of transferring comparatively small sums of money from one country to another through the agency of the Post Office or possibly an international bank (eg Barclays). Since only small amounts are involved, international money orders are best suited to small orders where the exporter asks for payment in advance since the small amount of money involved would perhaps not financially justify allowing credit to the buyer or the minimum bank charges associated with collections or letters of credit.

Chapter roundup

- We have looked at various methods of **cash management**, **cash transmission** and **international payment**.
- A **small company** may have little choice but to accept the range of services offered by their bank managers or the facilities offered by overseas suppliers. **Larger companies** and multinational enterprises are in a position to adopt a more active role in managing deposits, borrowings and foreign debtors.

Quick quiz

1. How do cash flow problems arise? (see para 1.2)
2. What cash management services are offered by banks? (1.7, 1.8)
3. What are the drawbacks of an inventory approach to cash management? (1.20)
4. Give a brief assessment of the usefulness of the Miller-Orr model of cash management. (1.27)
5. What is SWIFT? (3.2, 3.3)
6. What is BACS? (3.6)
7. What are the advantages and disadvantages of settling foreign debts by cheque? (3.8 - 3.10)

Question to try	Level	Marks	Time
17	Exam standard	20	36 mins

Part C
Investment decisions

Chapter 18

INVESTMENT APPRAISAL METHODS

Introduction

The managers of all businesses will find themselves faced, from time to time, by capital investment decisions. Indeed, such decisions are fundamental to the long-term profitability of the business. In this chapter, we begin our coverage of investment and decision-making by revising some of the principles of appraising a project.

Exam focus point

You should already be familiar with annuities and perpetuities, formulae and tables for which are included in the CIMA *Mathematical Tables*; these are covered in this chapter to refresh your memory.

1 CAPITAL INVESTMENT APPRAISAL 5/99

1.1 Most **capital investment decisions** will have a direct effect on future profitability either because they will result in an increase in revenue or because they will bring about an increase in efficiency and a reduction in costs. Whatever level of management authorises a capital expenditure, the proposed investment should be properly evaluated, and found to be worthwhile, before the decision is taken to go ahead with the expenditure.

1.2 Capital expenditures differ from day to day revenue expenditures for the following reasons. They often involve a bigger outlay of money. Also, the benefits will accrue over a long period of time, usually well over one year and often much longer, so that the benefits cannot all be set against costs in the current year's profit and loss account.

1.3 The planning steps in the process of developing a new programme of capital investment are as follows.

(a) Identification of an investment opportunity
(b) Consideration of the alternatives to the project being evaluated
(c) Acquiring relevant information
(d) Detailed planning
(e) Taking the investment decision

1.4 The identification of an investment opportunity is the most difficult part of the capital investment process. Indeed, for many businesses, and particularly small ones, it is the only stage; projects are undertaken without any form of sophisticated investment appraisal. There are often two or more ways of getting a job done, or achieving an objective. The different investment alternatives ought to be identified, and compared.

1.5 Acquiring the relevant data to form the basis for an informed decision is one of the most important aspects in practice. Large capital investments that turn out to be unprofitable can usually be abandoned only at a substantial loss, and therefore the time and effort spent in market research and acquiring data about relevant costs and benefits is rarely wasted. This activity helps to focus managers' minds on the reality of the projections as they are forecasting and so weed out poor projects at an early stage, before they are subjected to intensive financial scrutiny.

1.6 The principal methods of evaluating capital projects are as follows.

(a) The return on investment method, or accounting rate of return method

(b) The payback method

(c) Discounted cash flow (DCF):

(i) the net present value method (NPV)
(ii) the internal rate of return method (IRR)

Of these, DCF should be by far the most important, although (a) and (b) are used more in practice by small and medium-sized firms.

2 THE ACCOUNTING RATE OF RETURN METHOD

2.1 The **accounting rate of return method** of appraising a capital project is to estimate the accounting rate of return or return on investment (ROI) that the project should yield. If it exceeds a target rate of return, the project will be undertaken. Unfortunately, there are several different definitions of 'return on investment'. One of the most popular is as follows.

$$\text{ARR} = \frac{\text{Estimated average profits}}{\text{Estimated average investment}} \times 100\%$$

The others include:

$$\text{ARR} = \frac{\text{Estimated total profits}}{\text{Estimated initial investment}} \times 100\%$$

$$\text{ARR} = \frac{\text{Estimated average profits}}{\text{Estimated initial investment}} \times 100\%$$

2.2 There are arguments in favour of each of these definitions. The most important point is, however, that the method selected should be used consistently. For examination purposes we recommend the first definition unless the question clearly indicates that some other one is to be used.

2.3 EXAMPLE: ACCOUNTING RATE OF RETURN

A company has a target accounting rate of return of 20% (using the first definition in Paragraph 2.1 above), and is now considering the following project.

Capital cost of asset	£80,000
Estimated life	4 years
Estimated profit before depreciation	
Year 1	£20,000
Year 2	£25,000
Year 3	£35,000
Year 4	£25,000

The capital asset would be depreciated by 25% of its cost each year, and will have no residual value. Should the project be undertaken?

2.4 SOLUTION

The annual profits after depreciation and the mid-year net book value of the asset would be as follows.

Year	*Profit after depreciatiod*	*Mid-year net book value*	*ARR in the year*
	£	£	%
1	0	70,000	0
2	5,000	50,000	10
3	15,000	30,000	50
4	5,000	10,000	50

2.5 As the table shows, the ARR is low in the early stages of the project, partly because of low profits in Year 1 but mainly because the net book value of the asset is much higher early on in its life. The project does not achieve the target ARR of 20% in its first two years, but exceeds it in years 3 and 4. So should it be undertaken?

2.6 When the accounting rate of return from a project varies from year to year, it makes sense to take an overall or 'average' view of the project's return. In this case, we should look at the return as a whole over the four year period.

	£
Total profit before depreciation over four years	105,000
Total profit after depreciation over four years	25,000
Average annual profit after depreciation	6,250
Original cost of investment	80,000
Average net book value over the four year period $\frac{(80{,}000+0)}{2}$	40,000

The average ARR is 6,250 ÷ 40,000 = 15.625%.

The project would not be undertaken because it would fail to yield the target return of 20%.

The ARR and the comparison of mutually exclusive projects

2.7 The ARR method of capital investment appraisal can also be used to compare two or more projects which are mutually exclusive, which means that only one of the projects can be undertaken. The project with the highest ARR would be selected (provided that the expected ARR is higher than the company's target ARR).

2.8 EXAMPLE: ARR AND MUTUALLY EXCLUSIVE PROJECTS

Arrow Ltd wants to buy a new item of equipment which will be used to provide a service to customers of the company. Two models of equipment are available, one with a slightly higher capacity and greater reliability than the other. The expected costs and profits of each item are as follows.

	Equipment item X	*Equipment item Y*
Capital cost	£80,000	£150,000
Life	5 years	5 years
Profits before depreciation	£	£
Year 1	50,000	50,000
Year 2	50,000	50,000
Year 3	30,000	60,000
Year 4	20,000	60,000
Year 5	10,000	60,000
Disposal value	0	0

ARR is measured as the average annual profit after depreciation, divided by the average net book value of the asset. Which item of equipment should be selected, if any, if the company's target ARR is 30%?

2.9 SOLUTION

	Item X	*Item Y*
	£	£
Total profit over life of equipment		
Before depreciation	160,000	280,000
After depreciation	80,000	130,000
Average annual profit after depreciation	16,000	26,000
(Capital cost + disposal value)/2	40,000	75,000
ARR	40%	34.7%

Both projects would earn a return in excess of 30%, but since item X would earn a bigger ARR, it would be preferred to item Y, even though the profits from Y would be higher by an average of £10,000 a year.

The drawbacks to the ARR method of capital investment appraisal

2.10 The ARR method of capital investment appraisal has the serious drawback that it does not take account of the **timing** of the profits from an investment. Whenever capital is invested in a project, money is tied up until the project begins to earn profits which pay back the investment. Money tied up in one project cannot be invested anywhere else until the profits come in. Management should be aware of the benefits of early repayments from an investment, which will provide the money for other investments.

3 THE PAYBACK METHOD

KEY TERM

The CIMA's *Official Terminology* (1996) defines **payback** as 'the time required for the cash inflows from a capital investment project to equal the cash outflows'.

3.1 When deciding between two or more competing projects, the usual decision is to accept the one with the shortest payback. Payback is commonly used as a first screening method. That is, when a capital investment project is being considered, the first question to ask is: 'How long will it take to pay back its cost?' The organisation might have a target payback, and so it would reject a capital project unless its payback period is less than a certain number of years, perhaps five years, depending on the company policy.

3.2 However, a project should not be evaluated on the basis of payback alone. The payback method should be a first screening process, and if a project passes the payback test, it ought then to be evaluated using another investment appraisal technique.

3.3 The reason why payback should not be used on its own to evaluate capital investments should be clear if you look at the figures below for two mutually exclusive projects.

	Project P	*Project Q*
Capital expenditure	£60,000	£60,000
Cash inflows		
Year 1	£20,000	£50,000
Year 2	£30,000	£20,000
Year 3	£40,000	£5,000
Year 4	£50,000	£5,000
Year 5	£60,000	£5,000

3.4 Project P pays back in year 3 (about one quarter of the way through year 3). Project Q pays back half way through year 2. Using payback alone to judge capital investments, project Q would be preferred. But the returns from project P over its life are much higher than the returns from project Q. The payback period has provided a rough measure of liquidity and not of profitability.

(a) Project P will earn total profits after depreciation of £140,000, on an investment of £60,000.

(b) Project Q will earn total profits after depreciation of only £25,000, on an investment of £60,000.

3.5 Payback can be important, and long payback periods mean capital tied up and also high investment risk, but total project returns ought to be taken into consideration as well.

4 DISCOUNTED CASH FLOW 5/96, 5/97, 5/99

4.1 As noted above, the ARR method of project evaluation ignores the timing of cash flows and the opportunity cost of capital tied up. Payback considers the time it takes to recover the original investment cost, but ignores total profits over a project's life.

4.2 Discounted cash flow, or DCF for short, is an investment appraisal technique which takes into account both the time value of money and also total profitability over a project's life. DCF is therefore superior to both ARR and payback as a method of investment appraisal.

4.3 Two important points about DCF are as follows.

(a) DCF looks at the **cash flows** of a project, not the accounting profits. Like the payback technique, DCF is concerned with liquidity, not profitability. Cash flows are considered because they show the costs and benefits of a project when they occur. For example, the capital cost of a project will be the original cash outlay, and not the depreciation charge which is used to spread the capital cost over the asset's life in the financial accounts.

(b) The timing of cash flows is taken into account by discounting them. The effect of discounting is to give a bigger value per pound for cash flows that occur earlier, for example £1 earned after one year will be worth more than £1 earned after two years, which in turn will be worth more than £1 earned after three years and so on.

4.4 There are two methods of using DCF to evaluate capital investments.

(a) The **net present value (NPV) method**
(b) The **internal rate of return (IRR) method**, or DCF yield method

The net present value (NPV) method

4.5 Present value (PV) can be defined as the cash equivalent now of a sum of money receivable or payable at a stated future date, discounted at a specified rate of return.

4.6 Net present value or NPV is the value obtained by discounting all cash outflows and inflows of a capital investment project at a chosen target rate of return or cost of capital. The PV of cash inflows minus the PV of cash outflows is the NPV.

KEY TERM

Net present value (NPV): the difference between the sum of the projected discounted cash inflows and outflows attributable to a capital investment or other long-term project *(OT)*.

4.7 (a) **If the NPV is positive,** it means that the cash inflows from a capital investment will yield a return in excess of the cost of capital, and so the project should be undertaken if the cost of capital is the organisation's target rate of return.

(b) **If the NPV is negative,** it means that the cash inflows from a capital investment will yield a return below the cost of capital, and so the project should not be undertaken if the cost of capital is the organisation's target rate of return.

(c) **If the NPV is exactly zero,** the cash inflows from a capital investment will yield a return which is exactly the same as the cost of capital, and so if the cost of capital is the organisation's target rate of return, the project will be only just worth undertaking.

Discount tables for the PV of £1

4.8 The discount factor used in discounting is $\frac{1}{(1+r)^t} = (1+r)^{-t}$

where r is the discount rate
t is the number of periods

4.9 Discount tables for the present value of £1, for different values of r and t, are shown in the Appendix to this Study Text.

Question 1

LCH Ltd manufactures product X which it sells for £5 a unit. Variable costs of production are currently £3 a unit, and fixed costs 50p a unit. A new machine is available which would cost £90,000 but which could be used to make product X for a variable cost of only £2.50 a unit. Fixed costs, however, would increase by £7,500 a year as a direct result of purchasing the machine. The machine would have an expected life of four years and a resale value after that time of £10,000. Sales of product X are estimated to be 75,000 units a year. If LCH Ltd expects to earn at least 12% a year from its investments, should the machine be purchased? (Ignore taxation.)

Answer

Savings are 75,000 × £(3.00 – 2.50) = £37,500 a year.
Additional costs are £7,500 a year.
Net cash savings are therefore £30,000 a year.

It is assumed that the machine will be sold for £10,000 at the end of year 4.

Year	*Cash flow*	*PV factor*	*PV of cash flow*
	£	12%	£
0	(90,000)	1.000	(90,000)
1	30,000	0.893	26,790
2	30,000	0.797	23,910
3	30,000	0.712	21,360
4	40,000	0.636	25,440
		NPV	+7,500

The NPV is positive and so the project is expected to earn more than 12% a year and is therefore acceptable.

The timing of cash flows: conventions used in DCF

4.10 The following guidelines may be applied unless a question indicates that they should not be.

(a) A cash outlay to be incurred at the beginning of an investment project, that is now, occurs in year 0. The present value of £1 in year 0 is £1.

(b) A cash outlay, saving or inflow which occurs during the course of a time period (say, one year) is assumed to occur all at once at the end of the time period. Therefore receipts of £10,000 during the first year are taken to occur at the end of that year. That point in time is called 'year 1'.

(c) A cash outlay, saving or inflow which occurs at the beginning of a time period (say at the beginning of the second year) is taken to occur at the end of the previous year. Therefore a cash outlay of £5,000 at the beginning of the second year is taken to occur at year 1.

Annuity tables

KEY TERM

Annuity: a fixed periodic payment which continues either for a specified time, or until the occurrence of a specified event *(OT)*.

4.11 In the last exercise the calculations could have been simplified for years 1-3 to:

$$
\begin{array}{rl}
 & 30{,}000 \times 0.893 \\
+ & 30{,}000 \times 0.797 \\
+ & 30{,}000 \times 0.712 \\
= & 30{,}000 \times 2.402
\end{array}
$$

4.12 Where there is a constant cash flow from year to year (in this case £30,000 a year for years 1-3) it is quicker to calculate the present value by adding together the discount factors for the

individual years. These total factors are the cumulative present value factors or annuity factors, given by the following formula.

EXAM FORMULA

The value of an annuity of £1 per period for t year (t-year annuity factor) is: PV = $\frac{1}{r} - \frac{1}{r(1+r)^t}$

4.13 EXAMPLE: ANNUITY TABLES

The Woodstock Skyscraper Company Ltd takes on a three year lease of a building for which it pays £20,000 as a lump sum payment. It then sub-lets the building to Linus Ltd for the three years at a fixed annual rent. If the Woodstock Skyscraper Company Ltd expects to earn at least 16% per annum from its investments, what should the annual rental charge be?

4.14 SOLUTION

As the rent is fixed for three years, there will be a constant cash flow from year to year.

Let the annual rent be £R.

£R × (PV of £1 per annum for three years at 16%) = PV of the rent

The present value of the rent over the three year period must be at least £20,000.

The annuity factor for £1 at 16% for years 1-3 = 2.246, therefore:

$$R \times 2.246 = £20{,}000 \text{ (at least)}$$

$$R = \frac{20{,}000}{2.246} = £8{,}905$$

4.15 The rent should be £8,905 a year for the company to earn 16% per annum on its investment of £20,000. In practice, this rent would probably be rounded up to, say, £9,000.

Question 2

Elsie Ltd is considering the manufacture of a new product which would involve the use of both a new machine (costing £150,000) and an existing machine, which cost £80,000 two years ago and has a current net book value of £60,000. There is sufficient capacity on this machine, which has so far been under-used.

Annual sales of the product would be 5,000 units, selling at £32 a unit. Unit costs would be as follows.

	£
Direct labour (4 hours at £2)	8
Direct materials	7
Fixed costs including depreciation	9
	24

The project would have a five year life, after which the new machine would have a net residual value of £10,000. Because direct labour is continually in short supply, labour resources would have to be diverted from other work which currently earns a contribution of £1.50 per direct labour hour. The fixed overhead absorption rate would be £2.25 an hour (£9 a unit) but actual expenditure on fixed overhead would not alter.

Working capital requirements would be £10,000 in the first year, rising to £15,000 in the second year and remaining at this level until the end of the project, when it will all be recovered. The company's cost of capital is 20%. Ignore taxation.

Is the project worthwhile?

Answer

Working			£
Years 1-5	Contribution from new product		
		5,000 × £(32 – 15)	85,000
	Less contribution forgone		
		5,000 × (4 × £1.50)	30,000
			55,000

Year	Equipment	Working capital	Contribution	Net cash flow	Discount factor	PV of net cash flow
	£	£	£	£	20%	£
0	(150,000)	(10,000)		(160,000)	1.000	(160,000)
1		(5,000)		(5,000)	0.833	(4,165)
1-5			55,000	55,000	2.991	164,505
5	10,000	15,000		25,000	0.402	10,050
					NPV =	10,390

The NPV is positive and the project is worthwhile, although there is not much margin for error. Some risk analysis of the project is recommended.

Annual cash flows in perpetuity

KEY TERM

Perpetuity: A periodic payment continuing for a limitless period *(OT)*.

4.16 When the cost of capital is r, the cumulative PV of £1 a year for ever (a perpetuity) is £1/r.

EXAM FORMULA

The value of a perpetuity of £1 per year is: $PV = \frac{1}{r}$

4.17 For example, the PV of a perpetuity of £1 at a discount rate of 10% is £1/0.10 = £10.

Question 3

A company with a cost of capital of 14% is considering an investment in a project costing £500,000 that would yield annual cash inflows of £100,000 in perpetuity. Should the project be undertaken?

Answer

Year	Cash flow	Discount factor	Present value
	£	14%	£
0	(500,000)	1.000	(500,000)
1 – ∞	100,000	1/0.14 = 7.143	714,300
		Net present value	214,300

The NPV is positive and so the project should be undertaken.

4.18 **Gordon's growth model** gives the following growing perpetuity formula (included in the CIMA *Mathematical Tables*) for cash flows growing at constant rate g for ever.

EXAM FORMULA

If the initial cash flow is £1 at year 1 and if cash flows thereafter grow at a constant rate of g in perpetuity: $PV = \frac{1}{r-g}$

Other formulae

4.19 You may also find the following formulae useful.

(a) For **non-annual cash flows,** the period interest rate r is related to the annual interest rate R by the following formula.

$$r = \sqrt[n]{1+R} - 1$$

where n is the number of periods per annum.

For example, if the annual interest rate is 18%, the monthly interest rate $r = \sqrt[12]{1.18} - 1 = 0.0139$, ie 1.39%.

(b) **Changes in interest rate** can be reflected as in the following example.

In years 1, 2 and 3, the interest rate is 10%, 12% and 14% respectively.

$$\text{Then, Year 3 discount factor} = \frac{1}{(1+r_1)(1+r_2)(1+r_3)}$$

$$= \frac{1}{1.10 \times 1.12 \times 1.14} = 0.712$$

The profitability index

4.20 A measure of project profitability is provided by the **profitability index** (PI), which is defined in CIMA's *Official Terminology* as follows.

$$PI = \frac{\text{Present value of cash inflows}}{\text{Initial investment}}$$

The decision rule to apply when using the PI is to accept all projects with a PI of greater than 1.

4.21 **Advantages of the PI method**

- similar to the NPV method, usually giving the same result on individual projects
- can be used to rank divisible projects in conditions of capital rationing (see Chapter 19)

Disadvantages of the PI method

- PI indicates relative returns and is not an absolute measure
- The PI method may rank projects incorrectly. If cash is not rationed, it is preferable to look at the NPV, which is an absolute measure
- Establishing what is the initial investment may not be straightforward. The PI method works well only if the project has an outflow of cash at time 0, followed by cash inflows which may be at various times

The net terminal value (NTV)

4.22 The **net terminal value** is the cash surplus remaining at the end of a project after taking account of interest and capital repayments. The NTV discounted at the cost of capital will give the NPV of the project.

4.23 EXAMPLE: THE NET TERMINAL VALUE

A project has the following cash flows.

Year	£
0	(5,000)
1	3,000
2	2,600
3	6,200

The project has an NPV of £4,538 at the company's cost of capital of 10% (workings not shown).

Calculate the net terminal value of the project.

4.24 SOLUTION

The net terminal value can be determined directly from the NPV, or by calculating the cash surplus at the end of the project.

Assume that the £5,000 for the project is borrowed at an interest rate of 10% and that cash flows from the project are used to repay the loan.

	£
Loan balance outstanding at beginning of project	5,000
Interest over first year at 10%	500
Repaid at year 1	(3,000)
Balance outstanding at year 1	2,500
Interest over second year	250
Repaid at year 2	(2,600)
Balance outstanding at year 2	150
Interest over third year	15
Repaid at year 3	(6,200)
Cash surplus at end of project	6,035

The net terminal value is £6,035.

Check

NPV $= £6,035 \times 0.751$ (discount factor for year 3) $= £4,532$

Allowing for the rounding errors caused by using discount tables, this is the correct figure for the NPV.

The internal rate of return (IRR) method or DCF yield method

4.25 By the NPV method of discounted cash flow, present values are calculated by discounting at a target rate of return, or cost of capital, and the difference between the PV of costs and the PV of benefits is the NPV. In contrast, the **IRR method** is to calculate the exact rate of return which the project is expected to achieve, that is the discount rate at which the NPV is 0. If the expected rate of return exceeds the target rate of return, the project should be undertaken.

KEY TERM

Internal rate of return (IRR): the annual percentage return achieved by a project, at which the sum of the discounted cash inflows over the life of the project is equal to the sum of the discounted cash outflows *(OT)*.

4.26 The IRR is found approximately using interpolation. The first step is to calculate two net present values, both as close as possible to zero, using two rates for the cost of capital. Ideally, one NPV should be positive and the other negative. The method works with two positive NPVs or two negative NPVs, but the approximation may not be as good.

4.27 Choosing rates for the cost of capital which will give NPVs close to zero is a hit and miss exercise, and several attempts may be needed to find satisfactory rates. As a rough guide, try starting at a return figure which is two thirds of the accounting return on investment.

4.28 EXAMPLE: IRR

A company is trying to decide whether to buy a machine for £80,000 which will save £20,000 a year for five years and which will have a resale value of £10,000 at the end of year 5. What would the IRR of the investment project be?

4.29 SOLUTION

The return on investment is $\dfrac{20{,}000 - \text{depreciation of } 14{,}000}{\frac{1}{2} \text{ of } (80{,}000 + 10{,}000)} = \dfrac{6{,}000}{45{,}000} = 13.3\%$

Two thirds of this is 8.9% and so we can start by trying 9%.

The IRR is the rate for the cost of capital at which the NPV = 0.

Year	*Cash flow*	*PV factor*		*PV of cash flow*
	£	9%		£
0	(80,000)	1.000		(80,000)
1-5	20,000	3.890		77,800
5	10,000	0.650		6,500
			NPV	4,300

This is fairly close to zero. It is also positive, which means that the IRR is more than 9%. We will try 12% next.

Year	*Cash flow*	*PV factor*		*PV of cash flow*
	£	12%		£
0	(80,000)	1.000		(80,000)
1-5	20,000	3.605		72,100
5	10,000	0.567		5,670
			NPV	(2,230)

4.30 This is fairly close to zero and negative. The IRR is therefore greater than 9% but less than 12%. We shall now use the two NPV values to estimate the IRR, using the following formula.

Internal rate of return $= A + \left[\dfrac{X}{X-Y} \times (B-A)\right]$

where A is one rate of return
B is the other rate of return
X is the NPV at rate A
Y is the NPV at rate B

4.31 In this example:

$$\text{Internal rate of return} = 9 + \left[\frac{4{,}300}{4{,}300 - -2{,}230} \times (12 - 9)\right] = 10.98\%, \text{ say } 11\%$$

NPV or IRR?

4.32 Given that there are two methods of using DCF, the NPV method and the IRR method, the relative merits of each method have to be considered. Which is better?

4.33 The main advantage of the IRR method is that the information it provides is more easily understood by managers, especially non-financial managers. For example, it is fairly easy to understand the meaning of the following statement.

> 'The project has an initial capital outlay of £100,000, and will earn a yield of 25%. This is in excess of the target yield of 15% for investments.'

It is not so easy to understand the meaning of this statement.

> 'The project will cost £100,000 and have an NPV of £30,000 when discounted at the minimum required rate of 15%.'

4.34 In other respects, the IRR method has serious disadvantages.

(a) It might be tempting to confuse the IRR and the accounting ROCE. The accounting ROCE and the IRR are two completely different measures. If managers were given information about both ROCE (or ROI) and IRR, it might be easy to get their meanings and significance mixed up.

(b) It ignores the relative size of investments. Both the following projects have an IRR of 18%.

	Project A	*Project B*
	£	£
Cost, year 0	350,000	35,000
Annual savings, years 1-6	100,000	10,000

Clearly, project A is bigger (ten times as big) and so more profitable but if the only information on which the projects were judged were to be their IRR of 18%, project B would seem just as beneficial as project A.

(c) If the cash flows from a project are not conventional (with an outflow at the beginning resulting in inflows over the life of a project) there may be more than one IRR. This could be very difficult for managers to interpret. For example, the following project has cash flows which are not conventional, and as a result has two IRRs of approximately 7% and 35%.

Year	*Project X*
	£'000
0	(1,900)
1	4,590
2	(2,735)

(d) The IRR method should not be used to select between mutually exclusive projects. This follows on from point (b) and it is the most significant and damaging criticism of the IRR method.

4.35 EXAMPLE: MUTUALLY EXCLUSIVE OPTIONS

A company is considering two mutually exclusive options, option A and option B. The cash flows for each would be as follows.

Year		*Option A*	*Option B*
		£	£
0	Capital outlay	(10,200)	(35,250)
1	Net cash inflow	6,000	18,000
2	Net cash inflow	5,000	15,000
3	Net cash inflow	3,000	15,000

The company's cost of capital is 16%. Which option should be chosen?

4.36 SOLUTION

The NPV of each project is calculated below.

		Option A		*Option B*	
Year	*Discount factor*	*Cashflow*	*Present value*	*Cashflow*	*Present value*
	16%	£	£	£	£
0	1.000	(10,200)	(10,200)	(35,250)	(35,250)
1	0.862	6,000	5,172	18,000	15,516
2	0.743	5,000	3,715	15,000	11,145
3	0.641	3,000	1,923	15,000	9,615
		NPV	+610		+1,026

However, the IRR of option A is 20% and the IRR of option B is only 18% (workings not shown). On a comparison of NPVs, option B would be preferred but, on a comparison of IRRs, option A would be preferred.

4.37 Option B should be chosen. This is because the differences in the cash flows between the two options, when discounted at the cost of capital of 16%, show that the present value of the incremental benefits from option B compared with option A exceed the PV of the incremental costs. This can be re-stated in the following ways.

(a) The NPV of the differential cash flows (option B cash flows minus option A cash flows) is positive, and so it is worth spending the extra capital to get the extra benefits.

(b) The IRR of the differential cash flows exceeds the cost of capital of 16%, and so it is worth spending the extra capital to get the extra benefits.

The time value of money

4.38 DCF is a capital appraisal technique that is based on the concept of the time value of money, that £1 earned or spent sooner is worth more than £1 earned or spent later.

4.39 Various reasons could be suggested as to why a present £1 is worth more than a future £1.

(a) **Uncertainty**: the business world is full of uncertainty, and although there might be the promise of money to come in the future, it can never be certain that the money will be received until it has actually been received. This is an important argument, and risk must always be considered in investment appraisal. But this argument does not explain why the discounted cash flow technique should be used to reflect the time value of money. Other techniques can be used to allow for uncertainty and these are discussed in a later chapter.

(b) **Inflation:** because of inflation £1 now is worth more than £1 in the future. It is important however, that the problem of inflation should not confuse the meaning of

DCF, and even if there were no inflation at all, discounted cash flow techniques would still be used for investment appraisal. Ways of allowing for inflation are considered in a later chapter.

(c) An individual attaches more weight to current pleasures than to future ones, and would rather have £1 to spend now than £1 in a year's time. One reason suggested to justify the use of the discounted cash flow technique is this '**subjective time preference**' of individuals who have the choice of consuming or investing their wealth. It has been argued that the return from investments must therefore be sufficient to persuade individuals to prefer to invest now.

Future cash flows: relevant costs

4.40 The concept of cash flow is of vital importance to capital investment appraisal since the real cost to a business of any new investment project is the actual amount of cash that flows out of the business as a result of the investment decision, and the return to the business from the project will be the actual amount of cash earned from the project during its life.

4.41 In DCF, cash inflows and outflows are used to determine the benefits and costs of a project, and the concept of 'relevant costs' applies to capital investment decisions in the same way as it does to short-run decisions.

5 THE USE OF APPRAISAL METHODS IN PRACTICE

5.1 A survey of the use of capital investment evaluation methods in the UK carried out by RH Pike in 1992 produced the following results on the frequency of use of different methods by 100 large UK firms.

Capital investment evaluation methods in 100 large UK firms: frequency of use (1992)

	Total	*Always*	*Mostly*	*Often*	*Rarely*
Firms using	%	%	%	%	%
Payback	94	62	14	12	6
Accounting rate of return	56	21	5	13	17
Internal rate of return	81	54	7	13	7
Net present value	74	33	14	16	11

(Source: Pike & Neale, *Corporate Finance and Investment*)

5.2 Almost two-thirds of the firms surveyed by Pike used three or more appraisal techniques, indicating that DCF techniques complement rather than replace more traditional approaches.

5.3 The following points are worth noting.

(a) The **payback method** is used in the great majority (94%) of companies surveyed. Although it remains a traditional 'rule-of-thumb method' with limited theoretical justification because it ignores the profile of cash flows and cash flows beyond the payback period, it will provide in practice a fair approximation to the net present value method. Its widespread use is perhaps then not so reprehensible given the uncertainty of future cash flows and the tendency of cash flows following the payback period to be similar in form to earlier cash flows in most cases.

(b) In spite of its theoretical limitations (notably, its failure to take account of the time value of money), the **ARR method** was used in half of the companies surveyed. This is perhaps to be expected, given the importance in practice of the rate of return on capital as a financial goal.

(c) The data shows a preference for the **IRR method** over the **NPV method**. It would appear that, in spite of theoretical reasons for favour NPV, the IRR method is preferred by managers as a convenient way of ranking projects in percentage terms.

AMT and investment appraisal

5.4 There has been much criticism in recent management accounting literature of the short-term orientation of many organisations' investment appraisal systems and their effect of slowing down the adoption of **advanced manufacturing technology (AMT)** by British firms.

5.5 Some writers have criticised the short-term quantitative and financial orientation of many investment appraisal techniques. These techniques fail to consider the unquantifiable long-term benefits which are an implicit part of AMT projects.

5.6 **Strategic investment appraisal** has been defined as 'linking corporate strategy to costs and benefits associated with AMT adoption by combining both formal and informal evaluation procedures.' Formal appraisal methods may be of limited practical use when considering the acquisition of AMT, because of the strategic (often non-quantifiable) issues involved.

5.7 Management accountants are beginning to accept the need for a more external orientation and a consideration of the longer-term effects in investment appraisal generally, particularly in those organisations which operate in rapidly changing markets with a high level of uncertainty. You should by now be aware of the importance of combining formal and informal procedures, as well as short-term and long-term considerations, in effective capital investment appraisal.

6 PROJECT CONTROL

6.1 Once a capital project has been evaluated and given the go-ahead, project controls should be applied to ensure through a process of **continuous evaluation** that:

(a) capital spending does not exceed the amount authorised;
(b) the implementation of the project is not delayed;
(c) the anticipated benefits are eventually obtained.

6.2 Items (a) and (b) are probably easier to control than (c), because the controls can normally be applied soon after the capital expenditure has been authorised, whereas monitoring the benefits will span a longer period.

Controls over excess spending

6.3 Controls over capital expenditure can be applied as follows.

(a) The authority to make capital expenditure decisions must be formally assigned. There should be a proposer for the project who applies for approval of the spending.

(i) All spending over (for example) £250,000 must be authorised by the holding company's board. The spending would be proposed by a member of the board, or by another manager who is asked to make a submission to the board asking for approval of the spending.

(ii) Spending over (for example) £100,000 and up to (for example) £250,000 can be authorised by the subsidiary company's board. In the same way, the capital project would be proposed by a member of the board, or by another manager who is asked to make a submission to the board asking for approval of the project.

(iii) Spending over (for example) £10,000 and up to (for example) £100,000 can be authorised by heads of departments. Once again, a junior manager should submit a proposal for approval of the project, which the head of department would be asked to authorise.

(b) Capital expenditure decisions should be documented. The approval of the project should specify:

(i) which manager has been authorised to carry out the expenditure. The manager will be responsible for the successful implementation of the project;

(ii) how much expenditure has been authorised;

(iii) within what period of time the expenditure should take place.

(c) Some overspending above the amount authorised, say 5% or 10%, might be allowed. If the required expenditure exceeds the amount authorised by more than this amount, a fresh submission for re-authorisation of the project should be required.

(d) There should be a total capital budget, and the authorisation of any capital expenditure which would take total spending above the budget should be referred to board level for approval.

Control over the anticipated benefits

6.4 When a capital project has clearly defined costs, and clearly identifiable benefits, further control can be exercised over capital projects by monitoring the progress of the projects to ensure that the following occur.

(a) The anticipated benefits do actually materialise.
(b) The benefits are as big as anticipated.
(c) Running costs do not exceed expectation.

6.5 A difficulty with control of capital projects is that most projects are unique with no standard or yardstick to judge them against, and so if actual costs were to exceed the estimated costs, it might be impossible to tell just how much of the variance is due to bad estimating and how much is due to inefficiencies and poor cost control. In the same way, if benefits are below expectation, this might be because the original estimates were optimistic, or because management has been inefficient and failed to get the benefits they should have done.

6.6 Many capital projects do not have such clearly identifiable costs and benefits, for example decisions to purchase replacement assets or to acquire a new office building. The incremental benefits and costs of such schemes can be estimated for the purpose of the project evaluation, but it would need a very sophisticated management accounting system to be able to measure the actual benefits and many of the costs. Even so, some degree of monitoring and control can still be exercised by means of a post audit.

Post audits

6.7 A **post audit** or a **post-completion audit** is a review of the cash inflows to and outflows from a project after it has reached the end of its life, or at least some years after it began. As far as possible, the actual cash flows should be measured and compared with the estimates contained in the original capital expenditure appraisal. The manager responsible for the project should be asked to explain any significant variances.

KEY TERM

Post-completion audit: an objective and independent appraisal of the measure of success of a capital expenditure project in progressing the business as planned *(OT)*.

6.8 Post-audit checking cannot reverse the decision to make the capital expenditure, because the expenditure will already have taken place. However, it does have a certain control value.

(a) If a manager asks for and gets approval for a capital project, and knows that in due course the project will be subject to a post audit, then the manager will be more likely to pay attention to the benefits and the costs than if no post audit were threatened.

(b) If the post audit takes place before the project life ends, and if it finds that the benefits have been less than expected because of management inefficiency, steps can be taken to improve efficiency and earn greater benefits over the remaining life of the project. Alternatively, the post audit may highlight those projects which should be discontinued.

(c) A post audit can help to identify managers who have been good performers and those who have been poor performers.

(d) A post audit might identify weaknesses in the forecasting and estimating techniques used to evaluate projects, and so should help to improve the quality of forecasting for future investment decisions.

(e) A post audit might reveal areas where improvements can be made in methods so as to achieve better results from capital investments in general.

(f) The original estimates may be more realistic if managers are aware that they will be monitored, but post audits should not be unfairly critical.

6.9 It may be too expensive to post audit all capital expenditure projects, therefore managers may need to select a sample for a post audit. The selection will depend on the probability that the audit of any particular project will produce benefits, which is obviously difficult to determine. A reasonable guideline might be to audit all projects above a certain size, and a random sample of smaller projects.

6.10 There are a number of problems with post audits.

(a) There are many uncontrollable factors in long-term investments such as environmental changes. Since such factors are outside management control there may be little to gain by identifying the resulting variances.

(b) This means that it may not be possible to identify separately the costs and benefits of any particular project or, due to uncertainty, to identify the costs and benefits at all.

(c) Post audit can be a costly and time-consuming exercise. Labour, which maybe a scarce resource, is required to undertake the task.

(d) Applied punitively, post audit exercises may lead to managers becoming over cautious and unnecessarily risk averse.

(e) The strategic effects of a capital investment project may take years to materialise and it may never be possible to identify or quantify them effectively.

6.11 It has been found that 67% of companies carry out post audits in the UK (Pike and Wolfe, 1988) and 79% of quoted firms carry out post audit to some extent (Neal, 1990). Despite the growth in popularity of post audits, you should bear in mind the possible alternative control processes.

(a) Teams could be set up to manage a project from beginning to end, control being used before the project is started and during its life, rather than at the end of its life.

(b) More time could be spend choosing projects rather than checking completed projects.

Chapter roundup

- This chapter has provided some revision of the techniques for **evaluating capital expenditure decisions**.
- Your examination will call for some **advanced applications** of the techniques and with this in mind the next chapter will build on this introduction.

Quick quiz

1 What is the main drawback of the ARR method of capital investment appraisal? (see para 2.10)

2 Why is the payback method alone an inadequate investment appraisal technique? (3.5)

3 What is another name for the internal rate of return? (4.4)

4 What is the cumulative present value of £1 a year in perpetuity, given a cost of capital r? (4.16)

5 Outline the advantages and disadvantages of the profitability index (PI) method compared with the NPV method in investment appraisal. (4.21)

6 What are the disadvantages of using the IRR method? (4.333, 4.34)

7 What are the advantages of post audits and what problems can arise in carrying them out? (6.7, 6.10)

Question to try	Level	Marks	Time
18	Exam standard	20	36 mins

Chapter 19

APPLICATIONS OF DCF. COST BENEFIT ANALYSIS

	Chapter topic list	Syllabus reference	Ability required
1	Capital rationing	13 c(iv)	Knowledge
2	DCF and gradual annual sales growth	13 c(i)	Application
3	The annualised cost of a capital item	13 c(i)	Application
4	Asset replacement decisions	13 c(i)	Application
5	Cost benefit analysis	13 c(i)	Application

Introduction

In this chapter, we examine some **applications of discounted cash flow (DCF)** techniques revised in the previous chapter. An enterprise may be faced with more investment opportunities than it can finance, and we look first at how capital rationing may affect the investment decision.

Later in this chapter we look at ways of assessing the **social costs** and **social benefits** of investment decisions.

1 CAPITAL RATIONING 5/96

1.1 We saw in the last chapter that the decision rule with DCF techniques is to accept all projects which result in positive NPVs when discounted at the company's cost of capital. If a business suffers **capital rationing**, it will not be able to enter into all projects with positive NPVs because there is not enough capital for all the investments.

KEY TERM

Capital rationing: a situation in which a choice between different projects has to be made and where one of the limitations constraining the choice is the availability of funding *(OT)*.

1.2 Managers are therefore faced with the problem of deciding which projects to invest in. The decision technique to be applied will depend on the type of capital rationing. **Single period capital rationing** is where capital is limited for the current period only but will be freely available in the future. **Multi-period capital rationing** is where capital will be limited for several periods.

1.3 Before we look at some examples of capital rationing we need to distinguish between divisible projects and non-divisible projects. **Divisible projects** are those which can be undertaken completely or in fractions. Suppose that project A is divisible and requires the investment of £15,000 to achieve an NPV of £4,000. £7,500 invested in project A will earn an NPV of ½ × £4,000 = £2,000. **Indivisible projects** are those which must be undertaken completely or not at all. It is not possible to invest in a fraction of the project.

Single period rationing with divisible projects

1.4 With **single period capital rationing**, investment funds are a limiting factor in the current period. The total return will be maximised if management follows the decision rule of maximising the return per unit of the limiting factor. They should therefore select those projects whose cash inflows have the highest present value per £1 of capital invested. As stated in the previous chapter, according to the CIMA *Official Terminology* definition, the ratio of the present value of cash inflows to the initial investment gives the **profitability index (PI).** (The ratio of the NPV of the whole project - ie taking into account outlay as well as inflows - to the initial outlay is sometimes called the **benefit-cost ratio**. The benefit-cost ratio will always give the same ranking as the profitability index.)

1.5 EXAMPLE: SINGLE PERIOD RATIONING WITH DIVISIBLE PROJECTS

Short O'Funds Ltd has capital of £130,000 available for investment in the forthcoming period, at a cost of capital of 20%. Capital will be freely available in the future. Details of six projects under consideration are as follows. All projects are independent and divisible. Which projects should be undertaken and what NPV will result?

Project	*Investment required*	*Net present value at 20%*
	£'000	£'000
P	40	16.5
Q	50	17.0
R	30	18.8
S	45	14.0
T	15	7.4
U	20	10.8

1.6 SOLUTION

The first step is to rank the projects according to the return achieved from the limiting factor of investment funds.

Project	*NPV*	*Investment*	*NPV per £1 invested (PI)*	*Ranking*
	£'000	£'000	£	
P	16.5	40	0.41	4
Q	17.0	50	0.34	5
R	18.8	30	0.63	1
S	14.0	45	0.31	6
T	7.4	15	0.49	3
U	10.8	20	0.54	2

The available funds of £130,000 can now be allocated.

Project	*Investment*		*NPV*
	£'000		£'000
R	30		18.8
U	20		10.8
T	15		7.4
P	40		16.5
Q (balance)	25	(½)	8.5
	130	Maximum NPV =	62.0

Project S should not be undertaken and only half of project Q should be undertaken.

Single period rationing with indivisible projects

1.7 If the projects are not divisible then the method shown in the last paragraph may not result in the optimal solution. Another complication which arises is that there is likely to be a small amount of unused capital with each combination of projects. The best way to deal with this situation is to use trial and error and test the NPV available from different combinations of projects. This can be a laborious process if there are a large number of projects available. We will continue with the previous example to demonstrate the technique.

1.8 EXAMPLE: SINGLE PERIOD RATIONING WITH INDIVISIBLE PROJECTS

Short O'Funds Ltd now discovers that funds in the forthcoming period are actually restricted to £95,000. The directors decide to consider projects P, Q and R only. They wish to invest only in whole projects, but surplus funds can be invested to earn 25% per annum in perpetuity. Which combination of projects will produce the highest NPV at a cost of capital of 20%?

1.9 SOLUTION

The cumulative PV of £1 received per annum in perpetuity is £1/r. Therefore at a cost of capital of 20% the PV of the interest on £1 invested in perpetuity at 25% is $\frac{£1 \times 0.25}{0.20} = £1.25$

The net present value per pound invested is £1.25 less the original investment of £1. Therefore the NPV per pound invested is £0.25. The NPVs from all possible combinations of the three projects can now be tested.

Projects	*Required investment*	*Funds remaining for external investment*		*NPV of external investment*		*NPV from projects*	*Total NPV*
	£'000	£'000		£'000		£'000	£'000
P and Q	90	5	(× 0.25)	1.25	(16.5 + 17.0)	33.5	34.75
P and R	70	25		6.25	(16.5 + 18.8)	35.3	41.55
Q and R	80	15		3.75	(17.0 + 18.8)	35.8	39.55

The highest NPV will be achieved by undertaking projects P and R and investing the unused funds of £25,000 externally.

Multi period capital rationing with divisible projects

1.10 If capital rationing is expected to continue after the current period then the timing of the cash flows for each project becomes important. Management will still try to maximise the return from the limiting factor and since projects are divisible it is possible to use **linear programming** to find the optimal solution. You should be aware of how linear programming is performed (see the example below), although you will not be required to formulate the 'objective function' in the exam.

Exam focus point

Capital rationing will only be tested numerically using the profitability index.

1.11 EXAMPLE: MULTI PERIOD RATIONING WITH DIVISIBLE PROJECTS

X Ltd has the following six investment opportunities open to it.

Project			*Years*				*NPV at*
	0	*1*	*2*	*3*	*4*	*5*	*15%*
			Annual cash flows				
	£'000	£'000	£'000	£'000	£'000	£'000	£'000
A	–200	–100	–50	+200	+200	+200	20.53
B	–60	–80	+110	+110			25.94
C		–120	–50	+170	+210		89.69
D			–250	+240	+120	+110	92.07
E	–80	–100	+100	+150	+150	–100	43.33
F	–150	–150	+200	+180	+50		17.33

The company wishes to place a limit of £300,000 on the amount invested in projects in any one year. This investment limit cannot be supplemented with income from the projects. For example the cash inflow of £110,000 from project B in year 2 cannot be used for investment in another project. Projects are divisible and can be repeated more than once. Project timings cannot be advanced or delayed.

1.12 The objective is to maximise the NPV from the projects, and the **objective function** is as follows.

Maximise $20.53A + 25.94B + 89.69C + 92.07D + 43.33E + 17.33F$

where A, B, C, D, E and F are the proportions of each of the projects to be undertaken.

The £300,000 limit on funds does not matter in years 3 and 4 because there are no cash outflows in those years.

Constraints

Year 0:	200A	+ 60B			+ 80E	+ 150F	≤ 300
Year 1:	100A	+ 80B	+ 120C		+ 100E	+ 150F	≤ 300
Year 2:	50A		+ 50C	+ 250D			≤ 300
Year 5:					100E		≤ 300

Non-negativity: $A \geq 0, B \geq 0, C \geq 0, D \geq 0, E \geq 0, F \geq 0$

1.13 Once the objective function and the constraints have been established the problem can be solved using the simplex technique, which is not examinable and is not covered further here.

1.14 Many of the assumptions used when applying linear programming techniques to solve capital rationing problems are likely to be unrealistic and may therefore limit its usefulness.

(a) All cash flows are assumed to have linear relationships.
(b) Projects are assumed be infinitely divisible.
(c) It is assumed that cash flows are known with certainty.
(d) Projects and constraints are assumed to be independent.
(e) It is assumed that projects cannot be delayed.

Multi period capital rationing with indivisible projects

1.15 If it is not possible to invest in fractions of projects then the usual linear programming technique cannot be applied. In this situation, **integer programming** can be used. This is a form of linear programming in which variables can only take values 0 (reject the project) or 1 (accept the project).

Soft and hard capital rationing

1.16 Capital rationing may be necessary in a business due to internal factors (soft capital rationing) or external factors (hard capital rationing).

1.17 **Soft capital rationing** may arise for one of the following reasons.

(a) Management may be reluctant to issue additional share capital because of concern that this may lead to outsiders gaining control of the business.

(b) Management may be unwilling to issue additional share capital if it will lead to a dilution of earnings per share.

(c) Management may not want to raise additional debt capital because they do not wish to be committed to large fixed interest payments.

(d) There may be a desire within the organisation to limit investment to a level that can be financed solely from retained earnings.

(e) Capital expenditure budgets may restrict spending.

1.18 Note that whenever an organisation adopts a policy that restricts funds available for investment, such a policy may be less than optimal as the organisation may reject projects with a positive net present value and forgo opportunities that would have enhanced the market value of the organisation.

1.19 **Hard capital rationing** may arise for one of the following reasons.

(a) Raising money through the stock market may not be possible if share prices are depressed.

(b) There may be restrictions on bank lending due to government control.

(c) Lending institutions may consider an organisation to be to risky to be granted further loan facilities.

(d) The costs associated with making small issues of capital may be too great.

2 DCF AND GRADUAL ANNUAL SALES GROWTH

2.1 It is common for forecasts to assume that annual sales will increase over the life of a project. The following example shows how to apply DCF techniques in such cases.

2.2 EXAMPLE: GRADUAL ANNUAL SALES GROWTH

A consultancy firm is considering whether to set up a new fixed cost operation, providing specialist advice to clients. The operation would involve a capital outlay of £250,000. The project is to be evaluated over a period of five years, and discounted at a cost of capital of 14%. Running costs (cash outflows in pounds, with depreciation costs excluded) and demand as a percentage of maximum anticipated demand, are estimated as follows.

Year	*Costs*	*Demand as % of maximum*
	£	
1	50,000	40%
2	80,000	60%
3	100,000	80%
4	120,000	100%
5	120,000	100%

What are the minimum values of sales needed each year to justify the investment, on the assumption that growth in sales occurs at the forecast rate?

2.3 SOLUTION

Let maximum annual sales be £X.

Year	*Discount factor* 14%	*Costs* £	*PV of costs* £	*Revenues* £	*PV of revenues* £
0	1.000	(250,000)	(250,000)	0	0
1	0.877	(50,000)	(44,000)	0.4X	0.3508X
2	0.769	(80,000)	(61,600)	0.6X	0.4614X
3	0.675	(100,000)	(67,000)	0.8X	0.5400X
4	0.592	(120,000)	(70,800)	1.0X	0.5920X
5	0.519	(120,000)	(62,400)	1.0X	0.5190X
			(555,800)		2.4632X

To break even 2.4632X must equal £555,800.

$$X = \frac{£555,800}{2.4632} = £225,641, \text{ say } £226,000$$

The minimum sales are therefore as follows.

Year	£
1 (0.4X)	90,400
2 (0.6X)	135,600
3 (0.8X)	180,800
4	226,000
5	226,000

Question 1

A project would cost £120,000 immediately. The first year's contribution would be £35,000, and this would grow by 12% a year until the fourth and final year of the project. At a discount rate of 15%, is the project viable?

Answer

We can use a single rate to cover both the growth and the discounting. The present value of each year's contribution after the first year will be the present value of the previous year's contribution × 1.12/1.15.

Year	*Cash flow, growth and discounting*	*PV* £
0	£(120,000)	(120,000)
1	£35,000 × 1/1.15	30,435
2	£30,435 × 1.12/1.15	29,641
3	£29,641 × 1.12/1.15	28,868
4	£28,868 × 1.12/1.15	28,115
		(2,941)

The project is not viable.

---

3 THE ANNUALISED COST OF A CAPITAL ITEM 5/96

3.1 When an investment is being evaluated in terms of annual running costs, it may be appropriate to convert the capital cost into an annualised cost at the company's cost of capital. For example, when the capital expenditure is only a relatively small feature of a

project and annual running costs are a much more significant item, annual profitability is the key factor in the decision.

EXAM FORMULA

An asset with a life of t years has an equivalent annual cost of:

$$\frac{\text{PV costs}}{\text{t-year annuity factor}}$$

(a) 'PV costs' is the purchase cost, minus the present value of any subsequent disposal proceeds at the end of the item's life.

(b) The t-year annuity factor is at the company's cost of capital, for the number of years of the item's life.

3.2 EXAMPLE: ANNUALISED COST

A project is being considered which would involve a capital expenditure of £500,000 on equipment. The annual running costs and benefits would be as follows.

	£	£
Revenues		450,000
Costs		
Depreciation	100,000	
Other	300,000	
		400,000
Profit		50,000

The equipment would have a five year life, and no residual value, and would be financed by a loan at 12% interest per annum. Using annualised figures, assess whether the project is a worthwhile undertaking. Ignore risk and taxation.

3.3 SOLUTION

The annualised capital cost of the equipment is as follows.

$$\frac{\pounds 500{,}000}{\text{PV of } \pounds 1 \text{pa yrs } 1-5 \text{ at } 12\%} = \frac{\pounds 500{,}000}{3.605} = \pounds 138{,}504$$

Annual profit = £450,000 – £138,504 – £300,000 = £11,496

Depreciation is ignored because it is a notional cost and has already been taken into account in the annualised cost.

The project is a worthwhile undertaking, but only by about £11,000 a year for five years.

4 ASSET REPLACEMENT DECISIONS

4.1 A company may buy a new fixed asset to replace an existing, ageing asset or else to expand its business. Two types of asset replacement decision will be considered.

(a) The replacement of an existing asset with a new, but identical, asset. The problem is therefore simply one of deciding how frequently the asset should be replaced, that is of finding the optimum replacement cycle.

(b) The replacement of an existing asset with a different asset.

4.2 EXAMPLE: REPLACEMENT WITH AN IDENTICAL ASSET

Noel Hayter Ltd operates a machine which has the following costs and resale values over its four year life.

Purchase cost: £25,000.

	Year 1	*Year 2*	*Year 3*	*Year 4*
	£	£	£	£
Running costs (cash expenses)	7,500	10,000	12,500	15,000
Resale value (end of year)	15,000	10,000	7,500	2,500

How frequently should the asset be replaced? The company's cost of capital is 10%.

4.3 SOLUTION

There are three basic methods of finding the optimum replacement cycle: the **lowest common multiple method**; the **finite horizon method**; the **equivalent annual cost method**.

4.4 All three methods recognise that a replacement asset will eventually be replaced itself by an asset which will also in its turn be replaced. That is, replacements are assumed to occur into the indefinite future. The replacement options in our example are to replace the machine every one, two, three or four years.

To compare these options, we must assess the cost of each one over a comparable period of time.

The lowest common multiple method

4.5 The **lowest common multiple method** is as follows.

(a) Estimate the cash flows over a period of time which is the lowest common multiple of all the replacement cycles under consideration. Thus for replacement cycles of one, two, three or four years, the lowest common multiple is twelve years. In twelve years there would be:

(i) twelve complete replacement cycles of one year;
(ii) six complete replacement cycles of two years;
(iii) four complete replacement cycles of three years;
(iv) three complete replacement cycles of four years.

(b) Discount these cash flows over the lowest common multiple time period. The option with the lowest present value of cost will be the optimum replacement cycle.

4.6 In our example, we can calculate the annual cash flows as follows.

(a) **Replacement every year**

Year		£	£
0	Purchase		(25,000)
1	Running cost	(7,500)	
	Resale value	15,000	
	New purchase	(25,000)	
			(17,500)
2-11	Same as year 1		(17,500)
12	Running cost	(7,500)	
	Resale value	15,000	
			7,500

The new purchase at the end of year 12 is ignored, because this starts a new 12-year cycle for all four replacement options.

(b) **Replacement every two years**

Year		£	£
0	Purchase		(25,000)
1	Running cost		(7,500)
2	Running cost	(10,000)	
	Resale value	10,000	
	New purchase	(25,000)	
			(25,000)
3,5,7,9,11	Same as year 1		
4,6,8,10	Same as year 2		
12	Running cost	(10,000)	
	Resale value	10,000	
			0

(c) **Replacement every three years**

Year		£	£
0	Purchase		(25,000)
1	Running cost		(7,500)
2	Running cost		(10,000)
3	Running cost	(12,500)	
	Resale value	7,500	
	New purchase	(25,000)	
			(30,000)
4,7,10	Same as year 1		
5,8,11	Same as year 2		
6,9	Same as year 3		
12	Running cost	(12,500)	
	Resale value	7,500	
			(5,000)

(d) **Replacement every four years**

Year		£	£
0	Purchase		(25,000)
1	Running cost		(7,500)
2	Running cost		(10,000)
3	Running cost		(12,500)
4	Running cost	(15,000)	
	Resale value	2,500	
	New purchase	(25,000)	
			(37,500)
5,9	Same as year 1		
6,10	Same as year 2		
7,11	Same as year 3		
8	Same as year 4		
12	Running cost	(15,000)	
	Resale value	2,500	
			(12,500)

4.7 We can now calculate the present value for each replacement cycle.

	Replace every year		Replace every 2 years		Replace every 3 years		Replace every 4 years	
Year	Cash flow	PV at 10%	Cash flow	PV at 10%	Cash flow	PV at 10%	Cash flow	PV at 10%
	£	£	£	£	£	£	£	£
0	(25,000)	(25,000)	(25,000)	(25,000)	(25,000)	(25,000)	(25,000)	(25,000)
1	(17,500))		(7,500)	(6,818)	(7,500)	(6,818)	(7,500)	(6,818)
2	(17,500))		(25,000)	(20,650)	(10,000)	(8,260)	(10,000)	(8,260)
3	(17,500))		(7,500)	(5,633)	(30,000)	(22,530)	(12,500)	(9,388)
4	(17,500))		(25,000)	(17,075)	(7,500)	(5,123)	(37,500)	(25,613)
5	(17,500))		(7,500)	(4,658)	(10,000)	(6,210)	(7,500)	(4,658)
6	(17,500))	(113,663)	(25,000)	(14,100)	(30,000)	(16,920)	(10,000)	(5,640)
7	(17,500))		(7,500)	(3,848)	(7,500)	(3,848)	(12,500)	(6,413)
8	(17,500))		(25,000)	(11,675)	(10,000)	(4,670)	(37,500)	(17,513)
9	(17,500))		(7,500)	(3,180)	(30,000)	(12,720)	(7,500)	(3,180)
10	(17,500))		(25,000)	(9,650)	(7,500)	(2,895)	(10,000)	(3,860)
11	(17,500))		(7,500)	(2,625)	(10,000)	(3,500)	(12,500)	(4,375)
12	7,500	2,393	0	0	(5,000)	(1,595)	(12,500)	(3,988)
PV of costs		(136,270)		(124,912)		(120,089)		(124,706)

4.8 The cheapest policy would be to replace the machine every three years, because this has the lowest total present value of costs.

The finite horizon method

4.9 The lowest common multiple method can be tedious when the maximum life of the asset is more than about three years. If the maximum life were, say, seven years, there would be seven different replacement options and the lowest common multiple would be 420 years. The **finite horizon method** is to calculate the present value of costs for each option over a fairly long period (perhaps 15 or 20 years), because the present values of cash flows beyond this period are unlikely to affect the ranking of the replacement options.

The equivalent annual cost method

4.10 When there is no inflation, the **equivalent annual cost method** is the quickest method of deciding the optimum replacement cycle. It is necessary to calculate the present value of costs for each replacement cycle, but over one cycle only.

	Replace every year		Replace every 2 years		Replace every 3 years		Replace every 4 years	
Year	Cash flow	PV at 10%	Cash flow	PV at 10%	Cash flow	PV at 10%	Cash flow	PV at 10%
	£	£	£	£	£	£	£	£
0	(25,000)	(25,000)	(25,000)	(25,000)	(25,000)	(25,000)	(25,000)	(25,000)
1	7,500	6,818	(7,500)	(6,818)	(7,500)	(6,818)	(7,500)	(6,818)
2			0	0	(10,000)	(8,260)	(10,000)	(8,326)
3					(5,000)	(3,755)	(12,500)	(9,388)
4							(12,500)	(8,538)
PV of cost over one replacement cycle		(18,182)		(31,818)		(43,833)		(58,004)

4.11 These costs are not comparable, because they refer to different time periods. The equivalent annual cost method of comparing these cash flows is to calculate, for each length of replacement cycle, an equivalent annual cost. It is calculated as the present value of costs over one replacement cycle divided by the cumulative present value factor for the number of years in the cycle, ie using the formula given earlier:

$$\frac{\text{PV costs}}{\text{t-year annuity factor}}$$

4.12 In our example, given a discount rate of 10%, we have the following figures.

			Equivalent annual cost
(a)	Replacement every year		£
		$\frac{£(18{,}182)}{0.909}$	(20,002)
(b)	Replacement every two years		
		$\frac{£(31{,}818)}{1.36}$	(18,328)
(c)	Replacement every three years		
		$\frac{£(43{,}833)}{2.87}$	(17,625)
(d)	Replacement every four years		
		$\frac{£(58{,}004)}{3.170}$	(18,298)

The optimum policy is the one with the lowest equivalent annual cost, in this case to replace every three years (the same conclusion reached by the earlier lowest common multiple method).

4.13 The **equivalent annual cost method is recommended** because it is quicker and less cumbersome than the other methods described.

Question 2

A machine could be replaced every three years (amongst other possibilities), giving the following cash flows.

Year	*Cash flow*
	£
0	(10,000)
1	(1,000)
2	(1,200)
3	1,600

What is the equivalent annual cost of replacement every three years, using a discount rate of 15%?

Answer

Year	*Cash flow*	*Discount factor*	*PV*
	£	15%	£
0	(10,000)	1.000	(10,000)
1	(1,000)	0.870	(870)
2	(1,200)	0.756	(907)
3	1,600	0.658	1,052
			(10,725)

The equivalent annual cost is £10,725/2.283 = £4,698.

Non-identical replacement

4.14 When a machine will be replaced by a machine of a different type, there is a different replacement problem. The decision is now 'when should the existing asset be replaced?' rather than 'how frequently?' The optimum replacement cycle for the new machine may be calculated by one of the methods described previously. This does not resolve the further problem of whether the old machine should be replaced now, or in one year's time, two years' time, and so on.

4.15 EXAMPLE: NON-IDENTICAL REPLACEMENT

Suppose that the machine of Noel Hayter Ltd, in our previous example in Paragraph 4.2, is a new machine, which will be introduced to replace a non-identical existing machine, which is nearing the end of its life and has a maximum remaining life of only three years. The company wishes to decide when is the best time to replace the old machine, and estimates of relevant costs have been drawn up as follows.

Year	*Resale value of current machine*	*Extra expenditure and opportunity costs of keeping the existing machine in operation during the year*
	£	£
Now 0	8,500	0
1	5,000	9,000
2	2,500	12,000
3	0	15,000

When is the best time to replace the existing machine? The costs of the new machine will be those given in Paragraph 4.2, so that the optimum replacement cycle for the new machine will be three years as already calculated, with an equivalent annual cost of £17,625 (Paragraph 4.12(c)).

4.16 SOLUTION

The best time to replace the existing machine will be the option which gives the lowest NPV of cost in perpetuity, for both the existing machine and the machine which eventually replaces it. The present value of costs in perpetuity of the new machine is £17,625/0.1 = £176,250.

4.17 This present value of £176,250 relates to the beginning of the year when the first annual cash flow occurs, so that if replacement occurs now, the first payment is at year 1, and the PV is a year 0 value. If replacement occurs at the end of the first year the first payment is at year 2, and the PV is a year 1 value, and so on.

4.18 The total cash flows of the replacement decision may now be presented as follows. These cash flows show the PV of cost in perpetuity of the new machine and its replacements, the running costs of the existing machine, and the resale value of the existing machine, at the end of year 0, 1, 2 or 3 as appropriate.

	Time to replacement			
Year	*0 years*	*1 year*	*2 years*	*3 years*
	£	£	£	£
0	(176,250)	-	-	-
	8,500			
1	-	(176,250)		
		(9,000)	(9,000)	(9,000)
		5,000		
2	-	-	(176,250)	
			(12,000)	(12,000)
			2,500	
3	-	-	-	(176,250)
				(15,000)

	Year	Cash flow	Discount factor	Present value
		£	10%	£
Replace now	0	(176,250)		
		8,500		
		(167,750)	1.000	(167,750)
Replace in one year	1	(176,250)		
		(9,000)		
		5,000		
		(180,250)	0.909	(163,847)
Replace in two years	1	(9,000)	0.909	(8,181)
	2	(185,750)	0.826	(153,430)
				(161,611)
Replace in three years	1	(9,000)	0.91	(8,181)
	2	(12,000)	0.826	(9,912)
	3	(191,250)	0.751	(143,629)
				(161,722)

4.19 The optimum policy would be to replace the existing machine in three years' time, because this has the lowest total PV of cost in perpetuity.

5 COST BENEFIT ANALYSIS

Exam focus point

It is unlikely that cost benefit analysis will be tested quantitatively in the SFM examination, but you should understand the main principles behind it.

Social costs and social benefits **11/96**

KEY TERM

The CIMA *Official Terminology* defines **cost benefit analysis** as 'a comparison between the cost of the resources used, plus any other costs imposed by an activity (eg pollution, environmental damage) and the value of the financial and non-financial benefits derived'. However, the term 'cost benefit analysis' (or CBA) has developed a more specialised meaning, and is used to describe techniques for making investment decisions in a non profit making organisation, particularly a central or local government department.

5.1 In a profit making organisation, we know that investment decisions can be evaluated using DCF, and that if a project's economic benefits outweigh its economic costs, so that the project NPV is positive when cash flows are discounted at an appropriate cost of capital (discount rate) then it can be assumed that the project will add to the wealth of the organisation and its owners, and so should be undertaken.

5.2 In a non-profit making organisation, maximisation of the economic wealth of its owners may not be the prime objective. For example, if a government is wondering whether to build a new hospital, or a new school, the investment decision would not be based on whether or not the hospital or school would add to the nation's economic wealth. There are social objectives for investment decisions, and so investments ought to be measured in terms of social costs and social benefits.

5.3 **Social costs and benefits** can sometimes be expressed in economic terms, as follows.

(a) The social costs of putting resources into a project such as building a new power station, are their economic costs, for example building the station, and installing and testing the equipment.

(b) The social benefits can often be expressed in economic terms, for example in the case of a new power station, lower running costs and more efficient power generation, and so cheaper electricity.

5.4 There could well be some factors in an investment decision, particularly decisions by the government, which give rise to a social cost or a social benefit which does not have a market price. In the case of building a new power station, a social cost might be the increased pollution that the station would create. In the case of building a new road, the effect on the environment and the noise nuisance to local residents would be a social cost, but the greater ease of travelling for motorists would be a social benefit.

5.5 CBA is a technique which attempts to quantify these non-economic social costs and benefits, and to incorporate them into the evaluation of investment decisions. Investment decisions are still based largely on economic costs and benefits, in exactly the same way as investments would be evaluated in a profit-making organisation, but in addition one or several items of social cost or benefit are added into the financial arithmetic. This is done by putting money values on the non-economic social costs and benefits, treating them as cash flows and discounting both economic and social cost and benefit 'cash flows' at a suitable discount rate.

5.6 **Capital budgeting in the public sector** differs from capital budgeting in the private sector for several reasons.

(a) Relatively few public sector capital investments are made with the intention of earning a financial return. Nationalised industries may be expected to earn profits on their investments, but spending on roads, hospitals, schools, the defence forces and the police service, nuclear waste dumps and so on are not made with an eye to profit and return.

(b) When there are two or more ways of achieving the same objective the investment decision might be to prefer the option with the lowest present value of cost. And if a cost-saving capital item is being considered for purchase, the decision might be to buy the item provided that the present value of savings exceeds the present value of costs. In these ways, capital budgeting decisions in the public sector might be based on financial considerations alone.

However, rather than considering financial costs and benefits alone, capital budgeting decisions will often have regard to the social costs and the social benefits of investments.

(c) The cost of capital that is applied to project cash flows will not be a commercial rate of return, but one that is determined by the Treasury on behalf of the government.

5.7 For capital budgeting decisions in the public sector, where social costs and benefits are thought to be significant elements in the decision the following points should be noted.

(a) An attempt can be made to quantify the social costs and social benefits in monetary terms, and to treat them as cash flows.

(b) In choosing between mutually exclusive options (such as sites for a new airport) the option with the lowest total PV of costs would be preferred. For optional investments, the decision would be to go ahead with the investment if it had a positive NPV, taking both financial and social costs and benefits into account.

5.8 EXAMPLE: COST BENEFIT ANALYSIS

CBA could help the government to evaluate the social and environmental costs and benefits, as well as the economic costs, of building high standard inner city roads, to speed up traffic flow and so reduce traffic congestion and save travelling time for motorists. Cost benefit studies could help the decision-maker to make decisions such as the following.

(a) Should a road be built at all?
(b) If it should be built, where should it go?
(c) Should environmental protection be used to limit the environmental costs?

5.9 A cost benefit study of a road scheme would attempt to put a monetary value on the environmental costs. Monetary values would be assigned to:

(a) the costs to people who would have to be moved and rehoused because their home would be demolished, which would include:

 (i) statutory compensation payments from the government;

 (ii) loss of 'householders' surplus': the value of the householders' attachment to their homes and the neighbourhood;

(b) the costs to people whose homes would not be demolished, but who would decide to leave the area anyway;

(c) the nuisance and health hazards from car noise and fumes for people who stayed in the area.

5.10 Monetary values would also be assigned to the social benefits, such as the traffic benefits from faster travelling through the city, the ability of the road to carry a bigger volume of traffic than the old road, and the environmental benefits to other people in the city from the reduced traffic congestion.

Question 3

List three social costs and three social benefits of building a new state school.

Answer

Tutorial note. You could of course have listed costs and benefits other than those given here.

Costs

(a) The economic cost of construction
(b) Disturbance to local residents
(c) Adverse impact on nearby schools

Benefits

(a) More school places
(b) The provision of education near students' homes
(c) The provision of a building reflecting modern educational thinking

General principles of cost benefit analysis

5.11 CBA tries to establish trade-offs between:

(a) different types of effect, only some of which have money costs attached to them;
(b) present and future effects;
(c) effects on different groups of people.

These trade-offs are used to convert as many as possible of the effects into a common scale, usually a monetary present value of benefits minus costs. Of course, this process does not replace the need for judgement in decision making, even in the unlikely event that all significant effects have been expressed in the common scale.

5.12 The basis for establishing trade-offs for intangibles is generally derived from the principle that benefits are to be valued at what the beneficiaries would be prepared to pay for them, while costs are to be valued at the amount the sufferers would regard as sufficient compensation to induce them to accept the cost willingly.

5.13 For government decisions, investments by different government departments should be evaluated consistently, and so the future costs and benefits of all proposed investments should be converted into present values using the same 'test discount rate.' The discount rate to apply for all projects would be decided by the Treasury department.

5.14 With most investment decisions, some people will benefit and others will suffer losses in the cost benefit sums. It is usual to compare the costs and benefits of different groups of people on an equal footing: 'a pound to me is the same as a pound to you'. This assumption could be challenged on the social or political grounds that it is fairer for a wealthy section of the community to suffer a cost of £10m, say, than it would be for a poorer section of the community to suffer a cost of much less than this. Cost benefit analysis techniques do not go into such matters of distributive justice.

Concepts for measuring social costs and benefits

5.15 CBA thus attempts to measure the social costs and benefits of a plan, by translating them into monetary values. The tangible costs and benefits of such schemes are comparatively easy to express in monetary values. Intangible costs and benefits are more difficult to assess, and we will now look at some of the concepts and techniques that can be used.

5.16 CBA attempts to identify the social costs or social benefits of an investment, and the term **shadow price** can be used to describe the value of these costs and benefits.

(a) A social cost or benefit may be the fall or rise in property values as a result of a change in the environment, for example the presence of a motorway. The monetary value of such a cost or benefit is its shadow price.

(b) Social benefits might be:

  (i) unmeasurable in quantitative terms; or

  (ii) measurable in non-monetary terms, for example hours saved, educational qualifications conferred or number of crimes prevented. Where possible, a monetary value should be placed on these quantified social benefits, and the shadow price of an educational qualification or a crime prevented can be used in the cost benefit analysis.

5.17 Another example is the social benefit of a project that reduces unemployment in an area. Suppose that building a new college of further education in a town is expected to provide employment for people in the area, with an estimate being made of the number of long-term and short-term jobs it would create. How should the creation of jobs be valued?

5.18 The shadow price of a job could be any of the following.

(a) The gross wage or salary that the employers would have to pay their employees
(b) The net wage or salary that employees would receive
(c) A weighted average of the gross pay and net pay for the jobs

The social value of 'goods' with no market

5.19 One feature of cost benefit analysis is that a social cost or benefit might be established for goods which do not have a market or a market price. Examples are as follows.

(a) **The value of time**. A money value can be worked out for people's time, that is the time saved or the extra time incurred as a result of an investment. For example a decision to close down a branch railway line will have some consequence for the extra travelling time for passengers who are now forced to use a bus service or a car. This extra time will have a social cost. Similarly, building a faster road will save time for motorists and bus travellers, and this will have a social benefit, for which a money value can be established.

(b) **The value of amenities.** A value can be assigned to the introduction of new public amenities, such as the improvement of street lighting in an area, or environmental landscaping. In this case, the social value can be given a money value by estimating the increase in the market value of local housing affected by the introduction of the amenity.

5.20 The term **surrogate price** is sometimes used to describe the price consumers would be willing to pay if a market existed for the product. It might be possible, for example, to estimate a surrogate price for the provision of a mains water supply to a particular area, although a free market for water does not exist. The surrogate price might be established as the increase in house values arising as a consequence of introducing the amenity.

Cost effectiveness analysis

5.21 CBA is by no means widely established. Some writers have recommended that greater attention be given to the assessment of social benefits in **non-monetary terms**. By a careful analysis of benefits given in the past and an estimate of non-monetary benefits obtainable in the future from spending money on various different services, it might be possible to discover the most beneficial way of sharing out the limited funds of the organisation. They recommend **cost effectiveness analysis**, where costs and resources committed are measured in money terms, but benefits are assessed in a non-monetary way. Cost effectiveness analysis is a form of CBA, except that social benefits are not measured in monetary terms, on the grounds that social benefits involve too many value judgements, and monetary estimates of them cannot be reliable.

5.22 Cost effectiveness analysis tries to show:

(a) how a given level of benefit can be achieved at the minimum cost; or

(b) how to maximise the non-monetary benefits given a fixed limit to the amount of money investment available.

5.23 For example, cost effectiveness analysis might consider:

(a) the optimal location for a hospital, given that certain non-monetary benefits must be obtained (for example in terms of number of patient beds) but at a minimum cost;

(b) the optimal way of investing in medicine or surgery for a particular disease or illness, given a budget limit. For example, given a budget limit for what the government will spend on treating heart diseases, how should the spending be allocated between heart transplants work and other medical or surgical treatments of the same complaint, in order to maximise the overall medical (non-monetary) benefits?

Chapter roundup

- The **application of basic DCF techniques** and other investment evaluation techniques should not pose any particular difficulties provided that you learn the basic techniques thoroughly. Then, apply clear, sensible and logical reasoning to a problem, and state all your assumptions. As with all decision making problems, your recommendations should recognise the qualitative factors in the decision.
- **Cost benefit analysis** uses financial decision-making techniques (relevant costs and DCF) but includes some non-financial costs and benefits as money items within the cash flows. A test discount rate that ought to be a 'social' discount rate rather than a financial discount rate should be applied to the cash flows (although the financial and the social discount rates might well be assumed to be the same or similar).

Quick quiz

1 Distinguish between soft capital rationing and hard capital rationing. (see para 1.16)

2 How do you calculate the equivalent annualised cost of a capital item? (3.1)

3 What are the three methods of finding the optimum replacement cycle for a capital asset? (4.3)

4 What is cost benefit analysis? (Section 5)

5 What is the difference between cost benefit analysis and cost effectiveness analysis? (5.21)

Question to try	Level	Marks	Time
19	Introductory	25	45 mins

Chapter 20

FURTHER ISSUES IN INVESTMENT APPRAISAL

	Chapter topic list	Syllabus reference	Ability required
1	The cost of capital, the NPV of new projects and the value of shares	13 c(i); c(v)	Application
2	The CAPM and project appraisal	13 c(vi)	Skill
3	The adjusted present value method of project evaluation	13 c(ii)	Application
4	Allowing for inflation	13 c(i)	Application
5	Allowing for taxation	13 c(i)	Application

Introduction

We explained earlier the two aspects of the cost of capital: it is the **cost of funds** a company uses, but also it is the **minimum return** a company should be making on its investments. It is the latter aspect of the cost of capital to which we now turn. We will also be looking in this chapter at how to incorporate **inflation** and **taxation** into investment decisions.

1 THE COST OF CAPITAL, THE NPV OF NEW PROJECTS AND THE VALUE OF SHARES

1.1 Using the **dividend valuation model,** it can be argued that the total value of a company's shares will increase by the NPV of any project that is undertaken, provided that there is no change in the company's WACC. We shall begin by considering this argument for companies financed entirely by equity, so that the WACC and the cost of equity are the same.

1.2 Suppose that a company relying on equity as its only source of finance wishes to invest in a new project. If the money is raised by issuing new share capital to the existing shareholders and the inflows generated by the new project are used to increase dividends, then the project will have to show a positive net present value (NPV) at the shareholders' marginal cost of capital, because otherwise the shareholders would not agree to provide the new capital.

1.3 The gain to the shareholders after acceptance of the new project will be the difference between the market value of the company before acceptance of the new project and the market value of the company after acceptance of the new project less the amount of funds raised from the shareholders to finance the project.

The market value of the shares will increase by:

$$\frac{A_1}{(1+r)}+\frac{A_2}{(1+r)^2}+\frac{A_3}{(1+r)^3}+.....-(\text{Cost of project})$$

where A_1, A_2 ..... are the additional dividends at years 1, 2 and so on
r is the shareholders' marginal cost of capital.

This is the NPV of the project.

Investments financed by retained profits

1.4 If for some reason there is a limit to the number of new shares that a company can issue to its shareholders and a company could undertake many projects with positive net present values, then reducing its dividend payment would increase the supply of capital available. Even though in the short term dividends will be reduced, this will be more than compensated for in the long term by the fact that extra cash inflows generated by the investments will increase dividends in the future. Indeed, it can be argued that no dividends should be paid until all projects with positive net present values have been financed.

1.5 EXAMPLE: INCREASE IN THE MARKET VALUE OF SHARES

Hubble plc, which has just paid its current dividend, expects to pay dividends of £6,000 at year 1, £6,000 at year 2 and £8,000 a year from then onwards.

A new project has just been discovered which will require an outlay of £3,000 at year 1 and will yield cash inflows of £2,000 each year for two years. If the project is accepted, dividends will be adjusted accordingly. The shareholders' marginal cost of capital is estimated at 15%.

If the shareholders were told at year 0 that the project was going to be accepted and they were given full information about the project, what should be the theoretical increase in the market value of the company's shares?

1.6 SOLUTION

(a) The market value of company at year 0 before acceptance of the new project is:

$$\frac{£6,000}{1.15}+\frac{£6,000}{1.15^2}+\frac{£8,000}{1.15^3}+\frac{£8,000}{1.15^4}+\ldots\ (£8,000 \text{ pa in perpetuity})$$

The value at year 2 of £8,000 receivable each year from year 3 onwards is:

$$\frac{£8,000}{0.15}=£53,333$$ which means that the above computation can be simplified to

$$\frac{£6,000}{1.15}+\frac{£6,000}{1.15^2}+\frac{£53,333}{1.15^2}=£50,080$$

(b) The market value of the company at year 0 after acceptance of the new project is:

$$\frac{£3,000}{1.15}+\frac{£8,000}{1.15^2}+\frac{£10,000}{1.15^3}+\frac{£8,000}{1.15^4}+\ldots\ (£8,000 \text{ pa in perpetuity})$$

The year 1 dividend will be £3,000 lower than before and the years 2 and 3 dividends will be £2,000 higher than before.

$$\frac{£3,000}{1.15}+\frac{£8,000}{1.15^2}+\frac{£10,000}{1.15^3}+\frac{£53,333}{1.15^3}=£50,300$$

(c) The market value of the company at year 0 would increase by £220 (£50,300 – £50,080) after acceptance of the project. The £220 can be proved as follows.

(i) NPV of the project at year 1 $= \dfrac{£2,000}{1.15^2} + \dfrac{£2,000}{1.15} - £3,000$

$= £(1,512 + 1,739 - 3,000) = £251$

(ii) NPV at year 0 of £251 receivable at the end of year 1

$= \dfrac{£251}{1.15} = £218$

This NPV of £218 is the same as the increase in the market value of £220, allowing for a rounding error of £2.

1.7 In the example above the shareholders would in theory benefit from a sudden rise in the price equal to the net present value of the new project as soon as the project was accepted. In practice, however, this is unlikely to happen for the following reasons.

(a) It would only happen if there is a strong form efficient market, or if dividend forecasts are published and are believed.

(b) Shareholders do not necessarily make rational decisions, so market values may not in practice respond to changes in future dividend expectations.

Conclusions for ungeared companies

1.8 If an all equity company undertakes a project, and it is financed in such a way that its cost of capital remains unchanged, the total market value of ordinary shares will increase by the amount of the NPV of the project.

If the market has strong form efficiency the shares will increase in value as soon as details of the intended project become available in advance of extra profits actually being earned and extra dividends actually being received from the project.

Geared companies

1.9 The situation is the same if a company has debt capital in its capital structure.

1.10 EXAMPLE: GEARED COMPANY

Trubshaw plc is financed 50% by equity and 50% by debt capital. The cost of equity is 20% and the cost of debt is 14%. Ignoring tax, this means that Trubshaw's WACC is 17%.

The company currently pays out all its profits as dividends, and expected dividends are £800,000 a year into the indefinite future.

A project is under consideration which would cost £1,200,000, to be financed half by a new issue of equity and half by a new loan. It would increase annual profits before interest by £340,000. The costs of equity and debt capital would be unchanged.

(a) What is the NPV of the project?

(b) By how much would the value of equity increase if the project is undertaken?

(c) How should this project be financed, such that the debt/equity ratio of the company remains at 50%:50%?

1.11 SOLUTION

(a) The NPV of the project is as follows.

Year	*Cash flow*	*Discount factor*		*Present value*
	£	17%		£
0	(1,200,000)	1.0		(1,200,000)
1 - ∞	340,000	1/0.17		2,000,000
			NPV	800,000

(b) The market value of the company as a whole will increase by £2,000,000, which is the project's NPV plus the cost of the investment. Of this, £1,000,000 will be debt capital and £1,000,000 will be equity.

(c) To maintain the 50:50 debt:equity ratio, the cost of the investment will be financed by £1,000,000 debt capital and £200,000 equity. It would not be financed by £600,000 of each. This is because the NPV of £800,000 will add to the value of equity **only**, not to the value of the debt capital. If new equity of £200,000 is issued, the NPV of £800,000 will increase the market value of equity by £1,000,000 in total, which matches the new loan capital of £1,000,000.

The increased value of equity can be proved as follows.

	£
Annual profit from project, before interest	340,000
Less interest cost (£1,000,000 × 14%)	140,000
Increase in annual profits and dividends	200,000
Cost of equity	÷20%
Increase in the market value of equity	£1,000,000

1.12 This example illustrates that given an unchanged WACC, the value of equity will be increased by the NPV of any project which is undertaken (plus the extra funds invested in equity, in this case £200,000) with the NPV calculated using a discount rate equal to the WACC.

2 THE CAPM AND PROJECT APPRAISAL

2.1 The CAPM can be used instead of the dividend valuation model to establish an equity cost of capital to use in project appraisal. The cost of equity is $r_e = r_f + [r_m - r_f]\ \beta_e$ where β_e is the beta value for the company's equity capital.

2.2 EXAMPLE: CAPM AND PROJECT APPRAISAL (1)

A company is financed by a mixture of equity and debt capital, whose market values are in the ratio 3:1. The debt capital, which is considered risk-free, yields 10% before tax. The average stock market return on equity capital is 16%. The beta value of the company's equity capital is estimated as 0.95. The tax rate is 30%.

What would be an appropriate cost of capital to be used for investment appraisal of new projects with the same systematic risk characteristics as the company's current investment portfolio?

2.3 SOLUTION

An appropriate cost of capital to use, assuming no change in the company's financial gearing, is its WACC. However, the CAPM can be used to estimate the cost of the company's equity.

$r_e \quad = 10\% + (16 - 10) \times 0.95\% = 15.7\%$

The after tax cost of debt is 0.70 × 10% = 7%.

The WACC is therefore

$$(\tfrac{3}{4} \times 15.7\%) + (\tfrac{1}{4} \times 7.0\%) = 13.525\%.$$

The cost of capital to use in project appraisal is 13.525%.

How is the WACC different using the CAPM?

2.4 You might be wondering how the weighted average cost of capital (WACC) is different when we use the CAPM compared to the method of calculating the WACC which was described in the earlier chapter on the cost of capital. The only difference, in fact, is the method used to calculate the cost of the firm's equity: the dividend valuation model or the CAPM.

Question 1

See if you can explain why you think the two methods will produce different values, before reading the next paragraph.

2.5 Using the different techniques for measuring the cost of equity will produce two different values for these reasons.

(a) The dividend valuation model uses expectations of actual dividends and current share values. Dividends may include extra or lower returns caused by unsystematic risk variations, as well as systematic risk. Share prices might not be in equilibrium.

(b) The CAPM considers systematic risk only, and assumes equilibrium in the stock market.

2.6 If dividends reflect systematic risk only, and if stock market prices are in equilibrium, the dividend valuation model and the CAPM should produce roughly the same estimates for the cost of a firm's equity and for its WACC.

The use of the CAPM for capital investment decisions

2.7 The CAPM produces a required return based on the expected return of the market, expected project returns, the risk-free interest rate and the variability of project returns relative to the market returns. Its main advantage when used for investment appraisal is that it produces a discount rate which is based on the systematic risk of the individual investment. It can be used to compare projects of all different risk classes and is therefore superior to an NPV approach which uses only one discount rate for all projects, regardless of their risk.

2.8 The model was developed with respect to securities; by applying it to an investment within the firm, the company is assuming that the shareholder wishes investments to be evaluated as if they were securities in the capital market and thus assumes that all shareholders will hold diversified portfolios and will not look to the company to achieve diversification for them.

2.9 The greatest practical problems with the use of the CAPM in capital investment decisions are as follows.

(a) It is hard to estimate returns on projects under different economic environments, market returns under different economic environments and the probabilities of the various environments.

(b) The CAPM is really just a single period model. Few investment projects last for one year only and to extend the use of the return estimated from the model to more than one time period would require both project performance relative to the market and the economic environment to be reasonably stable.

In theory, it should be possible to apply the CAPM for each time period, thus arriving at successive discount rates, one for each year of the project's life. In practice, this would exacerbate the estimation problems mentioned above and also make the discounting process much more cumbersome.

(c) It may be hard to determine the risk-free rate of return. Government securities are usually taken to be risk-free, but the return on these securities varies according to their term to maturity.

3 THE ADJUSTED PRESENT VALUE METHOD OF PROJECT EVALUATION

5/98

3.1 We have seen that a company's gearing level has implications for both the value of its equity shares and its WACC. The viability of an investment project will depend partly on how the investment is financed, and how the method of finance affects gearing.

3.2 The net present value method of investment appraisal is to discount the cash flows of a project at a cost of capital. This cost of capital might be the WACC, but it could also be another cost of capital, perhaps one which allows for the risk characteristics of the individual project.

3.3 An alternative method of carrying out project appraisal is to use the **adjusted present value (APV) method**. The APV method involves two stages.

(a) Evaluate the project first of all as if it were all equity financed, and so as if the company were an all equity company to find the 'base case NPV'.

(b) Make adjustments to allow for the effects of the method of financing that has been used.

3.4 EXAMPLE: APV METHOD

A company is considering a project that would cost £100,000 to be financed 50% by equity (cost 21.6%) and 50% by debt (pre-tax cost 12%). The financing method would maintain the company's WACC unchanged. The cash flows from the project would be £36,000 a year in perpetuity, before interest charges. Corporation tax is at 30%.

Appraise the project using firstly the NPV method and secondly the APV method.

3.5 SOLUTION

We can use the **NPV method** because the company's WACC will be unchanged.

	Cost	*Weighting*		*Product*
	%			%
Equity	21.6	0.5		10.8
Debt (70% of 12%)	8.4	0.5		4.2
			WACC	15.0

Annual cash flows in perpetuity from the project are as follows.

	£
Before tax	36,000
Less tax (30%)	10,800
After tax	25,200

NPV of project = –£100,000 + (25,200 ÷ 0.15)
= –£100,000 + £168,000
= + £68,000

3.6 Since £100,000 of new investment is being created, the value of the company will increase by £100,000 + £68,000 = £168,000, of which 50% must be debt capital.

The company must raise 50% × £168,000 = £84,000 of 12% debt capital, and (the balance) £16,000 of equity. The NPV of the project will raise the value of this equity from £16,000 to £84,000 thus leaving the gearing ratio at 50:50.

3.7 The **APV approach** to this example is as follows.

(a) First, we need to know the cost of equity in an ungeared company. The MM formula we can use to establish this is:

$$r_E = r + (1 - T_c)[(r - r_D) \times \frac{D}{E}]$$

$$21.6\% = r + (0.70)[(r - 12\%) \times \frac{50}{50}]$$

$$21.6\% = r + 0.70r - 8.4\%$$

$$1.70r = 30\%$$

$$r = 17.5765\%$$

(b) Next, we calculate the NPV of the project as if it were all equity financed. The cost of equity would be 17.647%

$$NPV = \frac{£25{,}200}{0.17647} - £100{,}000 = +£42{,}800$$

(c) Next, we can use the MM formula for the relationship between the value of geared and ungeared companies, to establish the effect of gearing on the value of the project. £84,000 will be financed by debt.

$$V_g = V_u + DT_c$$

$$= + £42{,}000 + (£84{,}000 \times 0.30) = £68{,}000$$

3.8 The value DT_c represents the present value of the tax shield on debt interest, that is the present value of the savings arising from tax relief on debt interest.

Annual interest charge = 12% of £84,000	=	£10,080
Tax saving (30% × £10,080)	=	£3,024.00
Cost of debt (pre-tax)	=	12%
PV of tax savings in perpetuity	=	$\frac{£3{,}024}{0.12}$
	=	£25,200

DT_c = £84,000 × 0.30 = £25,200 is a quicker way of deriving the same value.

3.9 The APV and NPV approaches produce the same conclusion. However, the APV method can also be adapted to allow for financing which changes the gearing structure and the WACC.

In this respect, it is superior to the NPV method. Suppose, for example, that in the previous example, the entire project were to be financed by debt. The APV of the project would be calculated as follows.

(a) The NPV of project if all equity financed is:

$$\frac{£25,200}{0.17647} - £100,000$$

$$= + £42,800 \text{ (as before)}$$

(b) The adjustment to allow for the method of financing is the present value of the tax relief on debt interest in perpetuity.

$DT_c = £100,000 \times 0.30 = 30,000$

(c) APV = £42,800 + £33,000 = +£72,800

The project would increase the value of equity by £72,800.

Question 2

A project costing £100,000 is to be financed by £60,000 of irredeemable 12% debentures and £40,000 of new equity. The project will yield an annual cash flow of £21,000 in perpetuity. If it were all equity financed, an appropriate cost of capital would be 15%. The corporation tax rate is 30%. What is the project's APV?

Answer

	£
NPV if all equity financed: £21,000/0.15 – £100,000	40,000
PV of the tax shield: £60,000 × 12% × 30%/0.12	18,000
APV	58,000

The advantages and disadvantages of the APV method

3.10 The main advantage of the APV method is that it can be used to evaluate all the effects of the method of financing a project. The NPV technique can allow for the financing side-effects implicitly, by adjusting the discount rate used. In contrast, the APV technique allows for the financing side-effects explicitly.

3.11 The main difficulties with the APV technique are:

(a) establishing a suitable cost of equity, for the initial DCF computation as if the project were all equity financed;

(b) identifying all the costs associated with the method of financing.

Adjusting the cost of capital

3.12 As well as reflecting how the net present value of a project can be increased or decreased by the effects of how the project is financed, the APV approach suggests that it is possible to calculate an adjusted cost of capital for use in specific circumstances.

3.13 There are different approaches to calculating an adjusted cost of capital for a project, reflected by the formulae included in the CIMA *Mathematical Tables*:

(a) Modigliani-Miller (MM);
(b) Miles-Ezzell; and

(c) weighted average cost of capital (WACC).

Exam focus point

Of these alternative methods, you should understand how to apply the WACC approach (method (c)). Methods (a) and (b) are not often used in practice and are mainly of academic interest.

3.14 First of all, we can distinguish the opportunity cost of capital and the adjusted cost of capital.

(a) The **opportunity cost of capital** (r) is the expected rate of return available in capital markets on assets of equivalent risk. This depends on the risk of the project cash flows, and should be used if there are no significant side-effects arising from the method of financing.

(b) The **adjusted cost of capital** ($r^\star$) is an adjusted opportunity cost which reflects the financing side-effects of the project. A firm should accept projects which have a positive net present value (NPV) at the adjusted cost of capital $r^\star$.

3.15 The following explanations cover, with examples, the formulae for the three different approaches.

MM formula

3.16 The following is the formula for the adjusted cost of capital ($r^\star$) suggested by the work of Modigliani and Miller.

EXAM FORMULA

$r^\star = r(1 - T^\star L)$

where $T^\star$ is the net tax saving, expressed in pounds, of £1 of future debt interest payments

L is the marginal contribution of the project to the debt capacity of the firm, expressed as a proportion of the *present value of the project.*

3.17 EXAMPLE: MM FORMULA

Project X, requiring an investment of £1,000,000, adds £300,000 to a firm's debt capacity. The project leads to a constant annual saving of £210,000 indefinitely. The opportunity cost of capital is 20%. Assume that the tax shield on interest payments is $T^\star = 0.30$ (30 per cent). What is the adjusted cost of capital?

3.18 SOLUTION

$L = 300{,}000 \div 1{,}000{,}000 = 0.30$

Using the MM formula:

$$r^\star = r(1 - T^\star L)$$

$$= 0.20(1 - 0.30 \times 0.30) = 0.182, \text{ or } 18.2\%$$

3.19 In what circumstances may the MM formula be used? The MM formula works exactly for any project which is expected to generate a level cash flow in perpetuity and to support permanent debt. The formula also works as a reasonable approximation for projects with limited lives or irregular cash flow streams.

Miles-Ezzell formula

3.20 This second formula (below) for calculating an adjusted cost of capital addresses the problem that the future value and risk of the project are likely to change. If the value of the project increases, or decreases, for example due to a commodity price change, then we would expect the contribution to debt capacity also to increase or decrease respectively.

EXAM FORMULA

$$r^* = r - L\, r_D\, T^* \left(\frac{1+r}{1+r_D}\right)$$

where r_D is the rate of interest on borrowings.

3.21 The Miles-Ezzell formula assumes that the firm adjusts its borrowing to keep it at a constant proportion of the project's value (in the example above, 30%). Where this is so, the formula works exactly with any cash flow pattern or project life.

3.22 EXAMPLE: MILES-EZZELL FORMULA

Using the same 'Project X' details as the example used above to illustrate the MM formula, if the borrowing rate is 13% we have:

$$r^* \quad = 0.20 - 0.30 \times 0.13 \times 0.30 \times \frac{1.20}{1.13} = 0.188\text{, or } 18.8\%$$

Weighted average cost of capital (WACC) formula

3.23 The WACC formula for the adjusted cost of capital is as follows.

EXAM FORMULA

$$r^* = r_D\,(1 - T_C)\,\frac{D}{E+D} + r_E\,\frac{E}{E+D}$$

where

r_D is the firm's current borrowing rate

T_c is the marginal corporate tax rate

r_E is the expected rate of return on the firm's shares (which depends on the firm's business risk and its debt ratio)

D, E are the market values of currently outstanding debt and equity respectively

3.24 All of the variables in this formula refer to the firm as a whole, and therefore the formula only works for projects which are just like the firm which undertakes them. It will not work for projects with a different level of risk than the average of the firm's assets; nor will it work for projects which lead to the firm's debt ratio increasing or decreasing.

3.25 EXAMPLE: WACC FORMULA

Suppose that Project X is set up as an independent company (Project X Ltd). When the project is in place, the company will be worth the initial investment of £1,000,000 plus the APV of the project.

3.26 Discounting the cash flows of the project at the 18.8% rate given by the Miles-Ezzell formula (still assuming a constant debt ratio of 30%) gives a net present value as follows:

$$\text{NPV} = -£1{,}000{,}000 + \frac{210{,}000}{0.188}$$
$$= +£117{,}021$$

The balance sheet of Project X Ltd should be as follows.

	£
Assets (initial investment + APV)	1,117,021
Debt (D) (30%)	335,106
Equity (E) (70%)	781,915
	1,117,021

3.27 Shareholders will expect to receive the cash flow from the investment (C) less the interest payment on debt ($r_D D$) plus the interest tax shield ($T_c\, r_D D$).

Expected income for equity $= C - r_D\, D + T_c\, r_D\, D$

$= C - (1 - T_c)\, r_D\, D$

$= 210{,}000 - (1 - 0.30) \times 0.13 \times 335{,}106 = 179{,}505$

Expected equity return r_E $= \dfrac{\text{Expected equity income}}{E}$

$= \dfrac{179{,}505}{781{,}915}$

$= 0.230$, or 23%

3.28 Suppose that Project X Ltd comes across another investment opportunity with the same business risk and the same pattern of cash flows as the first project, but a different level of profitability. The company therefore plans to borrow 30% of the value of the project. For this project, it will be possible to use the WACC formula to find the appropriate adjusted discount rate.

$$r^* = r_D\,(1 - T_c)\,\frac{D}{E+D} + r_E\,\frac{E}{E+D}$$
$$= 0.13(1 - 0.30) \times 0.3 + 0.230 \times 0.7$$
$$= 0.0273 + 0.161 = 0.188, \text{ or } 18.8\%$$

3.29 Note that this is the same figure we calculated earlier, using the Miles-Ezzell formula.

4 ALLOWING FOR INFLATION 5/98

4.1 So far we have not considered the effect of inflation on the appraisal of capital investment proposals. As the inflation rate increases so will the minimum return required by an investor. For example, you might be happy with a return of 5% in an inflation-free world, but if inflation was running at 15% you would expect a considerably greater yield.

4.2 EXAMPLE: INFLATION (1)

A company is considering investing in a project with the following cash flows.

Time	*Actual cash flows*
	£
0	(15,000)
1	9,000
2	8,000
3	7,000

The company requires a minimum return of 20% under the present and anticipated conditions. Inflation is currently running at 10% a year, and this rate of inflation is expected to continue indefinitely. Should the company go ahead with the project?

4.3 Let us first look at the company's required rate of return. Suppose that it invested £1,000 for one year on 1 January, then on 31 December it would require a minimum return of £200. With the initial investment of £1,000, the total value of the investment by 31 December must therefore increase to £1,200. During the course of the year the purchasing value of the pound would fall due to inflation. We can restate the amount received on 31 December in terms of the purchasing power of the pound at 1 January as follows.

Amount received on 31 December in terms of the value of the pound at 1 January

$$= \frac{£1{,}200}{(1.10)^1} = £1{,}091$$

4.4 In terms of the value of the pound at 1 January, the company would make a profit of £91 which represents a rate of return of 9.1% in 'today's money' terms. This is known as the real rate of return. The required rate of 20% is a money rate of return (sometimes called a nominal rate of return). The money rate measures the return in terms of the pound which is, of course, falling in value. The real rate measures the return in constant price level terms. The two rates of return and the inflation rate are linked by the equation:

$$(1 + \text{money rate}) = (1 + \text{real rate}) \times (1 + \text{inflation rate})$$

where all the rates are expressed as proportions.

In our example:

$$(1 + 0.20) = (1 + 0.091) \times (1 + 0.10) = 1.20$$

Which rate is used in discounting?

4.5 We must decide which rate to use for discounting, the real rate or the money rate. The rule is as follows.

(a) If the cash flows are expressed in terms of the actual number of pounds that will be received or paid on the various future dates, we must use the money rate for discounting.

(b) If the cash flows are expressed in terms of the value of the pound at time 0 (that is, in constant price level terms), we must use the real rate.

4.6 The cash flows given in Paragraph 4.2 are expressed in terms of the actual number of pounds that will be received or paid at the relevant dates. We should, therefore, discount them using the money rate of return.

Time	Cash flow	Discount factor	PV
	£	20%	£
0	(15,000)	1.000	(15,000)
1	9,000	0.833	7,497
2	8,000	0.694	5,552
3	7,000	0.579	4,053
			2,102

The project has a positive net present value of £2,102.

4.7 The future cash flows can be re-expressed in terms of the value of the pound at time 0 as follows, given inflation at 10% a year.

Time	Actual cash flow	Cash flow at time 0 price level	
	£		£
0	(15,000)		(15,000)
1	9,000	$9{,}000 \times \frac{1}{1.10}$	= 8,182
2	8,000	$8{,}000 \times \frac{1}{(1.10)^2}$	= 6,612
3	7,000	$7{,}000 \times \frac{1}{(1.10)^3}$	= 5,259

4.8 The cash flows expressed in terms of the value of the pound at time 0 can now be discounted using the real rate of 9.1%.

Time	Cash flow	Discount factor	PV
	£	9.1%	£
0	(15,000)	1.000	(15,000)
1	8,182	$\frac{1}{1.091}$	7,500
2	6,612	$\frac{1}{(1.091)^2}$	5,555
3	5,259	$\frac{1}{(1.091)^3}$	4,050
		NPV	2,105

4.9 The NPV is the same as before (and the present value of the cash flow in each year is the same as before) apart from rounding errors with a net total of £3.

Costs and benefits which inflate at different rates

4.10 Not all costs and benefits will rise in line with the general level of inflation. In such cases, we can apply the money rate to inflated values to determine a project's NPV.

4.11 EXAMPLE: INFLATION (2)

Rice Ltd is considering a project which would cost £5,000 now. The annual benefits, for four years, would be a fixed income of £2,500 a year, plus other savings of £500 a year in year 1, rising by 5% each year because of inflation. Running costs will be £1,000 in the first year, but would increase at 10% each year because of inflating labour costs. The general rate of inflation is expected to be 7½% and the company's required money rate of return is 16%. Is the project worthwhile? (Ignore taxation.)

4.12 SOLUTION

The cash flows at inflated values are as follows.

Year	*Fixed income*	*Other savings*	*Running costs*	*Net cash flow*
	£	£	£	£
1	2,500	500	1,000	2,000
2	2,500	525	1,100	1,925
3	2,500	551	1,210	1,841
4	2,500	579	1,331	1,748

The NPV of the project is as follows.

Year	*Cash flow*	*Discount factor*	*PV*
	£	16%	£
0	(5,000)	1.000	(5,000)
1	2,000	0.862	1,724
2	1,925	0.743	1,430
3	1,841	0.641	1,180
4	1,748	0.552	965
			+ 299

The NPV is positive and the project would appear to be worthwhile.

Variations in the expected rate of inflation

4.13 If the rate of inflation is expected to change, the calculation of the money cost of capital is slightly more complicated.

4.14 EXAMPLE: INFLATION (3)

Mr Gable has just received a dividend of £1,000 on his shareholding in Gonwithy Windmills plc. The market value of the shares is £8,000 ex div. What is the (money) cost of the equity capital, if dividends are expected to rise because of inflation by 10% in years 1, 2 and 3, before levelling off at this year 3 amount?

4.15 SOLUTION

The money cost of capital is the internal rate of return of the following cash flows.

Year	*Cash flow*	*PV at 15%*	*PV at 20%*
	£	£	£
0	(8,000)	(8,000)	(8,000)
1	1,100	957	916
2	1,210	915	840
3 - ∞	1,331 pa	6,709	4,621
		581	(1,623)

The IRR is approximately 15% + $\left[\frac{581}{581 - -1{,}623} \times (20-15)\right]$ % = 16.3%, say 16%

Expectations of inflation and the effects of inflation

4.16 When managers evaluate a particular project, or when shareholders evaluate their investments, they can only guess at what the rate of inflation is going to be. Their expectations will probably be wrong, at least to some extent, because it is extremely difficult to forecast the rate of inflation accurately. The only way in which uncertainty about inflation can be allowed for in project evaluation is by risk and uncertainty analysis.

4.17 We stated earlier that costs and benefits may rise at levels different from the general rate of inflation: inflation may be **general,** affecting prices of all kinds, or **specific** to particular prices. Generalised inflation has the following effects.

(a) Since fixed assets, stocks and other working capital will increase in money value, the same quantities of assets or working capital must be financed by increasing amounts of capital.

  (i) If the future rate of inflation can be predicted, management can work out how much extra finance the company will need, and take steps to obtain it (for example by increasing retentions of earnings, or borrowing).

  (ii) If the future rate of inflation cannot be predicted with accuracy, management should guess at what it will be and plan to obtain extra finance accordingly. However, plans should also be made to obtain 'contingency funds' if the rate of inflation exceeds expectations. For example, a higher bank overdraft facility might be negotiated, or a provisional arrangement made with a bank for a loan.

(b) Inflation means higher costs and higher selling prices. The effect of higher prices on demand is not necessarily easy to predict. A company that raises its prices by 10% because the general rate of inflation is running at 10% might suffer a serious fall in demand.

(c) Inflation, because it affects financing needs, is also likely to affect gearing, and so the cost of capital.

5 ALLOWING FOR TAXATION

5.1 So far, in looking at project appraisal, we have ignored **taxation**. However, payments of tax, or reductions of tax payments, are cash flows and ought to be considered in DCF analysis.

Exam focus point

The tax rules might be simplified for an examination question and, as mentioned earlier, you should read any question carefully to establish what tax rules and rates to use.

5.2 Typical assumptions which may be stated in questions are as follows.

(a) Corporation tax is payable in the year following the one in which the taxable profits are made. Thus, if a project increases taxable profits by £10,000 in year 2, there will be a tax payment, assuming tax at (say) 30%, of £3,000 in year 3.

This is not always the case in examination questions. Look out for questions which state that tax is payable in the same year as that in which the profits arise.

(b) Net cash flows from a project should be considered as the taxable profits arising from the project (unless an indication is given to the contrary).

Capital allowances

5.3 Capital allowances are used to reduce taxable profits, and the consequent reduction in a tax payment should be treated as a cash saving arising from the acceptance of a project.

5.4 Writing down allowances are allowed on the cost of **plant and machinery** at the rate of 25% on a **reducing balance** basis. Thus if a company purchases plant costing £80,000, the subsequent writing down allowances would be as follows.

Year		*Capital allowance*	*Reducing balance*
		£	£
1	(25% of cost)	20,000	60,000
2	(25% of RB)	15,000	45,000
3	(25% of RB)	11,250	33,750
4	(25% of RB)	8,438	25,312

When the plant is eventually sold, the difference between the sale price and the reducing balance amount at the time of sale will be treated as:

(a) a taxable profit if the sale price exceeds the reducing balance; and

(b) a tax-allowable loss if the reducing balance exceeds the sale price. Examination questions often assume that this loss will be available immediately, though in practice the balance less the sale price continues to be written off at 25% a year as part of a pool balance unless the asset has been de-pooled.

The cash saving on the capital allowances (or the cash payment for the charge) is calculated by multiplying the allowance (or charge) by the corporation tax rate.

5.5 Assumptions about capital allowances could be simplified in an exam question. For example, you might be told that capital allowances can be claimed at the rate of 25% of cost on a straight line basis (that is, over four years), or a question might refer to 'tax allowable depreciation', so that the capital allowances equal the depreciation charge.

5.6 There are two possible assumptions about the time when capital allowances start to be claimed.

(a) It can be assumed that the first claim for capital allowances occurs at the start of the project (at year 0) and so the first tax saving occurs one year later (at year 1).

(b) Alternatively it can be assumed that the first claim for capital allowances occurs later in the first year, so the first tax saving occurs one year later, that is, year 2.

5.7 You should state clearly which assumption you have made. Assumption (b) is more prudent, because it defers the tax benefit by one year, but assumption (a) is also perfectly feasible. It is very likely, however that an examination question will indicate which of the two assumptions is required.

5.8 EXAMPLE: TAXATION

A company is considering whether or not to purchase an item of machinery costing £40,000 in 19X5. It would have a life of four years, after which it would be sold for £5,000. The machinery would create annual cost savings of £14,000.

The machinery would attract writing down allowances of 25% on the reducing balance basis which could be claimed against taxable profits of the current year, which is soon to end. A balancing allowance or charge would arise on disposal. The rate of corporation tax is 30%. Tax is payable one year in arrears. The after-tax cost of capital is 8%. Assume that tax payments occur in the year following the transactions.

Should the machinery be purchased?

5.9 SOLUTION

The first capital allowance is claimed against year 0 profits.

Cost: £40,000

Year	Allowance	Reducing balance (RB)	
	£	£	
(0) 19X5 (25% of cost)	10,000	30,000	(40,000 – 10,000)
(1) 19X6 (25% of RB)	7,500	22,500	(30,000 – 7,500)
(2) 19X7 (25% of RB)	5,625	16,875	(22,500 – 5,625)
(3) 19X8 (25% of RB)	4,219	12,656	(16,875 – 4,219)
(4) 19X9 (25% of RB)	3,164	9,492	(12,656 – 3,164)

	£
Sale proceeds, end of fourth year	5,000
Less reducing balance, end of fourth year	9,492
Balancing allowance	4,492

5.10 Having calculated the allowances each year, the tax savings can be computed. The year of the cash flow is one year after the year for which the allowance is claimed.

Year of claim	Allowance	Tax saved	Year of tax payment/saving
	£	£	
0	10,000	3,000	1
1	7,500	2,250	2
2	5,625	1,688	3
3	4,219	1,266	4
4	7,656	2,297	5
	35,000 *		

* Net cost £(40,000 – 5,000) = £35,000

These tax savings relate to capital allowances. We must also calculate the extra tax payments on annual savings of £14,000.

5.11 The net cash flows and the NPV are now calculated as follows.

Year	Equipment	Savings	Tax on savings	Tax saved on capital allowances	Net cash flow	Discount factor	Present value of cash flow
	£	£	£	£	£	8%	£
0	(40,000)				(40,000)	1.000	(40,000)
1		14,000		3,000	17,000	0.926	15,742
2		14,000	(4,200)	2,250	12,050	0.857	10,327
3		14,000	(4,200)	1,688	11,488	0.794	9,121
4	5,000	14,000	(4,200)	1,266	11,066	0.735	8,134
5			(4,200)	2,297	(1,903)	0.681	(1,296)
							2,028

The NPV is positive and so the purchase appears to be worthwhile.

An alternative and quicker method of calculating tax payments or savings

5.12 In the above example, the tax computations could have been combined, as follows.

Year	*0*	*1*	*2*	*3*	*4*
	£	£	£	£	£
Cost savings	0	14,000	14,000	14,000	14,000
Capital allowance	10,000	7,500	5,625	4,219	7,656
Taxable profits	(10,000)	6,500	8,375	9,781	6,344
Tax at 30%	3,000	(1,950)	(2,512)	(2,934)	(1,903)

5.13 The net cash flows would then be as follows.

Year	*Equipment*	*Savings*	*Tax*	*Net cash flow*
	£	£	£	£
0	(40,000)			(40,000)
1		14,000	3,000	17,000
2		14,000	(1,950)	12,050
3		14,000	(2,512)	11,488
4	5,000	14,000	(2,934)	11,066
5			(1,903)	(1,903)

The net cash flows are exactly the same as calculated previously in Paragraph 5.11.

Taxation and DCF

5.14 The effect of taxation on capital budgeting is theoretically quite simple. Organisations must pay tax, and the effect of undertaking a project will be to increase or decrease tax payments each year. These incremental tax cash flows should be included in the cash flows of the project for discounting to arrive at the project's NPV.

5.15 When taxation is ignored in the DCF calculations, the discount rate will reflect the pre-tax rate of return required on capital investments. When taxation is included in the cash flows, a post-tax required rate of return should be used.

Question 3

A company is considering the purchase of an item of equipment, which would earn profits before tax of £25,000 a year. Depreciation charges would be £20,000 a year for six years. Capital allowances would be £30,000 a year for the first four years. Corporation tax is at 30%.

What would be the annual net cash inflows of the project:

(a) for the first four years;
(b) for the fifth and sixth years,

assuming that tax payments occur in the same year as the profits giving rise to them, and there is no balancing charge or allowance when the machine is scrapped at the end of the sixth year?

Answer

(a)

	Years 1-4	*Years 5-6*
	£	£
Profit before tax	25,000	25,000
Add back depreciation	20,000	20,000
Net cash inflow before tax	45,000	45,000
Less capital allowance	30,000	0
	15,000	45,000
Tax at 30%	4,500	13,500

Years 1 - 4 Net cash inflow after tax £45,000 – £4,500 = £40,500

(b) Years 5 - 6 Net cash inflow after tax = £45,000 – £13,500 = £31,500

Question 4

A company is considering the purchase of a machine for £150,000. It would be sold after four years for an estimated realisable value of £50,000. By this time capital allowances of £120,000 would have been claimed. The rate of corporation tax is 30%.

What are the tax implications of the sale of the machine at the end of four years?

Answer

There will be a balancing charge on the sale of the machine of £(50,000 – (150,000 – 120,000)) = £20,000. This will give rise to a tax payment of 30% × £20,000 = £6,000.

5.16 We will end this section by considering an example which involves project appraisal, taxation and inflation.

5.17 EXAMPLE: TAXATION, INFLATION AND INVESTMENT DECISIONS

A project requires an initial investment in machinery of £300,000. Additional cash inflows of £120,000 at current price levels are expected for three years, at the end of which time the machinery will be scrapped. The machinery will attract writing down allowances of 25% on the reducing balance basis, which can be claimed against taxable profits of the current year, which is soon to end. A balancing charge or allowance will arise on disposal.

The rate of corporate tax is 50% and tax is payable one year in arrears. The pre-tax cost of capital is 22% and the rate of inflation is 10%. Tax payments occur in the year following the transactions. Assume that the project is 100% debt financed.

Required

Assess whether, in the circumstances described above, taxation acts as an incentive to invest.

5.18 SOLUTION

The project can be appraised on a pre-tax and a post-tax basis.

Pre-tax:

Year	*Purchase*	*Inflation factor*	*Cash flow after inflation*	*Discount factor*	*Present value*
	£	£	£	22%	£
0	(300,000)	1.000	(300,000)	1.000	(300,000)
1		1.100	132,000	0.820	108,240
2		1.210	145,200	0.672	97,574
3		1.331	159,720	0.551	88,006
				NPV =	(6,180)

Post-tax:

Year	*Purchase*	*Inflation factor*	*Cash flow after inflation*	*Tax on cash inflow*	*(W1-3) Tax saved on capital allowances*	*Net cash flow*	*Discount factor*	*Present value*
	£		£	£	£	£	11%	£
0	(300,000)	1.000	(300,000)			(300,000)	1.000	(300,000)
1		1.100	132,000		37,500	169,500	0.901	152,720
2		1.210	145,200	(66,000)	28,125	107,325	0.812	87,148
3		1.331	159,720	(72,600)	21,094	108,214	0.731	79,104
4		1.464		(79,860)	63,281	16,579	0.659	(10,926)
							NPV =	8,046

In these circumstances, taxation does act as an incentive to invest.

Workings

1 **Writing down allowance** (Initial cost £300,000)

Year		*WDA*	*Reducing balance (RB)*
		£	£
0	(25% at cost)	75,000	225,000
1	(25% of RB)	56,250	168,750
2	(25% of RB)	42,188	126,562
3	(25% of RB)	31,641	94,921

2 **Balancing allowance**

	£
Sale proceeds, end of third year	-
RB, end of third year	94,921
Balancing allowance	94,921

3 **Tax saved on capital allowances**

Year of claim	*Allowance claimed*	*Tax saved*	*Year of tax saving*
	£	£	
0	75,000	37,500	1
1	56,250	28,125	2
2	42,188	21,094	3
3	126,562	63,281	4
	300,000		

Chapter roundup

- Managers need to know the **cost of capital** for their company for several reasons. Of particular interest to the management accountant is the cost of capital to be used **for the purposes of investment appraisal**.
- The **risk** associated with a project must be taken into account when appraising that project. The **CAPM** assumes that the investor is only interested in being compensated for the systematic risk of the project.
- The **beta factor** used in the CAPM allows for systematic risk. It is a measure of the importance of **systematic risk** to the **required return** on an investment.
- The **APV** method suggests that it is possible to calculate an **adjusted cost of capital** for use in project appraisal, as well as indicating how the net present value of a project can be increased or decreased by project financing effects.
- **Inflation** is a feature of all economies, and it must be accommodated in financial planning. The mathematics of relating real and money rates of return are fairly straightforward. Do not, however, forget the very great practical difficulty of predicting the rate of inflation.
- **Taxation** is also a major practical consideration for businesses. It is vital to take it into account in making decisions.

Quick quiz

1 What is the difference between using the CAPM and using the dividend valuation model for calculating a cost of equity and a WACC? (see paras 2.4 - 2.6)

2 What are the practical problems in using the CAPM in making capital investment decisions? (2.9)

3 Outline the adjusted present value method of project evaluation. (3.3)

4 What is the relationship between the money rate of return, the real rate of return and the rate of inflation? (4.4)

5 Summarise briefly how taxation is taken into consideration in capital budgeting. (5.14, 5.15)

Question to try	Level	Marks	Time
20	Exam standard	20	36 mins

Chapter 21

RESTRUCTURING AND VALUATION OF COMPANIES

	Chapter topic list	Syllabus reference	Ability required
1	Amalgamations and takeovers	13 c(viii)	Application
2	Trends in takeover activity	13 c(viii)	Application
3	The conduct and financing of a takeover	13 b(iv); c(viii)	Application
4	The position of shareholders	13 c(viii)	Application
5	Other matters in takeovers	13 c(viii)	Application
6	Post-acquisition integration	13 c(viii)	Application
7	Demergers	13 c(viii)	Application
8	Management buyouts	13 c(viii)	Application
9	Capital reconstruction schemes	13 c(viii)	Application
10	Reasons for share valuations	13 c(vii)	Application
11	Methods of valuing shares	13 c(vii)	Application

Introduction

In this chapter, we are concerned with the issues of **business combinations** and **restructuring** from the point of view of financial management and financial strategy. It is often in such circumstances that **valuations** are needed.

1 AMALGAMATIONS AND TAKEOVERS 5/95, 11/97, 5/99

KEY TERMS

A **takeover** is the purchase of a controlling interest in one company by another company. Takeovers are also called acquisitions, and are a form of 'external' investment. An **amalgamation** is a **merger** between two separate companies to form a single company.

1.1 The distinction between amalgamations and takeovers is not always clear, for example when a large company 'merges' with another smaller company. The methods used for mergers are often the same as the methods used to make takeovers. In practice, the number of genuine mergers is small relative to the number of takeovers.

Knowledge brought forward from Paper 9

Accounting treatment of mergers and acquisitions

You should be able to demonstrate an understanding of the main provisions of relevant accounting standards that cover the accounting treatment of mergers and acquisitions.

These are:

- Financial Reporting Standard 6 *Acquisitions and Mergers*
- Financial Reporting Standard 7 *Fair values in acquisition accounting*

Exam focus point

Business amalgamations (mergers and takeovers) have always been a key topic for exam questions.

The reasons for an amalgamation or a takeover

1.2 When two or more companies join together, there should be a 'synergistic' effect. Synergy can be described as the 2 + 2 = 5 effect, whereby a group after a takeover achieves combined results that reflect a better rate of return than was being achieved by the same resources used in two separate operations before the takeover. If company A, which makes annual profits of £200,000 merges with company B, which also makes annual profits of £200,000, the combined annual profits of the merged companies should be more than £400,000.

1.3 The main reasons why one company may wish to acquire the shares or the business of another may be categorised as follows.

(a) **Operating economies**. There are many ways in which operating economies can be realised through a combination of companies. Duplicate (and competing) facilities can be eliminated.

(b) **Management acquisition**. It is sometimes recognised that a company neither has, nor is likely to obtain in the immediate future, a management team of sufficient quality to ensure continued growth. In these circumstances it may be best to seek an amalgamation with another company which has aggressive and competent management.

(c) **Diversification**. The management of many companies may feel that the long term interest of the shareholders will be best served by spreading risk through diversification.

(d) **Asset backing**. A company in a risky industry with a high level of earnings relative to the net assets may attempt to reduce its overall risk by acquiring a company with substantial assets.

(e) **The quality of earnings**. A company may reduce its risk by acquiring another with less risky earnings.

(f) **Finance and liquidity**. A company may be able to improve its liquidity and its ability to raise new finance through the acquisition of another more financially stable company.

(g) **Growth**. A company may achieve growth through acquisition more cheaply than through internal expansion.

(h) **Tax factors.** In exceptional cases, a cash-financed takeover may be a tax-efficient method of transferring cash out of the corporate sector. In the USA until recently, amalgamation provided a way of utilising tax losses by setting them against profits of another company: UK tax law precludes this possibility.

(i) **Defensive merger**. Companies may merge in order to prevent competitors from obtaining an advantage in some way.

1.4 The aim of a merger or acquisition should be to make profits in the long term as well as in the short term.

(a) Acquisitions may provide a means of entering a market at a lower cost than would be incurred if the company tried to develop its own resources, or a means of acquiring the business of a competitor. Acquisitions or mergers which might reduce or eliminate competition in a market may be prohibited by the Monopolies and Mergers Commission.

(b) Mergers, especially in Britain, have tended to be more common in industries with a history of little growth and low returns. Highly profitable companies tend to seek acquisitions rather than mergers.

Factors in a takeover decision

1.5 Several factors will influence a decision to try to take over a target business. These include the following.

Price factors

(a) What would the cost of acquisition be?

(b) Would the acquisition be worth the price?

(c) Alternatively, factors (a) and (b) above could be expressed in terms of:
What is the highest price that it would be worth paying to acquire the business?

The value of a business could be assessed in terms of:

(i) its earnings;
(ii) its assets;
(iii) its prospects for sales and earnings growth;
(iv) how it would contribute to the strategy of the 'predator' company.

The valuation of companies is covered in the next chapter of this Study Text.

Other factors

(a) Would the takeover be regarded as desirable by the predator company's shareholders and (in the case of quoted companies) the stock market in general?

(b) Are the owners of the target company amenable to a takeover bid? Or would they be likely to adopt defensive tactics to resist a bid?

(c) What form would the purchase consideration take? An acquisition is accomplished by buying the shares of a target company. The purchase consideration might be cash, but the purchasing company might issue new shares (or loan stock) and exchange them for shares in the company taken over. If purchase is by means of a share exchange, the former shareholders in the company taken over will acquire an interest in the new, enlarged company.

(d) How would the takeover be reflected in the published accounts of the predator company?

(e) Would there be any other potential problems arising from the proposed takeover, such as future dividend policy and service contracts for key personnel?

Question 1

Flycatcher Ltd wishes to make a takeover bid for the shares of an unquoted company, Mayfly Ltd. The earnings of Mayfly Ltd over the past five years have been as follows.

19X0	£50,000	19X3	£71,000
19X1	£72,000	19X4	£75,000
19X2	£68,000		

The average P/E ratio of quoted companies in the industry in which Mayfly Ltd operates is 10. Quoted companies which are similar in many respects to Mayfly Ltd are:

(a) Bumblebee plc, which has a P/E ratio of 15, but is a company with very good growth prospects;
(b) Wasp plc, which has had a poor profit record for several years, and has a P/E ratio of 7.

What would be a suitable range of valuations for the shares of Mayfly Ltd?

Answer

(a) **Earnings**. Average earnings over the last five years have been £67,200, and over the last four years £71,500. There might appear to be some growth prospects, but estimates of future earnings are uncertain.

A low estimate of earnings in 19X5 would be, perhaps, £71,500.

A high estimate of earnings might be £75,000 or more. This solution will use the most recent earnings figure of £75,000 as the high estimate.

(b) **P/E ratio**. A P/E ratio of 15 (Bumblebee's) would be much too high for Mayfly Ltd, because the growth of Mayfly Ltd earnings is not as certain, and Mayfly Ltd is an unquoted company.

On the other hand, Mayfly Ltd's expectations of earnings are probably better than those of Wasp plc. A suitable P/E ratio might be based on the industry's average, 10; but since Mayfly is an unquoted company and therefore more risky, a lower P/E ratio might be more appropriate: perhaps 60% to 70% of 10 = 6 or 7, or conceivably even as low as 50% of 10 = 5.

The valuation of Mayfly Ltd's shares might therefore range between:

high P/E ratio and high earnings: 7 × £75,000 = £525,000; and

low P/E ratio and low earnings: 5 × £71,500 = £357,500.

A strategic approach to takeovers

1.6 A strategic approach to takeovers would imply that acquisitions are only made after a full analysis of the underlying strengths of the acquirer company, and identification of candidates' 'strategic fit' with its existing activities. Possible strategic reasons for a takeover are matched with suggested ways of achieving the aim in the following list from a publication of 3i (Investors in Industry), which specialises in offering advice on takeovers.

Strategic opportunities	
Where you are	**How to get to where you want to be**
Growing steadily but in a mature market with limited growth prospects	Acquire a company in a younger market with a higher growth rate
Marketing an incomplete product range, or having the potential to sell other products or services to your existing customers	Acquire a company with a complementary product range
Operating at maximum productive capacity	Acquire a company making similar products operating substantially below capacity
Under-utilising management resources	Acquire a company into which your talents can extend
Needing more control of suppliers or customers	Acquire a company which is, or gives access to, a significant customer or supplier
Lacking key clients in a targeted sector	Acquire a company with the right customer profile
Preparing for flotation but needing to improve your balance sheet	Acquire a suitable company which will enhance earnings per share
Needing to increase market share	Acquire an important competitor
Needing to widen your capability	Acquire a company with the key talents and/or technology

2 TRENDS IN TAKEOVER ACTIVITY

UK takeover activity

2.1 There was a boom in takeover activity in the UK in the second half of the 1980s. As the increased level of expenditure on acquisitions took place at the same time as a surge in capital expenditure by industrial and commercial companies (ICCs), it appears that the increase in takeover activity must partly reflect a desire of companies to expand.

2.2 A more recent surge in takeover activity in the mid 1990s has included, for example, the £8.9 billion takeover of Wellcome by Glaxo, Europe's largest ever takeover by that time.

Some major UK takeovers	
Acquirer	**Acquiree**
Nestlé	Rowntree Mackintosh
British Petroleum	Britoil
HSBC	Midland Bank
Glaxo	Wellcome

International aspects of UK takeovers

2.3 Acquisition is one of the chief ways of carrying out **foreign direct investment** (FDI). Over the past fifteen years or so, approximately half of the UK's FDI was in the form of acquisition of share and loan capital overseas, of which a substantial proportion was related to takeovers.

2.4 A number of reasons for the expansion of UK companies into the **USA**, which occurred particularly during the late 1980s, can be identified.

(a) The same factors which led to the expansion in takeovers at home can be cited, especially the strong financial position of companies in this period.

(b) US capital markets are open and large bids, often hostile, can be made relatively easily.

(c) The US product markets are large and diverse.

(d) There is no language barrier.

(e) The depreciation of the dollar during the mid to late 1980s made acquisition targets more attractive.

2.5 Takeover transactions conducted by UK companies in the **European Union** (EU) have on average been much smaller (at around £10 million on average) than for takeovers in the USA in past years. However, the Single European Act and financial deregulation are factors contributing to a growth in importance in UK takeovers in the rest of the EU.

International comparisons of takeover activity

2.6 Official statistics for acquisitions are not available on a fully comparable basis internationally. It is clear that takeover activity was buoyant in the major OECD economies generally in the latter half of the 1980s, especially in the USA, Germany, France and Canada. However, distinctive features of the UK takeover boom have been the frequency of hostile bids (relative to other EU countries) and the greater emphasis on equity finance than in the USA. Hostile bids involve payment of a substantial premium over the pre-bid share price of the target firm and are therefore only feasible if the profitability of the joint assets can be improved to compensate for this premium.

Takeovers in the UK compared with other European countries

2.7 It has been suggested that UK companies are more vulnerable to takeover than their counterparts in other European countries. There are a number of reasons why this should be so.

2.8 Firstly, the equity markets in Britain are more highly developed than in other European countries and a greater proportion of companies are either quoted or are subsidiaries of quoted firms with publicly traded shares. In the rest of Europe by contrast there is a much greater proportion of firms in private ownership; this is especially true in Germany. Thus access to ownership in Britain is easier.

2.9 In addition, the capital structure of British firms is generally different to their European counterparts. In European firms there is frequently a large class of shares that do not have voting rights, unlike the ordinary shares that make up the major part of the equity for most UK companies. Thus in Europe there is a greater division between ownership and control, and access to the controlling shares is harder to obtain.

2.10 It has been argued that it is easier to build a stake in a UK firm due to the '3% rule' whereby a shareholder does not have to declare an interest until he holds 3% of the shares or 10% of any particular class of share. This is enhanced by the rule that a full bid need not be triggered until he owns 30%. It is difficult for a firm to mount a defence until a bid is declared, by which time the bidder already has a strong hand.

2.11 Government attitudes to the issues of ownership and control are also different to those in many other European countries. The prevalent non-interventionist policies mean that the government holds much fewer stakes and controlling interests in companies than say in France, and the 'national interest' lobby in the UK is also weaker.

2.12 Reporting requirements in the UK have been generally more rigorous than in Continental Europe. Annual reports contain more information and are more transparent than those of comparable European firms, and thus it is easier for a predator to obtain a meaningful preliminary valuation of a potential target. Although reporting rules in Europe have become stricter, enforcement is relatively weak, and annual accounts do not provide as full a picture of the company's position as in the UK.

Friendly and hostile takeovers: the UK, USA, Japan, Europe

2.13 In contrast to the UK and the USA, takeovers in Continental Europe and Japan are nearly always friendly. It has been argued that this difference results from different approaches to corporate governance in the Anglo-US markets compared with others.

2.14 In Continental Europe and Japan, the prevailing philosophy is that the objective of the organisation should be the maximisation of corporate wealth. In contrast to the Anglo-American emphasis on maximisation of shareholder wealth, this objective gives much more emphasis to the interests of other interest groups such as management, trade unions and suppliers. There are more often dual classes of voting shares, and strategic alliances (eg exchanges of shares between firms) and networks of close personal relationships play an important role. These factors mean that there are many more defences against unfriendly takeovers.

3 THE CONDUCT AND FINANCING OF A TAKEOVER

Will the bidding company's shareholders approve of a takeover?

3.1 When a company is planning a takeover bid for another company, its board of directors should give some thought to how its own shareholders might react to the bid. A company does not have to ask its shareholders for their approval of every takeover, but:

(a) when a large takeover is planned by a listed company involving the issue of a substantial number of new shares by the predator company (to pay for the takeover), Stock Exchange rules may require the company to obtain the formal approval of its shareholders to the takeover bid at a general meeting (probably an extraordinary general meeting, called specifically to approve the takeover bid);

(b) if shareholders, and the stock market in general, think the takeover is not a good one the market value of the company's shares is likely to fall. The company's directors have a responsibility to protect their shareholders' interests, and are accountable to them at the annual general meeting of the company.

3.2 A takeover bid might seem unattractive to shareholders of the bidding company because:

(a) it might reduce the EPS of their company;

(b) the target company is in a risky industry, or is in danger of going into liquidation;

(c) it might reduce the net asset backing per share of the company, because the target company will probably be bought at a price which is well in excess of its net asset value.

Will a takeover bid be resisted by the target company?

3.3 Quite often, a takeover bid will be resisted. Resistance comes from the target company's board of directors, who adopt defensive tactics, and ultimately the target company's shareholders, who can refuse to sell their shares to the bidding company.

3.4 Resistance can be overcome by offering a higher price. In cases where an **unquoted** company is the target company, if resistance to a takeover cannot be overcome, the takeover will not take place, and negotiations would simply break down. Where the target company is a **quoted company**, the situation is different. The target company will have many shareholders, some of whom will want to accept the offer for their shares, and some of whom will not. In addition, the target company's board of directors might resist a takeover, even though their shareholders might want to accept the offer.

3.5 Because there are likely to be major differences of opinion about whether to accept a takeover bid or not, the Stock Exchange has issued formal rules for the conduct of takeover bids, in the City Code on Takeovers and Mergers.

Contesting an offer: defensive tactics

3.6 The directors of a target company must act in the interests of their shareholders, employees and creditors. They may decide to contest an offer on several grounds.

(a) The offer may be unacceptable because the terms are poor. Rejection of the offer may lead to an improved bid.

(b) The merger or takeover may have no obvious advantage.

(c) Employees may be strongly opposed to the bid.

(d) The founder members of the business may oppose the bid, and appeal to the loyalty of other shareholders.

3.7 When a company receives a takeover bid which the board of directors considers unwelcome, the directors must act quickly to fight off the bid.

The steps that might be taken to thwart a bid or make it seem less attractive include:

(a) issuing a forecast of attractive future profits and dividends to persuade shareholders that to sell their shares would be unwise, that the offer price is too low, and that it would be better for them to retain their shares to benefit from future profits, dividends and capital growth. Such profit and dividend forecasts can be included in 'defence documents' circulated to shareholders, and in press releases;

(b) lobbying the Office of Fair Trading and/or the Department of Trade and Industry to have the offer referred to the Monopolies and Mergers Commission;

(c) launching an advertising campaign against the takeover bid. One technique is to attack the accounts of the predator company;

(d) finding a 'white knight', a company which will make a welcome takeover bid;

(e) making a counter-bid for the predator company. This can only be done if the companies are of reasonably similar size;

(f) arranging a management buyout.

(g) introducing a 'poison-pill' anti-takeover device (see below).

e.g

Case example

An example of a **poison pill** anti-takeover device was that used by Time Warner, the US media group in which Canada's Seagram drinks company had built up an 11 per cent stake, early in 1994. Seagram had announced plans to buy up to 15 per cent of Time Warner shares for investment purposes.

The Time Warner device was formally known as a 'shareholder rights plan' and is triggered if one investor buys more than 15 per cent of the company's stock. If that occurs, all other shareholders are given the right to buy stock at a large discount, thus diluting the 15 per cent shareholding. Time Warner pointed out that the device would not preclude a *bona fide* all-cash offer for the company which treated all shareholders equally; the 'poison pill' was designed to protect against 'abusive takeover tactics'. Seagram, on the other hand, questioned whether poison pills were in the best interests of shareholders, since they could interfere with choice and adversely affect share values.

Costs of contested takeover bids

3.8 Takeover bids, when contested, can be very expensive, involving:

(a) costs of professional services, eg merchant bank and public relations agency;
(b) advertising costs;
(c) underwriting costs;
(d) interest costs;
(e) possible capital loss on buying/selling the target company's shares.

Gaining the consent of the target company shareholders

3.9 A takeover bid will only succeed if the predator company can persuade enough shareholders in the target company to sell their shares. Shareholders will only do this if they are dissatisfied with the performance of their company and its shares, or they are attracted by a high offer and the chance to make a good capital gain.

The Monopolies and Mergers Commission

3.10 A company might have to consider whether its proposed takeover would be drawn to the attention of the Monopolies and Mergers Commission. Under the terms of the Monopolies and Mergers Act, the Office of Fair Trading (the OFT) is entitled to scrutinise all mergers and takeovers above a certain size. If the OFT thinks that a merger or takeover might be against the public interest, it can refer it to the Monopolies and Mergers Commission. Proposed mergers can be notified to the OFT in advance. If no referral is made to the Monopolies and Mergers Commission within (normally) 20 days, the merger can proceed without fear of a referral.

3.11 The function of the Commission is to advise the government. The Commission can make recommendations to the Department of Trade and Industry (or to any other body, including the companies involved in the bid).

3.12 The result of an investigation by the Commission might be:

(a) a withdrawal of the proposal for the merger or takeover, in anticipation of its rejection by the Commission;

(b) acceptance or rejection of the proposal by the Commission;

(c) acceptance of the proposal by the Commission subject to the new company agreeing to certain conditions laid down by the Commission, for example on prices, employment or arrangements for the sale of the group's products.

European Union regulations on mergers

3.13 In the past, EU competition policy was criticised for its limited scope. However, under a regulation introduced during 1990, the European Commission gained, for the first time, the power to intervene and to either block or authorise larger mergers. If the Commission finds that the merger raises serious doubts as to its compatibility with the European common market, it will initiate proceedings to block the merger.

The purchase consideration

3.14 The terms of a takeover will involve a purchase of the shares of the target company for cash or for 'paper' (shares, or possibly loan stock). A purchase of a target company's shares with shares of the predator company is referred to as a **share exchange**.

Cash purchases

3.15 If the purchase consideration is in cash, the shareholders of the target company will simply be bought out. For example, suppose that there are two companies.

	Big Ltd	*Small Ltd*
Net assets (book value)	£1,500,000	£200,000
Number of shares	100,000	10,000
Earnings	£2,000,000	£40,000

Big Ltd negotiates a takeover of Small Ltd for £400,000 in cash.

3.16 As a result, Big Ltd will end up with:

(a) net assets (book value) of
£1,500,000 + £200,000 – £400,000 cash = £1,300,000;

(b) 100,000 shares (no change);

(c) expected earnings of £2,040,000, minus the loss of interest (net of tax) which would have been obtained from the investment of the £400,000 in cash which was given up to acquire Small Ltd.

Purchases with paper

3.17 One company can acquire another company by issuing shares to pay for the acquisition. The new shares might be issued:

(a) in exchange for shares in the target company. Thus, if A plc acquires B Ltd, A plc might issue shares which it gives to B Ltd's shareholders in exchange for their shares. The B Ltd shareholders therefore become new shareholders of A plc. This is a takeover for a 'paper' consideration. Paper offers will often be accompanied by a cash alternative;

(b) to raise cash on the stock market, which will then be used to buy the target company's shares. To the target company shareholders, this is a cash bid.

3.18 Sometimes, a company might acquire another in a share exchange, but the shares are then sold immediately on a stock market to raise cash for the seller. For example, A plc might acquire B Ltd by issuing shares which it gives to B's shareholders; however A plc's stockbrokers arrange to 'place' these shares with other buyers, and so sell the newly issued shares for cash on behalf of the ex-shareholders of B Ltd. This sort of arrangement, which is a mixture of (a) and (b), is called a 'vendor placing.'

3.19 Whatever the detailed arrangements of a takeover with paper, the end result will be an increase in the issued share capital of the company making the takeover.

The choice between a cash offer and a paper offer

3.20 The choice between cash and paper offers (or a combination of both) will depend on how the different methods are viewed by the company and its existing shareholders, and on the attitudes of the shareholders of the target company. The factors that the directors of the bidding company must consider include the following.

(a) **The company and its existing shareholders**

(i) **Dilution of earnings per share**. A fall in the EPS attributable to the existing shareholders is undesirable but it might occur when the purchase consideration is in equity shares.

(ii) **The cost to the company**. The use of loan stock (or of cash borrowed elsewhere) will be cheaper to the acquiring company than equity as the interest will be allowable for tax purposes. A direct consequence of this is that dilution of earnings may be avoided. If convertible loan stock is used, the coupon rate could probably be slightly lower than with ordinary loan stock.

(iii) **Gearing**. A highly geared company may find that the issue of additional loan stock either as consideration or to raise cash for the consideration may be unacceptable to some or all of the parties involved.

(iv) **Control**. In takeovers involving a relatively large new issue of ordinary shares the effective control of the company can change considerably. This could be unpopular with the existing shareholders.

(v) **An increase in authorised share capital**. If the consideration is in the form of shares, it may be necessary to increase the company's authorised capital. This would involve calling a general meeting to pass the necessary resolution.

(vi) **Increases in borrowing limits**. A similar problem arises if a proposed issue of loan stock will require a change in the company's borrowing limit as specified in the Articles.

(b) **The shareholders in the target company**

(i) **Taxation**. If the consideration is in cash many investors may find that they face an immediate liability to tax on a realised capital gain, whereas the liability would be postponed if the consideration consisted of shares.

(ii) **Income**. Where the consideration is other than cash, it is normally necessary to ensure that existing income is at least maintained. A drop may, however, be accepted if it is compensated for by a suitable capital gain or by reasonable expectations of future growth.

(iii) **Future investments**. Shareholders in the target company might want to retain a stake in the business after the takeover, and so would prefer the offer of shares in the bidding company, rather than a cash offer.

(iv) **Share price**. If shareholders in the target company are to receive shares, they will want to consider whether the shares are likely to retain their value.

Mezzanine finance and takeover bids

3.21 When the purchase consideration in a takeover bid is cash, the cash must be obtained somehow by the bidding company, in order to pay for the shares that it buys. Occasionally,

the company will have sufficient cash in hand to pay for the target company's shares. More frequently, the cash will have to be raised, possibly from existing shareholders, by means of a rights issue or, more probably, by borrowing from banks or other financial institutions.

3.22 When cash for a takeover is raised by borrowing, the loans would normally be medium-term and secured.

3.23 However, there have been many takeover bids, with a cash purchase option for the target company's shareholders, where the bidding company has arranged loans that:

(a) are short-to-medium term;

(b) are unsecured (that is, 'junior' debt, low in the priority list for repayment in the event of liquidation of the borrower);

(c) because they are unsecured, attract a much higher rate of interest than secured debt (typically 4% or 5% above LIBOR);

(d) often, give the lender the option to exchange the loan for shares after the takeover.

This type of borrowing is called **mezzanine finance** (because it lies between equity and debt financing) - a form of finance which is also often used in **management buyouts** (which are discussed later in this chapter).

Services of a merchant bank and stockbroker

3.24 During the acquisition process, a company may be assisted in the following ways by its merchant bank and stockbroker, or by one financial institution fulfilling both roles.

The merchant bank

- may provide the initial lead in identifying suitable acquisition targets; provides information on such target companies;
- can provide advice on and checks compliance with the City Code on Mergers and Takeovers, which is important from the very start of negotiations;
- will engage other advisors (for example, lawyers and reporting accountants);
- will provide some advice on the valuation of target companies; however, the valuation can only be properly decided by the acquiring company's board and the advice given by the banker will tend to avoid legal liability;
- will advise on the best method of financing the issue - whether cash, or a share issue or loan stock issue, or a combination of these methods;
- will arrange the issue of finance;
- will handle much of the publicity surrounding the acquisition.

The stockbroker

- can sound out the opinions of major institutional investors on possible bids;
- can provide background stock market information, such as share prices, P/E ratios, equity beta factors;
- will deal with the detailed documentation for share issues, share exchanges and so on.

4 THE POSITION OF SHAREHOLDERS

The market values of the companies' shares during a takeover bid

4.1 Market share prices can be very important during a takeover bid. Suppose that Velvet plc decides to make a takeover bid for the shares of Noggin plc. Noggin plc shares are currently quoted on the market at £2 each. Velvet shares are quoted at £4.50 and Velvet offers one of its shares for every two shares in Noggin, thus making an offer at current market values worth £2.25 per share in Noggin. This is only the value of the bid so long as Velvet's shares remain valued at £4.50. If their value falls, the bid will become less attractive.

This is why companies that make takeover bids with a share exchange offer are always concerned that the market value of their shares should not fall during the takeover negotiations, before the target company's shareholders have decided whether to accept the bid.

4.2 If the market price of the target company's shares rises above the offer price during the course of a takeover bid, the bid price will seem too low, and the takeover is then likely to fail, with shareholders in the target company refusing to sell their shares to the bidder.

EPS before and after a takeover

4.3 If one company acquires another by issuing shares, its EPS will go up or down according to the P/E ratio at which the target company has been bought.

(a) If the target company's shares are bought at a higher P/E ratio than the predator company's shares, the predator company's shareholders will suffer a fall in EPS.

(b) If the target company's shares are valued at a lower P/E ratio, the predator company's shareholders will benefit from a rise in EPS.

4.4 EXAMPLE: AMALGAMATIONS AND TAKEOVERS (1)

Giant plc takes over Tiddler Ltd by offering two shares in Giant for one share in Tiddler. Details about each company are as follows.

	Giant plc	*Tiddler Ltd*
Number of shares	2,800,000	100,000
Market value per share	£4	-
Annual earnings	£560,000	£50,000
EPS	20p	50p
P/E ratio	20	

By offering two shares in Giant worth £4 each for one share in Tiddler, the valuation placed on each Tiddler share is £8, and with Tiddler's EPS of 50p, this implies that Tiddler would be acquired on a P/E ratio of 16. This is lower than the P/E ratio of Giant, which is 20.

4.5 If the acquisition produces no synergy, and there is no growth in the earnings of either Giant or its new subsidiary Tiddler, then the EPS of Giant would still be higher than before, because Tiddler was bought on a lower P/E ratio. The combined group's results would be as follows.

	Giant group
Number of shares (2,800,000 + 200,000)	3,000,000
Annual earnings (560,000 + 50,000)	610,000
EPS	20.33p

If the P/E ratio is still 20, the market value per share would be £4.07, which is 7p more than the pre-takeover price.

4.6 EXAMPLE: AMALGAMATIONS AND TAKEOVERS (2)

Redwood plc agrees to acquire the shares of Hawthorn Ltd in a share exchange arrangement. The agreed P/E ratio for Hawthorn's shares is 15.

	Redwood plc	*Hawthorn Ltd*
Number of shares	3,000,000	100,000
Market price per share	£2	-
Earnings	£600,000	£120,000
P/E ratio	10	

4.7 The EPS of Hawthorn Ltd is £1.20, and so the agreed price per share will be £1.20 × 15 = £18. In a share exchange agreement, Redwood would have to issue nine new shares (valued at £2 each) to acquire each share in Hawthorn, and so a total of 900,000 new shares must be issued to complete the takeover.

4.8 After the takeover, the enlarged company would have 3,900,000 shares in issue and, assuming no earnings growth, total earnings of £720,000. This would give an EPS of:

$$\frac{£720,000}{3,900,000} = 18.5\text{p}$$

The pre-takeover EPS of Redwood was 20p, and so the EPS would fall. This is because Hawthorne has been bought on a higher P/E ratio (15 compared with Redwood's 10).

Buying companies on a higher P/E ratio, but with profit growth

4.9 Buying companies on a higher P/E ratio will result in a fall in EPS unless there is profit growth to offset this fall. For example, suppose that Starving plc acquires Bigmeal plc, by offering two shares in Starving for three shares in Bigmeal. Details of each company are as follows.

	Starving plc	*Bigmeal plc*
Number of shares	5,000,000	3,000,000
Value per share	£6	£4
Annual earnings		
Current	£2,000,000	£600,000
Next year	£2,200,000	£950,000
EPS	40p	20p
P/E ratio	15	20

4.10 Starving plc is acquiring Bigmeal plc on a higher P/E ratio, and it is only the profit growth in the acquired subsidiary that gives the enlarged Starving group its growth in EPS.

		Starving group
Number of shares (5,000,000 + 2,000,000)		7,000,000
Earnings		
If no profit growth (2,000,000 + 600,000) £2,600,000	EPS would have been 37.24p	
With profit growth (2,200,000 + 950,000) £3,150,000	EPS will be 45p	

If an acquisition strategy involves buying companies on a higher P/E ratio, it is therefore essential for continuing EPS growth that the acquired companies offer prospects of strong profit growth.

Reverse takeovers

4.11 A reverse takeover occurs when the smaller company takes over the larger one, so that the 'predator' company has to increase its voting equity by over 100% to complete the takeover.

Further points to consider: net assets per share and the quality of earnings

4.12 It might be concluded from what has been said above that dilution of earnings must be avoided at all cost. However, there are three cases where a dilution of earnings might be accepted on an acquisition if there were other advantages to be gained.

(a) Earnings growth may hide the dilution in EPS as above.

(b) A company might be willing to accept earnings dilution if the quality of the acquired company's earnings is superior to that of the acquiring company.

(c) A trading company with high earnings, but with few assets, may want to increase its assets base by acquiring a company which is strong in assets but weak in earnings so that assets and earnings get more into line with each other. In this case, dilution in earnings is compensated for by an increase in net asset backing.

4.13 EXAMPLE: AMALGAMATIONS AND TAKEOVERS (3)

Intangible plc has an issued capital of 2,000,000 £1 ordinary shares. Net assets (excluding goodwill) are £2,500,000 and annual earnings average £1,500,000. The company is valued by the stock market on a P/E ratio of 8. Tangible Ltd has an issued capital of 1,000,000 ordinary shares. Net assets (excluding goodwill) are £3,500,000 and annual earnings average £400,000. The shareholders of Tangible Ltd accept an all-equity offer from Intangible plc valuing each share in Tangible Ltd at £4. Calculate Intangible plc's earnings and assets per share before and after the acquisition of Tangible Ltd.

4.14 SOLUTION

(a) Before the acquisition of Tangible Ltd, the position is as follows.

$$\text{Earnings per share (EPS)} = \frac{\pounds 1{,}500{,}000}{2{,}000{,}000} = 75\text{p}$$

$$\text{Assets per share (APS)} = \frac{\pounds 2{,}500{,}000}{2{,}000{,}000} = \pounds 1.25$$

(b) Tangible Ltd's EPS figure is 40p (£400,000 ÷ 1,000,000), and the company is being bought on a multiple of 10 at £4 per share. As the takeover consideration is being satisfied by shares, Intangible plc's earnings will be diluted because Intangible plc is valuing Tangible Ltd on a higher multiple of earnings than itself. Intangible plc will have to issue 666,667 shares valued at £6 each (earnings of 75p per share at a multiple of 8) to satisfy the £4,000,000 consideration. The results for Intangible plc will be as follows.

$$\text{EPS} = \frac{\pounds 1{,}900{,}000}{2{,}666{,}667} = 71.25\text{p (3.75p lower than the previous 75p)}$$

$$\text{APS} = \frac{\pounds 6{,}000{,}000}{2{,}666{,}667} = \pounds 2.25 \text{ (£1 higher than the previous £1.25)}$$

If Intangible plc is still valued on the stock market on a P/E ratio of 8, the share price should fall by approximately 30p (8 × 3.75p, the fall in EPS) but because the asset

backing has been increased substantially the company will probably now be valued on a higher P/E ratio than 8.

4.15 The shareholders in Tangible Ltd would receive 666,667 shares in Intangible plc in exchange for their current 1,000,000 shares, that is, two shares in Intangible for every three shares currently held.

		£
(a)	Earnings	
	Three shares in Tangible earn (3 × 40p)	1.200
	Two shares in Intangible will earn (2 × 71.25p)	1.425
	Increase in earnings, per three shares held in Tangible	0.225

		£
(b)	Assets	
	Three shares in Tangible have an asset backing of (3 × £3.5)	10.50
	Two shares in Intangible will have an asset backing of (2 × £2.25)	4.50
	Loss in asset backing, per three shares held in Tangible	6.00

The shareholders in Tangible Ltd would be trading asset backing for an increase in earnings.

Dividends and dividend cover

4.16 A further issue which may create some difficulties before a merger or takeover can be agreed is the level of dividends and dividend cover expected by shareholders in each of the companies concerned. Once the companies merge, a single dividend policy will be applied.

5 OTHER MATTERS IN TAKEOVERS

Service contracts for key personnel

5.1 When the target company employs certain key personnel, on whom the success of the company has been based, the predator company might want to ensure that these key people do not leave as soon as the takeover occurs. To do this, it might be necessary to insist as a condition of the offer that the key people should agree to sign service contracts, tying them to the company for a certain time (perhaps three years). Service contracts would have to be attractive to the employees concerned, perhaps through offering a high salary or other benefits such as share options in the predator company. Where key personnel are shareholders, they might be bound not to sell shares for a period.

The Takeover Panel and the City Code on Takeovers and Mergers

5.2 The **City Code on Takeovers and Mergers** is a code of behaviour which companies are expected to follow during a takeover or merger, as a measure of self-discipline. The code has no statutory backing, although it is administered and enforced by the Takeover Panel. Once adopted, the 13th Company Law Directive of the EU will have statutory power in EU member states, bringing an end to the non-statutory approach to the regulation of bids and takeover deals currently used in the UK.

5.3 The nature and purpose of the City code is described within the code itself as follows.

> 'The Code represents the collective opinion of those professionally involved in the field of takeovers on a range of business standards. It is not concerned with the financial or commercial advantages or disadvantages of a takeover, which are matters for the company and its shareholders, or with those wider questions which are the responsibility of the government, advised by the Monopolies and Mergers Commission.

> The Code has not, and does not seek to have, the force of law, but those who wish to take advantage of the facilities of the securities markets in the United Kingdom should conduct themselves in matters relating to takeovers according to the code. Those who do not so conduct themselves cannot expect to enjoy those facilities and may find that they are withheld.'

5.4 Companies subject to the code include all public companies (listed or unlisted) and also some classes of private company.

The City code: general principles

5.5 The City code is divided into general principles and detailed rules which must be observed by persons involved in a merger or takeover transaction. The general principles include the following.

(a) 'All shareholders of the same class of an offeree company must be treated similarly by an offeror.' In other words, a company making a takeover bid cannot offer one set of purchase terms to some shareholders in the target company, and a different set of terms to other shareholders holding shares of the same class in that company.

(b) 'During the course of a takeover, or when such is in contemplation, neither the offeror nor the offeree company ...may furnish information to some shareholders which is not made available to all shareholders.'

(c) 'Shareholders must be given sufficient information and advice to enable them to reach a properly informed decision and must have sufficient time to do so. No relevant information should be withheld from them.'

(d) 'At no time after a *bona fide* offer has been communicated to the board of an offeree company ... may any action be taken by the board of the offeree company in relation to the affairs of the company, without the approval of the shareholders in general meeting, which could effectively result in any *bona fide* offer being frustrated or in the shareholders being denied an opportunity to decide on its merits.' In other words, directors of a target company are not permitted to frustrate a takeover bid, nor to prevent the shareholders from having a chance to decide for themselves.

(e) 'Rights of control must be exercised in good faith and the oppression of a minority is wholly unacceptable.' For example, a holding company cannot take decisions about a takeover bid for one of its subsidiaries in such a way that minority shareholders would be unfairly treated.

(f) 'Where control of a company is acquired ... a general offer to all other shareholders is normally required.' Control is defined as a 'holding, or aggregate holdings, of shares carrying 30% of the voting rights of a company, irrespective of whether that holding or holdings gives *de facto* control.'

The City code: rules

5.6 In addition to its general principles, the City code also contains a number of detailed rules, which are intended to govern the conduct of the parties in a takeover bid. These rules relate to matters such as:

(a) how the approach to the target company should be made by the predator company;

(b) the announcement of a takeover bid;

(c) the obligation of the target company board to seek independent advice (eg from a merchant bank);

(d) conduct during the offer;

(e) a time barrier to re-bidding if an offer fails.

6 POST-ACQUISITION INTEGRATION

6.1 Failures of takeovers often result from inadequate integration of the companies after the takeover has taken place. There is a tendency for senior management to devote their energies to the next acquisition rather than to the newly-acquired firm. The particular approach adopted will depend upon the culture of the organisation as well as the nature of the company acquired and how it fits into the amalgamated organisation (eg horizontally, vertically, or as part of a diversified conglomerate).

6.2 P F Drucker has suggested Five Golden Rules for the process of post-acquisition integration.

Rule 1. There should be a 'common core of unity' shared by the acquiror and acquiree. The ties should involve overlapping characteristics such as shared technology and markets, and not just financial links.

Rule 2. The acquiror should ask 'What can we offer them?' as well as 'What's in it for us?'

Rule 3. The acquiror should treat the products, markets and customers of the acquired company with respect, and not disparagingly.

Rule 4. The acquiring company should provide top management with relevant skills for the acquired company within a year.

Rule 5. Cross-company promotions of staff should occur within one year.

6.3 C S Jones has proposed a five-step 'integration sequence'.

Step 1 is to decide on and to communicate initial reporting relationships. This will reduce uncertainty. The issue of whether to impose relationships at the beginning, although these may be subject to change, or to wait for the organisation structure to become more established (see Step 5 below) needs to be addressed.

Step 2 is to achieve rapid control of key factors, which will require access to the right accurate information. Control of information channels needs to be gained without dampening motivation. Note that it may have been poor financial controls which led to the demise of the acquiree company.

Step 3 is the resource audit. Both physical and human assets are examined in order to get a clear picture.

Step 4 is to re-define corporate objectives and to develop strategic plans, to harmonise with those of the acquiror company as appropriate, depending on the degree of autonomy managers are to have to develop their own systems of management control.

Step 5 is to revise the organisational structure.

6.4 Successful post-acquisition integration requires careful management of the 'human factor' to avoid loss of motivation. Employees in the acquired company will want to know how they and their company are to fit into the structure and strategy of the amalgamated enterprise. Morale can, hopefully, be preserved by reducing uncertainty and by providing appropriate performance incentives, staff benefits and career prospects.

7 DEMERGERS

7.1 Mergers and takeovers are not inevitably good strategy for a business. In some circumstances, strategies of internal growth, no growth or even demerger might be preferable.

7.2 A demerger is the opposite of a merger. It is the splitting up of a corporate body into two or more separate and independent bodies. For example, the ABC Group plc might demerge by selling its 100% shareholding in a subsidiary, C plc, to an outside buyer, who will then run C plc as an independent company. This would be a case of **disinvestment** by the group, withdrawing from its investment in C plc.

7.3 The reasons for demergers could be any of the following.

(a) An unprofitable subsidiary could be sold. The buyer might perhaps be a group of the subsidiary's managers, with the management buyout team being backed by venture capital finance.

(b) Subsidiaries which are not 'core businesses' and do not fit in with the group's strategic plans could be sold.

(c) A subsidiary with high risk in its operating cash flows could be sold, so as to reduce the business risk of the group as a whole.

(d) A subsidiary could be sold at a profit. Some companies have specialised in taking over large groups of companies, and then selling off parts of the newly-acquired groups, so that the proceeds of sales more than pay for the original takeovers.

7.4 The potential disadvantages with demergers are as follows.

(a) Economies of scale may be lost, where the demerged parts of the business had operations in common to which economies of scale applied.

(b) The smaller companies which result from the demerger will have lower turnover, profits and status than the group before the demerger.

(c) There may be higher overhead costs as a percentage of turnover, resulting from (b).

(d) The ability to raise extra finance, especially debt finance, to support new investments and expansion may be reduced.

(e) Vulnerability to takeover may be increased.

8 MANAGEMENT BUYOUTS

8.1 A **management buyout** is the purchase of all or part of a business from its owners by its managers. For example, the directors of a subsidiary company in a group might buy the company from the holding company, with the intention of running it as proprietors of a separate business entity. To the managers, the buyout would be a method of setting up in business for themselves. To the group, the buyout would be a method of **disinvestment**, selling off the subsidiary as a going concern.

The parties to a buyout

8.2 There are usually three parties to a management buyout.

- A **management team** wanting to make a buyout. This team ought to have the skills and ability to convince financial backers that it is worth supporting.

- **Directors** of a group of companies, who make the disinvestment decision.

- **Financial backers** of the buyout team, who will usually want an equity stake in the bought-out business, because of the venture capital risk they are taking. Often, several financial backers provide the venture capital for a single buyout.

8.3 The management team making the buyout would probably have the aims of setting up in business themselves, being owners rather than mere employees; or avoiding redundancy, when the subsidiary is threatened with closure.

8.4 A large organisation's board of directors may agree to a management buyout of a subsidiary for any of a number of different reasons.

(a) The subsidiary may be peripheral to the group's mainstream activities, and no longer fit in with the group's overall strategy.

(b) The group may wish to sell off a loss-making subsidiary, and a management team may think that it can restore the subsidiary's fortunes.

(c) The parent company may need to raise cash quickly.

(d) The subsidiary may be part of a group that has just been taken over and the new parent company may wish to sell off parts of the group it has just acquired.

(e) The best offer price might come from a small management group wanting to arrange a buyout.

(f) When a group has taken the decision to sell a subsidiary, it will probably get better co-operation from the management and employees of the subsidiary if the sale is a management buyout.

8.5 A private company's shareholders might agree to sell out to a management team because they need cash, they want to retire, or the business is not profitable enough for them.

8.6 To help convince a bank or other institution that it can run the business successfully, the management team should prepare a **business plan** and estimates of sales, costs, profits and cash flows, in reasonable detail.

The appraisal of proposed buyouts

How likely is a management buyout to succeed?

8.7 Management-owned companies seem to get better performance out of their company, probably because of:

(a) a favourable buyout price having been achieved;
(b) personal motivation and determination;
(c) quicker decision making and so more flexibility;
(d) keener decisions and action on pricing and debt collection;
(e) savings in overheads, eg in contributions to a large head office.

However, many management buyouts, once they occur, begin with some redundancies to cut running costs.

How should an institutional investor evaluate a buyout?

8.8 An institutional investor should evaluate a buyout before deciding whether or not to finance. Aspects of any buyout that ought to be checked are as follows.

(a) Does the management team have the full range of management skills that are needed (for example a technical expert and a finance director)? Does it have the right blend of experience? Does it have the commitment?

(b) Why is the company for sale? The possible reasons for buyouts have already been listed. If the reason is that the parent company wants to get rid of a loss-making subsidiary, what evidence is there to suggest that the company can be made profitable after a buyout?

(c) What are the projected profits and cash flows of the business? The prospective returns must justify the risks involved.

(d) What is being bought? The buyout team might be buying the shares of the company, or only selected assets of the company. Are the assets that are being acquired sufficient for the task? Will more assets have to be bought? When will the existing assets need replacing? How much extra finance would be needed for these asset purchases? Can the company be operated profitably?

(e) What is the price? Is the price right or is it too high?

(f) What financial contribution can be made by members of the management team themselves?

The financial arrangements in a typical buyout

8.9 Typically, the buyout team will have a minority of the equity in the bought-out company, with the financial backers holding a majority of the shares between them. A buyout might have several financial backers, each providing finance in exchange for some equity.

8.10 The financial institutions will regard their investment as a fairly long-term one, but they might hope that if the company is successful, it will eventually be floated on a stock market, perhaps the second tier market, thus giving a market value to their equity, and the option to sell their shares if they wish to realise their investment. Investors of venture capital usually want the managers to be financially committed. Individual managers could borrow personally from a bank, say £20,000 to £50,000.

8.11 The suppliers of equity finance might insist on investing part of their capital in the form of redeemable convertible preference shares. These often have voting rights should the preference dividend fall in arrears, giving increased influence over the company's affairs. They are issued in a redeemable form to give some hope of taking out part of the investment if it does not develop satisfactorily, and in convertible form for the opposite reason: to allow an increased stake in the equity of a successful company.

Possible problems with buyouts

8.12 A common problem with management buyouts is that the managers have little or no experience in financial management or financial accounting.

Other problems are:

(a) tax and legal complications;

(b) difficulties in deciding on a fair price to be paid;

(c) convincing employees of the need to change working practices;

(d) inadequate cash flow to finance the maintenance and replacement of tangible fixed assets;

(e) the maintenance of previous employees' pension rights;

(f) accepting the board representation requirement that many sources of funds will insist upon;

(g) the loss of key employees if the company moves geographically, or wage rates are decreased too far, or employment conditions are unacceptable in other ways;

(h) maintaining continuity of relationships with suppliers and customers.

Buy-ins

8.13 '**Buy-in**' is a term used when a team of **outside managers**, as opposed to managers who are already running the business, mount a takeover bid and then run the business themselves. A management buy-in might occur when a business venture is running into trouble, and a group of outside managers see an opportunity to take over the business and restore its profitability.

Sell-offs

8.14 A **sell-off** is a form of **divestment** involving the sale of part of a company to a third party, usually another company. Generally, cash will be received in exchange.

8.15 A company may carry out a sell-off for one of the following reasons.

(a) As part of its strategic planning, it has decided to restructure, concentrating management effort on particular parts of the business. Control problems may be reduced if peripheral activities are sold off.

(b) It wishes to sell off a part of its business which makes losses, and so to improve the company's future reported consolidated profit performance.

(c) In order to protect the rest of the business from takeover, it may choose to sell a part of the business which is particularly attractive to a buyer.

(d) The company may be short of cash.

Liquidations

8.16 The extreme form of a sell-off is where the entire business is sold off in a **liquidation**. In a voluntary dissolution, the shareholders might decide to close the whole business, sell off all the assets and distribute net funds raised to shareholders.

Spin-offs

8.17 In a **spin-off**, a new company is created whose shares are owned by the shareholders of the original company which is making the distribution of assets. There is no change in the ownership of assets, as the shareholders own the same proportion of shares in the new company as they did in the old company. Assets of the part of the business to be separated off are transferred into the new company, which will usually have different management from the old company. In more complex cases, a spin-off may involve the original company being split into a number of separate companies.

8.18 For a number of possible reasons such as those set out below, a spin-off appears generally to meet with favour from stock market investors.

(a) The change may make a merger or takeover of some part of the business easier in the future, or may protect parts of the business from predators.

(b) There may be improved efficiency and more streamlined management within the new structure.

(c) It may be easier to see the value of the separated parts of the business now that they are no longer hidden within a conglomerate.

(d) The requirements of regulatory agencies might be met more easily within the new structure, for example if the agency is able to exercise price control over a particular part of the business which was previously hidden within the conglomerate structure.

(e) After the spin-off, shareholders have the opportunity to adjust the proportions of their holdings between the different companies created.

Going private

8.19 A public company '**goes private**' when a small group of individuals, possibly including existing shareholders and/or managers and with or without support from a financial institution, buys all of the company's shares. This form of restructuring is relatively common in the USA and may involve the shares in the company ceasing to be listed on a stock exchange. In some cases, a small group of shareholders who prefer private company status buy the shares in a company from all the other shareholders.

8.20 Advantages in going private could include the following.

(a) The costs of meeting listing requirements can be saved.

(b) The company is protected from volatility in share prices which financial problems may create.

(c) The company will be less vulnerable to hostile takeover bids.

(d) Management can concentrate on the long-term needs of the business rather than the short-term expectations of shareholders.

(e) Shareholders are likely to be closer to management in a private company, reducing costs arising from the separation of ownership and control (the 'agency problem').

Case examples

e.g.

One example of going private was Richard Branson's repurchase of shares in the Virgin Company from the public and from financial institutions. Another example was SAGA the tour operator which changed status from public to private in 1990. While public, 63% of the company was owned by one family. The family raised finance to buy all of the shares, to avoid the possibility of hostile takeover bids and to avoid conflicts between the long-term needs of the business and the short-term expectations which institutional shareholders in particular are often claimed to have.

9 CAPITAL RECONSTRUCTION SCHEMES

9.1 A **capital reconstruction scheme** is a scheme whereby a company reorganises its capital structure. A reconstruction scheme might be agreed when a company is in danger of being put into liquidation, owing debts that it cannot repay, and so the creditors of the company agree to accept securities in the company, perhaps including equity shares, in settlement of their debts.

9.2 There are certain **general principles** that you should observe in designing a scheme of reconstruction.

(a) If a company is in difficulties, it will probably need more finance to keep going, eg an injection of capital from existing shareholders or from another source, such as a bank.

(b) Anyone providing extra finance for an ailing company must be persuaded that the expected return from the extra finance is attractive. A **profit forecast** and a **cash forecast** or a **funds flow forecast** will be needed to provide reassurance about the company's future, to creditors and to any financial institution that is asked to put new capital into the company.

(c) A scheme of reconstruction might involve the creation of new share capital of a different nominal value than existing share capital, or the cancellation of existing share capital.

(d) For a scheme of reconstruction to be acceptable it needs to treat all parties fairly (for example, preference shareholders must not be treated with disproportionate favour in comparison with equity shareholders), and it needs to offer creditors a better deal than if the company went into liquidation. If it did not, the creditors would press for a winding up of the company. A reconstruction might therefore include an arrangement to pay off the company's existing debts in full.

9.3 EXAMPLE: CAPITAL RECONSTRUCTION SCHEMES

Crosby and Dawson Ltd is a private company that has for many years been making mechanical timing mechanisms for washing machines. The management was slow to appreciate the impact that new technology would have and the company is now faced with rapidly falling sales.

In July 19X1, the directors decided that the best way to exploit their company's expertise in the future was to diversify into the high precision field of control linkages for aircraft, rockets, satellites and space probes. By January 19X2, some sales had been made to European companies and sufficient progress had been made to arouse considerable interest from the major aircraft manufacturers and from NASA in the USA. The cost, however, had been heavy. The company had borrowed £2,500,000 from the Vencap Merchant Bank plc and a further £500,000 from other sources. Its bank overdraft was at its limit of £750,000 and the dividend on its cumulative preference shares, which was due in December, had been unpaid for the fourth year in succession. On 1 February 19X2, the company has just lost another two major customers for its washing machine timers. The financial director presents the following information.

If the company remains in operation, the expected cash flows for the next five periods are as follows.

	9 months to 31.12.X2	*19X3*	*Years ending 31 December 19X4*	*19X5*	*19X6*
	£'000	£'000	£'000	£'000	£'000
Receipts from sales	8,000	12,000	15,000	20,000	30,000
Payments to suppliers	6,000	6,700	7,500	10,800	18,000
pPurchase of equipment	1,000	800	1,600	2,700	2,500
Other expenses	1,800	4,100	4,200	4,600	6,400
Interest charges	800	900	700	400	100
	9,600	12,500	14,000	18,500	27,000
Net	(1,600)	(500)	1,000	1,500	3,000

The above figures are based on the assumption that the present capital structure is maintained by further borrowings as necessary.

BALANCE SHEETS

	31.12.X0	31.12.X1	31.3.X2 Projected
	£'000	£'000	£'000
Assets employed			
Fixed assets			
Freehold property	2,780	2,770	2,760
Plant and machinery	3,070	1,810	1,920
Motor vehicles	250	205	200
Deferred development expenditure	-	700	790
Current assets			
Stock	890	970	1,015
Debtors	780	795	725
	1,670	1,765	1,740
Current liabilities			
Trade creditors	1,220	1,100	1,960
Bank overdraft (unsecured)	650	750	750
	1,870	1,850	2,710
	(200)	(85)	(970)
	5,900	5,400	4,700
Long-term liabilities			
10% debentures 19X8 (secured on freehold property)	(1,000)	(1,000)	(1,000)
Other loans (floating charges)	-	(3,000)	(3,000)
	4,900	1,400	700
Ordinary shares of £1	3,500	3,500	3,500
8% Cumulative preference shares	1,000	1,000	1,000
Accumulated reserves/(accumulated deficit)	400	(3,100)	(3,800)
	4,900	1,400	700

Other information

1. The freehold property was revalued on 31 December 19X0. It is believed that its net disposal value at 31 March 19X2 will be about £3,000,000.
2. A substantial quantity of old plant was sold during the second six months of 19X1 to help pay for the new machinery needed. It is estimated that the break up value of the plant at 31 March 19X2 will be about £1,400,000.
3. The motor vehicles owned at 31 March 19X2 could be sold for £120,000.
4. Much of the work done on the new control linkages has been patented. It is believed that these patents could be sold for about £800,000, which can be considered as the break-up value of development expenditure incurred to 31 March 19X2.
5. On liquidation, it is expected that the current assets at 31 March 19X2 would realise £1,050,000. Liquidation costs would be approximately £300,000.

Suggest a scheme of reconstruction that is likely to be acceptable to all the parties involved. The ordinary shareholders would be prepared to invest a further £1,200,000 if the scheme were considered by them to be reasonable.

A full solution follows. Complete the first step yourself as a short question.

Question 2

Ascertain the likely result of Crosby & Dawson Limited (see above) going into liquidation as at 31 March 19X2.

Answer

Break-up values of assets at 31 March 19X2	£'000
Freehold	3,000
Plant and machinery	1,400
Motor vehicles	120
Patents	800
Current assets	1,050
	6,370

Total liabilities at 31 March 19X2	£'000
Debentures	1,000
Other loans	3,000
Bank overdraft	750
Trade creditors	1,960
	6,710

9.4 SOLUTION TO REMAINDER OF THE EXAMPLE

If the company was forced into liquidation, the debentures and other loans would be met in full but that after allowing for the expenses of liquidation (£300,000) the bank and trade creditors would receive a total of £2,070,000 or 76p per pound. The ordinary and preference shareholders would receive nothing.

If the company remains in operation, the cash position will at first deteriorate but will improve from 19X4 onwards. By the end of 19X6 net assets will have increased by £11,800,000 before depreciation (plant £8,600,000 and cash £3,400,000). If the figures can be relied on and the trend of results continues after 19X6 the company will become reasonably profitable.

In the immediate future, after taking into account the additional amounts raised from the existing ordinary shareholders, the company will require finance of £400,000 in 19X2 and £500,000 in 19X3.

Vencap might be persuaded to subscribe cash for ordinary shares. It is unlikely that the company's clearing bank would be prepared to accept any shares, but as they would only receive 76p per pound on a liquidation they may be prepared to transfer part of the overdraft into a (say) five year loan whilst maintaining the current overdraft limit. It is unlikely that a suitable arrangement can be reached with the trade creditors as many would be prepared to accept 76p per pound, rather than agree to a moratorium on the debts or take an equity interest in the company.

A possible scheme might be as follows.

1 The existing ordinary shares to be cancelled and ordinary shareholders to be issued with £1,200,000 new £1 ordinary shares for cash.

2 The existing preference shares to be cancelled and the holders to be issued with £320,000 new £1 ordinary shares at par.

3 The existing debentures to be cancelled and replaced by £800,000 15% secured Debentures with a 15 year term and the holders to be issued with £400,000 of new £1 ordinary shares at par.

4 The loan 'from other sources' to be repaid.

5 The Vencap Bank to receive £2,000,000 15% secured debentures with a 15 year term in part settlement of the existing loan, to be issued £680,000 new ordinary shares in settlement of the balance and to subscribe cash for £800,000 of new ordinary shares.

6 The clearing bank to transfer the existing overdraft to a loan account repayable over five years and to keep the overdraft limit at £750,000. Both the loan and overdraft to be secured by a floating charge.

Comments

1 *Debenture holders*. The debentures currently have more than adequate asset backing, and their current nominal yield is 10%. If the reconstruction is to be acceptable to them, they must have either the same asset backing or some compensation in terms of increased nominal value and higher nominal yield. Under the scheme they will receive securities with a total nominal value of £1,200,000 (an increase of £200,000) and an increase in total yield before any ordinary dividends of £20,000. The new debentures issued to Vencap can be secured on the freehold property (see below).

2 *Loans from other sources*. It has been suggested that the 'loans from other sources' should be repaid as, in general, it is easier to arrange a successful reconstruction that involves fewer parties.

3 *Vencap*. Vencap's existing loan of £2,500,000 will, under the proposed scheme, be changed into £2,000,000 of 15% debentures secured on the property and £680,000 of ordinary shares. This gives total loans of £2,800,000 secured on property with a net disposal value of £3,000,000. This is low asset cover which might increase if property values were to rise. The scheme will increase the nominal value of Vencap's interest by £180,000 with an improvement in security on the first £2,000,000 to compensate for the risk involved in holding ordinary shares. It has also been suggested that Vencap should be asked to subscribe £800,000 for new ordinary shares. The money is required to repay the 'loans from other sources' and to provide additional working capital. The issue of share capital would give the bank a total of 1,480,000 ordinary shares or 43.5% of the equity. From the company's point of view issuing new equity is to be preferred to loan stock as it will improve the gearing position.

4 *The clearing bank*. In a liquidation now, the clearing bank would receive approximately £573,000. In return for the possibility of receiving the full amount owed to them they are being asked under the scheme to advance a further £750,000. By way of compensation, they are receiving the security of a floating charge.

5 *Preference shares*. In a liquidation at the present time, the preference shareholders would receive nothing. The issue of 320,000 £1 ordinary shares should be acceptable as it is equivalent to their current arrears of dividend. If the preference shares were left unaffected by the scheme, the full arrears of dividend would become payable on the company's return to profitability, giving preference shareholders an undue advantage.

6 *Ordinary shareholders*. In a liquidation, the ordinary shareholders would also receive nothing. Under the scheme, they will lose control of the company but, in exchange for their additional investment, will still hold about 35.3% of the equity in a company which will have sufficient funds to finance the expected future capital requirements.

7 *Cash flow forecast, on reconstruction*

	£'000
Cash for new shares from equity shareholders	1,200
Cash for new shares from Vencap	800
	2,000
Repayment of loan from other sources	(500)
Cash available	1,500

The overdraft of £750,000 is converted into a long-term loan, leaving the company with a further £750,000 of overdraft facility to use.

8 *Adequacy of funds*. The balance sheet below shows the company's position after the implementation of the scheme but before any repayments to creditors.

	£'000	£'000
Fixed assets		
Freehold property		2,760
Plant and machinery		1,920
Motor vehicles		200
Deferred development expenditure		790
		5,670
Current assets		
Stocks	1,015	
Debtors	725	
Cash	1,500	
	3,240	
Less current liabilities: Trade creditors	1,960	
		1,280
		6,950
Less long-term liabilities		
15% debentures		(2,800)
Loan from clearing bank		(750)
		3,400
Ordinary shares of £1		3,400

It would seem likely that the company will have to make a bigger investment in working capital (ignoring cash) for the following reasons.

- Presumably a substantial proportion of the sales will be exports which generally have a longer collection period than domestic sales.
- It is unlikely that the trade creditors will accept the current payment position (average credit takes over two months) in the long term.

9 *Will the reconstructed company be financially viable?*

Assuming that net current assets excluding cash and any overdraft will, by the end of 19X2, rise from –£220,000 to £500,000 and increase in proportion to sales receipts thereafter, that the equipment required in 19X2 and 19X3 will be leased on five year terms and that the interest charges (including the finance elements in the lease rentals) will be approximately the same as those given in the question, then the expected cash flows on implementation could be as shown below.

	9 months to 31.12.X2	19X3	19X4	19X5	19X6
	£'000	£'000	£'000	£'000	£'000
Receipts from sales	8,000	12,000	15,000	20,000	30,000
Purchase of equipment	-	-	1,600	2,700	2,500
Payments to suppliers	6,000	6,700	7,500	10,800	18,000
Other expenses	1,800	4,100	4,200	4,600	6,400
Interest charges	800	900	700	400	100
Lease rentals (excluding finance element) (say)	200	360	360	360	360
Bank loan repayment (say)	150	150	150	150	150
Invt. in working capital	720	250	190	310	630
	9,670	12,460	14,700	19,320	28,140
Net movement	(1,670)	(460)	300	680	1,860
Cash balance b/f	1,500	(170)	(630)	(330)	350
Cash balance c/f	(170)	(630)	(330)	350	2,210

These figures suggest that with an agreed overdraft limit of £750,000 the company will have sufficient funds to carry it through the next five years, assuming that the figures are reliable and that no dividends are paid until perhaps 19X4 at the earliest.

This scheme of reconstruction might not be acceptable to all parties, if the future profits of the company seem unattractive. In particular, Vencap and the clearing bank might be reluctant to agree to the scheme. In such an event, an alternative scheme of reconstruction must be designed, perhaps involving another provider of funds (such as another venture capitalist). Otherwise, the company will be forced into liquidation.

10 REASONS FOR SHARE VALUATIONS

10.1 Our main interest in this section is with methods of valuing the entire equity in a company, perhaps for the purpose of making a takeover bid, rather than with the value of small blocks of shares which an investor might choose to buy or sell on the stock market. Given quoted share prices on the Stock Exchange, why devise techniques for estimating the value of a share? A share valuation will be necessary:

(a) for **quoted companies**, when there is a takeover bid and the offer price is an estimated 'fair value' in excess of the current market price of the shares;

(b) for **unquoted companies**, when:

- (i) the company wishes to 'go public' and must fix an issue price for its shares;
- (ii) there is a scheme of merger;
- (iii) shares are sold;
- (iv) shares need to be valued for the purposes of taxation;
- (v) shares are pledged as collateral for a loan;

(c) for **subsidiary companies**, when the group's holding company is negotiating the sale of the subsidiary to a management buyout team or to an external buyer.

10.2 Valuing **unquoted companies** presents some special considerations. **It may not be sensible to use P/E ratios** of a quoted company for comparative purposes because the market value of a quoted company is likely to include a premium to reflect the marketability of its shares. A small unquoted company may be highly sensitive to the **loss of key employees** which may follow a merger or buyout. An arrangement to tie key employees in to the enterprise could be costly.

11 METHODS OF VALUING SHARES 5/95, 11/96, 11/97, 5/98, 5/99

11.1 **Common methods of valuing shares**, each giving a different share valuation:

- the earnings method (P/E ratio method)
- the accounting rate of return method
- the net assets method
- the dividend yield method
- use of the CAPM
- the super-profits method
- DCF-based valuations

Exam focus point

In an exam question as well as in practice, it is unlikely that one method would be used in isolation. Several valuations might be made, each using a different technique or different assumptions. The valuations could then be compared, and a final price reached as a compromise between the different values.

The P/E ratio (earnings) method of valuation

11.2 This is a common method of valuing a controlling interest in a company, where the owner can decide on dividend and retentions policy. The P/E ratio relates earnings per share to a share's value.

$$\text{Since P/E ratio} = \frac{\text{Market value}}{\text{EPS}},$$

Market value per share = EPS × P/E ratio

Case example

You will find frequent references to the P/E ratio in the financial press. For example, the *Financial Times* on 8 July 1997 reported the first day's trading in shares of the newly demutualised bank Woolwich plc as follows.

'"This is now the most expensive bank in Europe" said one analyst when Woolwich shares ended their first day of trading at 334p. By the close of trading, Woolwich stood at between 18 and 21 times prospective earnings. That compares with 16 times for Lloyds TSB and is considered unsustainable by many brokers unless a bid or merger offer appears.'

11.3 The P/E ratio produce an earnings-based valuation of shares. This is done by deciding a suitable P/E ratio and multiplying this by the EPS for the shares which are being valued. The EPS could be a historical EPS or a prospective future EPS. For a given EPS figure, a higher P/E ratio will result in a higher price. A high P/E ratio may indicate:

(a) **expectations** that the EPS will grow rapidly in the years to come, so that a high price is being paid for future profit prospects. Many small but successful and fast-growing companies are valued on the stock market on a high P/E ratio. Some stocks (for example those of some internet companies in the late 1990s) have reached high valuations before making any profits at all, on the strength of expected future earnings.

e.g.

Case examples

By April 1999, the internet 'portal' company 'Yahoo!', with only very limited assets, commanded a higher stock market value than Boeing the aircraft manufacturer. Amazon.com, the online bookseller, was valued at $20 billion but had yet to make a profit. eBay, the internet auctioneer was valued at 2,000 times prospective earnings.

Press comment suggests that private investors, many of them trading through the internet, are mainly responsible for the volatility in internet stocks. These are 'momentum investors' who seem to care little about the economic fundamentals underlying a business. If enough people pile in to buy stocks whose prices seem to rise inexorably, the prices are driven even higher perhaps until the 'bubble' bursts, and investors panic and sell *en masse*, when the price drops again sharply.

(b) **security of earnings.** A well-established low-risk company would be valued on a higher P/E ratio than a similar company whose earnings are subject to greater uncertainty;

(c) **status.** If a quoted company made a share-for-share takeover bid for an unquoted company, it would normally expect its own shares to be valued on a higher P/E ratio than the target company's shares. This is because a quoted company ought to be a lower-risk company; but in addition, there is an advantage in having shares which are quoted on a stock market: the shares can be readily sold. The P/E ratio of an unquoted company's shares might be around 50% to 60% of the P/E ratio of a similar public company with a full Stock Exchange listing (and perhaps 70% of that of a company whose shares are traded on the AIM).

11.4 EXAMPLE: EARNINGS METHOD OF VALUATION

Spider plc is considering the takeover of an unquoted company, Fly Ltd. Spider's shares are quoted on the Stock Exchange at a price of £3.20 and since the most recent published EPS of the company is 20p, the company's P/E ratio is 16. Fly Ltd is a company with 100,000 shares and current earnings of £50,000, 50p per share. How might Spider plc decide on an offer price?

11.5 SOLUTION

The decision about the offer price is likely to be based on deciding first of all what a reasonable P/E ratio would be.

(a) If Fly Ltd is in the same industry as Spider plc, its P/E ratio ought to be lower, because of its lower status as an unquoted company.

(b) If Fly Ltd is in a different industry, a suitable P/E ratio might be based on the P/E ratio that is typical for quoted companies in that industry.

(c) If Fly Ltd is thought to be growing fast, so that its EPS will rise rapidly in the years to come, the P/E ratio that should be used for the share valuation will be higher than if only small EPS growth is expected.

(d) If the acquisition of Fly Ltd would contribute substantially to Spider's own profitability and growth, or to any other strategic objective that Spider has, then Spider should be willing to offer a higher P/E ratio valuation, in order to secure acceptance of the offer by Fly's shareholders.

Of course, the P/E ratio on which Spider bases its offer will probably be lower than the P/E ratio that Fly's shareholders think their shares ought to be valued on. Some haggling over the price might be necessary.

Spider might decide that Fly's shares ought to be valued on a P/E ratio of 60% × 16 = 9.6, that is, at 9.6 × 50p = £4.80 each.

Fly's shareholders might reject this offer, and suggest a valuation based on a P/E ratio of, say, 12.5, that is, 12.5 × 50p = £6.25.

Spider's management might then come back with a revised offer, say valuation on a P/E ratio of 10.5, that is, 10.5 × 50p = £5.25.

The haggling will go on until the negotiations either break down or succeed in arriving at an agreed price.

General guidelines for a P/E ratio-based valuation

11.6 When a company is thinking of acquiring an **unquoted** company in a takeover, the final offer price will be agreed by negotiation, but a list of some of the factors affecting the valuer's choice of P/E ratio is given below.

(a) General economic and financial conditions.

(b) The type of industry and the prospects of that industry.

(c) The size of the undertaking and its status within its industry. If an unquoted company's earnings are growing annually and are currently around £300,000 or so, then it could probably get a quote in its own right on the USM and a higher P/E ratio should therefore be used when valuing its shares.

(d) Marketability. The market in shares which do not have a Stock Exchange quotation is always a restricted one and a higher yield is therefore required. Because of restrictions on transfer given in their Articles, any 'private' market in the shares of private companies is likely to be particularly small. It is not uncommon for a quoted company to have a P/E ratio twice the size of that attributed to a private company in the same industry. For examination purposes, you should normally take a figure around one half to two thirds of the industry average when valuing an unquoted company.

(e) The diversity of shareholdings and the financial status of any principal shareholders.

(f) The reliability of profit estimates and the past profit record.

(g) Asset backing and liquidity.

(h) The nature of the assets, for example whether some of the fixed assets are of a highly specialised nature, and so have only a small break-up value.

(i) Gearing. A relatively high gearing ratio will generally mean greater financial risk for ordinary shareholders and call for a higher rate of return on equity.

(j) The extent to which the business is dependent on the technical skills of one or more individuals.

11.7 A predator company may sometimes use their higher P/E ratio to value a target company. This assumes that the predator can improve the target's business, which is a dangerous assumption to make. It would be better to use an adjusted industry P/E ratio, or some other method.

Forecast growth in earnings

11.8 When one company is thinking about taking over another, it should look at the target company's forecast earnings, not just its historical results. Forecasts of the future earnings of a target company might be attempted by managers in the company which is planning to make the takeover bid. Quite commonly, however, the management of the predator company will make an initial approach to the board of directors of the target company, to sound them out about a possible takeover bid. If the target company's directors are amenable to a bid, they might agree to produce forecasts of their company's future earnings and growth. These forecasts (for the next year and possibly even further ahead) might then be used by the predator company in choosing an offer price.

11.9 Forecasts of earnings growth should only be used if:

(a) there are good reasons to believe that earnings growth will be achieved;
(b) a reasonable estimate of growth can be made;
(c) forecasts supplied by the target company's directors are made in good faith.

The accounting rate of return (ARR) method of share valuation

11.10 This method considers the accounting rate of return which will be required from the company whose shares are to be valued. It is therefore distinct from the P/E ratio method, which is concerned with the market rate of return required.

The following formula should be used.

$$\text{Value} = \frac{\text{Estimated future profits}}{\text{Required return on capital employed}}$$

11.11 For a takeover bid valuation, it will often be necessary to adjust the profits figure to allow for expected changes after the takeover. Those arising in an examination question might include:

(a) new levels of directors' remuneration;

(b) new levels of interest charges (perhaps because the predator company will be able to replace existing loans with new loans at a lower rate of interest, or because the previous owners had lent the company money at non-commercial rates);

(c) a charge for notional rent where it is intended to sell existing properties or where the rate of return used is based on the results of similar companies that do not own their own properties;

(d) the effects of product rationalisation and improved management.

11.12 EXAMPLE: ARR METHOD OF SHARE VALUATION

Chambers Ltd is considering acquiring Hall Ltd. At present Hall Ltd is earning, on average, £480,000 after tax. The directors of Chambers Ltd feel that after reorganisation, this figure could be increased to £600,000. All the companies in the Chambers group are expected to yield a post-tax accounting return of 15% on capital employed. What should Hall Ltd be valued at?

11.13 SOLUTION

$$\text{Valuation} = \frac{£600{,}000}{15\%} = £4{,}000{,}000$$

This figure is the maximum that Chambers should be prepared to pay. The first offer would probably be much lower.

11.14 An ARR valuation might be used in a takeover when the acquiring company is trying to assess the maximum amount it can afford to pay. This is because it is a measure of management efficiency and the rate used can be selected to reflect (among other things) the return which the acquiring company thinks should be obtainable after any post-acquisition reorganisation has been completed. A valuation on this basis should then be compared with the stock market price (for quoted companies) or a price arrived at using the P/E ratio of similar quoted companies.

The net assets method of share valuation

11.15 Using this method of valuation, the value of a share in a particular class is equal to the net tangible assets attributable to that class, divided by the number of shares in the class. Intangible assets (including goodwill) should be excluded, unless they have a market value (for example patents and copyrights, which could be sold).

(a) Goodwill, if shown in the accounts, is unlikely to be shown at a true figure for purposes of valuation, and the value of goodwill should be reflected in another method of valuation (for example the earnings basis, the dividend yield basis or the super-profits method).

(b) Development expenditure, if shown in the accounts, would also have a value which is related to future profits rather than to the worth of the company's physical assets.

11.16 EXAMPLE: NET ASSETS METHOD OF SHARE VALUATION

The summary balance sheet of Cactus Ltd is as follows.

	£	£	£
Fixed assets			
Land and buildings			160,000
Plant and machinery			80,000
Motor vehicles			20,000
			260,000
Goodwill			20,000
Current assets			
Stocks		80,000	
Debtors		60,000	
Short-term investments		15,000	
Cash		5,000	
		160,000	
Current liabilities			
Creditors	60,000		
Taxation	20,000		
Proposed ordinary dividend	20,000		
		(100,000)	
			60,000
			340,000
12% debentures			(60,000)
Deferred taxation			(10,000)
			270,000

	£
Ordinary shares of £1	80,000
Reserves	140,000
	220,000
4.9% preference shares of £1	50,000
	270,000

What is the value of an ordinary share using the net assets basis of valuation?

11.17 SOLUTION

If the figures given for asset values are not questioned, the valuation would be as follows.

		£	£
Total value of net assets			340,000
Less intangible asset (goodwill)			20,000
Total value of tangible assets (net)			320,000
Less:	preference shares	50,000	
	debentures	60,000	
	deferred taxation	10,000	
			120,000
Net asset value of equity			200,000
Number of ordinary shares			80,000
Value per share			£2.50

11.18 The difficulty in an asset valuation method is establishing the asset values to use. Values ought to be realistic. The figure attached to an individual asset may vary considerably depending on whether it is valued on a going concern or a break-up basis.

11.19 The following list should give you some idea of the factors that must be considered.

(a) Do the assets need professional valuation? If so, how much will this cost?

(b) Have the liabilities been accurately quantified, for example deferred taxation? Are there any contingent liabilities? Will any balancing tax charges arise on disposal?

(c) How have the current assets been valued? Are all debtors collectable? Is all stock realisable? Can all the assets be physically located and brought into a saleable condition? This may be difficult in certain circumstances where the assets are situated abroad.

(d) Can any hidden liabilities be accurately assessed? Would there be redundancy payments and closure costs?

(e) Is there an available market in which the assets can be realised (on a break-up basis)? If so, do the balance sheet values truly reflect these break-up values?

(f) Are there any prior charges on the assets?

When is the net assets basis of valuation used?

11.20 The net assets basis of valuation should be used:

(a) **as a measure of the 'security' in a share value**. A share might be valued using the earnings basis, and this valuation might be:

(i) higher than the net asset value per share. If the company went into liquidation, the investor could not expect to receive the full value of his shares when the underlying assets were realised;

(ii) lower than the net asset value per share. If the company went into liquidation, the investor might expect to receive the full value of his shares (perhaps much more) when the underlying assets were realised.

The asset backing for shares thus provides a measure of the possible loss if the company fails to make the expected earnings or dividend payments. It is often thought to be a good thing to acquire a company with valuable tangible assets, especially freehold property which might be expected to increase in value over time;

(b) **as a measure of comparison in a scheme of merger**. For example, if company A, which has a low asset backing, is planning a merger with company B, which has a high asset backing, the shareholders of B might consider that their shares' value ought to reflect this. It might therefore be agreed that a something should be added to the value of the company B shares to allow for this difference in asset backing.

For these reasons, it is always advisable to calculate the net assets per share.

The dividend yield method of share valuation

11.21 The **dividend yield method** of share valuation is suitable for the valuation of small shareholdings in unquoted companies. It is based on the principle that small shareholders are mainly interested in dividends, since they cannot control decisions affecting the company's profits and earnings. A suitable offer price would therefore be one which compensates them for the future dividends they will be giving up if they sell their shares. The simplest dividend capitalisation technique is based on the assumption that the level of dividends in the future will be **constant**. A dividend yield valuation would be:

$$\text{Value} = \frac{\text{Dividend in pence}}{\text{Expected dividend yield \%}}$$

11.22 It may be possible to use expected **future** dividends for a share valuation and to predict dividend growth. For this purpose, it is first necessary to predict future earnings and then to decide how changes in earnings will be reflected in the company's dividend policy.

11.23 The dividend growth model for share valuation, you should recall, can be expressed as follows.

$$p_o = \frac{d_0(1+g)}{(r-g)}$$

where p_o is the current market value ex dividend
d_0 is the current dividend
g is the expected annual growth in dividend, so $d_0(1+g)$ is the expected dividend next year
r is the return required.

Question 3

A company expects to pay no dividends in years 1, 2 or 3, but a dividend of 7.8p per share each year from year 4 in perpetuity. Value its shares on a dividend yield basis, assuming a required yield of 12%.

Answer

$$\frac{7.8\text{p}}{(1.12)^4} + \frac{7.8\text{p}}{(1.12)^5} + \ldots\ldots$$

$$= \frac{7.8\text{p}}{0.12} \times \frac{1}{(1.12)^3}$$

$$= \frac{65\text{p}}{(1.12)^3} = 46.26\text{p, say 46p}$$

The CAPM and share price valuations

11.24 The **capital asset pricing model (CAPM)** might be used to value shares, particularly when pricing shares for a stock market listing. The CAPM would be used to establish a required equity yield.

11.25 EXAMPLE: CAPM AND SHARE PRICE VALUATIONS

Suppose that Mackerel plc is planning to obtain a Stock Exchange listing by offering 40% of its existing shares to the public. No new shares will be issued. Its most recent summarised results are as follows.

	£
Turnover	120,000,000
Earnings	1,500,000
Number of shares	3,000,000

The company has low gearing.

It regularly pays 50% of earnings as dividends, and with reinvested earnings is expected to achieve 5% dividend growth each year.

Summarised details of two listed companies in the same industry as Mackerel plc are as follows.

	Salmon plc	*Trout plc*
Gearing (total debt/total equity)	45%	10%
Equity beta	1.50	1.05

The current Treasury bill yield is 7% a year. The average market return is estimated to be 12%. The new shares will be issued at a discount of 15% to the estimated post-issue market price, in order to increase the prospects of success for the share issue. What will the issue price be?

11.26 SOLUTION

Using the CAPM, we begin by deciding on a suitable β value for Mackerel's equity. We shall assume that since Mackerel's gearing is close to Trout's, a β of 1.05 is appropriate.

The cost of Mackerel equity is 7% + (12 – 7) × 1.05% = 12.25%

11.27 This can now be used in the dividend growth model. The dividend this year is 50% of £1,500,000 = £750,000.

The total value of Mackerel's equity is $\frac{£750,000(1.05)}{(0.1225-0.05)} = £10,862,068$

There are 3,000,000 shares, giving a market value per share of £3.62.

11.28 Since the shares that are offered to the public will be offered at a discount of about 15% to this value, the share price for the market launch should be about 85% of £3.62 = £3.08.

The super-profits method of share valuation

11.29 This method, which is rather out of fashion at present, starts by applying a 'fair return' to the net tangible assets and comparing the result with the expected profits. Any excess of profits (the super-profits) is used to calculate goodwill. The goodwill is normally taken as a fixed number of years super-profits. The goodwill is then added to the value of the target company's tangible assets to arrive at a value for the business.

11.30 EXAMPLE: SUPER-PROFITS METHOD OF SHARE VALUATION

Light Ltd has net tangible assets of £120,000 and present earnings of £20,000. Doppler Ltd wants to take over Light Ltd and considers that a fair return for this type of industry is 12%, and decides to value Light Ltd taking goodwill at three years super-profits.

	£
Actual profits	20,000
Less fair return on net tangible assets: 12% × £120,000	14,400
Super-profits	5,600
Goodwill: 3 × £5,600	£16,800
Value of Light Ltd: £120,000 + £16,800	£136,800

11.31 The principal drawbacks to this valuation method are as follows.

(a) The rate of return required is chosen subjectively.

(b) The number of years purchase of super-profits is arbitrary. In the example above, goodwill was valued at three years of super-profits, but it could have been, for example, two years or four years of super-profits.

The discounted future profits method of share valuation

11.32 This method of share valuation may be appropriate when one company intends to buy the assets of another company and to make further investments in order to improve profits in the future.

11.33 EXAMPLE: DISCOUNTED FUTURE PROFITS METHOD OF SHARE VALUATION

Diversification Ltd wishes to make a bid for Tadpole Ltd. Tadpole Ltd makes after-tax profits of £40,000 a year. Diversification Ltd believes that if further money is spent on additional investments, the after-tax cash flows (ignoring the purchase consideration) could be as follows.

Year	*Cash flow (net of tax)*
	£
0	(100,000)
1	(80,000)
2	60,000
3	100,000
4	150,000
5	150,000

The after-tax cost of capital of Diversification Ltd is 15% and the company expects all its investments to pay back, in discounted terms, within five years. What is the maximum price that the company should be willing to pay for the shares of Tadpole Ltd?

11.34 SOLUTION

The maximum price is one which would make the return from the total investment exactly 15% over five years, so that the NPV at 15% would be 0.

Year	Cash flows ignoring purchase consideration	Discount factor	Present value
	£	15%	£
0	(100,000)	1.000	(100,000)
1	(80,000)	0.870	(69,600)
2	60,000	0.756	45,360
3	100,000	0.658	65,800
4	150,000	0.572	85,800
5	150,000	0.497	74,550
Maximum purchase price			101,910

Free cash flow

11.35 One approach to the valuation of a business is to treat its value as the sum of future discounted free cash flows, where **free cash flow** is given by the following.

Free cash flow = Revenues – operating costs + depreciation – investment expenditure

11.36 This approach, however, presents the following problems when used in financial planning and strategy.

(a) Due to movement of working capital items, accounting information on revenues and operating costs may fail to reflect cash flows. For example, if sales increase, they may do so on longer credit terms than previously, and the cash flow effect may therefore be delayed. Also, stock building may have adverse effects on cash flows while having no effects on profits.

(b) The timing of tax payments in a particular year will be based on profits earned in previous time periods. As a result, the free cash flow for the current period less this year's tax liability does not equal cash flow for the current year.

11.37 These problems mean that estimating free cash flow involves not just forecasting sales, costs and profits, but also working capital movements and taxation.

Chapter roundup

- Buying another company is a substantial undertaking for a company. The target company's shareholders must be persuaded of the benefits of the takeover. **Takeover bids** are not infrequent, and it is worth following one or two in the financial press, to see how the considerations set out in this chapter translate into practice.
- **Management buyouts** are a special sort of transaction, involving several parties. A buyout cannot go ahead unless all the parties are satisfied with the arrangements.
- Any **capital reconstruction scheme** must be carefully designed. Such schemes are only required when companies have already got into difficulties. Some parties will already stand to lose money, and they will only be persuaded to risk more money if they can see really good prospects of eventual success.
- There are a number of different ways of **putting a value on a business**, or on shares in an unquoted company. It makes sense to use **several methods** of valuation, and to compare the values they produce. At the end of the day, however, what really matters is the final price that the buyer and the seller agree. The purchase price for a company will usually be discussed mainly in terms of:
  - P/E ratios, when a large block of shares, or a whole business is being valued;
  - alternatively, a DCF valuation;
  - to a lesser extent, the net assets per share.
- The **dividend yield method** is more relevant to small shareholdings.

Quick quiz

1. What might be the reasons for an amalgamation or takeover? (see paras 1.3, 1.4)
2. Why might the shareholders of the bidding company disapprove of a bid for a target company by their board of directors? (3.1, 3.2)
3. What factors might affect the choice between a cash offer and a paper offer in a takeover bid? (3.20)
4. What is mezzanine finance? (3.23)
5. If a bidding company issues shares to buy a target company on a *lower* P/E ratio than the bidding company shares are valued at, what will happen to the bidding company's own EPS after the takeover? (4.3)
6. What are the steps which should be followed in ensuring that an acquired company is successfully integrated into the enterprise? (6.2 - 6.4)
7. What are the reasons for demergers? (7.3)
8. How should an institutional investor evaluate a management buyout? (8.8)
9. What advantages are there in a public company 'going private'? (8.20)
10. What is a capital reconstruction scheme? (9.1)
11. What guidelines should help to determine the P/E ratio on which to base an offer price for shares in a target company? (11.6)

Question to try	Level	Marks	Time
21	Exam standard	40	72 mins

Part D

International financial management

Chapter 22

FOREIGN EXCHANGE AND RISK MANAGEMENT I

Chapter topic list	Syllabus reference	Ability required
1 Risk and risk management	13 d(ii)	Application
2 Exchange rate risk	13 d(i)	Skill
	13 d(ii)	Application
3 Direct risk reduction methods	13 d(i)	Skill
4 Forward exchange rates and contracts	13 d(iii)	Application

Introduction

The rôle of the treasurer is increasingly concerned with identifying and managing **risks** of various types. In this chapter and the next, we look risks relating in particular to **exchange rate fluctuations**.

1 RISK AND RISK MANAGEMENT

1.1 **Exposure** means being open to or vulnerable to risk. **Risk management** describes the policies which a firm may adopt and the techniques it may use to manage the risks it faces.

1.2 There are basically two ways in which exposure to risk may be reduced.

(a) **Pooling** of risks. This method underlies insurance, in which risks which may be unacceptable to individual policyholders are aggregated or 'pooled' by being taken on by the insurance company. Pooling of risk also underlies the diversification of a portfolio of investments.

(b) **Hedging** of risks. In the case of hedging, different parties come to an agreement which cancels one of the parties' risks against the other's. The different parties may be subject to similar but opposite risks which they wish to hedge. Alternatively, one party may wish to hedge a risk while the other party may be a speculator.

1.3 Two types of risk with which corporate risk management is concerned are **exchange rate risk** - the risk of exchange rate movements - and **interest rate risk** - the risk of adverse interest rate movements, which we considered earlier. The inherent risks of the trade or business can be managed within the company. Other risks, including interest rate risk and foreign exchange risk, are due to factors beyond the control of the enterprise and hedging ought therefore to be considered.

Choosing not to hedge

1.4 Risk minimisation is not the only possible strategy. As noted when we considered the treatment of a treasury department as a profit centre, a company may, instead of hedging, choose to remain exposed to risks, hoping to profit from its risk-taking positions. A company's shareholders may prefer a higher risk strategy in the hope of achieving higher returns.

2 EXCHANGE RATE RISK 11/95, 11/96, 11/97, 5/98, 11/98, 5/99

2.1 A company may become exposed to exchange rate risk in a number of ways, including the following:

(a) as an exporter of goods or services;
(b) as an importer of goods or services;
(c) through having an overseas subsidiary;
(d) through being the subsidiary of an overseas company;
(e) through transactions in overseas capital markets.

2.2 The following different types of foreign exchange risk (or 'currency risk') may be distinguished.

(a) **Transaction risk** is the risk of adverse exchange rate movements occurring in the course of normal international trading transactions. This arises when export prices are fixed in foreign currency terms, or imports are invoiced in foreign currencies. Below, we discuss various methods for reducing this type of exposure to risk.

(b) **Translation risk** arises from differences in the currencies in which assets and liabilities are denominated. If a company has different proportions of its assets and liabilities denominated in particular currencies, then exchange rate movements are likely to have varying effects on the value of these assets and liabilities. This could influence investors' and lenders' attitudes to the financial worth and creditworthiness of the company. Such risk can be reduced if assets and liabilities denominated in particular currencies can be held in balanced amounts.

(c) **Economic risk** refers to the effect of exchange rate movements on the international competitiveness of a company. For example, a UK company might use raw materials which are priced in US dollars, but export its products mainly within the European Union. A depreciation of sterling against the dollar or an appreciation of sterling against other EU currencies will both erode the competitiveness of the company. Economic exposure can be difficult to avoid, although diversification of the supplier and customer base across different countries may reduce this kind of exposure to risk.

Selling and buying currency

2.3 If an importer has to pay a foreign supplier in a foreign currency, he might ask his bank to sell him the required amount of the currency. For example, suppose that a bank's customer, a trading company, has imported goods for which it must now pay US$10,000.

(a) The company will ask the bank to sell it $10,000. If the company is buying currency, the bank is selling it.

(b) When the bank agrees to sell US$10,000 to the company, it will tell the company what the range of exchange will be for the transaction. If the bank's selling rate (known as the 'offer', or 'ask' price) is, say $1.7935, the bank will charge the company:

$$\frac{\$10{,}000}{\$1.7935 \text{ per } £1} = £5{,}575.69 \text{ for the currency}$$

2.4 Similarly, if an exporter is paid, say, US$10,000 by a customer in the USA, he may wish to exchange the dollars to obtain sterling. He will therefore ask his bank to buy the dollars from him. Since the exporter is selling currency to the bank, the bank is buying the currency.

If the bank quotes a buying rate (known as the 'bid' price) of, say $1.8075, the bank will pay the exporter:

$$\frac{\$10{,}000}{\$1.8075 \text{ per } £1} = £5{,}532.50 \text{ for the currency}$$

2.5 A bank expects to make a profit from selling and buying currency, and it does so by offering a rate for selling a currency which is different from the rate for buying the currency.

2.6 If a bank were to buy a quantity of foreign currency from a customer, and then were to re-sell it to another customer, it would charge the second customer more (in sterling) for the currency than it would pay the first customer. The difference would be profit. For example, the figures used for illustration in the previous paragraphs show a bank selling some US dollars for £5,575.69 and buying the same quantity of dollars for £5,532.50, at selling and buying rates that might be in use at the same time. The bank would make a profit of £43.19.

Spot rates

2.7 The **spot rate** is the rate of exchange on currency for immediate delivery. All the rates so far mentioned in this chapter have been spot rates.

Question 1

Calculate how much sterling exporters would receive or how much sterling importers would pay, ignoring the bank's commission, in each of the following situations, if they were to exchange currency and sterling at the spot rate.

(a) A UK exporter receives a payment from a French customer of FF150,000.
(b) A UK importer buys goods from a Japanese supplier and pays 1 million yen.

Spot rates are as follows.

	Bank sells (offer)		*Bank buys (bid)*
France FF/£	9.4340	-	9.5380
Japan Y/£	203.65	-	205.78

Answer

(a) The bank is being asked to buy the French francs and will give the exporter:

$$\frac{150{,}000}{9.5380} = £15{,}726.57 \text{ in exchange}$$

(b) The bank is being asked to sell the yen to the importer and will charge:

$$\frac{1{,}000{,}000}{203.65} = £4{,}910.39$$

Direct and indirect currency quotes

2.8 A **direct quote** is the amount of domestic currency which is equal to one foreign currency unit. An **indirect quote** is the amount of foreign currency which is equal to one domestic currency unit. In the UK indirect quotes are invariably used but, in most countries, direct quotes are more common. Currencies may be quoted in either direction. For example the US dollar and German mark may be quoted as DM/$ = 1.723 or $/DM = 0.580. In other words, DM1.723 = $1 and $0.580 = DM1. One rate is simply the reciprocal of the other.

2.9 A further complication to be aware of is that the offer rate in one country becomes the bid rate in the other. For example, Malaysian Ringgit (MR) are quoted in London like this:

	Bank sells (offer)		*Bank buys (bid)*
MR/£	4.0440	-	4.0910

However, in Kuala Lumpur you would see:

	Bank sells (offer)		*Bank buys (bid)*
MR/£	4.0910	-	4.0440

Exam focus point

The examination is not confined to the activities of British companies. Exchange rates given in the examination could be as quoted in foreign countries. Because of these complications you should always double-check which rate you are using when choosing between the bid or offer rate. One sure method is to recognise that the bank makes money out of the transaction and will therefore offer you the worse of the two possible rates!

Factors influencing the exchange rate for a currency

2.10 The exchange rate between two currencies - ie the buying and selling rates, both 'spot' and forward - is determined primarily by supply and demand in the foreign exchange markets. Demand comes from individuals, firms and governments who want to buy a currency and supply comes from those who want to sell it.

2.11 Supply and demand for currencies are in turn influenced by:

(a) the rate of inflation, compared with the rate of inflation in other countries;
(b) interest rates, compared with interest rates in other countries;
(c) the balance of payments;
(d) sentiment of foreign exchange market participants regarding economic prospects;
(e) speculation;
(f) government policy on intervention to influence the exchange rate.

2.12 Other factors influence the exchange rate through their relationship with the items identified above. For example:

(a) total income and expenditure (demand) in the domestic economy determines the demand for goods, including:

(i) imported goods;

(ii) goods produced in the country which would otherwise be exported if demand for them did not exist in the home markets;

(b) output capacity and the level of employment in the domestic economy might influence the balance of payments, because if the domestic economy has full employment already, it will be unable to increase its volume of production for exports;

(c) the growth in the money supply influences interest rates and domestic inflation.

Interest rate parity

2.13 The difference between spot and forward rates reflects differences in interest rates. If this were not so, then investors holding the currency with the lower interest rates would switch to the other currency for (say) three months, ensuring that they would not lose on returning to the original currency by fixing the exchange rate in advance at the forward rate. If enough investors acted in this way (known as **arbitrage**), forces of supply and demand would lead to a change in the forward rate to prevent such risk-free profit making.

2.14 The principle of **interest rate parity** links the foreign exchange markets and the international money markets. The principle can be stated as follows.

EXAM FORMULA

$$\frac{1 + r_{SFr}}{1 + r_{\$}} = \frac{f_{SFr/\$}}{s_{SFr/\$}}$$

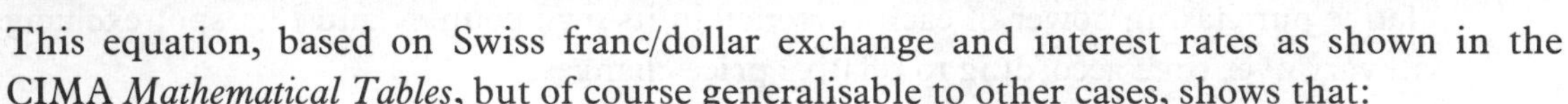

This equation, based on Swiss franc/dollar exchange and interest rates as shown in the CIMA *Mathematical Tables*, but of course generalisable to other cases, shows that:

Difference in interest rates = Difference between forward and spot rates

where r_{SFr} is the Swiss franc interest rate on a deposit for a certain time period
$r_{\$}$ is the dollar interest rate on a deposit for the same time period
$f_{SFr/\$}$ is the forward exchange rate SFr/$ for the same time period
$s_{SFr/\$}$ is the spot exchange rate SFr/$

2.15 EXAMPLE: INTEREST RATE PARITY

Exchange rates between two currencies, the Northland florin (NF) and the Southland dollar (S$) are listed in the financial press as follows.

Spot rates	4.7250	NF/$S
	0.21164	$S/NF
90 day rates	4.7506	NF/$S
	0.21050	$S/NF

The money market interest rate for 90 day deposits in Northland florins is 7.5% annualised. What is implied about interest rates in Southland?

Assume a 365 day year. (*Note*. In practice, foreign currency interest rates are often calculated on an alternative **360-day** basis, one month being treated as 30 days.)

2.16 SOLUTION

Today, $S1.000 buys NF4.7250.

NF4.7250 could be placed on deposit for 90 days to earn interest of NF(4.7250 × 0.075 × 90/365) = NF0.0874, thus growing to NF(4.7250 + 0.0874) = NF4.8124.

This is then worth $S 1.0130 at the 90 day exchange rate.

This tells us that the annualised expected interest rate on 90-day deposits in Southland is $0.013 \times 365/90 = 5.3\%$.

2.17 Alternatively, applying the formula given earlier, we have the following.

Northland interest rate on 90 day deposit = $r_n = 0.0874 + 4.7250 = 1.85\%$

Southland interest rate on 90 day deposit = r_s

90-day forward exchange rate = $f_{s/n} = 0.21050$

Spot exchange rate = $s_{s/n} = 0.21164$

$$\frac{1+r_s}{1+0.0185} = \frac{0.21050}{0.21164}$$

$$1 + r_s = 1.0185 \times 0.21050 \div 0.21164 = 1.013$$

$$r_s = 0.013\text{, or } 1.3\%$$

Annualised, this is $0.013 \times 365/90 = 5.3\%$

Purchasing power parity 11/98

2.18 Interest rate parity should not be confused with **purchasing power parity**. Purchasing power parity theory predicts that the exchange value of foreign currency depends on the relative purchasing power of each currency in its own country and that spot exchange rates will vary over time according to relative price changes.

Formally, purchasing power parity can be expressed in the formulae:

$$\frac{S_t - S_o}{S_o} = \frac{i_f - i_{uk}}{1 + i_{uk}} \quad \text{or} \quad S_t = S_o \times \frac{1+i_f}{1+i_{uk}}$$

where

S_o is the current spot exchange rate (at time 0)
S_t is the expected spot rate at time t
i_f is the expected inflation in the foreign country to time t (expressed as a decimal)
i_{uk} is the expected inflation in the home country to time t (expressed as a decimal)

2.19 EXAMPLE: PURCHASING POWER PARITY

The exchange rate between UK sterling and the French franc is £1 = 8.00 francs. Assuming that there is now purchasing parity, an amount of a commodity costing £110 in the UK will cost 880 French francs. Over the next year, price inflation in France is expected to be 5% while inflation in the UK is expected to be 8%. What is the expected spot exchange rate at the end of the year?

Using the first formula above:

$$\frac{S_t - 8.00}{8.00} = \frac{0.05 - 0.08}{1 + 0.08}$$

$$S_t - 8.00 = 8.00 \times \frac{-0.03}{1.08}$$

$$S_t = 8.00 - 0.22 = 7.78$$

or, using the second formula:

$$S_t = 8.00 \times \frac{1.05}{1.08} = 7.78$$

2.20 This is the same figure as we get if we compare the inflated prices for the commodity. At the end of the year:

UK price = £110 × 1.08 = £118.80

France price = FF880 × 1.05 = FF924

S_t = 924 ÷ 118.80 = 7.78

2.21 In the real world, exchange rates move towards purchasing power parity only over the long term. However, the theory is sometimes used to predict future exchange rates in investment appraisal problems where forecasts of relative inflation rates are available.

The Fisher effect

2.22 The term **Fisher effect** is sometimes used in looking at the relationship between interest rates and expected rates of inflation.

2.23 The rate of interest can be seen as made up of two parts: the real required rate of return plus a premium for inflation. Then:

(1+ nominal rate of interest) = (1 + real rate of interest) × (1 + expected rate of inflation)

2.24 Countries with relatively high rates of inflation will generally have high nominal rates of interest, partly because high interest rates are a mechanism for reducing inflation and partly because of the Fisher effect: higher nominal interest rates serve to allow investors to obtain a high enough real rate of return where inflation is relatively high.

2.25 According to the **international Fisher effect,** interest rate differentials between countries provide an unbiased predictor of future changes in spot exchange rates. The currency of countries with relatively high interest rates is expected to depreciate against currency's with lower interest rates, because the higher interest rates are considered necessary to compensate for the anticipated currency depreciation. Given free movement of capital internationally, this idea suggests that the real rate of return in different countries will equalise as a result of adjustments to spot exchange rates.

2.26 The Fisher effect can be expressed as:

$$\frac{1 + r_f}{1 + r_{uk}} = \frac{1 + i_f}{1 + i_{uk}}$$

where

r_f is the nominal interest rate in the foreign country

r_{uk} is the nominal interest rate in the home country

Question 2

Bulldog Ltd, a UK company, buys goods from Redland which cost 100,000 Reds (the local currency). The goods are re-sold in the UK for £32,000. At the time of the import purchase the exchange rate for Reds against sterling is 3.5650 - 3.5800.

Required

(a) What is the expected profit on the re-sale?

(b) What would the actual profit be if the spot rate at the time when the currency is received has moved to:

(i) 3.0800 - 3.0950
(ii) 4.0650 - 4.0800?

Ignore bank commission charges.

Answer

(a) Bulldog must buy Reds to pay the supplier, and so the bank is selling Reds. The expected profit is as follows.

	£
Revenue from re-sale of goods	32,000.00
Less cost of 100,000 Reds in sterling (÷ 3.5650)	28,050.49
Expected profit	3,949.51

(b) (i) If the actual spot rate for Bulldog to buy and the bank to sell the Reds is 3.0800, the result is as follows.

	£
Revenue from re-sale	32,000.00
Less cost (100,000 ÷ 3.0800)	32,467.53
Loss	(467.53)

(ii) If the actual spot rate for Bulldog to buy and the bank to sell the Reds is 4.0650, the result is as follows.

	£
Revenue from re-sale	32,000.00
Less cost (100,000 ÷ 4.0650)	24,600.25
Profit	7,399.75

---

3 DIRECT RISK REDUCTION METHODS 5/99

3.1 The forward exchange contract is perhaps the most important method of obtaining cover against risks, where a firm decides that it does not wish to speculate on foreign exchange. This is discussed later in the chapter. However, there are other methods of reducing risk which we shall consider first.

Currency of invoice

3.2 One way of avoiding exchange risk is for an exporter to invoice his foreign customer in the customer's domestic currency, or for an importer to arrange with his foreign supplier to be invoiced in his domestic currency. If a UK exporter is able to quote and invoice an overseas buyer in sterling, then the foreign exchange risk is in effect transferred to the overseas buyer. Similarly, a UK-based importer may be able to persuade the overseas supplier to invoice in sterling rather than in a foreign currency. Although either the exporter or the importer avoids exchange risk in this way, only one of them can. The other must accept the exchange risk, since there will be a period of time elapsing between agreeing a contract and paying for the goods (unless payment is made with the order).

3.3 An alternative method of achieving the same result is to negotiate contracts expressed in the foreign currency but specifying a fixed rate of exchange as a condition of the contract.

3.4 There is a possible marketing advantage to be obtained by proposing to invoice in the buyer's own currency, when there is competition for the sales contract. The foreign buyer, invoiced in his own currency, will not have the problem of deciding whether to protect himself against exchange risks.

(a) If the exporter believes that he is in danger of not winning the contract, owing to competition from other sellers overseas, and if the buyer's own currency is weak and likely to depreciate against sterling, the exporter might offer to invoice the buyer in his own (weak) currency in order to win the contract. The exporter would in effect be offering the buyer a price discount due to the probability of a movement in exchange rates favourable to the buyer and therefore unfavourable to the exporter.

(b) In some export markets, foreign currency (often the US dollar) is the normal trading currency, and so UK exporters might have to quote prices in that currency for customers to consider buying from them. By arranging to sell goods to customers in a foreign currency, a UK exporter might be able to obtain a loan in that currency at a lower rate of interest than in the UK, and at the same time obtain cover against exchange risks by arranging to repay the loan out of the proceeds from the sales in that currency.

3.5 There are certain other aspects to invoicing in foreign currency that an exporter might wish to consider.

(a) **Pricing and price lists**. If the exporter issues price lists in foreign currency, he should be aware of the need to revise price lists as the value of his domestic currency fluctuates against the value of the foreign currency. For example, if a UK exporter issues a price list in US dollars, and sterling strengthens against the US dollar, the exporter will earn less sterling when he sells his US dollar receipts, and so his profit margins will be cut. He might therefore need to raise his prices to maintain profit margins. On the other hand, if the US dollar strengthened against sterling, the UK exporter could cut his prices whilst still maintaining his sterling profit margins.

(b) **Customer relations**. A switch from invoicing in sterling to invoicing in a foreign currency might not be easy to achieve, at least not without giving adequate warning to the customer. The ability of an exporter to make a change might be thwarted by the resistance of a customer with bargaining strength.

(c) **Accounting systems**. Accounting procedures for invoicing in foreign currency, or borrowing in a foreign currency, are a little more complex than for invoicing and borrowing in sterling.

Matching receipts and payments

3.6 A company can reduce or eliminate its foreign exchange transaction risk exposure by matching receipts and payments. Wherever possible, a UK company that expects to make payments and have receipts in the same foreign currency should plan to offset its payments against its receipts in the currency.

3.7 The process of matching is made simpler by having **foreign currency accounts** with a bank. UK residents are allowed to have bank accounts in any foreign currency. Receipts of foreign currency can be credited to the account pending subsequent payments in the currency. (Alternatively, a company might invest its foreign currency income in the country of the currency - for example it might have a bank deposit account abroad - and make payments with these overseas assets/deposits). Since a company is unlikely to have exactly the same amount of receipts in a currency as it makes payments, it will still be exposed to the extent of the surplus of income, and so the company may wish to avoid exposure on this surplus by arranging forward exchange cover.

3.8 Offsetting (matching payments against receipts) will be cheaper than arranging a forward contract to buy currency and another forward contract to sell the currency, provided that receipts occur before payments, and the time difference between receipts and payments in the currency is not too long. Any differences between the amounts receivable and the amounts payable in a given currency should be covered by a forward exchange contract to buy/sell the amount of the difference.

Leads and lags

3.9 Companies might try to use:

(a) **lead payments:** payments in advance; or
(b) **lagged payments:** delaying payments beyond their due date

in order to take advantage of foreign exchange rate movements. With a lead payment, paying in advance of the due date, there is a finance cost to consider. This is the interest cost on the money used to make the payment.

3.10 EXAMPLE: LEADS AND LAGS

A company owes $30,000 to a US supplier, payable in 90 days. It might suspect that the US dollar will strengthen against sterling over the next three months, because the US dollar is quoted forward at a premium against sterling on the foreign exchange market. The spot exchange rate is $1.50 = £1.

(a) The company could pay the $30,000 now, instead of in 90 days time. This would cost £20,000 now, which is a payment that could have been delayed by 90 days.

(b) The cost of this lead payment would be interest on £20,000 for 90 days, at the company's borrowing rate or its opportunity cost of capital.

Matching long-term assets and liabilities

3.11 When an international company has an operating subsidiary abroad, it may try to finance the subsidiary's long-term assets with a matching long-term loan in the same currency. For example, suppose that a UK company with a French subsidiary decides to purchase extra premises in France which must be paid for in francs. The company may try to finance the purchase by raising a loan in francs, which it would then repay out of the operating profits (in francs) from the use of the French premises.

Money market hedges

3.12 An exporter who invoices foreign customers in a foreign currency can hedge against the exchange risk by:

(a) borrowing an amount in the foreign currency now;

(b) converting the foreign currency lent to it into domestic currency at the 'spot' rate;

(c) repaying the loan with interest out of the eventual foreign currency receipts from debtors.

3.13 For example, if an exporter knows that he will receive DM70,000 from a German customer in one year's time, he can cover the foreign exchange risk by borrowing DM70,000 now for one year and repaying the loan with the eventual receipts. (For simplicity, the interest charges are ignored in this example.) The DM70,000 can be converted into sterling at the spot rate, and so the exchange risk is avoided.

3.14 Similarly, if a company has to make a foreign currency payment in the future, it can buy the currency now at the spot rate and put it on deposit, using the principal and the interest earned to make the foreign currency payment when it falls due. These forms of **money market hedge** are an alternative method of covering foreign exchange risk to using forward exchange contracts (considered next).

3.15 Is one of these methods of cover likely to be cheaper than the other? The answer is perhaps, but not by much. There will be very little difference between borrowing in foreign currency and repaying the loan with currency receivables and borrowing in sterling and selling forward the currency receivables. This is because the premium or discount on the forward exchange rate reflects the interest differential between the two countries, as explained in the next section.

4 FORWARD EXCHANGE RATES AND CONTRACTS 5/97, 5/98

Forward exchange contracts

4.1 Foreign exchange transaction exposure may be overcome by means of a **forward exchange contract**, whereby the importer or exporter arranges for a bank to sell or buy a quantity of foreign currency at a future date, at a rate of exchange that is determined when the forward contract is made. Forward exchange contracts allow a trader who knows that he will have to buy or sell foreign currency at a date in the future, to make the purchase or sale at a predetermined rate of exchange. The trader will therefore know in advance either how much local currency he will receive (if he is selling foreign currency to the bank) or how much local currency he must pay (if he is buying foreign currency from the bank).

KEY TERM

A **forward exchange contract** is:

(a) an immediately firm and binding contract between a bank and its customer;

(b) for the purchase or sale of a specified quantity of a stated foreign currency;

(c) at a rate of exchange fixed at the time the contract is made;

(d) for performance (delivery of the currency and payment for it) at a future time which is agreed upon when making the contract. This future time will be either a specified date, or any time between two specified dates.

Forward rates and future exchange rate movements

KEY TERM

Forward exchange rate: an exchange rate set for the exchange of currencies at some future date *(OT)*.

4.2 A **forward price** is the spot price ruling on the day a forward exchange contract is made plus or minus the interest differential for the period of the contract. It is wrong to think of a forward rate as a forecast of what the spot rate will be on a given date in the future, and it will be a coincidence if the forward rate turns out to be the same as the spot rate on that future date. It is however likely that the spot rate will move in the direction indicated by the

forward rate. Currencies with high interest rates are likely to depreciate in value against currencies with lower interest rates: the attraction of higher interest persuades investors to hold amounts of a currency that is expected to depreciate.

Expectations theory of forward exchange rates

4.3 On the assumption that risk is absent, the **expectations theory of forward exchange rates** predicts that the percentage difference between forward and spot rates now equals the expected change in spot rates over the period. Thus, given expectations of interest rates and inflation rates, the spot rate three months from now is expected to equal the three-months forward rate quoted now, for example. Because on average the forward rate equals the future spot rate, and overestimates it about as often as it underestimates it, the forward market is said to be an **unbiased predictor** of exchange rates.

Fixed and option contracts

4.4 A forward exchange contract may be either **fixed** or **option**.

(a) 'Fixed' means that performance of the contract will take place on a specified date in the future. For example, a two months forward **fixed** contract taken out on 1 September will require performance on 1 November.

(b) 'Option' means that performance of the contract may take place, at the option of the customer, either

(i) at any date from the contract being made up to and including a specified final date for performance; or

(ii) at any date between two specified dates.

Option forward exchange contracts are different from **currency options**, which are explained later.

Premiums and discounts: quoting a forward rate

4.5 As you will already appreciate, a forward exchange rate might be higher or lower than the spot rate. If it is higher, the quoted currency will be cheaper forward than spot. For example, if in the case of Italian lire against sterling (i) the spot rate is 2,156 - 2,166 and (ii) the three months forward rate is 2,207 - 2,222:

(a) a bank would sell 2,000,000 lire:

(i) at the spot rate, now, for £927.64 $\left(\frac{2,000,000}{2,156}\right)$

(ii) in three months time, under a forward contract, for £906.21 $\left(\frac{2,000,000}{2,207}\right)$

(b) a bank would buy 2,000,000 lire:

(i) at the spot rate, now, for £923.36 $\left(\frac{2,000,000}{2,166}\right)$

(ii) in three months time, under a forward contract, for £900.09

$$\left(\frac{2{,}000{,}000}{2{,}222}\right)$$

4.6 In both cases, the quoted currency (lire) would be worth less against sterling in a forward contract than at the current spot rate. This is because it is quoted forward cheaper, or 'at a discount', against sterling.

4.7 Forward rates are not quoted independently, but are quoted as adjustments to the spot rates.

(a) If the forward rate for a currency is cheaper than the spot rate, it is quoted as a forward **discount** to the spot rate. The forward rate will be higher than the spot rate by the amount of the discount.

(b) If the forward rate for a currency is more expensive than the spot rate, it is quoted as a forward **premium** to the spot rate. The forward rate will be lower than the spot rate by the amount of the premium.

The rule for adding or subtracting discounts and premiums

4.8 A **discount** is therefore **added** to the spot rate, and a **premium** is therefore **subtracted** from the spot rate. The mnemonic 'ADDIS' may help you to remember that we ADD Discounts and so subtract premiums. The longer the duration of a forward contract, the larger will be the quoted premium or discount. Thus premiums or discounts will be larger three months forward than one month forward.

4.9 EXAMPLE: FORWARD EXCHANGE CONTRACTS (1)

A UK importer knows on 1 April that he must pay a foreign seller 26,500 Swiss francs in one month's time, on 1 May. He can arrange a forward exchange contract with his bank on 1 April, whereby the bank undertakes to sell the importer 26,500 Swiss francs on 1 May, at a fixed rate of say 2.64.

The UK importer can be certain that whatever the spot rate is between Swiss francs and sterling on 1 May, he will have to pay on that date, at this forward rate,

$$\frac{26{,}500}{2.64} = £10{,}037.88.$$

(a) If the spot rate is lower than 2.64, the importer would have successfully protected himself against a weakening of sterling, and would have avoided paying more sterling to obtain the Swiss francs.

(b) If the spot rate is higher than 2.64, sterling's value against the Swiss franc would mean that the importer would pay more under the forward exchange contract than he would have had to pay if he had obtained the francs at the spot rate on 1 May. He cannot avoid this extra cost, because a forward contract is binding.

Option forward exchange contracts

4.10 As we saw above, **option contracts** are forward exchange contracts where the customer has the option to call for performance of the contract:

(a) at any date from the contract being made up to a specified date in the future; or
(b) at any date between two dates both in the future.

The contract must be performed at some time: the customer cannot avoid performance altogether.

4.11 Option contracts are normally used to cover whole months straddling the likely payment date, where the customer is not sure of the exact date on which he will want to buy or sell currency. (The purpose of an option contract is to avoid having to renew a forward exchange contract and extend it by a few days, because extending a forward contract can be expensive.)

4.12 Option contracts can also be used bit by bit. For example, if a customer makes an option forward contract to sell DM 100,000 at any time between 3 July and 3 August, he might sell DM 20,000 on 5 July, DM 50,000 on 15 July and DM 30,000 on 1 August.

4.13 When a customer makes an option forward exchange contract with his bank, the bank will quote the rate which is most favourable to itself out of the forward rates for all dates within the option period. This is because the customer has the option to call for performance of the contract on any date within the period, and the bank will try to ensure that the customer does not obtain a favourable rate at the bank's expense.

What happens if a customer cannot satisfy a forward contract?

4.14 A customer might be unable to satisfy a forward contract for any one of a number of reasons.

(a) An importer might find that:

  (i) his supplier fails to deliver the goods as specified, so the importer will not accept the goods delivered and will not agree to pay for them;

  (ii) the supplier sends fewer goods than expected, perhaps because of supply shortages, and so the importer has less to pay for;

  (iii) the supplier is late with the delivery, and so the importer does not have to pay for the goods until later than expected.

(b) An exporter might find the same types of situation, but in reverse, so that he does not receive any payment at all, or he receives more or less than originally expected, or he receives the expected amount, but only after some delay.

Close-out of forward contracts

4.15 If a customer cannot satisfy a forward exchange contract, the bank will make the customer fulfil the contract.

(a) If the customer has arranged for the bank to buy currency but then cannot deliver the currency for the bank to buy, the bank will:

  (i) sell currency to the customer at the spot rate (when the contract falls due for performance);

  (ii) buy the currency back, under the terms of the forward exchange contract.

(b) If the customer has contracted for the bank to sell him currency, the bank will:

  (i) sell the customer the specified amount of currency at the forward exchange rate;
  (ii) buy back the unwanted currency at the spot rate.

4.16 Thus, the bank arranges for the customer to perform his part of the forward exchange contract by either selling or buying the 'missing' currency at the spot rate. These arrangements are known as **closing out** a forward exchange contract.

4.17 EXAMPLE: FORWARD EXCHANGE CONTRACTS (2)

Shutter Ltd arranges on 1 January with a US supplier for the delivery of a consignment of goods costing US$96,000. Shutter Ltd will have to pay for the goods in six months time, on 1 July. The company therefore arranges a forward exchange contract for its bank to sell it US$96,000 six months hence.

In the event, the size of the consignment is reduced, and on 1 July, Shutter Ltd only needs US$50,000 to pay its supplier. The bank will therefore arrange to close out the forward exchange contract for the US$46,000 which Shutter Ltd does not need. This is called a partial close-out.

Exchange rates between the US dollar and sterling are as follows.

1 January	
Spot	$1.5145 - 1.5155
6 months forward	0.95 - 0.85c pm
1 July	
Spot	$1.5100 - 1.5110

Compute the cost to Shutter Ltd of the whole transaction, ignoring commission.

4.18 SOLUTION

The bank will sell Shutter Ltd US$96,000, to fulfil the original forward contract. The six months forward rate on 1 January was as follows.

Spot rate	1.5145
Less premium	0.0095
Forward rate	1.5050

The bank will buy back the unwanted US$46,000 at the spot rate on 1 July, thus closing out the contract.

	£
Sale of US$96,000 at $1.5050	63,787.38
Purchase of US$46,000 at $1.5110	30,443.41
Cost to Shutter Ltd	33,343.97

Extensions of forward contracts

4.19 When a forward exchange contract reaches the end of its period, a customer might find that he has not yet received the expected currency from an overseas buyer, or does not yet have to pay an overseas seller. The customer still wants to buy or sell the agreed amount of currency in the forward exchange contract, but he wants to defer the delivery date for the currency under the contract. The customer can then ask the bank to close out the old contract at the appropriate spot rate, and ask for a new contract for the extra period, with the rate being calculated in the usual way.

4.20 An alternative would be for the bank to extend the contract, by changing the bank's selling or buying rate in the contract. The bank would then arrange a new forward exchange contract with the customer at a rate that is slightly more favourable to the customer than for an ordinary forward exchange contract. This type of arrangement is, however, frowned upon by the Bank of England as it might encourage companies to conceal losses, and banks will only permit it in the rarest of cases.

Chapter roundup

- There are a number of techniques for **exchange rate risk management**.
- **Hedging strategies** are possible involving various financial instruments including **options**, **swaps** and **futures**. We look at these alternatives in the next chapter.
- Examination questions may focus on the selection of the cheapest **appropriate** technique, so it is important to grasp not only the mathematics of these techniques but also what financial commitments are necessary to use each one.

Quick quiz

1 Distinguish and briefly explain the three types of currency risk. (see para 2.2)

2 What is the principle of interest rate parity? (2.14)

3 What is the principle of purchasing power parity? (2.18)

4 What does matching mean in the context of managing exposure to foreign exchange transaction risk? (3.6)

5 Define a forward exchange contract. (4.1)

6 What happens if a company cannot satisfy a forward exchange contract? (4.15)

Question to try	Level	Marks	Time
22	Introductory	25	45 mins

Chapter 23

FOREIGN EXCHANGE AND RISK MANAGEMENT II

Chapter topic list		Syllabus reference	Ability required
1	Choosing a hedging method	13 d(iii)	Application
2	Futures	13 d(iii)	Application
3	Options	13 c(iii); d(iii)	Application
4	Swaps	13 d(iii)	Application

Introduction

In this chapter, we extend our discussion of **foreign exchange risk management** and consider the choice of appropriate hedging methods as well as some of the plethora of **financial instruments** which are now available for managing **financial risks** of various kinds.

1 CHOOSING A HEDGING METHOD

1.1 When a company expects to receive or pay a sum of foreign currency in the next few months, it can choose between using the forward exchange market and the money market to hedge against the foreign exchange risk. Both of these methods were introduced in the previous chapter. The cheaper option available is the one that ought to be chosen. Other methods may also be possible, such as making lead payments.

1.2 EXAMPLE: CHOOSING THE CHEAPEST METHOD

Trumpton plc has bought goods from a US supplier, and must pay $4,000,000 for them in three months time. The company's finance director wishes to hedge against the foreign exchange risk, and the three methods which the company usually considers are:

(a) using forward exchange contracts;
(b) using money market borrowing or lending;
(c) making lead payments.

The following annual interest rates and exchange rates are currently available.

	US dollar		*Sterling*	
	Deposit rate	*Borrowing rate*	*Deposit rate*	*Borrowing rate*
	%	%	%	%
1 month	7	10.25	10.75	14.00
3 months	7	10.75	11.00	14.25

	\$/£ exchange rate (\$ = £1)
Spot	1.8625 - 1.8635
1 month forward	0.60c - 0.58c pm
3 months forward	1.80c - 1.75c pm

Which is the cheapest method for Trumpton plc? Ignore commission costs. (The bank charges for arranging a forward contract or a loan.)

1.3 SOLUTION

The three choices must be compared on a similar basis, which means working out the cost of each to Trumpton either now or in three months time. Here the cost to Trumpton now will be determined.

Choice 1: the forward exchange market

1.4 Trumpton must buy dollars in order to pay the US supplier. The exchange rate in a forward exchange contract to buy \$4,000,000 in three months time (bank sells) is:

	\$
Spot rate	1.8625
Less 3 months premium	0.0180
Forward rate	1.8445

The cost of the \$4,000,000 to Trumpton in three months time will be:

$$\frac{\$4,000,000}{1.8445} = £2,168,609.38$$

1.5 This is the cost in three months. To work out the cost now, we could say that by deferring payment for three months, the company is:

(a) saving having to borrow money now at 14.25% a year to make the payment now; or
(b) avoiding the loss of interest on cash on deposit, earning 11% a year.

The choice between (a) and (b) depends on whether Trumpton plc needs to borrow to make any current payment (a) or is cash rich (b). Here, assumption (a) is selected, but (b) might in fact apply.

1.6 At an annual interest rate of 14.25% the rate for three months is approximately 14.25/4 = 3.5625%. The 'present cost' of £2,168,609.38 in three months time is:

$$\frac{£2,168,609.38}{1.035625} = £2,094,010.27$$

Choice 2: the money markets

1.7 Using the money markets involves:

(a) borrowing in the foreign currency, if the company will eventually receive the currency;
(b) lending in the foreign currency, if the company will eventually pay the currency.

Here, Trumpton will pay \$4,000,000 and so it would lend US dollars.

1.8 It would lend enough US dollars for three months, so that the principal repaid in three months time plus interest will amount to the payment due of \$4,000,000.

(a) Since the US dollar deposit rate is 7%, the rate for three months is approximately 7/4 = 1.75%.

(b) To earn $4,000,000 in three months time at 1.75% interest, Trumpton would have to lend now:

$$\frac{\$4,000,000}{1.0175} = \$3,931,203.93$$

1.9 These dollars would have to be purchased now at the spot rate of (bank sells) $1.8625. The cost would be:

$$\frac{\$3,931,203.93}{1.8625} = £2,110,713.52$$

By lending US dollars for three months, Trumpton is matching eventual receipts and payments in US dollars, and so has hedged against foreign exchange risk.

Choice 3: lead payments

1.10 Lead payments should be considered when the currency of payment is expected to strengthen over time, and is quoted forward at a premium on the foreign exchange market.

Here, the cost of a lead payment (paying $4,000,000 now) would be $4,000,000 ÷ 1.8625 = £2,147,651.01.

1.11 In this example, the costs are as follows.

	£
Forward exchange contract	2,094,010.27 (cheapest)
Currency lending	2,110,713.52
Lead payment	2,147,651.01

2 FUTURES

KEY TERM

Futures contract: a contract relating to currencies, commodities or shares that obliges the buyer (issuer) to purchase (sell) the specified quantity of the item represented in the contract at a pre-determined price at the expiration of the contract *(OT)*.

2.1 Futures are a form of forward contract, which give a fixed rate for (eg) security prices, or exchange rates, or interest rates, at a future date. Futures markets exist for commodities, including sugar, gold, silver, wool and coffee, and serve the useful function of permitting suppliers and consumers to plan on the basis of known future prices. Futures markets also exist for various financial instruments. We looked at the use of interest rate futures in Chapter 17. Here, we concentrate our attention on currency futures.

2.2 Unlike with forward exchange contracts, a currency futures position can be (and most often is) 'closed out' by selling the futures contract in the market to realise any profit or loss without actually taking delivery of the underlying currency. (For some other types of future, eg stock index futures, delivery is not possible). It may help to think of a futures contract as being like a 'bet' on how exchange rates or other prices will move: however, like other derivatives, futures are of use to those who wish to hedge (reduce risk) as well as those who seek speculative risk-taking opportunities.

2.3 The purchaser of a futures contract must deposit a sum as collateral for the contract, known as the **margin,** which might be in the form of a bank letter of credit, Treasury bills or cash.

Changes in value of the contract must also be paid for daily by means of the **variation margin**. The size of the variation margin will be extremely volatile.

KEY TERM

Financial futures: Contracts to purchase or to sell a standard quantity of a financial instrument at a specific date in the future.

2.4 **Financial futures** in foreign exchange rates are traded on some formal futures exchanges, such as the Chicago Mercantile (CME), which has offices in Chicago, New York, Washington, London and Tokyo, with a trading partner in the Singapore International Monetary Exchange (SIMEX). The specialist division of the CME for trading in currency (and interest rate) futures is called the International Monetary Market Division (IMM). The London International Financial Futures and Options Exchange (LIFFE) does not trade in currency futures, and so a UK company wishing to buy or sell currency futures would need to use a foreign exchange such as the CME. Traders in foreign exchange rate futures (often banks) are dealers in large sums of money, seeking a way of hedging against exchange risks.

2.5 **Currency futures** are contracts to buy or sell a quantity of a foreign currency at a future date, and so in this respect they are similar to forward exchange contracts. Unlike forward contracts, however:

(a) they can be reversed quite simply;

(b) they are for fixed amounts of currency (eg £25,000 for a future against the US dollar, DM 125,000 against the US dollar, Swiss francs SF 125,000 against US dollars etc);

(c) they are traded on a formal exchange;

(d) traders in futures have to put up 'margin money' - pay money 'up front' - to the clearers of the Exchange, to ensure that they meet their future obligations.

2.6 Currency futures contracts can be used in a similar way to the non-standardised forward exchange contract to hedge exchange risks, although it may not be possible to match the total value of contracts entered into with the amount involved in an actual transaction.

2.7 EXAMPLE: CURRENCY FUTURES

A UK importer buys goods from a US supplier for US$320,000. The purchase takes place on 21 March but the goods do not have to be paid for until 21 April. The spot rate of exchange on 21 March between sterling and the US dollar is £1 = $1.60.

The UK importer can hedge against the currency risk (the risk of a fall in the value of sterling against the dollar in the credit period) with currency futures. The expected cost of the purchase in sterling on 21 March is 320,000/1.60 = £200,000.

2.8 Sterling futures must be bought and sold in blocks of £25,000 and so the UK importer could sell eight sterling futures contracts at the current rate of US$1.60 = £1. To do this, the importer must deposit £1,000 per contract, or £8,000 in total.

2.9 Suppose that on 21 April, when the UK importer must pay the $320,000:

(a) the spot rate of exchange is £1 = $1.50;

(b) the rate at which sterling futures can be closed out is £1 = $1.51.

2.10 On 21 April, the importer will:

(a) buy US$320,000 spot for $1.5000, at a cost of $\frac{320,000}{1.50}$ = £213,333.33.

This is £13,333.33 more than was expected on 21 March;

(b) close out the futures contract at £1 = $1.5100. The value is £211,920.52 giving a realised profit of £11,920.52.

The importer's net position is as follows.

	£
Loss on fall in value of sterling from $1.60 to $1.50	(13,333.33)
Profit on futures	11,920.52
Net loss	(1,412.81)

The importer has therefore been able to hedge his position with futures for only a small net cost, which might be less than the cost of hedging with a forward exchange contract.

3 OPTIONS

The nature of an option

KEY TERM

An **option** is an agreement giving the right to buy or sell a specific quantity something (eg shares) at a known or determinable price within a stated period.

3.1 Pure options are financial instruments such as share options which are created by exchanges rather than by the company. As with other types of option, share options can be used by investors either as a means of speculation or as a means of risk reduction (hedging). The financial manager seeking to hedge exchange rate risk or interest rate risk is however more likely to come across currency options or interest rate options, and we now look at these in more detail. We looked at the use of interest rate options in Chapter 17. Now, we turn to currency options.

Currency options

3.2 There is a major drawback to forward exchange contracts as a means of managing foreign exchange risk. A forward exchange contract is an agreement to buy or sell a given quantity of foreign exchange, which must be carried out because it is a binding contract. Some exporters might be uncertain about the amount of currency they will earn in several months time, and so would be unable to enter forward exchange contracts without the risk of contracting to sell more or less currency to their bank than they will actually earn when the time comes. An alternative method of obtaining foreign exchange cover, which overcomes much of the problem, is the **currency option**.

KEY TERM

A **currency option** is an agreement involving an option, but not an obligation, to buy or to sell a certain amount of currency at a stated rate of exchange (the exercise price) at some time in the future.

3.3 The exercise price for the option may be the same as the current spot rate, or it may be more favourable or less favourable to the option holder than the current spot rate. Options are '**at-the-money**', '**in-the-money**' or '**out-of-the-money**' accordingly.

3.4 Companies can choose whether to buy:

(a) a tailor-made currency option from a bank, suited to the company's specific needs. These are **over-the-counter** (OTC) or **negotiated** options;

(b) a standard option, in certain currencies only, from an options exchange. Such options are **traded** or **exchange-traded** options.

3.5 As with other types of option, buying a currency option involves paying a premium, which is the most the buyer of the option can lose. Selling (or 'writing') options, unless covered by other transactions, is extremely risky because the seller ('writer') bears the whole of the cost of the variation and can face potentially unlimited losses. Such risks received much publicity with the Barings Bank failure in 1995.

3.6 Currency options are not the same as forward exchange option contracts, although the similarity in names might seem confusing. An option can be purchased by an importer or an exporter, giving him the right to buy or sell a given quantity of currency at a stated rate of exchange at a future date, typically after three months. Unlike a forward exchange contract, an option does not have to be exercised. Instead, when the date for exercising the option arrives, the importer or exporter can either exercise the option or let the option lapse.

KEY TERMS

There are two types of currency option, both of which can be bought and sold.

(a) **Call options** give the buyer of the option the right to buy the underlying currency at a fixed rate of exchange (and the seller of the option would be required to sell the underlying currency at that rate).

(b) **Put options** give the buyer of the option the right to sell the underlying currency at a fixed rate of exchange (and the seller of the option would be required to buy the underlying currency at that rate).

The purpose of currency options

3.7 The purpose of currency options is to reduce or eliminate exposure to currency risks, and they are particularly useful for companies in the following situations:

(a) where there is uncertainty about foreign currency receipts or payments, either in timing or amount. Should the foreign exchange transaction not materialise, the option can be sold on the market (if it has any value) or exercised if this would make a profit;

(b) to support the tender for an overseas contract, priced in a foreign currency;

(c) to allow the publication of price lists for its goods in a foreign currency;

(d) to protect the import or export of price-sensitive goods. If there is a favourable movement in exchange rates, options allow the importer/exporter to profit from the favourable change (unlike forward exchange contracts, when the importer/exporter is tied to a fixed rate of exchange by the binding contract). This means that the gains can be passed on in the prices to the importer's or exporter's customers.

In both situations (b) and (c), the company would not know whether it had won any export sales or would have any foreign currency income at the time that it announces its selling prices. It cannot make a forward exchange contract to sell foreign currency without becoming exposed in the currency.

3.8 EXAMPLE: CURRENCY OPTIONS

Tartan plc has been invited to tender for a contract in Blueland with the bid priced in Blues (the local currency). Tartan thinks that the contract would cost £1,850,000. Because of the fierce competition for the bid, Tartan is prepared to price the contract at £2,000,000, and since the exchange rate is currently B2.80 = £1, it puts in a bid of B5,600,000. The contract will not be awarded until after six months.

3.9 What can happen to Tartan with the contract? There are two possible outcomes.

(a) Tartan plc decides to hedge against the currency risk, and on the assumption that it will be awarded the contract in six months time, it enters into a forward exchange contract to sell B5,600,000 in six months time at a rate of B2.8 = £1.

As it turns out, the company fails to win the contract and so it must buy B5,600,000 spot to meet its obligation under the forward contract. The exchange rate has changed, say, to B2.5 = £1.

	£
At the outset:	
Tartan sells B5,600,000 forward at B2.8 to £1	2,000,000
Six months later:	
Tartan buys B5,600,000 spot to cover the hedge, at B2.5 to £1	(2,240,000)
Loss	(240,000)

(b) Alternatively, Tartan plc might decide not to make a forward exchange contract at all, but to wait and see what happens. As it turns out, Tartan is awarded the contract six months later, but by this time, the value of the Blue has fallen, say, to B3.2 = £1.

Question 1

Have a go at calculating the outcome, before looking at the calculation below.

	£
Tartan wins the contract for B5,600,000, which has a sterling value of (B3.2 = £1)	1,750,000
Cost of the contract	(1,850,000)
Loss	(100,000)

A currency option would, for a fixed cost, eliminate these risks for Tartan plc. When it makes its tender for the contract, Tartan might purchase a currency option to sell B5,600,000 in six months time at B2.8 to £1, at a cost of £40,000.

3.10 The worst possible outcome for Tartan plc is now a loss of £40,000.

(a) If the company fails to win the contract, Tartan will abandon the option (unless the exchange rate has moved in Tartan's favour and the Blue has weakened against sterling so that the company can make a profit by buying B5,600,000 at the spot ate and selling it at B2.8 = £1).

(b) If the company wins the contract and the exchange rate of the Blue has weakened against sterling, Tartan will exercise the option and sell the Blues at 2.80.

	£	£
Proceeds from selling B5,600,000		2,000,000
Cost of contract	1,850,000	
Cost of currency option	40,000	
		1,890,000
Net profit		110,000

(c) If the Blue has strengthened against sterling, Tartan will abandon the option. For example, if Tartan wins the contract and the exchange rate has moved to B2.5 = £1, Tartan will sell the B5,600,000 at this rate to earn £2,240,000, and will incur costs, including the abandoned currency option, of £1,890,000.

	£	£
Proceeds from selling B5,600,000		2,240,000
Cost of contract	1,850,000	
Cost of currency option	40,000	
		1,890,000
Net profit		350,000

The drawbacks of currency options

3.11 The major drawbacks of currency options are as follows.

- The cost, which depends on the expected volatility of the exchange rate.
- Options must be paid for as soon as they are bought.
- Tailor-made options lack negotiability.
- Traded options are not available in every currency.

Options compared with futures

3.12 In the case of futures, both parties to the contract have an obligation to complete the transaction. This is different from options, which will simply lapse and not be exercised if they are 'out of the money'. Buyers of options pay at the outset of the contract (in the premium) for the fact that they can thus avoid sustaining a loss on the option. With futures, in contrast, the buyer might win or lose.

A graphical approach to options

3.13 A graphical approach to options may help you to understand options more fully and may provide a means of illustrating options in answers to exam questions. The examples illustrated below generally refer to share prices. In the case of other types of option (eg index options or currency options), then it will be the value or price of the particular underlying investment (eg the stock index or the currency) which is relevant.

3.14 Figure 1 shows the position of a **call option holder**.

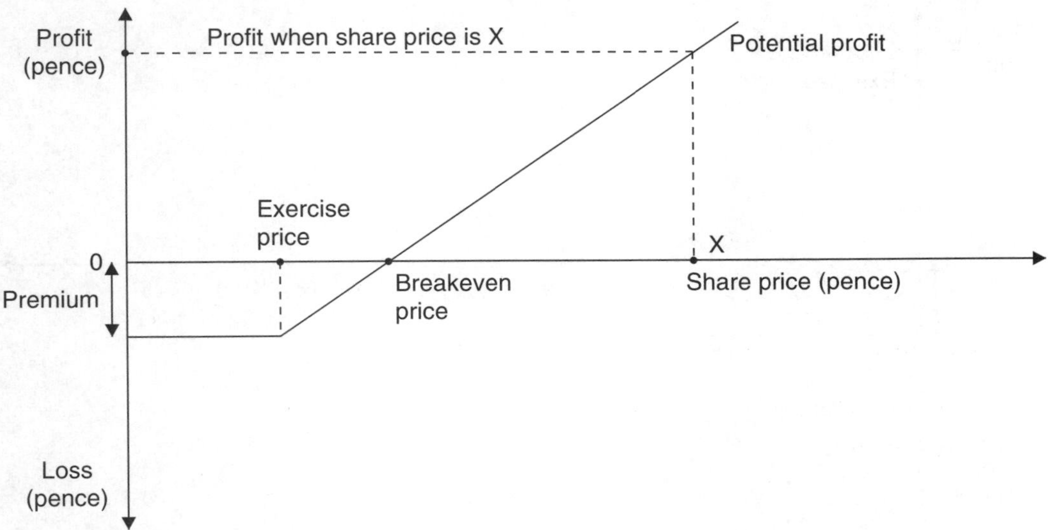

Figure 1 Call option holder ('long call position')

3.15 The holder of the call option will not exercise the option unless the share price is at least equal to the **exercise price** (or **strike price**) at the exercise date. If the share price is above that level, he can cut his losses (up to the break-even price) or make profits (if the share price is above the break-even price). Holding a call option is called having a **long position** in the option.

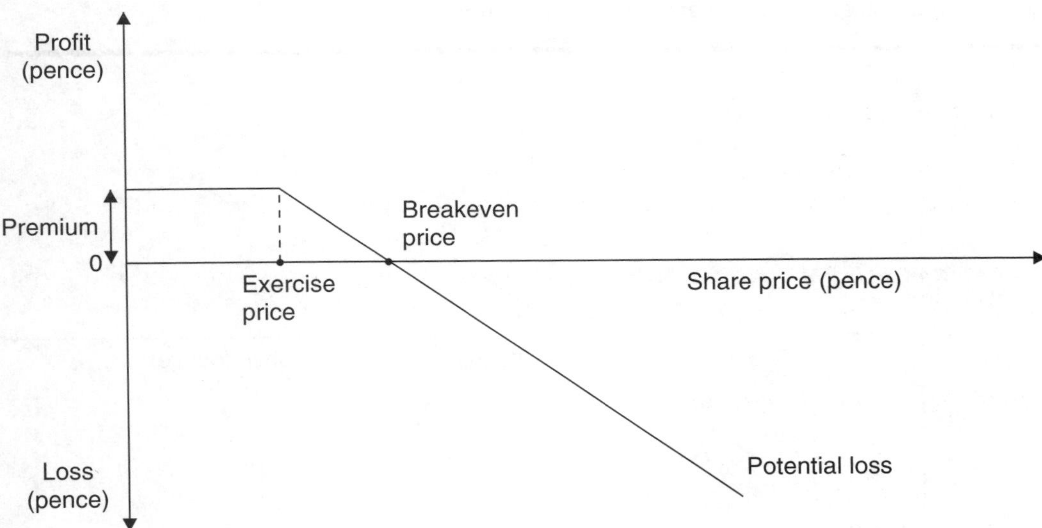

Figure 2 Call option writer ('short call position')

3.16 Any profit made by the holder of the option is reflected by the loss of the other party to the transaction - the writer of the option. Accordingly, Figure 2, illustrating the potential outcomes for the writer of the option, looks like a 'mirror image' of Figure 1. Selling or writing a call option is called taking a **short call position**. It can be seen from Figure 2 that the writer of the call option is exposed to potentially unlimited losses.

3.17 The position of the **buyer of a put option** is illustrated in Figure 3. The maximum potential profit is equal to the exercise price, which is the position if the share price falls to zero. Then, the put option holder has the option to sell worthless shares at the exercise price. You should be able to appreciate that the put option can be used to protect a holder of shares against a fall in their value. As Figure 3 shows, the loss on the option is limited to the size of the premium.

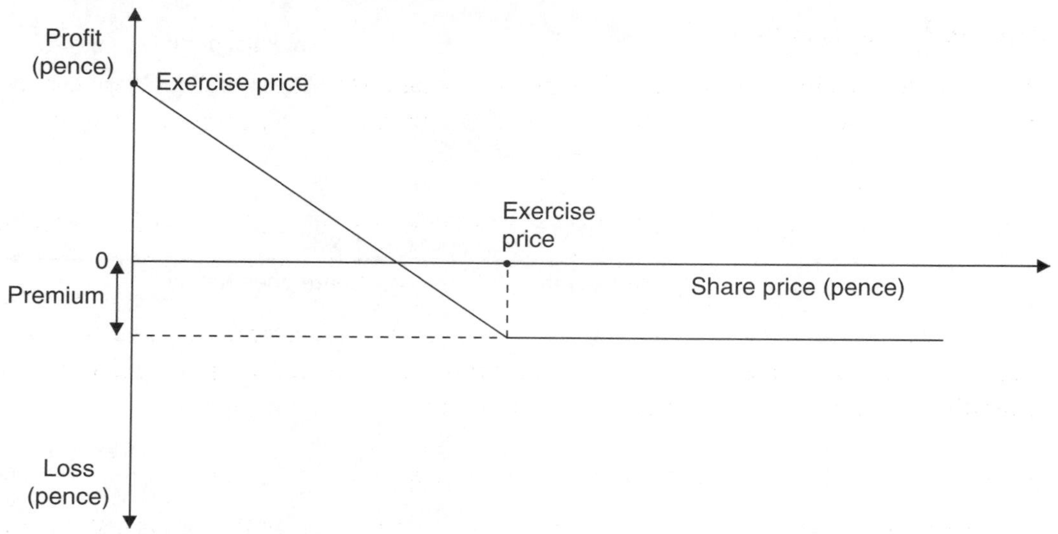

Figure 3 Put option holder ('long put position')

3.18 You will probably by now be able to guess what a graph illustrating the position of a put option writer will look like.

Question 2

See if you can sketch such a graph and then look at Figure 4.

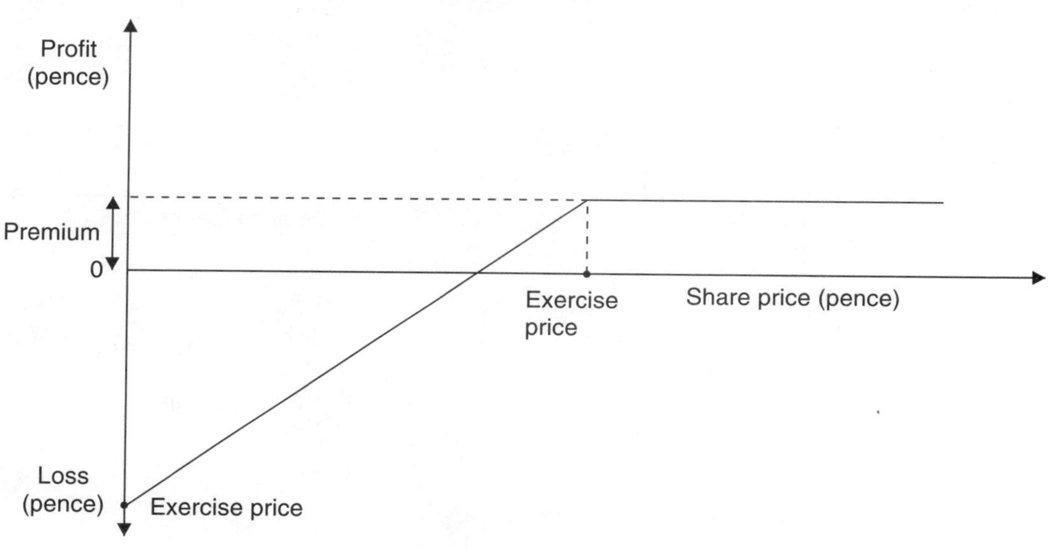

Figure 4 Put option writer ('short put position')

Question 3

Reasoning from what you have already learned about options, check that you can explain Figure 4. Note that the maximum loss for the writer or seller of the put option is the exercise price.

3.19 Figures 1 to 4 illustrate the basic positions which can be taken in options. It is also possible to combine different option positions in various ways, depending on the combination of risks and returns which are sought from different outcomes.

Time value and valuation of options

3.20 We need to consider the **time value of an option**. Holding a call option can be seen effectively as the deferred purchase of the underlying asset (eg shares), since the exercise price does not have to be paid until a later date.

3.21 The time value of an option will be affected by the level of interest rates. The higher the level of interest rates, the higher will be the value of the option as the present value of the exercise price of the option will be correspondingly lower. The longer the time to expiration, the higher will the value of the option be, as its present value will be lower. Furthermore, the longer is the period to expiration, the more opportunity there is for volatility in the markets to lead to higher share values.

3.22 We can illustrate the limits of valuation of options graphically (Figure 5).

(a) An upper limit to the value of an option is the value of the underlying share (or other asset). It will never be worthwhile to pay more for an option than the price of the asset which the option enables you to buy.

(b) The lower limit to the value of an option shown on Figure 5 represents the intrinsic value of the option - ie the extent to which it is 'in the money'. This lower limit is zero up to the exercise price and at higher share prices is the difference between the share price and the exercise price.

(c) In practice, the value of most options will lie somewhere between these limits, as illustrated by lines A, B and C in Figure 5.

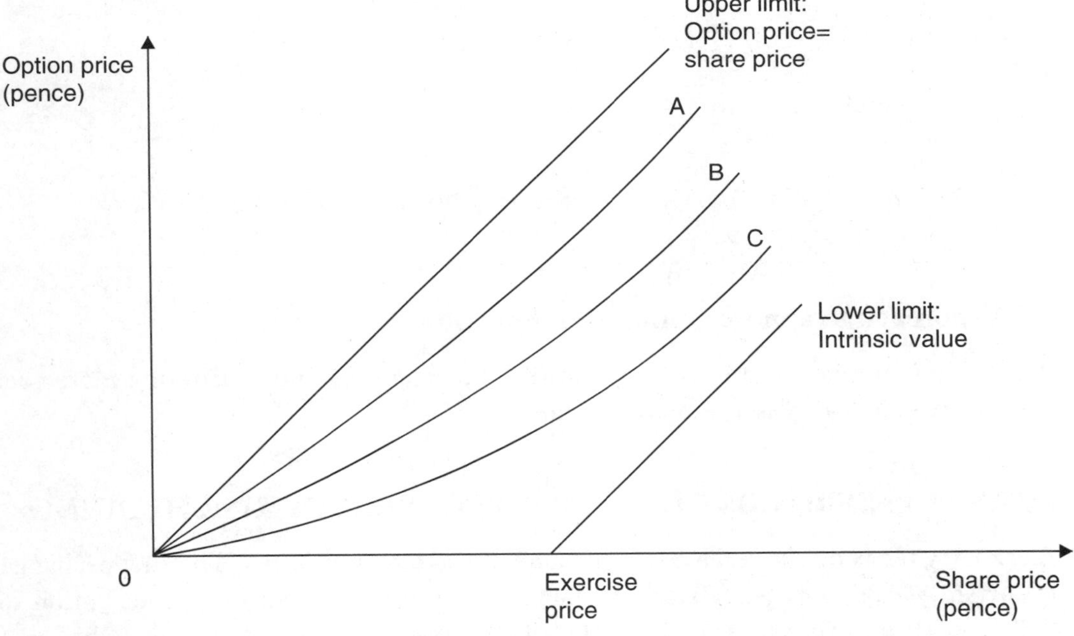

Figure 5 Limits to call option values

Graphical illustration of currency options

3.23 Above, we have used options on shares as the main type of example. A similar graphical approach can be used to illustrate other kinds of options, for example currency options.

Suppose that a UK-based company expects to receive an amount of export income in dollars ($) in three months' time. Figure 6 illustrates the profit/loss profile of different strategies.

(a) Selling dollars and buying sterling in the forward market eliminates all uncertainty. The outcome is represented by a horizontal line.

(b) Relying on the spot market results in a net gain or loss compared with the forward market if the spot exchange rate in three months' time turns out to be below or above $X per pound respectively.

(c) If a call option is used, it will not be exercised if the exchange rate is less than $X per pound. A currency call option reduces the potential gain compared with the spot market strategy (b) by the amount of the premium on the option, but has the advantage that potential losses are contained as they will not exceed the value of the premium.

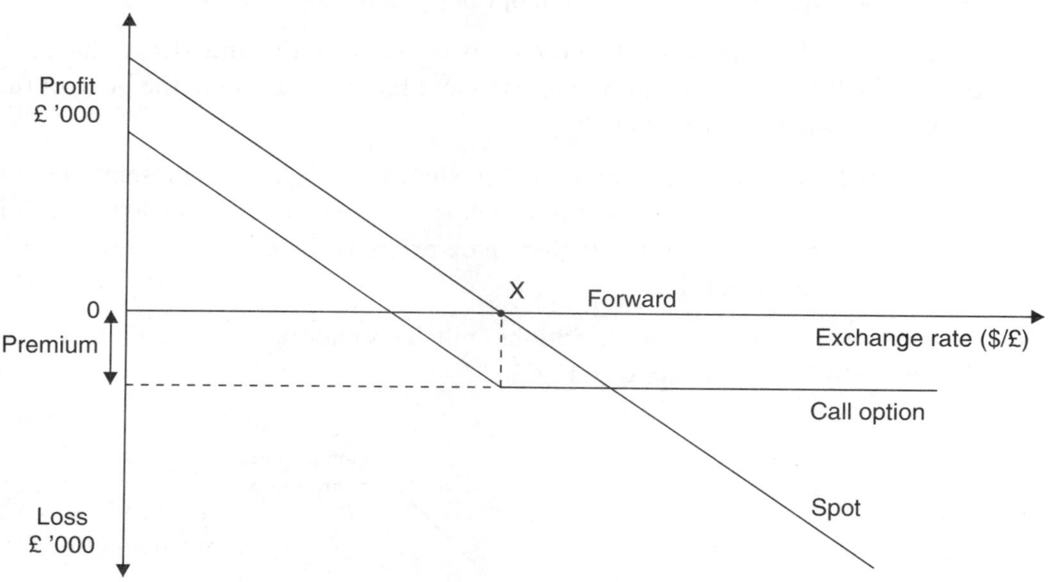

Figure 6 Currency call option, forward and spot markets: profit/loss profile

Graphical approach to a more complex option strategy

3.24 A graphical approach can also be helpful in understanding and illustrating more complex option strategies, such as a **zero cost collar**.

3.25 EXAMPLE: ZERO COST COLLAR FOR CURRENCY RISK HEDGING

Blackberry plc is due to receive US$ 400,000 in three months' time. The spot exchange rate is currently, say, 1.41 $/£. Blackberry plc chooses to purchase an OTC put option to sell dollars with an exercise price of $1.45 and a premium of 6 cents, exercisable in three months' time. At the same time, the company has the opportunity to **write** a put option to sell dollars to its bank at the lower rate of 1.40. If we assume that the premium on this latter option is also 6 cents, then the premium payable exactly matches the premium receivable, making the arrangement one of 'zero cost'.

3.26 The profit and loss profile for such an arrangement, illustrated in Figure 7, is called in option dealing jargon a **vertical bull spread** (one of the various terms for a variety of possible options dealing combinations).

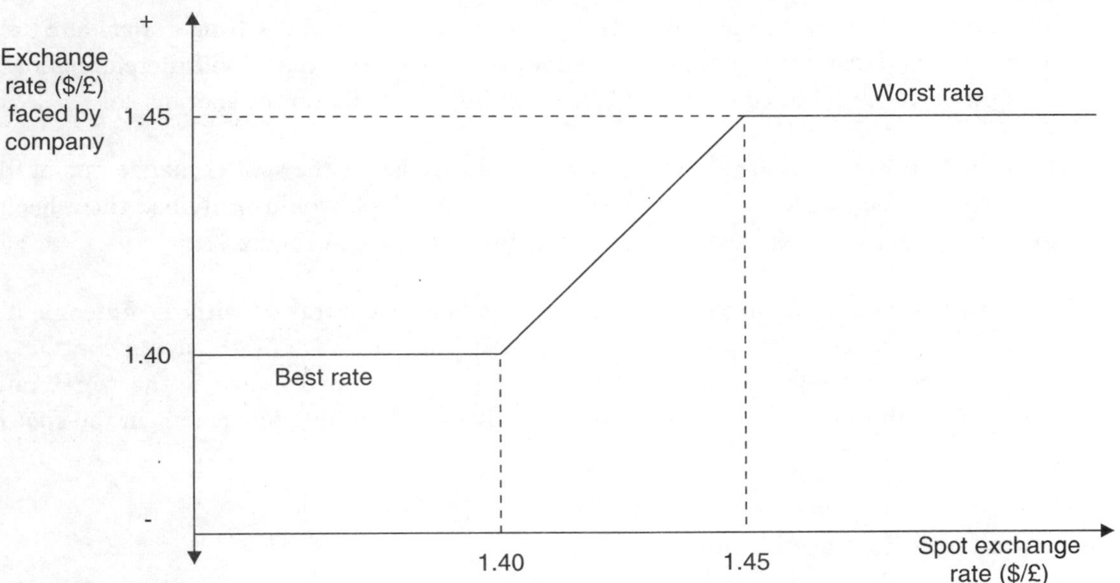

Figure 7 Vertical bull spread

3.27 Figure 7 illustrates the following points.

(a) If the spot exchange rate on expiry turns out to be between $1.40 and $1.45 to the pound, then the company will benefit from the favourable spot rate.

(b) The best rate which the company can receive from the arrangement is $1.40 while the worst it can receive is $1.45.

3.28 If the spot exchange rate is below $1.40 after the three month period has elapsed, then the bank will exercise its option to buy dollars from Blackberry plc at a rate of $1.40. Blackberry plc will thus have been prevented from taking advantage of the extent to which the $/£ exchange rate has fallen below $1.40. The company would allow its put option to lapse, since its exercise price of $1.45 is less favourable than the spot rate.

3.29 If the spot exchange rate is above $1.45, then the bank will allow its option to lapse since it could buy dollars at a more favourable rate in the spot market if it chooses to. Blackberry plc will choose to exercise its option and sell dollars at $1.45.

Question 4

Explain what the outcome will be if the spot exchange rate on expiry is between $1.40 and $1.45 to the pound. Consider whether each of Blackberry plc and the bank will exercise their options.

Answer

See the explanation below.

3.30 We have already noted that the company will benefit from the favourable spot rate if it falls between $1.40 and $1.45 to the pound. How is this so?

(a) The bank faces the choice between buying dollars at $1.40 to the pound by exercising the option or at a higher rate on the spot market. Therefore, the bank will allow the option to lapse.

(b) Blackberry plc faces the choice of exercising the option and selling dollars at $1.45 or selling dollars on the spot market at a lower rate. The company will therefore allow the option to lapse, preferring the choice of selling the dollar on the spot market.

3.31 Given that both options are allowed to lapse in the range for the spot exchange rate of $1.40 to $1.45, Blackberry plc then faces the exchange rate which would apply had there been no options contracts, as indicated by the 45° line for this range in Figure 7.

3.32 The **zero cost collar** employed by Blackberry plc may be contrasted with the outcome if the company had instead used a forward foreign exchange contract. With such a contract, the company would have faced a fixed single exchange rate, probably close to the 'worst' rate of $1.45 and would not be able to take advantage of any favourable movement in the spot rate below the forward rate.

Options theory and its applications

3.33 The widespread use of derivatives involving options has resulted in much attention being paid to the **valuation of options**. In this Study Text, we have looked at the use of interest rate and currency options in the hedging of interest rate risk and currency risk. Another common form of option is the share option, giving the right but not the obligation to buy or to sell a quantity of a company's shares at a specified price within a specified period.

3.34 Using share options as an example, the main variables which determine the value of a call option can be identified as:

(a) The current value of the share
(b) The exercise price of the option
(c) The time to expiry of the option
(d) Variability of the price of the share
(e) The risk-free rate of interest

3.35 Options theory can be applied to business decisions beyond the areas of financial instruments such as traded share options, currency options and interest rate options. The following are examples from the range of possible applications.

(a) **Convertible loan stock** provides a combination of a conventional loan with a call option. If the option is exercised, the loan is exchanged for a specified number of shares in the company.

(b) **Share warrants** provide the holder with an option to purchase shares from the company at a specified exercise price during a specified time period.

(c) **Government loan guarantees** effectively provide a put option to holders of risky loans, giving the holders an opportunity to exercise an option of obtaining reimbursement from the government if a borrower defaults.

(d) **Insurance** more generally is a form of put option which is exercised when an insurance claim is made.

(e) **Share purchase** at the prevailing market price can be seen as equivalent to the purchase of a call option combined with the sale of a put option, while putting the remaining amount on deposit at a risk-free rate of return over the option period.

(f) Option valuation theory which is used in valuing share options can be extended to various options which financial managers may meet in making **capital investment decisions.** We discuss this in more detail below.

Investments as options on future cash flows

Exam focus point

With effect from May 1998, a new topic on the syllabus has been the assessment of investments as options on future cash flows, including the option to abandon. Be prepared for this topic to be examined fairly early in the life of the new syllabus.

3.36 The application of option theory in the appraisal of capital investments is a relatively new development. To give one type of example, a business decision may amount to paying a specified price now - say, to develop a new production system - which gives the business wider flexibility in the future. Such a decision gives the business more **options** to exploit wider follow-on opportunities.

3.37 The most common types of 'real option' found in relation to capital projects are:

- The **option to make follow-on investments**: this is equivalent to a call option
- The **option to abandon** a project: equivalent to a put option
- The **option to wait** before making an investment: equivalent to a call option

Each of these types of scenario is discussed further below.

The value of follow-on investments

3.38 The discounted cash flow technique was originally developed for holdings of stocks and shares before being developed as a technique for investment appraisal. An investor in stocks and shares is usually a passive holder of assets, with no real influence over the interest or dividends paid on the asset. The managers of a business enterprise do not however 'hold' investment projects passively. Investing in a particular project may lead to other possibilities or options which managers can take advantage of, and which will not have been reflected in a conventional NPV analysis.

3.39 EXAMPLE: FOLLOW-ON INVESTMENTS AS OPTIONS

Cornseed Publishing Ltd is a publisher of study guides in a sector of the professional training market. Over the last ten years, it has built up a share of approximately 30% of its target market. The directors of the company are now considering a project which would involve producing its study guides on CD-ROM, to be called *CD Guides*. The new CD-ROMs would not simply duplicate the material in the study guides as they would involve some interactive features. However it is thought that in the future, *CD Guides* might be developed into a more innovative fully interactive format - provisionally called *CD Tutor* - which makes fuller use of the advantages of the CD-ROM format, but this would take much more time and would require greater software know-how than is currently available. The *CD Guides* project would involve employing additional staff to develop the CD-ROM material. It is thought that Cornseed's competitors are probably considering similar CD-ROM projects.

3.40 One of the directors, Mark Cornseed, has questioned whether the project is worthwhile. It has been calculated, using the NPV method, that the *CD Guides* project as proposed has a negative net present value of £50,000. 'Why invest in a negative NPV project?', he asks. 'CD-ROMs which are not fully interactive are not likely to be a success. Just because our competitors are putting money into them doesn't mean we should make the same mistake.'

3.41 Another director, Julia Cornseed, points out that if the project does not go ahead, Cornseed may be missing out on the opportunity to develop *CD Tutor.* If the *CD Guides* are developed, she argues, with the added expertise gained Cornseed will be able to pursue this follow-on option. It will have a 'call' on this follow-on investment: the option to 'buy' it at a future date, or alternatively not to buy it. The only downside is that the company, assuming it allows the option to lapse, is committing itself to a project with a negative NPV of £50,000. The possible upside is that, if conditions seem right at a future date for the *CD Tutor* option to be taken up, this follow-on project could be a great success.

3.42 The problem which now must be faced is that of putting a value on the option. In paragraph 3.39 above, we identified determinants of the value of a share option. Counterparts can be identified in valuing this follow-on investment, so that we could value the option in terms of:

(a) The present value of the future benefit streams of the follow-on project (counterpart to: the current value of the share)

(b) The initial cost of the follow-on project (counterpart to: the exercise price)

(c) The time within which the option must be exercised

(d) The variability of expected project returns (counterpart to: variability of the share price)

(e) The risk-free rate of interest

3.43 The formulae used to value options (such as the 'Black-Scholes model') are complex and you do not need to be able to use such formulae for the *SFM* exam. For our purposes, assume that a computer model shows that the follow-on investment *(CD Tutor)* has a value of £125,000. This reflects the fact that the project could be very profitable, but the company will not know if it is likely to be until the outcome of the *CD Guides* project is known. The *CD Guides* project carries an option value of £125,000 for an option 'premium' of £50,000 - the NPV of the initial project.

3.44 It needs to be borne in mind that quantifying the variables in valuing such investment options is not easy to do objectively. However, viewing strategic investment decisions from the 'options' perspective can offer insights to decision-makers. If the follow-on project is high-risk, this will **increase** the value of the call option. Analogously, the value of a share option is higher if the volatility of the share price is high.

The option to abandon

3.45 In the example above (Cornseed Publishing Ltd), we were looking at the valuation of an option to expand a business. Sometimes there is the converse problem - the value of an option to abandon a project.

3.46 It may be that a major capital investment cannot be abandoned. Once the initial investment is made, it may be impossible to do things differently. If the benefit streams from a project are highly uncertain, an option to abandon the project if things go wrong could be of great value.

3.47 The possibility of putting a value on the 'put' option of abandonment highlights the value of pursuing investments which offer flexibility. For example, a company may face a choice between:

(a) developing custom-designed plant to produce a single type of product; and
(b) buying lower-technology machine tools to produce the same product.

The NPV of Proposal (a) may be greater than the NPV for (b). But what if the product fails to sell? Abandonment in case (b) carries the value of a 'put' option, in that the company has the flexibility of using the low-technology equipment for other purposes.

The option to wait

3.48 A third type of option associated with investment decisions is the option to 'wait and see' in the expectation of gaining more relevant information before making a decision. This might seem like a justification for indefinite procrastination. The point to note is that, if we can make reasonable estimates of the determinants of the value of the option, then this could aid our strategic decision-making. Investments are rarely 'now-or-never' opportunities. More usually, there is some time period over which a project can be postponed, which corresponds to the period in which the option to invest can be exercised. During this period, new market information could emerge. Against this, we need to consider the cash inflows forgone in the period of postponement. Managers will need to balance this cost against the value of waiting.

Using computer models for practical option problems

3.49 As already mentioned, most practical option problems require the use of a computer model; using such a model effectively demands informed judgement. The binomial model for option valuation, for example, provides a basis for such a task and is basically a method of solving decision trees. The model involves starting at a future date and working back through the tree to the present time, determining the best future action at each decision point. Eventually, the various possible cash flows generated by future events are related back to establish a present value. In practice, such decision trees tend to be extremely complex: hence the need for computer power to solve them.

3.50 The application of option pricing theory such as the binomial model allows discounting to be carried out within decision trees. Standard discounted cash flow methods do not work within decision trees: there can be no single constant discount rate for options because the risk of the option changes as time progresses and the price of underlying assets change. Therefore, the market value of the future cash flows described by the decision tree needs to be calculated by option pricing methods.

4 SWAPS 11/96, 5/97

KEY TERM

A **swap** is 'an arrangement whereby two organisations contractually agree to exchange payments on different terms, eg in different currencies, or one at a fixed rate and the other at a floating rate' (*OT*).

4.1 We discussed the use of interest rate swaps in Chapter 17. Now we consider currency swaps.

Currency swaps

4.2 In a **currency swap**, the parties agree to swap equivalent amounts of currency for a period. This effectively involves the exchange of debt from one currency to another. As with interest rate swaps (discussed below), liability on the principal is not transferred and the parties are liable to counterparty risk: if the other party defaults on the agreement to pay

interest, the original borrower remains liable to the lender. This can present complicated legal problems, and some borrowers are unwilling to get involved in swap transactions for this reason.

4.3 The company should be able to obtain interest rates which are lower than it could get from a bank or from other investors, and may be able to structure the timing of payments so as to improve the matching of cash outflows with revenues. Swaps are easy to arrange and are flexible since they can be arranged in any size and are reversible. Transaction costs are low, only amounting to legal fees, since there is no commission or premium to be paid.

(a) The main benefit to the company is that it can gain access to debt finance in another country and currency where it is little known, and consequently has a poorer credit rating, than in its home country. It can therefore take advantage of lower interest rates than it could obtain if it arranged the loan itself.

(b) A further purpose of currency swaps is to restructure the currency base of the company's liabilities. This may be important where the company is trading overseas and receiving revenues in foreign currencies, but its borrowings are denominated in the currency of its home country. Currency swaps therefore provide a means of reducing exchange rate exposure.

(c) A third benefit of currency swaps is that at the same time as exchanging currency, the company may also be able to convert fixed rate debt to floating rate or vice versa. Thus it may obtain some of the benefits of an interest rate swap in addition to achieving the other purposes of a currency swap.

(d) A currency swap could be used to absorb excess liquidity in one currency which is not needed immediately, to create funds in another where there is a need.

4.4 A simple example would be one in which a UK company agrees with a US company to swap capital amounts at an agreed rate of exchange. Suppose a UK company is selling satellite equipment to NASA in the USA but will not be paid (in US dollars) for two years. The UK company could agree with another company to swap capital at an agreed rate of exchange in two years' time. The UK company will give the counterparty US dollars and receive sterling in return.

4.5 Consider a UK company X with a subsidiary in France which owns vineyards. Assume a spot rate of £1 = 10 French francs. Suppose the parent company wishes to raise a loan of 10 million French francs for the purpose of buying another French wine company. At the same time, the French subsidiary Y wishes to raise £1 million to pay for new up-to-date capital equipment imported from the UK. The UK parent company X could borrow the £1 million sterling and the French subsidiary Y could borrow the 10 million francs, each effectively borrowing on the other's behalf. This is known as a back-to-back loan.

KEY TERM

Back-to-back loan: a form of financing, whereby money borrowed in one country or currency is covered by lending an equivalent amount in another *(OT)*.

4.6 A variation on currency swaps is '**international interest arbitrage financing**' or **arbiloans**. This can be of value for an enterprise which operates in a country where interest rates are high and credit is hard to obtain. A subsidiary in a low-interest country borrows the amount required, converting it into the domestic currency of the parent company at the spot rate. The UK parent signs an agreement to repay the amount in the foreign currency at the end of the term, and purchases a forward contract for repayment at the same date.

4.7 In practice, most currency swaps are conducted between banks and their customers. An agreement may only be necessary if the swap were for longer than, say, one year.

4.8 EXAMPLE: HEDGING STRATEGY USING A SWAP

Adventurer Ltd, a UK company, is considering a contract to supply a telephone system to Blueland Telecom. All operating cash flows would be in the local currency, the Blue, as follows.

Time from start	*Cash flow*
	Blues
0	(700,000)
6 months	(400,000)
12 months	1,800,000

4.9 Because of high inflation in Blueland, the directors of Adventurer Ltd are very concerned about foreign exchange risk. However, the only available form of cover is a currency swap at a fixed rate of 9 Blues to the pound, for 1,100,000 Blues, to take effect in full at the start of the project and to last for a full year. The interest rate chargeable on the Blues would be 18% a year. This compares to a UK opportunity cost of capital for Adventurer Ltd of 22%.

4.10 The alternative to the swap is to convert between sterling and Blues at the spot rate, currently 10 Blues to the pound. The Blue floats freely on world currency markets. Inflation in Blueland and the UK over the year for which the project will last is forecast to be as follows.

UK	*Blueland*	*Probability*
%	%	
2	10	0.2
3	30	0.3
4	70	0.5

Required

Show whether or not Adventurer Ltd should use the available swap. Do not discount receipts and payments to a single time.

4.11 SOLUTION

The first step is to calculate the exchange rate in each of the different inflation scenarios. The rates can be found if we assume purchasing power parity between the two countries. Then, with inflation rates expressed as decimals:

$$\text{Exchange rate after a year} = \text{current spot rate} \times \frac{1+\text{Blueland inflation rate}}{1+\text{UK inflation rate}}$$

$$\text{Exchange rate after six months} = \text{current spot rate} \times \sqrt{\frac{1+\text{Blueland inflation rate}}{1+\text{UK inflation rate}}}$$

Month	Inflation Blueland	Inflation UK	Exchange rate B/£
0			10.00
6	0.10	0.02	10.38
12	0.10	0.02	10.78
0			10.00
6	0.30	0.03	11.23
12	0.30	0.03	12.62
0			10.00
6	0.70	0.04	12.79
12	0.70	0.04	16.35

4.12 The expected values will not be calculated since these have little real meaning. Instead, the swap will be evaluated using the currency markets for each of the three scenarios. The effects of the exchange rate on the investments and returns can now be calculated. It is assumed that Adventurer Ltd will have to borrow funds in the UK to finance the deal, and therefore interest will be calculated at the opportunity cost of funds, 22%. The interest rate for six months will be $\sqrt{1.22} - 1 = 0.1045 = 10.45\%$.

(a) **Using the currency markets**

(i) Inflation rates 2% and 10%:

	Blues	£	Interest £
Investment - month 0	(700,000)	(70,000)	(15,400)
Investment - month 6	(400,000)	(38,536)	(4,027)
		(108,536)	(19,427)
Interest		(19,427)	
Total cost		(127,963)	
Price received	1,800,000	166,976	
Net profit/(loss)		39,013	

(ii) Inflation rates 3% and 30%:

	Blues	£	Interest £
Investment - month 0	(700,000)	(70,000)	(15,400)
Investment - month 6	(400,000)	(35,619)	(3,722)
		(105,619)	(19,122)
Interest		(19,122)	
Total cost		(124,741)	
Price received	1,800,000	142,631	
Net profit/(loss)		17,890	

(iii) Inflation rates 4% and 70%:

	Blues	£	Interest £
Investment - month 0	(700,000)	(70,000)	(15,400)
Investment - month 6	(400,000)	(31,274)	(3,268)
		(101,274)	(18,668)
Interest		(18,668)	
Total cost		(119,942)	
Price received	1,800,000	110,092	
Net profit/(loss)		(9,850)	

(b) **Using the currency swap**

Adventurer Ltd will have to borrow sterling funds in the UK to finance the swap. The cost of funds in the UK is 22%. However, swaps involve the transfer of interest rate liabilities as well as of principal, and therefore the interest cost will be calculated at the swap rate of 18%.

It is assumed that no interest will be earned on the 400,000 Blues which will be lying idle until month 6. The sterling investment required before interest is £1,100,000/9 = £122,222.

The price received will depend on the inflation rates. 1,100,000 Blues will be at the swap rate of 9 Blues to the pound, yielding £122,222, equal to the initial sterling outlay; the balance (700,000 Blues) will be at the prevailing year end rate. The sterling value of interest payments (198,000 Blues) will also depend on the exchange rate. It is assumed that no interest will be paid until the end of the year.

Inflation rates	*Spot rate receipts*	*Interest*	*Profit*	*Profit/(loss) without swap*
	£'000	£'000	£'000	£'000
2% and 10%	64,935	18,367	46,568	39,013
3% and 30%	55,468	15,689	39,779	17,890
4% and 40%	42,813	12,110	30,703	(9,850)

4.13 Whatever the inflation rates, Adventurer Ltd will make a bigger profit with the swap than without it. It should therefore use the swap.

Chapter roundup

- A variety of financial instruments are available for reducing exposure to exchange rate risk. The markets for hedging instruments such as **futures**, **options** and **swaps** have undergone huge growth in recent years. Futures contracts have the practical disadvantage that they are for standardised amounts.
- Financial managers and strategists can use **options theory** in a variety of situations. However, where there is no market for the option concerned, such as there is with traded options, the exercise is likely to be a more subjective one involving a greater level of estimation to be made of the different factors affecting the value of the option.

Quick quiz

1. What are futures? (see para 2.1)
2. Define a currency future. (2.5)
3. What is a currency option and when might it be used? (3.2, 3.7)
4. Distinguish between a 'call option' and a 'put option' in the case of a currency option. (3.6)
5. Sketch a graph showing the position of a call option writer ('short call position'). (3.15)
6. Give examples of investment appraisal decision scenarios which could be viewed as call options. (3.37)
7. What are the benefits of a currency swap? (4.3)

Question to try	Level	Marks	Time
23	Exam standard	20	36 mins

Chapter 24

MULTINATIONAL OPERATIONS AND OVERSEAS TRADE

	Chapter topic list	Syllabus reference	Ability required
1	Multinational investment	13 d(iv)	Application
2	Financing overseas subsidiaries	13 d(iv)	Application
3	Obtaining returns from subsidiaries	13 d(iv)	Application
4	Reducing bad debt risk in foreign trade	13 d(iv)	Application
5	Countertrade	13 d(iv)	Application

Introduction

In this chapter, we examine the different **types of entity** which are available for international operations by a company. We also discuss various problems which companies face in relation to **foreign direct investment (FDI)** and **foreign trade**.

Exam focus point

Part of a question on appraisal of an international investment could ask you to discuss some of the issues covered in this chapter.

1 MULTINATIONAL INVESTMENT 11/95, 5/97

1.1 A **multinational company** or enterprise is one which owns or controls production facilities or subsidiaries or service facilities outside the country in which it is based. Thus, a company does not become 'multinational' simply by virtue of exporting or importing products: **ownership and control of facilities abroad** is involved.

The size and significance of multinationals

1.2 Multinational enterprises range from medium-sized companies having only a few facilities (or 'affiliates') abroad to giant companies having an annual turnover larger than the gross national product (GNP) of some smaller countries of the world. Indeed, the largest (the US multinationals Ford, General Motors and Exxon) each have a turnover larger than the GNPs of all but 14 countries of the world.

1.3 The size and significance of multinationals is increasing. Many companies in 'middle-income' countries such as Singapore are now becoming multinationals, and the annual growth in output of existing multinationals is in the range 10-15%.

1.4 The extensive activities of multinational enterprises, particularly the larger ones, raises questions about the problems of controlling them. Individual governments may be largely powerless if multinationals are able to exploit the tax regimes of 'tax haven' countries through transfer pricing policies or if the multinationals' production is switched from one country to another.

1.5 Most of the two-way traffic in investment by multinational companies ('foreign direct investment' or FDI) is between the developed countries of the world. While the present pattern of FDI can be traced back to the initial wave of investment in Europe by the USA following the Second World War, more recently Europe and Japan have become substantial overseas investors.

Changes in the pattern of FDI

1.6 There have been significant changes affecting the pattern of multinationals' activities over the last twenty years or so.

(a) The **destination countries** have changed. The focus has shifted from Canada and Latin America in the days when the USA was the major source of FDI to other areas, including the countries of South East Asia which receive significant direct investment from Japanese companies in particular. The group of 'newly industrialised countries' (NICs) - Taiwan, South Korea, the Philippines, Brazil and Mexico - have become significant recipients of FDI. For example, Taiwan's five largest electronic exporters are all US-owned companies.

(b) **Centralised control of production activities** within multinationals has increased, prompted partly by the need for strategic management of production planning and worldwide resource allocation. This process of centralisation has been facilitated by the development of sophisticated worldwide computer and telecommunications links.

Globalisation

1.7 Developments in international capital markets have provided an environment conducive to FDI. **Globalisation** describes the process by which the capital markets of each country have become internationally integrated. The process of integration is facilitated by improved telecommunications and the deregulation of markets in many countries (for example, the UK stock market's so-called Big Bang of 1986).

1.8 Securities issued in one country can now be traded in capital markets around the world. For example, shares in UK companies are traded in the USA. The shares are bought by US banks, which then issue ADRs (American depository receipts) which are a form in which foreign shares can be traded in US markets without a local listing.

1.9 For companies planning international investment activities, easy access to large amounts of funds denominated in foreign currencies can be very useful. Such funds are available in the eurocurrency markets, whose continued expansion during the 1980s, although slower than during the 1970s, encouraged FDI. The eurocurrency markets can also help to bypass official constraints on international business activities.

Reasons for undertaking FDI

1.10 FDI provides an alternative to growth restricted to a firm's domestic market. A firm might develop horizontally in different countries, replicating its existing operations on a global basis. Vertical integration might have an international dimension through FDI to acquire raw material or component sources overseas (backwards integration) or to establish final production and distribution in other countries (forward integration). Diversification might alternatively provide the impetus to developing international interests.

1.11 The **reasons** for foreign direct investment have changed over recent years. Previously the rationale may have been to supply local markets abroad or to exploit natural resources situated in the foreign country. Now FDI is likely to take place in the context of a worldwide corporate strategy which takes account of relative costs and revenues, tax considerations and **process specialisation** (specialisation of processes within particular production facilities). For example, some motor vehicle manufacturers locate labour-intensive processes in lower wage countries, leaving the final stage of the production process to be located nearer the intended market.

1.12 Different forms of expansion overseas are available to meet various strategic objectives.

(a) Firms may expand by means of new **'start-up' investments**, for example in manufacturing plants. This does allow flexibility, although it may be slow to achieve, expensive to maintain and slow to yield satisfactory results.

(b) A firm might **take over or merge with established firms abroad**. This provides a means of purchasing market information, market share and distribution channels. If speed of entry into the overseas market is a high priority, then acquisition may be preferred to start-up. However, enterprises available for takeover tend to be those which have high debt gearing, poor market performance and poor management. The better acquisitions will only be available at a premium.

(c) A **joint venture** with a local overseas partner might be entered into. A joint venture may be defined as 'the commitment, for more than a very short duration, of funds, facilities and services by two or more legally separate interests to an enterprise for their mutual benefit'. Different forms of joint venture are distinguished below.

Joint ventures

1.13 The two distinct types of joint venture are **industrial co-operation (contractual)**, and **joint-equity**. A contractual joint venture is for a fixed period and the duties and responsibility of the parties are contractually defined. A joint-equity venture involves investment, is of no fixed duration and continually evolves.

1.14 There is a growing trend towards a contractual form of joint venture as a consequence of the high research and development costs and the 'critical mass' necessary to take advantage of economies of scale in industries such as automobile engineering. Contractual joint ventures have become a common means of establishing a presence in the newly emerging mixed economies of Eastern Europe. As well as in the car industry, this form of joint venture is common in the aerospace industry. A joint-equity venture may however be the only way of establishing a presence in countries where full foreign ownership is discouraged, such as Nigeria, Japan and some Middle Eastern countries.

Alternatives to FDI

1.15 **Exporting** and **licensing** stand as alternatives to FDI. **Exporting** may be direct selling by the firm's own export division into the overseas markets, or it may be indirect through agents, distributors, trading companies and various other such channels. **Licensing** involves conferring rights to make use of the licensor company's production process on producers located in the overseas market in return for royalty payments.

1.16 Exporting may be unattractive because of tariffs, quotas or other import restrictions in overseas markets, and local production may be the only feasible option in the case of bulky products such as cement and flat glass. Licensing can allow fairly rapid penetration of overseas markets and has the advantage that substantial financial resources will not be required. Many multinationals use a combination of various methods of servicing international markets, depending on the particular circumstances.

Foreign subsidiaries

1.17 The basic structure of many multinationals consists of a parent company (a holding company) with subsidiaries in several countries. The subsidiaries may be wholly owned or just partly owned, and some may be owned through other subsidiaries. For example a UK parent company could own the holding company of a US group. Large multinationals have many subsidiaries in a large number of different countries and many of them are household names, for example Ford and Unilever.

The purpose of setting up subsidiaries abroad

1.18 The following are some reasons why a parent company might want to set up subsidiary companies in other countries.

(a) **The location of markets**. If, say, there is a big market in Australia for the products of a UK company, it might be cheaper for the UK company to establish a manufacturing subsidiary in Australia, in order to save the costs of shipping finished goods from the UK to Australia.

(b) **The need for a sales organisation**. Some subsidiaries are not manufacturing subsidiaries, but provide a sales and marketing organisation in their country for the parent company's goods. For example, a US parent company might set up a subsidiary in the UK, in order to sell goods in the UK which are shipped over from the USA.

(c) **The opportunity to produce goods more cheaply**. If labour costs are much lower in one country than in another, it might be profitable for a multinational to set up a manufacturing subsidiary in the low-cost country, provided that the labour force in that country has the skills that are needed to produce good quality output. For example, a UK company might design a new type of computer and set up a subsidiary in the Far East, where labour costs are lower, to manufacture the computers. They would then be shipped to the UK for sale in the UK market.

(d) **The need to avoid import controls**. When a country has regulations which restrict the import of certain goods, or impose high tariffs on imports, a multinational might decide to set up a manufacturing subsidiary in that country.

(e) **The need to obtain access to raw materials**, particularly in less developed countries (LDCs).

(f) **The availability of grants and tax concessions**.

1.19 Whatever the reason for setting up subsidiaries abroad, the aim is to increase the profits of the multinational's parent company. However there are different approaches to increasing profits that the multinational might take.

(a) At one extreme, the parent company might choose to get as much money as it can from the subsidiary, and as quickly as it can. This would involve the transfer of all or most of the subsidiary's profits to the parent company.

(b) At the other extreme, the parent company might encourage a foreign subsidiary to develop its business gradually, to achieve long-term growth in sales and profits. To encourage growth, the subsidiary would be allowed to retain a large proportion of its profits, instead of remitting the profits to the parent company. A further consequence is that the economy of the country in which the subsidiary operates should be improved, with higher output adding to the country's gross domestic product and increasing employment.

The risks of multinationals

1.20 Multinational companies, like any other companies, must accept the normal risks of business. However, compared with companies that trade entirely within one country, and even with companies that export from their base in one country, multinationals face additional risks, some of which we have already examined in earlier chapters of this Study Text.

1.21 To summarise, the main risks are as follows.

(a) **Foreign exchange risks.** As we have already seen, any company that exports or imports faces the risk of higher costs or lower revenues because of adverse movements in foreign exchange rates. Multinationals that trade between one country and another therefore face this risk. A company that owns assets in different countries (subsidiaries abroad) faces the risk of accounting losses due to adverse movements in exchange rates causing a fall in the value of those assets, as expressed in domestic currency.

(b) **Political risks and country risks.** A multinational can face risks of economic or political measures being taken by governments, affecting the operations of its subsidiaries abroad (see below).

(c) **Geographical separation.** The geographical separation of the parent company from its subsidiaries adds to the problems of management control of the group of companies as a whole.

KEY TERMS

Foreign exchange risk: risk of adverse movements in exchange rates affecting anticipated foreign exchange transactions.

Political risk: the risk that political action will affect the position and value of a company.

Country risk: the risk associated with undertaking transactions with, or holding assets in, a particular country. Sources of risk might be political, economic or regulatory instability affecting overseas taxation, repatriation of profits, nationalisation, currency instability etc (*OT*).

Government intervention

1.22 As stated above, when a multinational company invests in another country, by setting up a subsidiary, it may face a political risk of action by that country's government which restricts the multinational's freedom. The government of a country will almost certainly want to encourage the development and growth of commerce and industry, but it might also be suspicious of the motives of multinationals which set up subsidiaries in their country, perhaps fearing exploitation. The government might offer incentives to encourage new investment from abroad, for example by offering cash grants towards the building of factories or the purchase of equipment.

1.23 On the other hand, the government might try to prevent the exploitation of the country by multinationals, and the various measures it might take include the following.

(a) Import quotas could be used to limit the quantities of goods that a subsidiary can buy from its parent company and import for resale in its domestic markets.

(b) Import tariffs could make imports (such as from parent companies) more expensive and domestically produced goods therefore more competitive.

(c) Legal standards of safety or quality could be imposed on imported goods to prevent multinationals from selling goods through their subsidiary which have been banned as dangerous in other countries.

(d) Exchange control regulations could be applied (see below).

(e) A government could restrict the ability of foreign companies to buy domestic companies, especially those that operate in politically sensitive industries such as defence contracting, communications, energy supply and so on.

(f) A government could nationalise foreign-owned companies and their assets (with or without compensation to the parent company).

(g) A government could insist on a minimum shareholding in companies by residents. This would force a multinational to offer some of the equity in a subsidiary to investors in the country where the subsidiary operates.

Exchange controls

1.24 Exchange controls restrict the flow of foreign exchange into and out of a country, usually to defend the local currency or to protect reserves of foreign currencies. Exchange controls are generally more restrictive in developing and less developed countries although some still exist in developed countries. Typically, a government might enforce regulations:

(a) rationing the supply of foreign exchange. Anyone wishing to make payments abroad in a foreign currency will be restricted by the limited supply, which stops them from buying as much as they want from abroad;

(b) restricting the types of transaction for which payments abroad are allowed, for example by suspending or banning the payment of dividends to foreign shareholders, such as parent companies in multinationals, who will then have the problem of **blocked funds**.

KEY TERM

Blocked funds: funds affected by government regulations restricting flows of money out of a country.

Question

A management journal expressed (in 1989) the opinion that 'British investors have been bidding high for the acquisition of US companies. They are speculating on a scenario that an improved dollar will make the assets of those companies and the profit streams derived from them look cheap in the future.'

Required

Explain the above statement and discuss its validity, assuming that the exchange rate at the time of a particular acquisition was $1.50 = £1.

Answer

Consider a UK investor who is considering the purchase of a US company when the exchange rate is $1.50 = £1. The US company might cost $3,000,000 and generate annual income of $300,000. The cost would therefore be £2,000,000, and at present rates the annual income would be £200,000, a return of 10%.

If the dollar strengthened, so that the exchange rate became $1 = £1, the annual income would become £300,000, but the initial investment, having already been made at the old exchange rate, would be unaffected. The rate of return would thus rise to 15%.

While the calculations are sound, the statement in the question does not set out an easy way to achieve very high returns. Firstly, exchange rates are unpredictable; if the dollar weakened, the return on the sterling investment would fall rather than rise. Secondly, the sterling investment must be financed. It may well be that interest rates on sterling borrowings are higher than corresponding rates on US dollar borrowings, to reflect the scope for profitable investment overseas. This point will apply however the investment is to be financed, as high rates on borrowings imply high rates forgone on surplus cash not invested in the UK, and also high required rates of return on equity.

2 FINANCING OVERSEAS SUBSIDIARIES

2.1 The parent company will be largely financed in much the same way as any other large company, with share capital and reserves, loan capital and some short-term finance. But there are some differences in methods of financing:

(a) the parent company itself;
(b) the foreign subsidiaries.

2.2 The **parent company** itself is more likely than companies which have no foreign interests to raise finance in a foreign currency, or in its home currency from foreign sources.

2.3 The need to finance a **foreign subsidiary** raises the following questions.

(a) How much equity capital should the parent company put into the subsidiary?

(b) Should the subsidiary be allowed to retain a large proportion of its profits, to build up its equity reserves, or not?

(c) Should the parent company hold 100% of the equity of the subsidiary, or should it try to create a minority shareholding, perhaps by floating the subsidiary on the country's domestic stock exchange?

(d) Should the subsidiary be encouraged to borrow as much long term debt as it can, for example by raising large bank loans? If so, should the loans be in the domestic currency of the subsidiary's country, or should it try to raise a foreign currency loan?

(e) Should the subsidiary be encouraged to minimise its working capital investment by relying heavily on trade credit?

2.4 The method of financing a subsidiary will give some indication of the nature of the investment that the parent company is prepared to make. A sizeable equity investment (or long-term loans from the parent company to the subsidiary) would indicate a long-term investment by the parent company. In contrast, when a subsidiary is financed largely by debt capital and short-term liabilities (even if the trade creditor is the parent company, for goods supplied by the parent to the subsidiary), this would indicate a short-term investment policy.

2.5 When a UK company wishes to finance operations overseas, there may be a currency (foreign exchange) risk arising from the method of financing used. For example, if a UK company decides on an investment in the USA, to be financed with a sterling loan:

(a) the investment will provide returns in US dollars;
(b) the investors (the lenders) will want returns paid in sterling.

If the US dollar falls in value against sterling, the sterling value of the project's returns will also fall.

2.6 To reduce or eliminate the currency risk of an overseas investment, a company might finance it with funds in the same currency as the investment. The advantages of borrowing in the same currency as an investment are as follows.

(a) Assets and liabilities in the same currency can be matched, thus avoiding exchange losses on conversion in the group's annual accounts.

(b) Revenues in the foreign currency can be used to repay borrowings in the same currency, thus eliminating losses due to fluctuating exchange rates.

3 OBTAINING RETURNS FROM SUBSIDIARIES

Transfer pricing

3.1 When a foreign subsidiary makes a profit, the profit will be included in the total profits of the multinational group. The management of the parent company must decide, however:

(a) how the total profit of the group should be divided between the parent company and each of its subsidiaries, which is likely to depend on the transfer prices adopted;

(b) how the parent company should obtain the cash returns that it wants from each of its subsidiaries.

3.2 An example will show how shares of profits can be manipulated by accounting methods.

(a) Suppose that a US parent company ships some goods to a UK subsidiary. The goods cost US$40,000 to make, and they are sold in the UK by the subsidiary for £50,000, which is the equivalent, say, of US$75,000. The US multinational group will make a total profit of US$35,000. So how much profit from the US$35,000 has been earned by the US parent company, and how much has been earned by the UK subsidiary?

The answer depends on the transfer price at which the US parent sells the goods to its UK subsidiary.

(i) If the transfer price is US$45,000, the US parent company would make a profit of $5,000, leaving a profit of $30,000 for the UK subsidiary.

(ii) If the transfer price is US$70,000, the US parent company would make a profit of $30,000, leaving only a $5,000 profit for the UK subsidiary.

The transfer price will be set by management decision, so that the share of total profit between parent company and subsidiary can be manipulated to suit the preferences of management.

(b) The same choice of how to share total profits can be made in fixing a transfer price for goods made by a subsidiary and sold to the parent company or to another subsidiary.

3.3 The question of how profits are shared between parent company and subsidiary leads us on to the question of how a parent company obtains its returns in cash from its subsidiaries.

Different methods of obtaining cash returns

3.4 If a subsidiary earns a profit, but then retains and reinvests the profits, the parent company will not get any cash at all. Various ways of obtaining a cash return are as follows.

(a) The subsidiary could make a profit and pay a **dividend** out of profits.

(b) The parent company could sell goods or services to the subsidiary and obtain payment. The amount of this payment will depend on the volume of sales and also on the **transfer price** for the sales.

(c) A parent company which grants a subsidiary the right to make goods protected by patents can charge a **royalty** on any goods that the subsidiary sells. The size of any royalty can be adjusted to suit the wishes of the parent company's management.

(d) If the parent company makes a **loan** to a subsidiary, it can set the interest rate high or low, thereby affecting the profits of both companies. A high rate of interest on a loan, for example, would improve the parent company's profits to the detriment of the subsidiary's profits.

(e) **Management charges** may be levied by the parent company for costs incurred in the management of international operations.

3.5 When the subsidiary is in a country where there are exchange control regulations, the parent company may have difficulty in getting cash from the subsidiary.

Tax implications of transfer pricing

3.6 If a UK resident company makes investments abroad it will be liable to corporation tax on the profits made, the taxable amount being before the deduction of any foreign taxes. The profits may be any of the following.

(a) Profits of an overseas branch or agency
(b) Income from foreign securities, for example debentures in overseas companies
(c) Dividends from overseas subsidiaries
(d) Capital gains on disposals of foreign assets

3.7 In many instances, a company will be subject to overseas taxes as well as to UK corporation tax on the same profits. Double taxation relief is, however, usually available in respect of the foreign tax suffered.

Controlled foreign companies

3.8 A UK resident company may choose to trade abroad through an investment in a local company. Providing there are no exchange control problems and cash flow requirements do not call for the repatriation of all profits to the UK, there will generally be a tax benefit in accumulating income in a foreign company whose effective tax rate is lower than that of the UK company. (To prevent undue tax avoidance through the use of 'tax havens' in this way, there are complex tax rules for 'controlled foreign companies' (CFCs).)

The migration of companies

3.9 Because the overseas profits of a UK resident company are chargeable to corporation tax whereas the overseas profits of a non-UK resident company are not, UK companies might wish to transfer their residence in order to avoid paying UK corporation tax. A company may freely transfer its residence out of the UK provided that it gives notice to the Inland Revenue and pays an exit charge based on unrealised capital gains on its assets. Only companies incorporated abroad can emigrate, as companies incorporated in the UK are automatically UK resident.

Sales at artificial transfer prices

3.10 Where sales are made to a non-resident fellow group company at an undervalue, or purchases are made from such a company at an overvalue, the Inland Revenue will substitute a market price in computing the profits chargeable to corporation tax. However, no corresponding relief is given for sales at overvalue or purchases at undervalue by the UK company.

Trading abroad

3.11 The controlled foreign companies legislation may reduce the attractiveness of setting up a subsidiary in a tax haven, as opposed to a branch of the UK company. However, a bona fide group structure may still be designed, avoiding the CFC rules, with the result that UK tax can be minimised by controlling the timing and amounts of dividends paid by the foreign subsidiary. At worst, a trading company treated as a CFC would have to distribute half of its profits to avoid an apportionment. Where dividends are paid to the UK, there may be a cashflow advantage in that dividends will, if correctly timed, be assessed in a later accounting period than trading profits would have been.

3.12 If an overseas operation is expected to make losses at first and then become profitable, it may be sensible to start with a branch and then transfer the trade to a subsidiary. Provided all the assets (or all except cash) are transferred, and the consideration is in the form of shares, gains on the transfers of assets can be deducted from the value of the shares instead of being immediately taxable in the UK. Where the overseas country is a member state of the European Union, an alternative is to allow the gains to be taxable but to claim relief for tax which would have been payable overseas but for the EU Mergers directive (which gives certain reliefs from tax).

4 REDUCING BAD DEBT RISK IN FOREIGN TRADE

4.1 Methods of minimising credit risks are broadly similar to those for domestic trade. An exporting company should vet the creditworthiness of each customer, and grant credit terms accordingly.

KEY TERM

Credit risk: the risk that a borrower may default on his obligations *(OT)*.

4.2 Methods of reducing the risks of bad debts in foreign trade include:

- **export factoring**
- **forfaiting**

- **documentary credits**
- **international credit unions**
- **export credit insurance**

Export factoring

4.3 Export factoring is essentially the same as factoring domestic trade debts, which we discussed earlier. Factoring, as compared with forfaiting which we discuss below, is widely regarded as an appropriate mechanism for trade finance and collection of receivables for small to medium-sized exporters, especially where there is a flow of small-scale contracts.

4.4 A factoring service typically offers prepayment of up to 80% against approved invoices. Service charges vary between around 0.75% and 3% of total invoice value, plus finance charges at levels comparable to bank overdraft rates for those taking advantage of prepayment arrangements.

Forfaiting

4.5 Forfaiting is a method of providing medium-term (say, three to five years) export finance, which originated in Switzerland and Germany where it is still very common. It has normally been used for export sales involving capital goods (machinery etc), where payments will be made over a number of years. Forfaiting is also used as a short-term financing tool.

4.6 Forfaiting works as follows.

(a) An exporter of capital goods finds an overseas buyer who wants medium-term credit to finance the purchase. The buyer must be willing:

(i) to pay some of the cost (perhaps 15%) at once;

(ii) to pay the balance in **regular instalments** (perhaps every six months) normally for the next five years.

(b) The buyer will either:

(i) issue a series of promissory notes; or
(ii) accept a series of drafts

with a final maturity date, say, five years ahead but providing for regular payments over this time, in other words, a series of promissory notes maturing every six months, usually each for the same amount.

(c) If the buyer has a very good credit standing, the exporter might not ask for the promissory notes (or drafts) to be guaranteed. In most cases, however, the buyer will be required to find a bank which is willing to guarantee **(avalise)** the notes or drafts.

(d) At the same time, the exporter must find a bank that is willing to be a 'forfaiter'. Some banks specialise in this type of finance.

(e) Forfaiting is the business of **discounting (negotiating)** medium-term promissory drafts or bills. Discounting is normally at a fixed rate, notified by the bank (forfaiter) to the exporter when the financing arrangement is made. If the exporter arranges forfaiting with a bank before the export contract is signed with the buyer, the exporter will be able to incorporate the cost of discounting into the contract price.

(f) The exporter will deliver the goods and receive the avalised promissory notes or accepted bills. He will then sell them to the forfaiter, who will purchase them **without recourse to the exporter**. The forfaiter must now bear the following risks:

(i) risks of non-payment;

(ii) political risks in the buyer's country;

(iii) the transfer risk that the buyer's country might be unable to meet its foreign exchange obligations;

(iv) the foreign exchange risk. The forfaiter holds the promissory notes and has paid cash to the exporter, and therefore it is the forfaiter who accepts the exchange risk;

(v) the collection of payment from the avalising bank.

4.7 The following diagram should help to clarify the procedures.

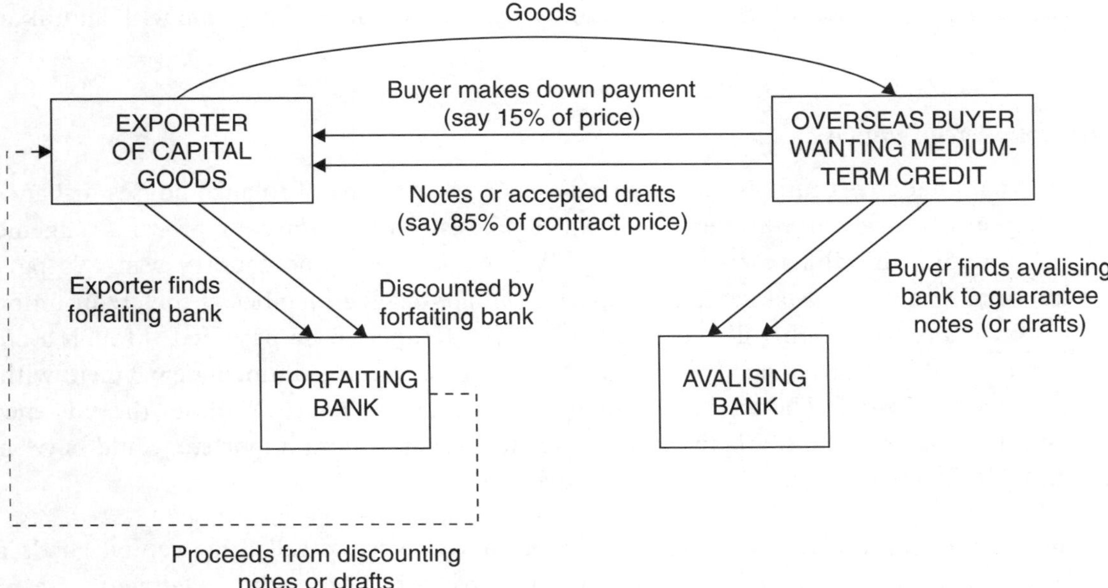

4.8 Forfaiting can be an expensive choice and arranging it takes time. However, it can be a useful way of enabling trade to occur in cases where other methods of ensuring payment and smooth cash flow are not certain, and in cases where trade may not be possible by other means.

Documentary credits

4.9 **Documentary credits ('letters of credit'**) provide a method of payment in international trade which gives the exporter a risk-free method of obtaining payment.

4.10 At the same time, documentary credits are a method of obtaining short-term finance from a bank, for working capital. This is because a bank might agree to discount or negotiate a bill of exchange, and so:

(a) the exporter receives immediate payment of the amount due to him, less the discount, instead of having to wait for payment until the end of the credit period allowed to the buyer;

(b) the buyer is able to get a period of credit before having to pay for the imports.

Banks may advance pre-shipment finance to help with manufacture.

4.11 The buyer (a foreign buyer, or a UK importer) and the seller (a UK exporter or a foreign supplier) first of all agree a contract for the sale of the goods, which provides for payment

through a documentary credit. The **buyer** then requests a bank in his country to issue a **letter of credit** in favour of the exporter. This bank which issues the letter of credit is known as the **issuing bank.** The buyer is known as the **applicant** for the credit and the exporter is known as the **beneficiary** (because he receives the benefits).

4.12 The issuing bank, by issuing its letter of credit, guarantees payment to the beneficiary. Banks are involved in the credits, not in the underlying contracts. The cost of issuing a letter of credit is usually borne by the buyer.

4.13 A documentary credit arrangement must be made between the exporter, the buyer and participating banks **before the export sale takes place**. Documentary credits are slow to arrange, and administratively cumbersome; however, they might be considered essential where the risk of non-payment is high, or when dealing for the first time with an unknown buyer.

International credit unions

4.14 International credit unions are organisations or associations of finance houses or banks in different countries (in Europe). The finance houses or banks have reciprocal arrangements for providing instalment credit finance. When a buyer in one country wants to pay for imported goods by instalments the exporter can approach a member of the credit union in his own country which will then arrange for the finance to be provided through a credit union member in the importer's country. The exporter receives immediate payment without recourse to himself. The buyer obtains instalment credit finance. Without the existence of international co-operation between members of a credit union, importers would have more difficulty in obtaining instalment credit finance.

4.15 Suppose, for example, that an exporter in the UK wishes to sell some capital goods to a customer in Germany and the customer wants to pay for the goods by instalment.

(a) The exporter can approach a member of an international credit union in the UK, and ask for the necessary instalment finance to be arranged through a German member of the credit union.

(b) Details of the proposed sale will be given to the German finance house or bank, which will then decide on the terms of instalment credit it will offer to the German buyer (in accordance with the German laws and practice).

(c) The UK finance house will receive full payment for the goods from the German finance house and pay the exporter. The German finance house is then left with a normal hire purchase agreement with the German buyer.

4.16 This type of scheme has advantages for small exporters who cannot afford to allow lengthy credit periods to its overseas customers. Examples of international credit unions are the European Credit Union and Eurocredit.

Export credit insurance

4.17 Export credit insurance is insurance against the risk of non-payment by foreign customers for export debts. Not all exporters take out export credit insurance because premiums are very high and the benefits are sometimes not fully appreciated; but, if they do, they will obtain an insurance policy from a private insurance company that deals in export credit insurance.

4.18 Although a number of private sector companies in the UK (such as Trade Indemnity) offer export credit insurance, the largest provider is NCM UK, which insures more than 6,000 British companies in trade with 200 countries. The UK government's **Export Credit Guarantee Department (ECGD)** also exists to providing long-term guarantees to banks on behalf of exporters.

4.19 Export credit insurance is not essential, eg when exporters are reasonably confident that all their customers are trustworthy. You might be wondering why export credit insurance should ever be necessary, when exporters can pursue non-paying customers through the courts in order to obtain payment. The answer is that:

(a) if a credit customer defaults on payment, the task of pursuing the case through the courts will be lengthy, and it might be a long time before payment is eventually obtained;

(b) there are various reasons why non-payment might happen. Export credit insurance provides insurance against non-payment for a variety of risks in addition to the buyer's failure to pay on time. The types of risk covered are described later.

The short-term guarantee

4.20 As already mentioned, NCM UK provides of credit insurance for short-term export credit business. A credit insurance policy for export trade on short-term credit (up to 180 days) or on cash terms is known as a short-term guarantee.

4.21 Exporters can choose to obtain credit insurance:

(a) for all their export business on a regular basis;
(b) for selected parts of their export business;
(c) for occasional, high-value export sales.

However, NCM UK prefers to provide comprehensive insurance for an exporter's entire export business. Cover is also available for UK manufacturers and merchants dealing in **foreign** goods, under an **endorsement** to the short-term guarantee, which was introduced in 1987. This is referred to as a **multi-sourcing endorsement**.

5 COUNTERTRADE

What is countertrade?

5.1 **Countertrade** is a general term used to describe a variety of commercial arrangements for reciprocal international trade or barter between companies or other organisations (eg state controlled organisations) in two or more countries.

> **KEY TERM**
>
> **Countertrade:** a form of trading activity based on other than an arm's-length goods for cash exchange *(OT)*.

5.2 Countertrade involving exchange of petroleum and manufacturing goods became popular in the early 1980s as such deals provided a way of avoiding OPEC export quotas for oil-producing countries. It is also common in deals with East European countries which are short of foreign exchange. The huge debts of many Third World and Eastern European

countries have contributed to the growth of countertrade as the only way of arranging international trade in the absence of cash or credit facilities to finance imports. It is now estimated that around 10% - 15% of international trade is conducted by some means of countertrade.

5.3 Countertrade is costly for the exporter; it creates lengthy and cumbersome administrative problems, just to set up a countertrade arrangement. It is fraught with uncertainty, and deals can easily collapse or go wrong. Small and medium-sized firms might be unable and unwilling to accept the costs and administrative burdens of exporting by means of countertrade arrangements. However, in some situations, countertrade might be the only way of securing export orders.

Problems with countertrade

5.4 Problems which may arise in countertrade include the following.

(a) The **costs** of countertrade (see below) might exceed the exporter's expectations. The exporter might increase the export price to cover the extra costs, or he might try to absorb the extra costs himself.

(b) The exporter might be pushed into agreeing to accept large quantities of **unmarketable goods** without any means of disposing of them.

(c) The importer's country might place an unrealistically high value on the goods they wish to countertrade (for example if British Steel were offered surgical instruments by India in a countertrade deal to export steel, the Indian government might place too high a value on what the Indian surgical instruments can really be sold for on the market).

(d) **Several parties** are likely to be involved in a countertrade arrangement, and this increases the risks of cancellation of the export order, due to one party failing to fulfil its contractual obligations.

What are the extra costs of countertrade?

5.5 The costs of countertrade include:

(a) fees of specialist consultants who advise on countertrade negotiations;

(b) the discount or 'disagio' necessary to dispose of the goods in countertrade. The size of the discount could vary from 2-3% for high grade materials and commodities to 25-30% (and sometimes as much as 40-50%) for low-quality manufactured goods;

(c) counterpurchase undertakings can be dealt with by assigning the counterpurchase obligations for a fee, to a third party trading house or broker;

(d) insurance costs;

(e) bank fees, where a bank provides advice and help on countertrade matters (for example on negotiations or disposal of countertraded goods).

Chapter roundup

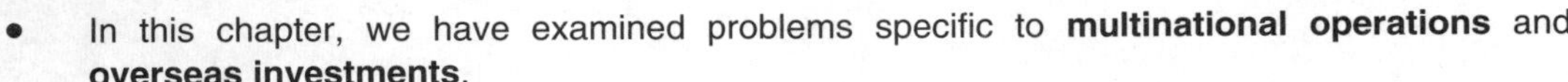

- In this chapter, we have examined problems specific to **multinational operations** and **overseas investments**.

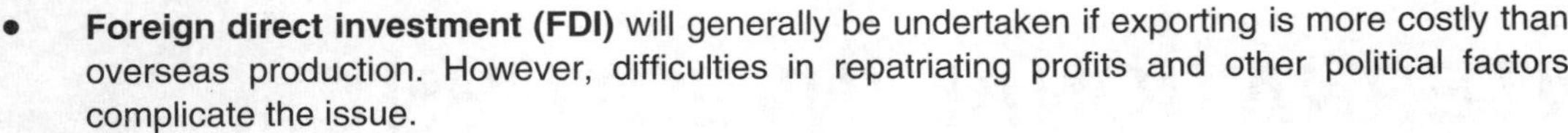

- **Foreign direct investment (FDI)** will generally be undertaken if exporting is more costly than overseas production. However, difficulties in repatriating profits and other political factors complicate the issue.
- **Transfer pricing** is of importance to multinational companies. There are legal provisions affecting transfer pricing which are aimed at preventing avoidance of tax. Different methods of transfer pricing also have different motivational effects on the cost centres involved.
- **Export factoring** provides all the advantages of factoring generally and is especially useful in assessing credit risk. **International credit unions** and forfaiting provide medium term finance for importers of capital goods. Various forms of **credit insurance** are available to exporters.
- The exporter can obtain some finance from the foreign buyer by insisting on **cash with order** and the importer can obtain finance from the foreign supplier by means of normal **trade credit**, perhaps evidenced by a term bill of exchange.
- **Countertrade** is a complex and possibly expensive means of trading with poor and less developed countries. It can take several forms.

Quick quiz

1. Outline the main changes in the pattern of multinationals' activities over the past twenty years or so. (see paras 1.6, 1.7)
2. What two different forms of joint venture can be distinguished? (1.13)
3. Why might a company set up subsidiaries abroad? (1.18)
4. What are the main risks faced by multinationals? (1.21)
5. What measures might a government take to control local subsidiaries of a multinational? (1.22)
6. By what different methods might a parent company extract cash from a subsidiary? (3.4)
7. In what type of situation might forfaiting be used? (4.8)
8. How are documentary credits used? (4.11 - 4.13)
9. What is the purpose of export credit insurance, and when is it needed? (4.17)
10. What is countertrade? (5.1)

Question to try	Level	Marks	Time
24	Exam standard	20	36 mins

Chapter 25

INTERNATIONAL INVESTMENT APPRAISAL

Chapter topic list		Syllabus reference	Ability required
1	International portfolio diversification	13 d(iv)	Application
2	Capital budgeting for foreign projects	13 d(iv)	Application
3	Taxation in the multinational environment	13 d(iv)	Application

Introduction

In this chapter, we look at aspects of **international investment decisions** in the light of **investment appraisal techniques** and **asset pricing theories** covered earlier in the Study Text.

Exam focus point

The Question 1 case study is likely to focus on one part of the syllabus, such as international FM, but will also include elements from other syllabus sections.

1 INTERNATIONAL PORTFOLIO DIVERSIFICATION

1.1 In Chapter 7, we saw how portfolio theory seeks to establish guidelines for building up a portfolio of investments. Given the increased liberalisation of domestic capital markets and the increasing internationalisation of the financial system, the investor seeking a diversified portfolio does not need to restrict choice of securities to domestic securities.

1.2 Approximately 7% of total world equities has been estimated to comprise cross-border holdings. Even so, it is arguable that there remains a domestic bias among many types of investor, which can be attributed to a number of **barriers** to international investment, including the following.

(a) Legal restrictions exist in some markets, limiting ownership of securities by foreign investors.

(b) Foreign exchange regulations may prohibit international investment or make it more expensive.

(c) Double taxation of income from foreign investment may deter investors.

(d) There are likely to be higher information and transaction costs associated with investing in foreign securities.

(e) Some types of investor may have a parochial 'home bias' for domestic investment.

1.3 There are a number of arguments in favour of international portfolio diversification.

Diversification of risk

1.4 A portfolio which is diversified internationally should in theory be less risky than a purely domestic portfolio. This is of advantage to any risk-averse investor. As with a purely domestic portfolio, the extent to which risk is reduced by international diversification will depend upon the degree of correlation between individual securities in the portfolio. The lower the degree of correlation between returns on the securities, the more risk can be avoided by diversification.

1.5 On the international dimension, a number of factors help to ensure that there is often low correlation between returns on securities in different countries and therefore enhance the potential for risk reduction, including the following.

(a) Different countries are often at different stages of the trade cycle at any one time.

(b) Monetary, fiscal and exchange rate policies differ internationally.

(c) Different countries have different endowments of natural resources and different industrial bases.

(d) Potentially risky political events are likely to be localised within particular national or regional boundaries.

On the other hand, for countries within the same region having closely linked economies, such as the USA and Canada, correlations are relatively high.

1.6 A study published in *Financial Analysts Journal* (1974) found that a fully diversified international portfolio had less than half the risk (measured as the variance of portfolio return ÷ variance of return on a typical security) of a fully diversified US domestic portfolio.

Risks and returns

1.7 Securities markets in different countries differ considerably in the combination of risk and return which they offer. For example, a study of fifteen major stock markets over the period 1973 to 1982 found that the Hong Kong, Singapore and UK stock markets were characterised by high risk but high returns while the US market displayed low risk and low returns.

Exchange rates

1.8 Exchange rate fluctuations will generally have implications for international portfolio diversification where the investment is in a country whose currency floats against that of the investor's own country's currency. Indeed, the volatility in exchange rates between major currencies in recent years is sometimes cited as a barrier to international investment.

1.9 Foreign exchange markets can often be almost as volatile as stock markets. Overall, fluctuations in exchange rates make international investment more risky, but this does not negate the fact that international portfolio diversification is worthwhile for investors wishing to reduce the risk of a portfolio.

Multinationals as diversified portfolios

1.10 Some of the costs and other barriers associated with international investment might be reduced if the investor is able to achieve international portfolio diversification by investing in the shares of a multinational company.

1.11 The evidence on this issue suggests that, unlike a portfolio of stocks drawn from different international markets, the share price behaviour of multinational companies closely reflects that of non-multinational domestic firms. It follows that the reduction of risk (ie the reduction in the variance of portfolio return) which international portfolio diversification can achieve is not likely to be gained through the strategy of investing in a domestically based multinational.

The international cost of capital

1.12 Earlier in this Study Text, we have examined the weighted average cost of capital (WACC) of a firm. The WACC, you should by now appreciate, is a weighted average of the required returns for the various providers of finance to the firm. The cost of capital is important for both the financing decision of the firm and for the investment decision.

The financing decision

1.13 The company will wish to keep the cost of funds after tax as low as possible within a reasonable level of risk, since the lower is the cost of capital the higher is the value of the firm. Multinational firms, having access to worldwide capital markets, are likely to be well placed to adjust the mix of the firm's finance so as to reduce the cost of capital.

1.14 There are various factors to consider in deciding the mix of finance.

(a) What are the relative costs of different types of fund? It must be borne in mind that an increase in one type of finance may have an effect on the cost (or return required) on other forms of finance.

(b) What is the appropriate mix of short-term and long-term finance?

(c) In the light of the arguments of Modigliani and Miller, what is the appropriate mix of debt and equity? The effect on risk for ordinary shareholders of increasing additional debt needs to be considered.

(d) Tax rules need to be considered. Because tax relief is available on debt interest, the mix of debt and equity can affect the tax liability of the firm.

The investment decision

1.15 It will be appropriate to adopt the firm's WACC as a discount rate if the following two conditions are satisfied.

(a) The systematic risk associated with the investment should be similar to that of the firm's other investments. In this context, we assume that the company's shareholders hold the shares within a well diversified portfolio.

(b) The method of financing of the project should not affect the level of gearing of the company.

1.16 An overseas project may alter the firm's total risk. Political risk and currency risk, both of which are unsystematic, are likely to increase. Total risk may be allowed for by:

(a) adjusting the discount rate for total risk; or

(b) accounting for risk in projected cash flows, using a discount rate adjusted for systematic business risk and financial risk as in the case of a domestic project.

1.17 In practice, it is common for firms to add a premium to the discount rate to account for risk. In comparing different approaches to adjusting for risk, the different characteristics of the special risks involved in international investment should be noted.

(a) **Political risk** is generally the risk of an adverse outcome in the form of possible expropriation of assets resulting from currently unforeseen changes in the political climate which may occur in the future. Since the risks cannot currently be foreseen, the effect is likely to be on future cash flows. If political risk were to be adjusted for through the discount rate, all cash flows would be affected.

(b) **Currency risk** can have either favourable or adverse effects on the project cashflows. Whether the effect is favourable or adverse depends on the direction of change in exchange rates and on whether the cash flows concerned are inflows or outflows. Instead of adjusting the discount rate, it is more appropriate to adjust for this 'two-way' risk by reflecting alternative outcomes in the cash flow forecasts themselves.

Effects of international portfolio diversification

1.18 As already discussed, internationalisation of a portfolio provides a means of reducing the risk of the portfolio. For a firm contemplating a foreign investment, the degree of correlation between the stock markets of the two countries involved provides an indication of the level of systematic risk associated with the investment: the lower is the correlation coefficient, the lower is the likely level of **systematic risk**.

1.19 The possibility of lowering systematic risk through international investment suggests that a lower discount rate is appropriate for overseas investments. However, whether this is reasonable depends upon whether it is true that shareholders will accept a lower return on their equity in an internationally diversified firm for the reason that there is a reduction in the domestic (home-country) systematic risk. This is likely to be the case if the multinational firm is enabling shareholders to achieve international diversification that they would not otherwise be able to achieve, perhaps because of regulatory restrictions.

1.20 If the multinational firm is investing in countries in which shareholders can readily invest themselves directly, or via a managed investment fund such as a unit trust or investment trust, then there is no reason to suppose that shareholders will gain from the diversification within the multinational firm. In this case, there would seem to be no reason for the firm to use a lower discount rate for the overseas investment.

2 CAPITAL BUDGETING FOR FOREIGN PROJECTS 5/95, 5/97, 5/99

2.1 Multinational capital budgeting can be based on similar concepts to those used in the purely domestic case which we have examined earlier in this Study Text:

(a) using **net present value (NPV) analysis**, project cash flows are discounted using the firm's weighted average cost of capital; or

(b) the **internal rate of return** which equates project cash flows with project costs is found.

2.2 Depending upon the information which is available, two alternative NPV methods are available. Both methods produce the NPV in domestic currency terms. For a UK company investing overseas, we can:

(a) convert the project cash flows into sterling and then discount at a sterling discount rate to calculate the NPV in sterling terms; or

(b) discount the foreign currency cash flows from the project at a discount rate for that currency and then convert the resulting NPV at the spot exchange rate.

2.3 There are, however, some special considerations in the international case, including the following.

(a) For the purpose of assessing how expected performance compares with potential performance, it is necessary to compare the project's net present value with those of similar host country projects. This involves measuring the cash flows in terms of the currency of the host country.

(b) A foreign project also needs to be evaluated on its net present value in respect of the funds which can be remitted to the parent. The purpose of this second stage is to evaluate whether the cash flow remitted justifies the cash invested from the home country.

(c) Cash flows from the subsidiary may come about through a variety of means, including licensing fees and payments for imports from the parent company.

(d) The possibility of differing national rates of inflation needs to be taken into account.

The APV method

2.4 The **adjusted present value (APV) method** may be used for a project which is financed differently from the parent company. However, although the APV is a feasible method of analysis for foreign projects, it is not used nearly as much in practice as the traditional weighted average cost of capital method.

Foreign exchange risk and overseas operations

2.5 When a UK company wishes to finance operations overseas, there may be a foreign exchange risk arising from the method of financing used. To reduce or eliminate the foreign exchange risk of an overseas investment, a company might finance it with funds raised in the same currency as the investment.

2.6 As you should appreciate from our earlier discussion of currency risk, there are advantages of borrowing in the same currency as an investment. Assets and liabilities in the same currency can be matched, thus avoiding exchange losses on conversion in the group's annual accounts. Revenues in the foreign currency can be used to repay borrowings in the same currency, thus eliminating losses due to fluctuating exchange rates.

Additional factors

2.7 Additional factors to be taken into account when appraising overseas investments are as follows.

(a) Political interference by overseas governments, including exchange controls, extra charges on the profits of overseas companies and employment legislation could be a danger.

(b) Differences in tax systems (and accounting practices) may be significant.

(c) Some countries offer special finance incentives for investment in that country.

(d) It might be better to export than to set up a foreign subsidiary.

Loans in foreign currencies

2.8 A UK company could borrow in a foreign currency to finance an investment in sterling. For example, a company could finance a project in the UK by borrowing in US dollars. The loan could be raised as a **eurocurrency loan** from a bank or, in the case of very large companies, as a eurobond issue.

2.9 The **reason** for financing a project in a foreign currency would be the availability of a lower interest rate than the current market rate for sterling loans. However, it is easy to be deceived by lower interest rates on eurocurrency loans, and foreign currency loans at a low interest rate could prove more expensive than a loan in domestic currency at a higher interest rate. Companies need to beware of this 'interest rate trap'. The project will pay back returns in sterling, but the loan, and interest on the loan, must be paid in the foreign currency. If the currency of the loan strengthens against sterling, the **sterling cost** of the loan interest and the loan repayment will increase.

2.10 For example, suppose that a UK company borrows $6,000,000 at an interest rate of 7%, when the exchange rate is $2 = £1. The loan would finance a UK investment costing £3,000,000. Annual interest on the loan would be $420,000, which would cost £210,000 if the exchange rate does not change. But if sterling falls in value against the dollar, to say $1.50 = £1, the loan interest will cost £280,000 a year, and the capital sum needed to repay the loan at the end of its term will be £4,000,000.

3 TAXATION IN THE MULTINATIONAL ENVIRONMENT

3.1 **Tax planning** for multinational companies is a complex area. (We looked at the tax implications of transfer pricing in Chapter 23.) Each country has its own range of taxes, and multinational enterprises must usually seek local advice in each country, which may be available through international accounting firms.

Foreign tax credits

3.2 In order to prevent the same income being taxed twice **(double taxation),** most countries give a tax credit for taxes on income paid to the host country. For example, a Japanese subsidiary of a US firm earns the equivalent of $500,000 in yen. The subsidiary pays 40% income tax ($200,000) in Japan. The US parent can claim a credit against US taxes of $200,000 when the earnings are remitted to the parent company. Foreign tax credits are also available for withholding taxes on sums paid to other countries as dividends, interest, royalties and in other forms.

Tax havens

3.3 **Tax havens** are used by some multinationals as a means of deferring tax on funds prior to their repatriation or reinvestment. A tax haven is likely to have the following characteristics.

(a) Tax on foreign investment or sales income earned by resident companies, and withholding tax on dividends paid to the parent, should be low.

(b) There should be a stable government and a stable currency.

(c) There should be adequate financial services support facilities.

Question

Donegal plc is considering whether to establish a subsidiary in the USA, at a cost of $2,400,000. This would be represented by fixed assets of $2,000,000 and working capital of $400,000. The subsidiary would produce a product which would achieve annual sales of $1,600,000 and incur cash expenditures of $1,000,000 a year.

The company has a planning horizon of four years, at the end of which it expects the realisable value of the subsidiary's fixed assets to be $800,000.

It is the company's policy to remit the maximum funds possible to the parent company at the end of each year.

Tax is payable at the rate of 35% in the USA and is payable one year in arrears. A double taxation treaty exists between the UK and the USA and so no UK taxation is expected to arise.

Tax allowable depreciation is at a rate of 25% on a straight line basis on all fixed assets.

Because of the fluctuations in the exchange rate between the US dollar and sterling, the company would protect itself against the risk by raising a eurodollar loan to finance the investment. The company's cost of capital for the project is 16%.

Calculate the NPV of the project.

Answer

The annual writing down allowance (WDA) is 25% of US$2,000,000 = $500,000, from which the annual tax saving would be (at 35%) $175,000.

Year	*Invest-ment*	*Contri-bution*	*Tax on contri-bution*	*Tax saving on WDA & tax on realisable value*	*Net cash flow*	*Discount factor*	*Present value*
	$m	$m	$m	$m	$m	16%	$m
0	(2.4)				(2.400)	1.000	(2.400)
1		0.6		0.175	0.775	0.862	0.668
2		0.6	(0.21)	0.175	0.565	0.743	0.420
3		0.6	(0.21)	0.175	0.565	0.641	0.362
4	1.2*	0.6	(0.21)	0.175	1.765	0.552	0.974
5			(0.21)	(0.28)**	(0.490)	0.476	(0.233)
							(0.209)

* Fixed assets realisable value $800,000 plus working capital $400,000

** It is assumed that tax would be payable on the realisable value of the fixed assets, since the tax written down value of the assets would be zero. 35% of $800,000 is $280,000.

The NPV is negative and so the project would not be viable at a discount rate of 16%.

Chapter roundup

- **International portfolio diversification** brings advantages resulting from differences in the economies of different countries.
- The **CAPM** can be extended to cover international portfolio risk, but in practice foreign exchange fluctuations and market imperfections also need to be considered.
- The **appraisal of foreign projects** involves a number of complexities which do not arise in the case of domestic projects, including international **tax complications** and **differential rates of inflation**.

Quick quiz

1 What barriers are there to international investment? (see para 1.2)

2 What factors ensure that there is low correlation between returns on securities in different national securities markets around the world? (1.5)

3 What special considerations are there in applying NPV analysis to the appraisal of foreign projects? (2.3)

4 Why might a multinational company make use of a tax haven, and what characteristics is a tax haven likely to have? (3.3)

Question to try	Level	Marks	Time
25	Exam standard	35	63 mins

Appendix

Mathematical tables, formulae and symbols

MATHEMATICAL TABLES

The tables below are included in CIMA's *Mathematical Tables* which is made available to candidates in the exam.

Present value table

Present value of 1 = $(1+r)^{-n}$ where r = discount rate, n = number of periods until payment.

Periods (n)	Discount rates (r) 1%	2%	3%	4%	5%	6%	7%	8%	9%	10%
1	0.990	0.980	0.971	0.962	0.952	0.943	0.935	0.926	0.917	0.909
2	0.980	0.961	0.943	0.925	0.907	0.890	0.873	0.857	0.842	0.826
3	0.971	0.942	0.915	0.889	0.864	0.840	0.816	0.794	0.772	0.751
4	0.961	0.924	0.888	0.855	0.823	0.792	0.763	0.735	0.708	0.683
5	0.951	0.906	0.863	0.822	0.784	0.747	0.713	0.681	0.650	0.621
6	0.942	0.888	0.837	0.790	0.746	0.705	0.666	0.630	0.596	0.564
7	0.933	0.871	0.813	0.760	0.711	0.665	0.623	0.583	0.547	0.513
8	0.923	0.853	0.789	0.731	0.677	0.627	0.582	0.540	0.502	0.467
9	0.914	0.837	0.766	0.703	0.645	0.592	0.544	0.500	0.460	0.424
10	0.905	0.820	0.744	0.676	0.614	0.558	0.508	0.463	0.422	0.386
11	0.896	0.804	0.722	0.650	0.585	0.527	0.475	0.429	0.388	0.350
12	0.887	0.788	0.701	0.625	0.557	0.497	0.444	0.397	0.356	0.319
13	0.879	0.773	0.681	0.601	0.530	0.469	0.415	0.368	0.326	0.290
14	0.870	0.758	0.661	0.577	0.505	0.442	0.388	0.340	0.299	0.263
15	0.861	0.743	0.642	0.555	0.481	0.417	0.362	0.315	0.275	0.239

Periods (n)	Discount rates (r) 11%	12%	13%	14%	15%	16%	17%	18%	19%	20%
1	0.901	0.893	0.885	0.877	0.870	0.862	0.855	0.847	0.840	0.833
2	0.812	0.797	0.783	0.769	0.756	0.743	0.731	0.718	0.706	0.694
3	0.731	0.712	0.693	0.675	0.658	0.641	0.624	0.609	0.593	0.579
4	0.659	0.636	0.613	0.592	0.572	0.552	0.534	0.516	0.499	0.482
5	0.593	0.567	0.543	0.519	0.497	0.476	0.456	0.437	0.419	0.402
6	0.535	0.507	0.480	0.456	0.432	0.410	0.390	0.370	0.352	0.335
7	0.482	0.452	0.425	0.400	0.376	0.354	0.333	0.314	0.296	0.279
8	0.434	0.404	0.376	0.351	0.327	0.305	0.285	0.266	0.249	0.233
9	0.391	0.361	0.333	0.308	0.284	0.263	0.243	0.225	0.209	0.194
10	0.352	0.322	0.295	0.270	0.247	0.227	0.208	0.191	0.176	0.162
11	0.317	0.287	0.261	0.237	0.215	0.195	0.178	0.162	0.148	0.135
12	0.286	0.257	0.231	0.208	0.187	0.168	0.152	0.137	0.124	0.112
13	0.258	0.229	0.204	0.182	0.163	0.145	0.130	0.116	0.104	0.093
14	0.232	0.205	0.181	0.160	0.141	0.125	0.111	0.099	0.088	0.078
15	0.209	0.183	0.160	0.140	0.123	0.108	0.095	0.084	0.074	0.065

Cumulative present value table

This table shows the present value of £1 per annum, receivable or payable at the end of each year for *n* years.

Periods (n)	Discount rates (r) 1%	2%	3%	4%	5%	6%	7%	8%	9%	10%
1	0.990	0.980	0.971	0.962	0.952	0.943	0.935	0.926	0.917	0.909
2	1.970	1.942	1.913	1.886	1.859	1.833	1.808	1.783	1.759	1.736
3	2.941	2.884	2.829	2.775	2.723	2.673	2.624	2.577	2.531	2.487
4	3.902	3.808	3.717	3.630	3.546	3.465	3.387	3.312	3.240	3.170
5	4.853	4.713	4.580	4.452	4.329	4.212	4.100	3.993	3.890	3.791
6	5.795	5.601	5.417	5.242	5.076	4.917	4.767	4.623	4.486	4.355
7	6.728	6.472	6.230	6.002	5.786	5.582	5.389	5.206	5.033	4.868
8	7.652	7.325	7.020	6.733	6.463	6.210	5.971	5.747	5.535	5.335
9	8.566	8.162	7.786	7.435	7.108	6.802	6.515	6.247	5.995	5.759
10	9.471	8.983	8.530	8.111	7.722	7.360	7.024	6.710	6.418	6.145
11	10.37	9.787	9.253	8.760	8.306	7.887	7.499	7.139	6.805	6.495
12	11.26	10.58	9.954	9.385	8.863	8.384	7.943	7.536	7.161	6.814
13	12.13	11.35	10.63	9.986	9.394	8.853	8.358	7.904	7.487	7.103
14	13.00	12.11	11.30	10.56	9.899	9.295	8.745	8.244	7.786	7.367
15	13.87	12.85	11.94	11.12	10.38	9.712	9.108	8.559	8.061	7.606

Periods (n)	Discount rates (r) 11%	12%	13%	14%	15%	16%	17%	18%	19%	20%
1	0.901	0.893	0.885	0.877	0.870	0.862	0.855	0.847	0.840	0.833
2	1.713	1.690	1.668	1.647	1.626	1.605	1.585	1.566	1.547	1.528
3	2.444	2.402	2.361	2.322	2.283	2.246	2.210	2.174	2.140	2.106
4	3.102	3.037	2.974	2.914	2.855	2.798	2.743	2.690	2.639	2.589
5	3.696	3.605	3.517	3.433	3.352	3.274	3.199	3.127	3.058	2.991
6	4.231	4.111	3.998	3.889	3.784	3.685	3.589	3.498	3.410	3.326
7	4.712	4.564	4.423	4.288	4.160	4.039	3.922	3.812	3.706	3.605
8	5.146	4.968	4.799	4.639	4.487	4.344	4.207	4.078	3.954	3.837
9	5.537	5.328	5.132	4.946	4.772	4.607	4.451	4.303	4.163	4.031
10	5.889	5.650	5.426	5.216	5.019	4.833	4.659	4.494	4.339	4.192
11	6.207	5.938	5.687	5.453	5.234	5.029	4.836	4.656	4.486	4.327
12	6.492	6.194	5.918	5.660	5.421	5.197	4.988	4.793	4.611	4.439
13	6.750	6.424	6.122	5.842	5.583	5.342	5.118	4.910	4.715	4.533
14	6.982	6.628	6.302	6.002	5.724	5.468	5.229	5.008	4.802	4.611
15	7.191	6.811	6.462	6.142	5.847	5.575	5.324	5.092	4.876	4.675

FORMULAE AND SYMBOLS

Section 15 of the CIMA *Mathematical Tables* contains the formulae and symbols set out below.

SECTION 15: FINANCIAL MATHEMATICS

GENERAL

Annuity

The value of annuity of £1 per period for t years (t-year annuity factor) is:

$$PV = \frac{1}{r} - \frac{1}{r(1+r)^t}$$

Perpetuity

The value of a perpetuity of £1 per year is:

$$PV = \frac{1}{r}$$

Growing perpetuity (Gordon model)

If the initial cash flow is £1 at year 1 and if cash flows thereafter grow at a constant rate of g in perpetuity

$$PV = \frac{1}{r-g}$$

Values and sums

The value, V, attained by a single sum X, after n periods at r% is $V = X(1 + r)^n$

The sum, S, of a geometric series of n terms, with first term A and common ratio R, is

$$S = A + AR + AR^2 + AR^3 + ... + AR^{n-1}$$

$$S = A\frac{(R^n - 1)}{R-1}$$

Equivalent annual cost

An asset with a life of t years has an equivalent annual cost of:

$$\frac{\text{PV costs}}{\text{t-year annuity factor}}$$

Interest rate parity

$$\frac{1+r_{SFr}}{1+r_{\$}} = \frac{f_{SFr/\$}}{s_{SFr/\$}}$$

Value of a right and ex-rights price

If N is the number of rights required to buy 1 share, the value of a right is:

$$\frac{\text{Rights-on price} - \text{issue price}}{N+1} = \frac{\text{ex-rights price} - \text{issue price}}{N}$$

The ex-rights price is:

$$\frac{1}{N+1}((N \times \text{rights-on price}) + \text{issue price})$$

Formulae and symbols

Value of a future *(see Note 1 below)*

$$\frac{\text{Futures price}}{(1+r_f)^t} = \text{spot price} + \text{PV(storage costs)} - \text{PV (convenience yield)}$$

Value of lease *(see Note 2)*

If LCF_t is the lease's cash outflow in period t, the value of an N-period lease of an asset costing INV is:

$$INV - \sum_{t=0}^{N} \frac{LCF_t}{[1+r(1-T_c)]^t}$$

COST OF CAPITAL

Cost of equity (r)

(i) *CAPM*

$$E(r_j) = r_f + [E(r_m) - r_f]\beta_j$$

(ii) *Dividend valuation model*

$$r = \frac{d_1}{p_o} + g$$

Adjusted cost of capital *(see Note 3)*

If r is the cost of capital under all-equity financing, the adjusted cost of capital ($r^\star$) is:

MM formula

$$r^\star = r(1 - T^\star L)$$

where L = project's marginal contribution to the firm's overall debt ratio
$T^\star$ = the net tax savings attached to debt interest payments

Miles-Ezzell formula

$$r^\star = r - Lr_D T^\star \frac{1+r}{1+r_D}$$

where r_D = the borrowing rate

Weighted average cost of capital formula

$$r^\star = r_D(1 - T_c)\frac{D}{E+D} + r_E \frac{E}{E+D}$$

where T_c = the marginal tax rate

RISK AND PORTFOLIO PERFORMANCE

Measures of risk

Variance of returns $= \sigma^2$

$= \text{expected value of } (\tilde{r} - r)^2$

Standard deviation of returns $= \sigma$

Covariance between returns of stocks 1 and 2

$= Cov_{1,2} = \text{expected value of } [(\tilde{r}_1 - r_1)(\tilde{r}_2 - r_2)]$

Correlation between returns of stock 1 and 2 $= \rho_{1,2} = \dfrac{Cov_{1,2}}{\sigma_1\sigma_2}$

Beta of stock i = $\beta_i = \dfrac{Cov_{i,m}}{\sigma^2_m}$

where $Cov_{i,m}$ is the covariance between stock i's return and the market return and $\sigma^2{}_m$ is the variance of the market return.

Variance of portfolio returns *(see Note 4)*

The variance of returns on a portfolio with proportion x_i invested in stock I is:

$$\sum_{i=1}^{N}\sum_{j=1}^{N} x_i\, x_j\, Cov_{i,j}$$

Capital asset pricing model

The expected risk premium on a risky investment is: $r - r_f = \beta(r_m - r_f)$

Capital asset pricing model (certainty-equivalent form) *(see Note 5)*

The present value of a one-period risky investment is:

$$PV = \frac{C_1 - \lambda Cov(\widetilde{C}_1, \widetilde{r}_m)}{1 + r_f}$$

where

$$\lambda = \frac{r_m - r_f}{\sigma_m{}^2}$$

Measures of portfolio performance *(see Note 6)*

Gain from picking stocks (Jensen's measure) = $(r - r_f) - \beta(r_m - r_f)$

Net gain from picking stocks = $(r - r_f) - \dfrac{\sigma}{\sigma_m}(r_m - r_f)$

OPTIONS

Value of a call and a put

Value of call + present value of exercise price = value of put + share price

Black-Scholes formula for value of a call *(see Note 7)*

Present value of call option

$$= PN(d_1) - EXe^{-r_f t} N(d_2)$$

where

$$d_1 = \frac{\log(P / EX) + r_f t + \sigma^2 t / 2}{\sigma\sqrt{t}}$$

$$d_2 = \frac{\log(P / EX) + r_f t - \sigma^2 t / 2}{\sigma\sqrt{t}}$$

N(d) = cumulative normal probability density function

EX = exercise price of option

t = time to exercise date

P = price of asset now

σ^2 = variance per period of (continuously compounded) rate of return on the asset

r_f = (continuously compounded) risk-free rate of interest

Binominal option valuation model *(see Note 7)*

Upside change = u = $e^{(\sigma\sqrt{h})} - 1$

Downside change = d = $e^{(-\sigma\sqrt{h})} - 1$

Probability of upside change in risk-neutral world = p = $\frac{r_f - d}{u - d}$

where σ = standard deviation of price changes per period

h = number of step jumps per period

Cash inventory models

Baumol model

Optimum amount of securities sold

$$= \sqrt{\frac{2 \times \text{annual cash disbursements} \times \text{cost per sale of securities}}{\text{Interest rate}}}$$

Miller-Orr model

Spread between upper and lower cash balance limits

$$= 3\left(\frac{\frac{3}{4} \times \text{transaction cost} \times \text{variance of cash flows}}{\text{Interest rate}}\right)^{1/3}$$

BPP Notes

Note 1. The *value of a future* formula applies to futures in *commodities*, which are beyond the scope of the current *SFM* syllabus.

Note 2. Most well prepared students will be able to do a leasing question without having to look up a formula. The *value of lease* formula is included in the *Mathematical Tables* for those who might have need of it.

Note 3. The Examiner has indicated that the *MM formula* given for *adjusted cost of capital* is unlikely to be used often in examinations and that, if it is, clear guidance will be given on its application.

Note 4. In an article in *CIMA Student*, the *SFM* Examiner has written as follows.

'It is unlikely that students will be asked to calculate portfolio variances as the calculations are tedious and time-consuming. However, a question may ask for an explanation of what portfolio variances are and how they might be interpreted. The formula may therefore aid students in their explanations.'

Note 5. The Examiner has commented that although the standard form of the CAPM will feature regularly in exams, the *certainty-equivalent form* of the CAPM is unlikely to be tested but is included in the *Mathematical Tables* for general information.

Note 6. The Examiner has stated that 'it is unlikely these formulae *[Measures of portfolio performance]* will be needed for the *SFM* examination ... although the Jensen measure could be used in discussion if the performance of share prices was the subject of a question and the measure could be introduced into the discussion'.

Note 7. Knowledge of the *Black-Scholes formula* and the *binomial option valuation model* is not required for the *SFM* syllabus.

Question and answer bank

Some questions of examination standard are given marks and time allocations.

1 EARNINGS PER SHARE

The main objective of a listed company is the maximisation of earnings per share. Discuss.

2 YIELD CURVE

(a) What is a yield curve?
(b) To what extent does the shape of the yield curve depend on expectations about the future?

3 SUBSIDIARIES *36 mins*

Your company has two subsidiaries, X Ltd and Y Ltd, both providing computer services, notably software development and implementation. The UK market for such services is said to be growing at about 20% a year. The business is seasonal, peaking between September and March.

You have available the comparative data shown in the Appendix to this question below. The holding company's policy is to leave the financing and management of subsidiaries entirely to the subsidiaries' directors.

Required

In the light of this information, compare the performance of the two subsidiaries.

It may be assumed that the difference in size of the two companies does not invalidate a comparison of the ratios provided.

Appendix

Data in this Appendix should be accepted as correct. Any apparent internal inconsistencies are due to rounding of the figures.

	X Ltd	*Y Ltd*
Turnover in most recent year (£'000)		
Home	2,856	6,080
Export	2,080	1,084
Total	4,936	7,164
Index of turnover 19X9 (19X6 = 100)		
Home	190%	235%
Export	220%	150%
Total	200%	220%
Operating profit 19X9 (£'000)	840	720
Operating capital employed 19X9 (£'000)	625	1,895

Ratio analysis		*X Ltd*			*Y Ltd*		
		19X9	*19X8*	*19X7*	*19X9*	*19X8*	*19X7*
Return on operating capital employed	%	134	142	47	38	40	52
Operating profit: Sales	%	17	16	6	10	8	5
Sales: Operating capital employed	×	8	9	8	4	5	10
Percentages to sales value:							
Cost of sales	%	65	67	71	49	49	51
Selling and distribution costs	%	12	11	15	15	16	19
Administration expenses	%	6	6	8	26	27	25
Number of employees		123	127	88	123	114	91
Sales per employee	£'000	40	37	31	58	52	47
Average remuneration per employee	£'000	13	13	12	16	4	13
Tangible fixed assets							
Turnover rate	×	20	21	14	9	11	14
Additions, at cost	%	57	47	58	303	9	124
Percentage depreciated	%	45	36	20	41	60	72
Product development costs carried forward as a percentage of turnover	%	0	0	0	10	8	6
Debtors : Sales	%	18	18	22	61	41	39
Stocks : Sales	%	0	1	0	2	2	1
Cash : Sales	%	7	9	2	1	1	0
Trade creditors : Sales	%	2	2	3	32	21	24
Trade creditors : Debtors	%	11	14	15	53	50	62
Current ratio (:1)		1.5	1.3	1.2	1.1	1.1	0.9
Liquid ratio (:1)		1.5	1.3	1.2	1.0	1.0	0.9
Liquid ratio excluding bank overdraft		0	0	0	1.4	1.5	1.2
Total debt : Total assets	%	61	71	109	75	72	84

Total Marks = 20

4 NEWBEGIN ENTERPRISES LTD *45 mins*

Newbegin Enterprises Ltd is considering whether to invest in a project which would entail immediate expenditure on capital equipment of £40,000. Expected sales from the project are as follows.

Probability	*Sales volume* (*Units*)
0.10	2,000
0.25	6,000
0.40	8,000
0.15	10,000
0.10	14,000

Once sales are established at a certain volume in the first year, they will continue at that same volume in later years. The unit price will be £10, the unit variable cost will be £6 and additional fixed costs will be £20,000. The project would have a life of six years, after which the equipment would be sold for scrap to earn £3,000. The company's cost of capital is 10%.

Required

(a) What is the expected value of the NPV of the project? **5 Marks**

(b) What is the minimum annual volume of sales required to justify the project? **5 Marks**

(c) Making whatever assumptions are necessary, describe (giving calculations) several different methods of analysing the risk or uncertainty in the project. **15 Marks**

Total Marks = 25

5 FINANCIAL FUNCTIONS

Discuss the possible advantages and disadvantages of centralising the financial functions of a group of companies.

6 TWO CLIENTS *45 mins*

Assume you are a newly recruited junior consultant with Q, Y and R, a large international firm of accountants and financial consultants. A number of its clients are currently examining the methods available for financing or re-financing their businesses. You have been asked to review two of Q, Y and R's clients. Only brief details are available at present. These are given below.

Client number 1: ABC Limited

ABC Limited is a software house in the south of England. The company was established four years ago by five telecommunications specialists who had been made redundant. The initial investment was £250,000 in equity and a bank loan of £250,000 repayable over 10 years at fixed rate of interest of 12%. The original five shareholders are still the only shareholders.

The company was formed to develop and market a range of specialist software for the telecommunications industry. At present, the company's main customers are in the United Kingdom and parts of western Europe. Extracts from the company's financial statements for last year and forecast for the current year are as follows.

PROFIT AND LOSS ACCOUNT (EXTRACTS) FOR YEARS

	19X3	*19X4*
	Actual	*Forecast*
	£'000	£'000
Turnover	2,350	3,250
Profit after tax	485	763
Dividends payable	440	563

BALANCE SHEET (EXTRACTS) AT END OF YEAR

	19X3	*19X4*
	Actual	*Forecast*
	£'000	£'000
Fixed assets (NBV)	250	350
Current assets	1,093	1,472
Current liabilities	(778)	(1,082)
Total net assets	565	740
Financed by:		
Issued share capital (ordinary £1 shares)	250	250
Reserves	165	365
Long-term loan (10-year bank loan)	150	125
Total financing	565	740

Notes

1 The fixed assets are primarily motor vehicles, furniture and fittings and computers. The company's premises are rented. The net book value is after charging depreciation of £100,000 and £150,000 in 19X3 and 19X4 respectively.

2 The tax charge for 19X3 was £220,000 and the forecast for 19X4 is £375,000.

3 Inflation, as it affects this company's business, has been negligible over the three-year period.

ABC Limited is now considering expanding its product range and moving into new international markets. These markets are highly competitive but expected to be very profitable in the long term. The company estimates it will need £2 million to establish local operations and support facilities in three main centres outside western Europe. If financing can be obtained and the expansion proceeds, turnover and profits could treble by 19X7.

The shares of listed companies trading in ABC Limited's industry are currently capitalised at P/E ratios between 16 and 20.

Client number 2: DEF plc

DEF plc is a clothes retailing company which has been established for over 50 years. It has shops mainly in small towns in the UK, selling to low-income families. The company has been listed on the Stock Exchange for over 30 years. Summary financial statistics for 19X3 and forecast for 19X4 are as follows.

PROFIT AND LOSS ACCOUNT (EXTRACTS) FOR YEARS

	19X3 Actual £million	*19X4 Forecast* £million
Turnover	1,250	1,450
Profit after tax	113	118
Dividends payable	60	72

BALANCE SHEET (EXTRACTS) AT END OF YEAR

	19X3 Actual £million	*19X4 Forecast* £million
Fixed assets (NBV)	925	915
Current assets	153	229
Current liabilities	(195)	(215)
Total net assets	883	929
Financed by:		
Issued share capital (ordinary 25p shares)	100	100
Reserves	573	619
Long-term debt 9% (redeemable in 19Y2)	210	210
Total financing	883	929
Share price (pence, average)	314	n/a

The company has recently launched a profit improvement programme: a number of cost-cutting measures have been implemented and the product range has been revised; a number of older products have been discontinued and new ones introduced. Overall, the company is moving into a higher priced section of the market and believes it can now open new shops in towns where it has no presence and where it will come into direct competition with the major retailing stores. It estimates it will require £250 million to undertake this expansion.

The current share price is 245 pence. Debt of similar risk and maturity to that in DEF plc's balance sheet is currently trading in the market at £125 per £100 nominal.

The methods of finance being considered by the two companies include, *but are not limited to*, the following:

- equity
- mortgage debt
- convertible debt
- debt with warrants
- leasing
- preference shares

Required

(a) Describe, very briefly, *three* of the methods of finance listed above. **5 Marks**

(b) Prepare, for discussion with the senior consultant, a set of briefing notes for *each* of your clients. These should contain reasoned arguments for an appropriate method, or methods, of financing taking into account the circumstances of each company. Make whatever assumptions you think necessary but state them clearly in your notes. **20 Marks**

Total Marks = 25

7 AB LTD *45 mins*

AB Ltd is a new company in the electrical industry. It has been formed by Mr A and Mr B, its joint managing directors, who have been made redundant by a major electrical manufacturer. They intend to employ a number of their former work colleagues who were also made redundant. Mr A and Mr B received a substantial amount of redundancy pay. This money, combined with their savings, will give them £300,000 towards the financing requirements of the company. The rest of their financing will need to be provided by debt and the directors approach their bank with a request for assistance.

The bank has asked for financial information and statements from the company in support of their request. The only information the two directors have available is an estimate of their first year's gross sales together with industry financial ratios/averages for the current year, obtained from the Inter Company Comparisons' (ICC) *Industrial Performance Analysis*. The information is as follows.

Estimated sales for 19X4	£1.4 million
Industry financial ratios/averages for 19X3	
Current ratio	1.83 times
Net operating profit	10%
Sales to capital employed	2.8 times
Average collection period	50 days
* Average payment period (Trade creditors)	60 days
Sales to stock	5.6 times
Fixed assets to capital employed	60%
Cost of sales to sales	60%
Operating expenses to sales	30%

* Assume that all cost of sales is on credit and all operating expenses are for cash.

Ignore taxation.

Required

(a) Draft a report for the bank based on the above information for inclusion in a formal request for financing. **9 Marks**

(b) State the assumptions necessary in your calculations and comment on other information which would be useful to support your request for finance. **5 Marks**

(c) Advise the company on alternative sources of short- and medium-term financing which could be considered if the bank refuses finance. **6 Marks**

(d) Comment on external sources of publicly available information, other than the ICC, which might be of use to the company in the preparation of its forecasts. **5 Marks**

Total Marks = 25

8 CAPITAL MARKETS

Explain the main advantages and disadvantages to a company of obtaining a quotation on the Stock Exchange for its ordinary shares.

9 GROWTH PLC

Growth plc, a company in the leisure industry with turnover of £20,000,000 in the year just ended, was formed six years ago. So far, the company has been financed by wealthy individual shareholders and by bank loans, but it is now clear that a wider range of investors will be needed to fund further expansion. Furthermore, some of the existing shareholders would like there to be a market for shares in the company, so that they could sell some shares.

Turnover and earnings have grown steadily since the company's formation, but it is recognised that the leisure industry is vulnerable to fluctuations in individuals' real earnings.

Required

Suggest a capital market to meet the requirements of the company and its shareholders, and discuss the advantages and disadvantages of your suggestion.

10 SHARE VALUES

(a) Outline the fundamental analysis theory of share values, giving numerical examples.

(b) To what extent is the validity of the fundamental analysis theory affected by the efficiency of the stock market?

11 CRYSTAL PLC *45 mins*

The following figures have been extracted from the most recent accounts of Crystal plc.

BALANCE SHEET AS ON 30 JUNE 19X9

	£'000	£'000
Fixed assets		10,115
Investments		821
Current assets	3,658	
Less current liabilities	1,735	
		1,923
		12,859
Ordinary share capital		
Authorised: 4,000,000 shares of £1		
Issued: 3,000,000 shares of £1		3,000
Reserves		6,542
Shareholders' funds		9,542
7% Debentures		1,300
Deferred taxation		583
Corporation tax		1,434
		12,859

Summary of profits and dividends

Year ended 30 June:	19X5	19X6	19X7	19X8	19X9
	£'000	£'000	£'000	£'000	£'000
Profit after interest and before tax	1,737	2,090	1,940	1,866	2,179
Less tax	573	690	640	616	719
Profit after interest and tax	1,164	1,400	1,300	1,250	1,460
Less dividends	620	680	740	740	810
Added to reserves	544	720	560	510	650

The current (1 July 19X9) market value of Crystal plc's ordinary shares is £3.27 per share cum div. An annual dividend of £810,000 is due for payment shortly. The debentures are redeemable at par in ten years time. Their current market value is £77.10 per cent. Annual interest has just been paid on the debentures. There have been no issues or redemptions of ordinary shares or debentures during the past five years.

The current rate of corporation tax is 30%, and the current basic rate of income tax is 25%. Assume that there have been no changes in the system or rates of taxation during the last five years.

Required

(a) Estimate the cost of capital which Crystal plc should use as a discount rate when appraising new investment opportunities. **20 Marks**

(b) Discuss any difficulties and uncertainties in your estimates. **5 Marks**

Total Marks = 25

12 CASTOR AND POLLUX *54 mins*

(a) Outline the Modigliani-Miller theory on the effect of gearing on the cost of capital to, and value of, the firm, in the absence of taxation. Explain how the theory is adjusted to take into account the effects of taxation. What are the principal weaknesses of this theory? **10 Marks**

(b) Castor plc and Pollux plc are two companies, operating in the same industry, which have reported identical net operating incomes. The stock market regards the net operating incomes of the two companies as being subject to the same degree of business risk.

Castor plc is financed entirely by equity, its share capital consisting of 20 million 50p shares with a market price of £4.80 per share (ex div). The cost of equity to Castor is estimated to be 18%. Pollux plc is financed by a combination of £20,000,000 12% irredeemable debenture stock (market price £120%) and 30 million £1 ordinary shares.

The risk free rate of interest is 10%. The market prices of Castor plc's shares and Pollux plc's debentures are considered to be in equilibrium.

Required

Using (where appropriate) the Modigliani-Miller propositions, calculate:

(i) the equilibrium market price of Pollux plc's shares;
(ii) the equilibrium cost of equity to Pollux plc; and
(iii) the weighted average cost of capital to Pollux plc.

Assume (I) no taxation; and (II) corporation tax at 25%. (Make separate calculations for each assumption.)

Ignore dividends and accrued interest on the stocks. **15 Marks**

Total Marks = 25

13 MOODY AND HART

Moody plc has an opportunity to invest in a project lasting one year.

Hart plc has three projects, each lasting one year, but in different industries.

The net cash flows (arising at the end of the year) and the beta factors for each of the projects are as follows.

	£'000	β
Moody plc	500	1.20
Hart plc	200	1.25
	100	0.80
	200	1.35

The market return is 12% and the risk-free rate of interest is 7%.

Required

(a) Suggest how portfolio diversification *by a company* can reduce the risk experienced by an investor.

(b) Calculate the total present value of the projects that can be undertaken by

(i) Moody plc;
(ii) Hart plc.

(c) Calculate the overall beta factor for Hart plc's projects, assuming that all three are undertaken.

(d) Using this information, discuss which company is likely to be valued more highly by investors.

14 INDUSTRIAL COMPANY *36 mins*

(a) What risks might an industrial company face as a result of interest rate movements? **10 Marks**
(b) Explain the main financial instruments which a company can use to reduce these risks. **10 Marks**

Total Marks = 20

15 ABC

The managing directors of three profitable listed companies discussed their company's dividend policies at a business lunch.

Company A has deliberately paid no dividends for the last five years.

Company B always pays a dividend of 50% of earnings after taxation.

Company C maintains a low but constant dividend per share (after adjusting for the general price index), and offers regular scrip issues and shareholder concessions.

Each managing director is convinced that his company's policy is maximising shareholder wealth.

Required

What are the advantages and disadvantages of the alternative dividend policies of the three companies? Discuss the circumstances under which each managing director might be correct in his

belief that his company's dividend policy is maximising shareholder wealth. State clearly any assumptions that you make.

16 H AND D

H Finance plc is prepared to advance 80% of D Ltd's sales invoicing, provided its specialist collection services are used by D Ltd. H Finance plc would charge an additional 0.5% of D Ltd's turnover for this service. D Ltd would avoid administration costs it currently incurs amounting to £80,000 per annum.

The history of D Ltd's debtors' ledgers may be summarised as follows:

	19X8	*19X9*	*19Y0*
Turnover (£'000)	78,147	81,941	98,714
% debtors at year end	17	20	22
% debtors of 90 + days (of turnover)	1.5	2	2.5
Bad debts (£'000)	340	497	615

D Ltd estimates that the aggressive collection procedures adopted by the finance company are likely to result in lost turnover of some 10% of otherwise expected levels.

Currently, each £1 of turnover generates 18 pence additional profit before taxation. D Limited turns its capital over, on average, three times each year. On receipt by H Finance plc of amounts due from D Ltd's customers, a further 15% of the amounts are to be remitted to D Ltd.

The cheapest alternative form of finance would cost 20% per annum.

Required

Calculate whether the factoring of D Ltd's debtors ledger would be worthwhile.

17 EXCESS CASH AND MONEY MARKET INSTRUMENTS *36 mins*

(a) The treasurer of B plc has forecast that, over the next year, the company will generate cash flows in excess of its requirements. List four possible reasons for such a surplus, and explain the circumstances under which the board of directors might decide to keep the excess in liquid form.

8 Marks

(b) The following table of London money rates shows the relationship between maturity and interest rates for four types of short-term investment, as published in the financial press.

	One month	*Three months*	*Six months*	*One year*
Sterling certificates of deposit	$9^7/_8$	$10^1/_{16}$	$10^3/_{16}$	$10^5/_{16}$
Local authority bonds	$9^7/_8$	10	$10^1/_4$	$10^1/_2$
Finance house deposits	10	$10^1/_8$	$10^3/_8$	$10^9/_{16}$
Treasury bills (buy)	$9^{11}/_{16}$	$9^3/_4$	-	-

Explain:

(i) the nature of the instruments listed; and
(ii) the main reasons for the differences in interest rate between the instruments and over time.

12 Marks

Total Marks = 20

18 COLLEGE BOOKSHOP *36 mins*

A college has an area of unused space available within its main entrance hall. The administrator has proposed that this should be used to accommodate a kiosk selling books, stationery and other student requirements. The hall is well lit and adequately heated and no additional cost would be involved for these services.

No other useful purpose is foreseen for the area. However, future major redevelopment is planned at the college so the facility is only likely to be available for five years.

A suitable lock-up kiosk together with fittings would cost £20,000 to build. The cost of capital for the college is 10% a year. A survey of sales potential and estimated costs has produced the following disappointing annual figures.

	£'000	£'000	£'000
Total sales			100
Cost of sales		80	
Staff salaries		13	
Interest on capital		2	
Depreciation of kiosk		4	
Share of existing college overheads			
Building repairs	3		
Heat and light	1		
Administration	1		
		5	
			104
Estimated annual loss			4

During discussion on supply prices, a local wholesaler has offered, in return for a five year tenancy, to pay half of the cost of building the kiosk and an annual rent of £4,000 inclusive of lighting and heating.

Required

(a) Critically review the administrator's figures. **5 Marks**

(b) Evaluate the two proposed methods of operating the kiosk. **10 Marks**

(c) Recommend a course of action you think should be taken using the data established in part (b) and stating any assumptions you make. **5 Marks**

Total Marks = 20

19 ANTARES PLC *45 mins*

Antares plc, a multi-product company, is considering four investment projects, details of which are given below.

Development costs already incurred on the projects are as follows.

A	*B*	*C*	*D*
£	£	£	£
100,000	75,000	80,000	60,000

Each project will require an immediate outlay on plant and machinery, the cost of which is estimated as follows.

A	*B*	*C*	*D*
£	£	£	£
2,100,000	1,400,000	2,400,000	600,000

In all four cases the plant and machinery has a useful life of five years at the end of which it will be valueless.

Unit sales per annum, for each project, are expected to be as follows.

A	*B*	*C*	*D*
£	£	£	£
150,000	75,000	80,000	120,000

Selling price and variable costs per unit for each project are estimated below.

	A	*B*	*C*	*D*
	£	£	£	£
Selling price	30.00	40.00	25.00	50.00
Materials	7.60	12.00	4.50	25.00
Labour	9.80	12.00	5.00	10.00
Variable overheads	6.00	7.00	2.50	10.50

The company charges depreciation on plant and machinery on a straight line basis over the useful life of the plant and machinery. Development costs of projects are written off in the year that they are incurred. The company apportions general administration costs to projects at a rate of 5% of selling price. None of the above projects will lead to any actual increase in the company's administration costs.

Working capital requirements for each project will amount to 20% of the expected annual sales value. In each case this investment will be made immediately and will be recovered in full when the projects end in five years time.

Funds available for investment are limited to £5,200,000. The company's cost of capital is estimated to be 18%.

Required

(a) Calculate the NPV of each project. **12 Marks**

(b) Calculate the profitability index for each project and advise the company which of the new projects, if any, to undertake. You may assume that each of the projects can be undertaken on a reduced scale for a proportionate reduction in cash flows. Your advice should state clearly your order of preference for the four projects, what proportion you would take of any project that is scaled down, and the total NPV generated by your choice. **5 Marks**

(c) Discuss the limitations of the profitability index as a means of dealing with capital rationing problems. **8 Marks**

Ignore taxation. **Total Marks = 25**

20 DINARD PLC *36 mins*

(a) Explain the difference between real rates of return and money rates of return and outline the circumstances in which the use of each would be appropriate when appraising capital projects under inflationary conditions **4 Marks**

(b) Dinard plc has just developed a new product to be called Rance and is now considering whether to put it into production. The following information is available.

(i) Costs incurred in the development of Rance amount to £480,000.

(ii) Production of Rance will require the purchase of new machinery at a cost of £2,400,000 payable immediately. This machinery is specific to the production of Rance and will be obsolete and valueless when that production ceases. The machinery has a production life of four years and a production capacity of 30,000 units per annum.

(iii) Production costs of Rance (at year 1 prices) are estimated as follows.

	£
Variable materials	8.00
Variable labour	12.00
Variable overheads	12.00

In addition, fixed production costs (at year 1 prices), including straight line depreciation on plant and machinery, will amount to £800,000 per annum.

(iv) The selling price of Rance will be £80.00 per unit (at year 1 prices). Demand is expected to be 25,000 units per annum for the next four years.

(v) The retail price index is expected to increase at 5% per annum for the next four years and the selling price of Rance is expected to increase at the same rate. Annual inflation rates for production costs are expected to be as follows.

	%
Variable materials	4
Variable labour	10
Variable overheads	4
Fixed costs	5

(vi) The company's weighted average cost of capital in money terms is expected to be 15%.

Required

Advise the directors of Dinard plc whether it should produce Rance on the basis of the information above. **16 Marks**

Notes

Unless otherwise specified all costs revenues should be assumed to rise at the end of each year.

Ignore taxation. **Total Marks = 20**

21 DIVESTMENT PLC *72 mins*

Divestment plc has recently received an offer from the managers of one of its fully owned subsidiaries for a management buyout of that subsidiary.

The accounts of the subsidiary for the year just ended are as follows.

Profit and loss account

	£'000		£'000
Purchases (stock adjusted)	4,000	Sales	10,000
Wages	3,000		
Depreciation	1,000		
Other expenses	1,500		
Net profit	500		-
	10,000		10,000

Balance sheet

		£'000		£'000
Land and buildings		2,000	Ordinary shares of £1	1,000
Plant and machinery			Retained profits	7,000
Cost	6,000			8,000
Depreciation	3,000		Bank overdraft	2,000
		3,000		
		5,000		
Stock	2,000			
Debtors	3,000			
		5,000		-
		10,000		10,000

The managers have carried out a feasibility study from which they have learned the following.

(i) The subsidiary is buying its materials from the parent company and is paying a price 25% higher than that at which the materials could be bought from a competitor. Stockholdings are also too high and could be reduced by one-quarter. Furthermore, the parent company requires payment on delivery, whereas the competitor would give three months credit.

(ii) The figure for other expenses includes a head office charge of £500,000, which would not be payable if the subsidiary were acquired.

(iii) 20% of the sales are to the parent company which takes six months credit. All sales are made evenly throughout the year and the credit period given to other customers is three months.

(iv) The land and buildings could be sold for £6m, the plant and machinery has a scrap value of £1m, the stock is worth £1m and the debtors would be likely to pay in full.

(v) If £2m were to be spent on advertising immediately, sales would rise to £12m for the foreseeable future. Material and wages usage would rise proportionately, and 'other expenses' would increase by £200,000.

(vi) The plant and machinery will not require replacement for the foreseeable future.

(vii) A return on capital of 30% would be required for an investment of this sort.

Required

(a) Write a report which

(i) explains the highest price which the management team should be prepared to pay for the subsidiary, and **20 Marks**

(ii) suggests a possible funding package for financing the acquisition. **10 Marks**

Ignore taxation and state clearly any assumptions which you make.

(b) *Required*

Explain the main reasons for which a company may decide to make a takeover bid. **10 Marks**

Total Marks = 40

22 OXLAKE PLC

45 mins

Oxlake plc has export orders from a company in Singapore for 250,000 china cups, and from a company in Indonesia for 100,000 china cups. The unit variable cost to Oxlake of producing china cups is 55. The unit sales price to Singapore is Singapore $2.862 and to Indonesia, 2,246 rupiahs. Both orders are subject to credit terms of 60 days, and are payable in the currency of the importers. Past experience suggests that there is 50% chance of the customer in Singapore paying 30 days late. The Indonesian customer has offered to Oxlake the alternative of being paid US $125,000 in 3 months time instead of payment in the Indonesian currency. The Indonesian currency is forecast by Oxlake's bank to depreciate in value during the next year by 30% (from an Indonesian viewpoint) relative to the US dollar.

Whenever appropriate, Oxlake uses option forward foreign exchange contracts.

Foreign exchange rates (mid rates)

	$Singapore/$US	*$US/£*	*Rupiahs/£*
Spot	2.1378	1.4875	2,481
1 month forward	2.1132	1.4963	No forward
2 months forward	2.0964	1.5047	market exists
3 months forward	2.0915	1.5105	

Assume that any foreign currency holding in the UK will be immediately converted into sterling.

	Money market rates (% per year)	
	Deposit	*Borrowing*
UK clearing bank	6	11
Singapore bank	4	7
Euro-dollars	7½	12
Indonesian bank	15	Not available
Euro-sterling	6½	10½
US domestic bank	8	12½

These interest rates are fixed rates for either immediate deposits or borrowing over a period of two or three months, but the rates are subject to future movement according to economic pressures.

Required

(a) Using what you consider to be the most suitable way of protecting against foreign exchange risk, evaluate the sterling receipts that Oxlake can expect from its sales to Singapore and to Indonesia, without taking any risks.

All contracts, including foreign exchange and money market contracts, may be assumed to be free from the risk of default. Transactions costs may be ignored. **13 Marks**

(b) If the Indonesian customer offered another form of payment to Oxlake, immediate payment in US dollars of the full amount owed in return for a 5% discount on the rupiah unit sales price, calculate whether Oxlake is likely to benefit from this form of payment. **7 Marks**

(c) Discuss the advantages and disadvantages to a company of invoicing an export sale in a foreign currency. **5 Marks**

Total Marks = 25

23 EXPORTERS PLC

36 mins

Exporters plc, a UK company, is due to receive 500,000 Northland dollars in six months' time for goods supplied. The company decides to hedge its currency exposure by using the forward market. The short-term interest rate in the UK is 12% per annum and the equivalent rate in Northland is 15%. The spot rate of exchange is 2.5 Northland dollars to the pound.

Required

(a) Calculate how much Exporters plc actually gains or loses as a result of the hedging transaction if, at the end of the six months, the pound, in relation to the Northland dollar, has (i) gained 4%, (ii) lost 2% or (iii) remained stable. You may assume that the forward rate of exchange simply reflects the interest differential in the two countries (ie it reflects the interest rate parity analysis of forward rates). **6 Marks**

(b) Explain the rationale behind the interest rate parity analysis of forward rates. **6 Marks**

(c) Compare a forward market currency hedge with (i) a currency futures hedge, (ii) a currency options hedge. Indicate in each of the three cases how the hedging facility is actually provided, the nature of the costs and the potential outcomes of the hedge. **8 Marks**

Total Marks = 20

24 AARDVARK LTD *36 mins*

Aardvark Ltd has been having some difficulty with the collection of debts from export customers. At present the company makes no special arrangements for export sales.

As a result the company is considering either:

(a) employing the services of a non-recourse export factoring company; or
(b) insuring its exports against non-payment through and insurer.

The two alternatives also provide possible ways of financing sales.

An export factor will, if required, provide immediate finance of 80% of export credit sales at an interest rate of 2% above bank base rate (the base rate is 8%). The service fee for debt collection is 3% of credit sales. If the factor is used, administrative savings of £35,000 a year should be possible.

A comprehensive insurance policy costs 35 pence per £100 insured and covers 90% of the risk of non-payment for exports. The insurer will probably allow Aardvark Ltd to assign its rights to a bank, in return for which the bank will provide an advance of 70% of the sales value of insured debts, at a cost of 1.5% above base rate.

Aardvark's annual exports total £1,000,000. Export sales are on open account terms of 60 days credit, but on average payments have been 30 days late. Approximately 0.5%, by value, of credit sales result in bad debts which have to be written off.

The company is able to borrow on overdraft from its bank, unsecured, at 2.5% above base rate. Assume a 360 day year.

Required

Determine which combination of export administration and financing Aardvark Ltd should use.

Total Marks = 20

25 FOREIGN MARKETS *63 mins*

(a) Explain briefly the advantages and disadvantages of exporting, licensing and foreign direct investment as alternative forms of involvement in foreign markets. **10 Marks**

(b) You have been appointed by Ranek plc to advise on the price that the company should tender for the construction of a small power station in a foreign country, Zmbland.

The company normally charges a price that gives a 20% markup on all directly attributable costs (which includes leasing and the current written-down value of assets less any residual value of assets expected at the end of the contract but excludes any tax effects of such costs).

The power station will take 15 months to construct. All costs are payable in pounds sterling. Wages totalling £380,000 are payable monthly in arrears in pounds sterling. Materials are purchased two months in advance of the month when they are to be used. One month's credit is taken on all materials purchases. Materials usage is expected to be £715,000 per month, payable in sterling. Other direct costs are expected to be £50,000 per month and the company will allocate central overhead to the project at £25,000 per month. No increases in costs are expected during the contract period.

Ranek already owns some plant and equipment that could be used in this project. These assets cost £3 million and have a written-down value of £1.8 million after deduction of tax allowable depreciation at 25% on a reducing balance basis. If the contract is not undertaken the existing plant and equipment will be sold immediately for £2 million. The realisable value of these assets at the end of 15 months is expected to be £900,000. Special equipment for the contract would be obtained through an operating lease at a quarterly cost of £620,000 payable in advance on the first day of the quarter.

Assume that corporate tax in the United Kingdom at the rate of 35% is payable on net cash flows six months after the end of the relevant tax year. No foreign tax liability is expected. Any tax effects associated with the disposal of assets also occur six months after the relevant year end. The end of Ranek's financial year occurs three months after the start of the project.

The tender price for the power station is to be in Zmbland dollars (Z$). Thirty per cent is payable immediately and the balance upon completion. The current exchange rate is Z$45.5-46.0/£ and the Zmbland dollar is expected to steadily depreciate in value relative to the pound by approximately 25% during the next 15 months. No forward foreign exchange market exists.

Ranek's managers estimate that the company's opportunity cost of capital is 1% per month. The company currently has spare capacity.

Required

(i) Estimate the tender price that would result from a 20% markup on sterling direct costs. Ignore the time value of money in the estimate of the required markup. **5 Marks**

(ii) Estimate the net present value of the proposed project and discuss and recommend the minimum price that the company should tender. State clearly any assumptions that you make. **20 Marks**

Total Marks = 35

1 EARNINGS PER SHARE

The fundamental assumption which underlies financial theory is that the sole purpose of the existence of a company is to increase the wealth of its owners by the maximum amount possible. In other words, the primary purpose is to increase the wealth of the ordinary shareholders. This proposal will be investigated to determine to what extent such an aim coincides with the maximisation of earnings per share.

Maximisation means that the directors will try to obtain the best possible results from a given situation and will not settle for a level of performance that is merely satisfactory (satisficing). It might appear that to aim at maximising rather than satisficing earnings will be in the interests of the ordinary shareholders. However, the effects of the aim of maximisation of earnings can only be evaluated in the context of the directors' attitude to risk. It might mean that very risky investments are being undertaken since they yield potentially the highest returns. However, this could have the side effect of depressing the share price and thereby the market value of the company, which in turn represents a fall in the wealth of the shareholders. Further, if new equity needs to be raised, a larger number of shares will need to be issued if the price is depressed, and thus in the long term, earnings per share could even be reduced.

The wealth of the shareholders can be increased in two ways: by a rise in the market price of the shares, or by means of a distribution of dividends.

An increase in earnings per share means that there will be more profits available for distribution as dividend, and that there will be more profits that can be retained within the firm to invest in further expansion and earnings growth. This implies that the financial worth of the company will be increased, and as a result, the market price of the shares can be expected to rise. In the long term, therefore, there will be a relationship between shareholder wealth and earnings per share, since a proportion of the earnings will be paid out as dividend and the remainder reinvested to provide future growth in profits and dividends. However, there is a risk that a company may seek to increase earnings per share in the short term at the expense of longer term development and therefore earnings. Thus the relationship is only valid if the directors take a long term view of maximising earnings per share in setting their targets.

The statement in the question implies the acknowledged fact that companies do not have one single objective, but operate within a matrix of different objectives, both financial and non- financial. These other objectives are frequently formulated with the aim of assisting the achievement of the main objective, for example, a division of the company may be set the target of achieving a minimum rate of return on capital employed of 20%. However, these subsidiary targets are frequently evaluated over a short-term period, typically six months to a year. Thus they can come into conflict with the primary aim of maximising earnings in the long term. Other objectives may act as a constraint on the primary objective. For example, a financial constraint might be that a ceiling is set on the permitted level of gearing in order to limit the financial risk of the company. In a more highly geared company, the proportion of equity is lower and therefore the potential level of earnings per share is higher, albeit with a higher level of risk of annual fluctuations as the interest rate varies.

Non-financial objectives include, for example, to act scrupulously in relationships with customers and suppliers; to operate fair and generous personnel policies; to have competitive remuneration levels and good training and development programmes; and to achieve the highest standards that can reasonably be maintained in environmental policies. These policies do not necessarily run counter to the aim of maximising earnings per share, and may even enhance it by improving the image of the firm in its operating environment. However they will act as at least a short-term constraint upon the maximisation of earnings per share and shareholder wealth.

To conclude, it has been shown that the timescale over which decisions are evaluated is important in deciding the degree to which the maximisation of earnings per share is successful in achieving the maximisation of shareholder wealth, the two becoming increasingly similar as the timescale lengthens. However, this situation will always be subject to important constraints imposed by subsidiary financial and non-financial objectives.

2 YIELD CURVE

(a) A yield curve is a curve that can be drawn showing the relationship between the yield on an asset (usually long-term government stocks) and the term to maturity of that same asset. It shows how the rate of interest (yield) varies with different maturities. To construct a yield curve you need to gather information about the interest rates on short-term stocks, medium-term stocks and long-

term stocks. These rates can then be plotted on a diagram against the maturity dates of those same stocks. A normal yield curve looks like Figure 1.

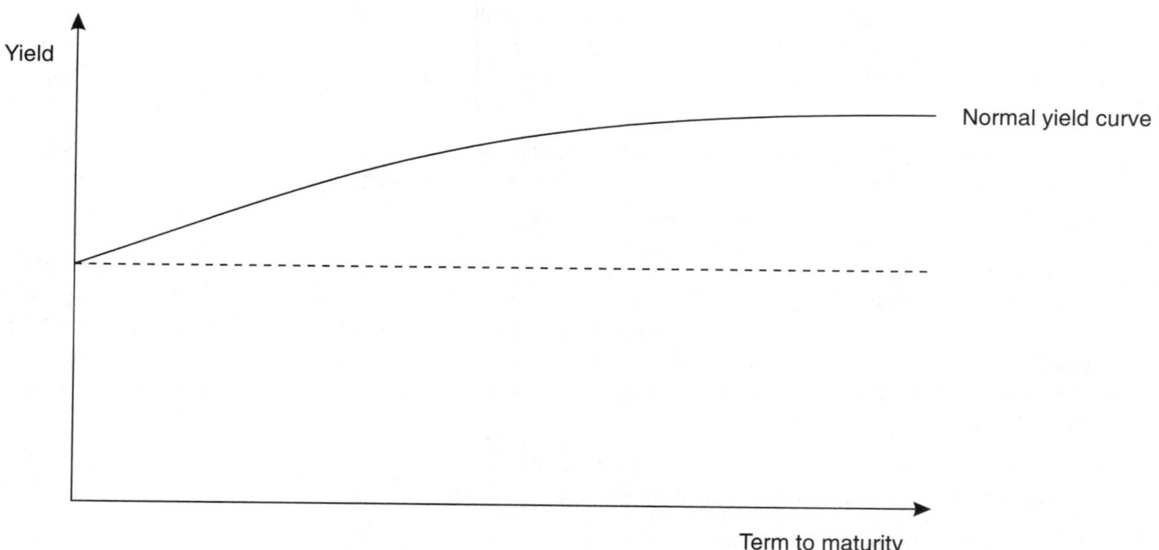

Figure 1

(b) The shape of the yield curve depends very much on expectations about the future. Reward for loss of liquidity is likely to remain fairly constant. Reward for possible default is likely to remain constant also. Reward for the risk of having to cash in before maturity and suffering a loss are also likely to stay fairly constant. The only factor which will vary widely is expectations - in particular, expectations about future short-term interest rates.

Expectations about the future level of short-term interest rates are the most important factor in determining the shape of the yield curve. Although the normal yield curve is upward sloping, with higher yields being expected for longer maturity periods, expectations of rises in future interest rates can cause the yield curve to be steeper than the normal curve. Expectations of falls in interest rates can cause the yield to flatten, or, if substantial falls are expected, to become downward-sloping (Figure 2).

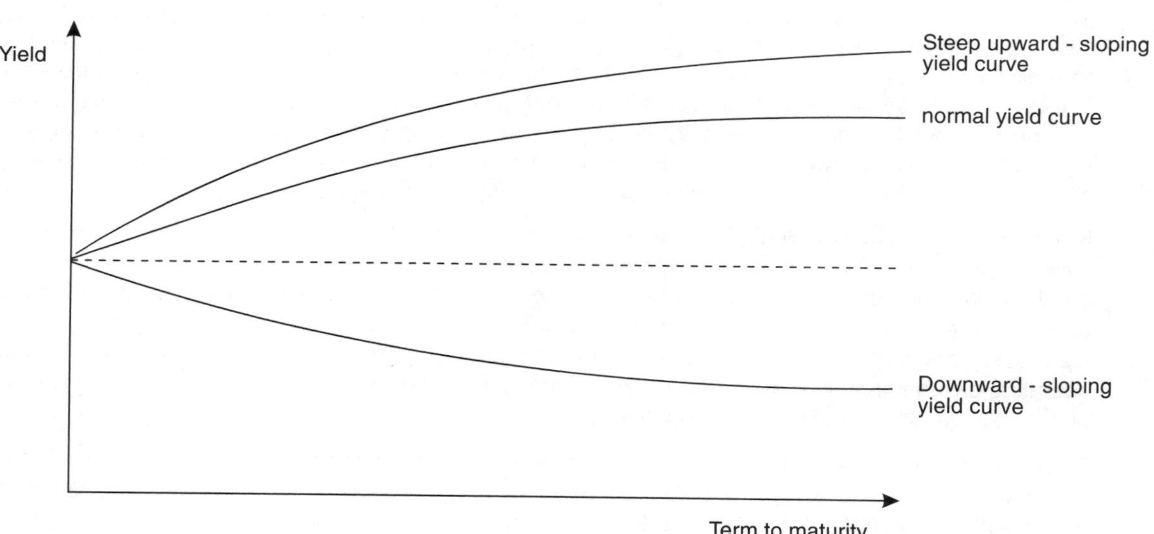

Figure 2

If interest rates are now expected to rise, investors will not wish to lock in to lower interest rates and will therefore sell short. Borrowers will wish to borrow at lower long-term rates to avoid exposure to the higher rates expected in the future. These demand and supply factors will result in a shortage of long-term funds, which will push up long-term money market rates, and to an excess supply of short-term funds, which will lead to a reduction in short-term rates. The resulting yield curve will be more steeply upward-sloping than the normal curve.

If there are new expectations that interest rates will fall, investors will prefer to lock in at higher long rates, while borrowers will not wish to be committed to higher long term rates and will prefer to borrow short. There will be an excess supply of funds at long maturities and a shortage of funds at short maturities. This will tend to lower the yield curve, possibly resulting in a flat curve or even in a downward-sloping curve.

Short-term interest rates are in turn determined partly by expectations of inflation rates in the near future. If high inflation is expected, investors will seek higher nominal rates of interest in order to achieve a real return. If people believe that inflation is falling, then they will not require such a high return.

3 SUBSIDIARIES

X Ltd is the more profitable company, both in absolute terms and in proportion to sales and to operating capital employed. This may indicate that X Ltd is much better managed than Y Ltd, but this is not the only possibility, and a study of the other data shows that Y Ltd's profitability, while at present lower, may be more sustainable.

A higher percentage of Y's sales are to the home market, while it has still achieved fairly substantial export sales. This suggests that Y could have done better in exploiting the export market, but also that Y is less exposed than X to exchange rate fluctuations and the possible imposition of trade barriers. The prospects for the home market appear good, and should give scope for adequate growth. Y has achieved higher growth in total turnover than X over the past three years.

While Y appears to be making worse use of its assets than X, with asset turnover ratios lower than X's and falling, this seems to be largely because Y has recently acquired substantial new assets. It may be that within the next few years X will have to undertake a major renewals programme, with consequent adverse effects on its asset turnover ratios.

While X may be making better use of its assets (subject to the reservations set out above), Y is making sales per employee about 50% higher than X, and has consistently done so over the past three years. X shows no sign of catching up, despite the fact that its total number of employees has recently fallen slightly. The modest rises in sales per employee over the past three years in both X and Y may be due largely to inflation.

Y seems to be significantly better than X at controlling the cost of sales (49% of sales in Y, and 65% in X), though X has made improvements over the past three years while there has been little change in Y. On the other hand, X's administration expenses have been only 6% of sales, while Y's have been 26% of sales. This contrast between the two types of cost suggests that different categorisations of costs may have been used. If we combine the cost of sales and administration expenses, then for X they total 71% of sales and for Y they total 75% of sales. There is thus little difference between the companies, though X has shown improved cost control while Y has not. X has also had lower selling and distribution costs. One must however bear in mind that X will have had a lower depreciation element in its costs than Y, because Y has recently invested substantially in fixed assets. Y's costs will also be increased by its higher salaries, which may pay off in better employee motivation and hence higher sales per employee. On the other hand, Y's costs have been kept down by the carrying forward of an increasing amount of product development costs, an accounting policy which may well be imprudent.

In working capital management, X has the edge. Y has very high debtors, and these have recently risen sharply as a proportion of turnover. Y also carries rather more stock than X, and has very little cash. While both companies have tolerable current and liquid ratios, X's are certainly safer. Y achieves a liquid ratio of 1:1 almost entirely by relying on debtors. If it suffers substantial bad debts, or if the bank should become concerned and call in the overdraft, Y could suffer serious liquidity problems. It also depends heavily on trade credit to finance debtors. While it is sensible to take advantage of trade credit offered, Y may depend too much on the continued goodwill of its suppliers. This may indicate the need for a fresh injection of equity.

On balance, X seems to be a sounder company than Y, with better financial management.

4 NEWBEGIN ENTERPRISES LTD

(a) The EV of annual sales volume is as follows.

Probability	*Sales volume*	*Expected value*
	Units	Units
0.10	2,000	200
0.25	6,000	1,500
0.40	8,000	3,200
0.15	10,000	1,500
0.10	14,000	1,400
		7,800

The EV of contribution will be 7,800 × £(10 – 6) = £31,200. The EV of additional cash profits each year will be £31,200 – £20,000 = £11,200.

Year	*Cash flow*	*Discount factor*	*Present value of cash flow*
	£	10%	£
0	(40,000)	1.000	(40,000)
1-6	11,200	4.355	48,776
6	3,000	0.564	1,692
			10,486

The expected value of the NPV of the project is £10,486.

(b) To justify the project the NPV must be at least zero. Assuming that the cost of the equipment and its residual value are known with certainty, we can calculate the minimum required PV of annual cash profits, as follows.

	Present value
	£
PV of capital outlay	40,000
Less PV of residual value	1,692
PV of annual cash profits required for NPV of zero	38,308

Discount factor of £1 pa for six years at 10% — 4.355

Annual cash profit required for NPV of zero = $\frac{£38,308}{4.355}$ = £8,796

Annual fixed costs	£20,000
Annual contribution required for NPV of zero	£28,796
Contribution per unit	£4

Annual sales required are $\frac{£28,796}{£4}$ = 7,199 units, say 7,200 units.

(c) Risk and uncertainty analysis can be carried out in several ways.

(i) Sensitivity analysis could be used to measure the percentage adverse change in estimates of cost or revenues which would make the NPV of the project negative.

The sales volume

Since the breakeven annual sales volume is about 7,200 units and expected sales are 7,800 units, the EV of sales volume could fall by 600 units or about 7.7% before the project ceases to be viable.

The price and fixed and variable costs

	£
EV of annual sales revenue (7,800 × £10)	78,000
EV of annual variable costs (7,800 × £6)	46,800
Annual fixed costs	20,000
PV of sales revenue over six years (× 4.355)	339,690
PV of variable costs over six years (× 4.355)	203,814
PV of fixed costs over six years (× 4.355)	87,100

A fall in NPV of £10,486 to £0 would occur, at an annual sales volume of 7,800 units, if:

(1) the sales price were $\frac{10,486}{339,690}$ = 3.1% lower

(that is, 31 pence less per unit, a price of £9.69 per unit)

(2) the variable costs were $\frac{10,486}{203,814}$ = 5.1% higher

(that is, 31 pence per unit higher, at £6.31 per unit)

(3) annual fixed costs were $\frac{10,486}{87,100}$ = 12.0% higher

(that is, £2,400 higher, at £22,400).

The capital cost of equipment

If the residual value is certain to be £3,000, the project would cease to be viable if the cost of the equipment were more than

$\frac{10,486}{40,000}$ or about 26.2% above the estimated cost.

(ii) To allow for risk, we could raise the discount rate from 10% to (say) 15%. If the NPV is still positive at 15%, we might then assume that the project is both viable and reasonably safe.

Year	*Cash flow*	*Discount factor*	*Present value of cash flow*
	£	15%	£
0	(40,000)	1.000	(40,000)
1-6	11,200	3.784	42,381
6	3,000	0.432	1,296
			3,677

(iii) To allow for the uncertainty of cash flows in the distant future, the cash flow each year could be adjusted to a 'certainty equivalent' and an NPV could be calculated on these adjusted cash flows.

(iv) Risk can be assessed by considering the worst (or best) possible outcome, and estimating the probability that this might occur.

If annual sales are only 2,000 units, there would be an annual contribution of £8,000 and an annual loss of £12,000. Similarly, if sales are 6,000 or 8,000 units, the annual profit would be £4,000 or £12,000 respectively.

		Sales 2,000		*Sales 6,000*		*Sales 8,000*	
Year	*Discount factor* 10%	*Cash flow* £	*Present value* £	*Cash flow* £	*Present value* £	*Cash flow* £	*Present value* £
0	1.000	(40,000)	(40,000)	(40,000)	(40,000)	(40,000)	(40,000)
1-6	4.355	(12,000)	(52,260)	4,000	17,420	12,000	52,260
6	0.564	3,000	1,692	3,000	1,692	3,000	1,692
Net present value			(90,568)		(20,888)		13,952
Probability			0.1		0.25		

There is a 35% probability that the NPV will be negative. The worst possible outcome (10% probability) is that the NPV will be £(90,568).

(v) The payback period could be considered.

The non-discounted payback period, assuming annual sales of 7,800 units, is

$\frac{40,000}{11,200}$ = 3.571 years.

The discounted payback period is where the cumulative discount factor of £1 pa at 10% equals 3.571.

The cumulative discount factor for four years at 10% is 3.170.
The cumulative discount factor for five years at 10% is 3.791.

The discounted payback period is between four and five years.

If this payback period is too long, the project should not be undertaken.

(vi) The standard deviation of the expected cash flows each year can be calculated as follows.

Probability	*Sales*	*Profit* (x)*	$(x - \bar{x})$	$p(x - \bar{x})^2$
	Units	£	£	
0.10	2,000	(12,000)	(23,200)	53.824
0.25	6,000	4,000	(7,200)	12.960
0.40	8,000	12,000	800	0.256
0.15	10,000	20,000	8,800	11.616
0.10	14,000	36,000	24,800	61.504
EV	7,800	11,200		140.160

* Contribution of £4 per unit minus fixed costs of £20,000.

The standard deviation is √140,160,000 = £11,839.

5 FINANCIAL FUNCTIONS

The following are advantages of centralising a group's financial functions.

(a) A centralised department for financial functions could probably afford to employ specialists (such as foreign currency dealers and tax specialists) which individual subsidiaries could not.

(b) Financial activities can be organised more efficiently in a variety of ways.

(i) There could be better co-ordination of foreign currency inflows and outflows. A centralised treasury function might be able to set up foreign currency bank accounts, and match inflows in one currency earned by one subsidiary with payments in the same currency by another subsidiary. This would eliminate foreign exchange risk in the currency, at little cost, in a way that individual subsidiaries could not do on their own. Centralised foreign exchange management would also avoid the risk that an individual subsidiary might allow itself to become over-exposed to foreign currency risk.

(ii) Better co-ordination of fund-raising would be possible. If several subsidiaries need extra finance, a centralised finance department should be able to provide it at a lower cost than individual subsidiaries could achieve on their own, for example by lending cash surpluses of one subsidiary to another in the group, or by raising a single large loan or making an equity issue, instead of leaving individual subsidiaries to obtain their own bank loans.

(iii) Centralised tax management would probably be beneficial for the group.

(iv) Cash surpluses of some subsidiaries can be pooled with cash deficits of others, so as to minimise bank overdraft requirements.

(c) The capital expenditure budget can be formulated, evaluated and approved on a group basis.

(d) Centralised financial control would allow the head office to monitor the performance of individual subsidiaries in the area of financial management. For example, there would be close central monitoring of credit management by subsidiaries.

(e) There might be some savings in administrative costs, with fewer staff needed in total in a centralised department than in a large number of decentralised departments.

There are some possible disadvantages to having a group's financial functions centralised.

(a) A centralised department might be slow moving and inefficient, if it is required to carry out many diverse functions.

(b) In a multinational group, financial staff at head office might be unaware of local conditions in the country that a subsidiary is operating in. Decision-making from head office could be inefficient. Subsidiaries in other countries would also need some measure of control over their cash, since it would be pointless to transfer funds from one country to another just for the sake of having centralised bank accounts.

(c) If key financial decisions are taken at head office, there is likely to be some loss of motivation among senior managers in the subsidiaries.

(d) Decisions are likely to be delayed when they are taken at head office. Where speedy decisions are needed, profit-making opportunities might be missed.

6 TWO CLIENTS

(a) (i) *Mortgage debt* takes the form of a loan to the company which is secured on specified assets (normally tangible). In the event of default the lender will be entitled to claim ownership of the assets which have been mortgaged. Interest will be calculated on either a fixed or floating rate basis and payments will be allowable against tax for the borrower.

(ii) *Convertible debt* takes the form of conventional debt such as a debenture, but has a call option attached. This option allows the debt to be exchanged for shares in the company at some time in the future. The conversion rate, ie the number of shares for which the debt may be exchanged, and the exercise period (dates between which the exchange may take place) are specified at the time of issue.

(iii) *Debt with warrants.* This is similar to convertible debt in that it is issued with a view to raising further equity in the future. The debt element is identical in form to other types of conventional debt. However it is issued with warrants attached which give the holder the right to purchase shares in the company at a predetermined future price (the exercise price) and during a specified future period (the exercise period). The exercise price will be pitched at a discount to the projected share price at the exercise date in order to make the warrants attractive. Once the debt has been issued, the warrants are detachable and can be traded separately.

(b) (i) *ABC Limited: Briefing notes*

The first stage is to assess the current operating position. The projected operating profit for 19X4 can be calculated as follows.

It is assumed that the bank loan is being repaid at the rate of £25,000 per year and that the balance outstanding is now £150,000.

		£
Profit after tax		763,000
Add:	Tax	375,000
	Interest (£150,000 × 12%)	18,000
Projected operating profit		1,156,000

This represents a return on sales of 35.6% which is extremely impressive, as is the return on assets. The way in which these profits will be applied can also be calculated.

Net assets have increased:

			£	£
19X3	Total net assets		565,000	
	Add:	Dividends	440,000	
		Tax	220,000	
	Operating assets			1,225,000
19X4	Total net assets		740,000	
	Add:	Dividends	563,000	
		Tax	375,000	
	Operating assets			1,678,000
Increase in operating assets				453,000

Thus the application of operating profits is as follows.

	£
Increased investment in operating assets	453,000
Dividends paid	440,000
Tax paid	220,000
Interest paid	18,000
Reduction in borrowings	25,000
	1,156,000

If the forecasts of performance in the new expansion are reliable, then this opportunity appears even more attractive then the existing operations. The trebling in profits is predicted on the basis of an increase of only 119% in the operating assets base. If this performance is achieved then the payback period will be very short, and ABC should therefore avoid taking on significant amounts of long-term debt. The options available depend to some extent on the long-term objectives and aspirations of the shareholders, but if it is assumed that they wish to maximise the value of their investment and to maintain control, then the possible courses of action include the following.

(1) To finance the investment as far as possible from retained earnings. The current level of dividends is high and is increasing. It is not known what the shareholders' remuneration policy is, nor the extent to which dividend forms a significant part of their total remuneration. However, the temporary restriction of dividends could provide significant internal funds for further investment.

(2) It appears that the shareholders have been withdrawing significant amounts of money from the business. This may mean that their personal financial situations will permit them to make significant individual borrowings for investment in the business either as debt or equity.

(3) The level of fixed assets is relatively low and the premises are leased and therefore it will not be possible to raise all the funds needed in the form of secured debt. However, further internal funds could be released by minimising the need for capital by leasing or hiring fixed assets, and by factoring debts or discounting invoices.

(4) It may be possible to find new investors to take a minority stake in the company. These could be friends, family, employees, customers, suppliers or even potential competitors who might wish to enter the new market through some form of joint venture.

(5) The company should be able to take on further short to medium term debt, possibly in the form of a bank loan.

(6) The company would be attractive to venture capitalists, and the amount of money required is appropriate for this form of investment. However, there would be some dilution of control, the venture capital company would be likely to demand representation on the board, and they would also expect to see returns continuing in excess of their target rate of return into the future. This would therefore be an expensive and demanding form of finance and would probably lock ABC in for longer than is strictly necessary.

(ii) *DEF plc: Briefing notes*

The operating position of DEF can be estimated, assuming a corporation tax rate of 30%, as follows.

19X4 forecast		£m
Profit after tax		118
Add back:	Tax at 30%	51
	Interest (210 × 9%)	19
Operating profit		188

Operating assets amount to £987m (£929m + £58m tax). The return on assets is therefore 19% (188/987), and the return on sales is 13.0% (188/1,450).

The equivalent calculations for 19X3 are:

		£m
Profit after tax		113
Add back:	Tax at 30%	48
	Interest	19
Operating profit		180

Operating assets were £938m (£883m + £55m). Return on assets was 19.2% (180/938) and return on sales was 14.4% (180/1,250).

It therefore appears that the profit improvement programme has not been forecast to have an impact on the 19X4 figures. Unfortunately, no projections have been provided as to the impact on profitability of the expansion programme, nor of the timescale over which the investment is to be made. It is therefore very difficult to provide DEF plc with appropriate financing advice. However, if it can be assumed that the return on the new investment will be similar to that on the existing operations, and that the performance of the existing operations will be unaffected, then some general suggestions can be made.

(1) If the new investment provides a return of approximately 20%, then the payback period will be relatively long and some form of long-term finance will be needed. DEF's gearing level is currently only 29.2% (£210m/(£100m + £619m)). It therefore has sufficient capacity to raise a part if not the whole of the required amount through debt. An additional £250m of debt would increase the gearing to 63.9%. If it is assumed that debt similar to that already held in the capital structure can be raised, then the effective

rated of interest will be 7.2% (9% ÷ 1.25), say 7.5%. If the return on the new investment is 20% ie £50m per annum, then the gross interest cover is 2.67 times (£50m/£18.75m) which appears to be quite acceptable. However it would be helpful to have more information on the volatility of DEF's earnings performance in order to make a better assessment of the likely cost of debt and of the level of risk involved.

The likely costs of the debt will also depend on the form in which it is raised. Since a large part of the investment is to be made in new shops it should be possible to secure a significant proportion of the finance on property and thus to obtain a better rate of interest than on a less well secured investment.

(2) An alternative approach would be to raise the new funds by means of a rights issue. This would be more expensive than the use of debt, partly because there has been a significant drop in the share price over the last few months, and partly because in these circumstances, and given the size of the new issue relative to the current market capitalisation (£2.45 × 400m = £980m), the issue would need to be underwritten. The new shares would need to be priced at a discount to the existing share price in order to make them attractive to investors (say a maximum price of 220p, this being a discount of 10%). Investors would also expect to see some projections of the financial performance of the expanded company. The directors would need to ensure that they had obtained the necessary authority to make such an issue.

(3) A combination approach could be used, perhaps in the form of some type of convertible debenture. This can be an attractive way of raising 'delayed equity' at a time when the share price is depressed and equity is relatively expensive. However, such an issue would need careful pricing which would have to be substantiated on the basis of detailed cash flow projections.

7 AB LTD

(a) AB LTD

FINANCIAL PROJECTIONS FOR YEAR 1

PROFIT AND LOSS ACCOUNT

	£'000
Sales	1,400
Direct costs (60% sales)	(840)
Gross profit	560
Operating expenses	420
Net profit	140
Contribution (%)	10%

BALANCE SHEET AT START OF YEAR 1

	£'000	£'000
Fixed assets ((1,400 × 0.6/2.8)		300
Current assets		
Stock (1,400/5.6)	250	
Debtors (1,400 × 50/365)	192	
		442
Less current liabilities		
Creditors (840 × 60/365)	(138)	
Bank overdraft (Note 1)	(104)	
		(242)
Net assets		500
Financed by		
Share capital		300
Bank loan (Note 2)		200
		500

Notes

1 The current ratio is 1.83. Current assets are £442,000, and therefore current liabilities must be £242,000. Creditors are £138,000, therefore the bank overdraft must be £104,000.

2 Since the overdraft is £104,000 and the net current assets are £500,000, it follows that a longer term loan of £200,000 will be required.

These figures have been calculated assuming that the level of sales in year one is £1.4m. The overdraft figure of £104,000 represents an 'average' level of short-term financing needs. In practice this figure is likely to vary due to variations in the timing of receipts and payments, and therefore a higher overdraft limit of say £120,000 might be more appropriate.

(b) The assumptions that have been used in arriving at these projections are as follows.

(i) AB Ltd will have an operating performance which closely matches the average for the industry. In practice this is unlikely to be the case in the first year of operations as the company gears up its level of activity from a zero base.

(ii) It is assumed that there are no marked cyclical changes in the level of activity. If there are, then allowance will need to be made in the projections.

(iii) The operating expenses are assumed to be wholly variable. This is unlikely to be true in practice.

Since the company is a new business it may be difficult to obtain the full 60 days trade credit from suppliers that is assumed in the projections. Initially at least, AB is likely to have more restrictive credit terms and this should be allowed for in the calculations.

It is not known how growth is expected to continue in subsequent years. If the rate of growth and the capital investment required will exceed the ability for funding from retentions, then it may be appropriate to consider a higher level of debt. Alternatively, the directors could consider approaching a venture capital institution for further equity funding.

It would be more appropriate to build up a budget based on projections specific to the business in terms of known customers, suppliers, premises and so on. Even though the margin of error is likely to be high, this will be more meaningful than industry averages, and will form a more helpful starting point when evaluating initial performance.

(c) If the bank refuses finance then AB Ltd could consider the following alternative sources of funds.

(i) Some additional form of equity, for example from a venture capital institution.

(ii) Loan finance from a different bank or banks. Some overseas banks are seeking to enter the UK commercial lending market and may be more willing to lend against limited security than a clearing bank.

(iii) An issue of convertible loan stock, or loan stock with warrants attached.

(iv) An issue of redeemable loan stock or debentures, possibly with a low coupon rate and at a discount in order to ease the servicing costs in the early years of trading.

(v) Debt finance secured on the fixed assets of the business. This could take the form of a mortgage, a lease, or in the case of plant and machinery, some form of hire purchase agreement.

(vi) Debt finance secured on the current assets of the business. Options include factoring of debtors, invoice discounting and loans secured against a floating charge on the current assets.

(vii) If the company is to be set up in an 'assisted area' it may be able to qualify for grant aid from one of the development agencies.

(d) Other sources of publicly available information include the following.

(i) Published accounts of other companies in the industry which might be expected to have a similar profile to AB Ltd.

(ii) Statistical information on industrial performance published by the government.

(iii) Surveys made by local chambers of commerce and trade associations.

(iv) Reports carried by the press which relate to other companies within the industry.

(v) Regular economic reports produced by the London Business School.

All the above sources are basically historical in nature. If AB wishes to take into account forecasts of likely developments in the industry, then it should also use the following sources.

(i) Press reports and surveys.

(ii) Information published by industrial consultancies and market research organisations such as Mintel.

(iii) Financial forecasts can be obtained from some of the major stockbroking firms.

(iv) Market forecasts can be obtained from some of the major banks.

8 CAPITAL MARKETS

The advantages of flotation include the following.

(a) The existing shareholders will benefit from the improved marketability of their shares.

(b) The shareholders will find inheritance tax planning easier since the valuation problems associated with unquoted shares are overcome.

(c) The fact that the company is listed is likely to improve the public perception of its financial soundness. It may similarly improve its credit rating thus making it easier to raise further debt. This improvement in status may also enhance the firm in the eyes of its customers and suppliers and result in new business being generated. Thus there is a 'virtuous circle' effect at work.

(d) It provides access to a much wider pool of capital, both at the time of flotation and in the future. This means that it may be able to expand at a faster rate if capital supply is no longer the primary constraint.

(e) The fact that the shares are more marketable and that perceived risk may be lower means that it is likely that the cost of equity will fall.

(f) If the company is planning to expand by acquisition and hopes to finance the purchase by means of a share issue, this will be much easier if it is publicly quoted.

(g) It will be possible to set up an approved share option scheme. This should make it easier to attract and retain staff.

The main disadvantages of flotation include the following.

(a) Flotation involves substantial expense.

(b) The company will have to comply with the Stock Exchange regulations. These are stringent and will involve the management in a significant amount of extra duties.

(c) The shareholders may not be happy with the dilution of their control. The company will become more vulnerable to takeover and a hostile bid will now be an option for a prospective purchaser.

(d) If the company has habitually relied on retained earnings as its principal source of finance it will have to consider the effect on its cash flow of having to pay regular dividends.

(e) It will no longer be possible to conceal a poor financial performance. The firm will be much more visible and the virtuous circle described above could easily be turned into a vicious circle in the event of performance not matching up to market expectations.

(f) If the flotation is being undertaken with the aim of raising the finance required to undertake a specific project, it will not be possible to guarantee that exactly the amount required will be raised. The success of the issue will depend in part on factors external to the company which can fluctuate from day to day, for example investor confidence, and although a minimum sum can be guaranteed by underwriters, the actual outcome cannot be predicted. The exception to this is if the float takes the form of a private placing; however in this case the issue price will have to be lower than for a public offer. Timing is important and the company will need a good profit record over the last two or three years as well as a clear plan for the future.

In conclusion, flotation will be most appropriate for the firm which has a good track record, good growth prospects and which has reached the point where its progress is being hampered by the lack of access to a large pool of finance. It has been shown that flotation is expensive and has a number of potential pitfalls and it should not be undertaken unless the firm has the resources and resilience to overcome such setbacks.

9 GROWTH PLC

The company is a substantial one, with a reasonably long trading record over which steady growth has been achieved. It should therefore apply for a full listing on the Stock Exchange. There seems to be little point in joining the Alternative Investment Market first, as the company would very soon want to

move on to a full listing. Over-the-counter markets are too small, too illiquid and too poorly regulated to be of any use to Growth plc.

Advantages to the company

The company will probably raise equity funds on joining the market, through an issue of new shares. Some shares will have to be issued in any case, so that at least 25% of the company's shares become available to the market, unless some existing shareholders wish to sell large parts of their holdings immediately.

Future equity issues will be easier if the company is listed than if it is not. It may also be easier to raise debt capital, because listed companies are generally thought of as less risky than unlisted companies.

The company may find it easier to take over other companies, because listed shares are often acceptable as consideration in a takeover.

Share option schemes as incentives to senior employees are more feasible for listed than for unlisted companies.

Advantages to the existing shareholders

When a company has a full listing, its shares are likely to be fairly readily marketable (although shares in some listed companies are not much traded). Shareholders wishing to sell shares should be able to do so, and shareholders needing a market value for their shares (perhaps for tax purposes) will be able to obtain one.

The status attached to being a listed company may itself lead to a rise in the value of the shares.

Disadvantages for the company

Joining the stock market can be expensive. Fees must be paid to professional advisers and to the Stock Exchange.

Once the company has obtained a listing, there will be further costs of compliance with Stock Exchange disclosure requirements, and also the Stock Exchange annual fee. Expenditure on public relations for the company as a whole (as opposed to the advertising of specific products) may also be needed.

The company will be expected to show reasonable results each year. If results are poor and it is suspected that bad management is to blame (rather than a general downturn in the leisure market), the company could become vulnerable to a hostile takeover bid. Because demand for the company's products is sensitive to individuals' real incomes, there is a serious risk of fluctuations in performance.

The company could become the victim of a 'bear raid', a campaign to drive the share price down by selling shares in order to profit by buying them back more cheaply.

Disadvantages for the existing shareholders

The shareholders will ultimately bear the costs of being listed which the company must pay.

Control of the company will be diluted, as shares must be made available to the market. A new investor, such as an insurance company, might build up a substantial stake by buying shares in the market. Such a shareholder could achieve effective control over the company even with a minority holding, if other large shareholders do not act in unison.

As mentioned above, the share price could be driven down in a bear raid; it could also fluctuate sharply on the publication of the company's results or other news relating to the company or its markets.

10 SHARE VALUES

(a) The fundamental analysis theory of share values states that the value of a share is the present value of the expected future dividends. No buyer would pay more for the share than this amount, because he would only have to invest this amount elsewhere to obtain the same income stream; and no seller would accept less than this amount, as to do so would involve an avoidable loss of wealth.

The theory assumes that there is a single discount rate applicable to all investors and potential investors in the shares (of one class) in a given company. This rate is applied to the expected future dividends to obtain a present value.

Examples

(i) X plc is expected to pay a dividend of 30p a share each year for ever, starting one year from now. An appropriate discount rate is 25%. The current market value per share (ex div) should be 30p/0.25 = £1.20.

(ii) Y plc is expected to pay a dividend of 21p a share one year from now. Thereafter, dividends are expected to rise by 3% a year. An appropriate discount rate is 15%. The current market value (taking into account the expected dividend growth) is:

$$\frac{21}{1.15} + \frac{21 \times 1.03}{1.15^2} + \frac{21 \times 1.03^2}{1.15^3} + \ldots = \frac{21}{0.15 - 0.03} = 175\text{p} = £1.75$$

The theory can be applied to the valuation of interest-bearing securities. The income stream from such securities is usually known with certainty, whereas future dividends from shares can only be estimated. With redeemable securities, not only the interest but also the amount due on maturity must be discounted in arriving at a present value.

(b) In an information-efficient stock market, no one investor dominates the market, transaction costs are not a significant deterrent to dealing and the prices at which shares are bought and sold reflect all available relevant information. Share prices will therefore be set in a rational way, taking account of the prospects for companies, and one would expect the fundamental analysis theory to apply. Exactly how it would apply would depend on the level of efficiency of the stock market, which is considered below.

If the stock market is inefficient, share prices may differ significantly and permanently from what the fundamental analysis theory would lead one to expect. A dominant investor or high dealing costs may distort prices; and if share prices do not reflect all available relevant information about companies, they may come to bear little relation to likely future dividends.

The level of efficiency of a stock market in this sense depends on the extent to which market prices reflect relevant information. Under weak form efficiency, only information about past price movements and their implications is reflected in current market prices; under semi-strong form efficiency, all publicly available information is reflected in current market prices; and under strong form efficiency, even confidential information (such as secret plans for new investments) is reflected in current market prices.

Information about a company, such as recent results or a proposed new investment, is normally known to only a few people at first. It is published, and after a while several investors will have dealt in the company's shares at prices which reflect the information. Thus whatever the level of efficiency of the stock market, if it is efficient at all then share prices will eventually reflect each item of relevant information about the company. Share prices should therefore be determined according to the principles of the fundamental analysis theory, although perhaps after some delay, even if the stock market shows only weak form efficiency.

11 CRYSTAL PLC

(a) The post-tax weighted average cost of capital should first be calculated.

(i)

Ordinary shares	£
Market value of shares cum div.	3.27
Less dividend per share (810 ÷ 3,000)	0.27
Market value of shares ex div.	3.00

The formula for calculating the cost of equity when there is dividend growth is:

$$r = \frac{d_0(1 + g)}{p_0} + g$$

where
r = cost of equity
d_o = current dividend
g = rate of growth
p_o = current ex div market value.

In this case we shall estimate the future rate of growth (g) from the average growth in dividends over the past four years.

$810 = 620 (1 + g)^4$

$$(1+g)^4 = \frac{810}{620} = 1.3065$$

$$1 + g = 1.069$$

$$g = 0.069, \text{ ie } 6.9\%$$

$$r = \frac{0.27 \times 1.069}{3} + 0.069 = 16.5\%$$

(ii) *7% Debentures*

In order to find the post-tax cost of the debentures, which are redeemable in ten years time, it is necessary to find the discount rate (IRR) that will give the future post-tax cash flows a present value of £77.10.

The relevant cash flows are:

(1) annual interest payments, net of tax, which are £1,300 × 7% × 70% = £63.70 (for ten years);

(2) a capital repayment of £1,300 (in ten years time).

It is assumed that tax relief on the debenture interest arises at the same time as the interest payment. In practice the cash flow effect is unlikely to be felt for about a year, but this will have no significant effect on the calculations.

		Present value
Try 8%		£'000
Current market value of debentures (1,300 at £77.10 per cent)		(1,002.3)
Annual interest payments net of tax 63.70 × 6.710 (8% for ten years)		427.4
Capital repayment £1,300 × 0.463 (8% in ten years time)		601.9
	NPV	27.0
Try 9%		£'000
Current market value of debentures		(1,002.3)
Annual interest payments net of tax 63.70 × 6.418		408.8
Capital repayment 1,300 × 0.422		548.6
	NPV	(44.9)

$$IRR = 8\% + \left[\frac{27.0}{27.0 - -44.9} \times (9-8)\right]\% = 8.38\%$$

(iii) *The weighted average cost of capital*

	Market value	*Cost*	*Product*
	£'000	%	
Equity	9,000	16.50	1,485
7% Debentures	1,002	8.38	84
	10,002		1,569

$$\frac{1,569}{10,002} \times 100 = 15.7\%$$

The above calculations suggest that a discount rate in the region of 16% might be appropriate for the appraisal of new investment opportunities.

(b) Difficulties and uncertainties in the above estimates arise in a number of areas.

(i) *The cost of equity.* The above calculation assumes that all shareholders have the same marginal cost of capital and the same dividend expectations, which is unrealistic. In addition, it is assumed that dividend growth has been and will be at a constant rate of 6.9%. In fact, actual growth in the years 19X5/6 and 19X8/9 was in excess of 9%, while in the year 19X7/8 there was no dividend growth. 6.9% is merely the average rate of growth for the past four years. The rate of future growth will depend more on the return from future projects undertaken than on the past dividend record.

(ii) *The use of the weighted average cost of capital.* Use of the weighted average cost of capital as a discount rate is only justified where the company in question has achieved what it believes to be the optimal capital structure (the mix of debt and equity) and where it intends to maintain this structure in the long term.

(iii) *The projects themselves.* The weighted average cost of capital makes no allowance for the business risk of individual projects. In practice some companies, having calculated the WACC, then add a premium for risk. In this case, for example, if one used a risk premium of 5% the final discount rate would be 21%. Ideally the risk premium should vary from project to project, since not all projects are equally risky. In general, the riskier the project the higher the discount rate which should be used.

12 CASTOR AND POLLUX

(a) Modigliani and Miller's theory of capital structure differs from the traditional view in its assumptions about shareholder behaviour. As a consequence they questioned the view that there is an optimal level of gearing that reduces the cost of capital and maximises the total market value of the firm. They showed that it is the income generated from the business activities of the firm which determines value and not the way in which this income is allocated between the providers of capital. If the shares of two firms with different levels of gearing but the same level of business risk are traded at different prices, then shareholders will switch their investment from the overvalued to the undervalued firm. At the same time they will adjust their level of personal borrowing through the market in order to maintain their overall level of business risk at the same level. This process which is called arbitrage will result in the firms having the same equilibrium total value.

The implications of the theory for the firm's cost of capital and total market value at different levels of gearing can best be illustrated graphically.

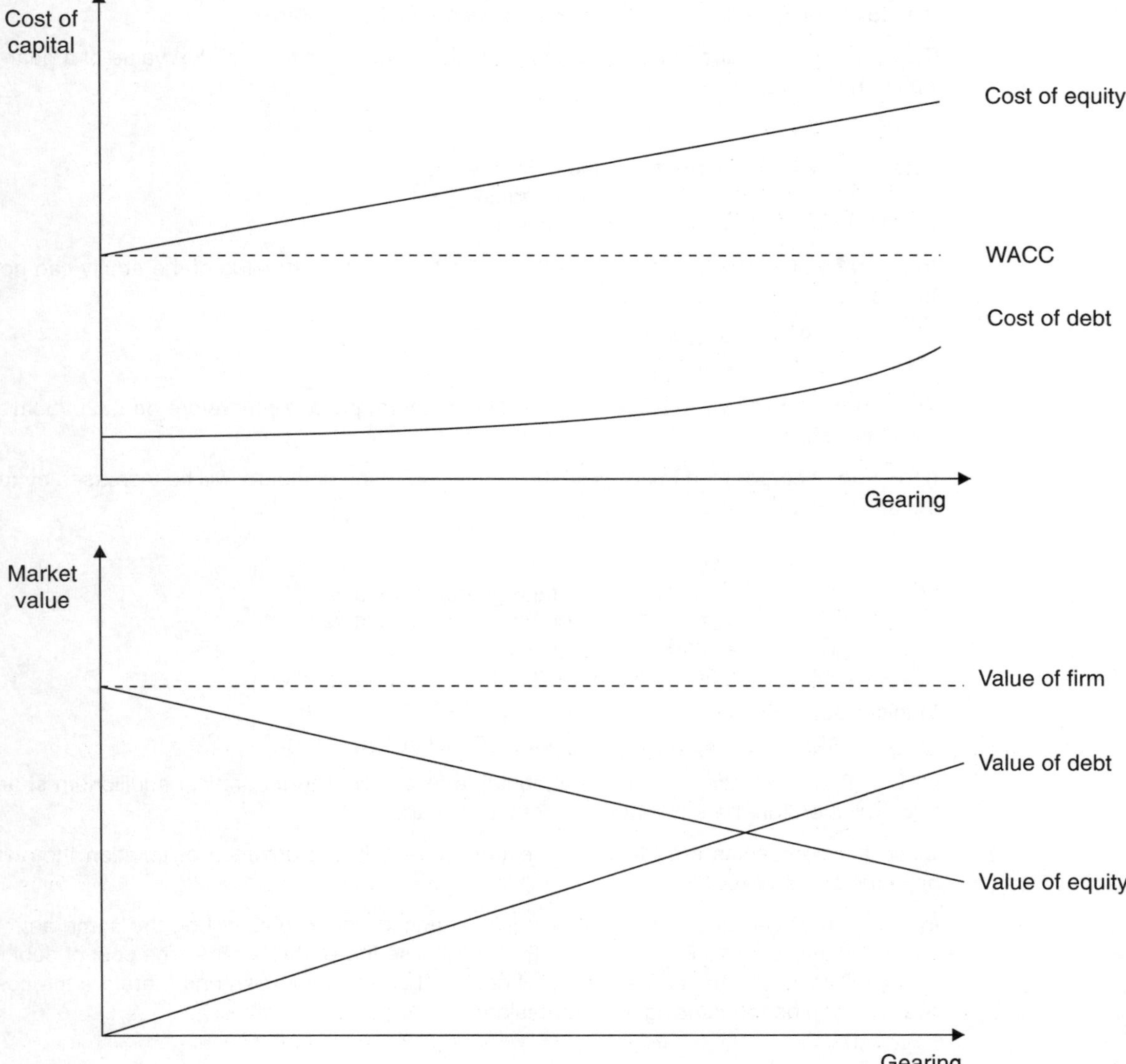

When taxation is introduced into the model, the total market value of the firm is no longer independent of its capital structure. This is because interest on debt is allowable against tax. The market value of the firm now increases with gearing, the amount of the increase being equal to the present value of the tax shield on the interest payments. This also means that the WACC declines as the gearing increases.

The main weaknesses of the theory arise from its simplifying assumptions.

(i) In defining the arbitrage process it is assumed that personal borrowing is a perfect substitute for corporate borrowing. This is unlikely to be true in practice since the private investor does not have the protection of limited liability and cannot usually negotiate such good rates as the corporate borrower.

(ii) It is assumed that all earnings are paid out as dividend. In practice a variable proportion of earnings is normally retained.

(iii) It is extremely difficult to identify firms with identical business risk and operating profiles.

(iv) It is assumed that investors' only criteria are risk and return. In practice, investors will also be concerned with other factors such as the ethical stance of the company, and they do not have perfect information about the market.

The theory begins to break down at very high levels of gearing since firms in this situation are normally heading for bankruptcy. For all these reasons, it has not been possible for the theory to be fully proved empirically.

(b) (i) Since the companies are identical in every respect apart from their level of gearing, in the absence of taxation their total market value will be equal.

The total market value of Castor = 20m shares × £4.80 = £96m

The total market value of Pollux is therefore also £96m. The total market value of a geared company is given by:

$$MV_p = E + D$$

where: MV_p = market value of Pollux
E = market value of equity
D = market value of debt

In the case of Pollux, D = £20m × 120% = £24m. The market value of the equity can now be found:

$$£96m = E + £24m$$
$$E = £72m$$

There are 30m shares in issue. The equilibrium share price will therefore be £72m/30m = £2.40 per share

If the rate of corporation tax is 25%, the total value of the company will be increased by the tax shield on the interest payments:

$$V_g = V_u + DT_c$$

where V_g = market value of the geared company
V_u = market value of the ungeared company
D = market value of debt
T_c = rate of corporation tax

In this case:

$$V_g = £96m + (£24m \times 0.25) = £102m$$

Of this, £78m (£102m – £24m) is attributable to equity. The theoretical equilibrium share price will therefore be £78m/30m = £2.60 per share.

(ii) Since the companies are identical in every respect, in the absence of taxation they will have the same WACC.

In the case of Castor which is totally equity financed, the WACC will be the same as the cost of equity, ie 18%. The WACC for Pollux will also therefore be 18%. The cost of debt is 10% (12%/120%). The market values of debt and equity are known and therefore the cost of equity can be found using the expression:

$$WACC = r_E \times \frac{E}{E+D} + r_D \times \frac{D}{E+D}$$

where:	r_E	=	cost of equity
	r_D	=	cost of debt
	E/(E+D)	=	72m/96m = 75%
	D/(E+D)	=	24m/96m = 25%
	18%	=	(r_E × 75%) + (10% × 25%)
	r_E	=	(18% – (10% × 25%))/75% = 20.67%

If taxation is to be taken into account, it has been shown that the total market value of the company will rise due to the PV of the tax shield on the debt interest. This increase in value will accrue to the ordinary shareholders. The level of dividends in the absence of tax can be calculated using the dividend valuation model:

$$r = d/p_o$$

where:	r	=	cost of equity
	d	=	annual level of dividends
	p_o	=	market value of equity
	20.67%	=	d/£72m
	d	=	£14.8824m

The annual value of the tax shield on the debt interest is £0.6m (£20m × 12% × 25%). The dividend valuation model can now be used again to find the cost of equity if this amount is added to the dividend total:

$$r = \frac{£14.8824m + £0.6m}{£78.0m} = 19.85\%$$

(iii) In the absence of taxation, the WACC of Pollux will be identical to that of Castor, ie 18%. If taxation is to be taken into account, then the WACC can be found using the expression:

$$WACC = r_E \times \frac{E}{E+D} + r_D(1-T_c) \times \frac{D}{E+D}$$

$$WACC = \frac{19.85\% \times 78}{78+24} + \frac{10\%(1-0.25) \times 24}{78+24}$$

13 MOODY AND HART

(a) Portfolio diversification reduces risk because the returns from projects will not be perfectly positively correlated, and diversification reduces risk more when project returns show little or no positive correlation (or even better, negative correlation). However, diversification by a company reduces the risk of insolvency for the company itself. But if corporate insolvency brings no added costs to the investor, diversification by a company should have no effect on the risks experienced by a well diversified investor.

(b) Project discount rates are as follows.

Moody plc		7% + (12 – 7) × 1.2%	= 13%
Hart plc	(1)	7% + (12 – 7) × 1.25%	= 13.25%
	(2)	7% + (12 – 7) × 0.8%	= 11%
	(3)	7% + (12 – 7) × 1.35%	= 13.75%

The net present values are as follows.

Moody plc $\frac{500}{1.13}$ = (in £'000) 442.48

				£'000
Hart plc	(1)	$\frac{200}{1.1325}$	=	176.60
	(2)	$\frac{100}{1.11}$	=	90.09
	(3)	$\frac{200}{1.1375}$	=	175.82
				442.51

Allowing for rounding errors, the present values of the three projects of Hart add up to the same amount as the present value of the project of Moody.

(c) Hart's overall beta factor is a weighted average of the beta factors of the three projects.

Project	*Value*	*β*	*Product*
(1)	200	1.25	250
(2)	100	0.80	80
(3)	200	1.35	270
	500		600

Overall beta factor = $\frac{600}{500}$ = 1.2

This is the same as Moody plc's project beta factor.

(d) Considering only the projects under review both companies have the same present value and the same systematic risk (the same beta factor). It follows that on the basis of these projects alone, both companies should be valued equally by investors.

It might be tempting to assume that since Hart plc is diversifying into three separate projects, whereas Moody is investing in only one project, investors should prefer the lower-risk Hart plc because Moody's unsystematic risk will be higher. But with CAPM theory, it is assumed that investors can eliminate unsystematic risk by diversifying their own investment portfolios, and do not have to rely on companies to diversify on their behalf.

14 INDUSTRIAL COMPANY

(a) There are a number of different risks facing commercial organisations. All businesses have to contend with the ups and downs of business life, booms and slumps, risky decisions about what to produce, what prices to charge, how and where to market their goods and so on. Firms which have borrowed money, or are about to borrow money in the near future, face the additional risk of exposure to interest rate changes.

If a company has a considerable amount of variable rate debt (for example a large overdraft or variable rate bank loan) then it faces the risk that interest rates may rise and its repayments increase. The effect of this on the business could be dramatic, reducing cashflow and profit and perhaps, if the rise in rates is a large one and the company highly geared (with a high proportion of debt), bringing the risk of liquidation.

Alternatively, a business with a large amount of fixed rate borrowing (for example a fixed rate loan or fixed interest preference shares or debentures) is exposed to a fall in interest rates. If the company has borrowed large sums at 10% fixed, and a short time later rates fall to 8%, it will be paying more for its debt than it needs to. Cashflow and profits could be better if only the debt were not at a fixed rate.

Companies thinking about borrowing in the near future also face risk. Should they borrow at a fixed rate now because they are worried about a rise in interest rates or should they wait in the hope that rates may fall shortly? A wrong decision could be costly.

Finally, there are companies with debt capital maturing that will need to be replaced. A company may have issued £5 million of debenture stock due to mature between 19X3 and 19X5. The company itself will have the choice as to exactly when they will repay the holders of the debt. If they think that interest rates are likely to be lower in 19X3 than in 19X5 they can repay the debenture holders early in 19X3 and replace the debt with a new issue of debentures then. If they think rates will be lower in 19X5 they can wait and replace the debt when it is cheaper to do so. Decisions like this are risky: making the wrong choice could cost millions of pounds.

(b) There are a number of ways that companies can reduce interest rate exposure.

(i) Large companies can make sure that they have a mix of both fixed and variable rate debt so that whichever way interest rates move they do not suffer too much.

(ii) A company may wish to take out a forward rate agreement (FRA) with their bank. If the company believes that it would be seriously affected by rates in excess of, say, 10% they may be able to 'fix' their borrowing at this rate. If rates actually rise above 10%, the bank pays the difference to the customer and if rates fall below 10%, the customer pays the difference to the bank. Although the company can never gain from interest rate movements through an FRA, it can remove the risk of rates rising.

(iii) It is possible to 'cap' an interest rate to reduce or remove the risk of a rate rise. A company can 'cap' its borrowing at say, 10%. This places an upper limit on the rate the company pays for borrowing a particular sum. Having bought a 'cap' they will use it if rates rise above 10% but if rates are currently 8% they have the advantage of actually borrowing at 8%. The 'cap' provides protection from rate rises whilst leaving the company free to enjoy the benefits of falling rates.

(iv) The opposite of a 'cap' is a 'floor'. If the company is worried about rates falling (because it has variable rate investments for example), it can purchase a 'floor'. Once rates fall below the floor the bank will pay the company the difference.

(v) Interest rate futures and options contracts may be purchased to hedge against the risk of interest rate movements. Large interest rate exposures can be hedged using a relatively small outlay on futures, whose price can be expected to reflect interest rate changes. Interest rate options (or 'interest rate guarantees') grant the buyer the right but not the obligation to deal at a specified interest rate at some future date.

(vi) Large companies may consider an interest rate 'swap'. A company worried about the fact that it has a lot of variable rate debt, and that rates will rise, may want to swap its variable rate debt for fixed rate debt. Similarly, a company with a lot of fixed rate debt that anticipates a fall in rates may want to 'swap' its fixed rate debt for floating rate. Matching up these two types of company will usually be the job of a bank or another intermediary. The bank will collect the payments of the two companies and ensure that the terms of the 'swap' are carried out.

15 ABC

Company A, which has deliberately avoided paying any dividends in the last five years, is pursuing a sensible policy for a rapidly growing company. All its post-tax profits are being reinvested in the company's business. By adopting this strategy, Company A reduces to a minimum its need to raise new capital from the market. Issue costs are reduced or eliminated and the company has greater flexibility in its investment programme since decision taking is not dependent on gaining market approval. Furthermore, since the company is probably investing heavily its taxation liability may well be small. Paying dividends would mean a UK company had to pay ACT too, which might not be recovered against the main company tax bill and so could cause a net cash outflow.

At first sight the policy pursued by Company B, of distributing 50% of post-tax profits, appears to offer the shareholders predictability. In fact, however, with changes in the company's operating profits and in the tax regime, the post-tax earnings may fluctuate considerably. Reducing the dividend of a quoted company normally causes its share price to fall sharply, since the market takes this as casting considerable doubt on its future earnings potential. But, the more mature and predictable that Company B's business is, the greater the merit in its dividend policy. A mature business usually needs less new capital investment than a growing one and so a higher level of dividend is justified. Distributing profits allows shareholders to make some adjustment to the risk and return profile of their portfolios without incurring the transaction costs of buying and selling.

Company C's policy falls between those of A and B in that a dividend is paid, albeit a small one. The predictability of the dividend will be welcomed by shareholders, since it allows them to make their financial plans with more certainty than would otherwise be possible. It also gives C part of A's advantage; retained earnings can be used as the principal source of investment capital. To the extent that they are relevant at all, scrip issues are likely to increase a company's market value, since they are often made to increase the marketability of the shares. Shareholder concessions are simply a means of attracting the 'small' shareholder who can benefit from them personally, and have no impact on dividend policy.

In addition to looking at the cash flows of each company, we must also consider the impact of these dividend policies on the after tax wealth of shareholders. Shareholders can be divided into groups or 'clienteles'. Different clienteles may be attracted to invest in each of the three firms, depending on their tax situation. It is worth noting that one clientele is as good as another in terms of the valuation it implies for the firm.

Company A would be particularly attractive to individuals who do not require an income stream from their investment and prefer to obtain a return through capital growth. Company B's clientele prefer a much higher proportion of their return to be in the form of income, although it would not be income on which they rely since it may be very variable from year to year. Tax exempt funds, such as pension funds, are indifferent between returns in the form of income or capital and might well invest in B since they need a flow of income to meet their day to day obligations. A large, diversified portfolio would reduce the effect of variability in the dividend. Company C is more likely to appeal to the private investor since most of the return is in the form of capital growth and there are shareholder concessions too.

So, each company may maximise the wealth of its shareholders. If the theorists are right, A, B and C all maximise shareholder wealth because the value of the companies is unaffected by dividend policy. Alternatively, each company's group of shareholders may favour their company's policy (and so their wealth is maximised) because the dividend policy is appropriate to their tax position and so maximises their post-tax returns.

16 H AND D

Assuming that the historical data presented is a reasonable guide to what will happen in the future, we can calculate whether the factoring of the debts on the debtors' ledger of D Ltd would be worthwhile as follows. The 19Y0 figures are assumed below to be typical.

The cost of the finance provided by the factor is 5% of sales, since 80% and then a further 15% is remitted by the factor. This is equivalent to around 23% of debtors (5 ÷ 0.22) based on the 19Y0 year end debtors' figure. However, it should be borne in mind that 15% of the finance is only received when the amounts due are received by the finance company: this delay of course makes the finance less attractive than if 95% were received straight away. In addition, there would be administration costs of 0.5% × 98.7m = £0.5 million which amounts to considerably more than the amount of £80,000 saved in D Ltd's own administration costs.

There may be some saving through a reduction in bad debts, which in 19Y0 amounted to 0.6% of turnover (£0.6m). However there is against this a loss of contribution amounting to 18% × 10% × £98.7m ≈ £1.8m as a result of the factor's aggressive collection procedures. This will outweigh any savings in the cost of bad debts.

Considering:

(a) the cost of the finance provided;
(b) the higher administration costs; and
(c) the loss in contribution from lost turnover;

it would appear that factoring is not justified on the basis of any of these three elements.

17 EXCESS CASH AND MONEY MARKET INSTRUMENTS

(a) Surplus cash flows will be earned by a company that is trading profitably, and does not have high capital expenditures or other outlays to use up the cash inflows. Four possible reasons for a cash surplus are:

(i) higher income from sales, due to an increase in sales turnover;

(ii) lower costs, due perhaps to a cost-cutting exercise or improved productivity;

(iii) lower capital expenditure, perhaps because of an absence of profitable new investment options;

(iv) income from selling off parts of the business.

The board of directors might keep the surplus in liquid form:

(i) to benefit from high interest rates that might be available from bank deposits, when returns on re-investment in the company appear to be lower;

(ii) to have cash available should a strategic opportunity arise, perhaps for the takeover of another company in which cash consideration might be needed;

(iii) to buy back shares from shareholders;

(iv) to pay an increased dividend to shareholders at some time in the future.

(b) (i) (1) *Sterling certificates of deposits (CDs)* are securities issued by a bank, acknowledging that a certain amount of sterling has been deposited with it for a certain period of time (usually, a short term). The CD is issued to the depositor, and attracts interest. The depositor will be another bank or a large commercial organisation. CDs are traded on the money market and so if a CD holder wishes to obtain immediate cash, he can sell the CD on the market at any time. This second-hand market in CDs makes them attractive, flexible investments for organisations with excess cash.

(2) *Local authority bonds* are short-term securities issued by local authorities to raise cash. They carry interest, and are repayable on maturity. They are traded secondhand in the money market, and so, like CDs, are a flexible investment for organisations with excess cash.

(3) *Finance house deposits* are non-negotiable time deposits with finance houses (usually subsidiaries of banks). Finance houses specialise in lending money, and have to raise the funds (much of them from the money market) for re-lending.

(4) *Treasury bills* are short-term debt instruments issued by the Bank of England, to raise cash for the government's spending needs. The bills are sold by tender, each week, at a price which is at a discount to their nominal value. They are redeemable at their nominal value, and so there is an implied rate of interest on the bill.

Treasury bills are bought initially by money market organisations with which the Bank of England has a special relationship, mainly the discount houses. The discount houses then carry out secondhand trading in Treasury bills (and other bills) on the discount market. Treasury bills are therefore negotiable.

(ii) *Differences in interest rates between instruments*

Some money market instruments carry a higher interest rate than others. The main reasons for this are differences in their relative marketability and risk.

(1) Treasury bills are government debt, and therefore the most secure form of short-term debt available. Interest rates on Treasury bills should therefore be lower than on other money market instruments. Interest rates at which the Bank of England deals in bills in the money market usually set the level of interest rates for all other money market instruments.

(2) Finance house deposits are not negotiable, and so are less marketable than the other money market instruments in the list. For this reason, interest rates on them are slightly higher. Similarly, CDs are more marketable than ordinary money market bank deposits, which are for a given (short) term; thus CD interest rates will be a bit lower than LIBID (the London inter-bank bid rate).

Differences in interest rates over time

Interest rates over time are affected by the supply and demand of funds, and by expectations of future changes in interest rates. Broadly speaking, interest rates on longer-term investments will be higher, and the 'yield curve' (a graph of interest rates against term to maturity) will normally be upward-sloping. In the data given, we see that interest rates are increased with the term of the deposit/bond/bill.

However, when there are expectations of a future fall in interest rates, because current rates are high, the yield curve may slope downwards, with yields on long term debt being lower than yields on shorter term debt.

18 COLLEGE BOOKSHOP

(a) The administrator's figures are not appropriate to the decision, for the following reasons.

(i) Apportioned costs have been included, which will be incurred even if the space is unused. The administrator should have considered the annual contribution of £1,000.

(ii) The figures ignore the time value of money, an important factor in a decision which will affect cash flows over five years.

(iii) The depreciation figure for the kiosk and fittings has assumed no residual value. Is this correct?

(iv) Staff salaries have been charged as an annual cost: is this an apportionment of salaries which would be incurred anyway? If so, the potential contribution is £14,000 a year.

(b) *Kiosk operated by the college*

Relevant annual cash flows

	£'000	£'000
Total sales		100
Cost of sales	80	
Staff salaries (assumed to be incremental)	13	
		93
		7

The net present value can now be calculated.

Year	*Cash flow*	*Discount factor*	*Present value*
	£	10%	£
0	(20,000)	1.000	(20,000)
1 - 5	7,000	3.791	26,537
		Net present value	6,537

The payback period for this option is just under three years.

The internal rate of return

The NPV at 20% is £7,000 × 2.991 – £20,000 = £937.
The NPV at 25% is £7,000 × 2.689 – £20,000 = –£1,177.

The IRR is approximately $\frac{937}{937 - -1,177} \times (25 - 20) = 22\%$.

Kiosk rented to wholesaler

Year	*Cash flow*	*Discount factor*	*Present value*
	£	10%	£
0	(10,000)	1.000	(10,000)
1 - 5	4,000	3.791	15,164
		Net present value	5,164

The payback period for this option is 2½ years.

The internal rate of return

The NPV at 25% is £4,000 × 2.689 – £10,000 = £756.
The NPV at 30% is £4,000 × 2.436 – £10,000 = – £256.

The IRR is approximately $25 + \frac{756}{756 - -256} \times (30 - 25) = 29\%$.

(c) Both options will generate a return which is well in excess of the cost of capital, and the highest internal rate of return would be earned by renting the kiosk to the wholesaler.

However, on the basis of the net present value calculations, the college should operate the kiosk itself, as this will generate the maximum wealth.

The assumptions have been made that there will be no residual value or dismantling costs concerning the kiosk, and that the cost of financing the stocks is negligible.

The risk involved is greater with this option because the cash flows are not guaranteed, but the college administrator should note these compensating advantages.

(i) The college will have greater control over the quality and range of books and stationery sold.

(ii) Pricing policies can be controlled by the college.

(iii) If the proposed major redevelopment is brought forward to an earlier date, the college will not be committed to renting the kiosk to the wholesaler.

19 ANTARES PLC

(a) The first step is to calculate the annual contribution from each project, together with the working capital cash flows. These cash flows, together with the initial outlay, can then be discounted at the cost of capital to arrive at the NPV of each project. Development costs already incurred are irrelevant. There are no additional administration costs associated with the projects, and depreciation is also irrelevant since it has no cash effect.

First, calculate annual contribution.

	A	*B*	*C*	*D*
Unit sales	150,000	75,000	80,000	120,000
	£	£	£	£
Selling price per unit	30.00	40.00	25.00	50.00
Material cost per unit	7.60	12.00	4.50	25.00
Labour cost per unit	9.80	12.00	5.00	10.00
Variable overheads per unit	6.00	7.00	2.50	10.50
	£'000	£'000	£'000	£'000
Sales per annum	4,500	3,000	2,000	6,000
Materials	1,140	900	360	3,000
Labour	1,470	900	400	1,200
Variable overheads	900	525	200	1,260
Annual contribution	990	675	1,040	540

	A	*B*	*C*	*D*
	£'000	£'000	£'000	£'000
Working capital requirement (20% annual sales value)	900	600	400	1,200

It is assumed that working capital will be recovered at the end of year 5. The initial outlay will be made in year 0.

The NPV of each project can now be calculated.

Cash flows

Year	*A* Gross	*A* Net	*B* Gross	*B* Net	*C* Gross	*C* Net	*D* Gross	*D* Net	*Discount factor*
	£'000	£'000	£'000	£'000	£'000	£'000	£'000	£'000	18%
0	(3,000)	(3,000)	(2,000)	(2,000)	(2,800)	(2,800)	(1,800)	(1,800)	1.000
1	990	840	675	572	1,040	882	540	458	0.848
2	990	711	675	485	1,040	747	540	388	0.718
3	990	603	675	411	1,040	633	540	329	0.609
4	990	511	675	348	1,040	537	540	279	0.516
5	1,890	826	1,275	557	1,440	629	1,740	760	0.437
Total NPV		491		373		628		414	

(b) The profitability index provides a means of optimising the NPV when there are more projects available which yield a positive NPV than funds to invest in them. The profitability index measures the ratio of the present value of cash inflows to the initial outlay and represents the net present value per £1 invested.

Project	*PV of inflows*	*Initial outlay*	*Ratio*	*Ranking*
	£'000	£'000		
A	3,491	3,000	1.164	4
B	2,373	2,000	1.187	3
C	3,428	2,800	1.224	2
D	2,214	1,800	1.230	1

Project D has the highest PI ranking and is therefore the first choice for investment. On this basis the funds available should be invested as follows.

Project	Initial outlay	Total NPV	% taken	Cumulative outlay	Actual NPV
	£'000	£'000		£'000	£'000
D	1,800	414	100	1,800	414
C	2,800	628	100	4,600	628
B	2,000	373	30	5,200	112
A	3,000	491	0	5,200	0
Total NPV generated					1,154

(c) The profitability index (PI) approach can be applied only if the projects under consideration fulfil certain criteria, as follows.

(i) There is only one constraint on investment, in this case capital. The PI ensures that maximum return per unit of scarce resource (capital) is obtained.

(ii) Each investment can be accepted or rejected in its entirety or alternatively accepted on a partial basis.

(iii) The NPV generated by a given project is directly proportional to the percentage of the investment undertaken.

(iv) Each investment can only be made once and not repeated.

(v) The company's aim is to maximise overall NPV.

(vi) If additional funds are available but at a higher cost, then the simple PI approach cannot be used since it is not possible to calculate unambiguous individual NPVs.

(vii) If certain of the projects that may be undertaken are mutually exclusive then sub-problems must be defined and calculations made for different combinations of projects. This can become a very lengthy process. These assumptions place limitations on the use of the ratio approach. It is not appropriate to multi-constraint situations when linear programming techniques must be used. Each project must be infinitely divisible and the company must accept that it may need to undertake a small proportion of a given project. This is frequently not possible in practice. It is also very unlikely that there is a simple linear relationship between the NPV and the proportion of the project undertaken; it is much more likely that there will be discontinuities in returns.

Possibly a more serious constraint is the assumption that the company's only concern is to maximise NPV. It is possible that there may be long-term strategic reasons which mean that an investment with a lower NPV should be undertaken instead of one with a higher NPV, and the ratio approach takes no account of the relative degrees of risk associated with making the different investments.

20 DINARD PLC

(a) The real rate of return is the rate of return which an investment would show in the absence of inflation. For example, if a company invests £100, inflation is 0%, and the investment at the end of the year is worth £110, then the real rate of return is 10%.

In reality however, there is likely to be an element of inflation in the returns due to the change in the purchasing power of money over the period. In the example above, if inflation was running at 5%, then to show a real rate of return of 10%, the investment would need to be worth £115.50 at the end of the year. In this case the money rate of return is 15.5% which is made up of the real return of 10% and inflation at 5%.

The relationship between the nominal ('money') rate of return and the real rate of return can be expressed as follows:

$$(1 + \text{nominal rate}) = (1 + \text{real rate}) \times (1 + \text{inflation rate})$$

The rate to be used in discounting cash flows for capital project appraisal will depend on the way in which the expected cash flows are calculated. If the cash flows are expressed in terms of the actual number of pounds that will be received or paid on the various future dates, then the nominal rate must be used. If however they are expressed in terms of the value of the pound at year 0, then the real rate must be used.

(b) *Workings*

	Year 1	Year 2	Year 3	Year 4
Sales volume	25,000	25,000	25,000	25,000
Unit price (£)	80	84	88	93
Variable material cost (£)	8.00	8.32	8.65	9.00
Variable labour cost (£)	12.00	13.20	14.52	15.97
Variable overhead (£)	12.00	12.48	12.98	13.50

Notes

(i) Development costs of £480,000 are sunk costs and will be excluded from the calculations.

(ii) Depreciation does not involve any movement of cash and will be excluded from the fixed overheads (£600,000 in year 1).

(iii) All figures have been adjusted for the appropriate rate of inflation. The investment will therefore be evaluated using the WACC expressed as a nominal rate of 15%.

Evaluation of investment

(All figures £'000)

	Year 0	Year 1	Year 2	Year 3	Year 4
Capital outlay	(2,400)				
Sales		2,000	2,100	2,205	2,315
Direct costs					
Materials		(200)	(208)	(216)	(225)
Labour		(300)	(330)	(363)	(399)
Overhead		(300)	(312)	(324)	(337)
Fixed overheads		(200)	(210)	(221)	(232)
Gross cash flow	(2,400)	1,000	1,040	1,081	1,122
Discount at 15%	1.000	0.870	0.756	0. 658	0.572
Present value	(2,400)	870	786	711	642
Cumulative PV	(2,400)	(1,530)	(744)	(33)	608

The investment yields a net present value at the end of four years of £608,000. In the absence of other factors such as capital rationing, production of the Rance should be undertaken.

21 DIVESTMENT PLC

(a) *A Company Ltd*

REPORT

To: Management team
From: Management Accountant — Date: 21 March 19X6
Subject: Management buyout - financial implications

Introduction

1 Following the feasibility study recently carried out it has been possible to prepare financial projections for the first year of trading following buyout. These figures are included as an Appendix to this report. As a result it is now possible to consider the price that could be considered for the buyout, together with means of raising the necessary finance.

Pricing of buyout

2 The figures show that the projected net profit before tax for the first year of trading is £1.36m. However this includes a one-off item of £2m in respect of advertising costs. The profits thereafter would be in the region of £3.36m per annum. As agreed, we require a return of 30% on our investment, and therefore it is possible to capitalise the projected revenue figure to arrive at the maximum price that could be paid for the assets of the company as follows:

Price = 3.36m / 0.30 = £11.2m

3 An alternative method of valuation is to calculate the fair value of the net assets of the firm as follows.

	£'000
Land and buildings at valuation	6,000
Plant and machinery at valuation	1,000
Stock at valuation	1,000
Debtors (assumed to be collectable)	3,000
Overdraft	(2,000)
	9,000

4 On this basis, the highest price that the team should be prepared to pay is £11.2m, based on the accounting rate of return method of valuation. Alternatively, it could be argued that the £2m advertising costs needed to achieve this should be deducted from the valuation, giving a top price of £9.2m.

5 It would also be worth establishing P/E ratios for other similar firms in this sector in order to look at an earnings based valuation.

Financing of buyout

6 Funding is required initially to finance the purchase price together with £2m to pay for the advertising costs. By the end of the first year of trading, the net assets (excluding the overdraft) should be in the region of £10.98m. Thus in round figures, we are looking for finance in the region of £11m, plus a further amount to cover week to week variations in the level of working capital.

7 It is conventional and prudent to match long-term assets to long-term funding, only using cheaper short term finance to fund short-term assets and working capital fluctuations. In this case, long-term assets consist of the fixed assets (£7m) plus a semi-permanent level of working capital (approximately £4m). The following sources should be considered for this long-term funding.

(i) Specialist venture capital organisations who will provide medium to long-term equity finance. However it must be recognised that they are likely to require a seat on the management board in return for their investment.

(ii) Personal funds raised and loans secured by the new directors. A venture capitalist is likely to want to see some personal commitment on behalf of the management team.

(iii) Grants from the local Enterprise Agency.

(iv) When the price is being negotiated with Divestment plc, it would be beneficial if payment can be staged in order to allow other financing to be negotiated without a tight deadline, and so that part of the payment can be made out of future profits.

(v) Consideration should be given to possible sale and leaseback of some of the fixed assets. If the current premises are not being fully utilised, then it may be possible to sell or lease a part of the land and buildings to another firm. Short-term funding will be required to finance working capital fluctuations and the immediate costs of advertising. A combination of medium-term loans and overdraft facilities from the bank are probably most appropriate for this.

Conclusions

8 The feasibility study figures now provide a basis for negotiations with Divestment plc on price, and also allow us to start to put together a financing package. It will also be necessary to give some consideration to other associated issues, such as the effect of the buyout on employees service contracts, and the setting up of acceptable alternative pension arrangements. These could well impact further upon the price negotiations.

Signed: Management Accountant

Appendix

Forecast profit and loss account following buyout - year 1

	£'000	£'000
Sales		12,000
Cost of sales:		
Purchases	(3,840)	
Wages	(3,600)	
Other expenses	(1,200)	
Advertising	(2,000)	
		(10,640)
Net profit		1,360

Forecast balance sheet following buyout (end of year 1)

	£'000	£'000
Fixed assets		
Land and buildings at valuation	6,000	
Plant and machinery at valuation	1,000	
		7,000
Current assets		
Stock	1,440	
Debtors	3,500	
		4,940
Current liabilities		
Bank overdraft	(620)	
Creditors	(960)	
		(1,580)
Net assets		10,360
Represented by:		
Ordinary shares		1,000
Reserves		9,360
		10,360

Notes

Purchases

Current cost is 40% of sales. If materials were bought from a competitor, this would reduce to 32% (40/1.25).

Expected cost = 12,000 × 0.32 = 3,840

Wages

Current cost is 30% of sales. This level would be maintained.

Expected cost = 12,000 × 0.30 = 3,600

Depreciation

Plant and machinery have been written down to scrap value. Since it is stated that they will not require replacement in the immediate future, no depreciation has been charged.

Other expenses should be adjusted as follows.

	£'000
Current level	1,500
Less head office charge	(500)
Effect of increased turnover	200
	1,200

Stock

Write off over-valuation of stocks of 1,000 against reserves.

Stock level is currently 50% of purchases. This could be reduced by 25%.

Expected stock level = 3,840 × 0.50 × 0.75 = 1,440

Debtors

It is assumed that the level of sales to the parent company would remain unchanged.

	£'000
Parent company debt (10,000 × 0.2 × 0.5)	1,000
Other debt ((10,000 × 0.8) + 2,000) × 0.25)	2,500
	3,500

Creditors

It is assumed that only purchases of materials are made on credit.

Expected creditors = 3,840 × 0.25 = £ 960,000.

Reserves	£'000
Retained profits	7,000
Add retained profit for year	1,360
Less stock write off	(1,000)
Add revaluation of land & buildings	4,000
Less plant & machinery write off	(2,000)
	9,360

Cash	£'000
Opening overdraft	(2,000)
Add net profit	1,360
Add reduction in stock	560
Less stock write off	(1,000)
Less increase in debtors	(500)
Add increase in creditors	960
	(620)

(b) A company may decide to make a takeover bid for one or a combination of reasons.

Market factors

Acquisition of competing products. The company may see the opportunity, particularly in a static or declining market, to reduce competition by acquiring the products of its competitors. One way to do this is to make a bid for the competing company. This will only be possible if the acquisition satisfies the Monopolies and Mergers Commission.

Entry to a new market. Where a company is seeking to enter a new market which is dissimilar to its own, the fastest and lowest cost method of achieving this may be to acquire an existing firm. The dangers of this are that the company may lack the expertise to value it accurately, or to integrate it effectively following takeover.

Operational factors

The opportunity to make economies of scale. One company may bid for another firm in a similar line of business to its own in the belief that in doing so it will be able to achieve economies of scale in one or more areas of its operations. For example, it may be able to concentrate production on key sites which can then work to capacity to supply the regional market. Alternatively, the two firms may be able to share and rationalise their transport and distribution systems or their sales operations. Where the same customer base is served with similar products, further economies of scale may be possible in administrative and research functions eg debt collection and product development.

Diseconomies of scale are also possible due to problems of management and the effective integration of operations.

Management acquisition. Cases arise where it becomes apparent that the management team is not of the calibre needed to take the company through a period of continued growth. In this situation, one option is to acquire a company with a competent team of managers already in place.

Access to innovation. A company which lacks its own research and development facilities and which is falling behind the market technically may see an acquisition as the best way to return to the forefront of innovation in its particular field.

Diversification

The directors may decide that it is in the best interests of the shareholders in the long term to reduce risk by conglomerate diversification. One of the most effective ways to achieve this is to take over an existing profitable firm in a different market sector - ideally one in which systematic risk is negatively correlated with that of the existing company. The new company can then be allowed to continue to operate under its existing management, provided that its performance is satisfactory.

Financial factors

Access to liquid funds. A company which needs a large amount of working capital may seek to improve this situation by the acquisition of a firm which is a cash generator. An example of this latter type of firm would be a chain of petrol stations, where goods are obtained by the company on credit and sold to its customers for cash.

Improved asset backing. Firms in a risky sector with high but volatile earnings levels in relation to the net assets may acquire companies with a high asset backing in order to attempt to improve the risk profile and assist in raising further funds through borrowing.

Growth in earnings per share. It may be cheaper for a company to achieve growth in earnings per share (or sales, dividends and market share) by acquisition than by organic growth. The bidding company may also perceive that due to poor management or lack of resources, the assets are not being used to their fullest capacity to generate earnings, and believe that it could use those assets more effectively itself.

Undervalued shares in the target company. The shares in the target company may appear to be undervalued, and the predator may see an opportunity to acquire the company at a discount. In this situation, the bidding company must make sure that the shares are truly undervalued due to the market having failed to take account of a publicly available piece of information, and not discounted due to expectations of poor performance in the future.

22 OXLAKE PLC

(a) *Receipts from export sales*

(i) *Sales to Singapore*

The value of the sales at the spot rate is:

$$250{,}000 \times \text{Singapore } \$2.862 \times \frac{1}{3.1800} \text{ (W1)} = £225{,}000$$

If Oxlake enters into a contract to sell 250,000 × 2.862 = Singapore $715,000, delivery between two and three months,

Anticipated sterling proceeds = Singapore $715,500 ÷ 3.1592 = £226,481

Oxlake can take out a forward option contract to sell Singapore dollars forward, for delivery between two and three months. This will hopefully overcome the uncertainty surrounding the timing of the receipt from Singapore. The exchange rate used is the least favourable quoted rate for delivery during the period (in this case the three month rate).

Alternatively, Oxlake can cover its foreign exchange risk via the money markets, as follows.

(1) Borrow Singapore $703,194 for three months (see W2).

(2) As required, convert to sterling at spot rate of 3.18 (W1).
The proceeds will be 703,194 ÷ 3.18 = £221,130.

(3) Invest sterling in the Eurosterling market for three months at 6½% pa.
The Eurosterling deposit will grow to £224,723.

(ii) *Sales to Indonesia*

The value of the sales at the spot rate is $100{,}000 \times \frac{2246}{2481} = £90{,}528$.

The first alternative is to compute the eventual proceeds using the £/US $ forward market, since payment has been offered in US dollars and no forward market exists in Rupiahs/£.

Using the US $/£ forward market, the contracted receipts from selling US $ 125,000 for delivery in three months are $\frac{125{,}000}{1.5105} = £82{,}754$

The second alternative is to use the money markets, as follows.

(1) Borrow US $ 121,359 for three months (W4)

(2) Convert US $121,359 into sterling at the spot rate of US $ 1.4875/£, giving $\frac{121{,}359}{1.4875}$ = £81,586

(3) Invest the sterling proceeds of £81,586 on the Eurosterling deposit market for three months at 6½% pa, yielding £81,586 × 1.01625 = £82,912.

Conclusion. The protection should be effected through the foreign exchange market for the sale to Singapore and through the money market for the sale to Indonesia.

(b)

	Rupiahs
Sales value (100,000 × 2,246)	224,600,000
Less 5% discount	(11,230,000)
Discounted sales value	213,370,000

Proceeds of sales = $\frac{213{,}370{,}000}{1{,}667.9\text{(W5)}}$ = \$127,927

The best US \$ deposit rate of interest is 8% pa in a US domestic bank.

The yield after three months is \$127,927 × 1.02 = \$130,486.

Converted into sterling, using the three month forward market, this is $\frac{\$130{,}486}{1.5105}$ = £86,386.

Alternatively, the US dollar proceeds could be converted immediately into sterling and then invested for three months in eurosterling. The calculation is as follows.

(i) Conversion of US \$127,927 (see above) into sterling yields

$\frac{127{,}927}{1.4875}$ = £86,001

(ii)

	£
Yield of eurosterling 3 month deposit (£86,001 × 6.5%/4)	1,398
Add principal	86,001
	87,399

Conclusion. The best yield without the offer of immediate payment was £82,912. Both the forward foreign exchange market and the money market yield better returns, with the money market's £87,399 as the better of the alternatives.

Workings

W1 *Cross rates, Singapore \$/£*

	Singapore \$/US\$	*US \$/£*	*Singapore \$/£*
Spot	2.1378	1.4875	3.1800
1 month forward	2.1132	1.4963	3.1620
2 months forward	2.0964	1.5047	3.1545
3 months forward	2.0915	1.5105	3.1592

W2 *Required Singapore \$ borrowings*

The interest rate in Singapore \$ is 7% pa or 1.75% for three months.

Thus the maximum borrowing which can be repaid from export sale proceeds is

Singapore \$ $\frac{715{,}000}{1.0175}$ = 703,194

W3 *Eurosterling deposit*

The interest rate for three months is 1.625%.

Thus the yield on the deposit is £221,130 × 1.01625 = £224,723.

W4 *Required US \$ borrowings*

US \$ interest rates (eurodollars) are 12% pa or 3% for three months.

Thus, the maximum borrowing which can be repaid from the sale proceeds is

$\frac{\$125{,}000}{1.03}$ = \$121,359

W5 *Cross rate, Rupiah/£*

	US \$/£	*Rupiah/US \$*	*Rupiah/£*
Spot	1.4875	1667.90	2,481

(c) When a company invoices sales in a currency other than its own, the amount of 'home' currency it will eventually receive is uncertain. There may be an advantage or a disadvantage, depending on changes in the exchange rate over the period between invoicing and receiving payment. With this in mind, invoicing in a foreign currency has the following advantages.

(i) The foreign customer will find the deal more attractive than a similar one in the exporter's currency, since the customer will bear no foreign exchange risk. Making a sale will therefore be that much easier.

(ii) The exporter can take advantage of favourable foreign exchange movements by selling the exchange receipts forward (for more of the home currency than would be obtained by conversion at the spot rate).

(iii) In some countries, the importer may find it difficult or even impossible to obtain the foreign exchange necessary to pay in the exporter's currency. The willingness of the exporter to sell in the importer's currency may therefore prevent the sale falling through.

The disadvantages of making export sales in foreign currency are the reverse of the advantages.

(i) The exporter (rather than the foreign customer) bears the foreign exchange risk.
(ii) If the exchange movement is unfavourable, the exporter's profit will be reduced.

23 EXPORTERS PLC

(a) First calculate the forward rate of exchange at which the hedging contract is made.

The company will receive $500,000 in six months' time.
Assuming an interest rate of 15%, this equates to $465,116.2 at today's date ($500,000 / 1.075).

$465,116.2 at the spot rate of $2.50 equates to £186,046.50.

£186,046.50 at an interest rate of 12% would be worth £197,209.30 in six months' time (£186,046.50 × 1.06).

The forward rate is therefore $2.5354 (500,000 / 197,209.30).

The effect on Exporters plc in the event of the pound moving in different ways over the six month period can now be calculated.

(i) If the pound gains 4%, the exchange rate will be $2.60 ($2.50 × 1.04). $500,000 would therefore buy only £192,307.70. Hedging has saved the company £4,901.60 (£197,209.30 – £192,307.70).

(ii) If the pound loses 2%, the exchange rate will be $2.45 ($2.50 × 0.98). $500,000 would therefore buy £204,081.60. Hedging has cost the company £6,872.30 (£204,081.60 – £197,209.30).

(iii) If the pound remains at $2.50, the transaction would realise £200,000. Hedging has therefore cost the company £2,790.70 (£200,000 – £197,209.30).

(b) The interest rate parity theory describes the relationship between the spot rate and the forward rate of exchange at any one time. The theory states that in equilibrium, the difference in interest rates between two countries equates to the difference between the forward and spot rates of exchange. All other things being equal, traders in the money market can invest or borrow in the currency that offers them the best interest rates; however they will lose on the currency side of the transaction since they will receive a lower exchange rate at the end of the period. This is because banks avoid leaving currency risks exposed so that when a trader sells a currency forward, the banker will borrow that currency to balance the transaction. The banker will pass the cost of the difference in interest rates available in the two currencies on to the trader through the exchange rate applied.

As recent events have shown however, traders who believe that a currency is going to be devalued can speculate against that currency, and even when artificially high interest rates are introduced in support of the exchange rate, they will continue to sell in the expectation that devaluation will eventually be inevitable. Thus factors other than differential interest rates can be seen to have an effect on the relationship between spot and forward exchange rates.

(c) A forward market currency hedge is a contract to buy or sell a specific amount of currency on a specific date at a specific price agreed in advance. Contracts can be arranged through the banks in most currencies. Since the outcome of the contract is known in advance, the company is able to plan its cash movements with some degree of certainty. However it runs the risk that the currency markets may move in a manner different to that expected and implied in the agreement, and it may therefore lose out against the spot rate.

(i) Currency futures are similar in principle to forward market currency hedges, however they are generally for standard amounts and restricted to the most frequently traded currencies. They cannot be provided by the bank but must be traded on separate markets. The risks of costs being incurred through exchange rates moving differently to expectations are similar to those associated with forward market hedges; however the trader is able to realise a profit if the market moves in his favour by taking out a further futures contract in the opposite direction.

(ii) An options hedge is a contract which provides the right to buy or sell a specific amount of currency on a specific date at a specific rate. However, unlike the forward exchange contract, there is no obligation to exercise the option on the due date. Thus in the case of Exporters plc, the company would be protected from the effects of the pound strengthening, but would be able to benefit from any weakening of the pound. The cost of this takes the form of a premium payable on the contract. Options are available either in a tailor-made form specific to the trader's requirements from the bank, or in a standard form in certain currencies only from an options exchange.

24 AARDVARK LTD

Aardvark Ltd has the following options.

(a) It can continue its existing policy.

(b) It can use the export factor, either in combination with its existing overdraft, or using the 80% finance offered by the factor.

(c) It can use the insurer with the assignment of policy rights (since cheaper finance is available at no extra cost.

It is assumed that all export debts will be financed by an overdraft or by special lending arrangements.

(a) *Use of the export factor for debt collection only*

	£
Service fee 3% × £1,000,000	(30,000)
Bad debts saved (by insurance) 0.5% × £1,000,000	5,000
Administration costs saved	35,000
Net saving	10,000

(b) *Use of the export factor for debt collection and finance*

There will be a saving in finance charges of 0.5% a year on 80% of the average debtors required.

	£
Service fee for debt collection	(30,000)
Interest costs saved (0.5% × 80% × £1,000,000 × 90/360)	1,000
Bad debts saved	5,000
Administrative costs saved	35,000
Net saving	11,000

(c) *Use of the insurer*

If the insurer was used, there is a saving of 1% on 70% of the finance required, since 70% of finance will be obtained at just 1.5% above base rate, instead of 2.5% above base rate.

	£
Insurance costs (0.35% × £1,000,000)	(3,500)
Savings in bank interest (1% × 70% × £1,000,000 × 90/360)	1,750
Savings in bad debts (90% × 0.5% × £1,000,000)	4,500
Net saving	2,750

Conclusion

Aardvark Ltd should use the services of the export factor, and obtain finance for 80% of export credit sales from the factor.

25 FOREIGN MARKETS

(a) Exporting may be direct selling by the firm's own export department into the overseas markets, or it may be indirect through channels such as agents, distributors or trading companies. Provided the product can travel, the main advantage of exporting is that it is the lowest risk option.

However, it may be difficult to establish a good customer support system if there is no operational base in the overseas countries. Other disadvantages may include high transport costs as well as tariffs, quotas and unfavourable tax regimes in the foreign countries. Consumers may also have a preference for locally made equipment.

Licensing involves conferring rights to make use of the licenser company's production process on producers located in the overseas market in return for royalty payments. Advantage of licensing over exporting and direct foreign investment include the following.

(i) It can permit rapid penetration of the new markets.

(ii) Set-up costs are low compared with foreign direct investment.

(iii) Political risks are lessened since the licensee will probably be a local firm, and it is a good option when the overseas country has high import barriers.

(iv) License fees allow funds to be remitted to the home country.

Disadvantages include the following.

(i) The licensee company may end up as a direct competitor once the agreement has expired.

(ii) Quality standards are difficult to enforce and may be compromised.

(iii) Since some profit must accrue to the licensee the financial returns on the agreement may be relatively low.

Foreign direct investment (FDI) may take a variety of forms, including the setting up of a wholly owned subsidiary in the overseas country, taking over an existing firm in that country, or some form of joint venture operation. Whatever the mechanism, however, the size of the investment required is likely to be relatively large and the risks of failure correspondingly greater. Reasons for FDI are diverse and include the following.

(i) Access to new markets where transportation time and costs make exporting difficult.

(ii) The relative costs of production may be cheaper due to access to cheaper local raw materials, lower labour costs etc.

(iii) FDI may overcome the problem of import quotas and tariffs.

(iv) Grants and tax concessions may exist to attract foreign inward investment.

(b) (i)

		£'000
Materials	715 × 15	10,725
Labour	380 × 15	5,700
Other direct costs	50 × 15	750
Leasing costs	620 × 5	3,100
Plant	1,800 – 900	900
		21,175
20% mark up		4,235
Sterling price		25,410

The present exchange rate is Z$46.0 to the pound, and this will change to Z$46.0 × 1.25 to the pound, or Z$57.5 to the pound, over the duration of the project. The tender price in Z$ based on a 20% markup is therefore found as x from:

$$\frac{x \times 0.3}{46} + \frac{x \times 0.7}{57.5} = 25.41 \text{ million}$$

$$(0.00652174 + 0.01217391)\ x = 25.41 \text{ million}$$

$$x = 25{,}410{,}000 \div 0.01869565 \cong \text{Z\$}1{,}359 \text{ million}$$

(ii) To find the net present value of the project, we must first work out the tax cash flows and then include these, along with all other relevant costs, in a discounted cash flow computation.

	Tax year 1	Tax year 2
	19X2	19X3
	£'000	£'000
Materials (4:11)	2,860	7,865
Labour (3:12)	1,140	4,560
Other direct costs (3:12)	150	600
Leasing costs	620	2,480
Capital allowances[1]	450	450
	5,220	15,955
Sales 1,359,000 × 30%/46	8,863	
1,359,000 × 70%/57.5		16,544
Taxable profit	3,643	589
Tax cash flow at 35%	1,275	206

[1] Year 1: £1.8m × 0.75 = £1.35m WDV, £450,000 allowance.
Year 2: £1.35m × 0.75 = £1.0125m WDV, £337,500 + £112,500 balancing allowance.

Net present value computation

Month	Item	Amount £'000	Discount factor (1%)	NPV £'000
0	Sales	8,863	1.000	8,863
15	Sales	16,544	0.861	14,244
1 - 15	Labour	(380)	13.870	(5,271)
0 - 14	Materials	(715)	14.000	(10,010)
1 - 15	Other direct costs	(50)	13.870	(693)
0	Lease	(620)	1.000	(620)
3	Lease	(620)	0.971	(602)
6	Lease	(620)	0.942	(584)
9	Lease	(620)	0.914	(567)
12	Lease	(620)	0.887	(550)
9	Taxation	(1,275)	0.914	(1,165)
21	Taxation	(206)	0.811	(167)
0	Plant not sold	1,936	1.000	(1,936)
15	Final sale of plant	900	0.861	775
				1,717

Plant not sold represents the opportunity cost of not selling the plant and equipment immediately. On immediate sale, a balancing charge of £2m – £1.8m = £200,000 would arise, with tax of £70,000 payable in Month 9. The present value of the tax payment is therefore £70,000 × 0.914 = £64,000. £2,000,000 – £64,000 = £1,936,000. The net present value of the project at the suggested tender price is approximately £1,717,000.

The minimum tender price

Unless there are special factors, such as a need to succeed at almost any cost because of the prestige and future business which this project would bring, the company should not tender at a price below that which will yield a net present value of zero. The price which will yield such a result may be estimated as follows.

Each Z$1,000,000 reduction in the tender price has the following effects.

Month	Item	Amount £'000	Discount factor (1%)	NPV £'000
0	Fall in sales (300/46)	6.52	1.000	6.5
15	Fall in sales (700/57.5)	12.17	0.861	10.5
9	Fall in taxation (35% × 6.52)	(2.28)	0.914	(2.1)
21	Fall in taxation (35% × 12.17)	(4.26)	0.811	(3.5)
Fall in net present value				11.4

The net present value would therefore fall to zero at a tender price of approximately 1,359 – (1,717 ÷ 11.4) = Z$ 1,208 million, and this should be the minimum tender price.

This estimate assumes that the cash flow estimates are accurate. However, they could all be subject to considerable error. No account has been taken of inflation in the costs payable in sterling, and it has been assumed that payment for the project will be received in full on time. This in turn depends on the project being completed on time to an acceptable standard. It has also been assumed that the project's risks are such that the company's usual cost of capital is an appropriate discount rate.

Lecturers' question bank

1 FINANCIAL PLANS *45 mins*

(a) Outline the factors that a company should consider when developing a long-term financial plan to cover three years or more.

Briefly describe the major types of financial model that might be used to assist in the preparation of such plans, and discuss the problems that companies face in long-term planning. **15 Marks**

(b) List and discuss briefly five reasons why companies in the same type of business might have different P/E ratios.

Comment on the view that the P/E ratio is 'an attempt to value a company in terms of its earnings'. **10 Marks**

Total Marks = 25

2 FINANCIAL OBJECTIVE *45 mins*

The primary objective in financial management is usually assumed to be the maximisation (or improvement) of the wealth of ordinary shareholders. One way this can be achieved is to obtain a consistent rate of growth in the earnings per share. The ability of a company to achieve such consistent growth depends to some extent on:

(a) the external environment of the company;
(b) the company's operating cost structure;
(c) the company's capital gearing and the cost of debt capital.

Required

(a) Show how these factors are relevant to a consistent growth in earnings per share, using the information provided below about two companies, X Ltd and Y Ltd. **8 Marks**

(b) Discuss the financial management of both companies, insofar as the information provided allows. **17 Marks**

	X Ltd				*Y Ltd*			
Year	*19X1*	*19X2*	*19X3*	*19X4*	*19X1*	*19X2*	*19X3*	*19X4*
	£'000	£'000	£'000	£'000	£'000	£'000	£'000	£'000
Profit & loss account								
Turnover	100	124	175	254	400	448	582	728
Variable costs	60	77	112	165	120	140	192	286
Fixed costs	26	31	42	58	180	196	230	256
Total costs	86	108	154	223	300	336	422	542
Earnings before interest and tax	14	16	21	31	100	112	160	186
Less interest	4	4	7	8	10	16	19	19
Earnings before tax	10	12	14	23	90	96	141	167
Less tax	4	5	6	11	40	44	70	83
Distributable profits	6	7	8	12	50	52	71	84
Less dividends	3	3	4	4	18	18	30	40
Retained earnings	3	4	4	8	32	34	41	44
Balance sheet								
Fixed assets	29	42	56	64	300	318	400	425
Net current assets	31	34	49	72	80	153	207	232
	60	76	105	136	380	471	607	657
Ordinary shares £1	20	20	20	25	200	200	250	250
Asset revaluation reserve	0	12	16	20	0	0	0	0
Reserves	15	19	23	31	100	134	175	225
Equity funds	35	51	59	76	300	334	425	475
Loans	25	25	46	60	80	137	182	182
	60	76	105	136	380	471	607	657
EPS (pence)	30.0	35.0	40.0	48.0	25.0	26.0	28.4	33.6

Note. Earnings per share (EPS) are the profits distributable to ordinary shareholders (after interest, tax and preference dividend) divided by the number of ordinary shares in issue. **Total Marks = 25**

3 BUTLER PLC *36 mins*

Butler plc has issued £500,000 of 12% convertible loan stock which is due for redemption on 31 January 19X8. Assume that it is now ten years before this date.

The issue was made to the general public at a price of £105 per £100 of stock. Its current market price is £134 per cent (interest having just been paid).

Non-convertible loan stock of a similar risk class currently yields 14% per annum.

The option to convert loan stock into shares can be taken by the security holders at any time up to 31 January 19X2 (four years from now). If the options are not taken up by this date, they will lapse. The rate of conversion is 20 shares per £100 of stock.

Ordinary shares of the company have a current market value of £5.70 (ex div), and the dividend paid recently was 57 pence per share (net).

You are the holder of £50,000 of the stock, and you wish to decide whether:

(a) to hold on to the stock until it matures;
(b) to convert the stock into shares;
(c) to sell the stock.

Ignore taxation.

Required

(a) What would be the value of the stock you hold, if it could not be converted into shares? **5 Marks**

(b) What would be the expected minimum annual growth rate in the market price of ordinary shares of the company to justify a decision to hold on to the stock for the moment with the intention of converting it into shares before the option period expires? **7 Marks**

(c) What would be your best investment decision? Explain your reasons, making whatever assumptions you think are necessary. **8 Marks**

Total Marks = 20

4 AGENCY THEORY *45 mins*

(a) Agency theory presents the firm as a combination of competing interest groups, two of which are shareholders and management.

Required

Discuss how the firm's attitude to risk might vary depending on whether shareholder objectives or management-oriented goals predominate in the firm's planning. **9 Marks**

(b) Outline the fundamental analysis theory of share values, giving numerical examples. **8 Marks**

(c) To what extent is the validity of the fundamental analysis theory affected by the efficiency of the stock market? **8 Marks**

Total Marks = 25

5 BETTALUCK PLC *27 mins*

Bettaluck plc has been enjoying a substantial net cash inflow, and until the surplus funds are needed to meet tax and dividend payments, and to finance further capital expenditure in several months time, they have been invested in a small portfolio of short-term equity investments.

Details of the portfolio, which consists of shares in four UK listed companies, are as follows.

Company	*Number of shares held*	*Beta equity coefficient*	*Market price per share*	*Latest dividend yield*	*Expected return on equity in the next year*
				%	%
Dashing plc	60,000	1.16	£4.29	6.1	19.5
Elegant plc	80,000	1.28	£2.92	3.4	24.0
Fantastic plc	100,000	0.90	£2.17	5.7	17.5
Gaudy plc	125,000	1.50	£3.14	3.3	23.0

The current market return is 19% a year and the Treasury bill yield is 11% a year.

Required

(a) On the basis of the data given, calculate the risk of Bettaluck plc's short-term investment portfolio relative to that of the market. **5 Marks**

(b) Recommend, with reasons, whether Bettaluck plc should change the composition of its portfolio. **10 Marks**

Total Marks = 15

6 HAMM PLC *36 mins*

Hamm plc is a company quoted on the Alternative Investment Market. It produces medical products which are sold to retailers for sale to the general public, and to hospitals.

The company currently makes no use of debt finance, although it could borrow from its bank at an annual rate of 18% before tax. It wishes now to install computerised equipment with a four year life which would involve an outlay of £5 million (residual value: nil). The Financial Director has carried out a study which shows that the project has a positive net present value when this is calculated using the shareholders' required rate of return as a discount rate.

Hamm plc has asked Castles Leasing Limited ('Castles'), a subsidiary of a major bank, for a quotation for the acquisition of the equipment on a leasing contract under which maintenance of the equipment would be provided by Castles.

Castles has quoted an annual rental of £1,800,000. The maintenance services would cost Hamm plc £190,000 annually if it had to obtain them from another source.

The following further information is available about Castles. Castles can finance purchase of the equipment by borrowing at 14% (before tax). The purchase would be timed to coincide with receipt of the first of the annual rental payments to be made by Hamm. Castles would be able to provide the maintenance service at no incremental cost by utilising spare capacity in its own maintenance division. Castles and Hamm both pay corporate tax at a rate of 30%, and the tax becomes payable 12 months after the relevant cash flow. A writing down allowance can be claimed on a 25% reducing balance basis.

Required

(a) Describe the key aspects of:

(i) Finance leases **2 Marks**
(ii) Hire purchase **2 Marks**
(iii) Sale and leaseback **2 Marks**

(b) By how much does the proposed rental exceed the rental level at which Castles would break even? (Assume that the rental is fully allowable against tax.) **6 Marks**

(c) Disregarding the savings in maintenance costs, evaluate whether Hamm plc should lease the equipment from Castles or borrow money to purchase the equipment itself. **6 Marks**

(d) Calculate whether a different evaluation should be made if the savings in maintenance costs for Hamm plc are accounted for. **2 Marks**

Total Marks = 20

7 MANAGEMENT *45 mins*

(a) The working capital (or operating) cycle of a business is the length of time between payment for materials entering into stock and receipt of the proceeds of sales.

The table below gives information extracted from the annual accounts of Management plc for the past three years.

Required

(i) Calculate the length of the working capital cycle year by year (assuming 365 days in the year).

(ii) List possible actions that might be taken to reduce the length of that cycle, and the possible disadvantages of each. **15 Marks**

Management plc - Extracts from annual accounts

	Year 1	Year 2	Year 3
	£	£	£
Stocks: raw materials	108,000	145,800	180,000
work in progress	75,600	97,200	93,360
finished goods	86,400	129,600	142,875
Purchases	518,400	702,000	720,000
Cost of goods sold	756,000	972,000	1,098,360
Sales	864,000	1,080,000	1,188,000
Debtors	172,800	259,200	297,000
Trade creditors	86,400	105,300	126,000

(b) The sales director of Management plc estimates that if the period of credit allowed to customers were reduced to 60 days, this would result in a 25% reduction in sales but would probably eliminate about £30,000 of bad debts a year. It would be necessary to spend an additional £20,000 a year on credit control. The company at present relies heavily on overdraft finance costing 9% a year.

Required

Make calculations showing the effect of these changes, and advise whether they would be financially justified. Base your answer on the Year 3 level of sales, and assume that purchases and stockholdings would be reduced proportionately to the reduction in sales value. **10 Marks**

Total Marks = 25

8 LEIVERS *36 mins*

(a) In recent years there has been a large increase in the number of management buyouts, often when a company is in financial distress. What are the possible financial advantages of a company's shares being sold to a group of managers rather than the company's being liquidated? **6 Marks**

(b) Five managers of Leivers Ltd are discussing the possibility of a management buy-out of the part of the company that they work for. The buy-out would require a total of £700,000, of which £525,000 would comprise the purchase cost, and £175,000 the funds for a small expansion in activity and for working capital. The managers believe that they could jointly provide £70,000.

Required

(i) Discuss possible sources of finance that the managers might use to raise the required funds. **7 Marks**

(ii) What are likely to be the major factors that a potential supplier of finance will consider before deciding whether to offer finance? What type of security or other conditions might providers of finance specify?

7 Marks

Total Marks = 20

9 KILLISICK AND HOLBECK *45 mins*

Killisick plc wishes to acquire Holbeck plc. The directors of Killisick are trying to justify the acquisition to the shareholders of both companies on the grounds that it will increase the wealth of all shareholders.

The supporting financial evidence produced by Killisick's directors is summarised below.

	Killisick	*Holbeck*
	£'000	£'000
Operating profit	12,400	5,800
Less interest payable	4,431	2,200
Profit before tax	7,969	3,600
Less taxation	2,789	1,260
Earnings available to ordinary shareholders	5,180	2,340

	Killisick	*Holbeck*
Earnings per share (pre-acquisition)	14.80 pence	29.25 pence
Market price per share (pre-acquisition)	222 pence	322 pence
Estimated market price (post-acquisition)	240 pence	
Estimated equivalent value of one old Holbeck share (post-acquisition)		360 pence

Payment is to be made with Killisick ordinary shares, at an exchange ratio of 3 Killisick shares for every 2 Holbeck shares.

Required

(a) Show how the directors of Killisick produced their estimates of post-acquisition value and, if you do not agree with these estimates, produce revised estimates of post-acquisition values. All calculations must be shown. State clearly any assumptions that you make. **10 Marks**

(b) If the acquisition is contested by Holbeck plc, using Killisick's estimate of its post-acquisition market price calculate the maximum price that Killisick could offer without reducing the wealth of its existing shareholders. **3 Marks**

(c) The board of directors of Holbeck plc later informally indicate that they are prepared to recommend to their shareholders a 2 for 1 share offer.

Further information regarding the effect of the acquisition on Killisick is given below.

(i) The acquisition will result in an increase in the total pre-acquisition after tax operating cash flows of £2,750,000 a year indefinitely.

(ii) Rationalisation will allow machinery with a realisable value of £7,200,000 to be disposed of at the end of the next year.

(iii) Redundancy payments will total £3,500,000 immediately and £8,400,000 at the end of the next year.

(iv) Killisick's cost of capital is estimated to be 14% a year.

All values are after any appropriate taxation. Assume that the pre-acquisition market values of Killisick and Holbeck shares have not changed.

Recommend, using your own estimates of post-acquisition values, whether Killisick should be prepared to make a 2 for 1 offer for the shares of Holbeck. **6 Marks**

(d) Disregarding the information in (c) above and assuming no increase in the total post-acquisition earnings, assess whether this acquisition is likely to have any effect on the value of debt of Killisick plc. **6 Marks**

Total Marks = 25

10 LAVIPILON PLC *45 mins*

The managing director of Lavipilon plc wishes to provide an extra return to the company's shareholders and has suggested these three possibilities.

(i) A 2 for 5 bonus issue (capitalisation issue) in addition to the normal dividend.
(ii) A 1 for 5 scrip dividend instead of the normal cash dividend.
(iii) A 1 for 1 share (stock) split in addition to the normal dividend.

SUMMARISED BALANCE SHEET OF LAVIPILON PLC
(AS AT THE END OF LAST YEAR)

	£m
Fixed assets	65
Current assets	130
Less current liabilities	(55)
	140
Ordinary shares (50 pence par value)	25
Share premium account	50
Revenue reserves	40
Shareholders' funds	115
11% debenture	25
	140

The company's shares are trading at 300 pence cum div and the company has £50,000,000 of profit from this year's activities available to ordinary shareholders of which £30,000,000 will be paid as a dividend if option (i) or option (iii) is chosen. None of the £40,000,000 revenue reserves would be distributed. This year's financial accounts have not yet been finalised.

Required

(a) For each proposal show the likely effect on the company's balance sheet at the end of *this* year, and the likely effect on the company's share price. **9 Marks**

(b) Comment upon how well these suggestions fulfil the managing director's objective of providing an extra return to the company's shareholders. **3 Marks**

(c) Discuss reasons why a company might wish to make:
  (i) a scrip dividend;
  (ii) a share (stock) split. **5 Marks**

(d) The managing director has heard that it is possible for the company to purchase its own shares. Explain why the purchase of its own shares might be useful to a company. **8 Marks**

Total Marks = 25

11 RATE OF RETURN *36 mins*

(a) (i) Assume that the opportunity rate of return on equity capital of companies in a particular risk class is 12½% and that this is also the rate at which surplus funds can be re-invested.

The equity of X plc is in this risk category and the company has a policy of paying annual dividends at the rate of 5% on the market value of shareholders' funds at the beginning of each year.

Calculate what annual rate of growth in share price X plc should achieve. **5 Marks**

(ii) X plc has under consideration a project costing £20,000, of similar risk to existing activities, to be financed by an issue of ordinary shares at par, and generating return cash flows of £10,500 at the end of year 1 and £13,500 at the end of year 2.

Demonstrate that this project will satisfy all the criteria derived from (a)(i) above, by preparing a calculation of the net terminal value of the project. Ignore taxation. **5 Marks**

(b) (i) Discuss whether all capital expenditure projects undertaken by an enterprise should be expected to yield the same rate of return.

5 Marks

(ii) Discuss whether the cost of equity capital used in appraising projects would be affected by an increase in the rate of interest at which surplus funds could be re-invested. **5 Marks**

Total Marks = 20

12 SOLDEN PLC

Solden plc is a UK company which is considering setting up a manufacturing operation to make ski-boot warmers in a country called Ober. The currency of Ober is the Gurgle and these are currently G16 to the pound sterling.

If the operation were to be set up the plant would be purchased in Ober costing G600,000 now and some equipment would be sent form the UK immediately. This equipment is fully written off in the UK but has a market value of £12,500 or G200,000. All plant and equipment is written off on a straight line basis by Solden plc over 5 years.

The ski-boot warmers will sell for an initial price of G160 but this price will increase in line with inflation in Ober which is expected to continue at its current rate of 10% pa. It is also expected that 4,000 ski-boot warmers will be sold in the first year increasing at a rate of 5% each year. The costs of making ski-boot warmers consist of local variable costs of G80 per unit and selling and administration costs of G40,000 pa, both of which will increase in line with inflation in Ober. The warmers also require some specialist parts sent over from the UK each year. These will be transferred at the beginning of the first year of production at a cost of G40,000 (£2,500) which includes a 25% mark up on cost. The transfer price and cost of these items are expected to increase by 5% pa, and they will be billed to the Ober operation at the beginning of the year and paid for at the end of the year. The working capital for this project will be required at the beginning of each year and will be equal to10% of the expected sales value for the year.

Solden plc estimates that it will lose some of its own exports worth £5,000 now and increasing by 5% pa due to the setting up of the operation in Ober. However, Solden plc will be receiving a licence fee from the Ober operation equal to 10% of sales each year.

Corporation tax in Ober is only 20% and operating costs, licence fees and depreciation at 25% on a straight line basis are all tax allowable expenses. Corporation tax in the UK is at 33%. There is a one year tax delay in both countries.

Solden plc wishes to assess this project from the point of view of both investors in Ober (required return 15%) and investors in the UK (required return 10%). The assessment will take place using Solden's usual 5 year time 'horizon' and valuing and Ober operation at three times its net cash inflow during the fifth year. If the operation were to be sold at this value, tax would be payable at 30% on the proceeds.

It is expected that the Gurgle will depreciate against the pound by 4% pa. Assume that all prices and exchange rates have just altered, and that all cash flows occur at the end of the year unless specified otherwise.

Required

(a) Prepare calculations (to the nearest 100 Gurgles) to show whether the operation would be worthwhile for investors based in Ober. **15 Marks**

(b) If all cash surpluses can be remitted to the UK calculate whether Solden plc should set up the operation. Assume no further UK tax is payable on income taxed on Ober. **5 Marks**

Total Marks = 20

List of Key Terms and Index

BPP
PUBLISHING

BPP
PUBLISHING

BPP
PUBLISHING

REVIEW FORM & FREE PRIZE DRAW

All original review forms from the entire BPP range, completed with genuine comments, will be entered into one of two draws on 31 January 2000 and 31 July 2000. The names on the first four forms picked out on each occasion will be sent a cheque for £50.

Name: ______________________ **Address:** ______________________

____

____

How have you used this Text?
(Tick one box only)

☐ Home study (book only)

☐ On a course: college ______________

☐ With 'correspondence' package

☐ Other ______________

Why did you decide to purchase this Text?
(Tick one box only)

☐ Have used BPP Texts in the past

☐ Recommendation by friend/colleague

☐ Recommendation by a lecturer at college

☐ Saw advertising

☐ Other ______________

During the past six months do you recall seeing/receiving any of the following?
(Tick as many boxes as are relevant)

☐ Our advertisement in CIMA *Student*

☐ Our advertisement in *Management Accounting*

☐ Our advertisement in *Pass*

☐ Our brochure with a letter through the post

Which (if any) aspects of our advertising do you find useful?
(Tick as many boxes as are relevant)

☐ Prices and publication dates of new editions

☐ Information on Text content

☐ Facility to order books off-the-page

☐ None of the above

Your ratings, comments and suggestions would be appreciated on the following areas

	Very useful	*Useful*	*Not useful*
Introductory section (Key study steps, personal study plan etc)	☐	☐	☐
Chapter introductions	☐	☐	☐
Key terms	☐	☐	☐
Explanations	☐	☐	☐
Case examples and examples	☐	☐	☐
Questions and answers	☐	☐	☐
Chapter roundups	☐	☐	☐
Quick quizzes	☐	☐	☐
Exam focus points	☐	☐	☐
Question bank	☐	☐	☐
Answer bank	☐	☐	☐
List of key terms and index	☐	☐	☐
Icons	☐	☐	☐

	Excellent	*Good*	*Adequate*	*Poor*
Overall opinion of this Text	☐	☐	☐	☐

Do you intend to continue using BPP Study Texts/Kits? ☐ Yes ☐ No

Please note any further comments and suggestions/errors on the reverse of this page.

Please return to: Alison McHugh, BPP Publishing Ltd, FREEPOST, London, W12 8BR

REVIEW FORM & FREE PRIZE DRAW (continued)

Please note any further comments and suggestions/errors below

FREE PRIZE DRAW RULES

1 Closing date for 31 January 2000 draw is 31 December 1999. Closing date for 31 July 2000 draw is 30 June 2000.

2 Restricted to entries with UK and Eire addresses only. BPP employees, their families and business associates are excluded.

3 No purchase necessary. Entry forms are available upon request from BPP Publishing. No more than one entry per title, per person. Draw restricted to persons aged 16 and over.

4 Winners will be notified by post and receive their cheques not later than 6 weeks after the relevant draw date. Lists of winners will be published in BPP's *focus* newsletter following the relevant draw.

5 The decision of the promoter in all matters is final and binding. No correspondence will be entered into.

See overleaf for information on other
BPP products and how to order

Mr/Mrs/Ms (Full name)

Daytime delivery address

Postcode

Daytime Tel

Date of exam (month/year)

CIMA Order

To BPP Publishing Ltd, Aldine Place, London W12 8AA

Tel: 020 8740 2211. Fax: 020 8740 1184

	7/99 Texts	1/99 Kits	1/99 Psscrds	1/99 Tapes	1/99 Videos	1999 CDs
STAGE 1						
1 Financial Accounting Fundamentals	£18.95 ☐	£8.95 ☐	£4.95 ☐	£12.95 ☐	£25.00 ☐	
2 Cost Accounting and Quantitative Methods	£18.95 ☐	£8.95 ☐	£4.95 ☐	£12.95 ☐	£25.00 ☐	
3 Economic Environment	£18.95 ☐	£8.95 ☐	£4.95 ☐	£12.95 ☐	£25.00 ☐	
4 Business Environment & Information Technology	£18.95 ☐	£8.95 ☐	£4.95 ☐	£12.95 ☐	£25.00 ☐	
STAGE 2						
5 Financial Accounting	£18.95 ☐	£9.95 ☐	£5.95 ☐	£12.95 ☐	£25.00 ☐	
6 Operational Cost Accounting	£18.95 ☐	£9.95 ☐	£5.95 ☐	£12.95 ☐	£25.00 ☐	£39.95 ☐
7 Management Science Applications	£18.95 ☐	£9.95 ☐	£5.95 ☐	£12.95 ☐	£25.00 ☐	£39.95 ☐
8 Business and Company Law	£18.95 ☐	£9.95 ☐	£5.95 ☐	£12.95 ☐	£25.00 ☐	
STAGE 3						
9 Financial Reporting	£19.95 ☐	£9.95 ☐	£5.95 ☐	£12.95 ☐	£25.00 ☐	£39.95 ☐
10 Management Accounting Applications	£19.95 ☐	£9.95 ☐	£5.95 ☐	£12.95 ☐	£25.00 ☐	
11 Organisational Management & Development	£19.95 ☐	£9.95 ☐	£5.95 ☐	£12.95 ☐	£25.00 ☐	
12 Business Taxation (FA 99)	£19.95 ☐	£9.95 ☐	£5.95 ☐	£12.95 ☐	£25.00 ☐	£39.95 ☐ (FA 98)
STAGE 4						
13 Strategic Financial Management	£20.95 ☐	£10.95 ☐	£5.95 ☐	£12.95 ☐	£25.00 ☐	
14 Strategic Management Accountancy & Mktg	£20.95 ☐	£10.95 ☐	£5.95 ☐	£12.95 ☐	£25.00 ☐	
15 Information Management	£20.95 ☐	£10.95 ☐	£5.95 ☐	£12.95 ☐	£25.00 ☐	
16 Management Accounting Control Systems	£20.95 ☐	£10.95 ☐	£5.95 ☐	£12.95 ☐	£25.00 ☐	
					£	

POSTAGE & PACKING

Study Texts

	First	Each extra	
UK	£3.00	£2.00	£
Europe*	£5.00	£4.00	£
Rest of world	£20.00	£10.00	£

Kits/Passcards/Success Tapes

	First	Each extra	
UK	£2.00	£1.00	£
Europe*	£2.50	£1.00	£
Rest of world	£15.00	£8.00	£

Master CDs/Breakthrough Videos

	First	Each extra	
UK	£2.00	£2.00	£
Europe*	£2.00	£2.00	£
Rest of world	£20.00	£10.00	£

Grand Total (Cheques to *BPP Publishing*) I enclose a cheque for (incl. Postage) £

Or charge to Access/Visa/Switch

Card Number

Expiry date Start Date

Issue Number (Switch Only)

Signature

We aim to deliver to all UK addresses inside 5 working days. Orders to all EU addresses should be delivered within 6 working days. All other orders to overseas addresses should be delivered within 8 working days.

* Europe includes the Republic of Ireland and the Channel Islands.